Electrical Power Systems

Electrical Power Systems

Analysis, Security and Deregulation

Second Edition

P. Venkatesh
Professor
Department of Electrical and Electronics Engineering
Thiagarajar College of Engineering, Madurai

B.V. Manikandan
Senior Professor
Department of Electrical and Electronics Engineering
Mepco Schlenk Engineering College, Sivakasi

S. Charles Raja
Associate Professor
Department of Electrical and Electronics Engineering
Thiagarajar College of Engineering, Madurai

A. Srinivasan
Professor
Department of Electrical and Electronics Engineering
Sethu Institute of Technology, Kariapatti

PHI Learning Private Limited
Delhi-110092
2025

In fond memory of ***Shri Asoke K. Ghosh*** *(October 1942 – February 2024), Founder Chairman and Managing Director of PHI Learning, whose vision endlessly inspires.*

The Legacy Continues....

Published by Pushpita Ghosh, PHI Learning Private Limited, Rimjhim House, 111, Patparganj Industrial Estate, Delhi-110092 and Printed by Multi Colour Services, I-45, DLF Industrial Area, Sector-32, Faridabad, Haryana-121003.

₹995.00

ELECTRICAL POWER SYSTEMS: Analysis, Security and Deregulation, Second Edition
P. Venkatesh, B.V. Manikandan, S. Charles Raja, and A. Srinivasan

ISBN-978-81-203-5330-5 (Print Book)
ISBN-978-93-90544-85-1 (e-Book)

The export rights of the book are vested solely with the publisher.

Contents

PART III DEREGULATION

Preface

The excellent response to the first edition of the book both by students and academicians of Indian and foreign universities has encouraged the authors to bring out the second edition to include the latest developments in the field of electrical power systems.

It has been the constant endeavour of the authors to understand the difficulties of their students in the classroom and accordingly prepare the lecture notes by referring various books on electrical power systems. The present book is an outcome of these notes and some research works, the authors carried out.

The book covers a very wide spectrum of electrical power systems studies which are normally not available in a single book. The book is so comprehensively written that at least three courses on power systems can be designed.

This edition comes with an improved approach in the sense that errors/mistakes are suitably corrected.

Some studies on sensitivity of network uncertainties on ATC determination are carried out especially for the Indian test system and it is explicitly given with suitable figures and tables.

MATLAB programs for the optimal power flow methods such as interior point method and Lagrange multiplier method add flavour to the book.

In the recent deregulated scenario, one of the important challenges is the transmission congestion management. Hence, it is added as a separate chapter with various classifications and reliving methodologies by rescheduling generation and possible load curtailment if needed on two different test systems.

All these additions would certainly enhance the utility of the book. The authors wish to thank all who have contributed through their useful and valuable suggestions in bringing out the second edition of the book.

P. Venkatesh
B.V. Manikandan
S. Charles Raja
A. Srinivasan

Preface

Preface to the First Edition

The features and structure of the modern power systems have assumed a great significance in recent years. Globally, the power system structure has changed a lot and different entities have come into the power system scenario. Hence a single book for electrical engineering students, covering the basic analysis of power systems, operational aspects of power systems and the vibrant restructuring concepts and issues in an integral manner, is the need of the hour. This book is written to meet this objective and hence it is also a fulfilment of our cherished desire to contribute our work aimed at furthering the students' understanding of electric energy systems.

The subject matter of the book is arranged in three parts in order to focus on three major areas in power systems, namely, analysis, security and deregulation. The book's audience mainly consists of undergraduate electrical and engineering students, postgraduate power engineering students as well as research scholars working in the field of power system engineering. The book contains explanations of important topics in power systems by providing suitable examples, working out solution to problems by MATLAB programs, and by illustrating the concepts and practices with the help of the state-of-the-art software tools, such as Power World Corporation's Power World Simulator (PWS) and Siemens' Power System Simulation for Engineers (PSS/E). The text material presented in this format is the outstanding feature of the book. In addition, care has been taken to introduce questions at the end of each chapter to reinforce the students' understanding of the concepts discussed. Students will be immensely benefited by executing the problems given in the chapters using the student version of PWS and PSS/E available free of cost.

Chapters one through five of Part I deal with analysis issues in power systems. Chapter 1 discusses the concepts of per unit system and different aspects of modelling of components in power systems. Various methods employed in power flow analysis are discussed in Chapter 2. Students will be really benefited because of several problems analyzed and solved here in three platforms, namely, MATLAB, PWS, and PSS/E. Chapters 3 and 4 discuss symmetrical and unsymmetrical fault calculations in power systems. Chapter 5 is devoted to stability study using suitable examples.

Part II discusses the security aspects in power systems under a vertically integrated environment. In any energy management/operations control centre, the knowledge of security analysis, state estimation and optimal power flow is essential. Chapter 6 discusses in detail the contingency analysis under various platforms. Different aspects such as estimation formula and bad measurement determination related to state estimation, are explained in Chapter 7. Optimal power flow (OPF) formulations, solution methods and unit commitment topics are described in Chapter 8.

Part III (Chapters 9–12) is focused on the need to restructure power systems from the vertically integrated into competitive ones. It incorporates topics such as international trends, Indian power scenario and power market operations. Two important technical challenges in the competitive environment, namely transmission pricing and available transfer capability, are discussed in detail in Chapter 9. Chapters 10 and 12 explain the operations in power market and ATC determination using PWS which is an added credit to the book. Chapter 11 describes the globally prevailing transmission pricing methods. Pricing methods in the context of Indian scenario are also discussed with an example problem using PSS/E.

We are indebted to our teachers who taught us power systems during our college days. We thank the management and the Principal of Thiagarajar College of Engineering, Madurai for making available to us the necessary facilities, in particular the software packages PWS and PSS/E software procured under the Department of Science and Technology-FIST scheme and University Grants Commission-MRP scheme. Finally, our heartfelt thanks go to our publisher PHI Learning for their cooperation in every endeavour in bringing out this book successfully.

Constructive criticism and suggestions for improvement of this book will be highly appreciated and gratefully acknowledged.

P. Venkatesh
B.V. Manikandan
S. Charles Raja
A. Srinivasan

Part I

Power System Analysis

CHAPTER 1

Introduction to Power System

1.1 Introduction

A power system consists of several subsystems such as generation, transmission, and distribution. The objectives of power system analysis are to model or to perform per phase analysis of power system components, to monitor the voltage at various buses, real and reactive power flow between buses, to design the circuit breakers, to plan future expansion of the existing system, to analyse the system under different fault conditions and to study the ability of the system to cope with small and large disturbances (stability studies).

1.2 Structure of Power Systems

An interconnected power system as shown in Figure 1.1 is a complex enterprise that may be subdivided into the following major subsystems:

- Generation
- Transmission and subtransmission subsystems
- Distribution subsystem
- Utilisation subsystem

Generators

An essential component of power systems is the three-phase ac generator known as synchronous generator or alternator. Its rotor is driven at synchronous speed and excited by the direct current. The other field is produced in the stator windings by the three-phase armature currents. The direct current for the rotor windings is provided by the excitation systems. In the older generators, the exciters were dc generators mounted on the same shaft, providing excitation through slip rings. The current systems use the ac generators with rotating rectifiers known as brushless excitation systems. The source of the mechanical power, commonly known as the prime mover, may be hydraulic turbines, steam turbines whose energy comes from the burning of coal, gas and nuclear fuel, gas turbines, or occasionally internal combustion engines burning oil.

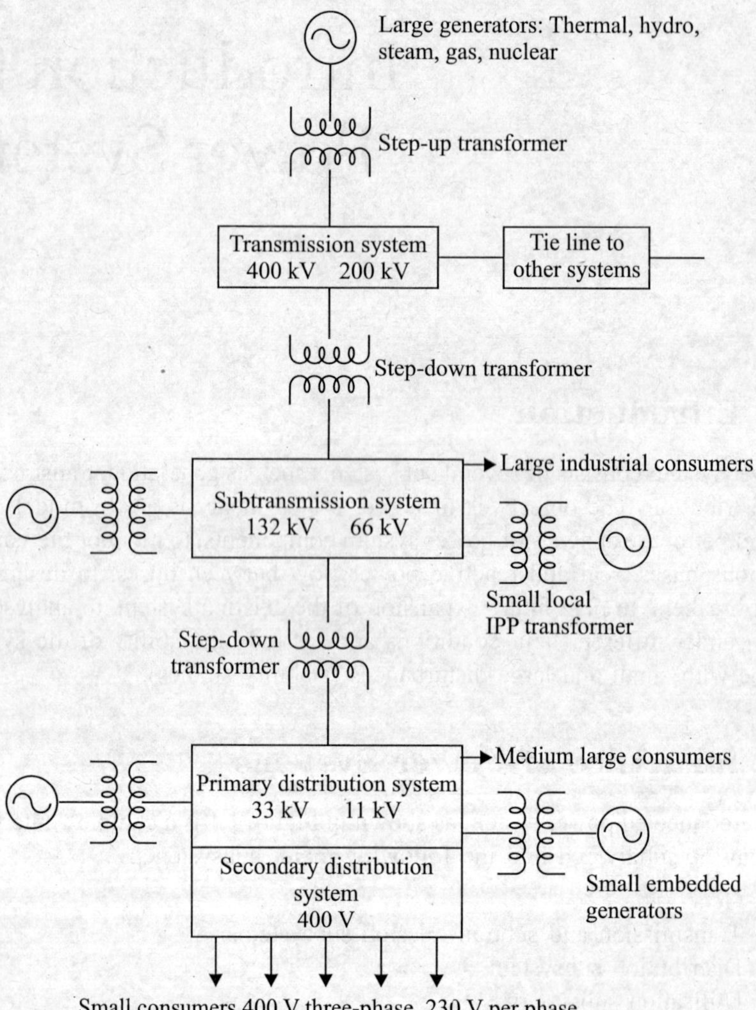

Figure 1.1 Structure of power system.

Transformers

The transformer transfers power with very high efficiency from one level of voltage to another. The power transferred to the secondary is almost the same as the primary, except for losses in the transformer. The use of a step-up transformer will reduce the losses in the transmission line, which makes the transmission of power over long distances possible.

Insulation requirements and the other practical design problems limit the generated voltage to low values, usually 11 kV. Thus, step-up transformers are used for transmission of power. At the receiving end of the transmission lines, step-down transformers are used to reduce the voltage to suitable values for distribution or utilisation. The electricity in an electric power system may undergo four or five transformations between the generator and the consumers.

Transmission and subtransmission subsystem

An overhead transmission network transfers electric power from the generating units to the distribution systems which ultimately supply the load centres at 220 kV or higher. Transmission level voltages are in the range of 66 kV to 400 kV.

As shown in Figure 1.1, electric power is generated in the range of 11 kV to 25 kV, which is increased by stepped-up transformers to the main transmission line voltage. At the substation, the connections between the various components are made, for example, lines and transformers and the arrangement for switching of these components is carried out.

The power supply network can be divided into two parts, namely, the transmission system and the distribution system. The transmission system may be further divided into primary and secondary transmission systems. The distribution system too, can be divided into primary and secondary distribution systems.

High voltage transmission lines are terminated in substations, which are called high-voltage substations, receiving substations, or primary substations. The function of some substations is switching circuits in and out of service; they are therefore referred to as switching stations. At the primary substation, the voltage is stepped down to a value more suitable for the next part of the flow towards the load. Very large industrial customers may be served directly from the primary sub-station.

The portion of the transmission system that connects the high-voltage substations through step-down transformers to the distribution substations is called the subtransmission network. Some large industrial customers may be served directly from the subtransmission system. Capacitor banks and reactor banks are usually installed in the substations for maintaining the transmission line voltage.

Distribution and utilisation subsystems

The distribution system connects the distribution substations to the consumers' service-entrance equipment. The primary distribution lines range from 3.3 to 11 kV and supply the load in a well-defined geographical area. Some small industrial customers are served directly by the primary feeders. The secondary distribution network reduces the voltage for utilisation by commercial and residential consumers. Lines and cables not exceeding a few hundred feet in length then deliver power to the individual consumers. The secondary distribution serves most of the customers at levels of 415/230 V, three phases, and four wires. The power for a typical home is derived from a transformer that reduces the primary feeder voltage to 240 V using a three-wire line. The distribution system utilises both overhead and underground conductors.

1.3 Modelling of Power System Components

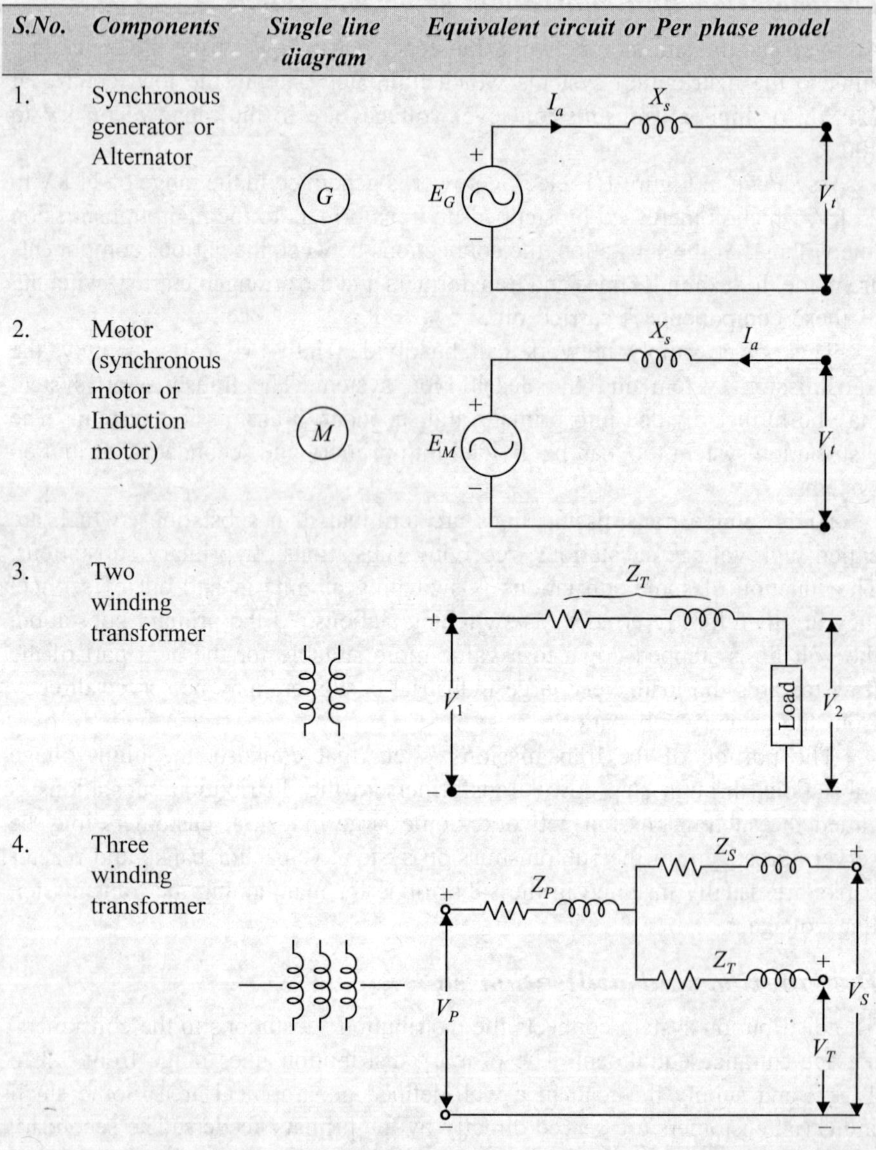

S.No.	*Components*	*Single line diagram*	*Equivalent circuit or Per phase model*
1.	Synchronous generator or Alternator	G	I_a, X_s, +, E_G, −, V_t
2.	Motor (synchronous motor or Induction motor)	M	X_s, I_a, +, E_M, −, V_t
3.	Two winding transformer		Z_T, +, V_1, −, Load, V_2
4.	Three winding transformer		Z_S, Z_P, Z_T, +, V_P, −, V_S, V_T

(*Contd.*)

(*Contd.*)

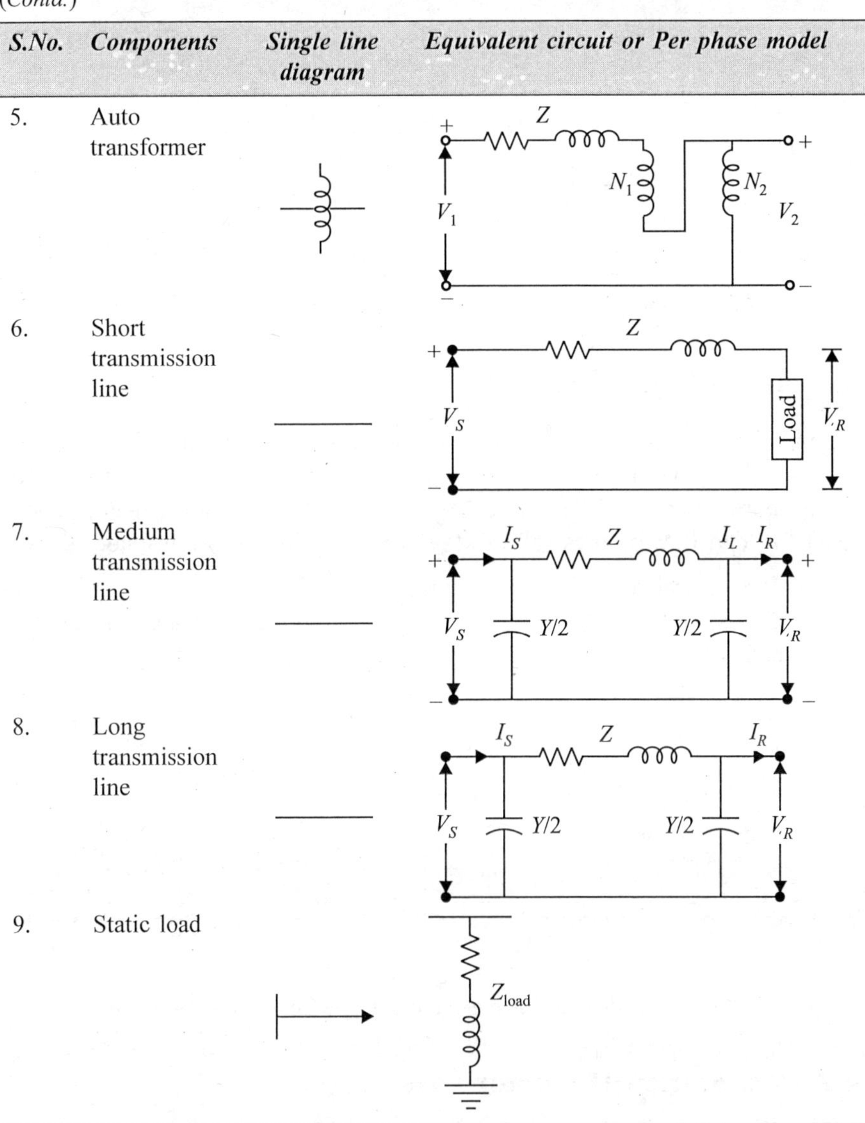

S.No.	*Components*	*Single line diagram*	*Equivalent circuit or Per phase model*
5.	Auto transformer		
6.	Short transmission line		
7.	Medium transmission line		
8.	Long transmission line		
9.	Static load		

1.4 Single Line Diagram or One Line Diagram

A single line diagram as shown in Figure 1.2 is a diagrammatic representation of a power system in which the components are represented by their symbols and the interconnections between them are shown by a straight line (even though the system might be a three-phase system). The ratings and the impedances of the components are also marked on the single line diagram. The purpose of the single line diagram is to supply the significant information about the system in a concise form.

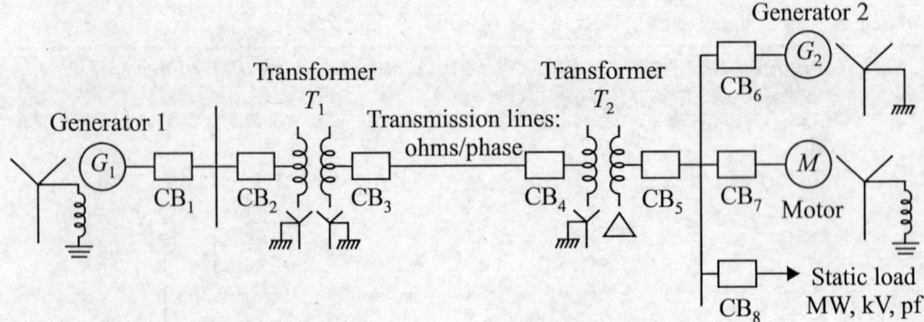

Figure 1.2 Single line representation of a representative power system.

1.4.1 Impedance Diagram

The impedance diagram (Figure 1.3) is the equivalent circuit of the power system in which the various components of the power system are represented by their approximate or simplified equivalent circuits. The impedance diagram is used for load flow studies. The following approximations are made:

(i) The neutral reactances are neglected.
(ii) The shunt branches in the equivalent circuits of transformers are neglected.

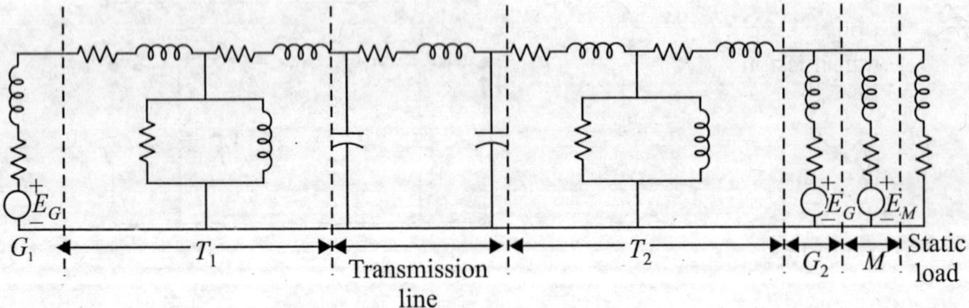

Figure 1.3 Impedance diagram of the representative power system of Figure 1.2.

1.4.2 Reactance Diagram

The reactance diagram (Figure 1.4) is the simplified equivalent circuit of the power system in which the various components of the power system are represented by their reactances. The reactance diagram can be obtained from the impedance diagram if all the resistive components are neglected. The reactance diagram is used for fault calculations. The following approximations are made:

(i) The neutral reactances are neglected.
(ii) The shunt branches in equivalent circuits of transformers are neglected.
(iii) The resistances are neglected.
(iv) All static loads are neglected.
(v) The capacitance of transmission lines is neglected.

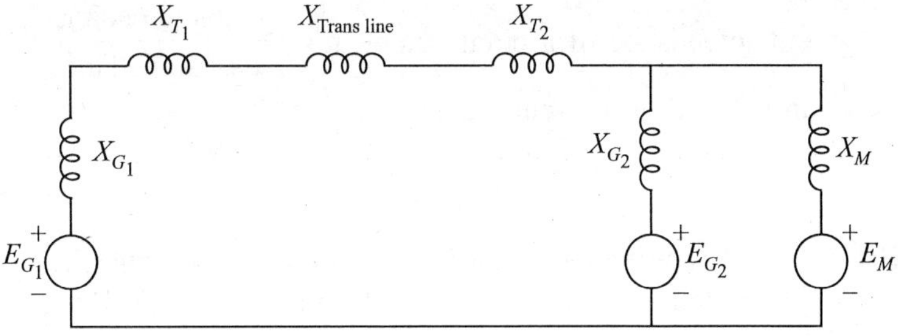

Figure 1.4 Reactance diagram of the representative power system of Figure 1.2.

1.5 Per Unit Value

The per unit value of any quantity is defined as the ratio of the actual value of that quantity to the base value of the same quantity as a decimal.

$$\text{Per unit value} = \frac{\text{Actual value}}{\text{Base value}} \tag{1.1}$$

Per phase analysis

A balanced three-phase system always analyses on per phase basis by considering one of the three-phase lines and the neutral.

Advantages of per unit system

(i) The comparison of characteristics of the various electrical apparatuses of different types of ratings is facilitated by expressing the value of reactances in per unit based on their ratings.
(ii) The per unit impedance of the transformer, whether referred to primary or secondary is the same.
(iii) The per unit system is ideal for the computerized analysis and simulation of complex power system problems.
(iv) The advantages of per unit impedance are more eagerly felt with a large number of circuits.

Single-phase system (1ϕ)

In a single phase system, suppose the base MVA and base kV ratings are given, then

$$\text{Base current (kA)} = \frac{\text{base MVA}}{\text{base kV}} \tag{1.2}$$

$$\text{Base impedance} = \frac{\text{base kV}}{\text{base kA}} = \frac{\text{base kV}}{\text{base MVA/base kV}} \tag{1.3}$$

$$\therefore \qquad \text{Base impedance} = \frac{(\text{base kV})^2}{\text{base MVA}} \tag{1.4}$$

$$\text{Per unit impedance of a circuit element} = \frac{\text{actual impedance}}{\text{base impedance}}$$

$\therefore$ Impedance of a circuit element in p.u.

$$= \frac{\text{actual impedance } Z \text{ (in ohms)} \times \text{base MVA}}{(\text{base kV})^2} \tag{1.5}$$

EXAMPLE 1.1 A single-phase transformer is rated at 110/440 V, 2.5 kVA, and its leakage reactance measured from L.T. side is 0.06 Ω. Determine the leakage reactance in p.u.

Solution: Given actual leakage reactance = 0.06 Ω

$$\text{Base impedance or reactance} = \frac{(\text{base kV})^2}{\text{base MVA}} = \frac{(110 \times 10^{-3})^2}{2.5 \times 10^{-3}} = 4.84\ \Omega$$

$$\therefore \quad \text{Per unit leakage reactance} = \frac{\text{actual reactance}}{\text{base reactance}} = \frac{0.06}{4.84} = 0.0124 \text{ p.u.}$$

Three-phase systems (3ϕ)

In a three-phase system, suppose the base MVA and the line-to-line base kV (L-L) ratings are given

Then, for star connection,

$$\text{Base voltage/phase} = \frac{\text{base kV (L-L)}}{\sqrt{3}} \tag{1.6}$$

$$\text{Base current/phase} = \frac{\left[\dfrac{\text{base MVA } (3\phi)}{3}\right]}{\left[\dfrac{\text{base kV (L-L)}}{\sqrt{3}}\right]} \tag{1.7}$$

$$= \frac{\text{base MVA } (3\phi)}{\sqrt{3} \times \text{base kV (L-L)}} \tag{1.8}$$

$$\text{Base impedance/phase} = \frac{\text{base voltage/phase}}{\text{base current/phase}} \tag{1.9}$$

$$= \frac{\left[\dfrac{\text{base kV (L-L)}}{\sqrt{3}}\right]}{\left[\dfrac{\text{base MVA } (3\phi)}{\sqrt{3} \times \text{base kV (L-L)}}\right]}$$

$$\therefore \quad \text{Base impedance/phase} = \frac{[\text{base kV (L-L)}]^2}{\text{base MVA } (3\phi)} \tag{1.10}$$

$$\text{Per unit impedance of a circuit element} = \frac{\text{actual impedance}}{\text{base impedance}}$$

$$\therefore \text{ Impedance in p.u.} = \frac{\text{actual impedance } Z \text{ (in ohms)} \times \text{base MVA } (3\phi)}{[\text{base kV (L-L)}]^2} \tag{1.11}$$

Change of base value

The components or various sections of power system may operate at different voltage and power levels. It will be convenient therefore for the purpose of analysis of power systems if the voltage, power, current and impedance ratings of components are expressed with reference to a common value called the base value.

$$Z_{\text{p.u.(given)}} = \frac{Z_{\text{actual}}}{(\text{base kV}_{\text{given}})^2} \times \text{base MVA}_{\text{given}} \tag{1.12}$$

Similarly, when expressed to the new base value

$$Z_{\text{p.u.(new)}} = \frac{Z_{\text{actual}}}{(\text{base kV}_{\text{new}})^2} \times \text{base MVA}_{\text{new}} \tag{1.13}$$

Dividing Eq. (1.13) by Eq. (1.12)

$$Z_{\text{p.u.(new)}} = Z_{\text{p.u.(given)}} \times \left[\frac{\text{base kV}_{\text{given}}}{\text{base kV}_{\text{new}}}\right]^2 \times \left[\frac{\text{base MVA}_{\text{new}}}{\text{base MVA}_{\text{given}}}\right] \tag{1.14}$$

For calculation of per unit values, the following points need to be noted:

1. A base kV and base MVA are selected in one part of the system. The base values for 3ϕ system are L-L kV and 3ϕ MVA.
2. The base MVA will be the same in all parts of the system.
3. For other parts of the system, i.e. on the other sides of transformers, the base kV for each part is determined using the L-L voltage ratios of the transformer.
4. The impedance values in per unit are calculated using the formulas.

EXAMPLE 1.2 Given

Generator 1: 100 MVA, 33 kV, reactance 10%
Generator 2: 150 MVA, 32 kV, reactance 8%
Generator 3: 110 MVA, 30 kV, reactance 12%

Determine the new per unit reactance of generators corresponding to the base values of 200 MVA and 35 kV.

Solution:

$$\text{Base MVA, MVA}_{\text{new}} = 200 \text{ MVA; Base kV, kV}_{\text{new}} = 35 \text{ kV}$$

Reactance of generator 1

$X_{\text{p.u.(given)}} = 10\% = 0.1$ p.u., $\text{MVA}_{\text{given}} = 100$ MVA, $\text{MVA}_{\text{new}} = 200$ MVA, $\text{kV}_{\text{given}} = 33$ kV, $\text{kV}_{\text{new}} = 35$ kV

$$Z_{\text{p.u.(new)}} = Z_{\text{p.u.(given)}} \times \left[\frac{\text{base kV}_{\text{given}}}{\text{base kV}_{\text{new}}}\right]^2 \times \left[\frac{\text{base MVA}_{\text{new}}}{\text{base MVA}_{\text{given}}}\right]$$

$$Z_{\text{p.u.(new)}} = 0.1 \times \left[\frac{33}{35}\right]^2 \times \left[\frac{200}{100}\right] = 0.178 \text{ p.u.}$$

Reactance of generator 2

$X_{\text{p.u.(given)}} = 8\% = 0.08$ p.u., $\text{MVA}_{\text{given}} = 150$ MVA, $\text{MVA}_{\text{new}} = 200$ MVA, $\text{kV}_{\text{given}} = 32$ kV, $\text{kV}_{\text{new}} = 35$ kV

$$Z_{\text{p.u.(new)}} = Z_{\text{p.u.(given)}} \times \left[\frac{\text{base kV}_{\text{given}}}{\text{base kV}_{\text{new}}}\right]^2 \times \left[\frac{\text{base MVA}_{\text{new}}}{\text{base MVA}_{\text{given}}}\right]$$

$$\therefore \quad Z_{\text{p.u.(new)}} = 0.08 \times \left[\frac{32}{35}\right]^2 \times \left[\frac{200}{150}\right] = 0.089 \text{ p.u.}$$

Reactance of generator 3

$X_{\text{p.u.(given)}} = 12\% = 0.12$ p.u., $\text{MVA}_{\text{given}} = 110$ MVA, $\text{MVA}_{\text{new}} = 200$ MVA, $\text{kV}_{\text{given}} = 30$ kV, $\text{kV}_{\text{new}} = 35$ kV

$$Z_{\text{p.u.(new)}} = Z_{\text{p.u.(given)}} \times \left[\frac{\text{base kV}_{\text{given}}}{\text{base kV}_{\text{new}}}\right]^2 \times \left[\frac{\text{base MVA}_{\text{new}}}{\text{base MVA}_{\text{given}}}\right]$$

$$\therefore \quad Z_{\text{p.u.(new)}} = 0.12 \times \left[\frac{30}{35}\right]^2 \times \left[\frac{200}{110}\right] = 0.16 \text{ p.u.}$$

EXAMPLE 1.3 Draw the per unit reactance diagram for the power system shown in Figure 1.5. Neglect the resistance and use a base of 100 MVA, 220 kV in a 50 Ω line. The ratings of the generator, motor and transformers are as follows:

G : 40 MVA, 25 kV, $X'' = 20\%$
M : 50 MVA, 11 kV, $X'' = 30\%$
T_1 : 40 MVA, 33Y/220Y kV, $X = 15\%$
T_2 : 30 MVA, 11 Δ/220Y kV, $X = 15\%$
Load : 11 kV, 50 MW + j68 MVAR

Determine the new per unit values of reactance of transmission line, and new values of per unit reactance of transformer T_1, generator G, transformer T_2 and motor M.

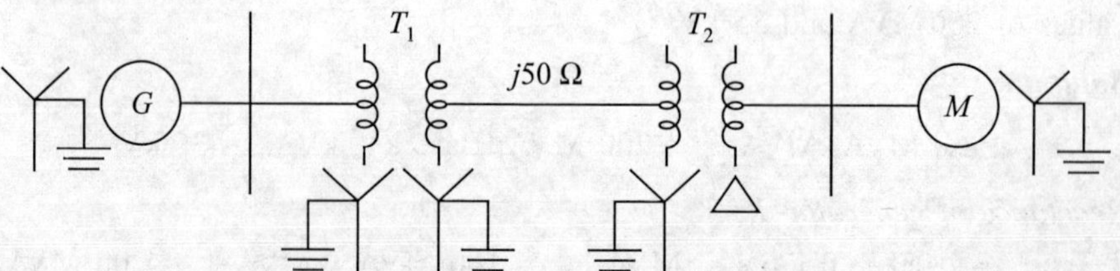

Figure 1.5 Single line diagram of Example 1.3.

Solution:

Base MVA, $MVA_{new} = 100$ MVA

Base kV, $kV_{new} = 220$ kV

Reactance of transmission line

$$\text{Per unit reactance of the transmission line} = \frac{\text{actual reactance, } \Omega}{\text{base reactance, } \Omega}$$

$$\text{Actual reactance} = 50\ \Omega$$

$$\text{Base reactance} = \frac{(kV_{new})^2}{MVA_{new}} = \frac{220^2}{100} = 484\ \Omega$$

$$\text{Per unit reactance of the transmission line} = \frac{\text{actual reactance, } \Omega}{\text{base reactance, } \Omega}$$

$$= \frac{50}{484} = 0.1033 \text{ p.u.}$$

Reactance of transformer T_1 (primary side)

$$X_{p.u.(new)} = X_{p.u.(given)} \times \left(\frac{kV_{given}}{kV_{new}}\right)^2 \times \left(\frac{MVA_{new}}{MVA_{given}}\right)$$

$X_{p.u.(given)} = 0.15$ p.u., $MVA_{given} = 40$, $MVA_{new} = 100$, $kV_{given} = 33$
$kV_{new} = ?$

Base kV on LT side of transformer T_1

$$= \text{base kV on HT side} \times \frac{\text{LT voltage rating}}{\text{HT voltage rating}}$$

$$\text{Base kV on LT side of transformer } T_1 = 220 \times \frac{33}{220} = 33 \text{ kV}$$

$$kV_{new} = 33 \text{ kV}$$

$$X_{p.u.(new)} = 0.15 \times \left(\frac{33}{33}\right)^2 \times \left(\frac{100}{40}\right) = 0.375 \text{ p.u.}$$

Reactance of the generator G

$$X_{p.u.(new)} = X_{p.u.(given)} \times \left(\frac{kV_{given}}{kV_{new}}\right)^2 \times \left(\frac{MVA_{new}}{MVA_{given}}\right)$$

$X_{p.u.(given)} = 0.2$ p.u., $MVA_{given} = 40$, $MVA_{new} = 100$, $kV_{given} = 25$,
$kV_{new} = 33$

$$X_{p.u.(new)} = 0.2 \times \left(\frac{25}{33}\right)^2 \times \left(\frac{100}{40}\right) = 0.287 \text{ p.u.}$$

Reactance of transformer T_2 (primary side)

$$X_{\text{p.u.(new)}} = X_{\text{p.u.(given)}} \times \left(\frac{\text{kV}_{\text{given}}}{\text{kV}_{\text{new}}}\right)^2 \times \left(\frac{\text{MVA}_{\text{new}}}{\text{MVA}_{\text{given}}}\right)$$

$X_{\text{p.u.(given)}} = 0.15$ p.u., $\text{MVA}_{\text{given}} = 30$, $\text{MVA}_{\text{new}} = 100$, $\text{kV}_{\text{given}} = 11$, $\text{kV}_{\text{new}} = ?$

$$\text{Base kV on LT side of transformer } T_2 = \text{base kV on HT side} \times \frac{\text{LT voltages rating}}{\text{HT voltage rating}}$$

$$\text{Base kV on LT side of transformer } T_1 = 220 \times \frac{11}{220} = 11\text{ kV}$$

$$\text{kV}_{\text{new}} = 11\text{ kV}$$

$$X_{\text{p.u.(new)}} = 0.15 \times \left(\frac{11}{11}\right)^2 \times \left(\frac{100}{30}\right) = 0.5\text{ p.u.}$$

Reactance of motor M

$$X_{\text{p.u.(new)}} = X_{\text{p.u.(given)}} \times \left(\frac{\text{kV}_{\text{given}}}{\text{kV}_{\text{new}}}\right)^2 \times \left(\frac{\text{MVA}_{\text{new}}}{\text{MVA}_{\text{given}}}\right)$$

$X_{\text{p.u.(given)}} = 0.3$ p.u., $\text{MVA}_{\text{given}} = 50$, $\text{MVA}_{\text{new}} = 100$, $\text{kV}_{\text{given}} = 11$, $\text{kV}_{\text{new}} = 11$

$$X_{\text{p.u.(new)}} = 0.3 \times \left(\frac{11}{11}\right)^2 \times \left(\frac{100}{50}\right) = 0.6\text{ p.u.}$$

Reactance diagram (Figure 1.6)

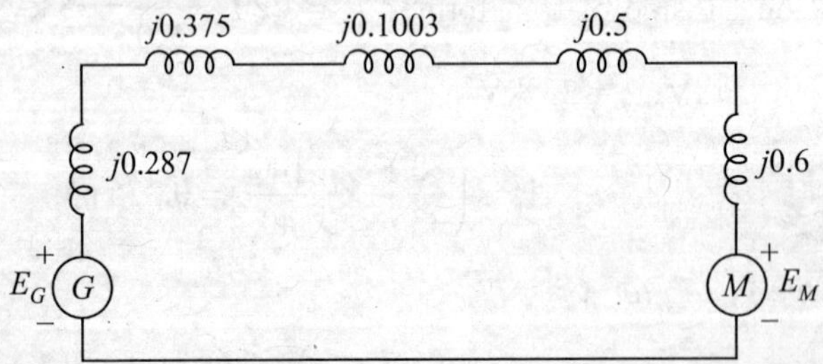

Figure 1.6 Reactance diagram of power system of Example 1.3.

EXAMPLE 1.4 Draw the reactance diagram for the power system shown in Figure 1.7. Neglect the resistance and use a base of 50 MVA and 13.8 kV on generator G_1.

G_1 : 20 MVA, 13.8 kV, $X'' = 20\%$

G_2 : 30 MVA, 18.0 kV, $X'' = 20\%$

G_3 : 30 MVA, 20.0 kV, $X'' = 20\%$

T_1 : 25 MVA, 220/13.8 kV, X = 10%
T_2 : 3 single phase unit each rated 10 MVA, 127/18 kV, X = 10%
T_3 : 35 MVA, 220/22 kV, X = 10%

Determine the new values of per unit reactance of G_1, T_1, transmission line 1, transmission line 2, T_2, G_2, T_3 and G_3.

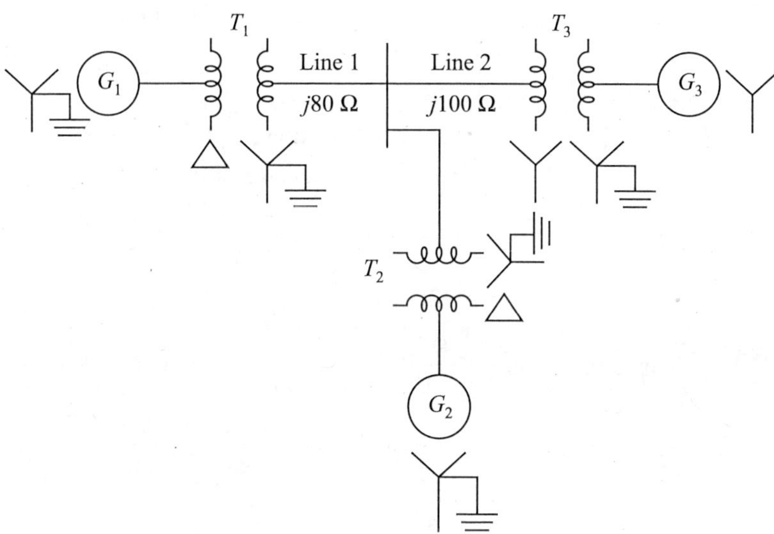

Figure 1.7 Single line diagram of Example 1.4.

Solution:

Base MVA, MVA_{new} = 50 MVA
Base kV, kV_{new} = 13.8 kV

Reactance of generator G_1

$$X_{p.u.(new)} = X_{p.u.(given)} \times \left(\frac{kV_{given}}{kV_{new}}\right)^2 \times \left(\frac{MVA_{new}}{MVA_{given}}\right)$$

$X_{p.u.(given)}$ =0.2 p.u., MVA_{given} = 20, MVA_{new} = 50, kV_{given} = 13.8, kV_{new} = 13.8

$$\therefore \qquad X_{p.u.(new)} = 0.2 \times \left(\frac{13.8}{13.8}\right)^2 \times \left(\frac{50}{20}\right) = j0.5 \text{ p.u.}$$

Reactance of transformer T_1 (primary side)

$$X_{p.u.(new)} = X_{p.u.(given)} \times \left(\frac{kV_{given}}{kV_{new}}\right)^2 \times \left(\frac{MVA_{new}}{MVA_{given}}\right)$$

$X_{p.u.(given)}$ = 0.1 p.u., MVA_{given} = 25, MVA_{new} = 50, kV_{given} = 13.8, kV_{new} = 13.8

$$X_{\text{p.u.(new)}} = 0.1 \times \left(\frac{13.8}{13.8}\right)^2 \times \left(\frac{50}{25}\right) = j0.2 \text{ p.u.}$$

Reactance of the transmission line j80 Ω

$$\text{Per unit reactance of the transmission line} = \frac{\text{actual reactance, } \Omega}{\text{base reactance, } \Omega}$$

$$\text{Actual reactance} = 80\ \Omega$$

$$\text{Base kV on HT side of transformer } T_1$$

$$= \text{base kV on LT side} \times \frac{\text{HT voltage rating}}{\text{LT voltage rating}}$$

$$\text{Base kV on HT side of transformer } T_1 = 13.8 \times \frac{220}{13.8} = 220 \text{ kV}$$

$$\text{kV}_{\text{new}} = 220 \text{ kV}$$

$$\text{Base impedance} = \frac{(\text{kV}_{\text{new}})^2}{\text{MVA}_{\text{new}}} = \frac{220^2}{50} = 968\ \Omega$$

$$\text{Per unit reactance of the transmission line} = \frac{\text{actual reactance, } \Omega}{\text{base reactance, } \Omega}$$

$$= \frac{80}{968} = j0.0826 \text{ p.u.}$$

Reactance of the transmission line j100 Ω

$$\text{Per unit reactance of the transmission line} = \frac{\text{actual reactance, } \Omega}{\text{base reactance, } \Omega}$$

$$\text{Actual reactance} = 100\ \Omega$$

$$\text{Base kV on HT side of transformer } T_1$$

$$= \text{base kV on LT side} \times \frac{\text{HT voltage rating}}{\text{LT voltage rating}}$$

$$\text{Base kV on HT side of transformer } T_1 = 13.8 \times \frac{220}{13.8} = 220 \text{ kV}$$

$$\text{kV}_{\text{new}} = 220 \text{ kV}$$

$$\text{Base impedance} = \frac{(\text{kV}_{\text{new}})^2}{\text{MVA}_{\text{new}}} = \frac{220^2}{50} = 968\ \Omega$$

$$\text{Per unit reactance of the transmission line} = \frac{\text{actual reactance, } \Omega}{\text{base reactance, } \Omega}$$

$$= \frac{100}{968} = j0.1033 \text{ p.u.}$$

Reactance of transformer T_2 (primary side)

$$X_{\text{p.u.(new)}} = X_{\text{p.u.(given)}} \times \left(\frac{\text{kV}_{\text{given}}}{\text{kV}_{\text{new}}}\right)^2 \times \left(\frac{\text{MVA}_{\text{new}}}{\text{MVA}_{\text{given}}}\right)$$

$$X_{\text{p.u.(given)}} = 0.1 \text{ p.u.}$$

Y/Δ connection; voltage rating: $\sqrt{3} \times \frac{127}{18} \text{ kV} = \frac{220}{18} \text{ kV}$

$\text{MVA}_{\text{given}} = 3 \times 10 = 30$, $\text{MVA}_{\text{new}} = 50$, $\text{kV}_{\text{given}} = 220$, $\text{kV}_{\text{new}} = 220$

$$X_{\text{p.u.(new)}} = 0.1 \times \left(\frac{220}{220}\right)^2 \times \left(\frac{50}{30}\right) = j0.1667 \text{ p.u.}$$

Reactance of generator G_2

$$X_{\text{p.u.(new)}} = X_{\text{p.u.(given)}} \times \left(\frac{\text{kV}_{\text{given}}}{\text{kV}_{\text{new}}}\right)^2 \times \left(\frac{\text{MVA}_{\text{new}}}{\text{MVA}_{\text{given}}}\right)$$

$X_{\text{p.u.(given)}} = 0.2$ p.u., $\text{MVA}_{\text{given}} = 30$, $\text{MVA}_{\text{new}} = 50$, $\text{kV}_{\text{given}} = 18$, $\text{kV}_{\text{new}} = ?$

Base kV on LT side of transformer T_2

$$= \text{base kV on HT side} \times \frac{\text{LT voltage rating}}{\text{HT voltage rating}}$$

Base kV on LT side of transformer $T_2 = 220 \times \frac{18}{220} = 18 \text{ kV}$

$$\text{kV}_{\text{new}} = 18 \text{ kV}$$

$$X_{\text{p.u.(new)}} = 0.2 \times \left(\frac{18}{18}\right)^2 \times \left(\frac{50}{30}\right) = j0.333 \text{ p.u.}$$

Reactance of transformer T_3 (secondary side)

$$X_{\text{p.u.(new)}} = X_{\text{p.u.(given)}} \times \left(\frac{\text{kV}_{\text{given}}}{\text{kV}_{\text{new}}}\right)^2 \times \left(\frac{\text{MVA}_{\text{new}}}{\text{MVA}_{\text{given}}}\right)$$

$X_{\text{p.u.(given)}} = 0.1$ p.u., $\text{MVA}_{\text{given}} = 35$, $\text{MVA}_{\text{new}} = 50$, $\text{kV}_{\text{given}} = 220$, $\text{kV}_{\text{new}} = 220$

$$X_{\text{p.u.(new)}} = 0.1 \times \left(\frac{220}{220}\right)^2 \times \left(\frac{50}{35}\right) = j0.1429 \text{ p.u.}$$

Reactance of generator G_3

$$X_{\text{p.u.(new)}} = X_{\text{p.u.(given)}} \times \left(\frac{\text{kV}_{\text{given}}}{\text{kV}_{\text{new}}}\right)^2 \times \left(\frac{\text{MVA}_{\text{new}}}{\text{MVA}_{\text{given}}}\right)$$

$X_{\text{p.u.(given)}} = 0.2$ p.u., $\text{MVA}_{\text{given}} = 30$, $\text{MVA}_{\text{new}} = 50$, $\text{kV}_{\text{given}} = 20$, $\text{kV}_{\text{new}} = ?$

Base kV on LT side of transformer T_3

$$= \text{base kV on HT side} \times \frac{\text{LT voltage rating}}{\text{HT voltage rating}}$$

$$\text{Base kV on LT side of transformer } T_3 = 220 \times \frac{22}{220} = 22 \text{ kV}$$

$$\text{kV}_{\text{new}} = 22 \text{ kV}$$

$$X_{\text{p.u.(new)}} = 0.2 \times \left(\frac{20}{22}\right)^2 \times \left(\frac{50}{30}\right) = j0.2755 \text{ p.u.}$$

Reactance diagram (Figure 1.8)

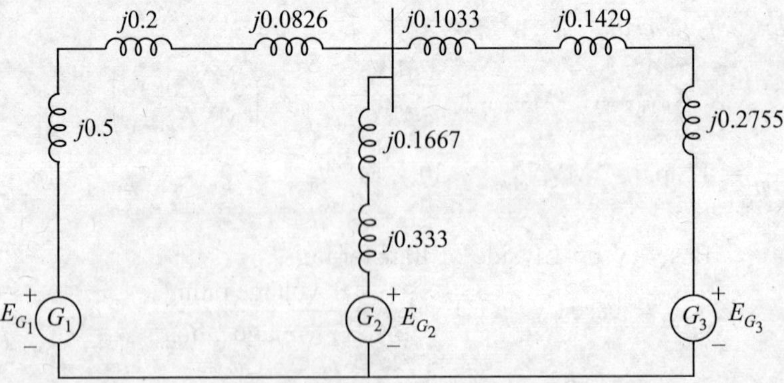

Figure 1.8 Reactance diagram of power system of Example 1.4.

EXAMPLE 1.5 A simple power system is shown in Figure 1.9. Redraw this system where the per unit reactance of the components is represented on a common 5000 VA base and common system base voltage of 250 V.

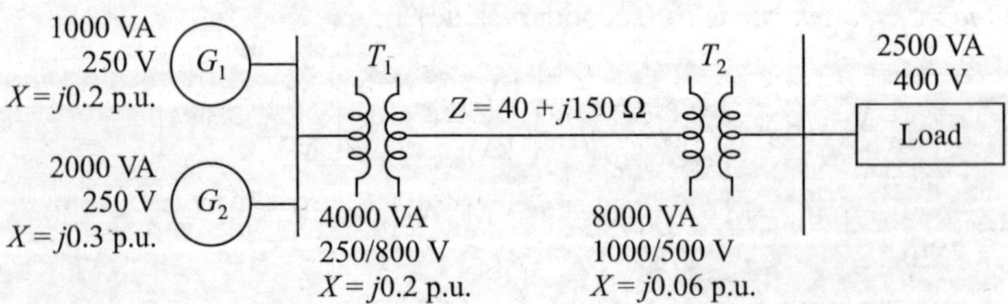

Figure 1.9 A simple power system of Example 1.5.

Determine the new values of per unit reactance of G_1, G_2, T_1, transmission line, T_2, and load.

Solution:

Base MVA, $\text{MVA}_{\text{new}} = 5000 \text{ VA} = 5 \text{ MVA}$

Base kV, $\text{kV}_{\text{new}} = 250 \text{ V} = 0.25 \text{ kV}$

Reactance of generator G_1

$$X_{\text{p.u.(new)}} = X_{\text{p.u.(given)}} \times \left(\frac{\text{kV}_{\text{given}}}{\text{kV}_{\text{new}}}\right)^2 \times \left(\frac{\text{MVA}_{\text{new}}}{\text{MVA}_{\text{given}}}\right)$$

$Z_{\text{p.u.(given)}} = 0.2$ p.u., $\text{MVA}_{\text{given}} = 1$, $\text{MVA}_{\text{new}} = 5$, $\text{kV}_{\text{given}} = 0.25$, $\text{kV}_{\text{new}} = 0.25$

$$Z_{\text{p.u.(new)}} = 0.2 \times \left(\frac{0.25}{0.25}\right)^2 \times \left(\frac{5}{1}\right) = j1.0 \text{ p.u.}$$

Reactance of generator G_2

$$X_{\text{p.u.(new)}} = X_{\text{p.u.(given)}} \times \left(\frac{\text{kV}_{\text{given}}}{\text{kV}_{\text{new}}}\right)^2 \times \left(\frac{\text{MVA}_{\text{new}}}{\text{MVA}_{\text{given}}}\right)$$

$Z_{\text{p.u.(given)}} = 0.3$ p.u., $\text{MVA}_{\text{given}} = 2$, $\text{MVA}_{\text{new}} = 5$, $\text{kV}_{\text{given}} = 0.25$, $\text{kV}_{\text{new}} = 0.25$

$$X_{\text{p.u.(new)}} = 0.3 \times \left(\frac{0.25}{0.25}\right)^2 \times \left(\frac{5}{2}\right) = j0.75 \text{ p.u.}$$

Reactance of transformer T_1 (primary side)

$$X_{\text{p.u.(new)}} = X_{\text{p.u.(given)}} \times \left(\frac{\text{kV}_{\text{given}}}{\text{kV}_{\text{new}}}\right)^2 \times \left(\frac{\text{MVA}_{\text{new}}}{\text{MVA}_{\text{given}}}\right)$$

$X_{\text{p.u.(given)}} = 0.2$ p.u., $\text{MVA}_{\text{given}} = 4$, $\text{MVA}_{\text{new}} = 5$, $\text{kV}_{\text{given}} = 0.25$, $\text{kV}_{\text{new}} = 0.25$

$$X_{\text{p.u.(new)}} = 0.2 \times \left(\frac{0.25}{0.25}\right)^2 \times \left(\frac{5}{4}\right) = j0.25 \text{ p.u.}$$

Impedance of transmission line $Z = 40 + j150\ \Omega$

$$\text{Per unit impedance of the transmission line} = \frac{\text{actual impedance, }\Omega}{\text{base impedance, }\Omega}$$

$$\text{Actual impedance} = (40 + j150)\ \Omega$$

$$\text{Base V on HT side of transformer } T_1 = \text{base V on LT side} \times \frac{\text{HT voltage rating}}{\text{LT voltage rating}}$$

$$\text{Base V on HT side of transformer } T_1 = 250 \times \frac{800}{250} = 800 \text{ V}$$

$$\text{V}_{\text{new}} = 800 \text{ V}$$

$$\text{Base impedance} = \frac{(\text{V}_{\text{new}})^2}{\text{VA}_{\text{new}}} = \frac{800^2}{5000} = 128\ \Omega$$

$$\text{Per unit impedance of the transmission line} = \frac{\text{actual impedance, }\Omega}{\text{base impedance, }\Omega}$$

$$= \frac{40 + j150}{128} = 0.3125 + j1.17 \text{ p.u.}$$

Reactance of transformer T_2 (primary side)

$$X_{\text{p.u.(new)}} = X_{\text{p.u.(given)}} \times \left(\frac{\text{kV}_{\text{given}}}{\text{kV}_{\text{new}}}\right)^2 \times \left(\frac{\text{MVA}_{\text{new}}}{\text{MVA}_{\text{given}}}\right)$$

Base kV on LT side of transformer T_2

$$= \text{Base kV on HT side} \times \frac{\text{LT voltage rating}}{\text{HT voltage rating}} = 800 \times \frac{500}{1000} = 400 = 0.4 \text{ kV}$$

$X_{\text{p.u.(given)}} = 0.06$ p.u., $\text{MVA}_{\text{given}} = 8$, $\text{MVA}_{\text{new}} = 5$, $\text{kV}_{\text{given}} = 0.5$, $\text{kV}_{\text{new}} = 0.4$

$$X_{\text{p.u.(new)}} = 0.06 \times \left(\frac{0.5}{0.4}\right)^2 \times \left(\frac{5}{8}\right) = j0.0585 \text{ p.u.}$$

Reactance diagram (Figure 1.10)

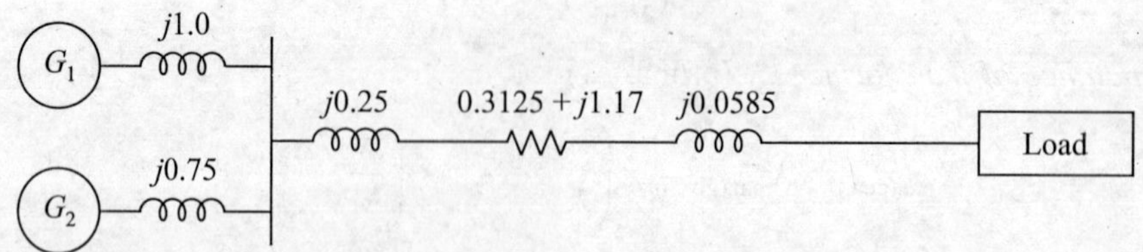

Figure 1.10 Reactance diagram of power system of Example 1.5.

EXAMPLE 1.6 The single line diagram of a three-phase power system is shown in Figure 1.11. Select a common base of 100 MVA and 13.8 kV on the generator side. Draw the per unit impedance diagram with new values per unit reactances.

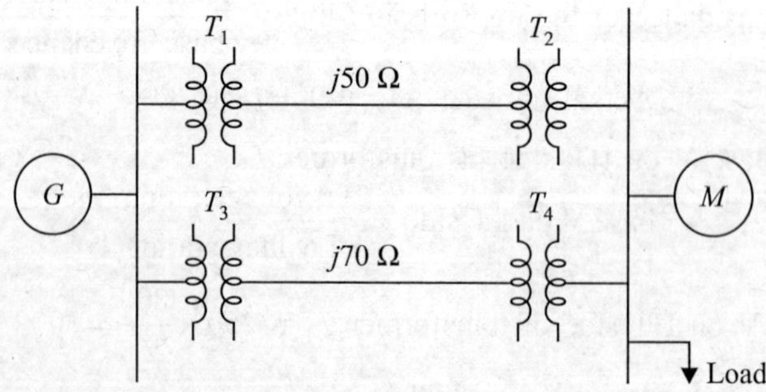

Figure 1.11 Single line diagram of power system of Example 1.6.

G : 90 MVA, 13.8 kV, $X = 18\%$

T_1 : 50 MVA, 13.8/220 kV, $X = 10\%$

T_2 : 50 MVA, 220/11 kV, $X = 10\%$

T_3 : 50 MVA, 13.8/132 kV, $X = 10\%$
T_4 : 50 MVA, 132/11 kV, $X = 10\%$
M : 80 MVA, 10.45 kV, $X = 20\%$
Load : 57 MVA, 0.8 p.f lagging at 10.45 kV
Line 1 = $j50\ \Omega$; Line 2 = $j70\ \Omega$

Solution:

Base MVA, $\text{MVA}_{\text{new}} = 100$ MVA
Base kV, $\text{kV}_{\text{new}} = 13.8$ kV

Reactance of generator G_1

$$X_{\text{p.u.(new)}} = X_{\text{p.u.(given)}} \times \left(\frac{\text{kV}_{\text{given}}}{\text{kV}_{\text{new}}}\right)^2 \times \left(\frac{\text{MVA}_{\text{new}}}{\text{MVA}_{\text{given}}}\right)$$

$X_{\text{p.u.(given)}} = 0.18$ p.u., $\text{MVA}_{\text{given}} = 90$, $\text{MVA}_{\text{new}} = 100$, $\text{kV}_{\text{given}} = 13.8$, $\text{kV}_{\text{new}} = 13.8$

$$X_{\text{p.u.(new)}} = 0.18 \times \left(\frac{13.8}{13.8}\right)^2 \times \left(\frac{100}{90}\right) = j0.2 \text{ p.u.}$$

Reactance of transformer T_1 (primary side)

$$X_{\text{p.u.(new)}} = X_{\text{p.u.(given)}} \times \left(\frac{\text{kV}_{\text{given}}}{\text{kV}_{\text{new}}}\right)^2 \times \left(\frac{\text{MVA}_{\text{new}}}{\text{MVA}_{\text{given}}}\right)$$

$X_{\text{p.u.(given)}} = 0.1$ p.u., $\text{MVA}_{\text{given}} = 50$, $\text{MVA}_{\text{new}} = 100$, $\text{kV}_{\text{given}} = 13.8$, $\text{kV}_{\text{new}} = 13.8$

$$X_{\text{p.u.(new)}} = 0.1 \times \left(\frac{13.8}{13.8}\right)^2 \times \left(\frac{100}{50}\right) = j0.2 \text{ p.u.}$$

Reactance of transmission line $j50\ \Omega$

$$\text{Per unit reactance of the transmission line} = \frac{\text{actual reactance, }\Omega}{\text{base reactance, }\Omega}$$

$$\text{Actual reactance} = 50\ \Omega$$

$$\text{Base kV on HT side of transformer } T_1 = \text{base kV on LT side} \times \frac{\text{HT voltage rating}}{\text{LT voltage rating}}$$

$$\text{Base kV on HT side of transformer } T_1 = 13.8 \times \frac{220}{13.8} = 220 \text{ kV}$$

$$\text{kV}_{\text{new}} = 220 \text{ kV}$$

$$\text{Base impedance} = \frac{(\text{kV}_{\text{new}})^2}{\text{MVA}_{\text{new}}} = \frac{220^2}{100} = 484\ \Omega$$

$$\text{Per unit reactance of the transmission line} = \frac{\text{actual reactance, } \Omega}{\text{base reactance, } \Omega}$$

$$= \frac{50}{484} = j0.1033 \text{ p.u.}$$

Reactance of transformer T_2 (secondary side)

$$X_{\text{p.u.(new)}} = X_{\text{p.u.(given)}} \times \left(\frac{\text{kV}_{\text{given}}}{\text{kV}_{\text{new}}}\right)^2 \times \left(\frac{\text{MVA}_{\text{new}}}{\text{MVA}_{\text{given}}}\right)$$

$X_{\text{p.u.(given)}} = 0.1$ p.u., $\text{MVA}_{\text{given}} = 50$, $\text{MVA}_{\text{new}} = 100$,
$\text{kV}_{\text{given}} = 220$,
$\text{kV}_{\text{new}} = 220$

$$X_{\text{p.u.(new)}} = 0.1 \times \left(\frac{220}{220}\right)^2 \times \left(\frac{100}{50}\right) = j0.2 \text{ p.u.}$$

Reactance of transformer T_3 (primary side)

$$X_{\text{p.u.(new)}} = X_{\text{p.u.(given)}} \times \left(\frac{\text{kV}_{\text{given}}}{\text{kV}_{\text{new}}}\right)^2 \times \left(\frac{\text{MVA}_{\text{new}}}{\text{MVA}_{\text{given}}}\right)$$

$X_{\text{p.u.(given)}} = 0.1$ p.u., $\text{MVA}_{\text{given}} = 50$, $\text{MVA}_{\text{new}} = 100$, $\text{kV}_{\text{given}} = 13.8$,
$\text{kV}_{\text{new}} = 13.8$

$$X_{\text{p.u.(new)}} = 0.1 \times \left(\frac{13.8}{13.8}\right)^2 \times \left(\frac{100}{50}\right) = j0.2 \text{ p.u.}$$

Reactance of transmission line $j70\ \Omega$

$$\text{Per unit reactance of the transmission line} = \frac{\text{actual reactance, } \Omega}{\text{base reactance, } \Omega}$$

$$\text{Actual reactance} = 70\ \Omega$$

Base kV on HT side of transformer T_3

$$= \text{base kV on LT side} \times \frac{\text{HT voltage rating}}{\text{LT voltage rating}}$$

$$\text{Base kV on HT side of transformer } T_3 = 13.8 \times \frac{132}{13.8} = 132 \text{ kV}$$

$$\text{kV}_{\text{new}} = 132 \text{ kV}$$

$$\text{Base impedance} = \frac{(\text{kV}_{\text{new}})^2}{\text{MVA}_{\text{new}}} = \frac{132^2}{100} = 174.24\ \Omega$$

$$\text{Per unit reactance of the transmission line} = \frac{\text{actual reactance, } \Omega}{\text{base reactance, } \Omega}$$

$$= \frac{70}{174.24} = j0.4017 \text{ p.u.}$$

Reactance of transformer T_4 (secondary side)

$$X_{\text{p.u.(new)}} = X_{\text{p.u.(given)}} \times \left(\frac{\text{kV}_{\text{given}}}{\text{kV}_{\text{new}}}\right)^2 \times \left(\frac{\text{MVA}_{\text{new}}}{\text{MVA}_{\text{given}}}\right)$$

$X_{\text{p.u.(given)}} = 0.1$ p.u., $\text{MVA}_{\text{given}} = 50$, $\text{MVA}_{\text{new}} = 100$, $\text{kV}_{\text{given}} = 132$;
$\text{kV}_{\text{new}} = 132$

$$X_{\text{p.u.(new)}} = 0.1 \times \left(\frac{132}{132}\right)^2 \times \left(\frac{100}{50}\right) = j0.2 \text{ p.u.}$$

Reactance of motor M

$$X_{\text{p.u.(new)}} = X_{\text{p.u.(given)}} \times \left(\frac{\text{kV}_{\text{given}}}{\text{kV}_{\text{new}}}\right)^2 \times \left(\frac{\text{MVA}_{\text{new}}}{\text{MVA}_{\text{given}}}\right)$$

$X_{\text{p.u.(given)}} = 0.2$ p.u., $\text{MVA}_{\text{given}} = 80$, $\text{MVA}_{\text{new}} = 100$,
$\text{kV}_{\text{given}} = 10.45$
$\text{kV}_{\text{new}} = ?$

$$\text{Base kV on LT side of transformer } T_4 = \text{base kV on HT side} \times \frac{\text{LT voltage rating}}{\text{HT voltage rating}}$$

$$\text{Base kV on LT side of transformer } T_4 = 132 \times \frac{11}{132} = 11 \text{ kV}$$

$$\text{kV}_{\text{new}} = 11 \text{ kV}$$

$$X_{\text{p.u.(new)}} = 0.2 \times \left(\frac{10.45}{11}\right)^2 \times \left(\frac{100}{80}\right) = j0.2256 \text{ p.u.}$$

The load at 0.8 p.f lagging is given by

$$S_L(3\phi) = 57\angle 36.87°$$

Load impedance is given by

$$Z_L = \frac{(V_{L-L})^2}{S_{L(3\phi)}} = \frac{10.45^2}{57\angle 36.87°} = (1.532 + j1.1495)\Omega$$

Base impedance for the load is given by

$$\text{Base impedance} = \frac{(\text{kV}_{\text{new}})^2}{\text{MVA}_{\text{new}}} = \frac{11^2}{100} = 1.21\,\Omega$$

$$\text{Per unit reactance of the transmission line} = \frac{\text{actual reactance, }\Omega}{\text{base reactance, }\Omega}$$

$$= \frac{1.532 + j1.1495}{1.21}$$

$$= (1.266 + j0.95) \text{ p.u.}$$

Reactance diagram (Figure 1.12)

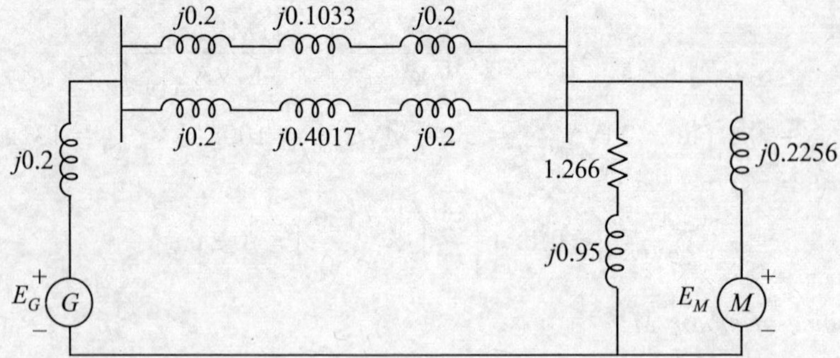

Figure 1.12 Reactance diagram of power system of Example 1.6.

1.6 Network Modelling

1.6.1 Bus Frame of Analysis

For a network with n number of nodes (buses) excluding the reference node, a set of following equations, one for each node can be written as

$$\begin{aligned} I_1 &= Y_{11}V_1 + Y_{12}V_2 + \cdots + Y_{1n}V_n \\ I_2 &= Y_{21}V_1 + Y_{22}V_2 + \cdots + Y_{2n}V_n \\ &\vdots \qquad\quad \vdots \qquad\qquad\quad \vdots \\ I_n &= Y_{n1}V_1 + Y_{n2}V_2 + \cdots + Y_{nn}V_n \end{aligned} \tag{1.15}$$

i.e.
$$I_i = \sum_{m=1}^{n} Y_{im}V_m \qquad i = 1, 2, 3 \ldots, n \tag{1.16}$$

where I_i is the current entering the ith bus

V_m is the voltage to reference of bus m

Y_{im} is the admittance between the buses i and m.

In matrix form,
$$\begin{bmatrix} I_1 \\ I_2 \\ \vdots \\ I_n \end{bmatrix} = \begin{bmatrix} Y_{11} & Y_{12} & \cdots & Y_{1n} \\ Y_{21} & Y_{22} & \cdots & Y_{2n} \\ \vdots & \vdots & \vdots & \vdots \\ Y_{n1} & Y_{n2} & \cdots & Y_{nn} \end{bmatrix} \begin{bmatrix} V_1 \\ V_2 \\ \vdots \\ V_n \end{bmatrix} \tag{1.17}$$

i.e.
$$I_{\text{bus}} = Y_{\text{bus}}\, V_{\text{bus}} \tag{1.18}$$

where Y_{bus} is the bus admittance matrix.

i.e.
$$Y_{\text{bus}} = \begin{bmatrix} Y_{11} & Y_{12} & \cdots & Y_{1n} \\ Y_{21} & Y_{22} & \cdots & Y_{2n} \\ \vdots & \vdots & \vdots & \vdots \\ Y_{n1} & Y_{n2} & \cdots & Y_{nn} \end{bmatrix} \tag{1.19}$$

Now,
$$V_{\text{bus}} = Z_{\text{bus}}\, I_{\text{bus}} \tag{1.20}$$

where Z_{bus} is the bus impedance matrix.

The diagonal elements of bus admittance matrix Y_{11}, Y_{22}, ..., Y_{nn} are called the short-circuit driving point admittances of the system bases, and the off-diagonal elements are called the short-circuit transfer admittances. Similarly, the diagonal elements of bus impedance matrices Z_{11}, Z_{22}, ..., Z_{nn} are called open circuit driving point impedances of the system bases, and the off-diagonal elements are known as open circuit transfer impedances.

To find out the elements of Z_{bus} and Y_{bus}, we need

1. Primitive network
2. Graph theory
3. Incidence matrices

1.6.2 Primitive Network

A network element may in general contain active and passive components. Network components are represented both in impedance form and in admittance form as shown in Figure 1.13.

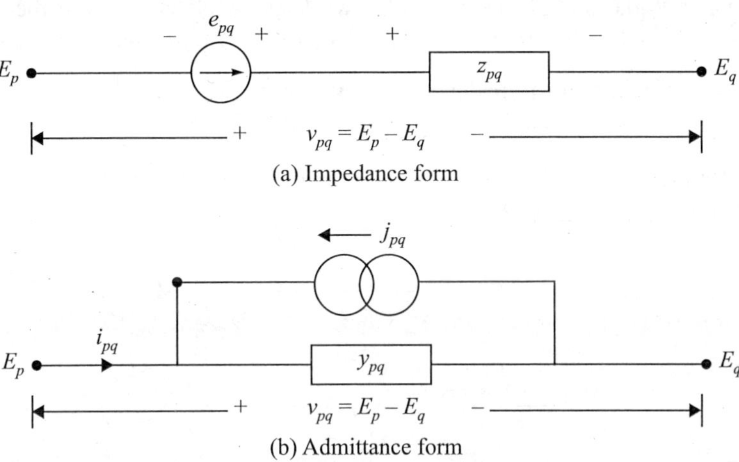

Figure 1.13 Primitive network.

In Figure 1.13, we have used the following notations:

v_{pq} = voltage across the element p-q
e_{pq} = voltage source in series with the element p-q
i_{pq} = current through the element p-q
z_{pq} = self impedance of the element p-q
j_{pq} = current source in parallel with the element p-q
y_{pq} = self admittance of the element p-q

In steady state condition, the variables v_{pq} and i_{pq} and the parameters of the elements z_{pq} and y_{pq} are real numbers for dc and complex numbers for ac.

The performance equation of the element in impedance form is

$$v_{pq} + e_{pq} = z_{pq} \times i_{pq} \tag{1.21}$$

The performance equation of the element in admittance form is

$$i_{pq} + j_{pq} = y_{pq} \times v_{pq} \tag{1.22}$$

The parallel current source in admittance form is related to the series voltage source in impedance form as

$$i_{pq} + j_{pq} = y_{pq} \times v_{pq}$$

or

$$j_{pq} = -i_{pq} + (y_{pq} \times v_{pq})$$

or

$$j_{pq} = -\left(\frac{v_{pq} + e_{pq}}{z_{pq}}\right) + (y_{pq} \times v_{pq})$$

∴

$$j_{pq} = -\, y_{pq} \times e_{pq} \tag{1.23}$$

A set of unconnected elements is defined as a primitive network. The performance equations of a primitive network can be derived from the above equations by expressing the variables as vectors and parameters as matrices.

The performance in impedance form $\mathbf{v} + \mathbf{e} = [z]\mathbf{i}$ (1.24)

The performance in admittance form $\mathbf{i} + \mathbf{j} = [y]\mathbf{v}$ (1.25)

Here $[z]$ and $[y]$ are primitive impedance and primitive admittance matrices, respectively, of the network.

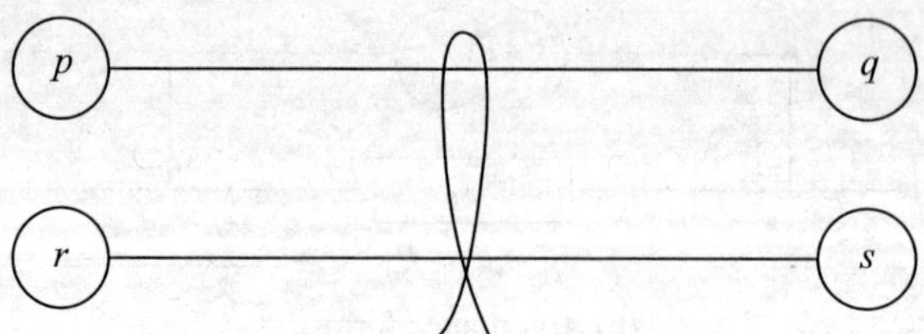

Figure 1.14 Mutual coupling between the elements *pq* and *rs*.

The mutual coupling between elements *pq* and *rs* is shown in Figure 1.14. The diagonal element of the matrix $[z]$ or matrix $[y]$ of the primitive network is the self impedance $z_{pq,pq}$ or self admittance $y_{pq,pq}$. The off-diagonal element is the mutual impedance $z_{pq,rs}$ or mutual admittance $y_{pq,rs}$ between the elements *pq* and *rs*.

1.6.3 Network Graph Theory

The geometrical structure of a network is sufficient to replace the network components by a single line segment irrespective of the characteristic of the components. These line segments are called ***element*** and their terminals are called ***nodes***. A node and an element are ***incident*** if the node is the terminal of the element. Nodes can be incident to one or more elements.

A ***graph*** shows the geometrical interconnection of the element of a network. The *rank of a graph* is $n - 1$, where n is the number of nodes in the graph. A ***subgraph*** is any subset of the graph. If each element of the connected graph is assigned a direction, it is then called ***oriented graph***. A graph is said to be ***planar***, if it can be drawn without crossover of edges, otherwise it is called non-planar.

Figure 1.15(a) shows the single line diagram of a simple power network consisting of generating stations, transformer, transmission lines and loads. Figure 1.15(b) shows the positive sequence network of the system depicted in Figure 1.15(a). The oriented connected graph is shown in Figure 1.16 for the same system.

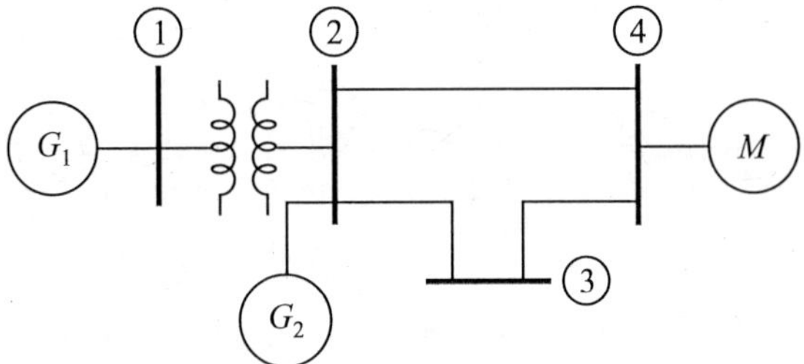

Figure 1.15(a) Sample single line diagram.

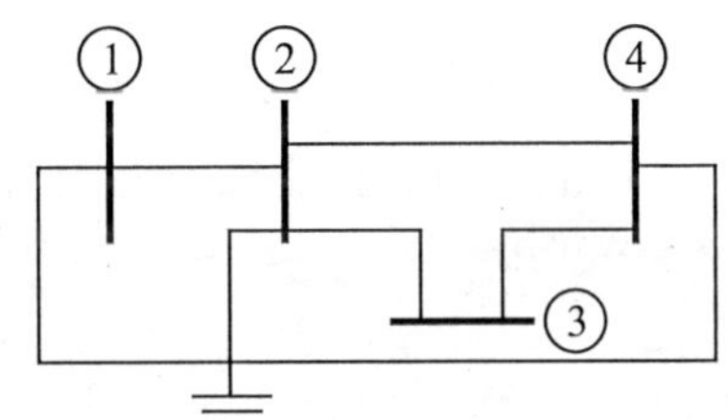

Figure 1.15(b) Positive sequence network diagram.

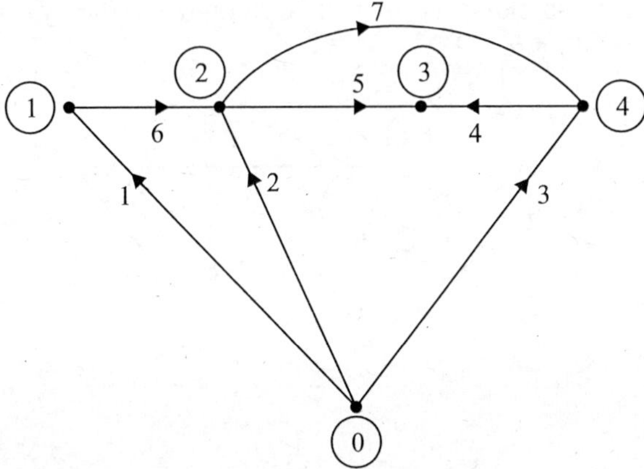

Figure 1.16 Oriented graph.

Tree and co-tree

A tree is a connected subgraph of a network which consists of all nodes of the original graph but no closed path. The graph of a network may have a number of trees. In general, if a tree contains n nodes, then it has $(n - 1)$ branches.

In forming a tree for a given graph, certain branches are removed. The branches thus opened are called links or link branches. The link for Figure 1.17, for example, is 5, 6 and 7. The set of all links of a given tree is called the co-tree of the graph.

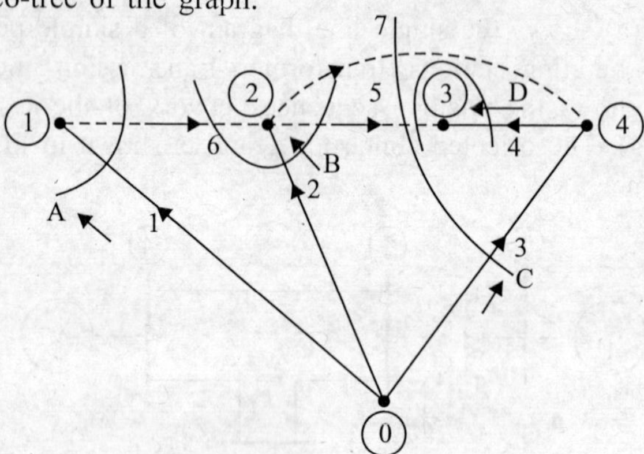

Figure 1.17 Tree of the representative power system of Figure 1.15(a).

The relation between the number of nodes and the number of branches in a tree is given by

$$b = n - 1 \tag{1.26}$$

If e is the total number of elements, then the number of links l of a connected graph with branches b is given by

$$l = e - b \tag{1.27}$$

Hence, from Eq. (1.26), the number of links l can be written as

$$l = e - n + 1 \tag{1.28}$$

A tree and the corresponding co-tree of the graph for the system are shown in Figure 1.17 and Figure 1.18.

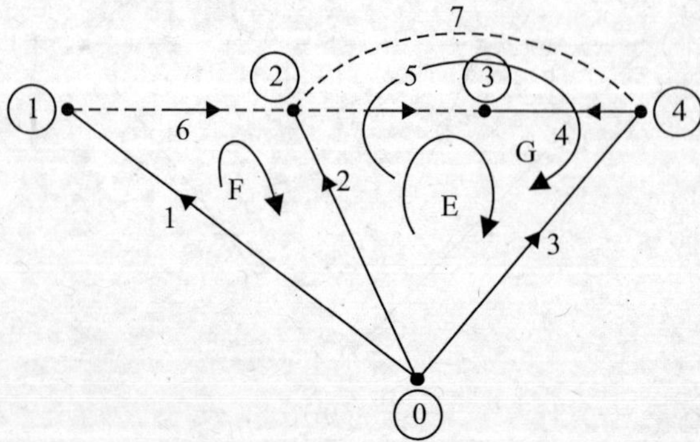

Figure 1.18 Co-tree of the representative power system of Figure 1.15(a).

1.6.4 Incidence Matrices

Incidence matrices are mostly used in graph theory. They are significant in developing the different networks matrices such as bus admittance matrix, bus impedance matrix using singular or non-singular transformation.

The following incidence matrices are of interest in power system analysis.

1. Element–node incidence matrices
2. Bus incidence matrix or element–bus incidence matrix
3. Basic loop incidence matrix
4. Basic cut-set incidence matrix

Element–node incidence matrices $(\bar{A})$

The incidence of elements to nodes in a connected graph is shown in Figure 1.15 by the element–node incidence matrix. The elements of the matrix are as follows:

$a_{ij} = 1$ if the ith element is incident to and oriented away from the jth node

$a_{ij} = -1$ if the ith element is incident to and oriented towards the jth node

$a_{ij} = 0$ if the ith element is not incident to the jth node

The dimension of the matrix $\bar{A}$ is $e \times n$, where $\boldsymbol{e}$ is the number of elements and n is the number of nodes in the graph.

$\bar{A} =$

e \ n	0	1	2	3	4
1	1	–1	0	0	0
2	1	0	–1	0	0
3	1	0	0	0	–1
4	0	0	0	–1	1
5	0	0	1	–1	0
6	0	1	–1	0	0
7	0	0	1	0	–1

Since

$$\sum_{j=0}^{4} a_{ij} = 0 \qquad i = 1, 2, 3, \ldots, n$$

The columns of $\bar{A}$ are linearly dependent. Hence, the rank of $\bar{A} < n$.

***Bus incidence matrix or element–bus incidence matrix* (A)**

Any node of a connected graph can be selected as the reference node. Then, the variables of the other nodes are referred to as buses. The matrix obtained from the element node incident matrix $(\bar{A})$ by deleting the columns corresponding to the reference node is the element bus incidence matrix or bus incidence matrix.

The dimension of the matrix A is $e \times (n - 1)$ or $e \times b$. Node **0** is the reference node.

e \ Bus	1	2	3	4
1	−1	0	0	0
2	0	−1	0	0
$A =$ 3	0	0	0	−1
4	0	0	−1	1
5	0	1	−1	0
6	1	−1	0	0
7	0	1	0	−1

Basic loop incidence matrix (C)

The incidence of elements to basic loops of a connected graph is shown in Figure 1.19 by the basic loop incidence matrix. The elements of this matrix are:

$C_{ij} = 1$ if the ith element is incident to and oriented in the same direction as the jth basic loop

$C_{ij} = -1$ if the ith element is incident to and oriented in the opposite direction as the jth basic loop

$C_{ij} = 0$ if the ith element is not incident to the jth basic loop

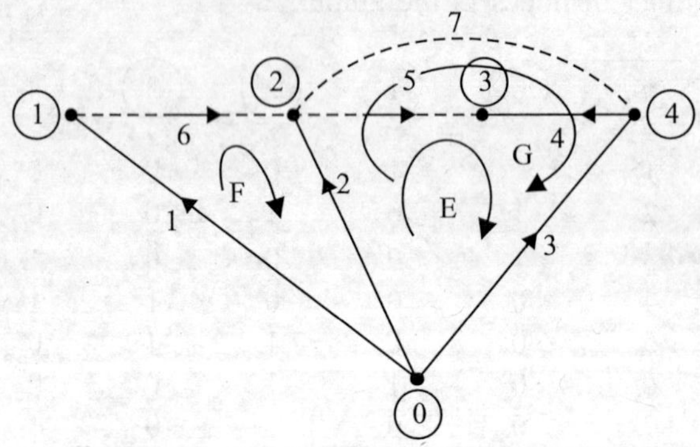

Figure 1.19 Basic loops E, F and G.

Element \ Basic loop	E	F	G
1	0	1	0
2	1	−1	1
$C =$ 3	−1	0	−1
4	−1	0	0
5	1	0	0
6	0	1	0
7	0	0	1

Basic cut-set incidence matrix (D)

The incidence of elements to basic cut-set of a connected graph is shown in Figure 1.20 by the basic cut-set incidence matrix. The elements of this matrix are:

$d_{ij} = 1$ if the ith element is incident to the jth basic cut-set and oriented in the same direction of the jth basic cut-set

$d_{ij} = 1$ if the ith element is incident to the jth basic cut-set and oriented in the opposite direction of the jth basic cut-set

$d_{ij} = 0$ if the ith element is not incident to the jth basic cut-set

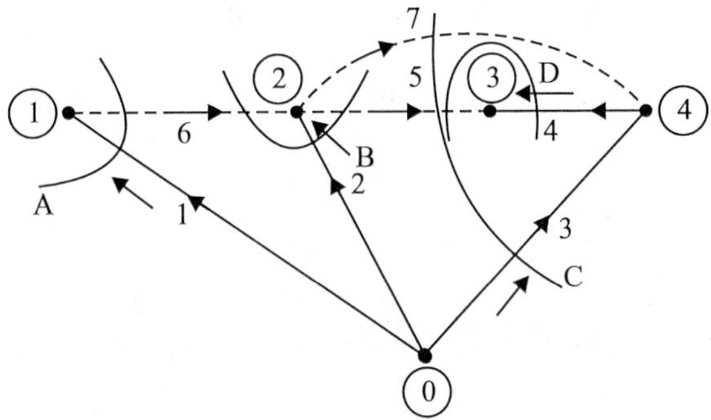

Figure 1.20 Basic cut-set of connected graph.

	Element \ Basic cut-set	A	B	C	D
	1	1	0	0	0
	2	0	1	0	0
	3	0	0	1	0
D =	4	0	0	0	1
	5	0	–1	1	1
	6	–1	1	0	0
	7	0	0	1	0

1.7 Formation of Bus Admittance Matrix [Y_{bus}]

The matrix consisting of the self admittance and the mutual admittance of the network of the power system is called the bus admittance matrix Y_{bus}. We will discuss here the following two methods by formulation of [Y_{bus}].

- Direct inspection method
- Singular transformation method (Primitive network)

1.7.1 Direct Inspection Method

Consider a simple three bus system (Figure 1.21).

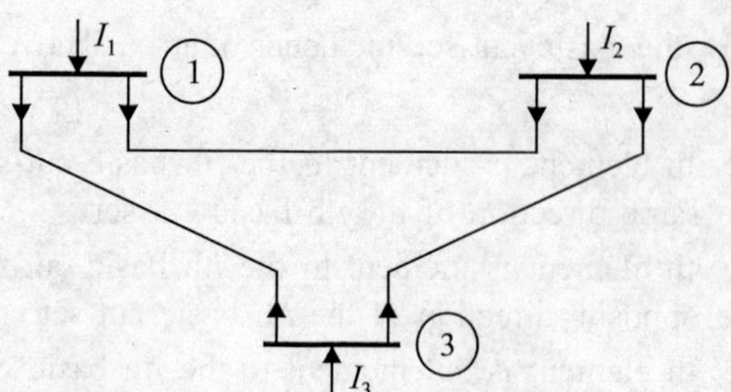

Figure 1.21 Simple three bus system.

Let I_1, I_2 and I_3 denote the current flowing into the buses. Applying KCL at each node:

At node 1:

$$I_1 = I_{11} + I_{12} + I_{13} \tag{1.29}$$

$$= y_{11}V_1 + (V_1 - V_2)y_{12} + (V_1 - V_3)y_{13}$$

$$= y_{11}V_1 + y_{12}V_1 - y_{12}V_2 + y_{13}V_1 - y_{13}V_3$$

$$= V_1(y_{11} + y_{12} + y_{13}) - y_{12}V_2 - y_{13}V_3$$

$$\therefore \quad I_1 = V_1Y_{11} + V_2Y_{12} + V_3Y_{13} \tag{1.30}$$

where

$$Y_{11} = y_{11} + y_{12} + y_{13} \quad \text{(Shunt charging admittance at bus)} \tag{1.31}$$

$$Y_{12} = -y_{12};\; Y_{13} = -y_{13} \tag{1.32}$$

At node 2:

$$I_2 = I_{22} + I_{21} + I_{23} \tag{1.33}$$

$$= y_{22}V_2 + (V_2 - V_1)y_{21} + (V_2 - V_3)y_{23}$$

$$= y_{22}V_2 + y_{21}V_2 - y_{21}V_1 + y_{23}V_2 - y_{23}V_3$$

$$= -y_{21}V_1 + V_2(y_{22} + y_{21} + y_{23}) - y_{23}V_3$$

$$\therefore \quad I_2 = V_1Y_{21} + V_2Y_{22} + V_3Y_{23} \tag{1.34}$$

where

$$Y_{22} = y_{21} + y_{22} + y_{23} \quad \text{(Shunt charging admittance at bus)} \tag{1.35}$$

$$Y_{21} = -y_{21};\; Y_{23} = -y_{23} \tag{1.36}$$

At node 3:

$$I_3 = I_{33} + I_{31} + I_{32} \tag{1.37}$$

$$= y_{33}V_3 + (V_3 - V_1)y_{31} + (V_3 - V_2)y_{32}$$

$$= y_{33}V_3 + y_{31}V_3 - y_{31}V_1 + y_{32}V_3 - y_{32}V_2$$

$$= -y_{31}V_1 - y_{32}V_2 + V_3(y_{33} + y_{31} + y_{32})$$

$$\therefore \quad I_3 = V_1Y_{31} + V_2Y_{32} + V_3Y_{33} \tag{1.38}$$

where

$$Y_{33} = y_{31} + y_{32} + y_{33} \quad \text{(Shunt charging admittance at bus)} \tag{1.39}$$

$$Y_{31} = -y_{31};\; Y_{32} = -y_{32} \tag{1.40}$$

The obtained nodal equations are now represented in matrix form as

$$\begin{bmatrix} I_1 \\ I_2 \\ I_3 \end{bmatrix} = \begin{bmatrix} Y_{11} & Y_{12} & Y_{13} \\ Y_{21} & Y_{22} & Y_{23} \\ Y_{31} & Y_{32} & Y_{33} \end{bmatrix} \begin{bmatrix} V_1 \\ V_2 \\ V_3 \end{bmatrix} \tag{1.41}$$

i.e.

$$[I_{\text{bus}}] = [Y_{\text{bus}}]\,[V_{\text{bus}}] \tag{1.42}$$

or

$$I_i = \sum_{j=1}^{n} Y_{ij} V_j \qquad i = 1, 2, 3, \ldots, n \tag{1.43}$$

Self admittance: The terms Y_{ii} are self admittance of respective nodes and represent the algebraic sum of all the admittances connected to that node. Each diagonal term in the $[Y_{\text{bus}}]$ matrix is the self admittance term.

$$Y_{ii} = \sum_{j=1}^{n} y_{ij} \tag{1.44}$$

Mutual admittance: The mutual admittance between two buses is the negative of the sum of all the admittances connected directly between these two buses. All the non-diagonal terms in the $[Y_{\text{bus}}]$ matrix are the mutual admittance terms.

$$Y_{ij} = -y_{ij} \tag{1.45}$$

EXAMPLE 1.7 Determine the bus admittance matrix $[Y_{\text{bus}}]$ of the representative power system shown in Figure 1.22. Data for this system is given in Table 1.1.

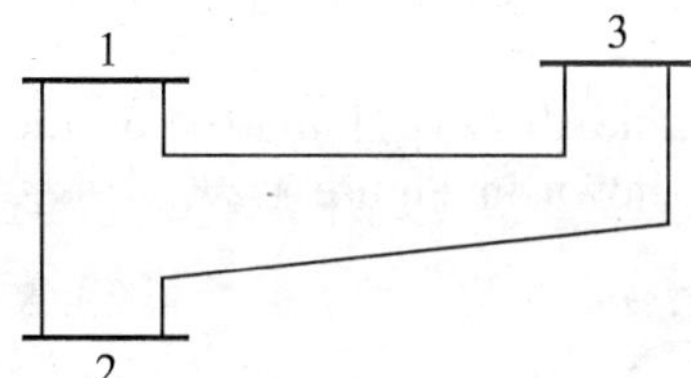

Figure 1.22 Representative power system: Example 1.7.

Table 1.1 Data for Example 1.7

Bus code i–k	*Impedance, Z_{ik}*	*Line charging $y_{ij}/2$*
1–2	$0.02 + j0.06$	$j0.03$
1–3	$0.08 + j0.24$	$j0.025$
2–3	$0.06 + j0.18$	$j0.020$

Solution:

$$y_{11} = \frac{y'_{12}}{2} + \frac{y'_{13}}{2} = j0.03 + j0.025 = j0.055$$

$$y_{22} = \frac{y'_{21}}{2} + \frac{y'_{23}}{2} = j0.03 + j0.020 = j0.050$$

$$y_{33} = \frac{y'_{31}}{2} + \frac{y'_{32}}{2} = j0.025 + j0.020 = j0.045$$

$$y_{12} = \frac{1}{z_{10}} = \frac{1}{0.02 + j0.06} = 5 - j15$$

$$y_{13} = \frac{1}{z_{13}} = \frac{1}{0.08 + j0.24} = 1.25 - j3.75$$

$$y_{23} = \frac{1}{z_{23}} = \frac{1}{0.06 + j0.18} = 1.667 - j5$$

$$Y_{11} = y_{11} + y_{12} + y_{13} = j0.055 + 5 - j15 + 1.25 - j3.75 = 6.25 - j18.695$$

$$Y_{12} = Y_{21} = -y_{12} = -5 + j15$$

$$Y_{13} = Y_{31} = -y_{13} = -1.25 + j3.75$$

$$Y_{22} = y_{22} + y_{21} + y_{23} = j0.050 + 5 - j15 + 1.667 - j5 = 6.667 - j19.95$$

$$Y_{23} = Y_{32} = -y_{23} = -1.667 + j5$$

$$Y_{33} = y_{33} + y_{31} + y_{32} = j0.045 + 1.25 - j3.75 + 1.667 - j5$$
$$= 2.917 - j8.705$$

$$\therefore \qquad Y_{bus} = \begin{bmatrix} Y_{11} & Y_{12} & Y_{13} \\ Y_{21} & Y_{22} & Y_{23} \\ Y_{31} & Y_{32} & Y_{33} \end{bmatrix}$$

$$= \begin{bmatrix} 6.25 - j18.695 & -5 + j15 & -1.25 + j3.75 \\ -5 + j15 & 6.667 - j19.95 & -1.667 + j5 \\ -1.25 + j3.75 & -1.667 + j5 & 2.917 - j8.705 \end{bmatrix}$$

EXAMPLE 1.8 Determine the $[Y_{bus}]$ matrix of the representative power system network diagram shown in Figure 1.23.

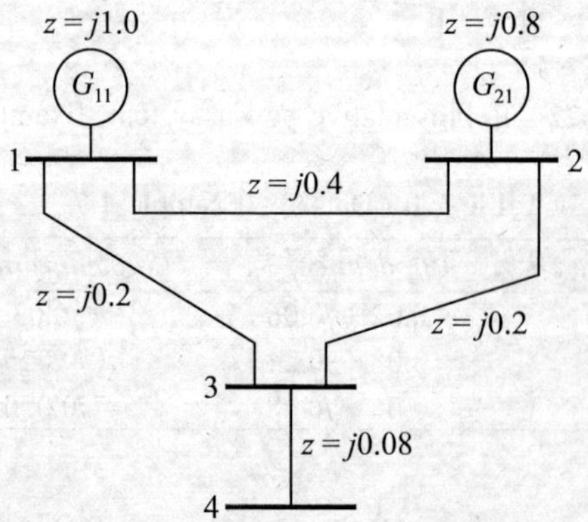

Figure 1.23 Representative power system: Example 1.8.

Solution:

$$y_{11} = \frac{1}{z_{11}} = \frac{1}{j1.0} = -j1.0$$

$$y_{22} = \frac{1}{z_{22}} = \frac{1}{j0.8} = -\,j1.25$$

$$y_{12} = \frac{1}{z_{12}} = \frac{1}{j0.4} = -\,j2.5$$

$$y_{13} = \frac{1}{z_{13}} = \frac{1}{j0.2} = -\,j5$$

$$y_{23} = \frac{1}{z_{23}} = \frac{1}{j0.2} = -\,j5$$

$$y_{34} = \frac{1}{z_{34}} = \frac{1}{j0.08} = -\,j12.5$$

$$Y_{11} = y_{10} + y_{12} + y_{13} = -j1.0 - j2.5 - j5 = -\,j8.5$$

$$Y_{12} = Y_{21} = -y_{12} = j2.5$$

$$Y_{13} = Y_{31} = -y_{13} = j5$$

$$Y_{22} = y_{20} + y_{21} + y_{23} = -j1.25 - j2.5 - j5 = -j8.75$$

$$Y_{23} = Y_{32} = -y_{23} = j5$$

$$Y_{33} = y_{31} + y_{32} + y_{34} = -j5 - j5 - j12.5 = -j22.5$$

$$Y_{44} = y_{43} = -j12.5$$

$$\therefore \qquad Y_{bus} = \begin{bmatrix} -j8.5 & j2.5 & j5 & 0 \\ j2.5 & -j8.75 & j5 & 0 \\ j5 & j5 & -j22.5 & -j12.5 \\ 0 & 0 & -j12.5 & -j12.5 \end{bmatrix}$$

EXAMPLE 1.9 Determine the $[Y_{bus}]$ matrix of the representative power system network diagram shown in Figure 1.24.

Verify the result using MATLAB program.

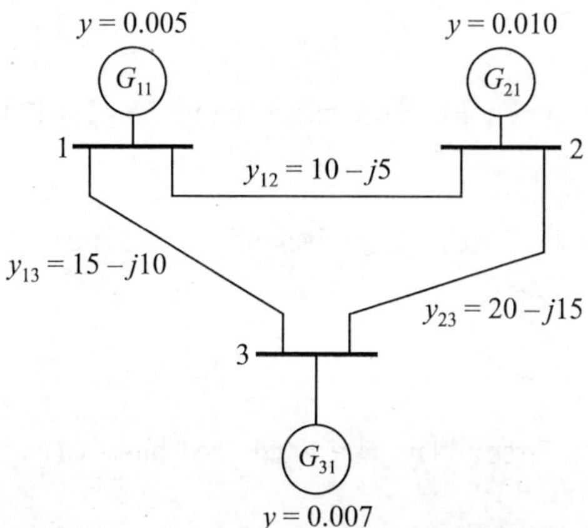

Figure 1.24 Representative power system: Example 1.9.

Solution:

$y_{11} = 0.005$

$y_{22} = 0.010$

$y_{33} = 0.007$

$y_{12} = 10 - j5$

$y_{13} = 15 - j10$

$y_{23} = 20 - j15$

$Y_{11} = y_{11} + y_{12} + y_{13} = 0.005 + 10 - j5 + 15 - j10 = 25.0050 - j15$

$Y_{22} = Y_{21} = -y_{12} = -10 + j5$

$Y_{13} = Y_{31} = -y_{13} = -15 + j10$

$Y_{22} = y_{22} + y_{21} + y_{23} = 0.010 + 10 - j5 + 20 - j15 = 30.010 - j20$

$Y_{23} = Y_{32} = -y_{23} = -20 + j15$

$Y_{33} = y_{33} + y_{31} + y_{32} = 0.007 + 15 - j10 + 20 - j15 = 35.0070 - j25$

$$\therefore \qquad Y_{\text{bus}} = \begin{bmatrix} 25.0050 - j15 & -10 + j5 & -15 + j10 \\ -10 + j5 & 30.010 - j20 & -20 + j15 \\ -15 + j10 & -20 + j15 & 35.0070 - j25 \end{bmatrix}$$

1.7.2 MATLAB Program for [Y_{bus}] Formation Using the Direct Inspection Method

```
clear all;
clc;
close all;
n=input('\n\n Enter the number of buses n=');
b=input('\n\n press your:\n>>1.for impedance  2.for admittance
\n');
if (b==2)
    fprintf('\n\n Enter the admittance value:');
end
if(b==1)
    fprintf('\n\n Enter the impedance value:');
end
for i=1:n
    for j=i+1:n
    a(i,j)=0;
    fprintf('\n Enter the bus %d to bus %d values:',i,j);
    a(i,j)=input('');
    if(b~=2&a(i,j)~=0)
      a(i,j)=1/a(i,j);
```

```
    end
    a(j,i)=a(i,j);
  end
end
d=input('\n\n   Is there any admittance value in source?\n
Press "1" for yes and "2" for no:');
if (d==1)
    for i=1:n
      fprintf('\n Enter for bus %d:',i);
      a(i,i)=input('');
    end
end
for i=1:n
      for j=1:n
        if(i~=j)
          a(i,i)=a(i,i)+a(i,j);
          y(i,j)=-a(i,j);
        end
      end
      y(i,i)=a(i,i);
end
fprintf('\n\n Y bus=:>>\n\n');
display(y);
```

```
output:
-----

Enter the number of buses n=3
    press your:
>>1.for impedance  2.for admittance
    2
    Enter the admittance value:
    Enter the bus 1 to bus 2 values:10-5j
    Enter the bus 1 to bus 3 values:15-10j
    Enter the bus 2 to bus 3 values:20-15j
      Is there any admittance value in source?
    Press "1" for yes and "2" for no:1
    Enter for bus 1:.005
    Enter for bus 2:.010
    Enter for bus 3:.007
    Y bus=:>>
y =
    25.0050 - 15.0000i - 10.0000 + 5.0000i - 15.0000 + 10.0000i
    -10.0000 + 5.0000i  30.0100 - 20.0000i - 20.0000 + 15.0000i
    -15.0000 + 10.0000i - 20.0000 + 15.0000i  35.0070 - 25.0000i
```

1.7.3 Formation of $[Y_{bus}]$ Using Power World Simulator

1. Start the Power World Simulator by clicking the icon
2. Go to file and click New Case and new window will open

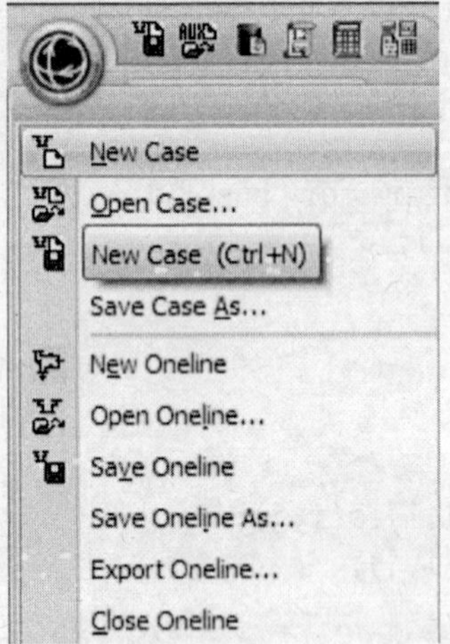

3. Select the draw tab which is on the top.

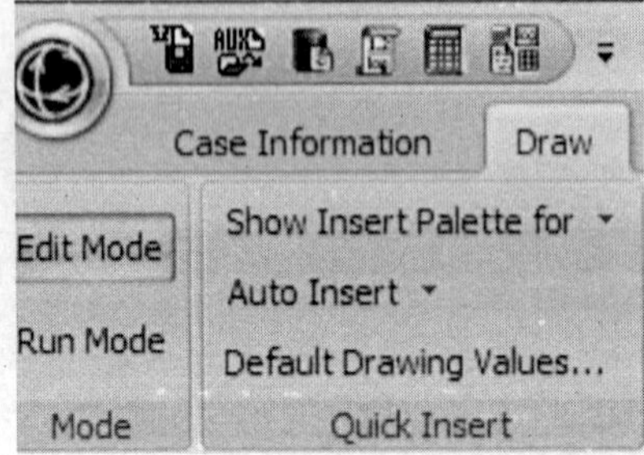

4. Using the option Network in the menu draw the one line diagram.

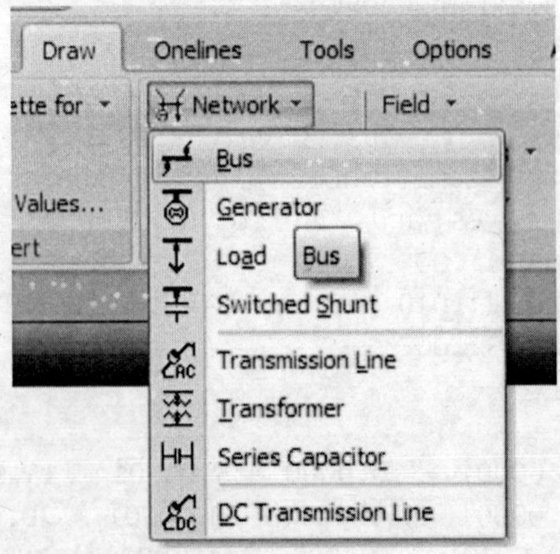

5. The input data for Buses, Generators, Loads, Transmission lines can be given by selecting the bus in the Network menu and left clicking the mouse in the new window opened.

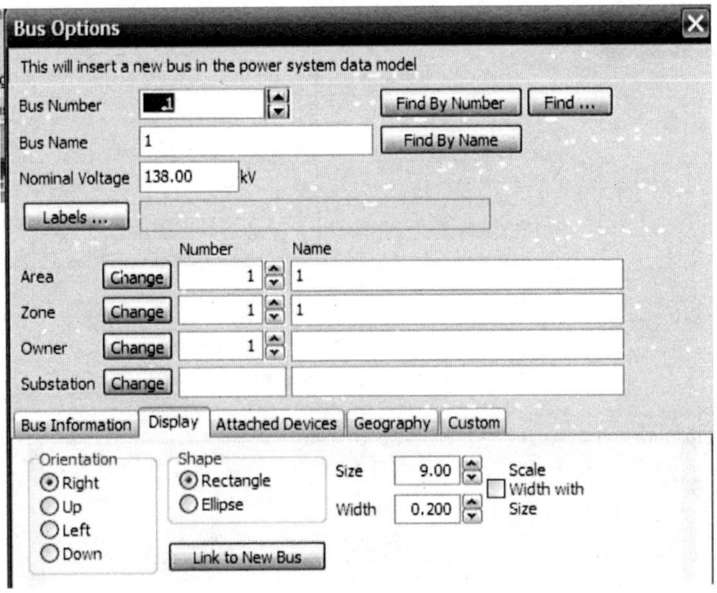

6. The bus can be shown as

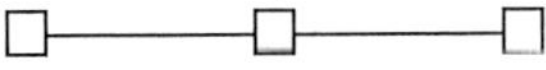

7. The same procedure is followed to draw generators, loads, etc.
8. Then the one line diagram for the 5 bus system can be obtained as

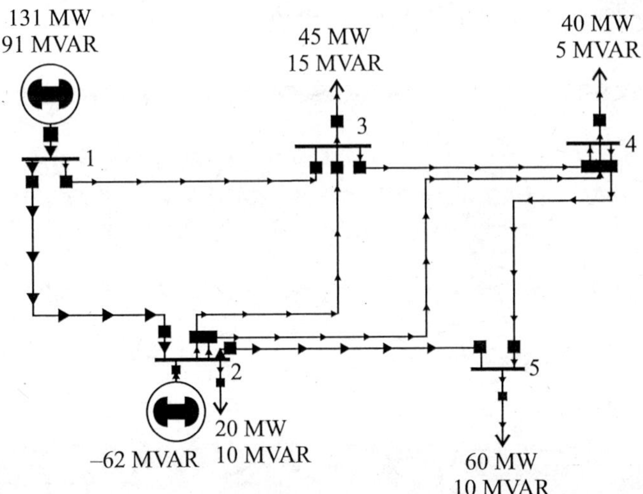

9. Go to Case information tab in the menu and select Solution details in the network tab, and select Y_{Bus}.

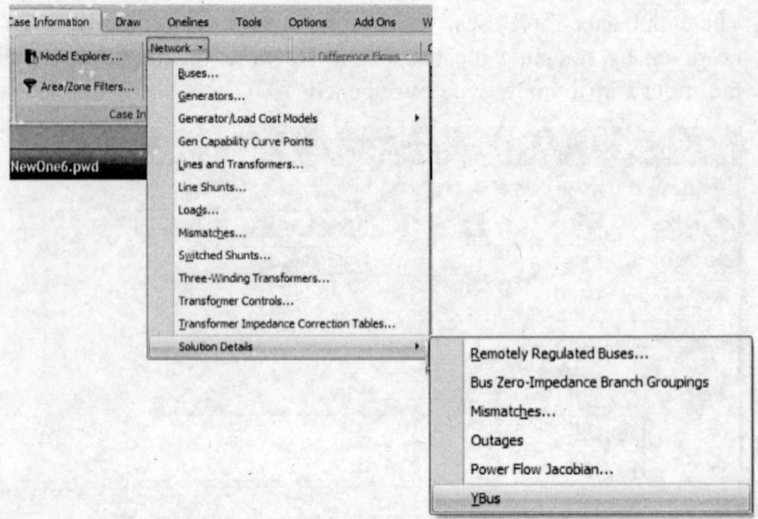

10. Then the matrix $[Y_{\text{bus}}]$ will be displayed as

	Number	Name	Bus 1	Bus 2	Bus 3	Bus 4	Bus 5
1	1	1	6.25 - j18.70	-5.00 + j15.00	-1.25 + j3.75		
2	2	2	-5.00 + j15.00	10.83 - j32.42	-1.67 + j5.00	-1.67 + j5.00	-2.50 + j7.50
3	3	3	-1.25 + j3.75	-1.67 + j5.00	12.92 - j38.70	-10.00 + j30.00	
4	4	4		-1.67 + j5.00	-10.00 + j30.00	12.92 - j38.70	-1.25 + j3.75
5	5	5		-2.50 + j7.50		-1.25 + j3.75	3.75 - j11.21

1.7.4 Formation of $[Y_{\text{bus}}]$ Using PSS/E

Let us consider a sample of 5 a bus system.

Bus data:

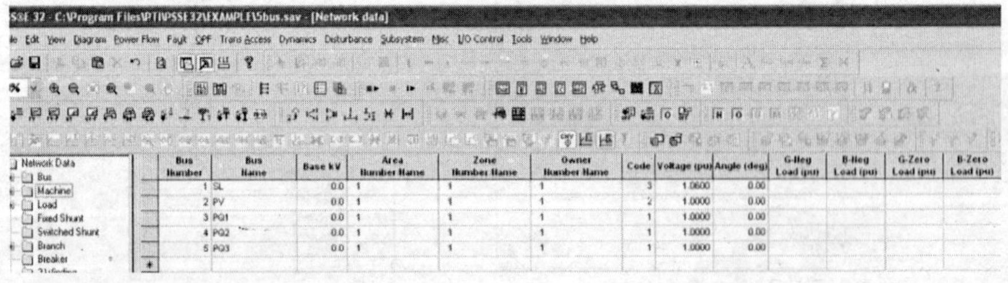

Bus Number	Bus Name	Base kV	Area Number Name	Zone Number Name	Owner Number Name	Code	Voltage (pu)	Angle (deg)	G-Neg Load (pu)	B-Neg Load (pu)	G-Zero Load (pu)	B-Zero Load (pu)
1	SL	0.0	1	1	1	3	1.0600	0.00				
2	PV	0.0	1	1	1	2	1.0000	0.00				
3	PQ1	0.0	1	1	1	1	1.0000	0.00				
4	PQ2	0.0	1	1	1	1	1.0000	0.00				
5	PQ3	0.0	1	1	1	1	1.0000	0.00				

Machine data:

Bus Number	Bus Name	Id	Code	VSched (pu)	Remote Bus	In Service	Pgen (MW)	Pmax (MW)	Pmin (MW)	Qgen (Mvar)	Qmax (Mvar)	Qmin (Mvar)	Mbase (MVA)	R Source (pu)	X Source (pu)	RTran (pu)
1	SL	1	3	1.0000	0	☑	0.0000	9999.0000	-9999.0000	0.0000	100.0000	90.0000	100.00	0.000000	1.000000	0.00000
2	PV	1	2	1.0000	0	☑	40.0000	9999.0000	-9999.0000	0.0000	-61.5900	-62.0000	100.00	0.000000	1.000000	0.00000

Load data:

	Bus Number	Bus Name	Id	Area Number Name	Zone Number Name	Owner Number Name	In Service	Scalable	Pload (MW)	Qload (Mvar)	IPload (MW)	IQload (Mvar)	YPload (MW)	YQload (Mvar)
	2	PV	1	1	1	1	✓	✓ Yes	20.0000	10.0000	0.0000	0.0000	0.0000	0.0000
	3	PQ1	1	1	1	1	✓	✓ Yes	45.0000	15.0000	0.0000	0.0000	0.0000	0.0000
	4	PQ2	1	1	1	1	✓	✓ Yes	40.0000	5.0000	0.0000	0.0000	0.0000	0.0000
	5	PQ3	1	1	1	1	✓	✓ Yes	60.0000	10.0000	0.0000	0.0000	0.0000	0.0000
*							✓	✓ Yes						

Bus | Plant | Machine | **Load** | Fixed Shunt | Switched Shunt | Branch | Breaker | 2 Winding | 3 Winding | Impedance table | FACTS | 2-Term DC | VSC DC | N-Term DC | Area

Branch data:

	From Bus Number	From Bus Name	To Bus Number	To Bus Name	Id	Line R (pu)	Line X (pu)	Charging (pu)	In Service	Metered	Rate A (I as MVA)	Rate B (I as MVA)	Rate C (I as MVA)	Line G From (pu)	Line B From (pu)	Line G To (pu)	Line To (p
	1	SL	2	PV	1	0.020000	0.060000	0.060000	✓	✓ From	0.0	0.0	0.0	0.00000	0.00000	0.00000	0.0
	1	SL	3	PQ1	1	0.080000	0.240000	0.050000	✓	✓ From	0.0	0.0	0.0	0.00000	0.00000	0.00000	0.0
	2	PV	3	PQ1	1	0.060000	0.180000	0.040000	✓	✓ From	0.0	0.0	0.0	0.00000	0.00000	0.00000	0.0
	2	PV	4	PQ2	1	0.060000	0.180000	0.040000	✓	✓ From	0.0	0.0	0.0	0.00000	0.00000	0.00000	0.0
	2	PV	5	PQ3	1	0.040000	0.120000	0.030000	✓	✓ From	0.0	0.0	0.0	0.00000	0.00000	0.00000	0.0
	3	PQ1	4	PQ2	1	0.010000	0.030000	0.020000	✓	✓ From	0.0	0.0	0.0	0.00000	0.00000	0.00000	0.0
	4	PQ2	5	PQ3	1	0.080000	0.240000	0.050000	✓	✓ From	0.0	0.0	0.0	0.00000	0.00000	0.00000	0.0
*									✓	✓ From							

Bus | Plant | Machine | Load | Fixed Shunt | Switched Shunt | **Branch** | Breaker | 2 Winding | 3 Winding | Impedance table | FACTS | 2-Term DC | VSC DC | N-Term DC | Area

In the network data we have to specify bus data, machine data, load data, fixed shunt data, etc., and save as six.sav file

Using slider file to create one line diagram

1. First we need to load a file as shown above.
2. Open **PSS/E.**
3. Go to file, and click new as shown below.

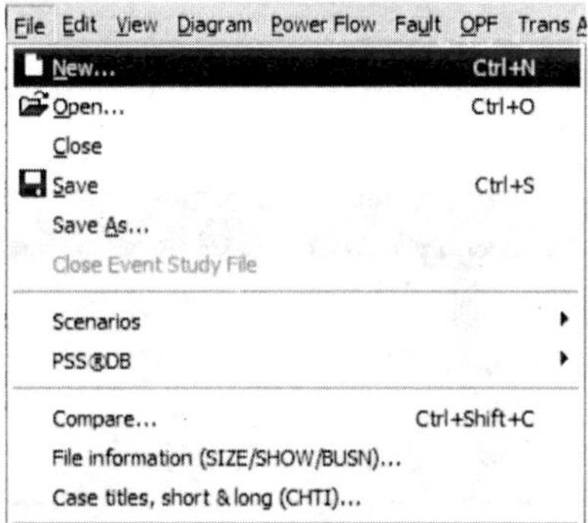

4. After clicking New the following will be displayed:

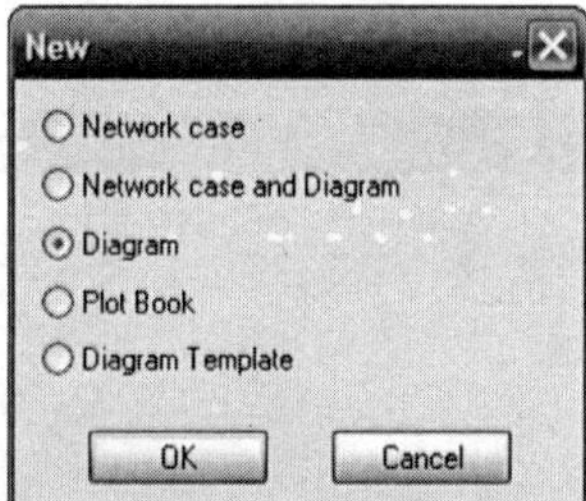

select **Diagram** and click **OK**.

5. A new diagram will be displayed.

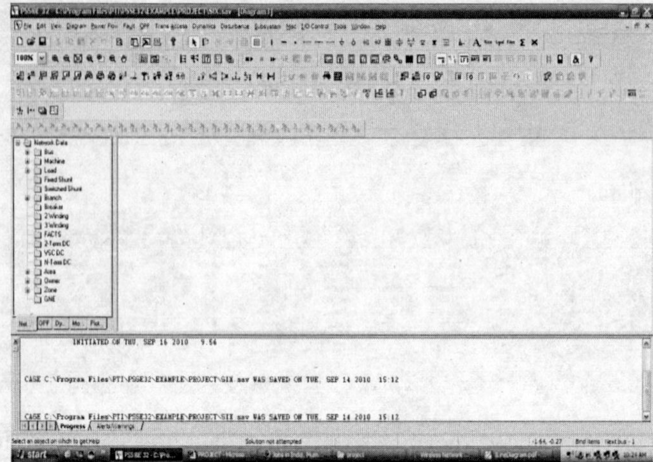

6. A bus can be imported from the data (*sav) file into the diagram. For this select **Auto Draw** function on the toolbar.

7. Click on an open place in a blank diagram, the following will be displayed:

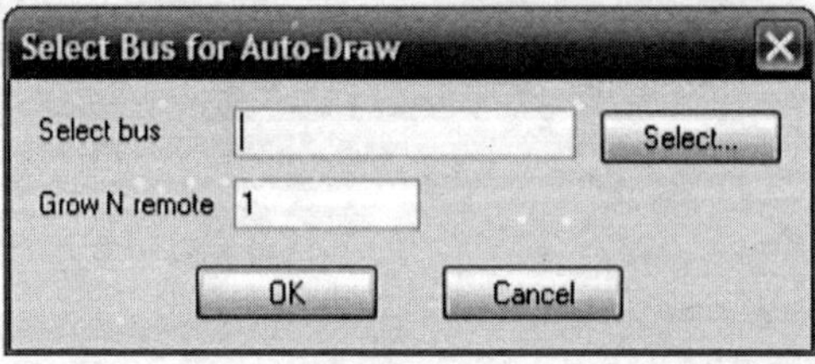

8. Next click **Select** in the select bus window or type the desired bus number from the *sav case file (In this case bus number 1 from six.sav file)

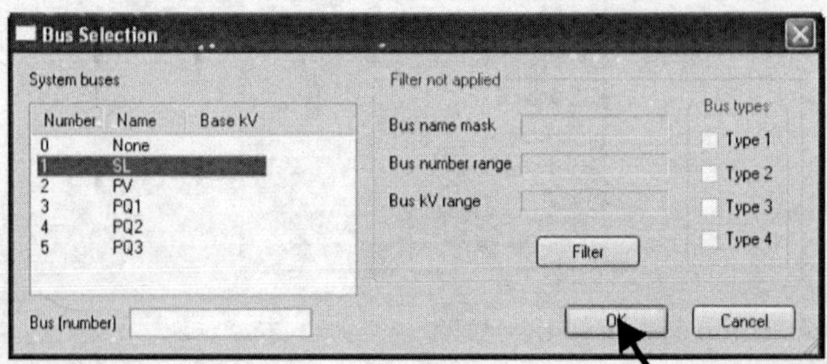

Click **OK** to return to the select bus window, which will show the bus selected.

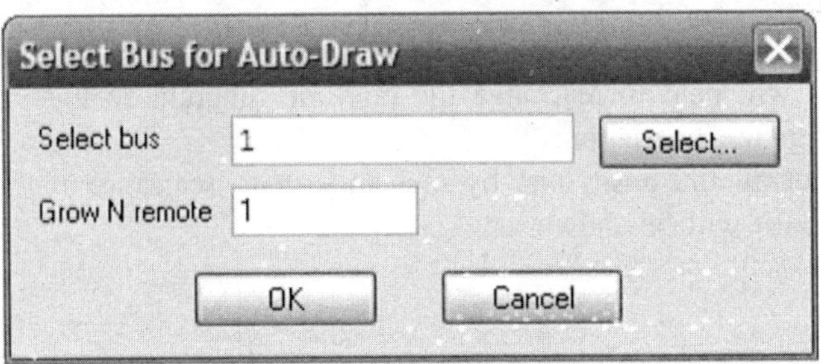

Click **OK.**

Note: As previously mentioned the bus can also be typed manually **to** skip the select bus window. If a bus number is not in a *.sav file, the following error message will be displayed.

click **OK** and enter any one of the bus numbers from *.sav file.

9. Select **bus number 1** and all devices connected to it are displayed as shown below:

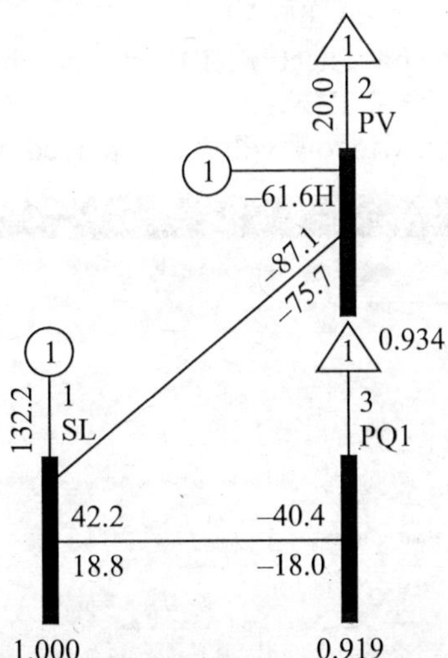

Select the **pointer** from the toolbar to exit out of the **AutoDraw** function.

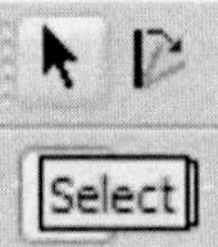

This will help to rearrange the one-line diagram so that no wires or ratings are overlapping.

10. Select all the buses one by one and try to rearrange them, the final diagram will be shown as:

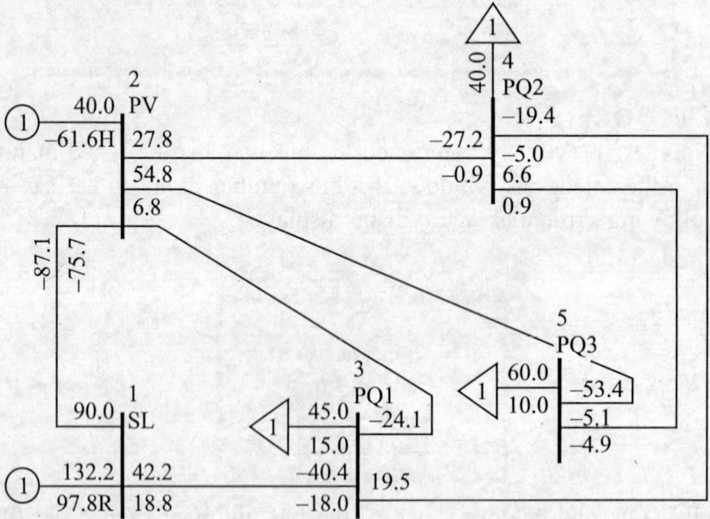

Formation of [Y_{bus}] using PSS/E

1. Load a file from a *.sav file.
2. Go to file menu and select **EXPORT** and then select **NETWORK ADMITTANCE MATRIX.**
3. Admittance matrix window will be displayed as

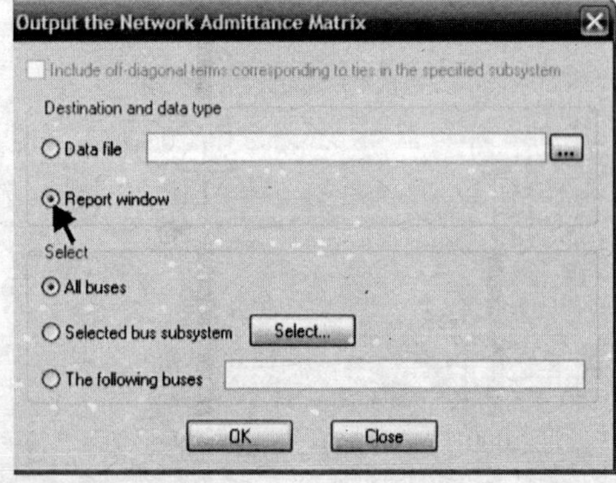

Select **REPORT WINDOW** and click **OK**.

4. $[Y_{\text{bus}}]$ matrix can be obtained in the report window as:

```
5,    5,  3.75000000000000     , -11.2099999999627
5,    4, -1.25000000000000     ,  3.75000000000000
5,    2, -2.50000000000000     ,  7.50000000000000
4,    4,  12.9166665077209     , -38.6950000002980
4,    5, -1.25000000000000     ,  3.75000000000000
4,    2, -1.66666650772095     ,  5.00000000000000
4,    3, -10.0000000000000     ,  30.0000000000000
2,    2,  10.8333330154419     , -32.4150000018999
2,    5, -2.50000000000000     ,  7.50000000000000
2,    4, -1.66666650772095     ,  5.00000000000000
2,    3, -1.66666650772095     ,  5.00000000000000
2,    1, -5.00000000000000     ,  15.0000000000000
3,    3,  12.9166665077209     , -38.6950000002980
3,    4, -10.0000000000000     ,  30.0000000000000
3,    2, -1.66666650772095     ,  5.00000000000000
3,    1, -1.25000000000000     ,  3.75000000000000
```

Progress | Alerts/Warnings | **Report**

1.7.5 Singular Transformation Method

The matrix $[Y_{\text{bus}}]$ can be determined by using the bus incidence matrix A and the related variable parameters of the primitive network quantities of the interconnected network.

From the primitive network equation,

$$i + j = [y]\overline{V} \tag{1.46}$$

Multiplying both sides of Eq. (1.46) by A^T, we get

$$A^T i + A^T j = A^T [y]\overline{V} \tag{1.47}$$

According to KCL, the algebraic sum of the currents meeting at any node is equal to zero. Thus,

$$A^T i = 0 \tag{1.48}$$

Similarly, $A^T j$ is equal to the sum of the current sources of an element incident at a node. It is a column vector. Thus,

$$A^T j = I_{\text{bus}} \tag{1.49}$$

Substituting Eqs. (1.48) and (1.49) in Eq. (1.47), we have

$$I_{\text{bus}} = A^T [y]\overline{V} \tag{1.50}$$

Power into the network is $(\overline{I}^*_{\text{bus}})^T \overline{E}_{\text{bus}}$ and equal to the sum of powers in the primitive network, i.e. $(j^*)^T \overline{V}$

The power in the primitive network

$$(\overline{I}^*_{\text{bus}})^T \overline{E}_{\text{bus}} = (j^*)^T \overline{V} \tag{1.51}$$

Taking conjugate transpose of Eq. (1.49),

$$(\overline{I}^*_{\text{bus}})^T = (A^T)^{*T} (j^*)^T$$

But A is a real matrix, so $A^* = A$

From the matrix property, $(A^T)^T = A$

Applying these two conditions in Eq. (1.51),

$$(\bar{I}^*_{\text{bus}})^T = A(j^*)^T \tag{1.52}$$

Substituting Eq. (1.52) into Eq. (1.51),

$$A(j^*)^T \bar{E}_{\text{bus}} = (j^*)^T \bar{V} \tag{1.53}$$

$$A\bar{E}_{\text{bus}} = \bar{V} \tag{1.54}$$

Substituting $\bar{V}$ from Eq. (1.54) into Eq. (1.50),

$$\bar{I}_{\text{bus}} = A^T[y]A\bar{E}_{\text{bus}} \tag{1.55}$$

$$\therefore \quad \frac{\bar{I}_{\text{bus}}}{\bar{E}_{\text{bus}}} = Y_{\text{bus}} = A^T[y]A \tag{1.56}$$

EXAMPLE 1.10 Form the matrix $[Y_{\text{bus}}]$ using the singular transformation method for the system shown in Figure 1.24. The impedance data is given in the Table 1.2. Take (1) as the reference node.

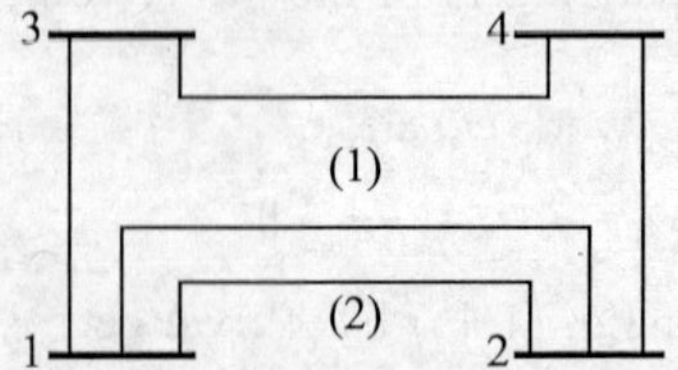

Figure 1.24 Sample power system of Example 1.10.

Table 1.2 Impedance data of Example 1.10

Element No.	*Self*	
	Bus code	***Impedance***
1	1–2 (1)	0.6
2	1–3	0.5
3	3–4	0.5
4	1–2 (2)	0.4
5	2–4	0.2

Solution: The oriented graph of the system is shown in Figure 1.25.

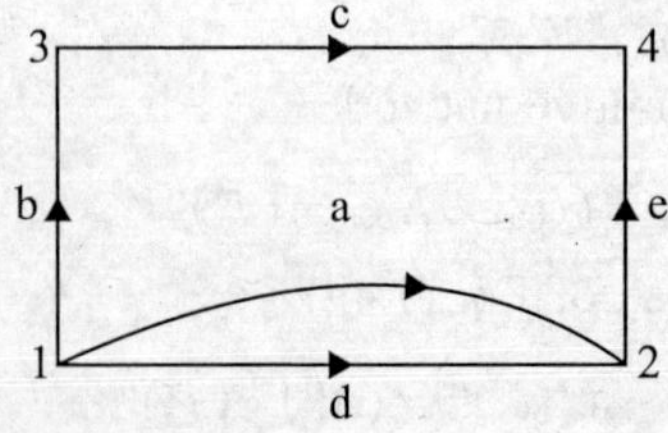

Figure 1.25 Oriented graph of the system shown in Figure 1.24.

Take (1) as the reference node,

$$\bar{A} = \begin{bmatrix} 1 & -1 & 0 & 0 \\ 1 & 0 & -1 & 0 \\ 0 & 0 & 1 & -1 \\ 1 & -1 & 0 & 0 \\ 0 & 1 & 0 & -1 \end{bmatrix}$$

Hence,

$$A = \begin{bmatrix} -1 & 0 & 0 \\ 0 & -1 & 0 \\ 0 & 1 & -1 \\ -1 & 0 & 0 \\ 1 & 0 & -1 \end{bmatrix}$$

and

$$A^T = \begin{bmatrix} -1 & 0 & 0 & -1 & 1 \\ 0 & -1 & 1 & 0 & 0 \\ 0 & 0 & -1 & 0 & -1 \end{bmatrix}$$

From the given impedance data,

$$Z_{\text{primitive}} = \begin{bmatrix} j0.6 & 0 & 0 & 0 & 0 \\ 0 & j0.5 & 0 & 0 & 0 \\ 0 & 0 & j0.5 & 0 & 0 \\ 0 & 0 & 0 & j0.4 & 0 \\ 0 & 0 & 0 & 0 & j0.2 \end{bmatrix}$$

Therefore,

$$Y_{\text{primitive}} = [Z_{\text{primitive}}]^{-1} = \begin{bmatrix} -j1.667 & 0 & 0 & 0 & 0 \\ 0 & -j2 & 0 & 0 & 0 \\ 0 & 0 & -j2 & 0 & 0 \\ 0 & 0 & 0 & -j2.5 & 0 \\ 0 & 0 & 0 & 0 & -j5 \end{bmatrix}$$

Hence

$$Y_{\text{bus}} = [A^T]\,[Y_{\text{primitive}}]\,[A]$$

Therefore,

$$Y_{\text{bus}} = \begin{bmatrix} -j9.167 & 0 & j5 \\ 0 & -j4 & j2 \\ j5 & j2 & -j7 \end{bmatrix}$$

EXAMPLE 1.11 Form the matrix $[Y_{\text{bus}}]$ using the singular transformation method for the system shown in Figure 1.26. The impedance data is given in Table 1.3. Take (1) as the reference node.

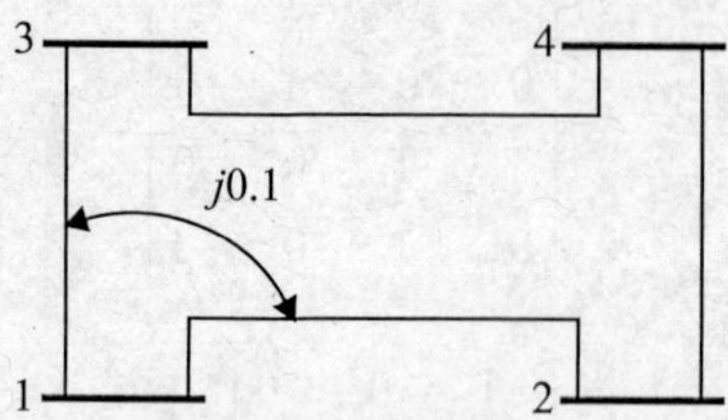

Figure 1.26 Sample power system of Example 1.11.

Table 1.3 Impedance data of Example 1.11

Element no.	*Self*		*Mutual*	
	Bus code	*Impedance*	*Bus code*	*Impedance*
1	1–2	0.5		
2	1–3	0.6	1–2	0.1
3	3–4	0.4		
4	2–4	0.3		

Solution: The oriented graph to the system is shown in Figure 1.27.

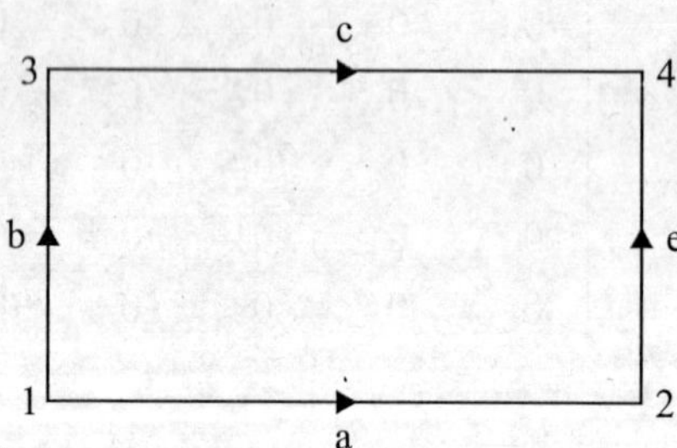

Figure 1.27 Oriented graph of the system shown in Figure 1.26.

Take (1) as the reference node,

$$\overline{A} = \begin{bmatrix} 1 & -1 & 0 & 0 \\ 1 & 0 & -1 & 0 \\ 0 & 0 & 1 & -1 \\ 0 & 1 & 0 & -1 \end{bmatrix}$$

Hence,

$$A = \begin{bmatrix} -1 & 0 & 0 \\ 0 & -1 & 0 \\ 0 & 1 & -1 \\ 1 & 0 & -1 \end{bmatrix}$$

and

$$A^T = \begin{bmatrix} -1 & 0 & 0 & 1 \\ 0 & -1 & 1 & 0 \\ 0 & 0 & -1 & -1 \end{bmatrix}$$

From the given impedance data,

$$Z_{\text{primitive}} = \begin{bmatrix} j0.5 & j0.1 & 0 & 0 \\ j0.1 & j0.6 & 0 & 0 \\ 0 & 0 & j0.4 & 0 \\ 0 & 0 & 0 & j0.3 \end{bmatrix}$$

Therefore,

$$Y_{\text{primitive}} = [Z_{\text{primitive}}]^{-1}$$

Consider the 2 × 2 matrix

$$\begin{bmatrix} j0.5 & j0.1 \\ j0.1 & j0.6 \end{bmatrix}^{-1} = \frac{1}{-0.29}\begin{bmatrix} j0.6 & -j0.1 \\ -j0.1 & j0.5 \end{bmatrix} = \begin{bmatrix} -j2.0689 & j0.3448 \\ j0.3448 & -j1.724 \end{bmatrix}$$

Hence,

$$Y_{\text{primitive}} = \begin{bmatrix} -j2.0689 & j0.3448 & 0 & 0 \\ j0.3448 & -j1.724 & 0 & 0 \\ 0 & 0 & -j2.5 & 0 \\ 0 & 0 & 0 & -j3.333 \end{bmatrix}$$

Now,

$$Y_{\text{bus}} = [A^T]\,[Y_{\text{primitive}}]\,[A]$$

Therefore,

$$Y_{\text{bus}} = \begin{bmatrix} -j5.4019 & j0.3448 & j3.333 \\ j0.3448 & -j4.224 & j2.5 \\ j3.333 & j2.5 & -j5.833 \end{bmatrix}$$

1.8 Solution Technique

The mathematical model of power system networks used for the purposes of load flow studies, short circuit studies and stabilities studies, is a set of linear or nonlinear algebraic equations or differential equations or both. But since the digital computer performs only four basic operations of addition, subtraction, multiplication and division, hence in order to solve these mathematical equations on the digital computer, it is necessary to transform these linear or nonlinear algebraic and differential equations to a set of four operations of addition, subtraction, multiplication and division with the help of numerical methods.

Solution of algebraic equations

There is a different numerical technique for the solution of algebraic equations. These algebraic equations can be expressed in the following form.

$$\left.\begin{aligned} f_1(x_1, x_2, ..., x_n) &= y_1 \\ f_2(x_1, x_2, ..., x_n) &= y_2 \\ \vdots \qquad & \quad \vdots \\ f_n(x_1, x_2, ..., x_n) &= y_n \end{aligned}\right\} \tag{1.57}$$

Here f_i are the functions relating the unknown variables x_i, with the known constants y_i. If any one of the f_i is nonlinear, the above algebraic equations form a set of nonlinear algebraic equations (equations involving power terms or the product of variables x_i). However, if all of the f_is are linear, then the above algebraic equations form a set of linear algebraic equations.

The linear algebraic equations can be expressed as follows:

$$[A]X = Y \tag{1.58}$$

where,

$[A]$ = the coefficient matrix of the physical system.
X = a column vector of unknowns
Y = a column vector of known constants.

Equation (1.58) can then be expressed as

$$\begin{bmatrix} a_{11} & a_{12} & \cdots & a_{1n} \\ a_{21} & a_{22} & \cdots & a_{2n} \\ \vdots & & & \vdots \\ a_{n1} & a_{n2} & \cdots & a_{nn} \end{bmatrix} \begin{bmatrix} x_1 \\ x_2 \\ \vdots \\ x_n \end{bmatrix} = \begin{bmatrix} y_1 \\ y_2 \\ \vdots \\ y_n \end{bmatrix} \tag{1.59}$$

In order to choose a numerical method to solve a set of algebraic equations on the digital computer, the following points must be considered:

(i) Number of steps needed to obtain the solution, i.e. speed at which the solution is obtained.
(ii) Resultant accuracy
(iii) Computer memory limitations.

The numerical techniques to solve a set of linear algebraic equations can be broadly classified into two main headings, namely.

(i) Direct method or exact method
(ii) Iterative technique

In the case of *direct method*, the solution can be obtained in a distinct number of steps. However, the number of steps required to obtain the solution depends upon the problem size, i.e. the order of the coefficient matrix [A] and the numerical method used. Hence before use, it is possible to compare different direct methods since the number of steps required to obtain the solution is known in advance. The only error is the loss of significant digits which is not bounded. The solution will be far from nominal solution because the round-off error goes on getting accumulated after each step. The round-off error results due to the subtraction or division by two numbers which are nearly equal. If the round-off error is bounded, the solution obtained will be nearly exact. This is why this method is also known as *exact method.*

Direct methods are:

(i) Cramer's rule
(ii) Gauss elimination method and
(iii) Gauss–Jordan elimination method

In the case of *iterative techniques*, the solution is obtained in an orderly fashion starting from its initial approximate solution, i.e. initial guess. Here we start with the initial approximate solution. Thus the rate of convergence, i.e. the number of steps needed to obtain solution depends upon the initial guess, problem size (number of equations) and the iterative the techniques used. Thus depending upon these factors, the approximate solution may converge to the nominal solution, diverge or oscillate about the nominal solution. The round-off error in this case goes on getting corrected in each step, .i.e. in each iteration.

The iterative techniques are:

(i) Gauss iterative technique
(ii) Gauss–Seidel iterative technique
(iii) Newton–Raphson method.

1.8.1 Sparse Matrix Techniques for Large-Scale Power Systems

The term "sparsity" is used to indicate the relative absence of certain problem interconnections. Mathematically, we can define:

Given a finite discrete sample space Ω *and a nonempty set of sample S such that the cardinality* $|S|$ *of S is small compared to cardinality* $|\Omega|$ *of* Ω, i.e. $|S| \ll |\Omega|$ *is then said to be sparse with respect to S.*

Let

$$n = |S|$$

$$N = |\Omega|$$

The efficient handling of sparse matrices is at the heart of almost every non-trivial power systems computational problem. Engineering problems have two stages. The first stage is an understanding and formulation of the problem in precise terms. The second stage is the solution of the problem. Many problems in power systems result in formulations that require the use of large sparse matrices. The well-known problems that fit into this category include three classic problems: power flow, short circuit, and transient stability. To this list we can also add numerous other important system problems: electromagnetic transients, economic dispatch, optimal power flows, state estimation, and contingency studies, just to name a few. In addition, the problems that require finite element or finite-difference methods for their solution invariably end up in mathematical formulations where sparse matrices are involved. Sparse matrices are also important for electronic circuits and numerous other engineering problems. We describe sparse matrices primarily from the perspective of power system network, though most of the ideas and results are readily applicable to more general sparse matrix problems.

The key idea behind sparse matrices is computational complexity. Storage requirements for a full matrix increase as order n^2. Computational requirements for many full matrix operations increase as order n^3. By the very definition of a sparse matrix, the storage and computational requirements for most sparse matrix operations increase only linearly or close to linearly. Faster computers will help solve larger problems, but unless the speedups are of order n^3 they will not keep pace with the advantages attainable from sparsity in the larger problems of the future. Thus, sparse matrices have become and will continue to be important. This introduction retraces some of the principal steps in the progress on sparse matrix theory.

Sparse system

Most of the discrete sample spaces are sparsely populated. Natural occurrences of sparsity are wide ranging. The following is a partial list of the sparse systems:

(i) Networks of all kinds such as electric power, electronics and communications, hydraulics, etc.
(ii) Space trusses and frames of structures.
(iii) Roads, highways and airways connecting all the important cities of the world.
(iv) Street connections among intersections within a city.
(v) Matrices associated with algebraic equations resulting from different methods in the solution of differential equations.
(vi) Matrices arising in the discrete analysis of continuous functions.

1.8.2 Optimally Ordered Triangular Factorization

Usually, the objective in the matrix analysis of networks is to obtain the inverse of the matrix of coefficients of a system of simultaneous linear network equations. However, for large sparse systems such as those which occur in many network problems, the use of the inverse is very inefficient. In general, the matrix of the equations formed from the given conditions of a network problem is sparse, whereas its inverse is full. By means of an appropriately ordered triangular decomposition, the inverse of a sparse matrix can be expressed as a product of sparse matrix factors, thereby gaining an advantage in computational speed, storage, and reduction of round-off error.

The method consists of two parts:

1. Recording the operations of triangular decomposition of a matrix such that repeated direct solutions based on the matrix can be obtained without repeating the triangularization
2. Ordering the operations that tends to conserve the sparsity of the original system.

Either part can be applied independently, but the greatest benefit is obtained from the combined application of both parts. The first part can be applied to any matrix. The application of the second part, i.e. ordering to conserve sparsity, is limited to sparse matrices in which the pattern of nonzero elements is symmetric and for which an arbitrary order of decomposition does not adversely affect numerical accuracy. Such matrices are usually characterized by a strong diagonal, and ordering to conserve sparsity increases the accuracy of the decomposition. A large class of network problems fulfils this condition. Generally it is not worth considering optimal ordering unless at least 80 per cent of the matrix elements are zero.

Factored direct solutions

The first part of the above method shows how to derive an array of numbers from a nonsingular matrix A that can be used to obtain the effects of any or all of the following: A, A^{-1}, A^{T}, (A^{T-1}), and certain two-way hybrid combinations of these matrices. The method is applicable to any nonsingular matrix, real or complex, sparse or full, symmetric or non-symmetric. This method is also applicable to mesh equations. Its greatest advantage is realized in problems involving large sparse matrices. The basic scheme is first presented for the most general case, a full non-symmetric matrix. Symmetry is then treated as a special case.

1.8.3 Triangular Decomposition—Gaussian Elimination

Triangular decomposition of a matrix by Gaussian elimination is described in many books on matrix analysis. Ordinarily, the decomposition is accomplished by the elimination of elements below the main diagonal in successive columns. For the purpose of computer programming for a sparse matrix, it is usually much more efficient to eliminate elements by successive rows. The development is based on the equation

$$AX = b \tag{1.60}$$

where A is a nonsingular matrix, X is a column vector of unknowns, and b is a known vector with at least one nonzero element, i.e.

$$\begin{bmatrix} a_{11} & a_{12} & \cdots & a_{1n} \\ a_{21} & a_{22} & \cdots & a_{2n} \\ \vdots & & & \vdots \\ a_{n1} & a_{n2} & \cdots & a_{nn} \end{bmatrix} \begin{bmatrix} x_1 \\ x_2 \\ \vdots \\ x_n \end{bmatrix} = \begin{bmatrix} b_1 \\ b_2 \\ \vdots \\ b_n \end{bmatrix}$$

In the computer algorithm, A is augmented by b as shown in Eq. (1.61) for an nth-order system.

$$\begin{bmatrix} a_{11} & a_{12} & \cdots & a_{1n} & b_1 \\ a_{21} & a_{22} & \cdots & a_{2n} & b_2 \\ \vdots & & & & \vdots \\ a_{n1} & a_{n2} & \cdots & a_{nn} & b_n \end{bmatrix} \tag{1.61}$$

The first step involves the division of the elements of the first row by a_{11}, as shown in Eq. (1.62).

$$\begin{aligned} a_{1j}^{(1)} &= \left(\frac{1}{a_{11}}\right) a_{1j} \qquad j = 2, n \\ b_1^{(1)} &= \left(\frac{1}{a_{11}}\right) b_1 \end{aligned} \tag{1.62}$$

The superscripts indicate the order of the derived system. The second step, as shown in Eqs. (1.63a) and (1.63b), involves elimination of a_{21}, from the second row by a linear combination with the derived first row, and then dividing the remaining derived elements of the second row by its derived diagonal element.

$$\begin{bmatrix} 1 & a_{12}^{(1)} & a_{13}^{(1)} & \cdots & a_{1n}^{(1)} & b_1^{(1)} \\ 0 & 1 & a_{23}^{(2)} & \cdots & a_{2n}^{(2)} & b_2^{(2)} \\ \vdots & \vdots & \vdots & \cdots & \vdots & \vdots \\ a_{n1} & a_{n2} & a_{n3} & \cdots & a_{nn} & b_n \end{bmatrix} \tag{1.63a}$$

$$\begin{aligned} a_{2j}^{(1)} &= a_{2j} - a_{21} a_{1j}^{(1)} \qquad j = 2, n \\ b_2^{(1)} &= b_2 - a_{21} b_1^{(1)} \\ a_{2j}^{(2)} &= \left(\frac{1}{a_{22}^{(1)}}\right) a_{2j}^{(1)} \qquad j = 3, n \\ b_2^{(2)} &= \left(\frac{1}{a_{22}^{(1)}}\right) b_2^{(1)} \end{aligned} \tag{1.63b}$$

The third step, as shown in Eqs. (1.64a) and (1.64b), involves elimination of elements to the left of the diagonal of the third row and dividing the remaining derived elements of the row by the derived diagonal element.

$$\begin{bmatrix} 1 & a_{12}^{(1)} & a_{13}^{(1)} & a_{14}^{(1)} & \cdots & a_{1n}^{(1)} & b_1^{(1)} \\ 0 & 1 & a_{23}^{(2)} & a_{24}^{(2)} & \cdots & a_{2n}^{(2)} & b_2^{(1)} \\ 0 & 0 & 1 & a_{34}^{(3)} & \cdots & a_{3n}^{(3)} & b_3^{(1)} \\ \vdots & \vdots & \vdots & \vdots & \cdots & \vdots & \vdots \\ a_{n1} & a_{n2} & a_{n3} & a_{n4} & \cdots & a_{nn} & b_n \end{bmatrix} \tag{1.64a}$$

$$
\begin{aligned}
a_{3j}^{(1)} &= a_{3j} - a_{31}a_{1j}^{(1)} \qquad j = 2, n\\
b_3^{(1)} &= b_3 - a_{31}b_1^{(1)}\\
a_{3j}^{(2)} &= a_{3j}^{(1)} - a_{32}^{(1)}\, a_{2j}^{(2)} \qquad j = 3, n\\
b_3^{(2)} &= b_3^{(1)} - a_{32}^{(1)}\, b_2^{(2)}\\
a_{3j}^{(3)} &= \left(\frac{1}{a_{33}^{(2)}}\right) a_{3j}^{(2)} \qquad j = 4, n\\
b_3^{(3)} &= \left(\frac{1}{a_{33}^{(2)}}\right) b_3^{(2)}
\end{aligned}
\tag{1.64b}
$$

Proceeding in this manner the nth derived system is obtained as shown below:

$$
\begin{bmatrix}
1 & a_{12}^{(1)} & \cdot & \cdot & \cdot & a_{1n}^{(1)} & b_1^{(1)}\\
 & 1 & \cdot & \cdot & \cdot & a_{2n}^{(2)} & b_2^{(1)}\\
 & & \cdot & \cdot & \cdot & \cdot & \cdot\\
 & & & \cdot & \cdot & \cdot & \cdot\\
 & & & & & 1 & b_n^{(n)}
\end{bmatrix}
\tag{1.65}
$$

It should be noted that at the end of the kth step, work on rows 1 to k gets completed and rows $k + 1$ to n have not yet entered the process in any way.

The solution can now be obtained by back substitution.

$$
\begin{aligned}
x_n &= b_n^{(n)}\\
x_{n-1} &= b_{n-1}^{(n-1)} - a_{n-1,n}^{(n-1)} \cdot x_n\\
x_i &= b_i^{(i)} - \sum_{j=i+1}^{n} a_{i,j}^{(i)} \cdot x_j
\end{aligned}
\tag{1.66}
$$

In programming, the x_i's replace the b_i's one-by-one as they are computed, starting with x_n, and working back to x_1. When A is full and n is large, it can be shown that the number of multiplication–addition operations for triangular decomposition is approximately $1/3n^3$ compared with n^3 for inversion.

It can be easily verified that triangularization in the same order by columns instead of rows would have produced identically the same result. Each eliminated element $a_{ij}^{(j-1)}$, $i > j$, would have been the same and the number of operations would have been the same. The back substitution also could have been accomplished by columns instead of rows in the same number of operations.

EXAMPLE 1.12 Solve the following equations using the Gauss elimination method:

$$
\begin{aligned}
2x_1 + x_2 + 3x_3 &= 6\\
2x_1 + 3x_2 + 4x_3 &= 9\\
3x_1 + 4x_2 + 7x_3 &= 14
\end{aligned}
$$

Solution: In the matrix form

$$\begin{bmatrix} 2 & 1 & 3 \\ 2 & 3 & 4 \\ 3 & 4 & 7 \end{bmatrix} \begin{bmatrix} x_1 \\ x_2 \\ x_3 \end{bmatrix} = \begin{bmatrix} 6 \\ 9 \\ 14 \end{bmatrix}$$

$$\therefore \qquad A = \begin{bmatrix} a_{11} & a_{12} & a_{13} \\ a_{21} & a_{22} & a_{23} \\ a_{31} & a_{32} & a_{33} \end{bmatrix} = \begin{bmatrix} 2 & 1 & 3 \\ 2 & 3 & 4 \\ 3 & 4 & 7 \end{bmatrix}$$

$$\text{Augmented matrix} = \begin{bmatrix} a_{11} & a_{12} & a_{13} & b_1 \\ a_{21} & a_{22} & a_{23} & b_2 \\ a_{31} & a_{32} & a_{33} & b_3 \end{bmatrix} = \begin{bmatrix} 2 & 1 & 3 & 6 \\ 2 & 3 & 4 & 9 \\ 3 & 4 & 7 & 14 \end{bmatrix}$$

$$= \begin{bmatrix} 1 & a_{12}^{(1)} & a_{13}^{(1)} & b_1^{(1)} \\ & 1 & a_{23}^{(2)} & b_2^{(2)} \\ & & 1 & b_3^{(3)} \end{bmatrix}$$

The first step is to divide the elements of the first row by a_{11},

$$a_{1j}^{(1)} = \left(\frac{1}{a_{11}}\right) a_{1j} \qquad j = 2, n$$

$$j = 2;\ a_{12}^{(1)} = \left(\frac{1}{a_{11}}\right) a_{12} = \left(\frac{1}{2}\right) 1 = 0.5$$

$$j = 3;\ a_{13}^{(1)} = \left(\frac{1}{a_{11}}\right) a_{13} = \left(\frac{1}{2}\right) 3 = 1.5$$

$$b_1^{(1)} = \left(\frac{1}{a_{11}}\right) b_1 = \left(\frac{1}{2}\right) \times 6 = 3$$

The second step is to eliminate a_{21}, from the second row by linear combination with the derived first row, and then to divide the remaining derived elements of the second row by its derived diagonal element.

$$a_{2j}^{(1)} = a_{2j} - a_{21} a_{1j}^{(1)} \qquad j = 2, n$$

$$j = 2;\ a_{22}^{(1)} = a_{22} - a_{21} a_{12}^{(1)} = 3 - 2 \times 0.5 = 2$$

$$j = 3;\ a_{23}^{(1)} = a_{23} - a_{21} a_{13}^{(1)} = 4 - 2 \times 1.5 = 1$$

$$b_2^{(1)} = b_2 - a_{21} b_1^{(1)} = 9 - 2 \times 3 = 3$$

$$a_{2j}^{(2)} = \left(\frac{1}{a_{22}^{(1)}}\right) a_{2j}^{(1)} \qquad j = 3, n$$

$$j = 3;\ a_{23}^{(2)} = \left(\frac{1}{a_{22}^{(1)}}\right) a_{23}^{(1)} = \left(\frac{1}{2}\right) \times 1 = 0.5$$

$$b_2^{(2)} = \left(\frac{1}{a_{22}^{(1)}}\right) b_2^{(1)} = \left(\frac{1}{2}\right) \times 3 = 1.5$$

The third step is to eliminate the elements to the left of the diagonal of the third row and to divide the remaining derived elements of the row by the derived diagonal element.

$$a_{3j}^{(1)} = a_{3j} - a_{31}a_{1j}^{(1)} \qquad j = 2, n$$

$$j = 2;\ a_{32}^{(1)} = a_{32} - a_{31}a_{12}^{(1)} = 4 - 3 \times 0.5 = 2.5$$

$$j = 3;\ a_{33}^{(1)} = a_{33} - a_{31}a_{13}^{(1)} = 7 - 3 \times 1.5 = 2.5$$

$$b_3^{(1)} = b_3 - a_{31}b_1^{(1)} = 14 - 3 \times 3 = 5$$

$$a_{3j}^{(2)} = a_{3j}^{(1)} - a_{32}^{(1)}a_{2j}^{(2)} \qquad j = 3, n$$

$$j = 3;\ a_{33}^{(2)} = a_{33}^{(1)} - a_{32}^{(1)}a_{23}^{(2)} = 2.5 - 2.5 \times 0.5 = 1.25$$

$$b_3^{(2)} = b_3^{(1)} - a_{32}^{(1)}b_2^{(2)} = 5 - 2.5 \times 1.5 = 1.25$$

$$a_{3j}^{(3)} = \left(\frac{1}{a_{33}^{(2)}}\right)a_{3j}^{(2)} \qquad j = 4, n$$

$$b_3^{(3)} = \left(\frac{1}{a_{33}^{(2)}}\right)b_3^{(2)} = \left(\frac{1}{1.25}\right) \times 1.25 = 1$$

$$\begin{bmatrix} 1 & a_{12}^{(1)} & a_{13}^{(1)} & b_1^{(1)} \\ & 1 & a_{23}^{(2)} & b_2^{(2)} \\ & & 1 & b_3^{(3)} \end{bmatrix} = \begin{bmatrix} 1 & 0.5 & 1.5 & 3 \\ & 1 & 0.5 & 1.5 \\ & & 1 & 1 \end{bmatrix}$$

The solution can now be obtained by back substitution.

$$x_n = b_n^{(n)}$$

$$n = 3;$$

$$x_3 = b_3^{(3)} = 1$$

$$x_3 = 1$$

$$x_{n-1} = b_{n-1}^{(n-1)} - a_{n-1,n}^{(n-1)} \cdot x_n$$

$$x_{3-1} = b_{3-1}^{(3-1)} - a_{3-1,3}^{(3-1)} \cdot x_3$$

$$x_2 = b_2^{(2)} - a_{2,3}^{(2)} \cdot x_3 = 1.5 - 0.5 \times 1 = 1$$

$$x_2 = 1$$

$$x_i = b_i^{(i)} - \sum_{j=i+1}^{n} a_{ij}^{(i)} \cdot x_j$$

$$x_1 = b_1^{(1)} - [a_{12}^{(1)}x_2 + a_{13}^{(1)}x_3] = 3 - [0.5 \times 1 + 1.5 \times 1] = 1$$

$$x_1 = 1$$

$$X = \begin{bmatrix} x_1 \\ x_2 \\ x_3 \end{bmatrix} = \begin{bmatrix} 1 \\ 1 \\ 1 \end{bmatrix}$$

1.8.4 Triangular Decomposition of Table of Factors

If the forward operations on b had been recorded so that they could be repeated, it is obvious that with this record and the upper triangle Eq. (1.65) for the back substitution, Eq. (1.60) could be solved for any vector b without repeating the triangularization. The recording of the forward operations, however, is trivial. Each forward operation is completely defined by the row and column coordinates and value of a single element $a_{ij}^{(j-1)}, i > j,$ that occurs in the process. Therefore, it is unnecessary to do anything to record these elements except to leave them.

The rules for recording the forward operations of triangularization are:

1. When a term $1/a_{ii}^{(i-1)}$ is computed, store it in the location ii.
2. Leave very derived term $a_{ij}^{(j-1)}, i > j,$ in the lower triangle Eq. (1.65).

Since the forward as well as the back substitution operations are recorded in this scheme, it is no longer necessary to include the vector b. The final result of triangularizing A and recording the forward operations is symbolized in Eq. (1.67).

$$\begin{array}{ccccc} d_{11} & u_{12} & u_{13} & \cdots & u_{1n} \\ l_{21} & d_{22} & u_{23} & \cdots & u_{2n} \\ l_{31} & l_{32} & d_{33} & \cdots & u_{3n} \\ \cdot & \cdot & \cdot & \cdots & \cdot \\ l_{n1} & l_{n2} & l_{n3} & \cdots & d_{nn} \end{array} \tag{1.67}$$

The elements of Eq. (1.67) defined in terms of the derived systems of A in Eq. (1.61) to Eq. (1.65), are:

$$\begin{aligned} d_{ii} &= \frac{1}{a_{ii}^{(i-1)}} \\ u_{ij} &= a_{ij}^{(i)} \qquad i < j \\ l_{ij} &= a_{ij}^{(j-1)} \qquad i > j \end{aligned} \tag{1.68}$$

The matrix brackets are omitted in Eq. (1.67) to emphasize that the array is not strictly a matrix in the same sense as the preceding examples, but only a scheme of recording. It will be referred to as the table of factors. In the literature this result is frequently shown as a factoring of the inverse matrix into the product of a lower and an upper triangular matrix, but it is more suitable for this discussion to consider it as a table of factors.

It is convenient in symbolizing the operations for obtaining direct solutions to define some special matrices in terms of the elements of the table of factors (1.67). The following nonsingular matrices differ from the unit matrix only in the row or column indicated.

$$
\begin{aligned}
&D_i\text{: Row } i = (0,0,\ldots\ 0,\ d_{ii},\ 0,\ \ldots\ 0,\ 0)\\
&L_i\text{: Col } i = (0,0,\ldots\ 0,1,\ -l_{i+1,i},\ -l_{i+2,i}\ \ldots\ -l_{n-1,i},\ -l_{n,i})^T\\
&L_i\text{: Row } i = (-l_{i,1},\ -l_{i,2}\ \ldots\ -l_{i,i-1},\ 1,\ 0,\ \ldots\ 0,\ 0) \qquad (1.69)\\
&U_i\text{: Row } i = (0,0,\ \ldots\ 0,\ 1,\ -u_{i,i+1},\ -u_{i,i+2}\ \ldots\ -u_{i,n-1},\ -u_{i,n})\\
&U_i\text{: Col } i = (-u_{1,i},\ -u_{2,i},\ \ldots\ -u_{i-1,i},\ 1,0,\ \ldots\ 0,0)^T
\end{aligned}
$$

The inverses of these matrices are trivial. The inverse of the matrix D_i involves only the reciprocal of the element d_{ii}. The inverses of the matrices L_i, L_i^*, U_i and U_i* involve only a reversal of algebraic signs of the off-diagonal elements.

The forward and back substitution operations on the column vector b that transform it to x can be expressed as premultiplications by matrices D_i, or L L_i^* and U_i or U_i^*. Thus the solution of $AX = b$ can be expressed as indicated in Eq. (1.70a) to 1.70d).

$$U_1U_2\ \ldots\ U_{n-2}U_{n-1}D_nL_{n-1}D_{n-1}L_{n-2}\ \ldots\ L_2D_2L_1D_1b\ = A^{-1}\ b = x \qquad (1.70a)$$

$$U_1U_2\ \ldots\ U_{n-2}U_{n-1}D_nL_n^*D_{n-1}L_{n-1}^*\ \ldots\ L_3^*D_2L_2^*D_1b\ = A^{-1}\ b = x \qquad (1.70b)$$

$$U_2^*U_3^*\ \ldots\ U_{n-1}^*U_n^*D_nL_{n-1}D_{n-1}L_{n-2}\ \ldots\ L_2D_2L_1D_1b\ = A^{-1}\ b = x \qquad (1.70c)$$

$$U_2^*U_3^*\ \ldots\ U_{n-1}^*U_n^*D_nL_n^*D_{n-1}L_{n-1}^*\ \ldots\ L_3^*D_2L_2^*D_1b\ = A^{-1}\ b = x \qquad (1.70d)$$

EXAMPLE 1.13 Solve the following equations using triangular decomposition with table of factors.

$$
\begin{aligned}
2x_1 + x_2 + 3x_3 &= 6\\
2x_1 + 3x_2 + 4x_3 &= 9\\
3x_1 + 4x_2 + 7x_3 &= 14
\end{aligned}
$$

Solution:

In the matrix form $\begin{bmatrix} 2 & 1 & 3\\ 2 & 3 & 4\\ 3 & 4 & 7 \end{bmatrix}\begin{bmatrix} x_1\\ x_2\\ x_3 \end{bmatrix} = \begin{bmatrix} 6\\ 9\\ 14 \end{bmatrix}$

$$\therefore \qquad A = \begin{bmatrix} a_{11} & a_{12} & a_{13}\\ a_{21} & a_{22} & a_{23}\\ a_{31} & a_{32} & a_{33} \end{bmatrix} = \begin{bmatrix} 2 & 1 & 3\\ 2 & 3 & 4\\ 3 & 4 & 7 \end{bmatrix}$$

and augmented matrix $\begin{bmatrix} a_{11} & a_{12} & a_{13} & b_1\\ a_{21} & a_{22} & a_{23} & b_2\\ a_{31} & a_{32} & a_{33} & b_3 \end{bmatrix} = \begin{bmatrix} 2 & 1 & 3 & 6\\ 2 & 3 & 4 & 9\\ 3 & 4 & 7 & 14 \end{bmatrix}$

Using the Gauss elimination method, we will get (from Example 1.12)

$$\begin{bmatrix} 1 & a_{12}^{(1)} & a_{13}^{(1)} & b_1^{(1)}\\ & 1 & a_{23}^{(2)} & b_2^{(2)}\\ & & 1 & b_3^{(3)} \end{bmatrix} = \begin{bmatrix} 1 & 0.5 & 1.5 & 3\\ & 1 & 0.5 & 1.5\\ & & 1 & 1 \end{bmatrix}$$

Table of factors

$$d_{ii} = \frac{1}{a_{ii}^{(i-1)}}$$

Therefore,

$$d_{11} = \frac{1}{a_{11}^{(0)}} = \left(\frac{1}{2}\right) = 0.5$$

$$d_{22} = \frac{1}{a_{22}^{(1)}} = \left(\frac{1}{2}\right) = 0.5$$

$$\therefore\ a_{22}^{(1)} \text{ value obtained from Example 1.12}$$

$$d_{33} = \frac{1}{a_{33}^{(2)}} = \left(\frac{1}{1.25}\right) = 0.8$$

$$\therefore\ a_{33}^{(2)} \text{ value obtained from Example 1.12}$$

$$u_{ij} = a_{ij}^{(i)} \qquad i < j$$

$$u_{12} = a_{12}^{(1)} = 0.5$$

$$u_{13} = a_{13}^{(1)} = 1.5$$

$$u_{23} = a_{23}^{(2)} = 0.5$$

$$l_{ij} = u_{ij}^{(j-1)} \qquad i > j$$

$$l_{21} = a_{21}^{(0)} = 2$$

$$l_{31} = a_{31}^{(0)} = 3$$

$$l_{32} = a_{32}^{(1)} = 2.5$$

$$\therefore\ a_{32}^{(1)} = a_{32} - a_{31}a_{12}^{(1)} = 4 - 3 \times 0.5 = 2.5$$

The table of factors for A is

$$\begin{matrix} d_{11} & u_{12} & u_{13} \\ l_{21} & d_{22} & u_{23} \\ l_{31} & l_{32} & d_{33} \end{matrix} = \begin{matrix} 0.5 & 0.5 & 1.5 \\ 2 & 0.5 & 0.5 \\ 3 & 2.5 & 0.0 \end{matrix}$$

With b given, the equation $AX = b$ can be solved for x using the equation below, which is based on Eq. (1.70a)

$$U_1U_2 \ldots U_{n-2}U_{n-1}D_nL_{n-1}D_{n-1}L_{n-2} \ldots L_2D_2L_1D_1b = A^{-1}\, b = x$$

For $n = 3$

$$U_1U_2D_3L_2D_2L_1D_1b = A^{-1}\, b = X$$

$$U_1 = \begin{bmatrix} 1 & -u_{12} & -u_{13} \\ & 1 & \\ & & 1 \end{bmatrix} = \begin{bmatrix} 1 & -0.5 & -0.5 \\ & 1 & \\ & & 1 \end{bmatrix}$$

$$U_2 = \begin{bmatrix} 1 & & \\ & 1 & -u_{23} \\ & & 1 \end{bmatrix} = \begin{bmatrix} 1 & & \\ & 1 & -0.5 \\ & & 1 \end{bmatrix}$$

$$D_3 = \begin{bmatrix} 1 & & \\ & 1 & \\ & & d_{33} \end{bmatrix} = \begin{bmatrix} 1 & & \\ & 1 & \\ & & 0.8 \end{bmatrix}$$

$$L_2 = \begin{bmatrix} 1 & & \\ & 1 & \\ & -l_{32} & 1 \end{bmatrix} = \begin{bmatrix} 1 & & \\ & 1 & \\ & -2.5 & 1 \end{bmatrix}$$

$$D_2 = \begin{bmatrix} 1 & & \\ & d_{22} & \\ & & 1 \end{bmatrix} = \begin{bmatrix} 1 & & \\ & 0.5 & \\ & & 1 \end{bmatrix}$$

$$L_1 = \begin{bmatrix} 1 & & \\ -l_{21} & 1 & \\ -l_{31} & & 1 \end{bmatrix} = \begin{bmatrix} 1 & & \\ -2 & 1 & \\ -3 & & 1 \end{bmatrix}$$

$$D_1 = \begin{bmatrix} d_{11} & & \\ & 1 & \\ & & 1 \end{bmatrix} = \begin{bmatrix} 0.5 & & \\ & 1 & \\ & & 1 \end{bmatrix}$$

$$b = \begin{bmatrix} 6 \\ 9 \\ 14 \end{bmatrix}$$

$$\overset{U_1}{\begin{bmatrix} 1 & -0.5 & -0.5 \\ & 1 & \\ & & 1 \end{bmatrix}} \overset{U_2}{\begin{bmatrix} 1 & & \\ & 1 & -0.5 \\ & & 1 \end{bmatrix}} \overset{D_3}{\begin{bmatrix} 1 & & \\ & 1 & \\ & & 0.8 \end{bmatrix}} \overset{L_2}{\begin{bmatrix} 1 & & \\ & 1 & \\ & -2.5 & 1 \end{bmatrix}} \overset{D_2}{\begin{bmatrix} 1 & & \\ & 0.5 & \\ & & 1 \end{bmatrix}}$$

$$\overset{L_1}{\begin{bmatrix} 1 & & \\ -2 & 1 & \\ -3 & & 1 \end{bmatrix}} \overset{D_1}{\begin{bmatrix} 0.5 & & \\ & 1 & \\ & & 1 \end{bmatrix}} \overset{b}{\begin{bmatrix} 6 \\ 9 \\ 14 \end{bmatrix}} = \overset{X}{\begin{bmatrix} 1 \\ 1 \\ 1 \end{bmatrix}}$$

EXAMPLE 1.14 Use the *LU* decomposition or triangular factorization method to solve the following simultaneous equations.

$$2x_1 + x_2 + 3x_3 = 6$$
$$2x_1 + 3x_2 + 4x_3 = 9$$
$$3x_1 + 4x_2 + 7x_3 = 14$$

Solution:

In the matrix form $\begin{bmatrix} 2 & 1 & 3 \\ 2 & 3 & 4 \\ 3 & 4 & 7 \end{bmatrix}\begin{bmatrix} x_1 \\ x_2 \\ x_3 \end{bmatrix} = \begin{bmatrix} 6 \\ 9 \\ 14 \end{bmatrix}$

$$A = L \quad U$$

$$\begin{bmatrix} a_{11} & a_{12} & a_{13} \\ a_{21} & a_{22} & a_{23} \\ a_{31} & a_{32} & a_{33} \end{bmatrix} = \begin{bmatrix} l_{11} & & \\ l_{21} & l_{22} & \\ l_{31} & l_{32} & l_{33} \end{bmatrix}\begin{bmatrix} 1 & u_{12} & u_{13} \\ & 1 & u_{23} \\ & & 1 \end{bmatrix}$$

$$\begin{aligned} a_{11} &= l_{11} & a_{12} &= l_{11}u_{12} & a_{13} &= l_{11}u_{13} \\ a_{21} &= l_{21} & a_{22} &= l_{21}u_{12} + l_{22} & a_{23} &= l_{21}u_{13} + l_{22}u_{23} \\ a_{31} &= l_{31} & a_{32} &= l_{31}u_{12} + l_{32} & a_{33} &= l_{31}u_{13} + l_{32}u_{23} + l_{33} \end{aligned}$$

$$\begin{bmatrix} 2 & 1 & 3 \\ 2 & 3 & 4 \\ 3 & 4 & 7 \end{bmatrix} = \begin{bmatrix} l_{11} & & \\ l_{21} & l_{22} & \\ l_{31} & l_{32} & l_{33} \end{bmatrix}\begin{bmatrix} 1 & u_{12} & u_{13} \\ & 1 & u_{23} \\ & & 1 \end{bmatrix}$$

The first row of the L & U matrices on the right side

$$a_{11} = l_{11} \Rightarrow l_{11} = a_{11} = 2$$

$$a_{12} = l_{11}u_{12} \Rightarrow u_{12} = \frac{a_{12}}{l_{11}} = \frac{1}{2} = 0.5$$

$$a_{13} = l_{11}u_{13} \Rightarrow u_{13} = \frac{a_{13}}{l_{11}} = \frac{3}{2} = 1.5$$

The second row of the L & U matrices on the right side

$$a_{21} = l_{21} \Rightarrow l_{21} = a_{21} = 2$$

$$a_{22} = l_{21}u_{12} + l_{22} \Rightarrow l_{22} = a_{22} - l_{21}u_{12} = 3 - 2 \times 0.5 = 2$$

$$a_{23} = l_{21}u_{13} + l_{22}u_{23} \Rightarrow u_{23} = \frac{a_{23} - l_{21}u_{13}}{l_{22}} = \frac{4 - 2 \times 1.5}{2} = 0.5$$

The third row of the L & U matrices on the right side

$$a_{31} = l_{31} \Rightarrow l_{31} = a_{31} = 3$$

$$a_{32} = l_{31}u_{12} + l_{32} \Rightarrow l_{32} = a_{32} - l_{31}u_{12} = 4 - 3 \times 0.5 = 2.5$$

$$\begin{aligned} a_{33} = l_{31}u_{13} + l_{32}u_{23} + l_{33} \Rightarrow l_{33} &= a_{33} - l_{31}u_{13} - l_{32}u_{23} \\ &= 7 - 3 \times 1.5 - 2.5 \times 0.5 = 1.25 \end{aligned}$$

$$L = \begin{bmatrix} l_{11} & & \\ l_{21} & l_{22} & \\ l_{31} & l_{32} & l_{33} \end{bmatrix} = \begin{bmatrix} 2 & & \\ 2 & 2 & \\ 3 & 2.5 & 1.25 \end{bmatrix}$$

$$U = \begin{bmatrix} 1 & u_{12} & u_{13} \\ & 1 & u_{23} \\ & & 1 \end{bmatrix} = \begin{bmatrix} 1 & 0.5 & 1.5 \\ & 1 & 0.5 \\ & & 1 \end{bmatrix}$$

$$[A]\ [x] = [b]$$

And if
$$[A] = [L]\ [U]$$

Then first solving
$$[L]\ [z] = [b]$$

$$\begin{bmatrix} 2 & & \\ 2 & 2 & \\ 3 & 2.5 & 1.25 \end{bmatrix} \begin{bmatrix} z_1 \\ z_2 \\ z_3 \end{bmatrix} = \begin{bmatrix} 6 \\ 9 \\ 14 \end{bmatrix}$$

$$2z_1 = 6$$

$$z_1 = 3$$

$$2z_1 + 2z_2 = 9$$

$$z_2 = 1.5$$

$$3z_1 + 2.5z_2 + 1.25z_3 = 14$$

$$z_3 = 1$$

And then
$$[U]\ [x] = [z]$$

$$\begin{bmatrix} 1 & 0.5 & 1.5 \\ & 1 & 0.5 \\ & & 1 \end{bmatrix} \begin{bmatrix} x_1 \\ x_2 \\ x_3 \end{bmatrix} = \begin{bmatrix} 3 \\ 1.5 \\ 1 \end{bmatrix}$$

$$x_3 = 1$$

$$x_2 + 0.5x_3 = 1.5$$

$$x_2 = 1$$

$$x_1 + 0.5x_2 + 1.5x_3 = 3$$

$$x_1 = 1$$

$$\therefore \qquad \begin{bmatrix} x_1 \\ x_2 \\ x_3 \end{bmatrix} = \begin{bmatrix} 1 \\ 1 \\ 1 \end{bmatrix}$$

1.8.5 Bi-factorization Method

If A is a sparse matrix, the set of n linear equations, $AX = b$, can be solved effectively by using the bi-factorization method. The inverse of A can be expressed by a multiple product of $2n$ factor matrices.

$$A^{-1} = R^{(1)}R^{(2)} \ldots R^{(n)}L^{(n)} \ldots L^{(2)}L^{(1)} \tag{1.71}$$

In order to find L and R, the following sequence of intermediate matrices is introduced.

$$A^{(0)} = A$$
$$A^{(1)} = L^{(1)}A^{(0)}R^{(1)}$$
$$\vdots$$
$$A^{(j)} = L^{(j)}A^{(j-1)}R^{(j)}$$
$$\vdots$$
$$A^{(j)} = L^{(j)}A^{(j-1)}R(j)$$
$$\vdots$$
$$A^{(n)} = L^{(n)}A^{(n-1)}R^{(n)} = I$$

where the reduced matrix $A^{(j)}$ has elements defined by the following equations

$$a_{jj}^{(j)} = 1 \quad ; \quad a_{ij}^{(j)} = a_{ik}^{(j)} = 0$$

$$a_{ik}^{(j)} = a_{ik}^{(j-1)} - \frac{a_{ij}^{(j-1)} \cdot a_{jk}^{(j-1)}}{a_{jj}^{(j-1)}}$$

j being the pivotal index and $i, k = (j + 1), ..., n$.
The left-hand factor matrices $L^{(j)}$ are very sparse and differ from the unity matrix in column j only.

$$L^{(j)} = \begin{bmatrix} 1 & & & & \\ & 1 & & & \\ & & L_{ij}^{(j)} & & \\ & & \vdots & 1 & \\ & & L_{nj}^{(j)} & & 1 \end{bmatrix}$$

where

$$L_{ij}^{(j)} = \frac{1}{a_{jj}^{(j-1)}}$$

and

$$L_{ij}^{(j)} = -\frac{a_{ij}^{(j-1)}}{a_{jj}^{(j-1)}} \qquad i = (j + 1), ..., n$$

The right-hand factor matrices $R^{(j)}$ are also very sparse and differ from the unity matrix in row j only.

$$R^{(j)} = \begin{bmatrix} 1 & & & & \\ & 1 & & & \\ & R_{j,j+1}^{(j)} & \cdots & R_{jn}^{(j)} & \\ & & 1 & & \\ & & & & 1 \end{bmatrix}$$

where

$$R_{jk}^{(j)} = -\frac{a_{jk}^{(j-1)}}{a_{jj}^{(j-1)}} \qquad k = (j + 1), ..., n$$

For a symmetric matrix A, the structures of left (L) and right (R) factor matrices are the same and can therefore be stored effectively in the matrix F as follows:

$$F = \begin{bmatrix} \ddots & & R \\ & \ddots & \\ L & & \ddots \end{bmatrix}$$

Solution to Eq. (1.71) can be written as

$$X = R^{(1)}R^{(2)} \ldots R^{(n)}L^{(n)} \ldots L^{(2)}L^{(1)}b \tag{1.72}$$

EXAMPLE 1.15 Solve the following simultaneous equations using the bi-factorization method.

$$2x_1 + x_2 + 3x_3 = 6$$
$$2x_1 + 3x_2 + 4x_3 = 9$$
$$3x_1 + 4x_2 + 7x_3 = 14$$

Solution: To find $X = R^{(1)}R^{(2)}L^{(3)}L^{(2)}L^{(1)}b$

In the matrix form $AX = b$

$$\begin{bmatrix} 2 & 1 & 3 \\ 2 & 3 & 4 \\ 3 & 4 & 7 \end{bmatrix} \begin{bmatrix} x_1 \\ x_2 \\ x_3 \end{bmatrix} = \begin{bmatrix} 6 \\ 9 \\ 14 \end{bmatrix}$$

$$A = A^{(0)} = \begin{bmatrix} a_{11}^{(0)} & a_{12}^{(0)} & a_{13}^{(0)} \\ a_{21}^{(0)} & a_{22}^{(0)} & a_{23}^{(0)} \\ a_{31}^{(0)} & a_{32}^{(0)} & a_{33}^{(0)} \end{bmatrix} = \begin{bmatrix} 2 & 1 & 3 \\ 2 & 3 & 4 \\ 3 & 4 & 7 \end{bmatrix}$$

Step 1:

$$L^{(1)}A^{(0)}R^{(1)} = A^{(1)}$$

$$\begin{bmatrix} L_{11}^{(1)} & . & . \\ L_{21}^{(1)} & 1 & . \\ L_{31}^{(1)} & . & 1 \end{bmatrix} \times A^{(0)} \times \begin{bmatrix} 1 & R_{12}^{(1)} & R_{13}^{(1)} \\ . & 1 & . \\ . & . & 1 \end{bmatrix} = \begin{bmatrix} 1 & 0 & 0 \\ 0 & a_{22}^{(1)} & a_{23}^{(1)} \\ 0 & a_{32}^{(1)} & a_{33}^{(1)} \end{bmatrix}$$

$$L_{11}^{(1)} = \frac{1}{a_{11}^{(0)}}$$

$$L_{11}^{(1)} = \frac{1}{2} = 0.5$$

$$L_{i1}^{(1)} = -\frac{a_{i1}^{(0)}}{a_{11}^{(0)}} \qquad (i = 2, 3)$$

$$i = 2;\ L_{21}^{(1)} = -\frac{a_{21}^{(0)}}{a_{11}^{(0)}} = \frac{-2}{2} = -1$$

$$i = 3;\ L_{31}^{(1)} = -\frac{a_{31}^{(0)}}{a_{11}^{(0)}} = \frac{-3}{2} = -1.5$$

$$R_{1i}^{(1)} = -\frac{a_{1i}^{(0)}}{a_{11}^{(0)}} \qquad (i = 2, 3)$$

$$i = 2;\ R_{12}^{(1)} = -\frac{a_{12}^{(0)}}{a_{11}^{(0)}} = \frac{-1}{2} = -0.5$$

$$i = 3;\ R_{13}^{(1)} = -\frac{a_{13}^{(0)}}{a_{11}^{(0)}} = \frac{-3}{2} = -1.5$$

$$a_{ij}^{(1)} = a_{ij}^{(0)} - \frac{a_{i1}^{(0)}\, a_{1j}^{(0)}}{a_{11}^{(0)}} \qquad (i = 2, 3 \text{ and } j = 2, 3)$$

$$i = 2;\ j = 2;\ a_{22}^{(1)} = a_{22}^{(0)} - \frac{a_{21}^{(0)} a_{12}^{(0)}}{a_{11}^{(0)}} = 3 - \frac{2 \times 1}{2} = 2$$

$$i = 2;\ j = 3;\ a_{23}^{(1)} = a_{23}^{(0)} - \frac{a_{21}^{(0)} a_{13}^{(0)}}{a_{11}^{(0)}} = 4 - \frac{2 \times 3}{2} = 1$$

$$i = 3;\ j = 2;\ a_{32}^{(1)} = a_{32}^{(0)} - \frac{a_{31}^{(0)} a_{12}^{(0)}}{a_{11}^{(0)}} = 4 - \frac{3 \times 1}{2} = 2.5$$

$$i = 3;\ j = 3;\ a_{33}^{(1)} = a_{33}^{(0)} - \frac{a_{31}^{(0)} a_{13}^{(0)}}{a_{11}^{(0)}} = 7 - \frac{3 \times 3}{2} = 2.5$$

$$L^{(1)} A^{(0)} R^{(1)} = A^{(1)}$$

$$\begin{bmatrix} L_{11}^{(1)} & . & . \\ L_{21}^{(1)} & 1 & . \\ L_{31}^{(1)} & . & 1 \end{bmatrix} \times A^{(0)} \times \begin{bmatrix} 1 & R_{12}^{(1)} & R_{13}^{(1)} \\ . & 1 & . \\ . & . & 1 \end{bmatrix} = \begin{bmatrix} 1 & 0 & 0 \\ 0 & a_{22}^{(1)} & a_{23}^{(1)} \\ 0 & a_{32}^{(1)} & a_{33}^{(1)} \end{bmatrix}$$

$$\begin{bmatrix} 0.5 & . & . \\ -1 & 1 & . \\ -1.5 & . & 1 \end{bmatrix} \times \begin{bmatrix} 2 & 1 & 3 \\ 2 & 3 & 4 \\ 3 & 4 & 7 \end{bmatrix} \times \begin{bmatrix} 1 & -0.5 & -1.5 \\ . & 1 & . \\ . & . & 1 \end{bmatrix} = \begin{bmatrix} 1 & . & . \\ . & 2 & 1 \\ . & 2.5 & 2.5 \end{bmatrix}$$

Step 2:

$$L^{(2)}A^{(1)}R^{(2)} = A^{(2)}$$

$$\begin{bmatrix} 1 & . & . \\ . & L_{22}^{(2)} & . \\ . & L_{32}^{(2)} & 1 \end{bmatrix} \times A^{(1)} \times \begin{bmatrix} 1 & . & . \\ . & 1 & R_{23}^{(1)} \\ . & . & 1 \end{bmatrix} = \begin{bmatrix} 1 & . & . \\ . & 1 & . \\ . & . & a_{33}^{(1)} \end{bmatrix}$$

$$L_{22}^{(2)} = \frac{1}{a_{22}^{(1)}}$$

$$L_{12}^{(2)} = \frac{1}{2} = 0.5$$

$$L_{i2}^{(2)} = -\frac{a_{i2}^{(1)}}{a_{22}^{(1)}} \qquad (i = 3,\ 4)$$

$$i = 3;\ L_{32}^{(2)} = -\frac{a_{32}^{(1)}}{a_{22}^{(1)}} = \frac{-2.5}{2} = -1.25$$

$$R_{2i}^{(2)} = -\frac{a_{2i}^{(0)}}{a_{22}} \qquad (i = 3,\ 4)$$

$$i = 3;\ R_{23}^{(2)} = -\frac{a_{23}^{(1)}}{a_{22}^{(1)}} = \frac{-1}{2} = -0.5$$

$$a_{ij}^{(2)} = a_{ij}^{(2)} - \frac{a_{i2}^{(1)} a_{2j}^{(1)}}{a_{22}^{(1)}} \qquad (i = 3 \text{ and } j = 3)$$

$$i = 3; j = 3;\ a_{33}^{(2)} = a_{33}^{(1)} - \frac{a_{32}^{(1)} a_{23}^{(1)}}{a_{22}^{(1)}} = 2.5 - \frac{2.5 \times 1}{2} = 1.25$$

$$L^{(2)}A^{(1)}R^{(2)} = A^{(2)}$$

$$\begin{bmatrix} 1 & . & . \\ . & L_{22}^{(2)} & . \\ . & L_{32}^{(2)} & 1 \end{bmatrix} \times A^{(1)} \times \begin{bmatrix} 1 & . & . \\ . & 1 & R_{23}^{(2)} \\ . & . & 1 \end{bmatrix} = \begin{bmatrix} 1 & 0 & 0 \\ 0 & 1 & . \\ 0 & . & a_{33}^{(2)} \end{bmatrix}$$

$$\begin{bmatrix} 1 & . & . \\ . & 0.5 & . \\ . & -1.25 & 1 \end{bmatrix} \times \begin{bmatrix} 1 & . & . \\ . & 2 & 1 \\ . & 2.5 & 2.5 \end{bmatrix} \times \begin{bmatrix} 1 & . & . \\ . & 1 & -0.5 \\ . & . & 1 \end{bmatrix} = \begin{bmatrix} 1 & . & . \\ . & 1 & . \\ . & . & 1.25 \end{bmatrix}$$

Step 3:

$$L^{(3)}A^{(2)}R^{(3)} = A^{(3)}$$

$$\begin{bmatrix} 1 & . & . \\ . & 1 & . \\ . & . & L_{33}^{(3)} \end{bmatrix}$$

$$L_{33}^{(3)} = \frac{1}{a_{33}^{(2)}} = \frac{1}{1.25} = 0.8$$

$$L^{(3)} = \begin{bmatrix} 1 & . & . \\ . & 1 & . \\ . & . & 0.8 \end{bmatrix}$$

$$X = \quad R^{(1)} \quad R^{(2)} \quad L^{(3)} \quad L^{(2)} \quad L^{(1)} \quad b$$

$$X = \begin{bmatrix} 1 & -0.5 & -1.5 \\ . & 1 & . \\ . & . & 1 \end{bmatrix} \begin{bmatrix} 1 & . & . \\ . & 1 & -0.5 \\ . & . & 1 \end{bmatrix} \begin{bmatrix} 1 & . & . \\ . & 1 & . \\ . & . & 0.8 \end{bmatrix} \begin{bmatrix} 1 & . & . \\ . & 0.5 & . \\ . & -1.25 & 1 \end{bmatrix} \begin{bmatrix} 0.5 & . & . \\ -1 & 1 & . \\ -1.5 & . & 1 \end{bmatrix} \begin{bmatrix} 6 \\ 9 \\ 14 \end{bmatrix}$$

$$X = \begin{bmatrix} 1 \\ 1 \\ 1 \end{bmatrix}$$

Comparison of methods for triangularization and bi-factorization

- These are identical methods based on removing Gauss.
- The number of arithmetic operations is equal in both methods.
- Since the factors raised by both the methods are different, the method of bi-factorization requires less memory, less indexing and simple arithmetic operations.
- In the triangular decomposition *LU*s are not symmetric. *LDU*s in the decomposition are symmetrical, but require a larger number of operations.
- The product of triangular matrices is also the matrix. The product of matrices is the matrix bifactors inverse, which facilitates the attainment of the solution.
- The bi-factorization is of particular interest for those sparse matrices, which have predominantly main diagonal elements, or arrays that are not symmetrical, but have a structure symmetric sparsity.

1.8.6 Sparsity and Optimal Ordering Scheme

When the matrix to be triangularized is sparse, the order in which rows are processed affects the number of nonzero terms in the resultant upper triangle.

If a programming scheme is used which processes and stores only the nonzero terms, a great savings in operations and computer memory can be achieved by keeping the table of factors as sparse as possible. The absolute optimal order of elimination would result in the least possible terms in the table of factors. An efficient algorithm for determining the absolute optimal order has not been developed, and it appears to be a practical impossibility. However, several effective schemes have been developed for determining the near-optimal orders.

Schemes for near-optimal ordering

The inspection algorithms for near-optimal ordering are applicable to sparse matrices that are symmetric in pattern of nonzero off-diagonal terms, i.e. if a_{ij} is nonzero, then a_{ji} also is nonzero but not necessarily equal to a_{ij}. These are the matrices that occur most frequently in network problems. From the standpoint of programming efficiency, the algorithms should be applied before, rather than during, the triangularization. It is assumed in what follows that the matrix rows are originally numbered according to some external criterion and then renumbered according to the inspection algorithm. Eliminations are then performed in ascending sequence of the renumbered system.

The descriptions of three schemes for renumbering in near-optimal order are the following. They are listed in increasing order of programming complexity, execution time, and optimality.

***Scheme* 1:** Number the rows of the coefficient matrix A according to the number of nonzero off-diagonal terms before elimination. In this scheme the rows with only one off-diagonal term are numbered first, those with two off-diagonal terms are numbered second, etc. and those with the most off-diagonal terms are numbered last.

From the network point of view, the nodes are numbered, starting with that having the fewest connected branches (i.e. minimum degree). This method does not take into account anything that happens during the elimination process but it is simple to program and fast to execute. The only information needed here is a list of the number of nonzero terms in each row of the original matrix.

***Scheme* 2:** Number the rows of the coefficient matrix A so that at each step of the process the next row to be operated upon is the one with the fewest nonzero terms. If more than one row meets this criterion, select anyone.

From the network point of view, the nodes are numbered, so that at each step of the elimination the next node to be eliminated is the one having the fewest connected branches (i.e. minimum degree). This method requires a simulation of elimination process to take into account the changes in the node branch connection effected at each. This scheme requires a simulation of the effects on the accumulation of nonzero terms of the elimination process. Input information is a list by rows of the column numbers of the nonzero off-diagonal terms, i.e. branches. This scheme, though takes longer time, is definitely better.

***Scheme* 3:** Number the rows so that at each step of the elimination process the next row to be operated upon is the one that will introduce the fewest new nonzero terms. If more than one row meets this criterion, select anyone.

From the network point of view, the nodes are numbered, such that at each step of the elimination process the next node to be eliminated is the one that will introduce the fewest row equivalent of every feasible alternative, i.e. new links at each step. Input information is the same as that of scheme (2).

Advantages of the above schemes: The comparative advantages of these schemes are influenced by the network topology and size and the number of direct solutions required. The only virtue of scheme (1) is its simplicity and speed. For nodal equations of power networks, scheme (2) is enough and better than scheme (1), to justify the additional time required for its execution. Scheme (3) does not appear to be enough, and not better than scheme (2) to justify its use for power networks, but it is known to be effective for other networks.

Comparative advantages for a sparse matrix

When A is a sparse matrix, the advantages of the factored form in addition to those previously listed are:

1. The table of factors can be obtained in a small fraction.
2. The storage requirement is small, permitting much larger systems to be solved.
3. Direct solutions can be obtained much faster unless the independent vector is extremely sparse.
4. Round-off error is reduced.
5. Modifications due to changes in the matrix can be made much faster.

The only **disadvantage** of the method is that it requires much more sophisticated programming techniques.

Review Questions

Part-A

1. What is power system?

2. What are the objectives of power system analysis?

3. What are the components of power system?

4. What is the modern power system?

5. What is complex power?

6. What is a bus?

7. Define per phase analysis.

8. Draw the per phase basis or modelling or representation of all components of power system.

9. What is an infinite bus bar?

10. What is single line diagram?
11. What is the purpose of using single line diagram?
12. What is impedance diagram? What are the approximations made in impedance diagram?
13. What is reactance diagram? What are the approximations made in reactance diagram?
14. Define per unit value.
15. What are the advantages of per unit system?
16. What is the need for base values?
17. Write the equation for per unit impedance if a change of base occurs.
18. A generator rated at 30 MVA, 11 kV has a reactance of 20%. Calculate its per unit reactance for a base of 50 MVA and 10 kV.
19. What is the new per unit impedance if the new base MVA is twice the old base MVA?
20. What is a primitive network?
21. What is a bus admittance matrix?
22. What are the methods available for forming the bus admittance matrix?
23. What is sparse matrix?
24. What are the advantages and disadvantages of sparse matrix?
25. Compare the methods of triangularization and bifactorization.

Part-B

1. The single line diagram of a three-phase power system is shown in the figure below. Draw its per unit impedance diagram.

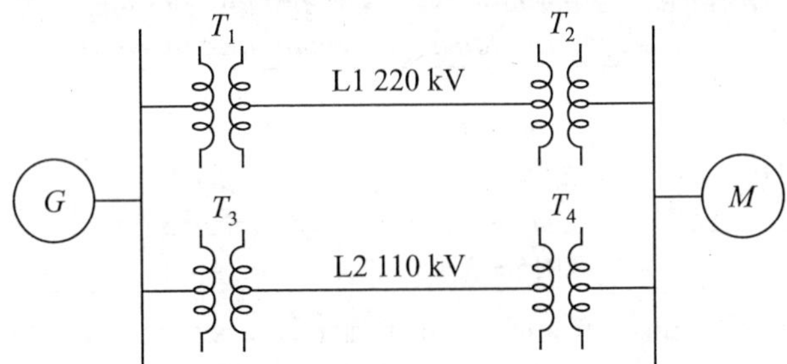

G: 100 MVA, 33 kV, $X = 20\%$
T_1: 50 MVA, 33/220 kV, $X = 10\%$
T_2: 40 MVA, 220/33 kV, $X = 5\%$
T_3: 30 MVA, 33/110 kV, $X = 5.2\%$
T_4: 40 MVA, 110/33 kV, $X = 5\%$
M: 80 MVA, 10.45 kV, $X = 20\%$
Line 1 = 115 Ω; Line 2 = 40 Ω
Motor: 60 MVA, 33 kV, $X = 20\%$

2. Form the matrix $[Y_{bus}]$ and compute the answer using the inspection method and singular transformation method. All the impedance values are in per unit.

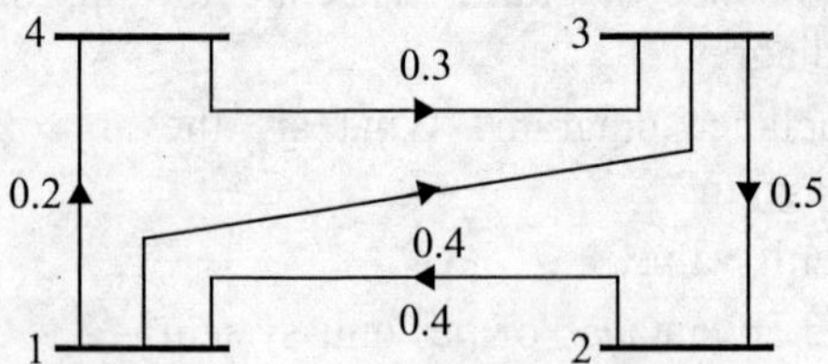

3. For a power system network with the following data, compute the bus admittance matrix.

System data

Line	*Start*	*End*	*X-value*
G_1	1	0	1
G_2	5	0	1.25
L_1	1	2	0.4
L_2	1	3	0.5
L_3	2	3	0.25
L_4	2	5	0.2
L_5	3	4	0.125
L_6	4	5	0.2

4. For the power system network with the following data, compute the bus incident matrix and form the bus admittance matrix by the singular transformation method.

Bus code	*Per unit line impedance*	*Half line charging admittance in per unit*
1–2	$0.05 + j0.12$	$j0.025$
2–3	$0.06 + j0.4$	---
3–4	$0.75 + j0.25$	$j0.02$
1–3	$0.045 + j0.45$	$j0.015$
1–4	$0.015 + j0{:}05$	---

5. Find the L and U triangular factors of the symmetric matrix.

$$M = \begin{bmatrix} 2 & 1 & 3 \\ 1 & 5 & 4 \\ 3 & 4 & 7 \end{bmatrix}$$

6. Solve the following equations using the Gauss elimination method and verify the result using the bi-factorization method:

$$\begin{aligned} 2x_1 + x_2 + 3x_3 &= 5 \\ 1x_1 + 5x_2 + 4x_3 &= 3 \\ 3x_1 + 4x_2 + 7x_3 &= 12 \end{aligned}$$

CHAPTER 2

Load Flow Analysis

2.1 Introduction

The load flow analysis is a very important and fundamental tool in power system analysis. Its results play the major role during the operational stages of any system for its control and economic schedule, as well as during the expansion and design stages. The purpose of any load flow analysis is to compute precise steady-state voltages and voltage angles of all buses in the network, the real and reactive power flows into every line and transformer, under the assumption of known generation and load. The load flow solution also gives the initial conditions of the system when the transient behaviour of the system is to be studied. In practice it will be required to carry out numerous power flow solutions under a variety of conditions.

2.2 Bus Classification

(i) **Load bus:** A bus where there is only load connected and no generation exists (both P_{Gi} and Q_{Gi} are zero) is called a load bus. At this bus real power (P_{Di}) and reactive power (Q_{Di}) are drawn from the supply. A load bus is also called a *PQ* bus, since the real power and reactive power are known values at this bus. The other two unknown quantities at a load bus are voltage magnitude ($|V_i|$) and its phase angle (δ_i) at the bus. In a power balance equation P_{Di} and Q_{Di} are treated as negative quantities since generated powers P_{Gi} and Q_{Gi} are assumed positive.

(ii) **Voltage controlled bus or generator bus:** A voltage controlled bus is any bus in the system where the voltage magnitude can be controlled. At each bus to which there is an alternator connected, the MW generation can be controlled by adjusting the prime mover. In other words, the phase angle of the rotor δ is directly related to the real power generated by the machine. The voltage magnitude can be controlled by adjusting generator excitation. Thus at a generator bus the real power generation (P_{Gi}) and the voltage magnitude ($|V_i|$) can be specified. The phase angle (δ_i) and the reactive power (Q_{Di}) are to be determined. The limits on the value of the reactive power are also specified. These buses are called *PV* buses.

(iii) Slack bus: In a power system network as load flows from the generators to the loads through transmission lines, the power loss occurs due to the losses in the transmission line conductors. These losses when included, we get the power balance relations:

$$P_L = \sum_{i=1}^{N} P_{Gi} - \sum_{i=1}^{N} P_{Di}$$

$$Q_L = \sum_{i=1}^{N} Q_{Gi} - \sum_{i=1}^{N} Q_{Di}$$

where P_{Gi} and Q_{Gi} are the total real and reactive power generations, P_{Di} and Q_{Di} are the total real and reactive power demands and P_L and Q_L are the power losses in the transmission network. The values of P_{Gi}, Q_{Gi}, P_{Di} and Q_{Di} are either known or estimated. For this reason, the slack bus is also known as the reference bus.

Types of Bus	*Specified quantities*	*Quantities to be determined*
Slack or swing or reference bus	$\|V\|, \delta$	P, Q
Generator or voltage controlled or *PV* bus	$P, \|V\|$	Q, δ
Load bus or *PQ* bus	P, Q	$\|V\|, \delta$

2.3 Load Flow Equation

The relationship between node current and voltage in the linear network can be described by the following node equation:

$$I = YV \tag{2.1}$$

or

$$I_i = \sum_{j=1}^{n} Y_{ij} V_j \qquad i = 1,2,3, ..., n \tag{2.2}$$

where I_i and V_j are the injected current at bus i and voltage at bus j, respectively. The voltage at a typical bus i of the system in polar coordinates is given by

$$V_i = |V_i| \angle \delta_i = |V_i| \,(\cos\,\delta_i + j\,\sin\,\delta_i) \tag{2.3}$$

Y_{ij} an element of the admittance matrix, is given by

$$Y_{ij} = |Y_{ij}| \angle \theta_{ij} = |Y_{ij}|\,\cos\,\theta_{ij} + j|Y_{ij}|\,\sin\,\theta_{ij} = G_{ij} + jB_{ij} \tag{2.4}$$

where n is the total number of nodes in the system.

The complex power injected by the source into the ith bus of a power system is

$$S_i = P_i + jQ_i = V_i I_i^* \qquad i = 1, 2, 3, \ldots, n \tag{2.5}$$

The complex conjugate of the above equation,

$$P_i - jQ_i = V_i^* I_i \qquad i = 1, 2, 3, \ldots, n \tag{2.6}$$

We know that

$$I_i = \sum_{j=1}^{n} Y_{ij} V_j$$

Equation (2.6) becomes

$$P_i - jQ_i = V_i^* \sum_{j=1}^{n} Y_{ij} V_j \tag{2.7}$$

Hence basically, real power

$$P_i = \text{real}\left[V_i^* \sum_{j=1}^{n} Y_{ij} V_j \right] \tag{2.8}$$

Reactive power,

$$Q_i = -\,\text{Im}\left[V_i^* \sum_{j=1}^{n} Y_{ij} V_j \right] \tag{2.9}$$

The power flow equations can also be written as follows.
Real power,

$$P_i = |V_i| \sum |V_j||Y_{ij}| \cos(\theta_{ij} + \delta_j - \delta_i) \tag{2.10}$$

Reactive power,

$$Q_i = -|V_i| \sum |V_j||Y_{ij}| \sin(\theta_{ij} + \delta_j - \delta_i) \tag{2.11}$$

Equations (2.10) and (2.11) comprise the polar form of the load flow equations or static load flow equations. They are usually expressed in the following forms as mathematical models of the load flow problem:

$$\Delta P_i = P_{i,\text{sch}} - P_{i,\text{calc}} = (P_{Gi} - P_{Di}) - P_{i,\text{calc}} \tag{2.12}$$

$$\Delta Q_i = Q_{i,\text{sch}} - Q_{i,\text{calc}} = (Q_{Gi} - Q_{Di}) - Q_{i,\text{calc}} \tag{2.13}$$

where $P_{i,\text{sch}}$, $Q_{i,\text{sch}}$ are the specified active and reactive powers at node i based on the above two simultaneous equations. The load flow problem can be roughly summarized as: for specified $P_{i,\text{sch}}$ and $Q_{i,\text{sch}}$, find the voltage vector $|V_i|$ and δ_i such that the magnitudes of the power errors ΔP_i and ΔQ_i are less than the acceptable tolerance.

The functions P_i and Q_i of Eqs. (2.10) and (2.11) are nonlinear functions of the state variables $|V_i|$ and δ_i. This static load flow equations are of such complexity that it is not possible to obtain the exact analytical solution. Hence, the power flow calculations usually employ iterative techniques.

2.4 Load Flow Methods

The iterative techniques are:

1. Gauss–Seidel method
2. Newton–Raphson method
3. Fast decoupled method

2.5 Gauss–Seidel Method

The load flow problem formulated as a set of nonlinear algebraic equations can be solved by an iterative algorithm called the Gauss–Seidel method.

2.5.1 Gauss–Seidel Method When *PV* Buses are Absent

We have chosen the Gauss–Seidel method first because of its simplicity. Now we shall consider the case when the generator buses or voltage controlled buses or *PV* buses are absent. This means we have $n - 1$ load buses or *PQ* buses, the remaining one being the slack bus.

Computational procedure

1. Form the bus admittance matrix of the network by direct inspection method, selecting the ground as reference [formation of Y_{bus}].
2. If the slack bus is not specified, select one of the generator buses as the slack bus. The voltage at the slack bus is assumed as $V_i = V + j0.0$ [selection of the slack bus].
3. Assume initial values of voltages for all buses except the slack bus. $V_i^{(0)} = 1 + j0.0$ (flat start voltage).
4. Set convergence criterion = ε, i.e. if the largest of absolute of the residues exceeds the convergence criterion the process is repeated, otherwise it is terminated.
5. Set iteration count $k = 0$.
6. Bus count $i = 1$. If i is the slack bus, then there will be an increment in the bus count.
7. Solve the voltage equation for bus i as we know that

$$P_i - jQ_i = V_i^* \sum_{j=1}^{n} Y_{ij} V_j$$

$$\frac{P_i - jQ_i}{V_i^*} = V_i \sum_{j=0}^{n} Y_{ij} - \sum_{j=1}^{n} Y_{ij} V_j \quad j \neq i$$

$$V_i = \frac{1}{Y_{ii}} \left[\frac{P_i - jQ_i}{V_i^*} - \sum_{\substack{j=1 \\ j \neq i}}^{n} Y_{ij} V_j \right]$$

or

$$V_i = \frac{1}{Y_{ii}}\left[\frac{P_i - jQ_i}{V_i^*} - \sum_{j=1}^{i-1} Y_{ij}V_j - \sum_{j=i+1}^{n} Y_{ij}V_j\right]$$

$$(V_i)^{k+1} = \frac{1}{Y_{ii}}\left[\frac{P_i - jQ_i}{(V_i^k)^*} - \sum_{j=1}^{i-1} Y_{ij}(V_j)^{k+1} - \sum_{j=i+1}^{n} Y_{ij}(V_j)^k\right] \quad (2.14)$$

8. Calculate the change in bus voltage

$$\Delta V_i^{k+1} = (V_i)^{k+1} - (V_i)^k \quad (2.15)$$

9. Acceleration of convergence: The process of convergence in the Gauss–Seidel method is slow as it requires larger number of iterations to obtain the solution. In this method, convergence can be increased by using the acceleration factor, denoted by α. In power flow studies, α is generally set about 1.6 and cannot exceed 2 if convergence is to occur. Therefore,

$$V_{i,\text{acc}}^{k+1} = (V_i)^k + \alpha\, \Delta V_i^{k+1} \quad (2.16)$$

Calculate the bus voltages, i.e. V_i^{k+1} for all the buses except the slack bus, where $i = 1, 2, 3, ..., n$.

10. Repeat the iterating process until change in voltage (ΔV_i) for all the buses are within the specified or within the tolerance.
11. Finally calculate the power flow and power losses.

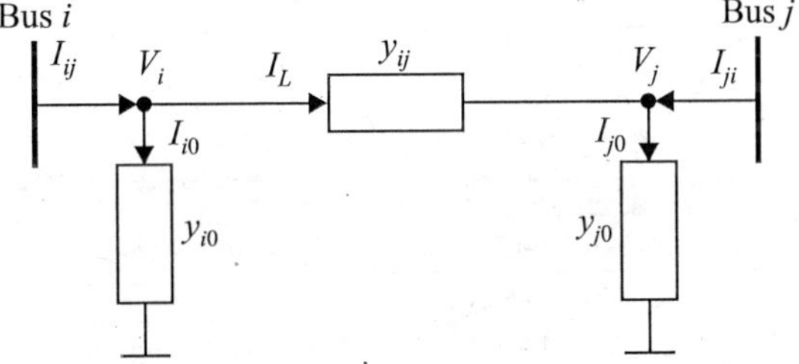

Current and power flows

$$i \rightarrow j$$

$$I_{ij} = I_L + I_{i0} = y_{ij}(V_i - V_j) + y_{i0}V_i$$
$$S_{ij} = V_i I_{ij}^* = V_i^2 (y_{ij} + y_{i0})^* - V_i y_{ij}^* V_j^*$$

$$j \rightarrow i$$

$$I_{ji} = -I_L + I_{j0} = y_{ij}(V_j - V_i) + y_{j0}V_j$$
$$S_{ji} = V_j I_{ij}^* = V_j^2 (y_{ij} + y_{j0})^* - V_j y_{ij}^* V_i^*$$

Power loss

$$S_{\text{loss}ij} = S_{ij} + S_{ji}$$

This completes the load flow study. Finally, in Figure 2.1 all the computational steps are summarized in the detailed flow chart.

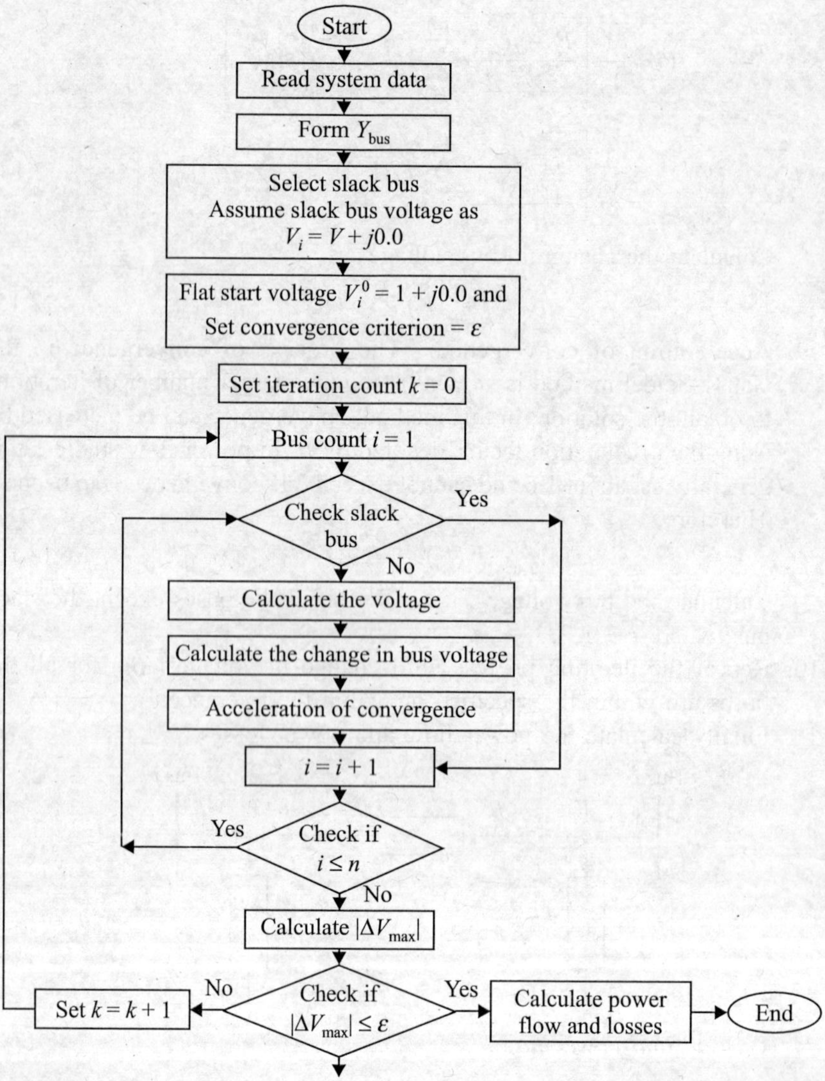

Figure 2.1 Flow chart for Gauss–Seidel method when *PV* buses are absent.

EXAMPLE 2.1 The per unit admittances are indicated at the diagram and the bus data are given in Table 2.1. Determine the voltages at buses 2 and 3 after the first iteration using the Gauss–Seidel method. Assume $\alpha = 1.6$.

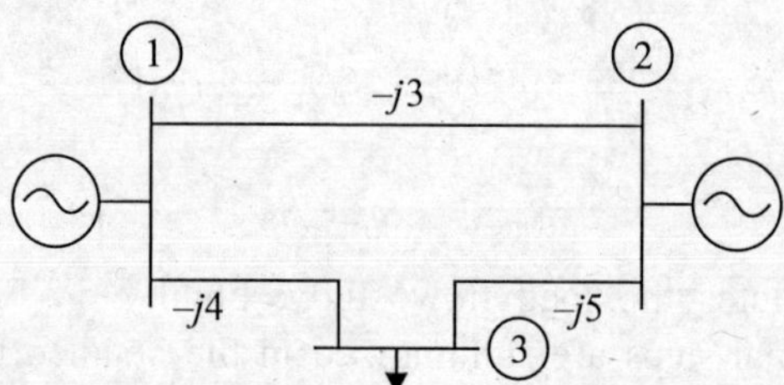

Table 2.1 Bus data

Bus No.	*Bus type*	*Generation (per unit)*		*Load (per unit)*		*Bus voltage*	
		P_G	Q_G	P_D	Q_D	V	δ
1	Slack	—	—	—	—	1.02	0
2	*PQ*	0.25	0.15	0.5	0.25	—	—
3	*PQ*	0	0	0.6	0.3	—	—

Solution: Form the Y_{bus}

$$Y_{11} = y_{12} + y_{13} = -j3 + (-j4) = -j7$$
$$Y_{12} = Y_{21} = -y_{12} = -(-j3) = j3$$
$$Y_{13} = Y_{31} = -y_{13} = -(-j4) = j4$$
$$Y_{22} = y_{21} + y_{23} = -j3 + (-j5) = -j8$$
$$Y_{23} = Y_{32} = -y_{23} = -(-j5) = j5$$
$$Y_{33} = y_{31} + y_{32} = -j4 + (-j5) = -j9$$

$$Y_{\text{bus}} = j\begin{bmatrix} -7 & 3 & 4 \\ 3 & -8 & 5 \\ 4 & 5 & -9 \end{bmatrix}$$

At bus 2,
$$P_2 = P_{G2} - P_{D2} = 0.25 - 0.5 = -0.25 \text{ p.u.}$$
$$Q_2 = Q_{G2} - Q_{D2} = 0.15 - 0.25 = -0.1 \text{ p.u.}$$

At bus 3,
$$P_3 = P_{G3} - P_{D3} = 0 - 0.6 = -0.6 \text{ p.u.}$$
$$Q_3 = Q_{G3} - Q_{D3} = 0 - 0.3 = -0.3 \text{ p.u.}$$

First iteration

Set $k = 0$, bus 1 is the slack bus.

$$\therefore \qquad V_1^0 = V_1^1 = V_1^2 = V_1^3 = \cdots = 1.02 + j0.0$$

Assume a flat start voltage for *PQ* buses.

$$V_2^0 = 1\angle 0; V_3^0 = 1\angle 0$$

The voltage at bus 2 is

$$(V_2)^1 = \frac{1}{Y_{22}}\left[\frac{P_2 - jQ_2}{(V_2^0)^*} - Y_{21}V_1 - Y_{23}(V_3)^0\right]$$

$$= \frac{1}{-j8}\left[\frac{-0.25 + j0.1}{1\angle 0} - j3\times 1.02\angle 0 - j5\times 1\angle 0\right]$$

$$= 0.995 - j0.03125$$

$$\Delta V_2^1 = (V_2)^1 - (V_2)^0 = (0.995 - j0.03125) - (1 + j0.0) = -0.005 - j0.03125$$

$$V_{2,\text{acc}}^1 = (V_2)^0 + \alpha\,\Delta V_2^1 = (1 + j0.0) + 1.6 \times (-0.005 - j0.03125)$$
$$= 0.992 - j0.0499$$

The voltage at bus 3 is

$$(V_3)^1 = \frac{1}{Y_{33}}\left[\frac{P_3 - jQ_3}{(V_3^0)^*} - Y_{31}V_1 - Y_{32}(V_2)^1\right]$$

$$= \frac{1}{-j9}\left[\frac{-0.6 + j0.3}{1\angle 0} - j4 \times 1.02\angle 0 - j5 \times (0.992 - j0.0499)\right]$$

$$= 0.971 - j0.0944$$

$$\Delta V_3^1 = (V_3)^1 - (V_3)^0 = (0.971 - j0.0944) - (1 + j0.0) = -0.029 - j0.0944$$

$$V_{3,\text{acc}}^1 = (V_3)^0 + \alpha\,\Delta V_3^1 = (1 + j0.0) + 1.6 \times (-0.029 - j0.0944)$$

$$= 0.9536 - j0.1514$$

The bus voltages at the end of the first iteration are

$$V_1^1 = 1.02 + j0$$

$$V_2^1 = 0.992 - j0.0499$$

$$V_3^1 = 0.9536 - j0.1514$$

EXAMPLE 2.2 The system data for a load flow solution are given in Tables 2.2 and 2.3. Determine the voltages at the end of the first iteration using the Gauss–Seidel method. Take $\alpha = 1.6$.

Table 2.2 Line admittances

Bus code	*Admittance*
1–2	2 – j8.0
1–3	1 – j4.0
2–3	0.666 – j2.664
2–4	1 – j4.0
3–4	2 – j8.0

Table 2.3 Schedule of active and reactive powers

Bus code	*P in* p.u.	*Q in* p.u.	*V in* p.u.	*Remarks*
1	—	—	1.06	Slack
2	0.5	0.2	1 + j0.0	PQ
3	0.4	0.3	1 + j0.0	PQ
4	0.3	0.1	1 + j0.0	PQ

Solution:

$$Y_{11} = y_{12} + y_{13} = (2 - j8) + (1 - j4) = 3 - j12$$

$$Y_{12} = Y_{21} = -y_{12} = -(2 - j8) = -2 + j8$$

$$Y_{13} = Y_{31} = -y_{13} = -(1 - j4) = -1 + j4$$

$$Y_{22} = y_{21} + y_{23} + y_{24} = (2 - j8) + (0.666 - j2.664) + (1 - j4)$$

$$= 3.666 - j14.664$$

$$Y_{23} = Y_{32} = -y_{23} = -(0.666 - j2.664) = -0.666 + j2.664$$

$$Y_{24} = Y_{42} = -y_{24} = -(1 - j4) = -1 + j4$$

$$Y_{33} = y_{31} + y_{32} + y_{34} = (1 - j4) + (0.666 - j2.664) + (2 - j8)$$

$$= 3.666 - j14.664$$

$$Y_{34} = Y_{43} = -y_{34} = -(2 - j8) = -2 + j8$$

$$Y_{44} = y_{42} + y_{43} = (1 - j4) + (2 - j8) = 3 - j12$$

$$Y_{\text{bus}} = \begin{bmatrix} 3 - j12 & -2 + j8 & -1 + j4 & 0 \\ -2 + j8 & 3.666 - j14.664 & -0.666 + j2.664 & -1 + j4 \\ -1 + j4 & -0.666 + j2.664 & 3.666 - j14.664 & -2 + j8 \\ 0 & -1 + j4 & -2 + j8 & 3 - j12 \end{bmatrix}$$

At bus 2, $P_2 = P_{G2} - P_{D2} = 0 - 0.5 = -0.5$ p.u.

$Q_2 = Q_{G2} - Q_{D2} = 0 - 0.2 = -0.2$ p.u.

At bus 3, $P_3 = P_{G3} - P_{D3} = 0 - 0.4 = -0.4$ p.u.

$Q_3 = Q_{G3} - Q_{D3} = 0 - 0.3 = -0.3$ p.u.

At bus 4, $P_4 = P_{G4} - P_{D4} = 0 - 0.3 = -0.3$ p.u.

$Q_4 = Q_{G4} - Q_{D4} = 0 - 0.1 = -0.1$ p.u.

First iteration

Set $k = 0$, bus 1 is slack bus.

$$\therefore \quad V_1^0 = V_1^1 = V_1^2 = V_1^3 = \cdots = 1.06 + j0.0$$

Assume a flat start voltage for PQ buses

$$V_2^0 = 1 \angle 0; V_3^0 = 1 \angle 0; V_4^0 = 1 \angle 0$$

The voltage at bus 2 is

$$(V_2)^1 = \frac{1}{Y_{22}}\left[\frac{P_2 - jQ_2}{(V_2^0)^*} - Y_{21}V_1^1 - Y_{23}V_3^0 - Y_{24}V_4^0\right]$$

$$V_2^1 = \frac{1}{3.666 - j14.664}\left[\frac{-0.5 + j0.2}{1 - j0.0} - 1.06(-2 + j8)\right.$$

$$\left. -1.0(-0.666 + j2.664) - (-1 + j4)1.0\right]$$

$$= 1.01187 - j0.02888$$

$$\Delta V_2^1 = (V_2)^1 - (V_2)^0 = (1.01187 - j0.02888) - (1 + j0.0)$$

$$= 0.01187 - j0.02888$$

$$V_{2,\text{acc}}^1 = (V_2)^0 + \alpha\, \Delta V_2^1 = (1 + j0.0) + 1.6 \times (0.01187 - j0.02888)$$

$$= 1.01896 - j0.04621$$

The voltage at bus 3 is

$$(V_3)^1 = \frac{1}{Y_{33}}\left[\frac{P_3 - jQ_3}{(V_3^0)^*} - Y_{31}V_1^1 - Y_{32}V_2^1 - Y_{34}V_3^0\right]$$

$$V_3^1 = \frac{1}{3.666 - j14.664}\left[\frac{-0.4 + j0.3}{1 - j0} - (-1 + j4)(1.06)\right.$$

$$\left. - (-0.666 + j2.664)(1.01187 - j0.02888) - (-2 + j8)(1)\right]$$

$$= 0.9926 - j0.026$$

$$\Delta V_3^1 = (V_3)^1 - (V_3)^0 = (0.9926 - j0.026) - (1 + j0.0)$$

$$= -7.4 \times 10^{-3} - j0.026$$

$$V_{3,\text{acc}}^1 = (V_3)^0 + \alpha\,\Delta V_3^1 = (1 + j0.0) + 1.6 \times (-7.4 \times 10^{-3} - j0.026)$$

$$= 0.988 - j0.0416$$

The voltage at bus 4 is

$$(V_4)^1 = \frac{1}{Y_{44}}\left[\frac{P_4 - jQ_4}{(V_4^0)^*} - Y_{41}V_1^1 - Y_{42}V_2^1 - Y_{43}V_3^1\right]$$

$$V_4^1 = \frac{1}{3 - j12}\left[\frac{-0.3 + j0.1}{1 - j0} - (0)(1.06) - (-1 + j4)(1.01187 - j0.02888)\right.$$

$$\left. - (-2 + j8)(0.988 - j0.0416)\right]$$

$$= 0.9825 - j0.06$$

$$\Delta V_4^1 = (V_4)^1 - (V_4)^0 = (0.9825 - j0.06) - (1 + j0.0)$$

$$= -0.0175 - j0.06$$

$$V_{4,\text{acc}}^1 = (V_4)^0 + \alpha\,\Delta V_4^1 = (1 + j0.0) + 1.6 \times (-0.0175 - j0.06)$$

$$= 0.9721 - j0.096$$

The bus voltages at the end of the first iteration are

$$V_1^1 = 1.06 + j0$$

$$V_2^1 = 1.01896 - j0.04621$$

$$V_3^1 = 0.988 - j0.0416$$

$$V_4^1 = 0.9721 - j0.096$$

EXAMPLE 2.3 Figure 2.2 shows the one line diagram of a simple three bus system with generation at bus 1. The magnitude of voltage at a bus 1 is adjusted to 1.05 p.u. The scheduled loads at buses 2 and 3 are as marked in the diagram. The line impedances are marked in p.u. on a 100 MVA base and the line charging susceptances are neglected.

(a) Using the Gauss–Seidel method, determine the phasor values of the voltages at the load buses 2 and 3 (*P-Q* buses) accurate to decimal places.
(b) Verify the result with Power World Simulator and PSS/E.

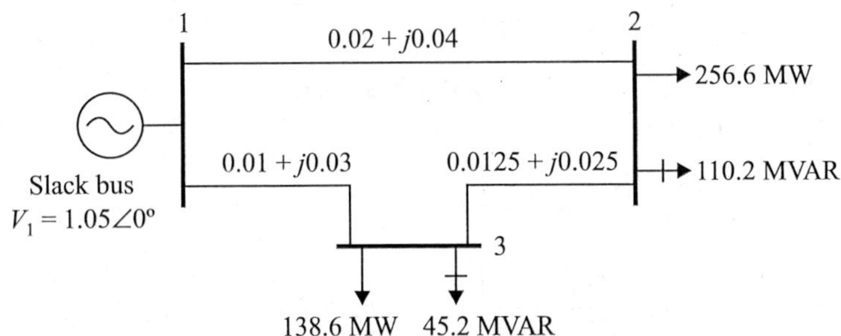

Figure 2.2 One line diagram of a simple three bus system.

Solution: (a) To form the Y_{bus}

$$y_{12} = \frac{1}{z_{12}} = \frac{1}{0.02 + j0.04} = 10 - j20$$

$$y_{13} = \frac{1}{z_{13}} = \frac{1}{0.01 + j0.03} = 10 - j30$$

$$y_{23} = \frac{1}{z_{23}} = \frac{1}{0.0125 + j0.025} = 16 - j32$$

$$Y_{11} = y_{12} + y_{13} = (10 - j20) + (10 - j30) = 20 - j50$$

$$Y_{12} = Y_{21} = -y_{12} = -(10 - j20) = -10 + j20$$

$$Y_{13} = Y_{31} = -y_{13} = -(10 - j30) = -10 + j30$$

$$Y_{22} = y_{21} + y_{23} = (10 - j20) + (16 - j32) = 26 - j52$$

$$Y_{23} = Y_{32} = -y_{23} = -(16 - j32) = -16 + j32$$

$$Y_{33} = y_{31} + y_{32} = (10 - j30) + (16 - j32) = 26 - j62$$

$$Y_{\text{bus}} = \begin{bmatrix} 20 - j50 & -10 + j20 & -10 + j30 \\ -10 + j20 & 26 - j52 & -16 + j32 \\ -10 + j30 & -16 + j32 & 26 - j62 \end{bmatrix}$$

At bus 2,

$$P_2 = P_{G2} - P_{D2} = 0 - \frac{256.6}{100} = -2.566 \text{ p.u.}$$

$$Q_2 = Q_{G2} - Q_{D2} = 0 - \frac{110.2}{100} = -1.102 \text{ p.u.}$$

At bus 3,

$$P_3 = P_{G3} - P_{D3} = 0 - \frac{138.6}{100} = -1.386 \text{ p.u.}$$

$$Q_3 = Q_{G3} - Q_{D3} = 0 - \frac{45.2}{100} = -0.452 \text{ p.u.}$$

First iteration

Set $k = 0$, bus 1 is the slack bus.

$$\therefore \qquad V_1^0 = V_1^1 = V_1^2 = V_1^3 = \cdots = 1.05 + j0.0$$

Assume a flat start voltage for *PQ* buses

$$V_2^0 = 1\angle 0; V_3^0 = 1\angle 0$$

The voltage at bus 2 is

$$(V_2)^1 = \frac{1}{Y_{22}}\left[\frac{P_2 - jQ_2}{(V_2^0)^*} - Y_{21}V_1^1 - Y_{23}V_3^0 - Y_{24}V_4^0\right]$$

$$V_2^1 = \frac{1}{26 - j52}\left[\frac{-2.566 + j1.102}{1 - j0.0} - (-10 + j20)1.05 - (-16 + j32)1.0\right]$$

$$= 0.9825 - j0.0310$$

The voltage at bus 3 is

$$(V_3)^1 = \frac{1}{Y_{33}}\left[\frac{P_3 - jQ_3}{(V_3^0)^*} - Y_{31}V_1^1 - Y_{32}V_2^1\right]$$

$$V_3^1 = \frac{1}{26 - j62}\left[\frac{-1.386 + j0.452}{1 - j0} - (-10 + j30)(1.05) - (-16 + j32)(0.9825 - j0.0310)\right] = 1.0011 - j0.0353$$

The bus voltages at the end of the first iteration are

$$V_1^1 = 1.05 + j0$$

$$V_2^1 = 0.9825 - j0.0310$$

$$V_3^1 = 1.0011 - j0.0353$$

(b) **Verify the result using Power World Simulator (PWS):** The one line diagram of a simple bus system is drawn in PWS, which is shown in Figure 2.3.

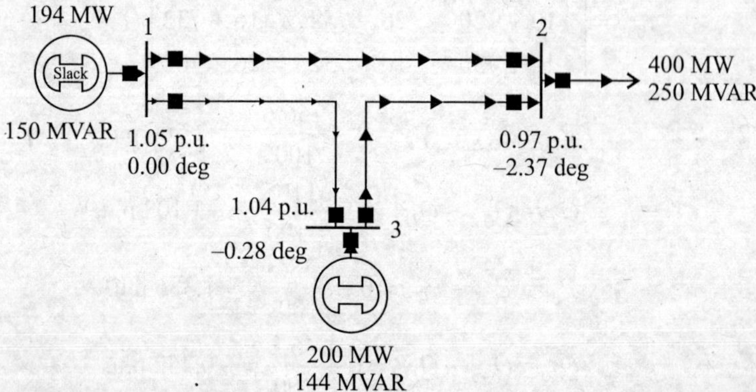

Figure 2.3 One line diagram of a simple three bus system (in PWS).

The first step is the formation of $[Y_{bus}]$ using the inspection method. The calculated $[Y_{bus}]$ values are given in Figure 2.4. Since the given problem is a three bus system, the size of $[Y_{bus}]$ is 3×3 matrix.

Y Bus (Bus Admittance Matrix)

Records ▾ Geo ▾ Set ▾ Columns ▾ f(x) ▾

Filter Advanced ▾ Bus ▾ Find... Remove

	Number	Name	Bus 1	Bus 2	Bus 3
1	1	1	20.00 - j50.00	-10.00 + j20.00	-10.00 + j30.00
2	2	2	-10.00 + j20.00	26.00 - j52.00	-16.00 + j32.00
3	3	3	-10.00 + j30.00	-16.00 + j32.00	26.00 - j62.00

Figure 2.4 Y_{bus} result.

There are three possible methods for executing load flow studies in Power World Simulator (PWS).

Gauss–Seidel method

Before executing this method, the number of iterations is to be fixed as 1 in *simulator options ribbon* to get the first iteration result. This method is executed by pressing the icon *Gauss–Seidel power flow* available in *tools ribbon*. The power flows and voltages are given in Figure 2.5 for the 1st iteration.

Bus Power Flows - Case: book_sample.PWB Status: Paused | Simulator ...

Case Information Draw Onelines Tools Options Add Ons Window

Edit Mode | Run Mode | Mode — Model Explorer... | Area/Zone Filters... | Limit Monitoring... — Network ▾ | Aggregation ▾ | Solution Details ▾ — Case Information — Difference Flows ▾ | Simulator Options... — Case Description... | Case Summary... | Custom Case Info... — Power Flow List... | Quick Power Flow List... | AUX Export Format Desc... — Case Data — Bus View... | Substation View... | Open Windows ▾ — Views

Records ▾ Geo ▾ Set ▾ Columns ▾ f(x) ▾ Power Flow List

```
                                   Bus Flows
BUS        1 1         138.0    MW      Mvar      MVA    % 1.0500    0.00    1 1
 GENERATOR 1                  193.85  149.73R   244.9
 TO        2 2         1      167.41  123.50    208.0   0
 TO        3 3         1       26.44   26.23     37.2   0
 **** Mismatch ****           193.85  149.73
BUS        2 2         138.0    MW      Mvar      MVA    % 0.9719   -2.37    1 1
 LOAD 1                       400.00  250.00    471.7
 TO        1 1         1     -159.56 -107.80    192.6   0
 TO        3 3         1     -223.06 -150.52    269.1   0
 **** Mismatch ****           -17.39    8.32
BUS        3 3         138.0    MW      Mvar      MVA    % 1.0400   -0.28    1 1
 GENERATOR 1                  200.00  143.83R   246.3
 TO        1 1         1      -26.32  -25.85     36.9   0
 TO        2 2         1      232.64  169.68    287.9   0
 **** Mismatch ****           193.68  143.83
```

Figure 2.5 Power flow results and voltages—1st iteration.

Now change the number of iterations as 2 in *simulator options ribbon* for getting the results of the second iteration and execute *Gauss–Seidel power flow*. The results are shown in Figure 2.6 for iteration 2.

```
BUS        1 1            138.0    MW      Mvar        MVA   % 1.0500    0.00    1 1
 GENERATOR 1                208.07  144.78R  253.5
 TO        2 2           1  174.39  120.92   212.2   0
 TO        3 3           1   33.68   23.87    41.3   0
 **** Mismatch ****         208.07  144.78
BUS        2 2            138.0    MW      Mvar        MVA   % 0.9717   -2.56    1 1
 LOAD 1                     400.00  250.00   471.7
 TO        1 1           1 -166.22 -104.58   196.4   0
 TO        3 3           1 -226.67 -149.32   271.4   0
 **** Mismatch ****          -7.11    3.90
BUS        3 3            138.0    MW      Mvar        MVA   % 1.0400   -0.40    1 1
 GENERATOR 1                200.00  145.42R  247.3
 TO        1 1           1  -33.52  -23.40    40.9   0
 TO        2 2           1  236.42  168.83   290.5   0
 **** Mismatch ****         197.10  145.42
```

Figure 2.6 Power flow results and voltages—2nd iteration.

Figure 2.6 indicates that there are mismatches in all three bus voltages. So, the execution should be continued until converged solution is obtained. This method gives converged results after 8th iterations for this problem. Before executing the program, the numbers of iterations have to be changed as 10. This is shown in Figure 2.7.

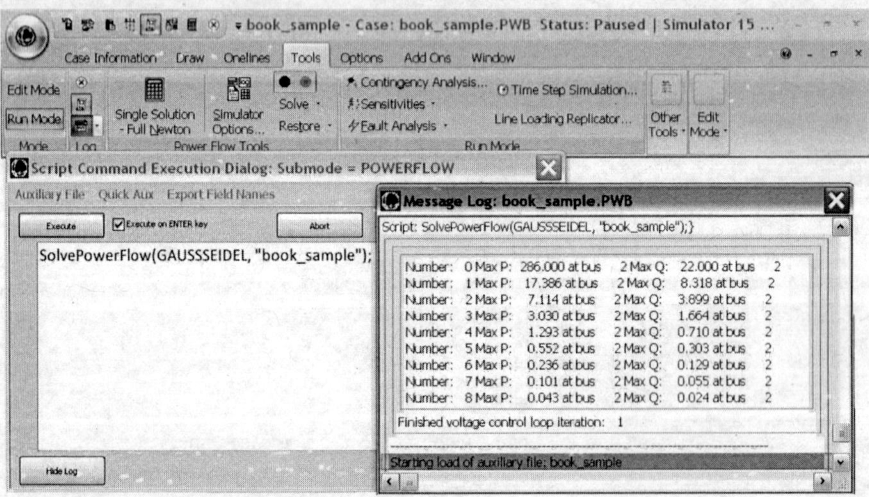

Figure 2.7 Details of convergence and iterations.

The final solutions are obtained after 8th iterations and it is shown in Figure 2.8.

Bus Power Flows - Case: book_sample.PWB Status: Paused | Simulator ...

BUS	1 1	138.0	MW	Mvar	MVA	%	1.0500	0.00	1 1
GENERATOR	1		218.36	140.88R	259.9				
TO	2 2	1	179.33	118.75	215.1	0			
TO	3 3	1	39.03	22.13	44.9	0			
**** Mismatch ****			218.36	140.88					
BUS	2 2	138.0	MW	Mvar	MVA	%	0.9717	-2.70	1 1
LOAD 1			400.00	250.00	471.7				
TO	1 1	1	-170.94	-101.96	199.0	0			
TO	3 3	1	-229.02	-148.06	272.7	0			
BUS	3 3	138.0	MW	Mvar	MVA	%	1.0400	-0.50	1 1
GENERATOR	1		200.00	146.17R	247.7				
TO	1 1	1	-38.85	-21.58	44.4	0			
TO	2 2	1	238.86	167.75	291.9	0			
**** Mismatch ****			199.98	146.17					

Figure 2.8 Converged power flow results and voltages.

PSS/E

The same problem is taken and drawn in PSS/E software and it is given in Figure 2.9.

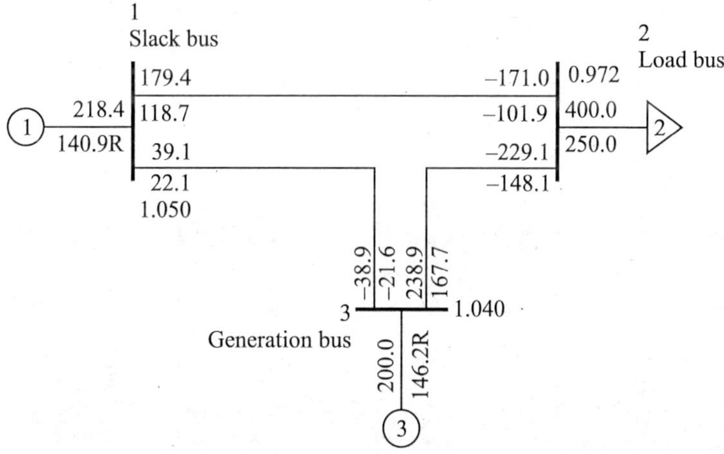

Figure 2.9 One line diagram of a simple three bus system (in PSS/E).

Once the data are entered in the software it can be executed by the above three power flow methods. Figure 2.10 shows the converged results obtained by the Gauss–Seidel method. This window is generated from *bus based report*.

2.5.2 Gauss–Seidel Method When *PV* Buses are Present

Some of the buses in an n bus power system are PV buses where P and V are specified but Q and δ are unknowns. The calculation strategy of Load flow solution with PV buses is different for PQ buses. Let the bus be numbered as

```
        PTI INTERACTIVE POWER              MON, JUN 27  2011    11:58    %MVA FOR TRANSFORMERS
      SYSTEM SIMULATOR--PSS®E                                   RATING   %I     FOR NON-TRANSFORMER BRANCHES
                                                                SET A
BUS     1 SLACK BUS    CKT     MV      MVAR     MVA   % 1.0500PU  0.00  X---LOSSES---X  X---AREA----X  X---ZONE---X  1
  FROM GENERATION             218.4   140.9R   260.0  260      kV          MV    MVAR         1              1
  TO    2 LOAD BUS       1    179.3   118.8    215.1                       8.39  16.79        1              1
  TO    3 GEN BUS        1     39.1    22.2     44.9                       0.18   0.55        1              1

BUS     2 LOAD BUS     CKT     MV      MVAR     MVA   % 0.9717PU -2.70  X---LOSSES---X  X---AREA----X  X---ZONE---X  2
                                                               kV          MV    MVAR         1              1
  TO LOAD-PQ                  400.0   250.0    471.7
  TO    1 SLACK BUS      1   -171.0  -102.0    199.1                       8.39  16.79        1              1
  TO    3 GEN BUS        1   -229.0  -148.1    272.7                       9.84  19.69        1              1

BUS     3 GEN BUS      CKT     MV      MVAR     MVA   % 1.0400PU -0.50  X---LOSSES---X  X---AREA----X  X---ZONE---X  3
  FROM GENERATION             200.0   146.1R   247.7  248      kV          MV    MVAR         1              1
  TO    1 SLACK BUS      1    -38.9   -21.6     44.5                       0.18   0.55        1              1
  TO    2 LOAD BUS       1    238.9   167.8    291.8                       9.84  19.69        1              1
                                                                                          Report
```

Figure 2.10 Converged results using Gauss–Seidel method.

$i = 1$ slack bus

$i = 2, 3, 4, \ldots, n$ *PQ* buses

$i = n + 1, n + 2, \ldots, n$ *PV* buses

Computational procedure

At the voltage controlled buses, bus voltages are specified and reactive power limits are also specified, i.e. $|V_i| = |V_i|_{\text{spec}}$; $Q_{i,\min} < Q_i < Q_{i,\max}$

1. Form the bus admittance matrix of the network by the direct inspection method, selecting the ground as reference [formation of Y_{bus}].
2. If slack bus is not specified, select one of the generator buses as the slack bus. The voltage at the slack bus is assumed as $V_i = V + j0.0$ [selection of the slack bus].
3. Assume initial values of voltages for all buses except the slack bus.

$$V_i^{(0)} = 1 + j0.0$$

4. For *PV* buses only angles $\delta_i^{(0)}$ have to be assumed.
5. Set convergence criterion = ε, i.e. if the largest of absolute of the residues exceeds the convergence criterion the process is repeated, otherwise it is terminated.
6. Set iteration count $k = 0$.
7. Bus count $i = 1$.
8. Check type of buses

   (a) If *i*th bus is *PQ* bus, go to step 10.
   (b) If *i*th bus is *PV* bus, go to the next step.

   Set $|V_i^k| = |V_i|_{\text{spec}}$
9. Calculate the reactive power of generator bus using the following equation

$$Q_i^{k+1} = -\,\text{im}\left[(V_i^k)^* \sum_{j=1}^{i-1} Y_{ij}(V_j)^{k+1} - (V_i^k)^* \sum_{j=1}^{n} Y_{ij}(V_j)^k \right] \tag{2.17}$$

   (a) If the calculated reactive power is within limits, then this bus can be treated as *PV* bus and set $Q_i = Q_i^{k+1}$.
   (b) If the calculated reactive power violates the limits, then this bus can be treated as *PQ* bus and set if

      (i) $Q_i^{k+1} < Q_{i,\min}$, then $Q_i = Q_{i,\min}$
      (ii) $Q_i^{k+1} > Q_{i,\max}$, then $Q_i = Q_{i,\max}$
10. Solve the voltage equation for bus *i* as, we know that

$$P_i - jQ_i = V_i^* \sum_{j=1}^{n} Y_{ij} V_j$$

$$\frac{P_i - jQ_i}{V_i^*} = V_i \sum_{j=0}^{n} Y_{ij} - \sum_{j=1}^{n} Y_{ij} V_j \qquad j \neq i$$

$$V_i = \frac{1}{Y_{ii}} \left[\frac{P_i - jQ_i}{V_i^*} - \sum_{\substack{j=1 \\ j \neq i}}^{n} Y_{ij} V_j \right]$$

or

$$V_i = \frac{1}{Y_{ii}} \left[\frac{P_i - jQ_i}{V_i^*} - \sum_{j=1}^{i-1} Y_{ij} V_j - \sum_{j=i+1}^{n} Y_{ij} V_j \right]$$

Equation (2.14) can be rewritten as

$$(V_i)^{k+1} = \frac{1}{Y_{ii}} \left[\frac{P_i - jQ_i}{(V_i^k)^*} - \sum_{j=1}^{i-1} Y_{ij} (V_j)^{k+1} - \sum_{j=i+1}^{n} Y_{ij} (V_j)^k \right]$$

11. Calculate the change in bus voltage

$$\Delta V_i^{k+1} = (V_i)^{k+1} - (V_i)^k$$

12. *Acceleration of convergence:* The process of convergence in the Gauss–Seidel method is slow as it requires larger number of iterations to obtain the solution. In this method, convergence can be increased by using the acceleration factor, denoted by α. In power flow studies, α is generally set about 1.6 and cannot exceed 2 if convergence is to occur. Therefore

$$V_{i,\text{acc}}^{k+1} = (V_i)^k + \alpha \, \Delta V_i^{k+1}$$

Calculate the bus voltages, i.e. V_i^{k+1} for all the buses except the slack bus, where $i = 1, 2, 3, \ldots, n$.

13. Repeat the iterating process until change in voltage (ΔV_i) for all the buses are within the specified or within the tolerance.
14. Finally calculate the power flow and power losses.

Current and power flows

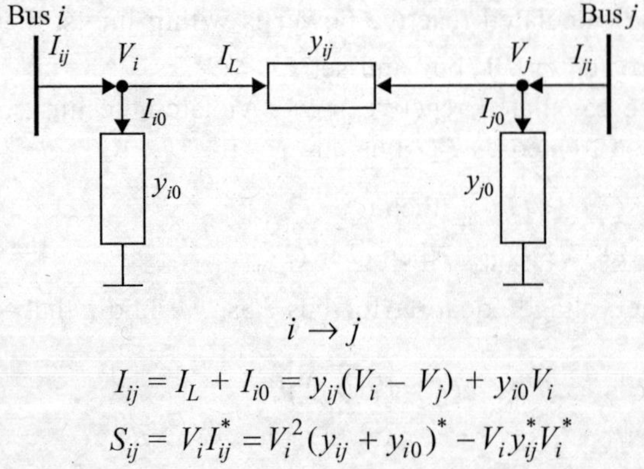

$$i \rightarrow j$$

$$I_{ij} = I_L + I_{i0} = y_{ij}(V_i - V_j) + y_{i0} V_i$$

$$S_{ij} = V_i I_{ij}^* = V_i^2 (y_{ij} + y_{i0})^* - V_i y_{ij}^* V_i^*$$

$$j \to i$$

$$I_{ji} = I_L + I_{j0} = y_{ij}(V_j - V_i) + y_{j0}V_j$$

$$S_{ji} = V_j I_{ij}^* = V_j^2 (y_{ij} + y_{j0})^* - V_j y_{ij}^* V_i^*$$

Power loss

$$S_{\text{loss}ij} = S_{ij} + S_{ji}$$

This completes the load flow study. Finally, in Figure 2.11 all the computational steps are summarized in the detailed flow chart.

Advantages and Disadvantages of Gauss–Seidel Method

Advantages

- The calculations are simple and so there is less programming task to perform.
- The memory requirement is small.
- Useful for the small systems.

Disadvantages

- Requires a large number of iterations to converge.
- Not suitable for large systems.
- Convergence time increases with the size of the system.

EXAMPLE 2.4 A three-bus power system is shown in Figure 2.12. The system parameters are given in Table 2.4 and the generation and demand data in Table 2.5. The voltage at bus 2 is maintained at 1.04 p.u. The maximum and minimum reactive power limits of the generation at bus 2 are 35 and 0 MVAR respectively. Determine one iteration of the load flow solution using the Gauss–Seidel iterative method. Assume bus 1 as slack bus and acceleration factor $\alpha = 1.6$.

Table 2.4 Bus code and impedance

Bus code	*Impedance in* p.u.	*Bus code*	*Line charging admittance* $\frac{y'_{ij}}{2}$
1–2	$0.06 + j0.18$	1	$j0.05$
1–3	$0.02 + j0.06$	2	$j0.06$
2–3	$0.04 + j0.12$	3	$j0.06$

Table 2.5 Scheduled bus voltages, real and reactive powers of generation and demand

Bus no.	*Bus voltage*	*Generation*		*Demand*	
		MW	MVAR	MW	MVAR
1	$1.06 + j0.0$	—	—	0	0
2	$1.04 + j0.0$	20	—	0	0
3	—	0	0	60	25

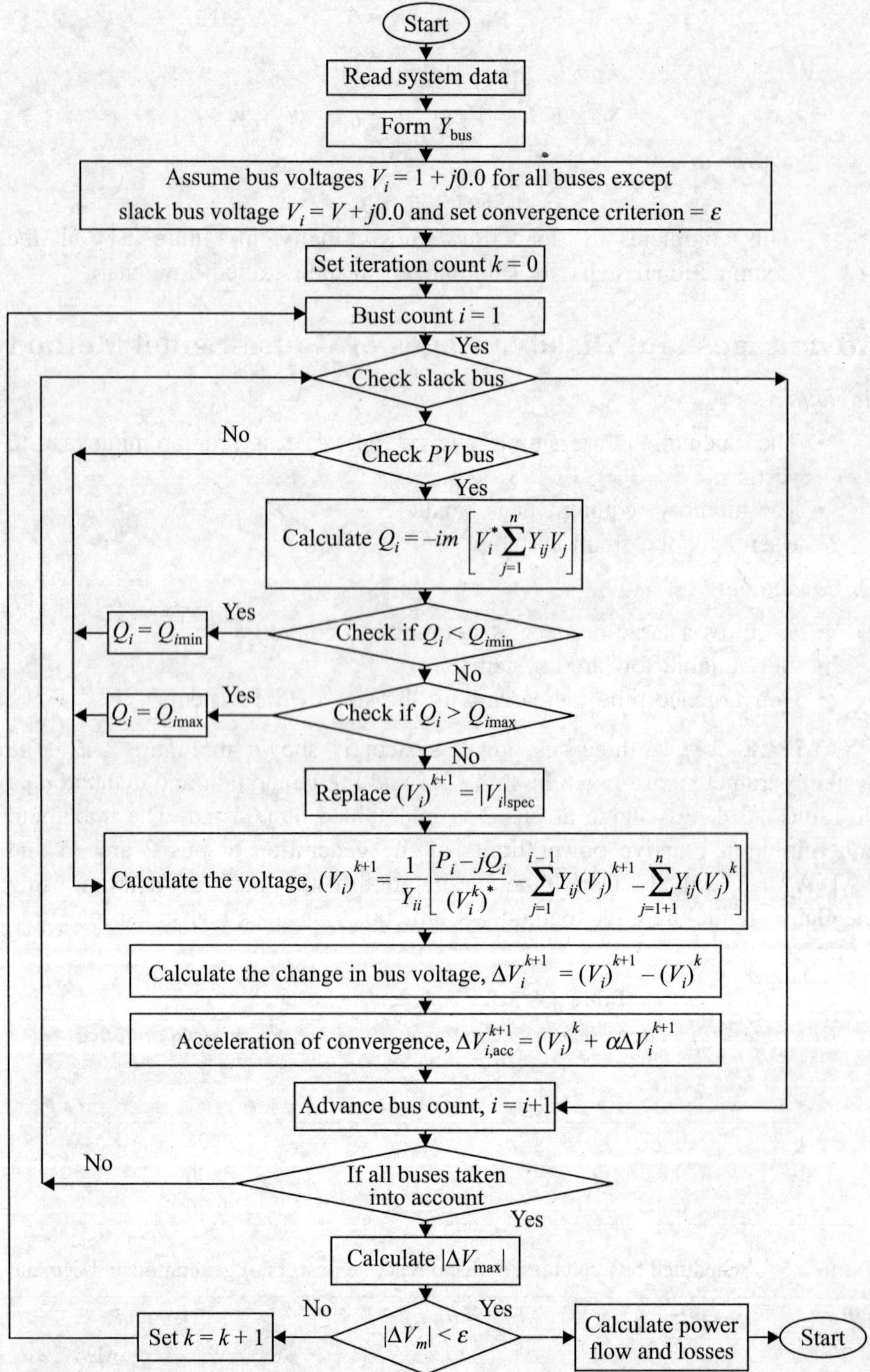

Figure 2.11 Flow chart for Gauss–Seidel method when PV buses are present.

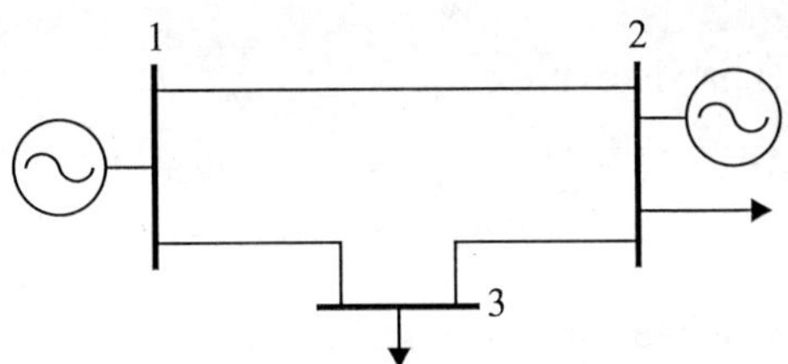

Figure 2.12 Three bus power system.

Solution: To form the Y_{bus}

$$y_{10} = \frac{y'_{12}}{2} + \frac{y'_{13}}{2} = j0.05 + j0.06 = j0.11$$

$$y_{20} = \frac{y'_{21}}{2} + \frac{y'_{22}}{2} = j0.05 + j0.06 = j0.11$$

$$y_{30} = \frac{y'_{31}}{2} + \frac{y'_{32}}{2} = j0.06 + j0.06 = j0.12$$

$$y_{12} = \frac{1}{z_{12}} = \frac{1}{0.06 + j0.18} = 1.67 - j5$$

$$y_{13} = \frac{1}{z_{13}} = \frac{1}{0.02 + j0.06} = 5 - j15$$

$$y_{23} = \frac{1}{z_{23}} = \frac{1}{0.04 + j0.12} = 2.5 - j7.5$$

$$Y_{11} = y_{10} + y_{12} + y_{13} = j0.11 + (1.67 - j5) + (5 - j15) = 6.67 - j19.89$$

$$Y_{12} = Y_{21} = -y_{12} = -(1.67 - j5) = -1.67 + j5$$

$$Y_{13} = Y_{31} = -y_{13} = -(5 - j15) = -5 + j15$$

$$Y_{22} = y_{20} + y_{21} + y_{23} = j0.11 + (1.67 - j5) + (2.5 - j7.5) = 4.17 - j12.39$$

$$Y_{23} = Y_{32} = -y_{23} = -(2.5 - j7.5) = -2.5 + j7.5$$

$$Y_{33} = y_{30} + y_{31} + y_{32} = j0.12 + (5 - j15) + (2.5 - j7.5) = 7.5 - j22.38$$

$$Y_{\text{bus}} = \begin{bmatrix} 6.67 - j19.89 & -1.67 + j5 & -5 + j15 \\ -1.67 + j5 & 4.17 - j12.39 & -2.5 + j7.5 \\ -5 + j15 & -2.5 + j7.5 & 7.5 - j22.38 \end{bmatrix}$$

At bus 2,

$$P_2 = P_{G2} - P_{D2} = \frac{20}{100} - 0 = 0.2 \text{ p.u.}$$

$$Q_2 = Q_{G2} - Q_{D2} = ? - 0 = ? \text{ p.u.}$$

At bus 3,

$$P_3 = P_{G3} - P_{D3} = 0 - \frac{60}{100} = -0.6 \text{ p.u.}$$

$$Q_3 = Q_{G3} - Q_{D3} = 0 - \frac{25}{100} = -0.25 \text{ p.u.}$$

First iteration

Set $k = 0$, Bus 1 is slack bus.

$$\therefore \quad V_1^0 = V_1^1 = V_1^2 = V_1^3 = \cdots = 1.06 + j0.0$$

$$V_2^{\,0} = 1.04\angle 0$$

Assume a flat start voltage for PQ buses

$$V_3^{\,0} = 1\angle 0$$

Determine the voltage at bus 2.

Given the reactive power limit:

$$0 \text{ MVAR} < Q_{G2} < 35 \text{ MVAR or } 0 \text{ p.u.} < Q_{G2} < 0.3 \text{ p.u.}$$

So to find V_2^1, first Q_2^1 is calculated.

$$(Q_i)^{k+1} = -\text{im}\left[(V_i^k)^* \sum_{j=1}^{i-1} Y_{ij}(V_j)^{k+1} - (V_i^k)^* \sum_{j=1}^{n} Y_{ij}(V_j)^k \right]$$

$$Q_2^1 = -\text{im}\,[(V_2^0)^* Y_{21} V_1^1 + (V_2^0)^* (Y_{22}V_2^0 + Y_{23}V_3^0)]$$

$$Q_2^1 = -\text{im}\,[(V_2^0)^* (Y_{21}V_1^1 + Y_{22}V_2^0 + Y_{23}V_3^0)]$$

$$Q_2^1 = -\text{im}\ [(1.04 - j0)\,(-1.67 + j5)\,(1.06 + j0.0) + (4.17 - j12.4)\,(1.04 - j0) + (-2.5 + j7.5)\,(1 + j0.0)]$$

$$Q_2^1 = -\text{im}\ [0.06947 - j0.09984]$$

$$Q_2^1 = 0.09984$$

The value of Q_2^1 is within the limits and so the reactive power limit is not violated. Therefore bus 2 can be treated as PV bus.

Now to find V_2^1

$$V_2^1 = \frac{1}{Y_{22}}\left[\frac{P_2 - jQ_2^1}{(V_2^0)^*} - Y_{21}V_1^1 - Y_{23}V_3^0 \right]$$

$$V_2^1 = \frac{1}{4.17 - j12.4}\left[\frac{0.2 - j0.09984}{1.04 - j0.0} - (-1.67 + j5)\,1.06 - (-2.5 + j7.5)\,(1.0) \right]$$

$$= 1.0432\angle 0.4985°$$

$$\delta_2^1 = \angle\, 0.4985°$$

We get $|V_2^1| = |V_2^1|_{\text{spec}}\angle\delta_2^1 = 1.01\angle 0.4985° = 1.0399 + j0.009$

The voltage at bus 3 (PQ bus) is

$$(V_3)^1 = \frac{1}{Y_{33}}\left[\frac{P_3 - jQ_3}{(V_3^0)^*} - Y_{31}V_2^1 - Y_{32}V_2^1 \right]$$

$$V_3^1 = \frac{1}{7.5 - j22.38}\left[\frac{-0.6 + j0.25}{1 - j0} - (5 + j15)(1.06) - (-2.5 + j7.5)(1.0399 + j0.009)\right]$$

$$= 0.9499 + j0.0109$$

$$\Delta V_3^1 = (V_3)^1 - (V_3)^0 = (0.9499 + j0.0109) - (1 + j0.0)$$

$$= -0.0501 + j0.0109$$

$$V_{3,\text{acc}}^1 = (V_3)^0 + \alpha \Delta V_3^1 = (1 + j0.0) + 1.6 \times (-0.0501 + j0.0109)$$

$$= 0.91984 - j0.01744$$

The bus voltages at the end of the first iteration are

$$V_1^1 = 1.06 + j0$$

$$V_2^1 = 1.0399 + j0.009$$

$$V_3^1 = 0.91984 - j0.01744$$

EXAMPLE 2.5 If the reactive power constraint on generator 2 is 0.2 p.u. < Q_{G2} < 0.5 p.u. in the Example 2.4, then find the bus voltages at the end of the first iteration. Assume the acceleration factor is 1.6.

Solution: In the previous example we have calculated Q_2^1 as

$$Q_2^1 = 0.09984$$

This value of reactive power violates the lower limit of Q_{G2}. Therefore Q_{G2} is fixed at 0.2 p.u. Hence the bus 2 is considered as a load bus.

Now

At bus 2,
$$P_2 = P_{G2} - P_{D2} = \frac{20}{100} - 0 = 0.2 \text{ p.u.}$$

$$Q_2 = Q_{G2} - Q_{D2} = 0.2 - 0 = 0.2 \text{ p.u.}$$

At bus 3,
$$P_3 = P_{G3} - P_{D3} = 0 - \frac{60}{100} = -0.6 \text{ p.u.}$$

$$Q_3 = Q_{G3} - Q_{D3} = 0 - \frac{25}{100} = -0.25 \text{ p.u.}$$

First iteration

Set $k = 0$, bus 1 is the slack bus.

$$\therefore \quad V_1^0 = V_1^1 = V_1^2 = V_1^3 = \cdots = 1.06 + j0.0$$

Assume a flat start voltage for PQ buses

$$V_2^0 = 1\angle 0$$

$$V_3^0 = 1\angle 0$$

The voltage at bus 2 (*PQ* bus) is

$$V_2^1 = \frac{1}{Y_{22}}\left[\frac{P_2 - jQ_2^1}{(V_2^0)^*} - Y_{21}V_1^1 - Y_{23}V_3^0\right]$$

$$V_2^1 = \frac{1}{4.17 - j12.4}\left[\frac{0.2 - j0.2}{(1 - j0.0)} - (-1.67 + j5)1.06 - (-2.5 + j7.5)(1.0)\right]$$

$$= 1.0508 + j0.00713$$

$$\Delta V_2^1 = (V_2)^1 - (V_2)^0 = (1.0508 + j0.00713) - (1 + j0.0)$$

$$= 0.0508 + j0.00713$$

$$V_{2,\text{acc}}^1 = (V_2)^0 + \alpha\,\Delta V_2^1 = (1 + j0.0) + 1.6 \times (0.0508 + j0.00713)$$

$$= 1.08128 + j0.0114$$

The voltage at bus 3 (*PQ* bus) is

$$(V_3)^1 = \frac{1}{Y_{33}}\left[\frac{P_3 - jQ_3}{(V_3^0)^*} - Y_{31}V_2^1 - Y_{32}V_2^1\right]$$

$$V_3^1 = \frac{1}{7.5 - j22.38}\left[\frac{-0.6 + j0.25}{1 - j0} - (5 + j15)(1.06) - (-2.5 + j7.5)(1.08128 + j0.0114)\right]$$

$$= 0.963 + j0.0117$$

$$\Delta V_3^1 = (V_3)^1 - (V_3)^0 = (0.963 + j0.0117) - (1 + j0.0)$$

$$= -0.037 + j0.0117$$

$$V_{3,\text{acc}}^1 = (V_3)^0 + \alpha\,\Delta V_3^1 = (1 + j0.0) + 1.6 \times (-0.037 + j0.0117)$$

$$= 0.9421 - j0.01872$$

The bus voltages at the end of the first iteration are

$$V_1^1 = 1.06 + j0$$

$$V_2^1 = 1.08128 + j0.0114$$

$$V_3^1 = 0.9421 - j0.01872$$

2.6 Newton–Raphson Load Flow Method

2.6.1 Introduction

The Newton–Raphson method is a competent algorithm to solve nonlinear equations. It transforms the procedure of solving nonlinear equations into the procedure of repeatedly solving linear equations. This sequential linearization process is the core of the Newton–Raphson method.

$$f(x) = 0 \tag{2.18}$$

Let us assume that $f(x)$ is continuous and differential at a point $x(0)$, the initial guess for the sought root. Assume the real solution x is close to $x(0)$,

$$x = x^{(0)} - \Delta x^{(0)} \tag{2.19}$$

where $\Delta x^{(0)}$ is a correction value of $x^{(0)}$. The following equation embraces to

$$f(x^{(0)} - \Delta x^{(0)}) = 0 \tag{2.20}$$

Now expanding the above equation in a Taylor series expansion about point $x^{(0)}$ yields:

$$f(x^{(0)} - \Delta x^{(0)}) = f(x^{(0)}) - f'(x^{(0)})\,\Delta x^{(0)} + f''(x^{(0)})\frac{(\Delta x^{(0)})^2}{2!} - \cdots + (-1)^n f^n(x^{(0)})\frac{(\Delta x^{(0)})^n}{n!} + \cdots = 0 \tag{2.21}$$

where $f'(x^{(0)})$, ..., $f^n(x^{(0)})$ are the different order partial derivatives of $f(x)$ at $x(0)$. If the initial guess is sufficiently close to the actual solution, the higher order terms of the Taylor series expansion could be neglected. Equation (2.21) becomes

$$f(x^{(0)}) - f'(x^{(0)})\,\Delta x^{(0)} = 0 \tag{2.22}$$

This is a linear equation in $\Delta x^{(0)}$ and can be easily solved.

Using $\Delta x^{(0)}$ to modify $x^{(0)}$, we can get $x^{(1)}$

$$x^{(1)} = x^{(0)} - \Delta x^{(0)} \tag{2.23}$$

$x^{(1)}$ may be close to the actual solution. Then using $x^{(1)}$ as the new guess value, we solve the following equation similar to Eq. (2.22)

$$f(x^{(1)}) - f'(x^{(1)})\,\Delta x^{(1)} = 0 \tag{2.24}$$

Thus $x^{(2)}$ is obtained.

$$x^{(2)} = x^{(1)} - \Delta x^{(1)} \tag{2.25}$$

Repeat this procedure to establish the correction equation in the kth iteration:

$$f(x^{(k)}) - f'(x^{(k)})\,\Delta x^{(k)} = 0 \tag{2.26}$$

or

$$f(x^{(k)}) = f'(x^{(k)})\,\Delta x^{(k)} \tag{2.27}$$

The left-hand of the above equation can be considered as the error produced by the approximate solution $x^{(k)}$. When $f(x^{(k)}) \Rightarrow 0$, Eq. (2.18) is satisfied, so $x^{(k)}$ is the solution of the equation.

Now we will extend the Newton's method to simultaneous nonlinear equations. Assume the nonlinear equations with variables $x_1, x_2, \ldots, x_n$:

$$\left.\begin{aligned} f_1(x_1, x_2, \ldots, x_n) &= 0 \\ f_2(x_1, x_2, \ldots, x_n) &= 0 \\ &\vdots \\ f_n(x_1, x_2, \ldots, x_n) &= 0 \end{aligned}\right\} \tag{2.28}$$

Specify the initial guess values of all variables $x_1^{(0)}, x_2^{(0)}, \ldots, x_n^{(0)}$. Let $\Delta x_1^{(0)}$, $\Delta x_2^{(0)}$, $\Delta x_3^{(0)}$, ..., $\Delta x_n^{(0)}$ be the correction values to satisfy the following equations:

$$\left.\begin{aligned} f_1(x_1^{(0)} - \Delta x_1^{(0)}, x_2^{(0)} - \Delta x_2^{(0)}, \ldots, x_n^{(0)} - \Delta x_n^{(0)}) = 0 \\ f_2(x_1^{(0)} - \Delta x_1^{(0)}, x_2^{(0)} - \Delta x_2^{(0)}, \ldots, x_n^{(0)} - \Delta x_n^{(0)}) = 0 \\ \vdots \qquad\qquad \\ f_n(x_1^{(0)} - \Delta x_1^{(0)}, x_2^{(0)} - \Delta x_2^{(0)}, \ldots, x_n^{(0)} - \Delta x_n^{(0)}) = 0 \end{aligned}\right\} \tag{2.29}$$

Expanding the above equations via the multivariate Taylor series and neglecting the higher order terms, we have the following equations:

$$\left.\begin{aligned} f_1(x_1^{(0)}, x_2^{(0)}, \ldots, x_n^{(0)}) \left[\left(\frac{\partial f_1}{\partial x_1}\right)^{(0)} \Delta x_1^{(0)} + \left(\frac{\partial f_1}{\partial x_2}\right)^{(0)} \Delta x_2^{(0)} + \cdots + \left(\frac{\partial f_1}{\partial x_n}\right)^{(0)} \Delta x_n^{(0)}\right] = 0 \\ f_2(x_1^{(0)}, x_2^{(0)}, \ldots, x_n^{(0)}) \left[\left(\frac{\partial f_2}{\partial x_1}\right)^{(0)} \Delta x_1^{(0)} + \left(\frac{\partial f_2}{\partial x_2}\right)^{(0)} \Delta x_2^{(0)} + \cdots + \left(\frac{\partial f_2}{\partial x_n}\right)^{(0)} \Delta x_n^{(0)}\right] = 0 \\ \vdots \qquad\qquad\qquad\qquad \vdots \qquad\qquad\qquad\qquad \\ f_n(x_1^{(0)}, x_2^{(0)}, \ldots, x_n^{(0)}) \left[\left(\frac{\partial f_n}{\partial x_1}\right)^{(0)} \Delta x_1^{(0)} + \left(\frac{\partial f_n}{\partial x_2}\right)^{(0)} \Delta x_2^{(0)} + \cdots + \left(\frac{\partial f_n}{\partial x_n}\right)^{(0)} \Delta x_n^{(0)}\right] = 0 \end{aligned}\right\} \tag{2.30}$$

Here $(\partial f_1/\partial x_2)^{(0)}$ is the partial derivative of function $f_1(x_1, x_2, \ldots, x_n)$ over independent variable x_j at the point $(x_1^{(0)}, x_2^{(0)}, \ldots, x_n^{(0)})$. Rewrite the above equation in the matrix form.

$$\begin{bmatrix} f_1(x_1^{(0)}, x_2^{(0)}, \ldots, x_n^{(0)}) \\ f_2(x_1^{(0)}, x_2^{(0)}, \ldots, x_n^{(0)}) \\ \vdots \qquad \vdots \\ f_n(x_1^{(0)}, x_2^{(0)}, \ldots, x_n^{(0)}) \end{bmatrix} = \begin{bmatrix} \left(\frac{\partial f_1}{\partial x_1}\right)^{(0)} & \left(\frac{\partial f_1}{\partial x_2}\right)^{(0)} & \cdots & \left(\frac{\partial f_1}{\partial x_n}\right)^{(0)} \\ \left(\frac{\partial f_2}{\partial x_1}\right)^{(0)} & \left(\frac{\partial f_2}{\partial x_2}\right)^{(0)} & \cdots & \left(\frac{\partial f_2}{\partial x_n}\right)^{(0)} \\ \vdots & \vdots & \cdots & \vdots \\ \left(\frac{\partial f_n}{\partial x_1}\right)^{(0)} & \left(\frac{\partial f_n}{\partial x_2}\right)^{(0)} & \cdots & \left(\frac{\partial f_n}{\partial x_n}\right)^{(0)} \end{bmatrix} \begin{bmatrix} \Delta x_1^{(0)} \\ \Delta x_2^{(0)} \\ \vdots \\ \Delta x_n^{(0)} \end{bmatrix} \tag{2.31}$$

After solving $\Delta x_1^{(0)}, \Delta x_2^{(0)}, \cdots, \Delta x_n^{(0)}$ from the above equation, we get

$$\left.\begin{aligned} x_1^{(1)} = x_1^{(0)} - \Delta x_1^{(0)} \\ x_2^{(1)} = x_2^{(0)} - \Delta x_2^{(0)} \\ \vdots \qquad \\ x_n^{(1)} = x_n^{(0)} - \Delta x_n^{(0)} \end{aligned}\right\} \tag{2.32}$$

$x_1^{(1)}, x_2^{(1)}, \ldots, x_n^{(1)}$ will approach the actual solution more closely. The updated values are used as the new guess to solve the correction equation (2.31) and to further correct the variables. In this way the iterative process of the Newton–Raphson method is formed.

Generally, the correction in the kth iteration can be written as

$$\begin{bmatrix} f_1(x_1^{(k)}, x_2^{(k)}, \ldots, x_n^{(k)}) \\ f_2(x_1^{(k)}, x_2^{(k)}, \ldots, x_n^{(k)}) \\ \vdots \\ f_n(x_1^{(k)}, x_2^{(k)}, \ldots, x_n^{(k)}) \end{bmatrix} = \begin{bmatrix} \left(\frac{\partial f_1}{\partial x_1}\right)^{(k)} & \left(\frac{\partial f_1}{\partial x_2}\right)^{(k)} & \cdots & \left(\frac{\partial f_1}{\partial x_n}\right)^{(k)} \\ \left(\frac{\partial f_2}{\partial x_1}\right)^{(k)} & \left(\frac{\partial f_2}{\partial x_2}\right)^{(k)} & \cdots & \left(\frac{\partial f_2}{\partial x_n}\right)^{(k)} \\ \vdots & \vdots & \cdots & \vdots \\ \left(\frac{\partial f_n}{\partial x_1}\right)^{(k)} & \left(\frac{\partial f_n}{\partial x_2}\right)^{(k)} & \cdots & \left(\frac{\partial f_n}{\partial x_n}\right)^{(k)} \end{bmatrix} \begin{bmatrix} \Delta x_1^{(k)} \\ \Delta x_2^{(k)} \\ \vdots \\ \Delta x_n^{(k)} \end{bmatrix} \tag{2.33}$$

The above equation can be expressed in the matrix form as

$$\mathbf{F} = \mathbf{JC} \tag{2.34}$$

where,

$$\mathbf{F} = \begin{bmatrix} f_1(x_1^{(k)}, x_2^{(k)}, \ldots, x_n^{(k)}) \\ f_2(x_1^{(k)}, x_2^{(k)}, \ldots, x_n^{(k)}) \\ \vdots \\ f_n(x_1^{(k)}, x_2^{(k)}, \ldots, x_n^{(k)}) \end{bmatrix} \tag{2.35}$$

is the error vector in the kth iteration.

$$\mathbf{J} = \begin{bmatrix} \left(\frac{\partial f_1}{\partial x_1}\right)^{(k)} & \left(\frac{\partial f_1}{\partial x_2}\right)^{(k)} & \cdots & \left(\frac{\partial f_1}{\partial x_n}\right)^{(k)} \\ \left(\frac{\partial f_2}{\partial x_1}\right)^{(k)} & \left(\frac{\partial f_2}{\partial x_2}\right)^{(k)} & \cdots & \left(\frac{\partial f_2}{\partial x_n}\right)^{(k)} \\ \vdots & \vdots & \cdots & \vdots \\ \left(\frac{\partial f_n}{\partial x_1}\right)^{(k)} & \left(\frac{\partial f_n}{\partial x_2}\right)^{(k)} & \cdots & \left(\frac{\partial f_n}{\partial x_n}\right)^{(k)} \end{bmatrix} \tag{2.36}$$

is the first derivative matrix and it is called **Jacobian matrix**.

$$\mathbf{C} = \begin{bmatrix} \Delta x_1^{(k)} \\ \Delta x_2^{(k)} \\ \vdots \\ \Delta x_n^{(k)} \end{bmatrix} \tag{2.37}$$

is the correction value vector in the kth iteration.

We also have the equation similar to Eq. (2.32)

$$X^{(k+1)} = X^{(k)} - \Delta X^{(k)} \tag{2.38}$$

The state update vector $\Delta X^{(k)}$ is calculated from Eq. (2.33) by taking the inverse of the Jacobian matrix. Thus we get

$$X^{(k)} = -[J]^{-1}F \tag{2.39}$$

With Eqs. (2.34) and (2.38) solved alternately in each iteration, $X^{(k+1)}$ gradually approaches the actual solution. Convergence can be evaluated by the norm of the correction value,

$$|\Delta X^{(k)}| < \varepsilon \tag{2.40}$$

2.6.2 Load Flow Solution Using Newton–Raphson Method

For large interconnected power systems among the numerous solution methods available for load flow analysis, the Newton–Raphson method is considered to be the most important. Many advantages are attributed to the Newton–Raphson approach. Its convergence characteristics are relatively powerful compared to the alternative processes, and very low computing times are achieved when sparse network equations are solved by the technique of sparsity programmed ordered elimination. The reliability of the Newton–Raphson method is comparatively good, since it can solve cases that lead to divergence with the other popular processes, but the method is by no means reliable. Failure does not occur on some ill-conditioned problems.

The number of iterations required to obtain a solution is independent of the system size, but more functional evaluations are required at each iteration. Since in the load flow problem real power and magnitude of bus voltage are specified for the PV buses, the load flow equation is formulated in the polar form.

The load flow equations can be rewritten as follows.

Real power

$$P_i^{(k)} = |V_i| \sum_{j=1}^{n} |V_j||Y_{ij}| \cos(\theta_{ij} + \delta_j - \delta_i) \tag{2.41}$$

Reactive power

$$Q_i^{(k)} = -|V_i| \sum_{j=1}^{n} |V_j||Y_{ij}| \sin(\theta_{ij} + \delta_j - \delta_i) \tag{2.42}$$

We have two equations for each load bus, given by Eqs. (2.41) and (2.42), and one equation for each voltage controlled bus, given by Eq. (2.41). Expanding Eqs. (2.41) and (2.42) in Taylor's series about the initial estimate and neglecting all higher order terms result in the following set of linear equations.

$$\begin{bmatrix} \Delta P_2^{(k)} \\ \vdots \\ \Delta P_n^{(k)} \\ \Delta Q_2^{(k)} \\ \vdots \\ \Delta Q_n^{(k)} \end{bmatrix} = \begin{bmatrix} \frac{\partial P_2^{(k)}}{\partial \delta_2} & \cdots & \frac{\partial P_2^{(k)}}{\partial \delta_n} & \frac{\partial P_2^{(k)}}{\partial |V_2|} & \cdots & \frac{\partial P_2^{(k)}}{\partial |V_n|} \\ \vdots & \ddots & \vdots & \vdots & \ddots & \vdots \\ \frac{\partial P_n^{(k)}}{\partial \delta_2} & \cdots & \frac{\partial P_n^{(k)}}{\partial \delta_n} & \frac{\partial P_n^{(k)}}{\partial |V_2|} & \cdots & \frac{\partial P_n^{(k)}}{\partial |V_n|} \\ \frac{\partial Q_2^{(k)}}{\partial \delta_2} & \cdots & \frac{\partial Q_2^{(k)}}{\partial \delta_n} & \frac{\partial Q_2^{(k)}}{\partial |V_2|} & \cdots & \frac{\partial Q_2^{(k)}}{\partial |V_n|} \\ \vdots & \ddots & \vdots & \vdots & \ddots & \vdots \\ \frac{\partial Q_n^{(k)}}{\partial \delta_2} & \cdots & \frac{\partial Q_n^{(k)}}{\partial \delta_n} & \frac{\partial Q_n^{(k)}}{\partial |V_2|} & \cdots & \frac{\partial Q_n^{(k)}}{\partial |V_n|} \end{bmatrix} \begin{bmatrix} \Delta \delta_2^{(k)} \\ \vdots \\ \Delta \delta_n^{(k)} \\ \Delta |V_2^{(k)}| \\ \vdots \\ \Delta |V_n^{(k)}| \end{bmatrix} \tag{2.43}$$

In the above equation, bus 1 is assumed to be the slack bus. The Jacobian matrix gives the linearised relationship between small changes in voltage angle $\Delta\delta_i^{(k)}$ and voltage magnitude $\Delta|V_i^{(k)}|$ with the small changes in real and reactive powers $\Delta P_i^{(k)}$ and $\Delta Q_i^{(k)}$ respectively. The elements of the Jacobian matrix are the partial derivatives of Eqs. (2.41) and (2.42), calculated at $\Delta\delta_i^{(k)}$ and $\Delta|V_2^{(k)}|$.

The above equation can be written as

$$\begin{bmatrix} \Delta P \\ \Delta Q \end{bmatrix} = \begin{bmatrix} J_1 & J_2 \\ J_3 & J_4 \end{bmatrix} \begin{bmatrix} \Delta\delta \\ \Delta|V| \end{bmatrix} \tag{2.44}$$

For the PV buses, the voltage magnitudes are known. Therefore, if m buses of the system are voltage controlled equations involving ΔQ and ΔV, and the corresponding columns of the Jacobian matrix are eliminated, then there are $(n - 1)$ real power constraints and $(n - 1 - m)$ reactive power constraints, and the order of the complete Jacobian matrix is $(2n - 2 - m) \times (2n - 2 - m)$.

Order of Jacobian matrix $\mathbf{J}_1$ is $(n - 1) \times (n - 1)$.
Order of Jacobian matrix $\mathbf{J}_2$ is $(n - 1) \times (n - 1 - m)$.
Order of Jacobian matrix $\mathbf{J}_3$ is $(n - 1 - m) \times (n - 1)$.
Order of Jacobian matrix $\mathbf{J}_4$ is $(n - 1 - m) \times (n - 1 - m)$.

Elements of Jacobian matrix $\mathbf{J}_1$

(i) the diagonal elements are

$$\frac{\partial P_i}{\partial \delta_i} = \sum_{j \neq i} |V_i||V_j||Y_{ij}| \sin(\theta_{ij} - \delta_i + \delta_j) \tag{2.45}$$

(ii) the off-diagonal elements are

$$\frac{\partial P_i}{\partial \delta_j} = -|V_i||V_j||Y_{ij}| \sin(\theta_{ij} - \delta_i + \delta_j) \qquad j \neq i \tag{2.46}$$

Elements of Jacobian matrix $\mathbf{J}_2$

(i) the diagonal elements are

$$\frac{\partial P_i}{\partial |V_i|} = 2|V_i||Y_{ii}|\cos\theta_{ii} + \sum_{j \neq i} |V_j||Y_{ij}|\cos(\theta_{ij} - \delta_i + \delta_j) \tag{2.47}$$

(ii) the off-diagonal elements are

$$\frac{\partial P_i}{\partial |V_j|} = |V_i||Y_{ij}|\cos(\theta_{ij} - \delta_i + \delta_j) \qquad j \neq i \tag{2.48}$$

Elements of Jacobian matrix $\mathbf{J}_3$

(i) the diagonal elements are

$$\frac{\partial Q_i}{\partial \delta_i} = \sum_{j \neq i} |V_i||V_j||Y_{ij}|\cos(\theta_{ij} - \delta_i + \delta_j) \tag{2.49}$$

(ii) the off-diagonal elements are

$$\frac{\partial Q_i}{\partial \delta_j} = -|V_i||V_j||Y_{ij}|\cos(\theta_{ij} - \delta_i + \delta_j) \qquad j \neq i \tag{2.50}$$

Elements of Jacobian matrix $\mathbf{J}_4$

(i) the diagonal elements are

$$\frac{\partial Q_i}{\partial |V_i|} = -2|V_i||Y_{ii}|\sin\theta_{ii} - \sum_{j \neq i} |V_j||Y_{ij}|\sin(\theta_{ij} - \delta_i + \delta_j \tag{2.51}$$

(ii) the off-diagonal elements are

$$\frac{\partial Q_i}{\partial |V_j|} = -|V_i||Y_{ij}|\sin(\theta_{ij} - \delta_i + \delta_j) \qquad j \neq i \tag{2.52}$$

Difference in scheduled to calculated power (power residuals) is given by

$$\Delta P_i^{[k]} = P_{i,\text{sch}} - P_i^{[k]} \tag{2.53}$$

$$\Delta Q_i^{[k]} = Q_{i,\text{sch}} - Q_i^{[k]} \tag{2.54}$$

The new estimates for the voltage magnitude and angle

$$\delta_i^{[k+1]} = \delta_i^{[k]} + \Delta\delta_i^{[k]} \tag{2.55}$$

$$|V_i^{[k+1]}| = |V_i^{[k]}| + \Delta|V_i^{[k]}| \tag{2.56}$$

Computation procedure

1. Set flat start

   - For load buses, set the voltages equal to the slack bus or $1\angle 0°$.
   - For generator buses, set the angles equal to the slack bus or $0°$.

2. Calculate power mismatch
   - For load buses, calculate $P_i^{[k]}$ (Eq. (2.41)) and $Q_i^{[k]}$ (Eq. (2.42)) injections using the known and estimated system voltages.
   - For generator buses, calculate $P_i^{[k]}$ (Eq. (2.41)) and $\Delta P_i^{[k]}$ (Eq. (2.53)).
3. Form the Jacobian matrix
   - Use the various equations for the partial derivatives with respect to the voltage angle and magnitudes (form the Jacobian matrix).
   - The elements of Jacobian matrix ($\mathbf{J}_1$, $\mathbf{J}_2$, $\mathbf{J}_3$ and $\mathbf{J}_4$) calculated from Eqs. (2.45) to (2.52).
4. Find the matrix solution
   - Inverse the Jacobian matrix and multiply by the mismatch power.
   - Compute $\Delta\delta$ and $\Delta|V|$.
5. Difference in scheduled to calculated power

$$\Delta P_i^{[k]} = P_{i,\text{sch}} - P_i^{[k]}$$

$$\Delta Q_i^{[k]} = Q_{i,\text{sch}} - Q_i^{[k]}$$

6. Find the new estimates for the voltage magnitude and angle

$$\delta_i^{[k+1]} = \delta_i^{[k]} + \Delta\delta_i^{[k]}$$

$$|V_i^{[k+1]}| = |V_i^{[k]}| + \Delta|V_i^{[k]}|$$

7. Repeat the process until the mismatch (residuals) is less than the specified accuracy

$$|\Delta P_i^{[k]}| \le \varepsilon$$

$$|\Delta Q_i^{[k]}| \le \varepsilon$$

8. After solving for bus voltages and angles, power flows and losses on the network branches are calculated
   - Transmission lines and transformers are network branches.
   - The direction of positive current flow is defined for a branch element (demonstrated on a medium length line).
   - Power flow is defined for each end of the branch.
   - Example: The power leaving bus i and flowing to bus j as shown below.

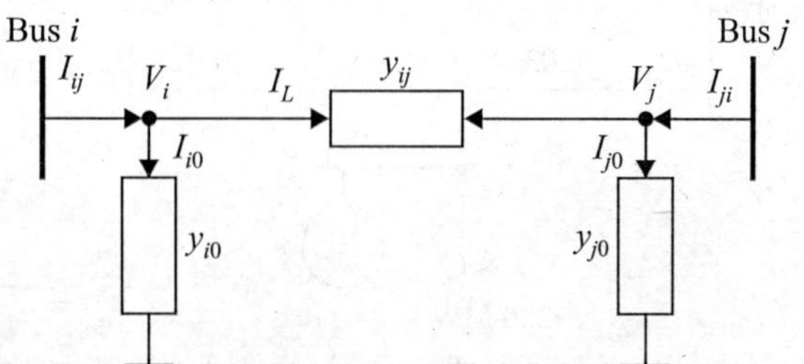

Current and power flows

$$i \rightarrow j$$

$$I_{ij} = I_L + I_{i0} = y_{ij}(V_i - V_j) + y_{i0}V_i$$

$$S_{ij} = V_i I_{ij}^* = V_i^2 (y_{ij} + y_{i0})^* - V_i y_{ij}^* V_i^*$$

$$j \rightarrow i$$

$$I_{ji} = -I_L + I_{j0} = y_{ij}(V_j - V_i) + y_{j0}V_j$$

$$S_{ji} = V_j I_{ij}^* = V_j^2 (y_{ij} + y_{j0})^* - V_j y_{ij}^* V_i^*$$

Power loss

$$S_{\text{loss}ij} = S_{ij} + S_{ji}$$

This completes the load flow study. Finally, in Figure 2.13 all the computational steps are summarized in the detailed flow chart.

2.6.3 Advantages and Disadvantages of Newton–Raphson Method

Advantages

Faster, more reliable and yields accurate results, requires less number of iterations.

Disadvantages

Program as well as memory is more complex.

EXAMPLE 2.6 Figure 2.14 shows the one line diagram of a simple three-bus system with generation at bus 1. The magnitude of voltage at bus 1 is adjusted to 1.05 p.u. The scheduled loads at buses 2 and 3 are given in the diagram. Line impedances are marked in p.u. on a 100 MVA base and the line charging susceptances are neglected.

(a) Using the Newton–Raphson method, determine the phasor values of the voltages at the load buses 2 and 3(PQ buses) accurate to decimal places.

(b) Verify the result with Power World Simulator.

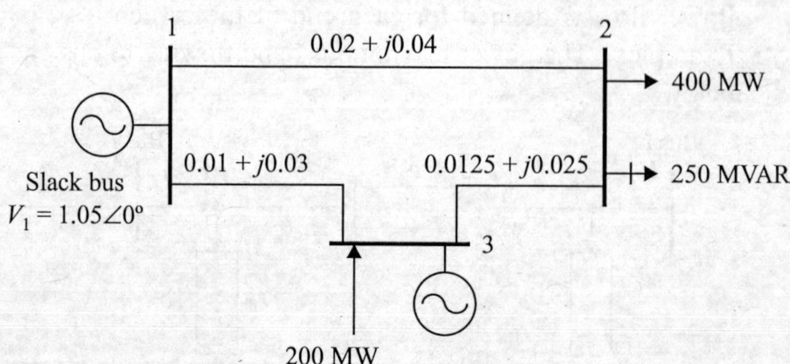

Figure 2.14 One line diagram of a simple three-bus system Example 2.6.

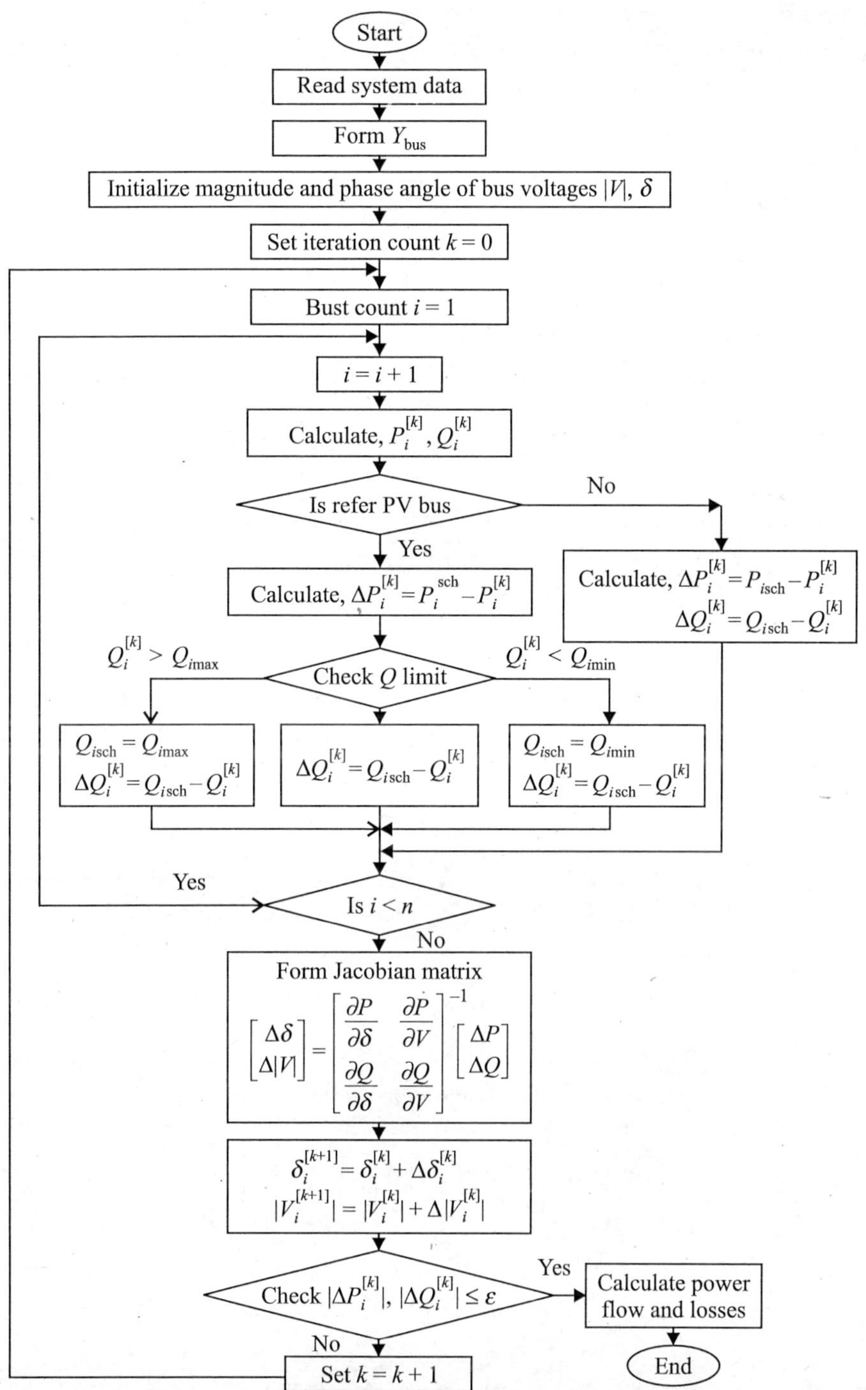

Figure 2.13 Flow chart for Newton–Raphson method.

Solution:

(a) Form the Y_{bus}

$$y_{12} = \frac{1}{z_{12}} = \frac{1}{0.02 + j0.04} = 10 - j20$$

$$y_{13} = \frac{1}{z_{13}} = \frac{1}{0.01 + j0.03} = 10 - j30$$

$$y_{23} = \frac{1}{z_{23}} = \frac{1}{0.0125 + j0.025} = 16 - j32$$

$$Y_{11} = y_{12} + y_{13} = (10 - j20) + (10 - j30) = 20 - j50$$

$$Y_{12} = Y_{21} = -y_{12} = -(10 - j20) = -10 + j20$$

$$Y_{13} = Y_{31} = -y_{13} = -(10 - j30) = -10 + j30$$

$$Y_{22} = y_{21} + y_{23} = (10 - j20) + (16 - j32) = 26 - j52$$

$$Y_{23} = Y_{32} = -y_{23} = -(16 - j32) = -16 + j32$$

$$Y_{33} = y_{31} + y_{32} = (10 - j30) + (16 - j32) = 26 - j62$$

$$Y_{bus} = \begin{bmatrix} 20 - j50 & -10 + j20 & -10 + j30 \\ -10 + j20 & 26 - j52 & -16 + j32 \\ -10 + j30 & -16 + j32 & 26 - j62 \end{bmatrix}$$

$$Y_{bus} = \begin{bmatrix} 53.85165\angle -1.9029 & 22.36068\angle 2.0344 & 31.62278\angle 1.8925 \\ 22.36068\angle 2.0344 & 58.13777\angle -1.1071 & 35.77709\angle 2.0344 \\ 31.62278\angle 1.8925 & 35.77709\angle 2.0344 & 67.23095\angle -1.1737 \end{bmatrix}$$

$$Y_{bus} = \begin{bmatrix} 53.85165\angle -68.2 & 22.36068\angle 116.6 & 31.62278\angle 108.4 \\ 22.36068\angle 116.6 & 58.13777\angle -63.4 & 35.77709\angle 116.6 \\ 31.62278\angle 108.4 & 35.77709\angle 116.6 & 67.23095\angle -67.2 \end{bmatrix}$$

Initialize magnitude and angle of bus voltage

$$|V_1| = 1.05, \ \delta_1 = 0.0 \text{ rad}$$

$$|V_2|^{(0)} = 1, \ \delta_2^{(0)} = 0.0 \text{ rad}$$

$$|V_3|^{(0)} = 1.04, \ \delta_3^{(0)} = 0.0 \text{ rad}$$

In the matrix form

$$\begin{bmatrix} \delta_1^{(0)} \\ V_1^{(0)} \end{bmatrix} = \begin{bmatrix} 0 \\ 1.05 \end{bmatrix}; \ \begin{bmatrix} \delta_2^{(0)} \\ V_2^{(0)} \end{bmatrix} = \begin{bmatrix} 0 \\ 1 \end{bmatrix}; \ \begin{bmatrix} \delta_3^{(0)} \\ V_3^{(0)} \end{bmatrix} = \begin{bmatrix} 0 \\ 1.04 \end{bmatrix}$$

Scheduled powers are

At bus 2, $\quad P_{2,\text{sch}} = P_{G2} - P_{D2} = 0 - \dfrac{400}{100} = -4 \text{ p.u.}$

$$Q_{2,\text{sch}} = Q_{G2} - Q_{D2} = 0 - \frac{250}{100} = -2.5 \text{ p.u.}$$

At bus 3, $\quad P_{3,\text{sch}} = P_{G3} - P_{D3} = \dfrac{200}{100} - 0 = 2 \text{ p.u.}$

The real power at buses 2 and 3 and reactive power at bus 2 are

$$P_2 = |V_2||V_1||Y_{21}| \cos(\theta_{21} - \delta_2 + \delta_1) + |V_2^2||Y_{22}| \cos\theta_{22}$$
$$+ |V_2||V_3||Y_{23}| \cos(\theta_{23} - \delta_2 + \delta_3)$$

$$P_2 = (1)\,(1.05)\,(22.36068) \cos(116.6 - 0 + 0) + (1)^2(58.13777) \cos(-63.4)$$
$$+ (1)\,(1.04)\,(35.77709) \cos(116.6 - 0 + 0) = -1.1414$$

$$P_3 = |V_3||V_1||Y_{31}| \cos(\theta_{31} - \delta_3 + \delta_1) + |V_3||V_2||Y_{32}| \cos(\theta_{32} - \delta_3 + \delta_2)$$
$$+ |V_3^2||Y_{33}| \cos\theta_{33}$$

$$P_3 = (1.04)\,(1.05)\,(31.62278) \cos(108.4 - 0 + 0)$$
$$+ (1.04)(1)(35.77709) \cos(116.6 - 0 + 0) + (1.04)^2(67.23095) \cos(-67.2)$$
$$= 0.5616$$

$$Q_2 = -|V_2||V_1||Y_{21}| \sin(\theta_{21} - \delta_2 + \delta_1) - |V_2^2||Y_{22}| \sin\theta_{22}$$
$$- |V_2||V_3||Y_{23}| \sin(\theta_{23} - \delta_2 + \delta_3)$$

$$Q_2 = -(1)\,(1.05)\,(22.36068) \sin(116.6 - 0 + 0) - (1)^2(58.13777) \sin(-63.4)$$
$$- (1)\,(1.04)\,(35.77709) \sin(116.6 - 0 + 0) = -2.28$$

Difference in scheduled to calculated power

$$\Delta P_2^{[0]} = P_{2,\text{sch}} - P_{2,\text{calc}}^{(0)} = -4 - (-1.1414) = -2.8586$$
$$\Delta P_3^{[0]} = P_{3,\text{sch}} - P_{3,\text{calc}}^{(0)} = 2 - (0.5616) = 1.43846$$
$$\Delta Q_2^{[0]} = Q_{2,\text{sch}} - Q_{2,\text{calc}}^{(0)} = -2.5 - (-2.28) = -0.22$$

The Jacobian matrix is given by

$$\begin{bmatrix} \Delta P_2 \\ \Delta P_3 \\ \Delta Q_2 \end{bmatrix} = \begin{bmatrix} \dfrac{\partial P_2}{\partial \delta_2} & \dfrac{\partial P_2}{\partial \delta_3} & \dfrac{\partial P_2}{\partial |V_2|} \\ \dfrac{\partial P_3}{\partial \delta_2} & \dfrac{\partial P_3}{\partial \delta_3} & \dfrac{\partial P_3}{\partial |V_2|} \\ \dfrac{\partial Q_2}{\partial \delta_2} & \dfrac{\partial Q_2}{\partial \delta_3} & \dfrac{\partial Q_2}{\partial |V_2|} \end{bmatrix} \begin{bmatrix} \Delta \delta_2 \\ \Delta \delta_3 \\ \Delta |V_2| \end{bmatrix}$$

$$\frac{\partial P_2}{\partial \delta_2} = |V_2||V_1||Y_{21}| \sin(\theta_{21} - \delta_2 + \delta_1) + |V_2||V_3||Y_{23}| \sin(\theta_{23} - \delta_2 + \delta_3)$$
$$= (1)\,(1.05)\,(22.36068) \sin(116.6 - 0 + 0)$$
$$+ (1)\,(1.04)\,(35.77709) \sin(116.6 - 0 + 0) = 54.2634$$

$$\frac{\partial P_2}{\partial \delta_3} = -|V_1||V_3||Y_{23}| \sin(\theta_{23} - \delta_2 + \delta_3)$$
$$= -(1)\,(1.04)\,(35.77709) \sin(116.6 - 0 + 0) = -33.2698$$

$$\frac{\partial P_2}{\partial |V_2|} = |V_1||Y_{21}| \cos(\theta_{21} - \delta_2 + \delta_1) + 2|V_2||Y_{22}| \cos\theta_{22}$$
$$+ |V_3||Y_{23}| \cos(\theta_{23} - \delta_2 + \delta_3)$$

$$= (1.05)\,(22.36068)\cos(116.6 - 0 + 0) + 2(1)\,(58.13777)\cos(-63.4)$$
$$+ (1.04)\,(35.77709)\cos(116.6 - 0 + 0) = 24.890$$

$$\frac{\partial P_3}{\partial \delta_2} = -|V_3||V_2||Y_{32}|\sin(\theta_{32} - \delta_3 + \delta_2)$$
$$= -(1.04)\,(1)\,(35.77709)\sin(116.6 - 0 + 0) = -33.2698$$

$$\frac{\partial P_3}{\partial \delta_3} = |V_3||V_1||Y_{31}|\sin(\theta_{31} - \delta_3 + \delta_1) + |V_3||V_2||Y_{32}|\sin(\theta_{32} - \delta_3 + \delta_2)$$
$$= (1.04)\,(1.05)\,(31.62278)\sin(108.4 - 0 + 0)$$
$$+ (1.04)\,(1)\,(35.77709)\sin(116.6 - 0 + 0) = 66.0365$$

$$\frac{\partial P_3}{\partial |V_2|} = |V_3||Y_{32}|\cos(\theta_{32} - \delta_3 + \delta_2)$$
$$= (1.04)\,(35.77709)\cos(116.6 - 0 + 0) = -16.663$$

$$\frac{\partial Q_2}{\partial \delta_2} = |V_2||V_1||Y_{21}|\cos(\theta_{21} - \delta_2 + \delta_1) + |V_2||V_3||Y_{23}|\cos(\theta_{23} - \delta_2 + \delta_3)$$
$$= (1)\,(1.05)\,(22.36068)\cos(116.6 - 0 + 0)$$
$$+ (1)\,(1.04)\,(35.77709)\cos(116.6 - 0 + 0) = -27.1731$$

$$\frac{\partial Q_2}{\partial \delta_3} = -|V_2||V_3||Y_{23}|\cos(\theta_{23} - \delta_2 + \delta_3)$$
$$= -(1)\,(1.04)\,(35.77709)\cos(116.6 - 0 + 0) = 16.663$$

$$\frac{\partial Q_2}{\partial |V_2|} = -|V_1||Y_{21}|\sin(\theta_{21} - \delta_2 + \delta_1) - 2|V_2||Y_{22}|\sin(\theta_{22})$$
$$- |V_3||Y_{23}|\sin(\theta_{23} - \delta_2 + \delta_3)$$
$$= -(1.05)\,(22.36068)\sin(116.6 - 0 + 0) - 2(1)\,(58.13777)\sin(-63.4)$$
$$- (1.04)\,(35.77709)\sin(116.6 - 0 + 0) = 49.707$$

$$\begin{bmatrix} -2.8586 \\ 1.43846 \\ -0.22 \end{bmatrix} = \begin{bmatrix} 54.2634 & -33.2698 & 24.890 \\ -33.2698 & 66.0365 & -16.663 \\ -27.1731 & 16.663 & 49.707 \end{bmatrix} \begin{bmatrix} \Delta\delta_2^{(0)} \\ \Delta\delta_3^{(0)} \\ \Delta|V_2|^{(0)} \end{bmatrix}$$

$$\begin{bmatrix} \Delta\delta_2^{(0)} \\ \Delta\delta_3^{(0)} \\ \Delta|V_2|^{(0)} \end{bmatrix} = \begin{bmatrix} 54.2634 & -33.2698 & 24.890 \\ -33.2698 & 66.0365 & -16.663 \\ -27.1731 & 16.663 & 49.707 \end{bmatrix}^{-1} \begin{bmatrix} -2.8586 \\ 1.43846 \\ -0.22 \end{bmatrix}$$

$$\begin{bmatrix} \Delta\delta_2^{(0)} \\ \Delta\delta_3^{(0)} \\ \Delta|V_2|^{(0)} \end{bmatrix} = \begin{bmatrix} 0.0231 & 0.0134 & -0.0071 \\ 0.0137 & 0.0219 & 0.0005 \\ 0.0081 & 0.0000 & 0.0161 \end{bmatrix} \begin{bmatrix} -2.8586 \\ 1.43846 \\ -0.22 \end{bmatrix}$$

$$\begin{bmatrix} \Delta\delta_2^{(0)} \\ \Delta\delta_3^{(0)} \\ \Delta|V_2|^{(0)} \end{bmatrix} = \begin{bmatrix} -0.0452 \\ -0.0077 \\ -0.0266 \end{bmatrix}$$

New bus voltages and angles in the first iteration are

$$\delta_i^{[k+1]} = \delta_i^{[k]} + \Delta\delta_i^{[k]}$$

$$\delta_2^{[1]} = \delta_2^{[0]} + \Delta\delta_2^{[0]} = 0 + (-0.0452) = -0.0452$$

$$\delta_3^{[1]} = \delta_3^{[0]} + \Delta\delta_3^{[0]} = 0 + (-0.0077) = -0.0077$$

$$|V_i^{[k+1]}| = |V_i^{[k]}| + \Delta|V_i^{[k]}|$$

$$|V_2^{[1]}| = |V_2^{[0]}| + \Delta|V_2^{[0]}| = 1 + (-0.0266) = 0.9734$$

(b) Verify the result using Power World Simulator (PWS): The one line diagram of a simple bus system is drawn in PWS, which is shown in Figure 2.15.

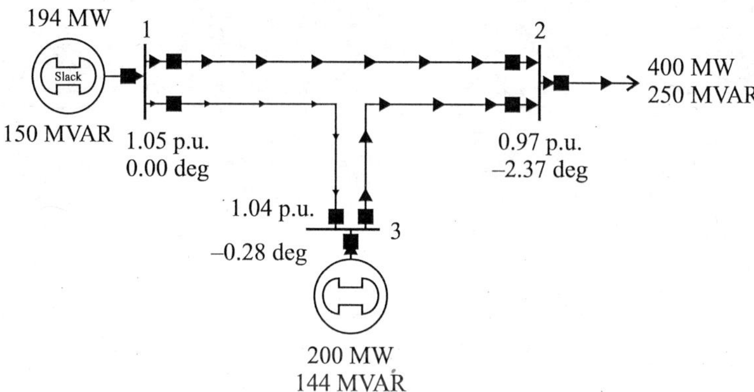

Figure 2.15 One line diagram of a simple three-bus system.

The first step is the formation of $[Y_{\text{bus}}]$ using the inspection method. The calculated $[Y_{\text{bus}}]$ values are given in Figure 2.16. Since the given problem is a three-bus system, the size of $[Y_{\text{bus}}]$ is 3×3 matrix.

Y Bus (Bus Admittance Matrix)

Records Geo Set Columns f(x)

Filter Advanced Bus Find... Remove

	Number	Name	Bus 1	Bus 2	Bus 3
1	1	1	20.00 - j50.00	-10.00 + j20.00	-10.00 + j30.00
2	2	2	-10.00 + j20.00	26.00 - j52.00	-16.00 + j32.00
3	3	3	-10.00 + j30.00	-16.00 + j32.00	26.00 - j62.00

Figure 2.16 Y_{bus} result.

Newton–Raphson method

This method is executed by pressing the icon *Newton–Raphson power flow* available in *tools ribbon*. Before executing this method, the number of iterations is to be fixed as 1 in *simulator options ribbon*. The Jacobian values and power flow results are given in Figure 2.17 and Figure 2.18 for the 1st iteration.

Power Flow Jacobian

	Number	Name	Jacobian Equation	Angle Bus 2	Angle Bus 3	Volt Mag Bus 2	Volt Mag Bus 3
1	2	2	Real Power	51.71	-31.76	21.24	-16.80
2	3	3	Real Power	-33.03	65.71	-15.32	28.99
3	2	2	Reactive Power	-28.66	17.47	48.23	-30.53
4	3	3	Voltage Magnitude				1.00

Figure 2.17 Jacobian values.

```
                                  Bus Flows
BUS         1 1          138.0     MW      Mvar       MVA    % 1.0500    0.00    1 1
 GENERATOR 1                    213.54   136.29R   253.3
 TO         2 2            1    177.35   113.36    210.5    0
 TO         3 3            1     36.18    22.94     42.8    0
 **** Mismatch ****             213.54   136.29
BUS         2 2          138.0     MW      Mvar       MVA    % 0.9741   -2.70    1 1
 LOAD 1                         400.00   250.00    471.7
 TO         1 1            1   -169.32   -97.28    195.3    0
 TO         3 3            1   -229.08  -139.14    268.0    0
 **** Mismatch ****              -1.60   -13.58
BUS         3 3          138.0     MW      Mvar       MVA    % 1.0400   -0.45    1 1
 GENERATOR 1                    200.00   135.63R   241.6
 TO         1 1            1    -36.01   -22.44     42.4    0
 TO         2 2            1    238.54   158.07    286.2    0
 **** Mismatch ****             197.47   135.62
```

Figure 2.18 Power flow results and voltages—1st iteration.

The details of convergence are shown in Figure 2.19. The mismatches of real powers and reactive power for each iteration are also clearly indicated. This method takes 2 iterations to converge power flows. The converged values of Jacobian and Power flow results are given in Figure 2.20 and Figure 2.21.

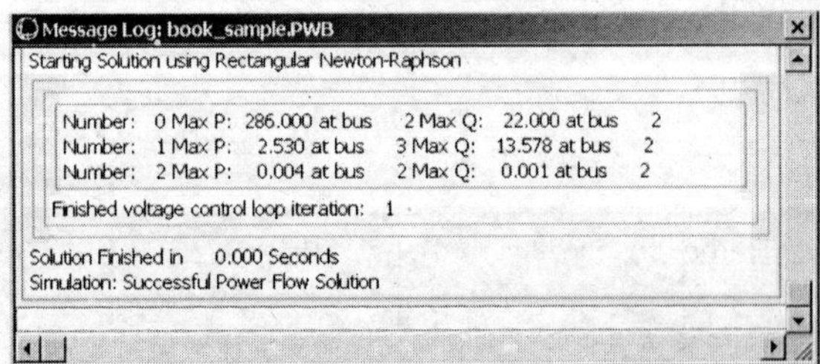

Message Log: book_sample.PWB

Starting Solution using Rectangular Newton-Raphson

Number: 0 Max P: 286.000 at bus 2 Max Q: 22.000 at bus 2
Number: 1 Max P: 2.530 at bus 3 Max Q: 13.578 at bus 2
Number: 2 Max P: 0.004 at bus 2 Max Q: 0.001 at bus 2

Finished voltage control loop iteration: 1

Solution Finished in 0.000 Seconds
Simulation: Successful Power Flow Solution

Figure 2.19 Details of convergence.

Power Flow Jacobian

	Number	Name	Jacobian Equation	Angle Bus 2	Angle Bus 3	Volt Mag Bus 2	Volt Mag Bus 3
1	2	2	Real Power	51.60	-31.69	21.15	-16.73
2	3	3	Real Power	-32.93	65.60	-15.35	28.96
3	2	2	Reactive Power	-28.55	17.40	47.95	-30.47
4	3	3	Voltage Magnitude				1.00

Figure 2.20 Jacobian values.

```
BUS          1 1         138.0    MW      Mvar       MVA   % 1.0500    0.00    1 1
 GENERATOR 1                   218.42  140.85R   259.9
 TO          2 2          1    179.36  118.73    215.1   0
 TO          3 3          1     39.06   22.12     44.9   0
 **** Mismatch ****            218.42  140.85
BUS          2 2         138.0    MW      Mvar       MVA   % 0.9717   -2.70    1 1
 LOAD 1                        400.00  250.00    471.7
 TO          1 1          1   -170.97 -101.95    199.1   0
 TO          3 3          1   -229.03 -148.05    272.7   0

BUS          3 3         138.0    MW      Mvar       MVA   % 1.0400   -0.50    1 1
 GENERATOR 1                   200.00  146.18R   247.7
 TO          1 1          1    -38.87  -21.57     44.5   0
 TO          2 2          1    238.88  167.75    291.9   0
 **** Mismatch ****            200.00  146.18
```

Figure 2.21 Converged power flow results and voltages.

PSS/E

The same problem is taken and drawn in PSS/E software and it is given in Figure 2.22.

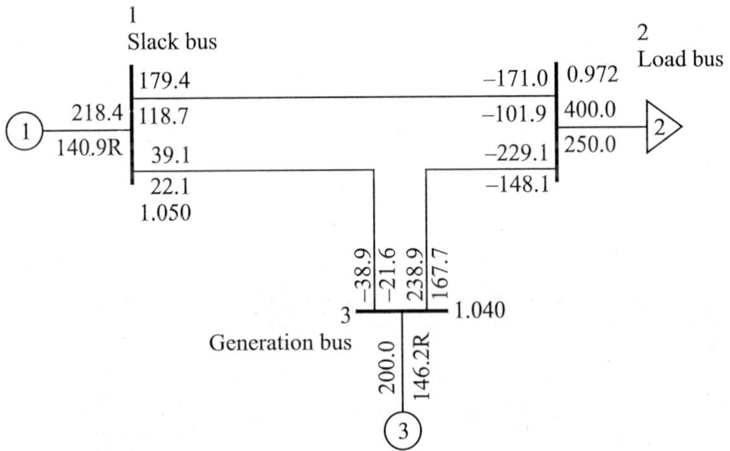

Figure 2.22 One line diagram of a simple three-bus system.

Once the data are entered in the software it can be executed by the above three power flow methods. Figure 2.23 shows the converged results obtained by the Gauss–Seidel method. This window is generated from ***bus based report***.

The Newton–Raphson method is executed and the power flow results are shown in Figure 2.23.

2.7 Fast Decoupled Load Flow Method

The Fast Decoupled Load Flow (FDLF) method is one of the improved methods, which was based on the simplification of the Newton–Raphson method and reported by Stott and Alsac in 1974. This method due to its simplifications

```
      PTI INTERACTIVE POWER                 Mon, JUN 27 2011   11:50    %MVA FOR TRANSFORMERS
   SYSTEM SIMULATOR--PSS®E                                     RATING   %I     FOR NON-TRANSFORMER BRANCHES
                                                                SET A
BUS    1 SLACK BUS   CKT    MW      MVAR     MVA   %  1.050PU   0.00   X---LOSSES---X  X---AREA----X  X---ZONE---X  1
  FROM GENERATION          218.4   140.8R   259.9  260      kV          MW      MVAR        1              1
  TO    2 LOAD BUS     1   179.3   118.7    215.1                       8.39    16.78       1              1
  TO    3 GEN BUS      1    39.1    22.1     44.9                       0.18     0.55       1              1

BUS    2 LOAD BUS    CKT    MW      MVAR     MVA   % 0.9717PU  –2.70   X---LOSSES---X  X---AREA----X  X---ZONE---X  2
                                                            kV          MW      MVAR        1              1
  TO LOAD-PQ               400.0   250.0    471.7
  TO    1 SLACK BUS    1  –171.0  –101.9    199.0                       8.39    16.78       1              1
  TO    3 GEN BUS      1  –229.0  –148.0    272.7                       9.85    19.69       1              1

BUS    3 GEN BUS     CKT    MW      MVAR     MVA   % 1.0400PU  –0.50   X---LOSSES---X  X---AREA----X  X---ZONE---X  3
  FROM GENERATION          200.0   146.2R   247.7  248      kV          MW      MVAR        1              1
  TO    1 SLACK BUS    1   –38.9   –21.6     44.5                       0.18     0.55       1              1
  TO    2 LOAD BUS     1   238.9   167.7    291.9                       9.85    19.69       1              1
```

Report

Figure 2.23 Converged results using Newton–Raphson method.

of calculations, fast convergence and reliable results became the most widely used method in load flow analysis.

However, FDLF for some cases, where high R/X ratios or heavy loading (low voltage) at some buses are present, does not converge well. For these cases, many efforts and developments have been made to overcome these convergence obstacles. Some of them targeted the convergence of systems with high R/X ratios, others those with low voltage buses. However, one of the most recent developments is a Robust Fast Decoupled Load Flow developed by Wang and Li; it is based on heuristic justification and general voltage normalization methods and solves both high R/X ratios and low bus voltage problem simultaneously.

This method exploits the property of the power system wherein real power flow-voltage angle ($P = (V_1V_2/X_1)\sin\delta$) and reactive power flow-voltage magnitude are loosely ($Q = (V_1V_2/X)\cos\delta - (V_2^2/X)$) coupled.

As the FDLF is derived from the Newton–Raphson method, we will start from the matrix representation of Newton–Raphson and apply some simplifications and approximations to reach the equations of the FDLF.

The matrix representation of the Newton–Raphson method is:

$$\begin{bmatrix} \Delta P \\ \Delta Q \end{bmatrix} = \begin{bmatrix} J_1 & J_2 \\ J_3 & J_4 \end{bmatrix} \begin{bmatrix} \Delta\delta \\ \Delta|V| \end{bmatrix} \tag{2.57}$$

Elements of Jacobian matrix $\mathbf{J}_1$

(i) the diagonal elements are

$$\frac{\partial P_i}{\partial \delta_i} = \sum_{j\neq i} |V_i||V_j||Y_{ij}|\sin(\theta_{ij} - \delta_i + \delta_j) \tag{2.58}$$

(ii) the off-diagonal elements are

$$\frac{\partial P_i}{\partial \delta_j} = -|V_i||V_j||Y_{ij}|\sin(\theta_{ij} - \delta_i + \delta_j) \qquad j \neq i \tag{2.59}$$

Elements of Jacobian matrix $\mathbf{J}_2$

(i) the diagonal elements are

$$\frac{\partial P_i}{\partial |V_i|} = 2|V_i||Y_{ii}|\cos\theta_{ii} + \sum_{j\neq i} |V_j||Y_{ij}|\cos(\theta_{ij} - \delta_i + \delta_j) \tag{2.60}$$

(ii) the off-diagonal elements are

$$\frac{\partial P_i}{\partial |V_j|} = |V_i||Y_{ij}|\cos(\theta_{ij} - \delta_i + \delta_j) \qquad j \neq i \tag{2.61}$$

Elements of Jacobian matrix $\mathbf{J}_3$

(i) the diagonal elements are

$$\frac{\partial Q_i}{\partial \delta_i} = \sum_{j\neq i} |V_i||V_j||Y_{ij}|\cos(\theta_{ij} - \delta_i + \delta_j) \tag{2.62}$$

(ii) the off-diagonal elements are

$$\frac{\partial Q_i}{\partial \delta_j} = -|V_i||V_j||Y_{ij}|\cos(\theta_{ij} - \delta_i + \delta_j) \qquad j \neq i \tag{2.63}$$

Elements of Jacobian matrix $\mathbf{J}_4$

(i) the diagonal elements are

$$\frac{\partial Q_i}{\partial |V_i|} = -2|V_i||Y_{ii}|\sin\theta_{ii} - \sum_{j\neq i}|V_j||Y_{ij}|\sin(\theta_{ij} - \delta_i + \delta_j) \tag{2.64}$$

(ii) the off-diagonal elements are

$$\frac{\partial Q_i}{\partial |V_j|} = -|V_i||Y_{ij}|\sin(\theta_{ij} - \delta_i + \delta_j) \qquad j \neq i \tag{2.65}$$

Now, for typical power system branches:

$$X/R \gg 1 \text{ and } \theta_{ij} < 20° \tag{2.66}$$

These two approximations will cause a weak coupling between ΔP and ΔV, and between ΔQ and $\Delta\delta$, hence $\mathbf{J}_2$ and $\mathbf{J}_3$ entries of the initial matrix of equation (2.57) can be ignored leading to the following decoupled equations:

$$\begin{bmatrix} \Delta P \\ \Delta Q \end{bmatrix} = \begin{bmatrix} J_1 & 0 \\ 0 & J_4 \end{bmatrix} \begin{bmatrix} \Delta\delta \\ \Delta|V| \end{bmatrix} \tag{2.67}$$

$$[\Delta P] = [J_1][\Delta\delta] = \left[\frac{\partial P}{\partial \delta}\right][\Delta\delta] \tag{2.68}$$

$$[\Delta Q] = [J_4][\Delta|V|] = \left[\frac{\partial Q}{\partial |V|}\right][\Delta|V|] \tag{2.69}$$

Equations (2.68) and (2.69) show that the matrix equations are separated into two decoupled equations requiring considerably less time to solve compared to the time required for the solution of Eq. (2.57).

Furthermore, considerable simplifications can be made to eliminate the need for recalculating $\mathbf{J}_1$ and $\mathbf{J}_4$ during iteration.

The elements of Jacobian matrix $\mathbf{J}_1$ are as follows.

The diagonal elements are

$$\frac{\partial P_i}{\partial \delta_j} = \sum_{j=1}^{n}|V_i||V_j||Y_{ij}|\sin(\theta_{ij} - \delta_i + \delta_j) - |V_i|^2|Y_{ii}|\sin(\theta_{ii})$$

$$\frac{\partial P_i}{\partial \delta_j} = -Q_i - |V_i|^2|Y_{ii}|\sin(\theta_{ii})$$

$$\frac{\partial P_i}{\partial \delta_j} = -Q_i - |V_i|^2 B_{ii}$$

Now, the diagonal elements of $\mathbf{J}_1$ can be written as

$$\frac{\partial P_i}{\partial \delta_i} = -Q_i - |V_i|^2 B_{ii} \tag{2.70}$$

where $B_{ii} = |Y_{ii}| \sin\theta_{ii}$ is the imaginary part of the diagonal elements of the bus admittance matrix Y_{bus}.

Further simplifications can be applied to Eq. (2.70), by considering

$$B_{ii} \gg Q_i \text{ and } |V_i|^2 \approx |V_i|$$

$$\frac{\partial P_i}{\partial \delta_i} = -|V_i| B_{ii} \tag{2.71}$$

Also, as under normal operating conditions $\delta_j - \delta_i$ is quite small, therefore $\theta_{ij} - \delta_i + \delta_j \approx \theta_{ij}$ and $|V_j| \approx 1$.

The off-diagonal elements of $\mathbf{J}_1$ can be written as

$$\frac{\partial P_i}{\partial \delta_j} = -|V_i||V_j||Y_{ij}| \sin(\theta_{ij} - \delta_i + \delta_j) \qquad \therefore |V_j| \approx 1$$

$$= -|V_i||Y_{ij}| \sin(\theta_{ij})$$

$$\frac{\partial P_i}{\partial \delta_j} = -|V_i| B_{ij} \tag{2.72}$$

Similarly, the diagonal elements of $\mathbf{J}_4$ may be written as

$$\frac{\partial Q_i}{\partial |V_i|} = -|V_i||Y_{ii}| \sin\theta_{ii} - \sum_{j=1}^{n} |V_j||Y_{ij}| \sin(\theta_{ij} - \delta_i + \delta_j)$$

Multiplying the above equation by $|V_i|$, we get

$$|V_i| \times \frac{\partial Q_i}{\partial |V_i|} = -|V_i|^2 |Y_{ii}| \sin\theta_{ii} - \sum_{j=1}^{n} |V_i||V_j||Y_{ij}| \sin(\theta_{ij} - \delta_i + \delta_j) = -|V_i|^2 B_{ii} + Q_i$$

Again, since $B_{ii} \gg Q_i$, Q_i may be neglected

$$\frac{\partial Q_i}{\partial |V_i|} = -|V_i| B_{ii} \tag{2.73}$$

The off-diagonal elements of $\mathbf{J}_4$ are

$$\frac{\partial Q_i}{\partial |V_j|} = -|V_i||Y_{ij}| \sin(\theta_{ij} - \delta_i + \delta_j)$$

Again assume $\theta_{ij} - \delta_i + \delta_j \approx \theta_{ij}$

$$\frac{\partial Q_i}{\partial |V_j|} = -|V_i||Y_{ij}| \sin\theta_{ij}$$

$$\frac{\partial Q_i}{\partial |V_j|} = -|V_i| B_{ij} \tag{2.74}$$

Applying these assumptions to Eqs. (2.68) and (2.69), we get

$$\frac{\partial P_i}{\partial \delta_i} = -|V_i| B_{ii} \quad \text{or} \quad \frac{\Delta P_i}{\Delta \delta_i} = -|V_i| B_{ii}$$

$$\frac{\Delta P_i}{|V_i|} = -B_{ii} \Delta \delta_i$$

$$\frac{\Delta P}{|V_i|} = -B' \Delta \delta_i \tag{2.75}$$

Similarly,

$$\frac{\partial Q_i}{\partial |V_i|} = -|V_i| B_{ii} \quad \text{or} \quad \frac{\Delta Q_i}{\Delta |V_i|} = -|V_i| B_{ii}$$

$$\frac{\Delta Q_i}{\Delta |V_i|} = -B_{ii} \Delta |V_i|$$

$$\frac{\Delta Q}{|V_i|} = -B'' \Delta |V_i| \tag{2.76}$$

where, B' and B'' are the imaginary part of the bus admittance matrix Y_{bus}, such that B' contains all buses admittance except those related to the slack bus, and B'' is B' deprived from all voltage controlled buses related admittances.

Finally, all these approximations and simplifications lead to the following successive voltage magnitude and voltage angle updating equations.

$$\Delta \delta = -[B']^{-1} \frac{\Delta P}{|V|} \tag{2.77}$$

$$\Delta V = -[B'']^{-1} \frac{\Delta Q}{|V|} \tag{2.78}$$

FDLF technique is very useful in contingency analysis where numerous outages are to be simulated or a load flow solution is required for online control.

The algorithm written according to the equations derived in the previous section is as follows:

Step 1: Create the bus admittance matrix $[Y_{\text{bus}}]$.

Step 2: Detect all kinds and numbers of buses and setting all bus voltages to an initial value of 1 p.u., all voltage angles to 0, and the iteration counter *iter* to 0.

Step 3: Create the matrices B' and B'' according to Eqs. (2.75) and (2.76).

Step 4: *If* max $(\Delta P, \Delta Q) \leq$ accuracy

$$\Delta P_i^{[k]} = P_{i,\text{sch}} - P_i^{[k]}$$

$$\Delta Q_i = Q_{i,\text{sch}} - Q_i^{[k]}$$

then go to Step 6

else

(i) Calculate $\mathbf{J}_1$ and $\mathbf{J}_4$ elements of Eqs. (2.71), (2.72), (2.73) and (2.74).

$$\frac{\partial P_i}{\partial \delta_i} = -|V_i|B_{ii} \qquad \frac{\partial P_i}{\partial \delta_j} = -|V_i|B_{ij}$$

$$\frac{\partial Q_i}{\partial |V_i|} = -|V_i|B_{ii} \qquad \frac{\partial Q_i}{\partial |V_j|} = -|V_i|B_{ij}$$

(ii) Calculate the real and reactive powers at each bus, and check if MVAR of generator buses are within the limits, otherwise update the voltage magnitude at these buses by ± 2 %.

If $Q_{i,\min} < Q_i < Q_{i,\max}$, calculate $P_i^{(k)}$

If $Q_i^{[k]} > Q_{i,\max}$, $\quad Q_{i,\text{sch}} = Q_{i,\max}$

If $Q_i^{[k]} < Q_{i,\min}$, $\quad Q_{i,\text{sch}} = Q_{i,\min}$

The *PV* bus will act as *PQ* bus.

(iii) Calculate the power residuals, ΔP and ΔQ.

$$\Delta P_i^{[k]} = P_{i,\text{sch}} - P_i^{[k]}$$

$$\Delta Q_i^{[k]} = Q_{i,\text{sch}} - Q_i^{[k]}$$

(iv) Calculate the bus voltage and voltage angle updates ΔV and $\Delta\delta$.

$$[\Delta\delta_i]^{(k)} = -[B']^{-1}\frac{\Delta P_i^{[k]}}{|V_i|}$$

$$[\Delta V_i]^{(k)} = -[B'']^{-1}\frac{\Delta Q_i^{[k]}}{|V_i|}$$

(v) Update the voltage magnitude V and the voltage angle δ at each bus.

$$\delta_i^{[k+1]} = \delta_i^{[k]} + \Delta\delta_i^{[k]}$$

$$|V_i^{[k+1]}| = |V_i^{[k]}| + \Delta|V_i^{[k]}|$$

(vi) Increment of the iteration counter *iter* = *iter* + 1

Step 5: If iter $\leq$ maximum number of iteration

$$|\Delta P_i^{[k]}| \leq \varepsilon$$

$$|\Delta Q_i^{[k]}| \leq \varepsilon$$

then go to Step 4

else print out 'Solution did not converge' and go to Step 6.

Step 6: Print out of the power flow solution, computation and display of the line flow and losses.

This completes the load flow study. Finally, in Figure 2.24 all the computational steps are summarized in the detailed flow chart.

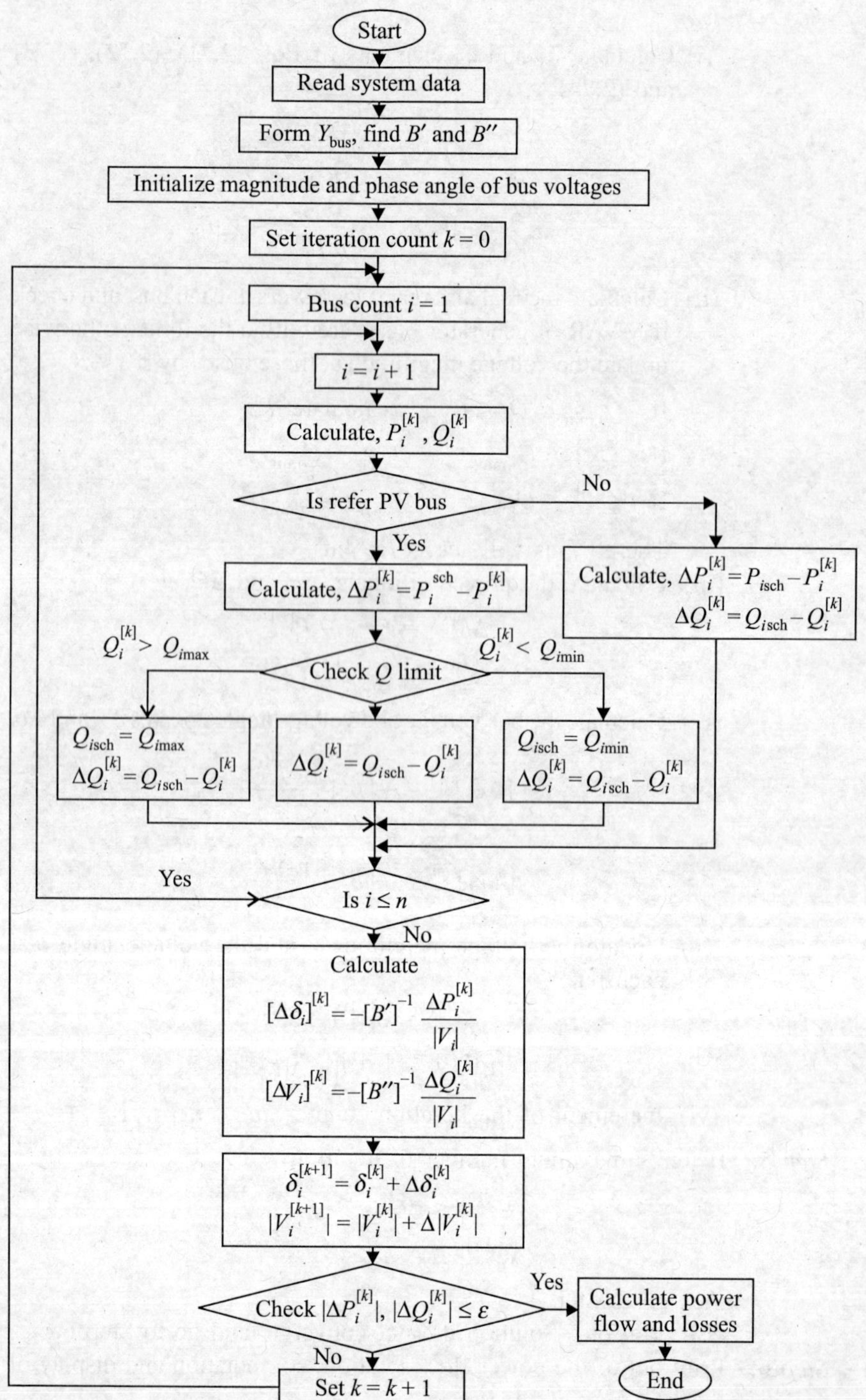

Figure 2.24 Flow chart for FDLF method.

EXAMPLE 2.7 Figure 2.25 shows the one line diagram of a simple three-bus system with generation at bus 1. The magnitude of voltage at bus 1 is adjusted to 1.05 p.u. The scheduled loads at buses 2 and 3 are given in the diagram. Line impedances are marked as *n* p.u. on a 100 MVA base and the line charging susceptances are neglected.

(a) Using the fast decoupled load flow method, determine the phasor values of the voltages at the load buses 2 and 3(*PQ* bus) accurate to decimal places.

(b) Verify the result with Power World Simulator and PSS/E.

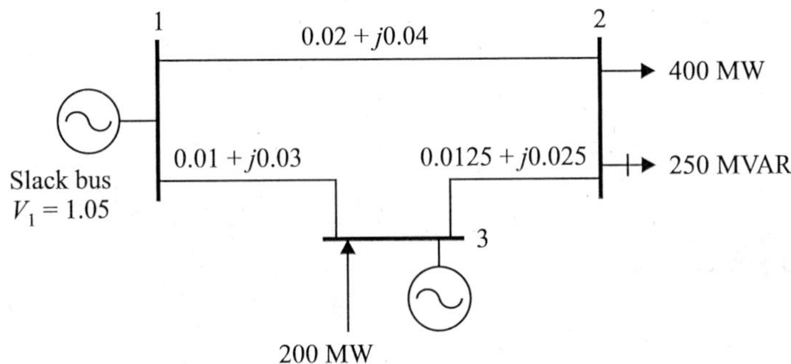

Figure 2.25 One line diagram of a simple three-bus system.

Solution: (a) Form the Y_{bus}

$$y_{12} = \frac{1}{z_{12}} = \frac{1}{0.02 + j0.04} = 10 - j20$$

$$y_{13} = \frac{1}{z_{13}} = \frac{1}{0.01 + j0.03} = 10 - j30$$

$$y_{23} = \frac{1}{z_{23}} = \frac{1}{0.0125 + j0.025} = 16 - j32$$

$$Y_{11} = y_{12} + y_{13} = (10 - j20) + (10 - j30) = 20 - j50$$

$$Y_{12} = Y_{21} = -y_{12} = -(10 - j20) = -10 + j20$$

$$Y_{13} = Y_{31} = -y_{13} = -(10 - j30) = -10 + j30$$

$$Y_{22} = y_{21} + y_{23} = (10 - j20) + (16 - j32) = 26 - j52$$

$$Y_{23} = Y_{32} = -y_{23} = -(16 - j32) = -16 + j32$$

$$Y_{33} = y_{31} + y_{32} = (10 - j30) + (16 - j32) = 26 - j62$$

$$Y_{bus} = \begin{bmatrix} 20 - j50 & -10 + j20 & -10 + j30 \\ -10 + j20 & 26 - j52 & -16 + j32 \\ -10 + j30 & -16 + j32 & 26 - j62 \end{bmatrix}$$

Bus 1 is slack bus and the corresponding bus susceptance matrix for evaluation of phase angle $\Delta\delta_2$ and $\Delta\delta_3$ is

$$B' = \begin{bmatrix} -52 & 32 \\ 32 & -62 \end{bmatrix}$$

The inverse of the above matrix is

$$[B']^{-1} = \begin{bmatrix} -0.028182 & -0.014545 \\ -0.014545 & -0.023636 \end{bmatrix}$$

Initialize magnitude and angle of bus voltage

$$|V_1| = 1.05, \ \delta_1 = 0.0 \text{ rad}$$

$$|V_2|^{(0)} = 1, \ \delta_2^{(0)} = 0.0 \text{ rad}$$

$$|V_3|^{(0)} = 1.04, \ \delta_3^{(0)} = 0.0 \text{ rad}$$

In the matrix form

$$\begin{bmatrix} \delta_1^{(0)} \\ V_1^{(0)} \end{bmatrix} = \begin{bmatrix} 0 \\ 1.05 \end{bmatrix}; \ \begin{bmatrix} \delta_2^{(0)} \\ V_2^{(0)} \end{bmatrix} = \begin{bmatrix} 0 \\ 1 \end{bmatrix}; \ \begin{bmatrix} \delta_3^{(0)} \\ V_3^{(0)} \end{bmatrix} = \begin{bmatrix} 0 \\ 1.04 \end{bmatrix}$$

Scheduled powers are

at bus 2, $$P_{2,\text{sch}} = P_{G2} - P_{D2} = 0 - \frac{400}{100} = -4 \text{ p.u.}$$

$$Q_{2,\text{sch}} = Q_{G2} - Q_{D2} = 0 - \frac{250}{100} = -2.5 \text{ p.u.}$$

at bus 3, $$P_{3,\text{sch}} = P_{G3} - P_{D3} = \frac{200}{100} - 0 = 2 \text{ p.u.}$$

The real power at buses 2 and 3 and reactive power at bus 2 are

$$P_2 = |V_2||V_1||Y_{21}| \cos(\theta_{21} - \delta_2 + \delta_1) + |V_2^2||Y_{22}| \cos\theta_{22} + |V_2||V_3||Y_{23}| \cos(\theta_{23} - \delta_2 + \delta_3)$$

$$P_2 = (1)\,(1.05)\,(22.36068) \cos(116.6 - 0 + 0) + (1)^2 (58.13777) \cos(-63.4) + (1)\,(1.04)\,(35.77709) \cos(116.6 - 0 + 0) = -1.1414$$

$$P_3 = |V_3||V_1||Y_{31}| \cos(\theta_{31} - \delta_3 + \delta_1) + |V_3||V_2||Y_{32}| \cos(\theta_{32} - \delta_3 + \delta_2) + |V_3^2||Y_{33}| \cos\theta_{33}$$

$$P_3 = (1.04)\,(1.05)\,(31.62278) \cos(108.4 - 0 + 0) + (1.04)(1)(35.77709) \cos(116.6 - 0 + 0) + (1.04)^2 (67.23095) \cos(-67.2) = 0.5616$$

$$Q_2 = -|V_2||V_1||Y_{21}| \sin(\theta_{21} - \delta_2 + \delta_1) - |V_2^2||Y_{22}| \sin\theta_{22} - |V_2||V_3||Y_{23}| \sin(\theta_{23} - \delta_2 + \delta_3)$$

$$Q_2 = -(1)\,(1.05)\,(22.36068) \sin(116.6 - 0 + 0) - (1)^2 (58.13777) \sin(-63.4) - (1)\,(1.04)\,(35.77709) \sin(116.6 - 0 + 0) = -2.28$$

Difference in scheduled to calculated power

$$\Delta P_2^{[0]} = P_{2,\text{sch}} - P_{2,\text{calc}}^{(0)} = -4 - (-1.1414) = -2.8586$$

$$\Delta P_3^{[0]} = P_{3,\text{sch}} - P_{3,\text{calc}}^{(0)} = 2 - (0.5616) = 1.43846$$

$$\Delta Q_2^{[0]} = Q_{2,\text{sch}} - Q_{2,\text{calc}}^{(0)} = -2.5 - (-2.28) = -0.22$$

The FDLF algorithm given by Eq. (2.77) becomes

$$[\Delta\delta_i]^{(k)} = -[B']^{-1} \frac{\Delta P_i^{[k]}}{|V_i|}$$

$$\begin{bmatrix} \delta_2^{(0)} \\ \delta_3^{(0)} \end{bmatrix} = -[B']^{-1} \begin{bmatrix} \dfrac{\Delta P_2^{[0]}}{|V_2|} \\ \dfrac{\Delta P_3^{[0]}}{|V_3|} \end{bmatrix}$$

$$\begin{bmatrix} \delta_2^{(0)} \\ \delta_3^{(0)} \end{bmatrix} = -\begin{bmatrix} -0.028182 & -0.014545 \\ -0.014545 & -0.023636 \end{bmatrix} \begin{bmatrix} \dfrac{-2.8586}{1.0} \\ \dfrac{1.43846}{1.04} \end{bmatrix}$$

$$= \begin{bmatrix} -0.028182 & -0.014545 \\ -0.014545 & -0.023636 \end{bmatrix} \begin{bmatrix} -2.8586 \\ 1.3831 \end{bmatrix}$$

$$= \begin{bmatrix} -0.060483 \\ -0.008909 \end{bmatrix}$$

Since bus 3 is a regulated bus, the corresponding row and column of B' are eliminated and we get

$$B'' = [-52]$$

$$[B'']^{-1} = \frac{-1}{52} = -0.01923$$

$$[\Delta V_i]^{(k)} = -[B'']^{-1} \frac{\Delta Q_i^{[k]}}{|V_i|}$$

$$[\Delta V_2]^{(0)} = -[B'']^{-1} \frac{\Delta Q_0^{[0]}}{|V_2|}$$

$$[\Delta V_2]^{(0)} = -(-0.01923)\left[\frac{-0.22}{1.0}\right] = -0.0042308$$

The new bus voltages and the angles in the first iteration are

$$\delta_i^{[k+1]} = \delta_i^{[k]} + \Delta\delta_i^{[k]}$$

$$\delta_2^{[1]} = \delta_2^{[0]} + \Delta\delta_2^{[0]} = 0 + (-0.060483) = -0.060483$$

$$\delta_3^{[1]} = \delta_3^{[0]} + \Delta\delta_3^{[0]} = 0 + (-0.008909) = -0.008909$$

$$|V_i^{[k+1]}| = |V_i^{[k]}| + \Delta|V_i^{[k]}|$$

$$|V_2^{[1]}| = |V_2^{[0]}| + \Delta|V_2^{[0]}| = 1 + (-0.0042308) = 0.99577$$

(b) Verify the result using Power World Simulator: The one line diagram of a simple bus system drawn in PWS is shown in Figure 2.26.

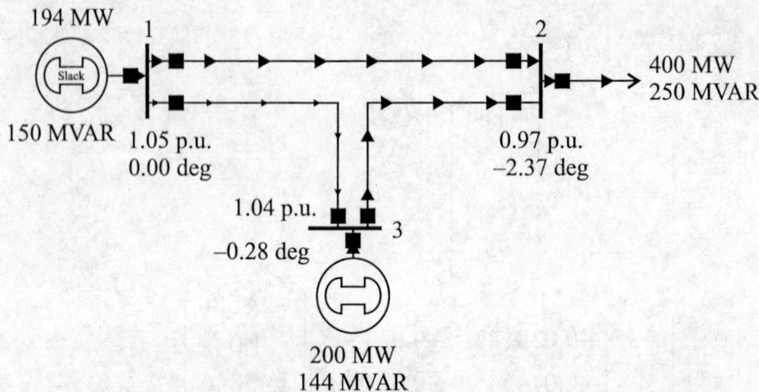

Figure 2.26 One line diagram of a simple three-bus system.

The first step is the formation of $[Y_{bus}]$ using the inspection method. The calculated $[Y_{bus}]$ values are given in Figure 2.27. Since the given problem is a three-bus system, the size of $[Y_{bus}]$ is 3×3 matrix.

Y Bus (Bus Admittance Matrix)

	Number	Name	Bus 1	Bus 2	Bus 3
1	1	1	20.00 - j50.00	-10.00 + j20.00	-10.00 + j30.00
2	2	2	-10.00 + j20.00	26.00 - j52.00	-16.00 + j32.00
3	3	3	-10.00 + j30.00	-16.00 + j32.00	26.00 - j62.00

Figure 2.27 Y_{bus} result.

This method is executed by pressing the icon *fast decoupled* available in *tools ribbon*. Before executing this method, the number of iterations is to be fixed as 1 in *simulator options ribbon.*

The same problem has been executed by the fast decoupled method. The converged results are given in Figure 2.28. The converged power flow results for Gauss–Seidel, Newton–Raphson and fast decoupled are shown in Figures 2.8, 2.21 and 2.28. The power flow results are the same for all methods, but the results are converged quickly by Newton–Raphson method, i.e. by two iterations.

Bus Power Flows - Case: book_sample.PWB Status: Running (PF) | Simu...

Bus Flows

BUS	1 1		138.0 MW	Mvar	MVA	% 1.0500	0.00	1 1
GENERATOR 1			218.35	140.91R	259.9			
TO	2 2	1	179.35	118.77	215.1	0		
TO	3 3	1	39.00	22.14	44.8	0		
**** Mismatch ****			218.35	140.91				
BUS	2 2		138.0 MW	Mvar	MVA	% 0.9717	-2.70	1 1
LOAD 1			400.00	250.00	471.7			
TO	1 1	1	-170.95	-101.98	199.1	0		
TO	3 3	1	-229.07	-148.08	272.8	0		
BUS	3 3		138.0 MW	Mvar	MVA	% 1.0400	-0.50	1 1
GENERATOR 1			200.00	146.19R	247.7			
TO	1 1	1	-38.82	-21.59	44.4	0		
TO	2 2	1	238.92	167.78	291.9	0		
**** Mismatch ****			199.90	146.19				

Figure 2.28 Converged power flow results and voltages.

PSS/E

The same problem is taken and drawn in PSS/E software and it is given in Figure 2.29.

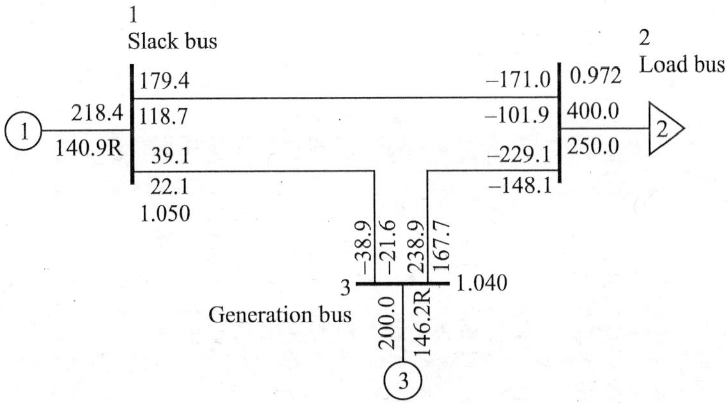

Figure 2.29 One line diagram of a simple three-bus system.

Once the data are entered in the software it can be executed by the above three power flow methods. Figure 2.30 shows the converged results obtained by the fast decoupled method. This window is generated from *bus based report*.

The fast decoupled method is executed and the power flow results are shown in Figure 2.30.

```
     PTI INTERACTIVE POWER              Mon, JUN 27 2011   12:00     %MVA FOR TRANSFORMERS
    SYSTEM SIMULATOR--PSS®E                                RATING    %I    FOR NON-TRANSFORMER BRANCHES
                                                           SET A

BUS    1 SLACK BUS    CKT    MW      MVAR     MVA    %  1.050PU   0.00   X---LOSSES---X  X---AREA----X  X---ZONE---X  1
  FROM GENERATION           218.4    140.9R   259.9  260     kV           MW     MVAR        1               1
  TO   2 LOAD BUS      1    179.4    118.7    215.1                       8.39   16.79       1               1
  TO   3 GEN BUS       1     39.0     22.1     44.9                       0.18    0.55       1               1

BUS    2 LOAD BUS     CKT    MW      MVAR     MVA    %  0.9717PU  -2.70  X---LOSSES---X  X---AREA----X  X---ZONE---X  2
                                                          kV              MW     MVAR        1               1
  TO LOAD-PQ                400.0    250.0    471.7
  TO   1 SLACK BUS     1   -171.0   -102.0    199.1                       8.39   16.79       1               1
  TO   3 GEN BUS       1   -229.0   -148.1    272.7                       9.85   19.69       1               1

BUS    3 GEN BUS      CKT    MW      MVAR     MVA    %  1.0400PU  -0.50  X---LOSSES---X  X---AREA----X  X---ZONE---X  3
  FROM GENERATION           200.0    146.2R   247.7  248     kV           MW     MVAR        1               1
  TO   1 SLACK BUS     1    -38.9    -21.6     44.5                       0.18    0.55       1               1
  TO   2 LOAD BUS      1    238.9    167.7    291.9                       9.85   19.69       1               1
```

Figure 2.30 Converged results using fast decoupled method.

2.8 Comparison of the Gauss–Seidel, Newton–Raphson and Fast Decoupled Methods of Load Flow Study

S.No.	*Gauss–Seidel*	*Newton–Raphson*	*Fast decoupled*
1.	Requires a large number of iterations to reach convergence.	Requires a less number of iterations to reach convergence.	Requires a more number of iterations than Newton–Raphson method.
2.	Computation time per iteration is less.	Computation time per iteration is more.	Computation time per iteration is less.
3.	It has linear convergence characteristics.	It has quadratic convergence characteristics.	—
4.	The number of iterations required for convergence increases with the size of the system.	The number of iterations are independent of the size of the system.	The number of iterations does not depend on the size of the system.
5.	Less memory required.	More memory required.	Less memory required than Newton–Raphson method.

Review Questions

Part-A

1. What is the power flow study or load flow study?
2. What are the scraps of information that are obtained from the load flow study?
3. What is the need for load flow study?
4. What are the quantities associated with each bus in a system?
5. What are the different types of buses in a power system? Or, how are the buses classified and what are its types?
6. What is the need for slack bus?
7. Why do we go for iterative methods to solve the load flow problems?
8. What are the methods mainly used for the solution of load flow study?
9. What do you mean by a flat voltage start?
10. Discuss the effect of acceleration factor in load flow study.
11. When is the generator bus treated as load bus?
12. What are the advantages and disadvantages of Gauss–Seidel method?
13. What are the advantages and disadvantages of Newton–Raphson method?
14. Compare the Gauss–Seidel and the Newton–Raphson methods of load flow study.

Part-B

1. The system data for a load flow solution are given in the following tables. Determine the voltages at the end of first iteration by Gauss–Seidel method. Take $\alpha = 1.6$. Verify the result with Power World Simulator.

Bus code	*R* in p.u.	*X* in p.u.
1–2	0.05	0.15
1–3	0.10	0.30
1–4	0.20	0.40
2–4	0.10	0.30
3–4	0.05	0.15

Bus code	*P*	*Q*	*V*	*Remarks*
1	—	—	1.05	Slack bus
2	0.5	−0.2	—	*PQ* bus
3	−1.0	0.5	—	*PQ* bus
4	0.3	−0.1	—	*PQ* bus

2. The system contains six buses. The bus data, branch data and generator data are given below. The system data are prepared and the power flows are solved by Newton–Raphson method using **Power World Simulator**.

Bus data

Bus	*Type*	*V* p.u.	δ *degree*	P_g MW	Q_g p.u.	P_L p.u.	Q_L p.u.	*Nominal voltage in* kV
1	Swing	1.05	0	—	—	—	—	230
2	Generator	1.05	—	66.368	0	0.0	0.0	230
3	Generator	1.07	—	77.473	—	0.0	0.0	230
4	Load	1.00	—	0	0	70	70	230
5	Load	1.00	—	0	0	70	70	230
6	Load	1.00	—	0	0	70	70	230

Line data

From Bus	*To bus*	*R* p.u.	*X* p.u.	*B* p.u.	*Max. MVA* p.u.
1	2	0.20	0.20	0.02	40
1	4	0.05	0.20	0.02	60
1	5	0.08	0.30	0.03	40
2	3	0.05	0.25	0.03	40
2	4	0.05	0.10	0.01	60
2	5	0.10	0.30	0.02	30
2	6	0.07	0.20	0.025	90
3	5	0.12	0.26	0.025	70
3	6	0.02	0.10	0.01	80
4	5	0.20	0.40	0.04	20
5	6	0.10	0.30	0.03	40

3. A one line diagram of the system is shown in the figure below. The system contains seven buses. The bus data, branch data and generator data are given below. The system data are prepared and the power flows are solved by Newton–Raphson method or fast decoupled method using **Power World Simulator software.**

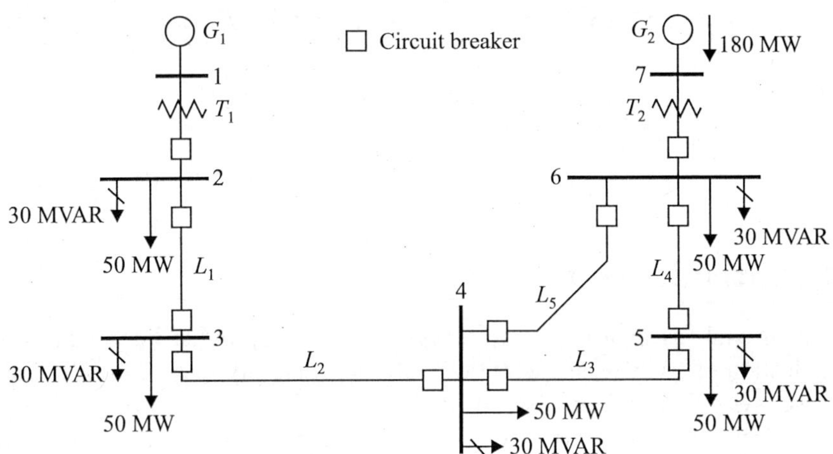

Generator ratings

G_1: 100 MVA, 13.8 kV, $X'' = 0.12$, $X_2 = 0.14$, $X_0 = 0.05$ p.u.
G_2: 100 MVA, 13.8 kV, $X'' = 0.12$, $X_2 = 0.14$, $X_0 = 0.05$ p.u.

Generator neutrals are solidly grounded.

Transformer ratings

T_1: 100 MVA, 13.8 kVΔ/230 kV Y, $X = 0.1$ p.u.
T_2: 200 MVA, 15 kVΔ/230 kV Y, $X = 0.1$ p.u.

Generator neutrals are solidly grounded

Transmission line ratings

All lines: 230 kV, $Z_1 = 0.08 + j0.5$ Ω/km, $Z_0 = 0.2 + j1.5$ Ω/km, $y_1 = j3.3 \times 10^{-6}$ s/km
$L_1 = 15$ km, $L_2 = 25$ km, $L_3 = 40$ km, $L_4 = 15$ km, $L_5 = 50$ km

Power flow data

Bus 1: Swing bus, $V_1 = 13.8$ kV
Buses 2, 3, 4, 5, and 6: Load buses
Bus 7: Voltage control bus, $V_7 = 15$ kV, $P_{G7} = 180$ MW, $-87 \text{ MVAR} < Q_{G7} < +87$ MVAR

System base quantities

$S_{base} = 100$ MVA, three phase, $V_{base} = 13.8$ kV in the zone of G_1

CHAPTER 3

Symmetrical Fault Analysis

3.1 Introduction

The fault analysis of a power system is required to provide information for the selection of switchgear, setting of relays and stability of system operation. A power system is not static but changes during the operation (switching on or off of generators and transmission lines) and planning (addition of generators and transmission lines). Thus fault studies need to be routinely performed by the utility engineers.

Faults usually occur in a power system due to

- insulation failure of equipment.
- flashover of lines initiated by a lighting stroke.
- permanent damage to conductors and towers or accidental faulty operations.

Faults may either be three-phases in nature involving all three-phases in a symmetrical manner, or may be asymmetrical where usually only one or two phases may be involved. Faults may also be caused either by short-circuits to earth, between live conductors, or by broken conductors in one or more phases. Sometimes simultaneous faults may occur involving both short-circuit and broken conductor faults (also known as open-circuit fault).

3.2 Types of Faults

(i) Series fault or open-circuit fault

- One open conductor fault
- Two open conductor fault

(ii) Shunt fault or short-circuit fault

- Symmetrical fault or balanced fault
  - — Three-phase fault

- Unsymmetrical fault or unbalanced fault
  - Line-to-ground (L-G) fault
  - Line-to-line (L-L) fault
  - Double line-to-ground (L-L-G) fault

A three-phase fault is a condition where either (a) all the three-phases of the system are short-circuited to each other, or (b) all the three-phases of the system are earthed. This type of fault is defined as the simultaneous short-circuited fault which occurs at all the three-phases and gives rise to symmetrical current. It occurs infrequently, but it is the most severe type. This fault current is determined by the internal emf of the machine in the system, the internal impedances and the impedance in the network between machine and fault.

The balanced three-phase faults may be analysed using per phase basis analysis or equivalent single-phase circuit. With asymmetrical three-phase faults, the use of symmetrical components helps to reduce the complexity of the calculations as transmission lines and components are by and large symmetrical, although the fault may be asymmetrical.

Fault analysis is usually carried out in per-unit quantities as they give solutions which are somewhat consistent over different voltage and power ratings, and operate on values of the order of unity.

This, in general, is a balanced condition, and we just need to know the positive-sequence network to analyse faults. Further, the single line diagram can be used, as all the three-phases carry equal currents displaced by 120°.

Typically, only 5% of the initial faults in a power system are three-phase faults with or without earth. Of the unbalanced faults, 80% are line-earth and 15% are double line faults with or without earth and which can often deteriorate to three-phase fault. Broken conductor faults account for the rest.

A fault represents a structural network change equivalent with that caused by the addition of impedance at the place of a fault. If the fault impedance is zero, the fault is referred to as bolted fault or solid fault.

3.3 Transient (Short-circuit) on Power System Components

A modern large interconnected power system components have inductive property which gives rise to transients when there is a sudden change in current.

3.3.1 Transient (Short-circuit) on a Transmission Line

Let us consider the short-circuit transient on a transmission line. Certain simplifying assumptions are made at this stage. The line is fed from the constant voltage source. Short-circuit takes place when the line is unloaded and the line capacitance is negligible.

Consider the series R–L circuit as shown in Figure 3.1. The closing of switch (SW) at $t = 0$ represents a first approximation of a three-phase short-circuit at the terminals of an unloaded transmission line. The current is assumed to be zero before switch closes, and the source angle α determines the source voltage at $t = 0$. Now the Kirchhoff's voltage law equation for the circuit

$$Ri(t) + L\frac{di(t)}{dt} = \sqrt{2}V \sin(\omega t + \alpha) \qquad t \geq 0 \tag{3.1}$$

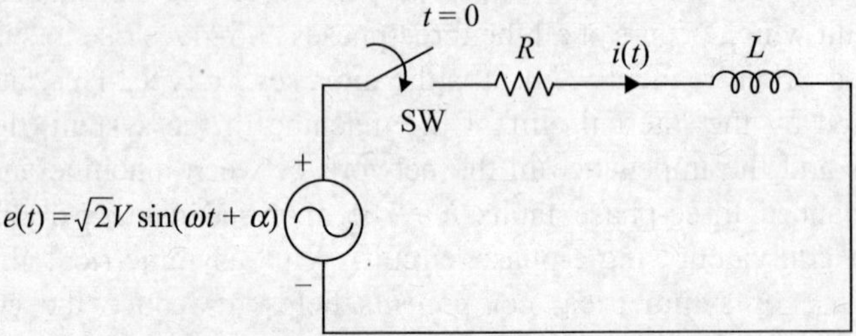

Figure 3.1 Simple series R–L circuit.

The solution to the above equation is as follows.

Total short-circuit current

$$i(t) = i_{ac}(t) + i_{dc}(t)$$

$$i(t) = \frac{\sqrt{2}V}{|Z|} \sin(\omega t + \alpha - \theta) + \frac{\sqrt{2}V}{|Z|} \sin(\theta - \alpha)\, e^{-(R/L)t} \tag{3.2}$$

where symmetrical short-circuit current,

$$i_{ac}(t) = \frac{\sqrt{2}V}{|Z|} \sin(\omega t + \alpha - \theta) \tag{3.3}$$

dc offset current,

$$i_{dc}(t) = \frac{\sqrt{2}V}{|Z|} \sin(\theta - \alpha)\, e^{-(R/L)t} \tag{3.4}$$

Impedance of the transmission line

$$Z = \sqrt{R^2 + (\omega L)^2} \tag{3.5}$$

$$\theta = \tan^{-1}\left(\frac{\omega L}{R}\right) \tag{3.6}$$

The total short-circuit current in Eq. (3.2) is plotted in Figure 3.2 along with two components. The symmetrical short-circuit current given by Eq. (3.3) is a sinusoidal. The dc offset current, given by Eq. (3.4), decays exponentially with time constant.

The total short-circuit current $i(t)$, the value corresponding to the first peak, is called maximum momentary short-circuit current i_{mm}. If the decay of the transient current in this short time is neglected, then

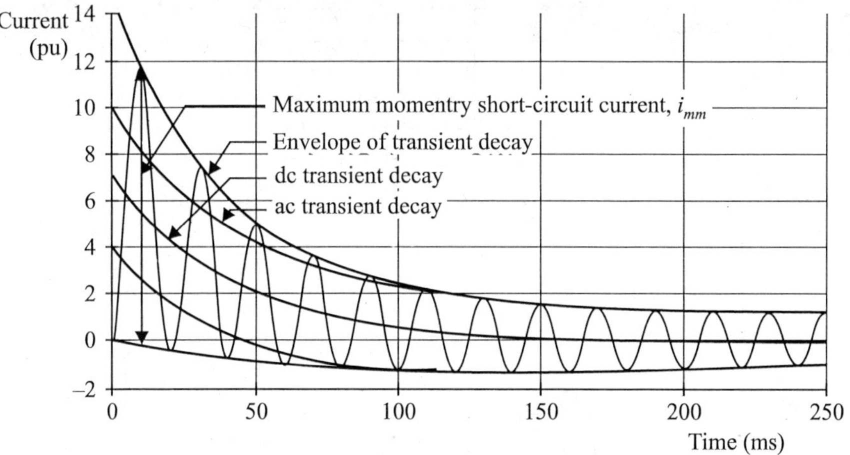

Figure 3.2 Waveform of a short-circuit current on a transmission line.

$$i_{mm} = \frac{\sqrt{2}V}{|Z|}\sin(\theta - \alpha) + \frac{\sqrt{2}V}{|Z|} \tag{3.7}$$

Since the transmission line resistance is small, $\theta \cong 90°$.

Therefore,

$$i_{mm} = \frac{\sqrt{2}V}{|Z|}\cos\alpha + \frac{\sqrt{2}V}{|Z|} \tag{3.8}$$

From Eq. (3.8), i_{mm} has the maximum possible value when $\alpha = 0$. This implies that the effect of short-circuit will be severe if the fault occurs when the voltage wave is going through zero. Thus

$$i_{mm\,(\text{max possible})} = \frac{\sqrt{2}V}{|Z|} + \frac{\sqrt{2}V}{|Z|} = \frac{2\sqrt{2}V}{|Z|} = \text{doubling effect} \tag{3.9}$$

For the selection of circuit breakers, the momentary short-circuit current is taken corresponding to its maximum possible value.

3.3.2 Transient (Short-circuit) on a Synchronous Machine

As mentioned earlier, the current flowing in the power system network during a fault depends on the machines connected to the system. Due to the effect of the armature current on the flux that generates the voltage, the current flowing in a synchronous machine differs immediately after the occurrence of the fault, a few cycles later, and under sustained or steady state conditions. Further there is an exponentially decaying dc component caused by the instantaneous value at the instant of fault occurring. These are shown in Figure 3.3. Figures 3.3(a) and 3.3(b) depict the steady state current waveform and the transient waveform of a simple *R–L* circuit to show the decay in the dc component.

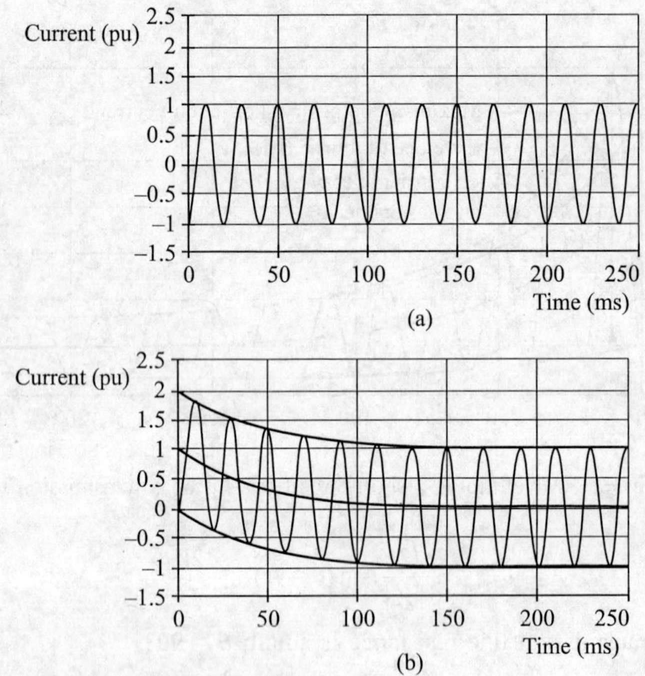

Figure 3.3 Steady state and transient waveform of transmission line.

In addition to this, in the synchronous machine, the magnitude of the ac current peak also changes with time as shown in Figure 3.4, with the unidirectional component of the transient waveform removed. Due to the initial low back emf at the instant of fault resulting in high current, the effective impedance is very low. Even when the dc transient component is not present, the initial current can be several times the steady state value.

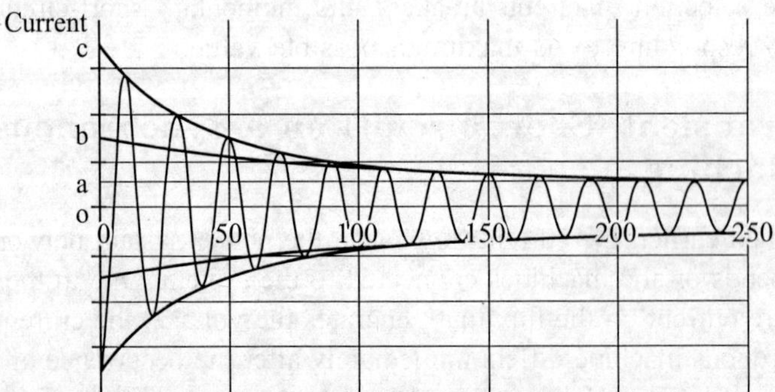

Figure 3.4 Symmetrical short-circuit armature current in synchronous machine.

Thus the three regions are identified for determining the reactance. These are the subtransient reactance X_d'' for the first 10 to 20 ms of fault, the transient reactance X'_d for up to about 500 ms, and the steady state reactance X_d (synchronous reactance).

Under the steady state three-phase short-circuit condition, the armature reaction of an alternator produces a demagnetizing flux. This effect is represented as a reactance called armature reaction reactance, X_a. The combined of armature reactance, X_a and leakage reactance, X_l is called synchronous reactance, X_s. In case of a salient pole alternator, the synchronous reactance is called direct axis reactance, X_d.

Direct axis subtransient reactance (X''_d): At the instant of short-circuit, the dc offset current appears in all the three-phases of stator. This dc offset current can induce current in rotor field winding and damper winding by the transformer action. The increase in field current and damper winding current will set up flux in a direction to augment the main flux. This effect can be represented by two reactances in parallel with X_a as shown in Figure 3.5. Here X_f represents the flux created by induced current in the field winding and X_{dw} indicates the flux created by induced current in the damper winding. The combined effect of all the three reactances is to reduce the total reactance of the machine and so the short-circuit current is very high in this state which is called subtransient state. That is, the total reactance under this condition is subtransient reactance.

$$X''_d = X_l + \frac{1}{\dfrac{1}{X_a} + \dfrac{1}{X_f} + \dfrac{1}{X_{dw}}} \tag{3.10}$$

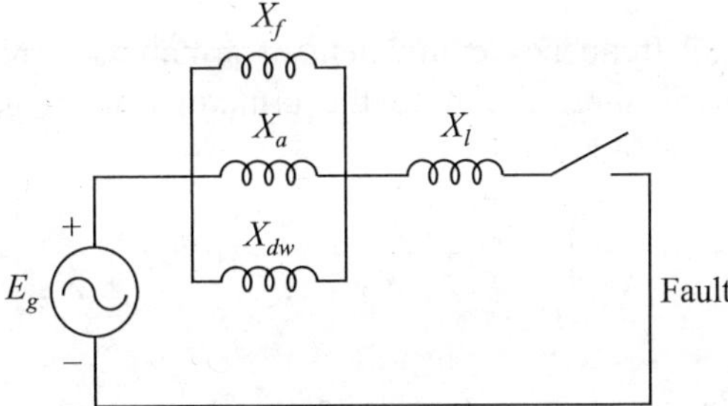

Figure 3.5 Circuit model of subtransient reactance.

Direct axis transient reactance (X'_d): The reactance is effective after the damper winding currents have died out, i.e. the transient reactance of the machine as shown in Figure 3.6 is given by

$$X'_d = X_l + (X_a \parallel X_f)$$

or

$$X'_d = X_l + \frac{1}{\dfrac{1}{X_a} + \dfrac{1}{X_f}} \tag{3.11}$$

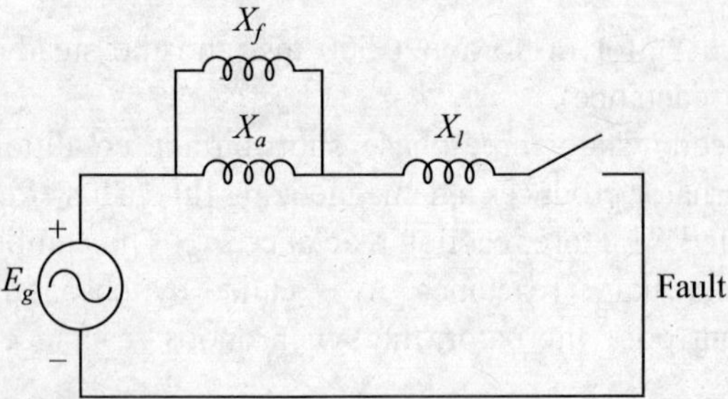

Figure 3.6 Circuit model of transient reactance.

Direct axis synchronous reactance or steady state condition reactance: The transient state will exist for a few cycles and then the steady state conditions are achieved as the effect of field winding current will also die out in short time depending on its time constant. Thus the steady state total reactance as shown in Figure 3.7 is given by the sum of X_a and X_l.

$$X_d = X_a + X_l \tag{3.12}$$

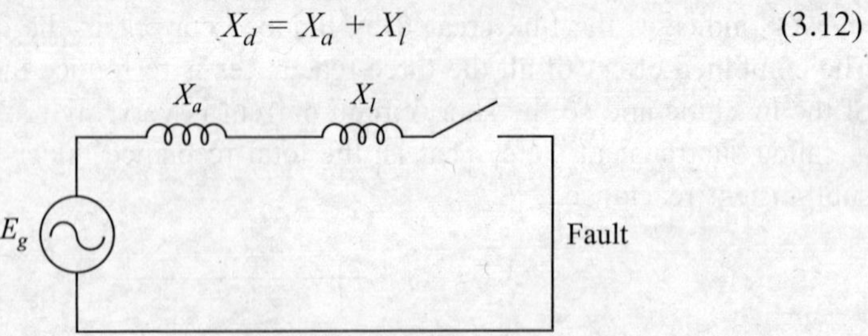

Figure 3.7 Circuit model of steady state reactance.

The fundamental frequency component of armature current following the sudden application of short-circuit to the armature of an initially unloaded machine can be expressed as

$$i_{ac}(t) = \sqrt{2}E_g\left[\left(\frac{1}{X''_d}-\frac{1}{X'_d}\right)e^{-t/\tau''_d}+\left(\frac{1}{X'_d}-\frac{1}{X_d}\right)e^{-t/\tau'_d}+\frac{1}{X_d}\right]\sin\left(\omega t+\alpha-\frac{\pi}{2}\right) \tag{3.13}$$

where E_g is the rms line to lone neutral pre-fault terminal voltage of the unloaded synchronous machine. The armature resistance is neglected in the above equation.

Note that at time $t = 0$, when the fault occurs the rms value of current

$$i_{ac}(0) = I'' = \frac{E_g}{X''_d} \tag{3.14}$$

which is called the rms subtransient fault current, I''. The duration of I'' is determined by the time constant τ''_d, which is called the direct axis short-circuit subtransient time constant.

At a later time, when t is large compared to τ''_d, but small compared to the direct axis short-circuit transient time constant τ'_d, the first exponential term in Eq. (3.13) has decayed almost to zero, but the second exponential has not decayed significantly. The rms ac fault current then equals to the rms transient fault current and given by

$$I' = \frac{E_g}{X'_d} \tag{3.15}$$

when t is much larger than τ'_d, the rms ac fault current approaches its steady state value, given by

$$I = \frac{E_g}{X_d} \tag{3.16}$$

After a fault occurs, the subtransient, transient, and steady state periods are characterized by the subtransients reactance X''_d, the transient reactance X'_d and steady state reactance X_d respectively. These reactances have increasing values ($X''_d < X'_d < X_d$) and the corresponding components of the short-circuit current have decreasing magnitudes ($|I''| > |I'| > |I|$). With dc component removed, the initial symmetrical rms current is the rms value of the ac component of the fault current immediately after the fault occurs.

Internal voltages of loaded machines under fault conditions

Let us consider a generator that is loaded when a fault occurs. Figure 3.8 shows the equivalent circuit of generator that has a balanced three-phase load.

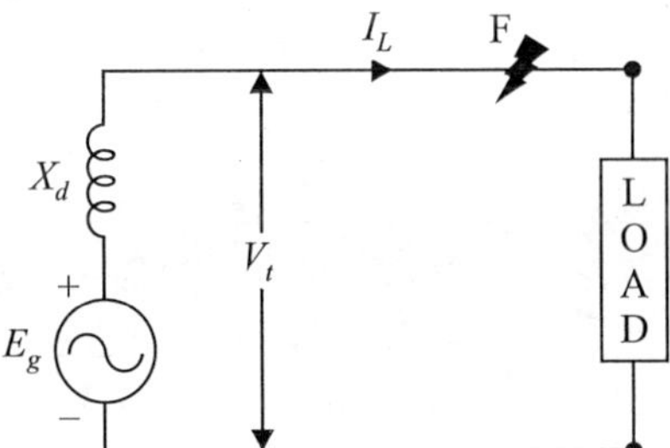

Figure 3.8 Equivalent circuit of a loaded generator under steady state condition.

I_L is the current delivered by the generator. The circuit model of a synchronous generator operating under steady state condition supplying a load current I_L is shown in Figure 3.8.

$$E_g = V_t + jI_L X_d \tag{3.17}$$

where E_g is the induced emf under loaded condition

X_d is the direct axis synchronous reactance of the machine.

V_t is the terminal voltage of the generator.

If a three-phase fault or short-circuit occurs at point F, we see that a short-circuit from F to neutral in the equivalent circuit does not satisfy the conditions for calculating subtransient current, for the reactance of the generator.

Now to study the subtransient state, E_g and X_d of Figure 3.8 should be replaced by E_g'' and X_d'' as shown in Figure 3.9.

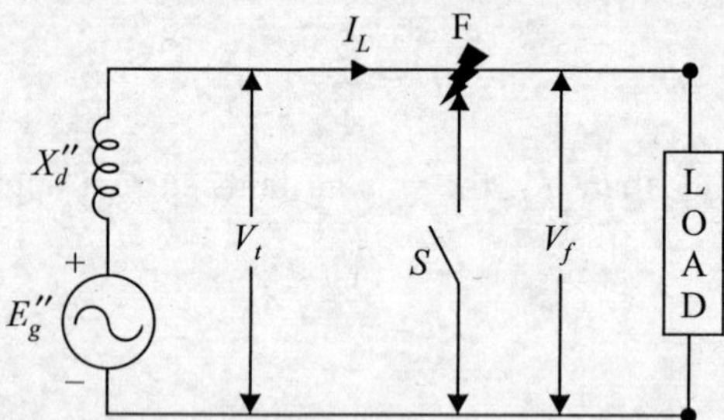

Figure 3.9 Equivalent circuit of a loaded generator under subtransient condition.

$$E_g'' = V_t + jI_L X_d'' = V_f + jI_L X_d'' \tag{3.18}$$

where E_g'' is the subtransient internal voltage.

In order to study the transient state, E_g and X_d of Figure 3.8 should be replaced by E_g' and X_d' as shown in Figure 3.10.

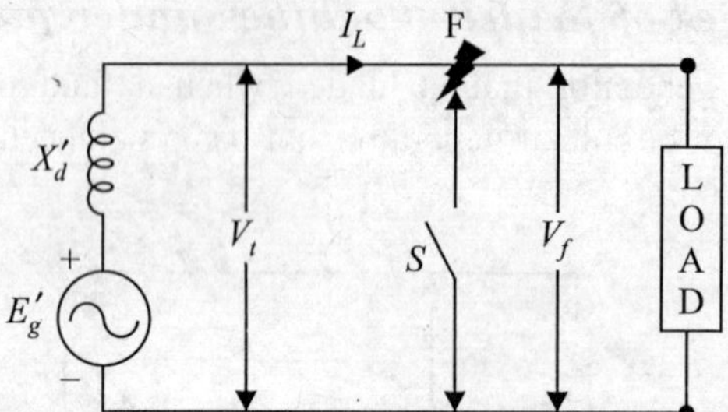

Figure 3.10 Equivalent circuit of a loaded generator transient condition.

$$E_g' = V_t + jI_L X_d' = V_f + jI_L X_d' \tag{3.19}$$

where E_g' is the transient internal voltage.

The **synchronous motors** have internal emfs and reactances similar to that of generator except that the current direction is reversed.

$$E_g'' = V_t - jI_L X_d'' \tag{3.20}$$

$$E_g' = V_t - jI_L X_d' \tag{3.21}$$

3.4 Symmetrical Short-circuit Current Calculation Through Thevenin's Theorem

An alternative method of computing short-circuit current is through the Thevenin's theorem. This method is faster and easily adapted to systematic computation for large networks.

Consider a synchronous generator feeding a synchronous motor over a transmission line and the fault occurs at motor terminals as shown in Figure 3.11. The fault current and the bus voltage and the line current during the fault can be determined and the fault voltage and current can be obtained by using the prefault voltage and current.

3.4.1 Procedure for Symmetrical Short-circuit Current Calculation Through Thevenin's Theorem

1. Assume all prefault voltage magnitudes are 1.0 per unit and all prefault currents are zero.
2. Draw the single line diagram (Figure 3.11).

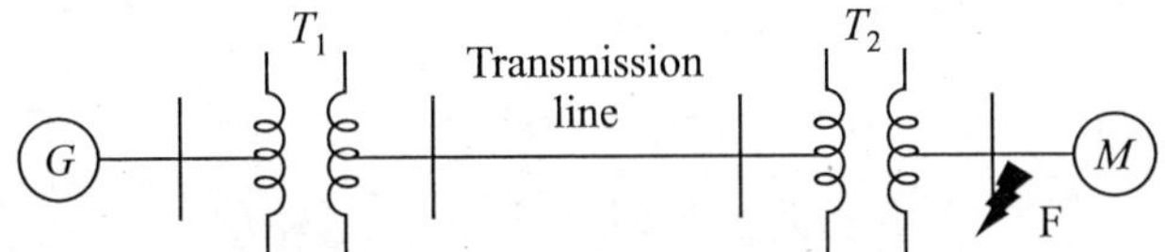

Figure 3.11 Single line diagram of representative power system.

3. Draw the reactance diagram. The per unit reactance values are determined from the per unit analysis (Figures 3.12 and 3.13).

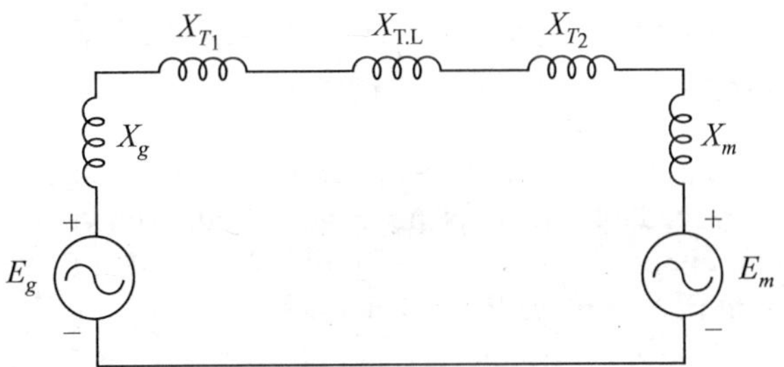

Figure 3.12 Reactance diagram of power system.

4. Prefault bus voltage and current are obtained from the result of load flow analysis.
5. Replace the reactances of synchronous machines by their subtransient/transient values.
6. Short-circuited all the emf sources. The result is the passive Thevenin's network (Figure 3.13).

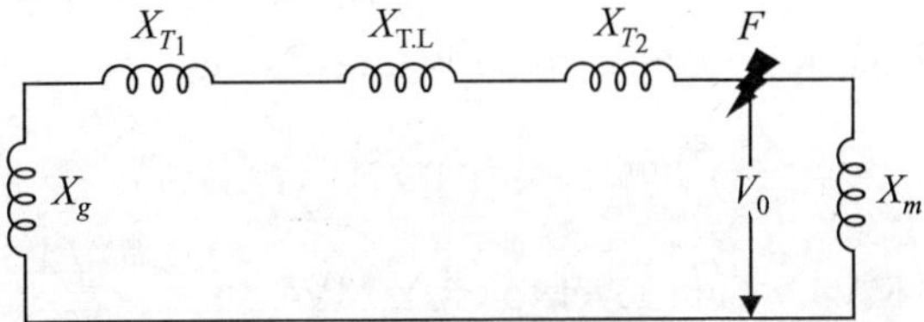

Figure 3.13 Reactance diagram of power system.

7. Draw Thevenin's equivalent circuit viewed from the faulted bus.
8. Find the fault current

$$I_f = \frac{E_{th}}{j(X_{th} + X_f)} \tag{3.22}$$

where, E_{th} or $V°$ is the prefault voltage
Thevenin reactance, $X_{th} = (X_g + X) \parallel X_m$
X_f is the fault reactance.

$$X = X_{T1} + X_{TL} + X_{T2}$$

9. Determine the current contributed by the generator and motor, etc.

$$I_G = \frac{jX_m}{j(X_g + X + X_m)} I_f\,; \quad I_M = \frac{j(X_g + X)}{j(X_g + X + X_m)} I_f \tag{3.23}$$

10. Determine the postfault voltage using

$$V_{i(f)} = V_{i(0)} + \Delta V = V_{i(0)} + (-jX_{th} I_f) \tag{3.24}$$

11. Determine the postfault line flows

$$I_{ij(f)} = \frac{(V_{i(f)} - V_{j(f)})}{z_{ij}} \tag{3.25}$$

3.4.2 Short-circuit Capacity (SCC) or Short-circuit MVA or Fault Level Calculations

In a power system, the maximum fault current (or fault MVA) that can flow into a zero impedance fault is necessary to be known for switch gear solution. This can either be the balanced three-phase value or the value at an asymmetrical condition. The fault level defines the value for the symmetrical condition. The fault level is usually expressed in MVA (or the corresponding per unit value), with the maximum fault current value being converted using the nominal voltage rating.

The short-circuit capacity (SCC) is defined by the product of magnitude of prefault bus voltage and postfault current.

$$\text{Short-circuit capacity} = |E_{th}| \times |I_f| \tag{3.26}$$

$$\text{Short-circuit capacity} = E_{th} \times \frac{E_{th}}{Z_{th}} \quad (Z_f = 0) = \frac{E_{th}^2}{Z_{th}}$$

The per unit voltage for nominal value is unity, so that

$$\text{Fault level (p.u.)} = \frac{1}{Z_{th}} \tag{3.27}$$

$$\text{Fault MVA} = \text{fault level (p.u.)} \times \text{MVA}_{\text{base}} = \frac{\text{MVA}_{\text{base}}}{Z_{th}} \tag{3.28}$$

$$\text{Base current} = \frac{\text{MVA}_{\text{base}}}{\sqrt{3}\ \text{kV}_{\text{b}}} \times 10^3 \tag{3.29}$$

$$\text{Fault current in } A = \text{fault current in p.u. } (I_f) \times \text{base current} \tag{3.30}$$

The SCC of a busbar is the fault level of the busbar. The strength of a busbar (or the ability to maintain its voltage) is directly proportional to its SCC. An infinitely strong bus (or infinite busbar) has an infinite SCC, with zero equivalent impedance and will maintain its voltage under all conditions.

The magnitude of short-circuit current is time dependant due to synchronous generators. It is initially at its largest value and decreasing to steady value. These higher fault levels tax circuit breakers (CBs) adversely so that current limiting reactors can be used.

The short-circuit MVA is a better indicator of the stress on CBs than the short-circuit current as CB has to withstand recovery voltage across breaker following arc interruption. The current flowing during a fault is determined by the internal emfs of machines in the network, the impedances of the machines, and the impedances between the machines and the fault.

3.5 Selection of Circuit Breaker

The circuit breakers are protective devices which are used in power system to automatically open the faulty part of the system in the event of a fault. In normal working condition they can be used as a switch. Hence the two functions of CBs are as follows:

- To act as switch for normal load conditions
- To automatically isolate the faulty part in the event of a fault

Two of the CB ratings which require the computation of SC current are:

1. Rated momentary current and
2. Rated symmetrical interrupting current.

Symmetrical short-circuit current is obtained by using subtransient reactance for synchronous machines. Momentary current (rms) is then calculated by multiplying the symmetrical momentary current by a factor of 1.6 to account for the presence of dc offset current.

The CB for a particular application is selected on the basis of the following ratings.

1. Normal working power level specified as rated interrupting current or rated interrupting kVA.
2. The fault level specified as either the rated short-circuit interrupting current or rated short-circuit current interrupting MVA.
3. Momentary current rating
4. Normal working voltage
5. Speed of CB

The symmetrical current to be interrupted is computed by using subtransient reactances for synchronous generators and transient reactances for synchronous motors. The dc offset value to be added to obtain the current to be interrupted is accounted for by multiplying the symmetrical SC current by a factor as tabulated below.

Speed of CB	*Multiplying factor*
8 cycles or more	1.0
5 cycles	1.1
3 cycles	1.2
2 cycles	1.4
1½ cycles	1.5

$$\text{Short-circuit current interrupting MVA} = \sqrt{3} \times |V_{pf\,L}| \times |I_{f\,L}| \quad (3.31)$$

$$\text{Short-circuit current interrupting in p.u} = \sqrt{3} \times |V_{pf\,\text{p.u.}}| \times |I_{f\,\text{p.u.}}| \times \text{MVA}_b \quad (3.32)$$

EXAMPLE 3.1 Generators G_1 and G_2 are identical and rated 11 kV, 20 MVA and have a transient reactance of 0.25 p.u. at own MVA base. The transformers T_1 and T_2 are also identical and are rated 11/66 kV, 5 MVA and have a reactance of 0.06 p.u. to their own MVA base. A 50 km long transmission line is connected between the two generators. Calculate the three-phase fault current, when fault occurs at the middle of the line as shown in Figure 3.14.

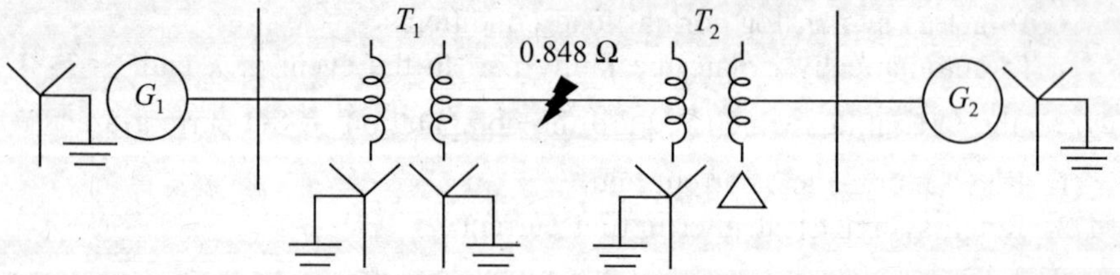

Figure 3.14 Single line diagram.

Solution:

$$\text{Base MVA, MVA}_{\text{new}} = 20 \text{ MVA}$$

$$\text{Base kV, kV}_{\text{new}} = 11 \text{ kV}$$

Reactance of generator G_1

$X_{\text{p.u.(given)}} = 0.25$ p.u., $\text{MVA}_{\text{given}} = 20$, $\text{MVA}_{\text{new}} = 20$, $\text{kV}_{\text{given}} = 11$, $\text{kV}_{\text{new}} = 11$

$$X_{\text{p.u.(new)}} = 0.25 \times \left(\frac{11}{11}\right)^2 \times \left(\frac{20}{20}\right) = 0.25 \text{ p.u.}$$

Reactance of transformer T_1 (Primary side)

$X_{\text{p.u.(given)}} = 0.06$ p.u., $\text{MVA}_{\text{given}} = 5$, $\text{MVA}_{\text{new}} = 20$, $\text{kV}_{\text{given}} = 11$, $\text{kV}_{\text{new}} = 11$

$$X_{\text{p.u.(given)}} = j0.06 \times \left(\frac{11}{11}\right)^2 \times \left(\frac{20}{5}\right) = j0.24 \text{ p.u.}$$

Reactance of transmission line

Middle of the line, (25 km long), actual reactance = 0.848 × 25 = 21.2 Ω

Base kV on HT side of transformer T_1

$$= \text{base kV on LT side} \times \frac{\text{HT voltage rating}}{\text{LT voltage rating}}$$

$$\text{Base kV on HT s ide of transformer } T_1 = 11 \times \frac{66}{11} = 66 \text{ kV}$$

$$\text{kV}_{\text{new}} = 66 \text{ kV}$$

$$\text{Base impedance} = \frac{(\text{kV}_{\text{new}})^2}{\text{MVA}_{\text{new}}} = \frac{66^2}{20} = 217.8\,\Omega$$

Per unit reactance of the transmission line

$$= \frac{\text{actual reactance, }\Omega}{\text{base reactance, }\Omega} = \frac{21.2}{217.8} = j0.0973 \text{ p.u.}$$

Reactance of transformer T_2 (Primary side)

$X_{\text{p.u.(given)}} = 0.06$ p.u., $\text{MVA}_{\text{given}} = 5$, $\text{MVA}_{\text{new}} = 20$, $\text{kV}_{\text{given}} = 11$ $\text{kV}_{\text{new}} = 11$

$$X_{\text{p.u.(given)}} = j0.06 \times \left(\frac{11}{11}\right)^2 \times \left(\frac{20}{5}\right) = j0.24 \text{ p.u.}$$

Reactance of generator G_2

$X_{\text{p.u.(given)}} = 0.25$ p.u., $\text{MVA}_{\text{given}} = 20$, $\text{MVA}_{\text{new}} = 20$, $\text{kV}_{\text{given}} = 11$, $\text{kV}_{\text{new}} = ?$

Base kV on LT side of transformer T_2

$$= \text{base kV on HT side} \times \frac{\text{LT voltage rating}}{\text{HT voltage rating}}$$

$$\text{Base kV on LT side of transformer } T_2 = 66 \times \frac{11}{66} = 11 \text{ kV}$$

$$\text{kV}_{\text{new}} = 11 \text{ kV}$$

$$X_{\text{p.u.(new)}} = 0.25 \times \left(\frac{11}{11}\right)^2 \times \left(\frac{20}{20}\right) = j0.25 \text{ p.u.}$$

Prefault reactance diagram of Example 3.1

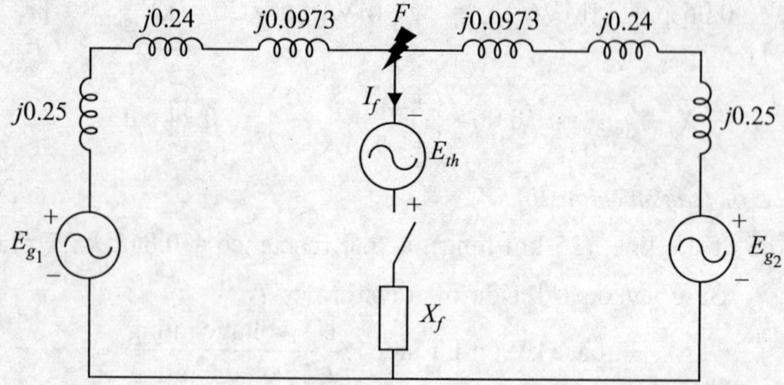

The above diagram is reduced to $j0.25 + j0.24 + j0.0973 = j0.5873$.

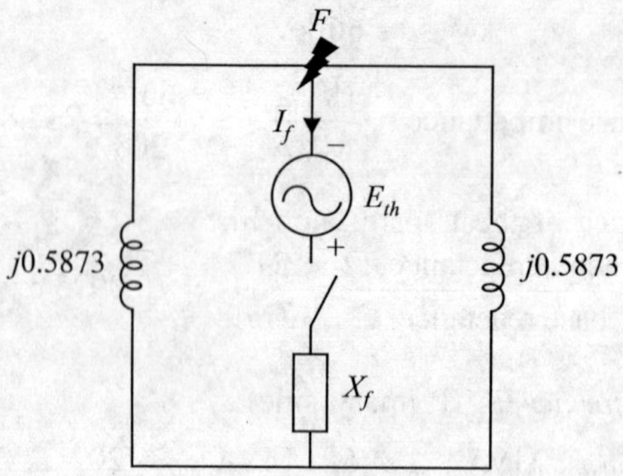

Thevenin equivalent network of Example 3.1

F

I_f

E_{th}

$j0.29365$

Thevenin equivalent impedance, X_{th} is $j0.5873 \parallel j0.5873$

$$\therefore \qquad Z_{th} \text{ or } X_{th} = \frac{j0.5873 \times j0.5873}{j0.5873 + j0.5873} = j0.29365 \text{ p.u.}$$

Prefault voltage or Thevenin voltage, $E_{th} = 1\angle 0°$

Fault reactance or impedance, $X_f = 0$

Fault current

$$I_f = \frac{E_{th}}{j(X_{th} + X_f)} = \frac{1\angle 0°}{j0.29365} = -j3.405 \text{ p.u.}$$

$$\text{Base current} = \frac{\text{MVA}_{\text{Base}}}{\sqrt{3}\ \text{kV}_\text{b}} \times 10^3 = \frac{20}{\sqrt{3} \times 11} \times 10^3 = 1049.73 \text{ A}$$

Fault current in A = fault current in p.u. (I_f) × base current

Fault current in A, $|I_f| = 3.405 \times 1049.73 = 3574.32$ A

EXAMPLE 3.2 A synchronous generator and synchronous motor each rated 30 MVA, 13.2 kV and both have subtransient reactance of 20% and the line reactance of 12% on a base of machine ratings. The motor is drawing 25 MW at 0.85 p.f. leading. The terminal voltage is 12 kV when a three-phase short-circuit fault occurs at motor terminals. Determine the subtransient current in generator, motor and at the fault point.

Solution: Single line diagram

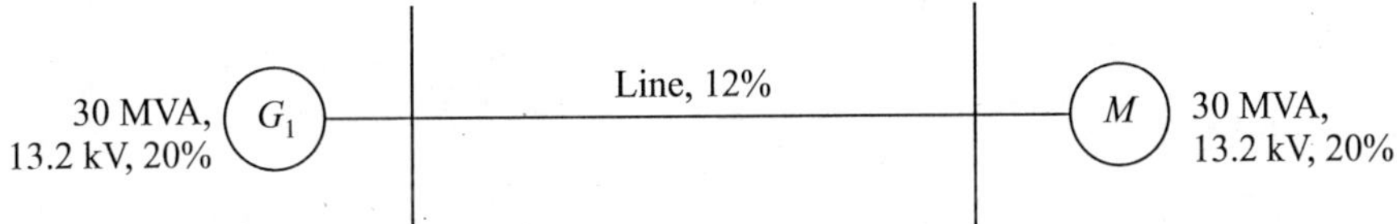

Base MVA, $\text{MVA}_{\text{new}} = 30$ MVA
Base kV, $\text{kV}_{\text{new}} = 13.2$ kV

Reactance of generator G_1

$X_{\text{p.u.(given)}} = 0.2$ p.u., $\text{MVA}_{\text{given}} = 30$, $\text{MVA}_{\text{new}} = 30$, $\text{kV}_{\text{given}} = 13.2$
$\text{kV}_{\text{new}} = 13.2$

$$X_{\text{p.u.(new)}} = 0.2 \times \left(\frac{13.2}{13.2}\right)^2 \times \left(\frac{30}{30}\right) = 0.2 \text{ p.u.}$$

Reactance of transmission line

$$\text{Actual reactance} = 12\% = 0.12\ \Omega$$

Reactance of motor M

$X_{\text{p.u.(given)}} = 0.2$ p.u., $\text{MVA}_{\text{given}} = 30$, $\text{MVA}_{\text{new}} = 30$, $\text{kV}_{\text{given}} = 13.2$
$\text{kV}_{\text{new}} = 13.2$

$$X_{\text{p.u.(new)}} = 0.2 \times \left(\frac{13.2}{13.2}\right)^2 \times \left(\frac{30}{30}\right) = 0.2 \text{ p.u.}$$

Prefault reactance diagram of Example 3.2

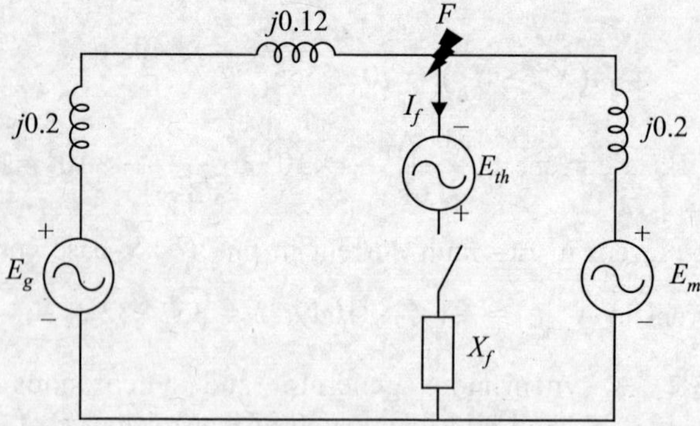

The above diagram is reduced to $j0.2 + j0.12 = j0.32$

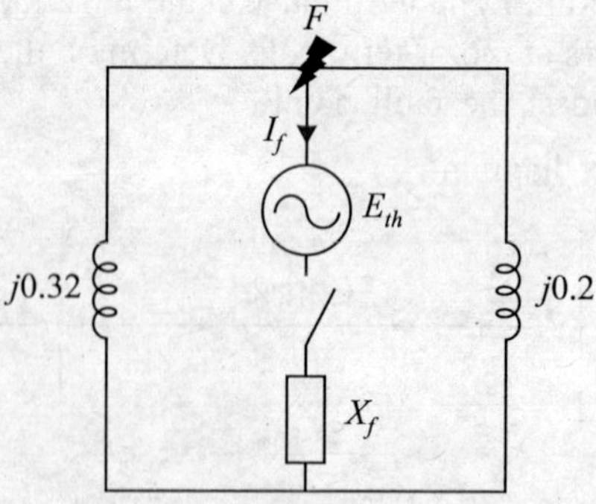

Thevenin equivalent network of Example 3.2

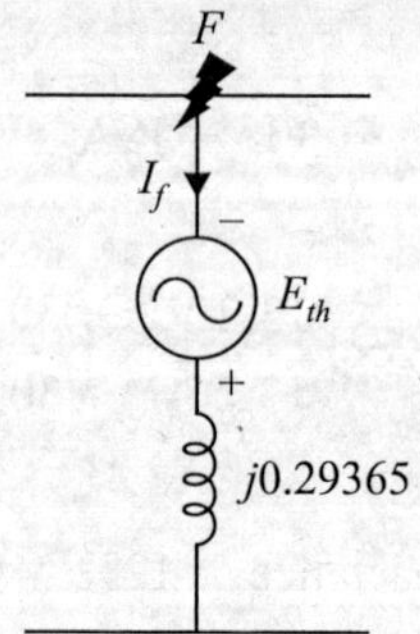

Thevenin equivalent impedance, X_{th} is $j0.32 \parallel j0.2$

$$\therefore \qquad Z_{th} \text{ or } X_{th} = \frac{j0.32 \times j0.2}{j0.32 + j0.2} = j0.1231 \text{ p.u.}$$

Actual prefault voltage at fault point = 12 V

Base kV, kV_{new} = 13.2 kV

Per unit prefault voltage or Thevenin voltage, $E_{th} = \dfrac{12}{13.2} = 0.9091\angle 0°$

Fault reactance or impedance, $X_f = 0$

(i) *Subtransient fault current*

$$I_f = \frac{E_{th}}{j(X_{th} + X_f)} = \frac{0.9091\angle 0°}{j0.1231} = \frac{0.9091\angle 0°}{0.1231\angle 90°} = 7.385\angle -90° \text{ p.u.}$$

$$\text{Base current} = \frac{\text{MVA}_{\text{base}}}{\sqrt{3}\text{kV}_b} \times 10^3 = \frac{30}{\sqrt{3} \times 13.2} \times 10^3 = 1312.16 \text{ A}$$

Fault current in kA = fault current in p.u.(I_f) × base current

$$\text{Fault current in kA } |I_f| = 7.385\angle -90° \times 1312.16$$
$$= 9.690\angle -90° \text{ kA}$$

(ii) *Subtransient fault current contributed by generator and motor*

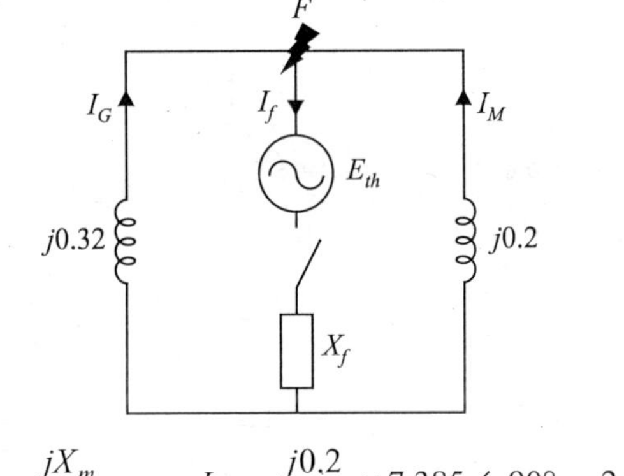

$$I_G = \frac{jX_m}{j(X_g + X + X_m)} I_f = \frac{j0.2}{j0.52} \times 7.385\angle -90° = 2.840\angle -90°$$

$$I_M = \frac{j(X_g + X)}{j(X_g + X + X_m)} I_f = \frac{j0.32}{j0.52} \times 7.385\angle -90° = 4.545\angle -90°$$

EXAMPLE 3.3 The two-bus system is shown in Figure 3.15. Determine the total three-phase fault current and the fault current supplied by each generator at the faulted point.

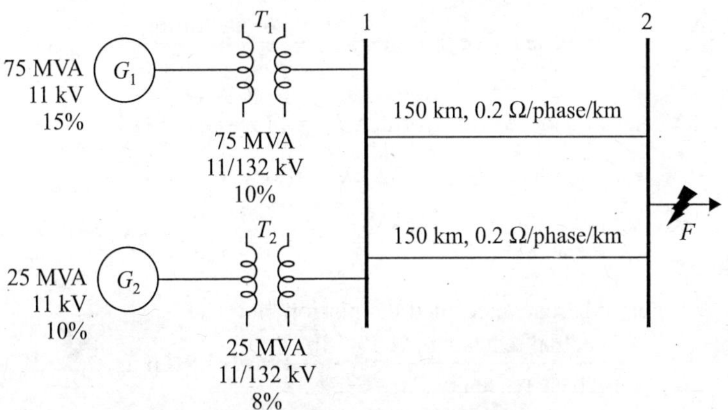

Figure 3.15 Single line diagram.

Solution:

Base MVA, MVA_{new} = 75 MVA
Base kV, kV_{new} = 11 kV

Reactance of generator G_1

$X_{p.u.(given)} = 0.15$ p.u., $MVA_{given} = 75$, $MVA_{new} = 75$, $kV_{given} = 11$, $kV_{new} = 11$

$$X_{p.u.(new)} = 0.15 \times \left(\frac{11}{11}\right)^2 \times \left(\frac{75}{75}\right) = j0.15 \text{ p.u}$$

Reactance of generator G_2

$X_{p.u.(given)} = 0.1$ p.u., $MVA_{given} = 25$, $MVA_{new} = 75$, $kV_{given} = 11$, $kV_{new} = 11$

$$X_{p.u.(new)} = 0.1 \times \left(\frac{11}{11}\right)^2 \times \left(\frac{75}{25}\right) = j0.3 \text{ p.u.}$$

Reactance of transformer T_1: (primary side)

$X_{p.u.(given)} = 0.1$ p.u., $MVA_{given} = 75$, $MVA_{new} = 75$, $kV_{given} = 11$, $kV_{new} = 11$

$$X_{p.u.(new)} = j0.1 \times \left(\frac{11}{11}\right)^2 \times \left(\frac{75}{75}\right) = j0.1 \text{ p.u.}$$

Reactance of transformer T_2: (primary side)

$X_{p.u.(given)} = 0.08$ p.u., $MVA_{given} = 25$, $MVA_{new} = 75$, $kV_{given} = 11$, $kV_{new} = 11$

$$X_{p.u.(new)} = j0.08 \times \left(\frac{11}{11}\right)^2 \times \left(\frac{75}{25}\right) = j0.24 \text{ p.u.}$$

Reactance of the transmission line

150 km long, actual reactance = 0.2 × 150 = 30 Ω

Base kV on HT side of transformer T_1

$$= \text{base kV on LT side} \times \frac{\text{HT voltage rating}}{\text{LT voltage rating}}$$

$$\text{Base kV on HT side of transformer } T_1 = 11 \times \frac{132}{11} = 132 \text{ kV}$$

$$kV_{new} = 132 \text{ kV}$$

$$\text{Base impedance} = \frac{(kV_{new})^2}{MVA_{new}} = \frac{132^2}{75} = 232.32\ \Omega$$

Per unit reactance of transmission line

$$= \frac{\text{actual reactance, }\Omega}{\text{base reactance, }\Omega} = \frac{30}{232.32} = j0.1291 \text{ p.u.}$$

Prefault reactance diagram of Example 3.3

Thevenin reactance network of Example 3.3

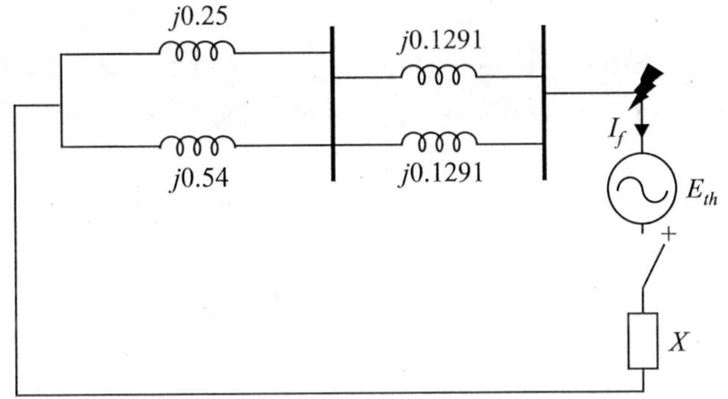

Thevenin equivalent network of Example 3.3

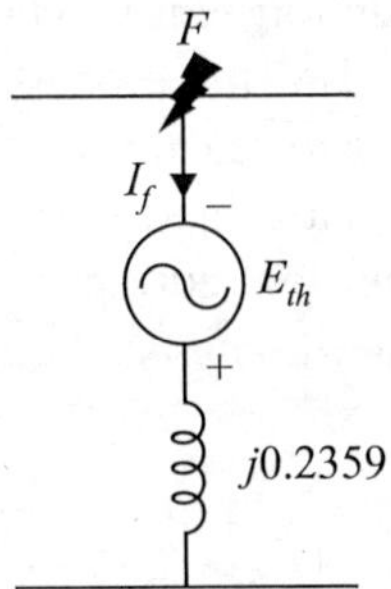

Thevenin equivalent impedance, X_{th} is $(j0.25 \parallel j0.54) + (j0.1291 \parallel j0.1291)$

$$\therefore \qquad Z_{th} \text{ or } X_{th} = \frac{j0.25 \times j0.54}{j0.25 + j0.54} + \frac{j0.1291 \times j0.1291}{j0.1291 + j0.1291}$$

$$= j0.1708 + j0.065 = j0.2358 \text{ p.u.}$$

Per unit prefault voltage or Thevenin voltage, $E_{th} = 1\angle 0°$

Fault reactance or impedance, $X_f = 0$

Fault current

$$I_f = \frac{E_{th}}{j(X_{th} + X_f)} = \frac{1\angle 0^\circ}{j0.2358} = -j4.241 \text{ p.u.}$$

$$\text{Base current} = \frac{\text{MVA}_{\text{base}}}{\sqrt{3}\text{kV}_b} \times 10^3 = \frac{75}{\sqrt{3} \times 132} \times 10^3 = 328.04 \text{ A}$$

Actual value of fault current in kA = fault current in p.u.(I_f) × base current

Actual value of fault current in $|I_f|$ = 4.241 × 328.04 = 1391.22 A

Fault current supplied by each generator

$$\text{Base current for primary side of transformer} = \frac{\text{MVA}_{\text{base}}}{\sqrt{3}\text{kV}_b} \times 10^3$$

$$= \frac{75}{\sqrt{3} \times 11} \times 10^3 = 3936.5 \text{ A}$$

Actual value of fault current = fault current in p.u.(I_f) × base current

Actual value of fault current = $-j4.241 \times 3936.5 = -j16{,}694.6$ A

$$I_{G1} = \frac{jX_{g2}}{j(X_{g1} + X_{g2})} I_f = \frac{j0.54}{j(0.25 + 0.54)} \times -j16{,}694.6 = -j11{,}411.5$$

$$I_{G2} = \frac{jX_{g1}}{j(X_{g1} + X_{g2})} I_f = \frac{j0.25}{j(0.25 + 0.54)} \times -j16{,}694.6 = -j5283.10$$

EXAMPLE 3.4 A 25 MVA, 11 kV generator with 20% subtransient reactance is connected through a transformer to a bus which supplies four identical motors, as shown in Figure 3.16. The subtransient reactance X_d'' of each motor is 20% on a base of 5 MVA, 6.6 kV. The three-phase rating of the transformer is 25 MVA, 11/6.6 kV, with a leakage reactance of 10%. The bus voltage at the motors is 6.6 kV when a three-phase fault occurs at the point F. For the fault specified, calculate (i) the subtransient current in the fault, (ii) the subtransient current in breaker A and (iii) the momentary current in breaker A.

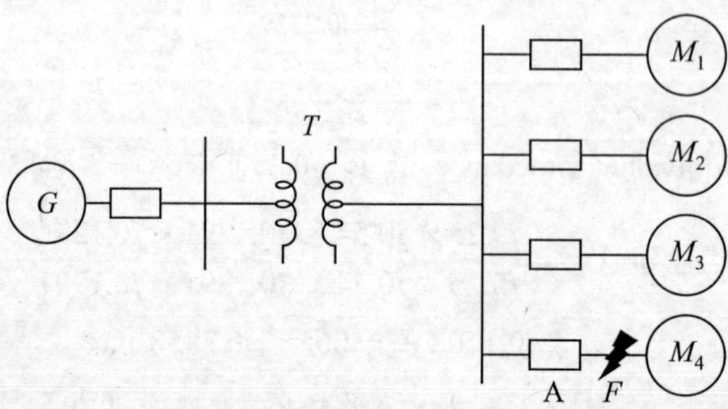

Figure 3.16 Single line diagram.

Solution:

Base MVA, $\text{MVA}_{\text{new}} = 25$ MVA
Base kV, $\text{kV}_{\text{new}} = 11$ kV

Reactance of generator G

$X_{\text{p.u.(given)}} = 0.2$ p.u., $\text{MVA}_{\text{given}} = 25$, $\text{MVA}_{\text{new}} = 25$, $\text{kV}_{\text{given}} = 11$, $\text{kV}_{\text{new}} = 11$

$$X_{\text{p.u.(new)}} = 0.2 \times \left(\frac{11}{11}\right)^2 \times \left(\frac{25}{25}\right) = 0.2 \text{ p.u.}$$

Reactance of transformer T_1 (Primary side)

$X_{\text{p.u.(given)}} = 0.1$ p.u., $\text{MVA}_{\text{given}} = 25$, $\text{MVA}_{\text{new}} = 25$, $\text{kV}_{\text{given}} = 11$, $\text{kV}_{\text{new}} = 11$

$$X_{\text{p.u.(new)}} = j0.1 \times \left(\frac{11}{11}\right)^2 \times \left(\frac{25}{25}\right) = j0.1 \text{ p.u.}$$

Reactance of motor

$X_{\text{p.u.(given)}} = 0.2$ p.u., $\text{MVA}_{\text{given}} = 5$, $\text{MVA}_{\text{new}} = 25$, $\text{kV}_{\text{given}} = 6.6$, $\text{kV}_{\text{new}} = ?$

Base kV on LT side of transformer T_1

$$= \text{base kV on HT side} \times \frac{\text{LT voltage rating}}{\text{HT voltage rating}}$$

Base kV on HT side of transformer $T_1 = 11 \times \dfrac{6.6}{11} = 6.6 \text{ kV}$

$$\text{kV}_{\text{new}} = 6.6 \text{ kV}$$

$$X_{\text{p.u.(new)}} = j0.2 \times \left(\frac{6.6}{6.6}\right)^2 \times \left(\frac{25}{5}\right) = j1.0 \text{ p.u.}$$

Prefault reactance diagram of Example 3.4

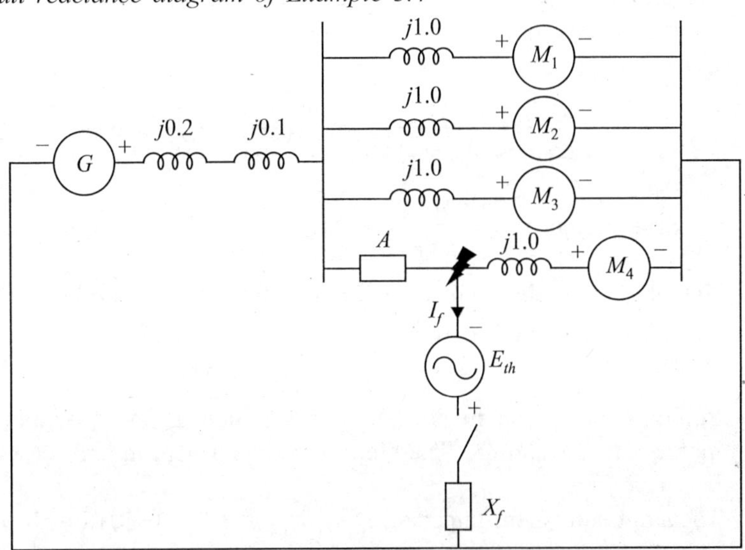

(i) *Subtransient state:* The prefault reactance diagram is shown above. The system being initially on no load, therefore, the generator and the motor induced emfs are each equal to $1\angle 0°$ p.u. The prefault reactance diagram can be reduced to Thevenin equivalent network as shown below.

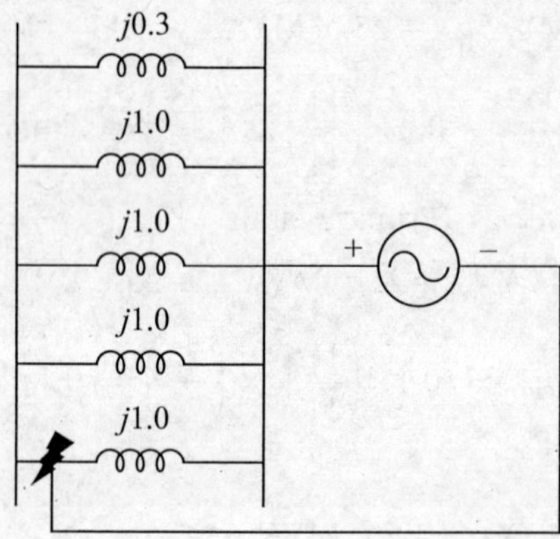

Thevenin equivalent impedance, X_{th} is

$$(j0.3 \parallel j1.0 \parallel j1.0 \parallel j1.0 \parallel j1.0)$$

$$\therefore \qquad \frac{1}{Z_{th}} \text{ or } \frac{1}{X_{th}} = \frac{1}{j0.3} + \frac{1}{j1} + \frac{1}{j1} + \frac{1}{j1} + \frac{1}{j1}$$

$$\frac{1}{X_{th}} = -j3.3 - j1 - j1 - j1 - j1 = -j7.33 \text{ p.u.}$$

$$X_{th} = \frac{1}{-j7.33} = j0.1364$$

Per unit prefault voltage or Thevenin voltage, $E_{th} = 1\angle 0°$

Fault reactance or impedance, $X_f = 0$

Fault current

$$I_f = \frac{E_{th}}{j(X_{th} + X_f)} = \frac{1\angle 0°}{j0.1364} = -j7.33 \text{ p.u.}$$

$$\text{Base current} = \frac{\text{MVA}_{\text{base}}}{\sqrt{3}\,\text{kV}_b} \times 10^3 = \frac{25}{\sqrt{3} \times 6.6} \times 10^3 = 2186.93 \text{ A}$$

Actual value of fault current = fault current in p.u.(I_f) × base current

Actual value of fault current $|I_f|$ = 7.33 × 2186.93

= 16030.2 A

(ii) Subtransient current in breaker *A* is supplied by the generator and motors M_1, M_2 and M_3. Therefore, the subtransient in breaker *A* may be written as.

Thevenin equivalent impedance, X_{th} is $(j0.3 \parallel j1.0 \parallel j1.0 \parallel j1.0)$

$$\therefore \quad \frac{1}{Z_{th}} \text{ or } \frac{1}{X_{th}} = \frac{1}{j0.3} + \frac{1}{j1} + \frac{1}{j1} + \frac{1}{j1}$$

$$\frac{1}{X_{th}} = -j3.3 - j1 - j1 - j1 = -j6.33 \text{ p.u.}$$

$$X_{th} = \frac{1}{-j6.33} = j0.15798$$

Per unit prefault voltage or Thevenin voltage, $E_{th} = 1\angle 0°$

Fault reactance or impedance, $X_f = 0$

Fault current

$$I_f = \frac{E_{th}}{j(X_{th} + X_f)} = \frac{1\angle 0°}{j0.15798} = -j6.33 \text{ p.u.}$$

$$\text{Base current} = \frac{\text{MVA}_{\text{base}}}{\sqrt{3}\,\text{kV}_b} \times 10^3 = \frac{25}{\sqrt{3} \times 6.6} \times 10^3 = 2186.93 \text{ A}$$

Actual value of fault current = fault current in p.u.(I_f) × base current

Actual value of fault current $|I_f|$ = 6.33 × 2186.93

= 13843.08 A

(iii) For finding momentary current through breaker A, we must add the dc offset current to the symmetrical subtransient obtained above in part (ii). A factor 1.6 is taken into account for dc component.

Thus the momentary current through breaker A = 1.6 × 13843.08

= 22148.9 A

3.6 Fault Calculation Using Bus Impedance Matrix

The three-phase short-circuit fault current calculation used in the last chapter is not efficient and is not applicable to a large interconnected network.

Consider a sample n bus system network as shown in Figure 3.17. It is assumed that the system is operating under balanced condition and a per phase

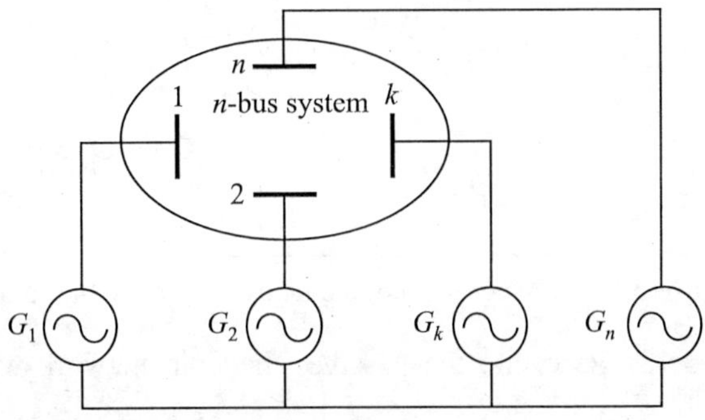

Figure 3.17 Sample n-bus system.

circuit model is used. A balanced three fault is to be applied at bus k through fault impedance.

The first step in the short-circuit study is to determine the prefault bus voltage and line current using the load flow study.

$$\text{Prefault bus voltage can be defined as } V_{\text{bus}}^0 = \begin{bmatrix} V_1^0 \\ V_2^0 \\ \vdots \\ V_k^0 \\ \vdots \\ V_n^0 \end{bmatrix} \tag{3.33}$$

where, V_1^0, V_2^0, V_k^0 and V_n^0 are the prefault bus voltages.

Let bus k be the faulted bus and Z_f be the fault impedance. The postfault bus voltage vector is given by

$$V_{\text{bus}}^f = V_{\text{bus}}^0 + \Delta V \tag{3.34}$$

where ΔV is the change in bus voltage caused by the fault and is given by

$$\Delta V = \begin{bmatrix} \Delta V_1 \\ \Delta V_2 \\ \vdots \\ \Delta V_n \end{bmatrix} \tag{3.35}$$

Figure 3.18 shows the Thevenin's network of the system with generator replaced by transient/subtransient reactance with their emfs shorted.

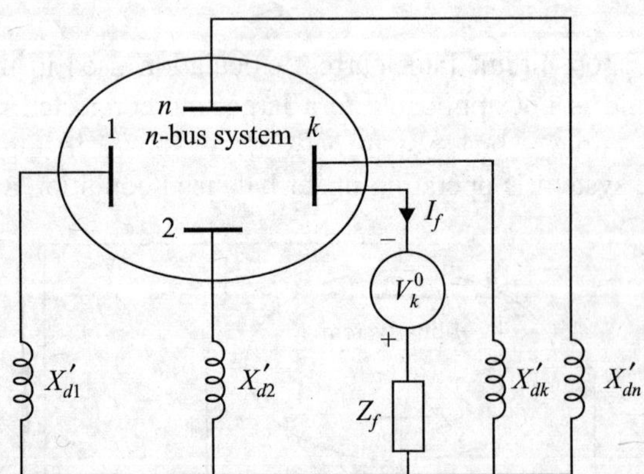

Figure 3.18 Changes in bus voltages caused by the fault.

In Figure 3.18, we excite the passive Thevenin network with $-V_k^0$ is in series with Z_f.

Now

$$\Delta V = Z_{bus} C_f \tag{3.36}$$

where $[Z_{bus}]$ is the bus impedance matrix of the passive thevenin network and is given by

$$Z_{bus} = \begin{bmatrix} Z_{11} & \cdots & Z_{1n} \\ \vdots & \ddots & \vdots \\ Z_{n1} & \cdots & Z_{nn} \end{bmatrix} \tag{3.37}$$

and C_f is the bus current injection vector. The network is injected with current $-I_f$ only at the *kth* bus, we have

$$C_f = \begin{bmatrix} 0 \\ 0 \\ \vdots \\ I_k = -I_f \\ \vdots \\ 0 \end{bmatrix} \tag{3.38}$$

From Eqs. (3.36) and (3.38)

$$\Delta V_k = -Z_{kk} I_f \tag{3.39}$$

The voltage at the *kth* bus under fault is

$$V_{k(f)} = V_k^0 + \Delta V_k = V_k^0 - Z_{kk} I_f \tag{3.40}$$

$$V_{k(f)} = Z_f I_f \tag{3.41}$$

$$Z_f I_f = V_k^0 - Z_{kk} I_f \tag{3.42}$$

$$I_f = \frac{V_k^0}{Z_{kk} + Z_f} \tag{3.43}$$

Using Eq. (3.39), at the *ith* bus ($k = i$)

$$\Delta V_i = -Z_{ii} I_f \tag{3.44}$$

Similarly from Eq. (3.40)

$$V_{i(f)} = V_i^0 + \Delta V_i = V_i^0 - Z_{ik} I_f \tag{3.45}$$

Substituting for I_f, the bus voltage during the fault at bus i becomes

$$V_{i(f)} = V_i^0 - \frac{Z_{ik}}{(Z_{kk} + Z_f)} V_k^0 \tag{3.46}$$

For $i = k$, Eq. (3.46) becomes

$$V_{k(f)} = V_i^0 - \frac{Z_{kk}}{(Z_{kk} + Z_f)} V_k^0$$

$$V_{k(f)} = \frac{Z_{kk}}{(Z_{kk} + Z_f)} V_k^0 \tag{3.47}$$

Note that V_i^0 are the prefault bus voltage and can be obtained from the load flow study. Z_{bus} matrix for the short-circuit study can be obtained by inversing Y_{bus} matrix. Also note that synchronous motors must be included in Z_{bus} formulation for the short-circuit study. However, in formulating short-circuit study network, load impedances are ignored, because these are very much larger than the impedances of generators and transmission lines.

Fault current flowing from bus i to bus j with impedance z_{ij} is given by

$$I_{ij(f)} = \frac{(V_{i(f)} - V_{j(f)})}{z_{ij}} = Y_{ij}(V_{i(f)} - V_{j(f)}) \tag{3.48}$$

Prefault generator current can be obtained by referring Figure 3.19(a).

Prefault generator $= P_{Gi} + jQ_{Gi}$

$$\therefore \qquad I_{Gi(0)} = \frac{P_{Gi} + jQ_{Gi}}{V_{i(0)}} \tag{3.49}$$

From Figure 3.19(a), we get

$$E'_{Gi} = V_{i(0)} + jX'_{Gi} I_{Gi(0)} \tag{3.50}$$

From the short-circuit study, $V_{i(f)}$ is obtained, from Figure 3.19(b)

$$I_{Gi(f)} = \frac{E'_{Gi} - V_{i(f)}}{jX'_{Gi}} \tag{3.51}$$

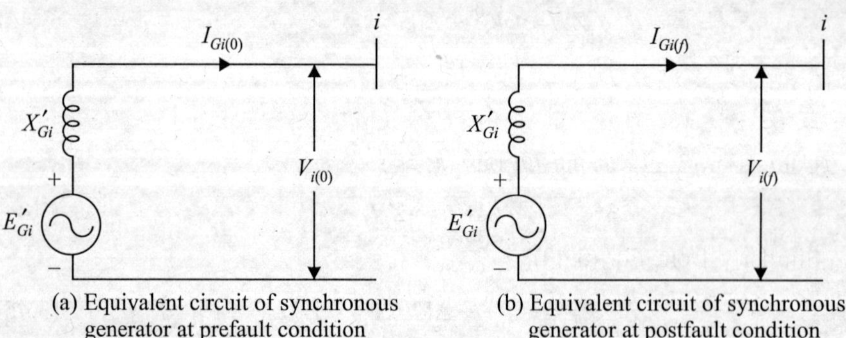

(a) Equivalent circuit of synchronous generator at prefault condition

(b) Equivalent circuit of synchronous generator at postfault condition

Figure 3.19

EXAMPLE 3.5 Consider the three bus system as shown in Figure 3.20. Each generator is represented by an emf behind the transient reactance. All impedances are expressed in per unit on a common 100 MVA base. A three-phase fault with a fault impedance $Z_f = j0.15$ p.u. occurs at bus 3 using the bus impedance matrix method; calculate the fault current, the bus voltages, and the line current during the fault.

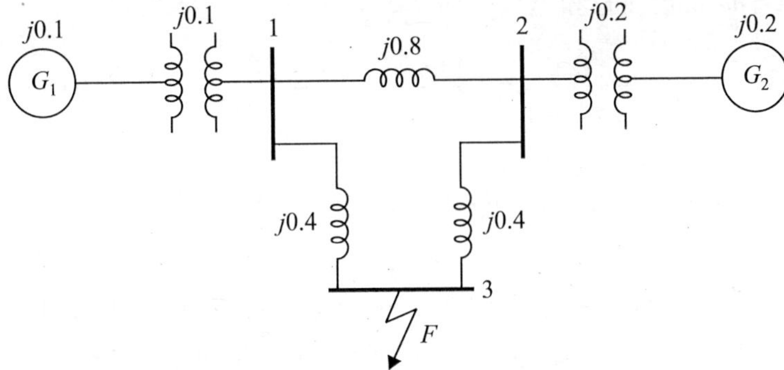

Figure 3.20 Single line diagram.

Solution:

Step 1 Determine the bus admittance matrix using the direct inspection method.

$$Y_{11} = \frac{1}{j0.2} + \frac{1}{j0.8} + \frac{1}{j0.4} = -j8.75$$

$$Y_{12} = Y_{21} = \frac{-1}{j0.8} = j1.25$$

$$Y_{13} = Y_{31} = \frac{-1}{j0.4} = j2.5$$

$$Y_{22} = \frac{1}{j0.4} + \frac{1}{j0.8} + \frac{1}{j0.4} = -j6.25$$

$$Y_{23} = Y_{32} = \frac{-1}{j0.4} = j2.5$$

$$Y_{33} = \frac{1}{j0.4} + \frac{1}{j0.4} = -j5.0$$

$$Y_{\text{bus}} = \begin{bmatrix} -j8.75 & j1.25 & j2.5 \\ j1.25 & -j6.25 & j2.5 \\ j2.5 & j2.5 & -j5.0 \end{bmatrix}$$

Step 2 Determine the bus impedance matrix $Z_{\text{bus}} = \dfrac{1}{Y_{\text{bus}}}$.

$$Z_{\text{bus}} = \begin{bmatrix} j0.16 & j0.08 & j0.12 \\ j0.08 & j0.24 & j0.16 \\ j0.12 & j0.16 & j0.34 \end{bmatrix}.$$

Step 3 Determine the fault current.

For a fault at bus 3 ($k = 3$) with fault impedance $Z_f = j0.15$ p.u.

Prefault voltages of all buses, $V_{1(0)} = V_{2(0)} = V_{3(0)} = 1.0$ p.u.

The fault current is

$$I_f = \frac{V_{k(0)}}{Z_{kk} + Z_f} = \frac{V_{3(0)}}{Z_{33} + Z_f} = \frac{1.0}{j0.34 + j0.15} = -\,j2.041 \text{ p.u.}$$

Step 4 Determine the bus voltages.
The bus voltages during the fault are:

$$V_{i(f)} = V_{i(0)} - Z_{ik} I_f$$

$$V_{1(f)} = V_{1(0)} - Z_{13} I_f = 1.0 - (j0.12) \times (-j0.2041) = 0.7551 \text{ p.u.}$$

$$V_{2(f)} = V_{2(0)} - Z_{23} I_f = 1.0 - (j0.16) \times (-j0.2041) = 0.6734 \text{ p.u.}$$

$$V_{3(f)} = V_{3(0)} - Z_{33} I_f = 1.0 - (j0.34) \times (-j0.2041) = 0.3060 \text{ p.u.}$$

Step 5 Determine the line current during the fault.

$$I_{ij(f)} = \frac{V_{i(f)} - V_{j(f)}}{z_{ij}}$$

$$I_{12(f)} = \frac{V_{1(f)} - V_{2(f)}}{z_{12}} = \frac{0.7551 - 0.6734}{j0.8} = -\,j0.102 \text{ p.u.}$$

$$I_{13(f)} = \frac{V_{1(f)} - V_{3(f)}}{z_{13}} = \frac{0.7551 - 0.3060}{j0.4} = -\,j1.122 \text{ p.u.}$$

$$I_{23(f)} = \frac{V_{2(f)} - V_{3(f)}}{z_{23}} = \frac{0.6734 - 0.3061}{j0.4} = -\,j0.918 \text{ p.u.}$$

EXAMPLE 3.6 The bus impedance matrix of a four-bus network with values in per unit is

$$Z_{\text{bus}} = j\begin{bmatrix} 0.15 & 0.08 & 0.04 & 0.07 \\ 0.08 & 0.15 & 0.06 & 0.09 \\ 0.04 & 0.06 & 0.13 & 0.05 \\ 0.07 & 0.09 & 0.05 & 0.12 \end{bmatrix}$$

The generators connected to buses 1 and 2 have their subtransient reactances included in Z_{bus}. If the prefault current is neglected, determine the subtransient current in per unit in the fault for a three-phase fault on bus 4. Assume the voltage at the fault is $1.0\angle 0°$ p.u. before the fault occurs. Find also the per unit current from generator 2, whose subtransient reactance is 0.2 p.u.

Solution: Fault at bus 4 ($k = 4$) with fault impedance, $Z_f = 0$ p.u.
Prefault voltages of all buses, $V_{1(0)} = V_{2(0)} = V_{3(0)} = V_{4(0)} = 1.0$ p.u.
The fault current is

$$I_f = \frac{V_{k(0)}}{Z_{kk} + Z_f} = \frac{V_{4(0)}}{Z_{44} + Z_f} = \frac{1.0}{j0.12} = -\,j8.33 \text{ p.u.}$$

$$V_{2(f)} = V_{2(0)} - Z_{24}I_f = 1.0 - (j0.09) \times (-j8.33) = 0.2503 \text{ p.u.}$$

Per unit current from generator 2,

$$I_{Gi(f)} = \frac{E'_{Gi} - V_{i(f)}}{jX'_{Gi}}$$

$$I_2 = \frac{1.0 - V_{2(f)}}{j0.2} = \frac{1.0 - 0.2503}{j0.2} = -\,j3.75 \text{ p.u.}$$

EXAMPLE 3.7 Consider the three bus network as shown in Figure 3.21. Determine the subtransient current in p.u. from generator 1 and in line 1–2 and voltages at buses 1 and 3 for three-phase fault on bus 2. Use the bus impedance matrix.

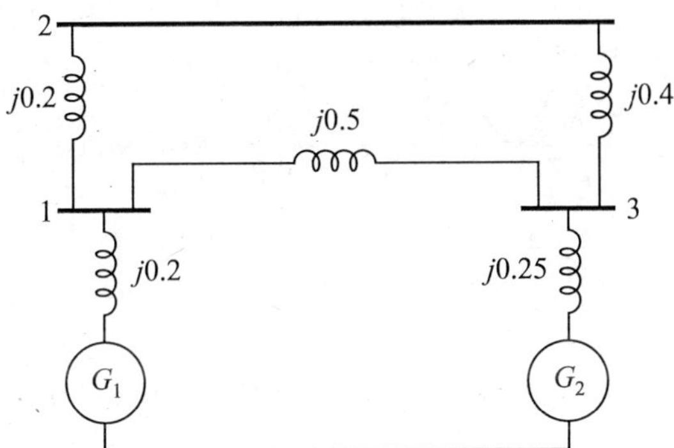

Figure 3.21 Three bus network for Example 3.7.

Solution:

Step 1 Determine the bus admittance matrix using the direct inspection method.

$$Y_{11} = \frac{1}{j0.2} + \frac{1}{j0.2} + \frac{1}{j0.5} = -\,j12$$

$$Y_{12} = Y_{21} = \frac{-1}{j0.2} = j5$$

$$Y_{13} = Y_{31} = \frac{-1}{j0.5} = j2$$

$$Y_{22} = \frac{1}{j0.2} + \frac{1}{j0.4} = -\,j7.5$$

$$Y_{23} = Y_{32} = \frac{-1}{j0.4} = j2.5$$

$$Y_{33} = \frac{1}{j0.25} + \frac{1}{j0.4} + \frac{1}{j0.5} = -\,j8.5$$

$$Y_{\text{bus}} = \begin{bmatrix} -j12 & j5 & j2 \\ j5 & -j7.5 & j2.5 \\ j2 & j2.5 & -j8.5 \end{bmatrix}$$

Step 2 Determine the bus impedance matrix $Z_{\text{bus}} = \dfrac{1}{Y_{\text{bus}}}$.

$$Z_{\text{bus}} = \begin{bmatrix} j0.1447 & j0.1195 & j0.0692 \\ j0.1195 & j0.2465 & j0.1006 \\ j0.0692 & j0.1006 & j0.1631 \end{bmatrix}.$$

Step 3 Determine the fault current.
For a fault at bus 2 ($k = 2$) with fault impedance $Z_f = 0$ p.u.
Prefault voltages of all buses, $V_{1(0)} = V_{2(0)} = V_{3(0)} = 1.0$ p.u.
The fault current is

$$I_f = \frac{V_{k(0)}}{Z_{kk} + Z_f} = \frac{V_{2(0)}}{Z_{22} + Z_f} = \frac{1.0}{j0.2465} = -\,j4.057 \text{ p.u.}$$

Step 4 Determine the bus voltages.
Bus voltages during the fault are:

$$V_{i(f)} = V_{i(0)} - Z_{ik} I_f$$

$$V_{1(f)} = V_{1(0)} - Z_{12} I_f = 1.0 - (j0.1195) \times (-j4.057) = 0.515 \text{ p.u.}$$

$$V_{2(f)} = V_{2(0)} - Z_{22} I_f = 1.0 - (j0.2465) \times (-j4.057) = 5 \times 10^{-5} \text{ p.u.}$$

$$V_{3(f)} = V_{3(0)} - Z_{32} I_f = 1.0 - (j0.1006) \times (-j4.057) = 0.592 \text{ p.u.}$$

Step 5 Determine the line current during the fault.

$$I_{ij(f)} = \frac{V_{i(f)} - V_{j(f)}}{z_{ij}}$$

$$I_{12(f)} = \frac{(V_{1(f)} - V_{2(f)})}{z_{12}} = \frac{0.515 - 5 \times 10^{-5}}{j0.2} = -\,j2.575 \text{ p.u.}$$

$$I_{Gi(f)} = \frac{E'_{Gi} - V_{i(f)}}{jX'_{Gi}}$$

$$I_1 = \frac{1.0 - 0.515}{j0.2} = -\,j2.43 \text{ p.u.}$$

3.7 Algorithm for Formation of the Bus Impedance Matrix

The bus impedance algorithm is a step by step procedure which proceeds branch by branch. The main advantage of this method is that any modification of the network elements does not require complete rebuilding of $[Z_{\text{bus}}]$ matrix.

The bus impedance matrix can be build up starting with a single element and the process is continued until all the nodes and elements are included. Let us assume that the Z_{bus} matrix exists for a partial network having n buses and a reference bus is as shown in the figure below. It is proposed to add a new element one at a time to this network and get modified $[Z_{\text{bus}}]$ matrix in the following four ways or four modifications.

Type 1 modification: Add an element with impedance Z_b, connected between the reference node 0 and a new node p

Type 2 modification: Add an element with impedance Z_b, connected between the existing node i and a new node p

Type 3 modification: Add an element with impedance Z_b, connected between the existing node i and a reference node 0

Type 4 modification: Add an element with impedance Z_b, connected between the existing nodes i and j

1. Add an element with impedance Z_b, connected between the reference node 0 and a new node p.

   In this case the addition of a new bus p to the reference node through impedance Z_b without a connection to any of the buses of the original network cannot alter the original bus voltage when a current is injected at the new bus.

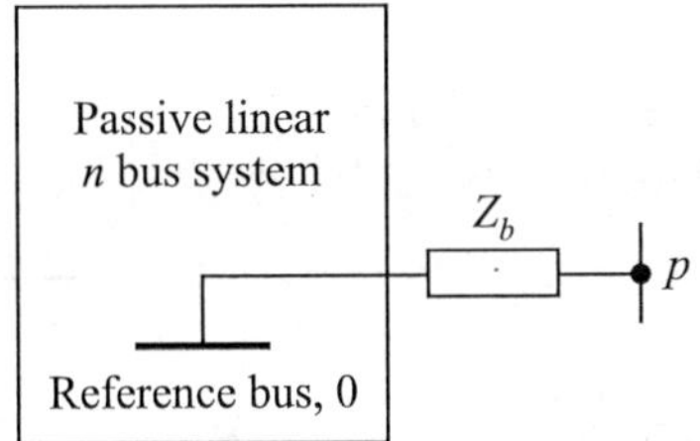

The modified $[Z_{\text{bus}}]$ matrix is given by

$$Z_{\text{bus}}^{\text{new}} = \left[\begin{array}{cccc|c} & & & & 0 \\ & & & & 0 \\ & & Z_{\text{bus}}^{\text{old}} & & \vdots \\ & & & & 0 \\ \hline 0 & 0 & \cdots & 0 & Z_b \end{array}\right] \tag{3.52}$$

2. Add an element with impedance Z_b, connected between the existing node i and a new node p.

   Consider impedance Z_b, connected between the existing node i and the new node p. The addition of bus will increase the order of the bus impedance matrix by one.

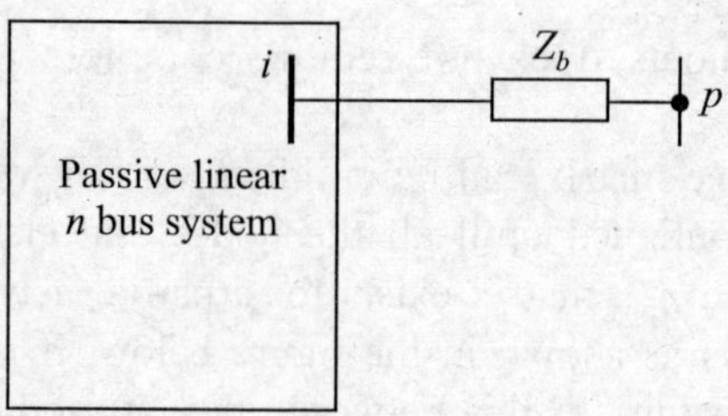

The modified $[Z_{\text{bus}}]$ matrix is given by

$$Z_{\text{bus}}^{\text{new}} = \left[\begin{array}{cccc|c} & & & & Z_{1i} \\ & & & & Z_{2i} \\ & Z_{\text{bus}}^{\text{old}} & & & \vdots \\ & & & & Z_{ni} \\ \hline Z_{i1} & Z_{i2} & \cdots & Z_{in} & Z_{ii} + Z_b \end{array}\right] \tag{3.53}$$

3. Add an element with impedance Z_b, connected between the existing node i and the reference node 0.

   To find the new $[Z_{\text{bus}}]$, the first step is to add an element in between the existing node i and a fictitious node $(n + 1)$ (instead of the reference node) and calculate the modified $[Z_{\text{bus}}]$ matrix of dimension $(n + 1) \times (n + 1)$ by using the matrix type 2 modification. The second step is to connect the fictitious node $(n + 1)$ by zero impedance link to the reference node whose voltage is zero.

   The new modified $[Z_{\text{bus}}]$ matrix of dimension $n \times n$ is obtained by applying Kron's reduction formula to the last row and column using the following relation.

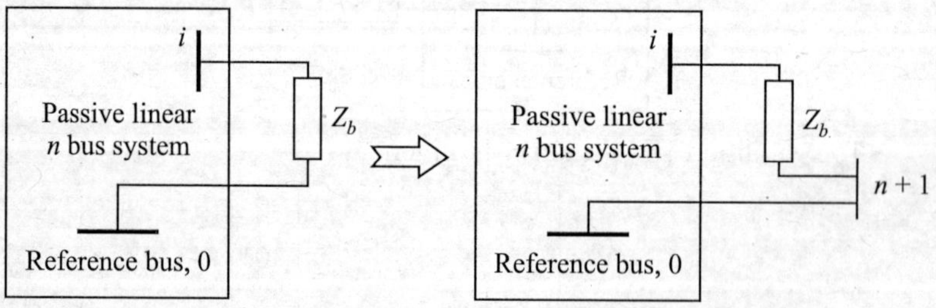

$$Z_{jk}^{\text{new}} = Z_{jk}^{\text{old}} - \frac{Z_{j(n+1)} \times Z_{(n+1)k}}{Z_{(n+1)(n+1)}} \qquad j, k = 1, 2, \ldots, n \tag{3.54}$$

   Here the size of the matrix will not change because no new node is added.

4. Add an element with impedance Z, connected between the existing nodes i and j.

   Consider an element Z_b, connected between two existing nodes i and j, the new modified Z_{bus} matrix is given by

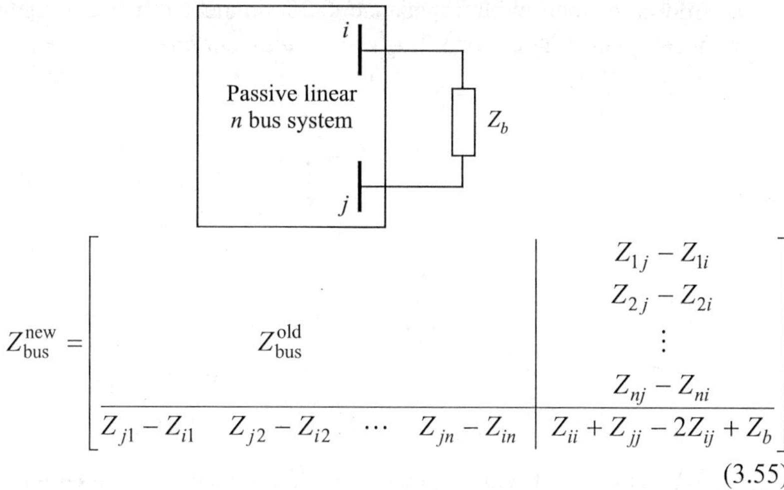

$$Z_{bus}^{new} = \left[\begin{array}{cccc|c} & & & & Z_{1j} - Z_{1i} \\ & & & & Z_{2j} - Z_{2i} \\ & Z_{bus}^{old} & & & \vdots \\ & & & & Z_{nj} - Z_{ni} \\ \hline Z_{j1} - Z_{i1} & Z_{j2} - Z_{i2} & \cdots & Z_{jn} - Z_{in} & Z_{ii} + Z_{jj} - 2Z_{ij} + Z_b \end{array}\right] \quad (3.55)$$

Now the size of the matrix becomes $(n + 1) \times (n + 1)$. The new modified $[Z_{bus}]$ matrix of dimension $(n \times n)$ is obtained by applying Kron's reduction formula to the last row and column using the following relation.

$$Z_{jk}^{new} = Z_{jk}^{old} - \frac{Z_{j(n+1)} \times Z_{(n+1)k}}{Z_{(n+1)(n+1)}} \qquad j, k = 1, 2, ..., n$$

EXAMPLE 3.8 The impedance matrix $[Z_{bus}]$ as shown in Figure 3.22.

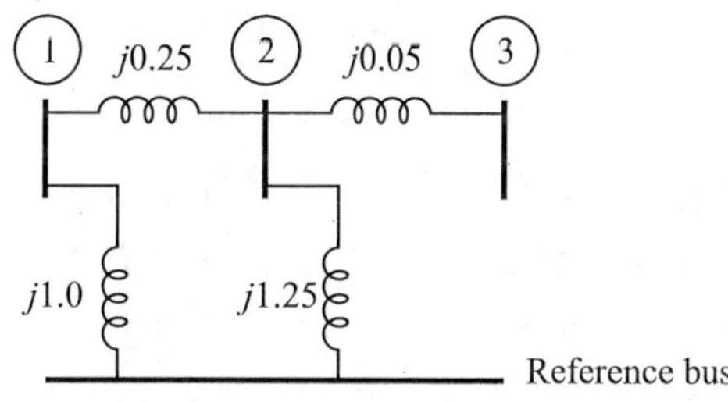

Figure 3.22

Solution:

1. Add an element with impedance $j1.0$, connected between the reference node 0 and a new node 1. (*Type* 1 *modification*)

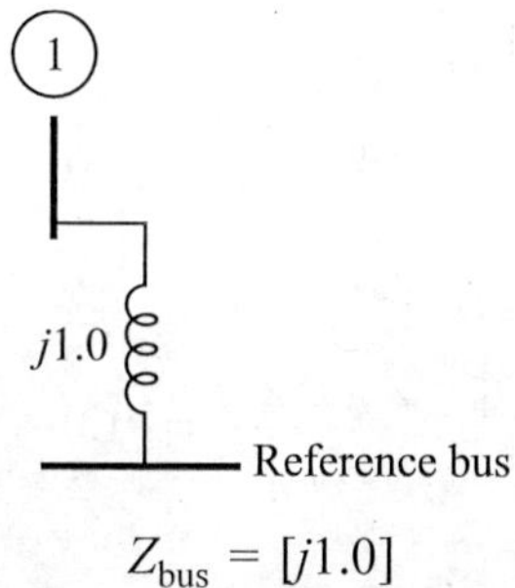

$$Z_{bus} = [j1.0]$$

2. Add an element with impedance $j0.25$, connected between the existing node 1 and a new node 2. (*Type 2 modification*)

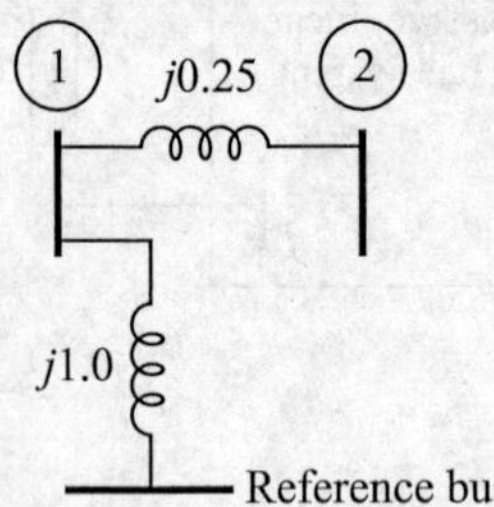

$$Z_{\text{bus}} = \begin{bmatrix} j1.0 & j1.0 \\ j1.0 & j1.0 + j0.25 \end{bmatrix} = \begin{bmatrix} j1.0 & j1.0 \\ j1.0 & j1.25 \end{bmatrix}$$

3. Add an element with impedance $j1.25$, connected between the existing node 2 and the reference node 0. (*Type 3 modification*)

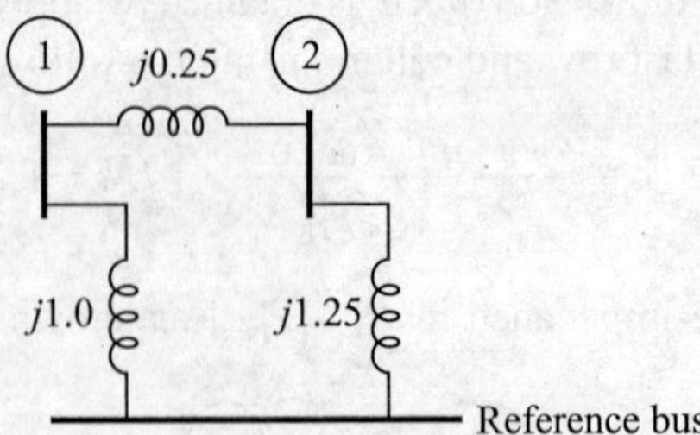

(a) To obtain $[Z_{\text{bus}}]$ matrix use type 2 modification

$$Z_{\text{bus}} = \begin{bmatrix} j1.0 & j1.0 & j1.0 \\ j1.0 & j1.25 & j1.25 \\ j1.0 & j1.25 & j1.25 + j1.25 \end{bmatrix} = \begin{bmatrix} j1.0 & j1.0 & j1.0 \\ j1.0 & j1.25 & j1.25 \\ j1.0 & j1.25 & j2.50 \end{bmatrix}$$

(b) Now apply Kron's reduction formula

$$Z_{jk}^{\text{new}} = Z_{jk}^{\text{old}} - \frac{Z_{j(n+1)} \times Z_{(n+1)k}}{Z_{(n+1)(n+1)}}$$

$j, k = 1, 2$ and $(n + 1) = 0$ (reference node)

$j = 1$; $k = 1$ and $(n + 1) = 0$

$$Z_{11}^{\text{new}} = Z_{11}^{\text{old}} - \frac{Z_{10} \times Z_{01}}{Z_{00}} = j1.0 - \frac{j1.0 \times j1.0}{j2.50} = j0.6$$

$j = 1$; $k = 2$ and $(n + 1) = 0$

$$Z_{12}^{\text{new}} = Z_{12}^{\text{old}} - \frac{Z_{10} \times Z_{02}}{Z_{00}} = j1.0 - \frac{j1.0 \times j1.25}{j2.50} = j0.5$$

$j = 2;\ k = 1$ and $(n + 1) = 0$

$$Z_{21}^{\text{new}} = Z_{21}^{\text{old}} - \frac{Z_{20} \times Z_{01}}{Z_{00}} = j1.0 - \frac{j1.25 \times j1.0}{j2.50} = j0.5$$

$j = 2;\ k = 2$ and $(n + 1) = 0$

$$Z_{22}^{\text{new}} = Z_{22}^{\text{old}} - \frac{Z_{20} \times Z_{02}}{Z_{00}} = j1.25 - \frac{j1.25 \times j1.25}{j2.50} = j0.625$$

$$Z_{\text{bus}} = \begin{bmatrix} j0.6 & j0.5 \\ j0.5 & j0.625 \end{bmatrix}$$

4. Add an element with impedance $j0.05$, connected between the existing node 2 and a new node 3. (*Type 2 modification*)

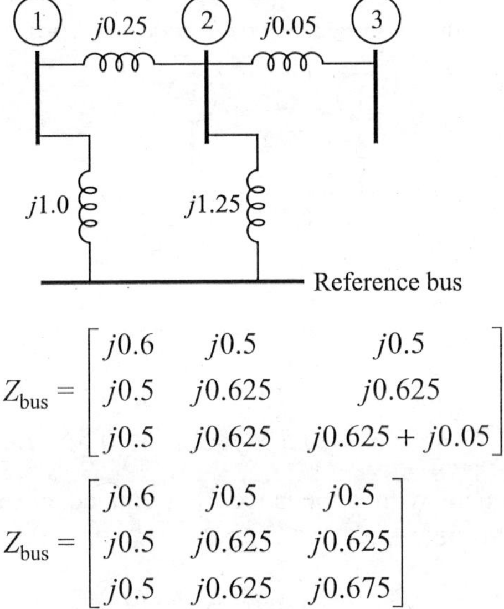

$$Z_{\text{bus}} = \begin{bmatrix} j0.6 & j0.5 & j0.5 \\ j0.5 & j0.625 & j0.625 \\ j0.5 & j0.625 & j0.625 + j0.05 \end{bmatrix}$$

$$Z_{\text{bus}} = \begin{bmatrix} j0.6 & j0.5 & j0.5 \\ j0.5 & j0.625 & j0.625 \\ j0.5 & j0.625 & j0.675 \end{bmatrix}$$

EXAMPLE 3.9 Obtain the bus impedance matrix $[Z_{\text{bus}}]$ as shown in Figure 3.23 using Z_{bus} building algorithm.

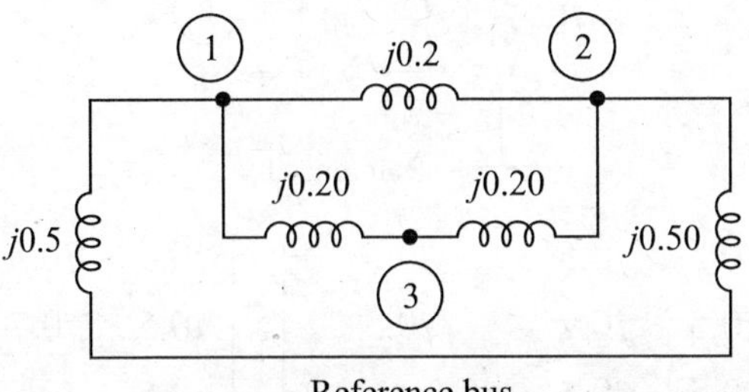

Figure 3.23

Solution:

1. Add an element with impedance $j0.5$, connected between the reference node 0 and a new node 1. (*Type* 1 *modification*)

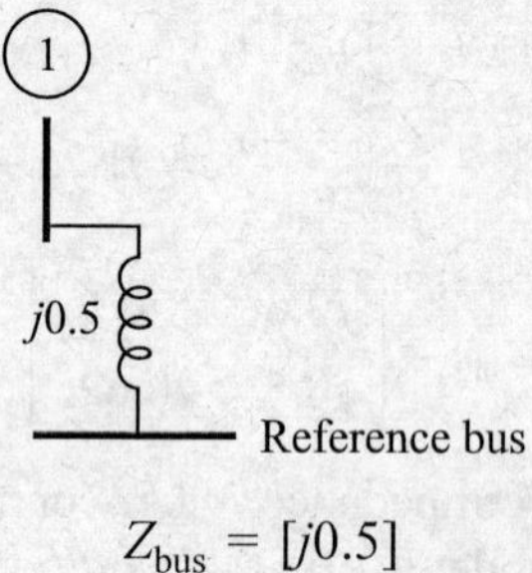

$$Z_{bus} = [j0.5]$$

2. Add an element with impedance $j0.2$, connected between the existing node 1 and a new node 2. (*Type* 2 *modification*)

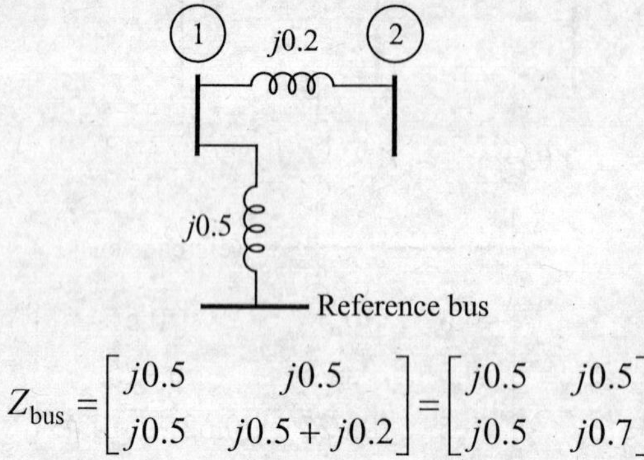

$$Z_{bus} = \begin{bmatrix} j0.5 & j0.5 \\ j0.5 & j0.5 + j0.2 \end{bmatrix} = \begin{bmatrix} j0.5 & j0.5 \\ j0.5 & j0.7 \end{bmatrix}$$

3. Add an element with impedance $j0.2$, connected between the existing node 1 and a new node 3. (*Type* 2 *modification*)

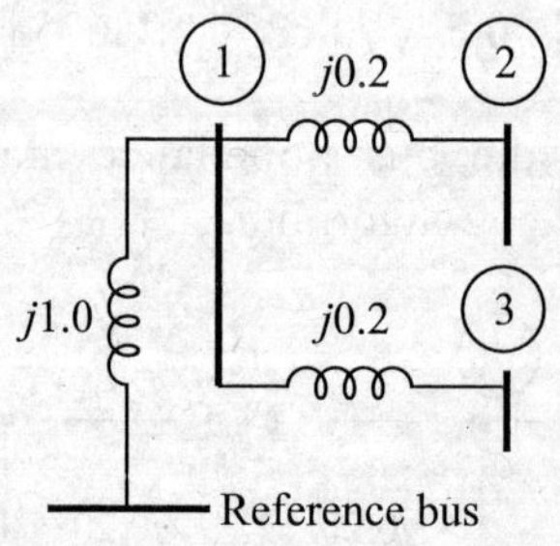

$$Z_{bus} = \begin{bmatrix} j0.5 & j0.5 & j0.5 \\ j0.5 & j0.7 & j0.5 \\ j0.5 & j0.5 & j0.5 + j0.2 \end{bmatrix} = \begin{bmatrix} j0.5 & j0.5 & j0.5 \\ j0.5 & j0.7 & j0.5 \\ j0.5 & j0.5 & j0.7 \end{bmatrix}$$

4. Add an element with impedance $j0.2$, connected between the existing nodes 2 and 3. (*Type* 4 *modification*)

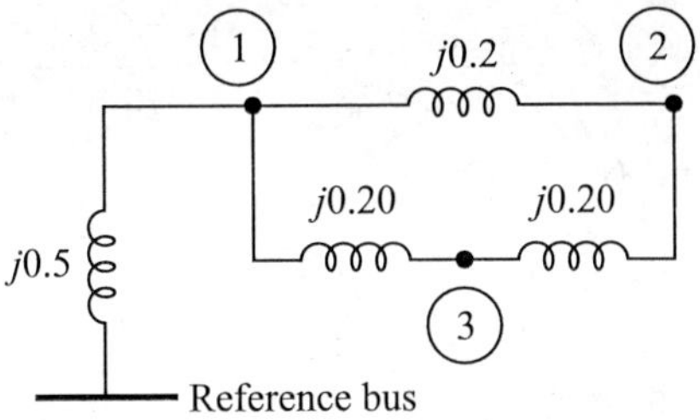

j0.2
j0.20
j0.20
j0.5
Reference bus

$$Z_{bus}^{new} = \left[\begin{array}{cccc|c} & & & & Z_{1j} - Z_{1i} \\ & & & & Z_{2j} - Z_{2i} \\ & Z_{bus}^{old} & & & \vdots \\ & & & & Z_{nj} - Z_{ni} \\ \hline Z_{j1} - Z_{i1} & Z_{j2} - Z_{i2} & \cdots & Z_{jn} - Z_{in} & Z_{ii} + Z_{jj} - 2Z_{ij} + Z_b \end{array}\right]$$

$i = 2; j = 3$

$$Z_{bus}^{new} = \left[\begin{array}{cccc|c} & & & & Z_{13} - Z_{12} \\ & & & & Z_{23} - Z_{22} \\ & Z_{bus}^{old} & & & \vdots \\ & & & & Z_{33} - Z_{32} \\ \hline Z_{31} - Z_{21} & Z_{32} - Z_{22} & \cdots & Z_{33} - Z_{23} & Z_{22} + Z_{33} - 2Z_{23} + Z_b \end{array}\right]$$

$$Z_{bus} = \begin{bmatrix} j0.5 & j0.5 & j0.5 & j0.5 - j0.5 \\ j0.5 & j0.7 & j0.5 & j0.5 - j0.7 \\ j0.5 & j0.5 & j0.7 & j0.7 - j0.5 \\ j0.5 - j0.5 & j0.5 - j0.7 & j0.7 - j0.5 & j0.7 + j0.7 - 2 \times j0.5 + j0.2 \end{bmatrix}$$

$$Z_{bus} = \begin{bmatrix} j0.5 & j0.5 & j0.5 & 0 \\ j0.5 & j0.7 & j0.5 & -j0.2 \\ j0.5 & j0.5 & j0.7 & j0.2 \\ 0 & -j0.2 & j0.2 & j0.6 \end{bmatrix}$$

Now apply Kron's reduction formula

$$Z_{jk}^{new} = Z_{jk}^{old} - \frac{Z_{j(n+1)} \times Z_{(n+1)k}}{Z_{(n+1)(n+1)}}$$

$j, k = 1, 2, 3$ and $(n + 1) = 0$ (reference node)

$j = 1; k = 1$ and $(n + 1) = 0$

$$Z_{11}^{new} = Z_{11}^{old} - \frac{Z_{10} \times Z_{01}}{Z_{00}} = j0.5 - \frac{0 \times 0}{j0.6} = j0.5$$

$j = 1; k = 2$ and $(n + 1) = 0$

$$Z_{12}^{\text{new}} = Z_{12}^{\text{old}} - \frac{Z_{10} \times Z_{02}}{Z_{00}} = j0.5 - \frac{0 \times (-j0.2)}{j0.6} = j0.5$$

$j = 1;\ k = 3$ and $(n + 1) = 0$

$$Z_{13}^{\text{new}} = Z_{13}^{\text{old}} - \frac{Z_{10} \times Z_{03}}{Z_{00}} = j0.5 - \frac{0 \times (j0.2)}{j0.6} = j0.5$$

$j = 2;\ k = 1$ and $(n + 1) = 0$

$$Z_{21}^{\text{new}} = Z_{21}^{\text{old}} - \frac{Z_{20} \times Z_{01}}{Z_{00}} = j0.5 - \frac{(-j0.2) \times 0}{j0.6} = j0.5$$

$j = 2;\ k = 2$ and $(n + 1) = 0$

$$Z_{22}^{\text{new}} = Z_{22}^{\text{old}} - \frac{Z_{20} \times Z_{02}}{Z_{00}} = j0.7 - \frac{(-j0.2) \times (-j0.2)}{j0.6} = j0.633$$

$j = 2;\ k = 3$ and $(n + 1) = 0$

$$Z_{23}^{\text{new}} = Z_{23}^{\text{old}} - \frac{Z_{20} \times Z_{03}}{Z_{00}} = j0.5 - \frac{(-j0.2) \times (j0.2)}{j0.6} = j0.567$$

$j = 3;\ k = 1$ and $(n + 1) = 0$

$$Z_{31}^{\text{new}} = Z_{31}^{\text{old}} - \frac{Z_{30} \times Z_{01}}{Z_{00}} = j0.5 - \frac{(j0.2) \times 0}{j0.6} = j0.5$$

$j = 3;\ k = 2$ and $(n + 1) = 0$

$$Z_{32}^{\text{new}} = Z_{32}^{\text{old}} - \frac{Z_{30} \times Z_{02}}{Z_{00}} = j0.5 - \frac{(j0.2) \times (-j0.2)}{j0.6} = j0.567$$

$j = 3;\ k = 3$ and $(n + 1) = 0$

$$Z_{33}^{\text{new}} = Z_{33}^{\text{old}} - \frac{Z_{30} \times Z_{03}}{Z_{00}} = j0.7 - \frac{(j0.2) \times (j0.2)}{j0.6} = j0.633$$

$$Z_{\text{bus}} = \begin{bmatrix} j0.5 & j0.5 & j0.5 \\ j0.5 & j0.633 & j0.567 \\ j0.5 & j0.567 & j0.633 \end{bmatrix}$$

6. Add an element with impedance $j0.5$, connected between the existing node 2 and the reference node 0. (*Type* 3 *modification*)

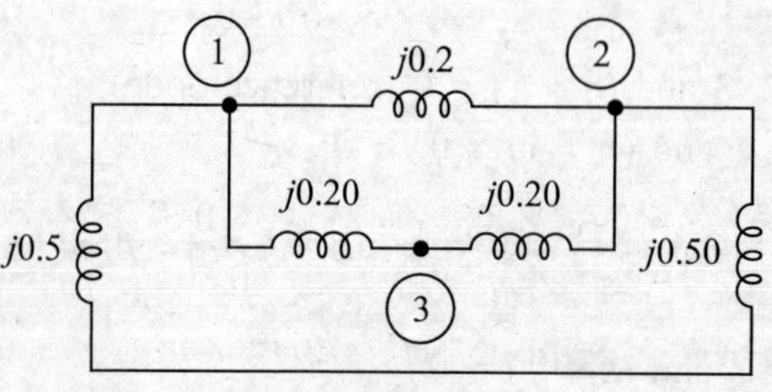

(a) To obtain $[Z_{bus}]$ matrix use type 2 modification

$$Z_{bus} = \begin{bmatrix} j0.5 & j0.5 & j0.5 & j0.5 \\ j0.5 & j0.633 & j0.567 & j0.633 \\ j0.5 & j0.567 & j0.633 & j0.567 \\ j0.5 & j0.633 & j0.567 & j0.633 + j0.5 \end{bmatrix}$$

$$Z_{bus} = \begin{bmatrix} j0.5 & j0.5 & j0.5 & j0.5 \\ j0.5 & j0.633 & j0.567 & j0.633 \\ j0.5 & j0.567 & j0.633 & j0.567 \\ j0.5 & j0.633 & j0.567 & j1.133 \end{bmatrix}$$

(b) Now apply Kron's reduction formula

$$Z_{jk}^{\text{new}} = Z_{jk}^{\text{old}} - \frac{Z_{j(n+1)} \times Z_{(n+1)k}}{Z_{(n+1)(n+1)}}$$

$j, k = 1, 2, 3$ and $(n + 1) = 0$ (reference node)

$j = 1;\ k = 1$ and $(n + 1) = 0$

$$Z_{11}^{\text{new}} = Z_{11}^{\text{old}} - \frac{Z_{10} \times Z_{01}}{Z_{00}} = j0.5 - \frac{j0.5 \times j0.5}{j1.133} = j0.2793$$

$j = 1;\ k = 2$ and $(n + 1) = 0$

$$Z_{12}^{\text{new}} = Z_{12}^{\text{old}} - \frac{Z_{10} \times Z_{02}}{Z_{00}} = j0.5 - \frac{j0.5 \times (j0.633)}{j1.133} = j0.2206$$

$j = 1;\ k = 3$ and $(n + 1) = 0$

$$Z_{13}^{\text{new}} = Z_{13}^{\text{old}} - \frac{Z_{10} \times Z_{03}}{Z_{00}} = j0.5 - \frac{j0.5 \times (j0.567)}{j1.133} = j0.2498$$

$j = 2;\ k = 1$ and $(n + 1) = 0$

$$Z_{21}^{\text{new}} = Z_{21}^{\text{old}} - \frac{Z_{20} \times Z_{01}}{Z_{00}} = j0.5 - \frac{(j0.633) \times j0.5}{j1.133} = j0.2206$$

$j = 2;\ k = 2$ and $(n + 1) = 0$

$$Z_{22}^{\text{new}} = Z_{22}^{\text{old}} - \frac{Z_{20} \times Z_{02}}{Z_{00}}$$

$$= j0.633 - \frac{(j0.633) \times (j0.633)}{j1.133} = j0.2793$$

$j = 2;\ k = 3$ and $(n + 1) = 0$

$$Z_{23}^{\text{new}} = Z_{23}^{\text{old}} - \frac{Z_{20} \times Z_{03}}{Z_{00}}$$

$$= j0.567 - \frac{(j0.633) \times (j0.567)}{j1.133} = j0.2502$$

$j = 3$; $k = 1$ and $(n + 1) = 0$

$$Z_{31}^{\text{new}} = Z_{31}^{\text{old}} - \frac{Z_{30} \times Z_{01}}{Z_{00}} = j0.5 - \frac{(j0.567) \times (j0.5)}{j1.133} = j0.2498$$

$j = 3$; $k = 2$ and $(n + 1) = 0$

$$Z_{32}^{\text{new}} = Z_{32}^{\text{old}} - \frac{Z_{30} \times Z_{02}}{Z_{00}}$$

$$= j0.567 - \frac{(j0.567) \times (j0.633)}{j1.133} = j0.2502$$

$j = 3$; $k = 3$ and $(n + 1) = 0$

$$Z_{33}^{\text{new}} = Z_{33}^{\text{old}} - \frac{Z_{30} \times Z_{03}}{Z_{00}}$$

$$= j0.633 - \frac{(j0.567) \times (j0.567)}{j1.133} = j0.3492$$

$$Z_{\text{bus}} = \begin{bmatrix} j0.2793 & j0.2206 & j0.2498 \\ j0.2206 & j0.2793 & j0.2502 \\ j0.2498 & j0.2502 & j0.3492 \end{bmatrix}$$

Review Questions

Part-A

1. What is meant by a fault?
2. Why do faults occur in a power system?
3. List the various types of faults.
4. Write the relative frequency of occurrence of various types of faults.
5. State and explain the symmetrical fault or balanced three-phase fault.
6. What is the need for short-circuit studies or fault analysis?
7. What is bolted fault or solid fault?
8. What is the reason for transients during short-circuit?
9. What is meant by doubling effect?
10. Define dc offset current.
11. What is synchronous reactance or steady state condition reactance?
12. What is subtransient reactance?
13. What is transient reactance?
14. Define the short-circuit capacity of power system or fault level.
15. Find the fault current as given in the figure, if the prefault voltage at the fault point is 0.97 p.u.?

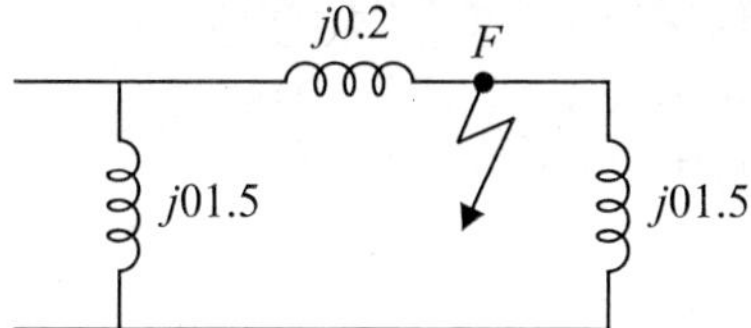

16. What is the bus impedance matrix?
17. Give the methods available for forming the bus impedance matrix.

Part-B

1. A synchronous generator and a synchronous motor each rated 20 MVA, 12.66 kV having 15% reactance are connected through transformers and a line as shown in the figure below. The transformers are rated 20 MVA, 12.66/66 kV and 66/12.66 kV with leakage reactance of 10% each. The line has a reactance of 8% on base of 20 MVA, 66 kV. The motor is drawing 10 MW at 0.8 leading power factors and a terminal voltage 11 kV when symmetrical three-phase fault occurs at the motors terminals. Determine the generator and motor currents. Also determine the fault current.

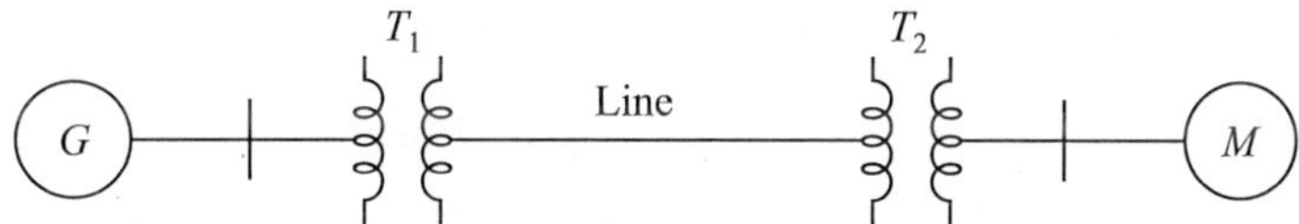

2. A 4-bus sample power system is shown in the figure. Perform the short-circuit analysis for a three-phase solid fault on bus 4. Data are given below.

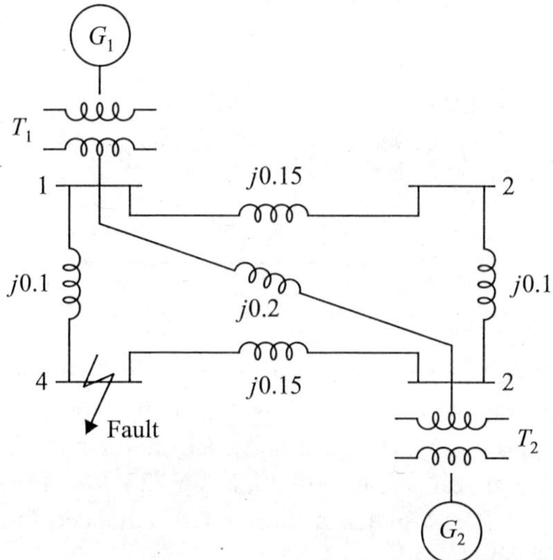

G_1: 11.2 kV, 100 MVA, $X = 0.08$ p.u.
G_2: 11.2 kV, 100 MVA, $X = 0.08$ p.u.
T_1: 11/110 kV, 100 MVA, $X = 0.06$ p.u.
T_2: 11/110 kV, 100 MVA, $X = 0.06$ p.u.

Assume the prefault voltage is 1.0 p.u. and the prefault current is zero.

3. Two generators G_1 and G_2 are rated 15 MVA, 11 kV and 10 MVA, 11 kV respectively. The generators are connected to a transformer as shown in the figure. Calculate the subtransient current in each generator when a three-phase fault occurs on the high voltage side of the transformer.

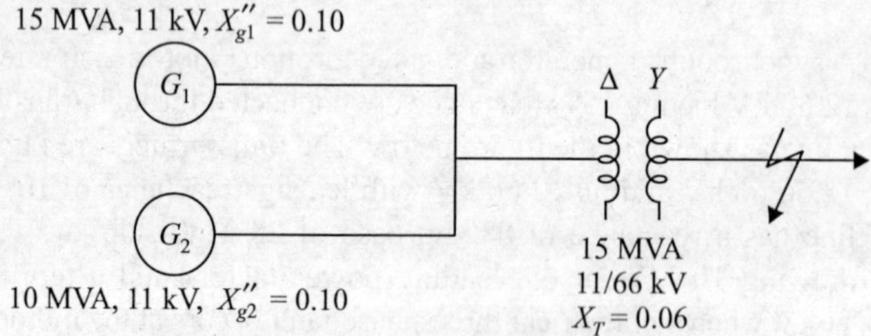

4. A radial power system network is shown in the figure below. A three-phase balanced fault occurs at F. Determine the fault current and the line voltage at 11.8 kV bus under the fault condition.

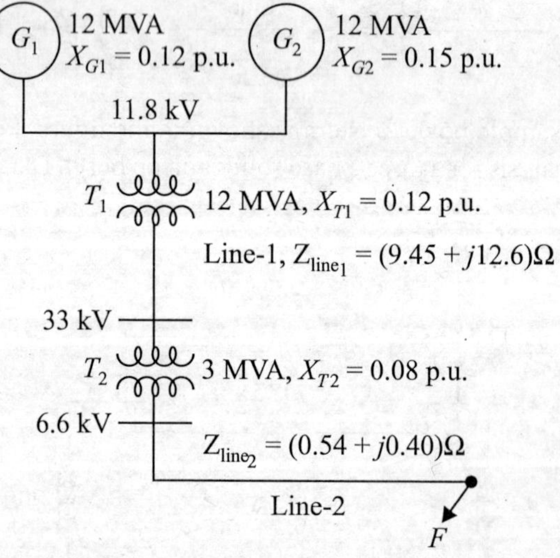

5. A 100 MVA, 11 kV generator with $X'' = 0.20$ p.u. is connected through a transformer to a bus bar that supplies three identical motors as shown in the figure and each motor has $X'' = 0.20$ p.u and $X' = 0.25$ p.u. on a base of 20 MVA, 33 kV. The bus voltage at the motors is 33 kV when a three-phase balanced fault occurs at the point F. Calculate

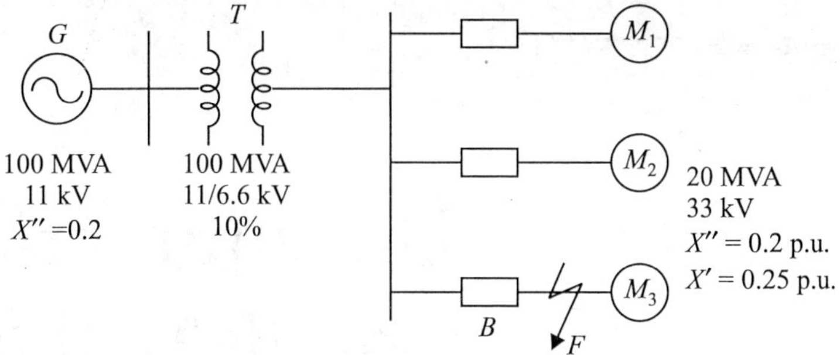

(a) the subtransient current in the fault.
(b) the subtransient current in the circuit breaker B.
(c) the momentary current in the circuit breaker B.
(d) the current to be interrupted by circuit breaker B in (i) 2 cycles, (ii) 3 cycles, (iii) 5 cycles and (iv) 8 cycles.

6. Determine the impedance matrix Z_{bus} as shown in the figure below.

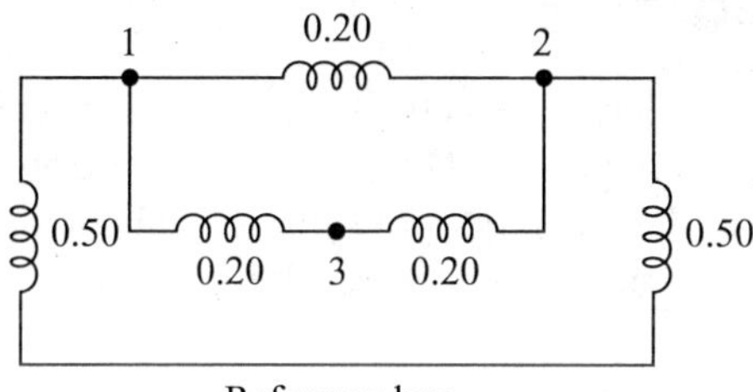

CHAPTER 4

Unsymmetrical Fault Analysis

4.1 Introduction

Practical systems rarely have perfectly balanced loads, currents, voltages or impedances in all the three phases. The analysis of unbalanced cases is greatly simplified by the use of the techniques of symmetrical components. The method of symmetrical components was developed by C.L. Fortescue prior to 1920.

4.2 Symmetrical Components

Symmetrical components or Fortescue theorem: It has been proven that an unbalanced system of n related phasors can be resolved into n systems of balanced phasors referred to as symmetrical components of the original phasors.

4.2.1 Sequence Operator 'a'

The phase sequence of the phasors or vectors is the order in which they pass through a positive maximum. Thus phase sequence abc implies that the maximum occur in the order a, b, c or R, Y, B.

When the balanced components are considered, we see that the most frequently occurring angle is 120°.

In complex number theory, we defined j as the complex operator which is equal to $\sqrt{-1}$ and a magnitude of unity, and more importantly, when operated on any complex number rotates it anticlockwise by an angle of 90°, i.e. $j = \sqrt{-1} = 1\angle 90°$.

Similarly, we define a new complex operator a which has a magnitude of unity and when operated on any complex number rotates it anticlockwise by an angle of 120°.

i.e. $a = 1\angle 120° = -0.5 + j\ 0.866$

Some properties of a

$a = 1\angle 120°$

$a^2 = 1\angle 240°$ or $1\angle -120° = -0.5 - j0.866$

$a^3 = 1\angle 360°$ or 1

$1 + a + a^2 = 0$

4.2.2 Types of Symmetrical Components

The unbalanced three-phase systems can be split up into the three balanced components, namely

- Positive sequence components
- Negative sequence components
- Zero sequence components

Positive sequence components: It consists of three phasors which are equal in magnitude, equally displaced 120° from each other and having the same phase sequence *abc*.

Let V_{a1}, V_{b1} and V_{c1} be the positive sequence voltages and I_{a1}, I_{b1} and I_{c1} be the positive sequence currents. It is assumed that the subscript 1 refers to the positive sequence.

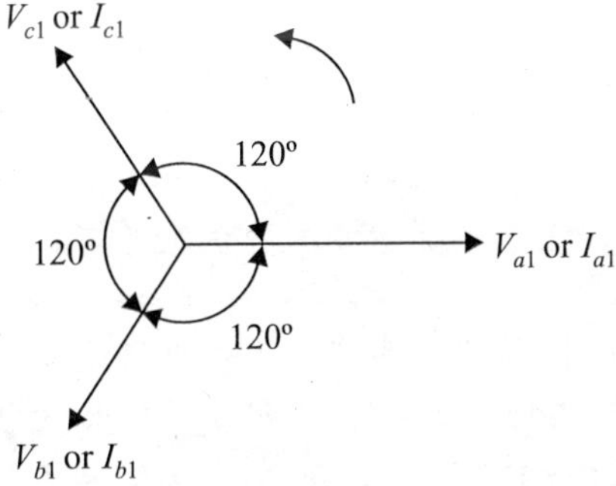

(a) Positive sequence components

$V_{a1} = V_{a1}\angle 0°$

$V_{b1} = V_{a1}\angle 240°$ or $V_{a1}\angle -120°$

$V_{c1} = V_{a1}\angle 120°$

$I_{a1} = I_{a1}\angle 0°$

$I_{b1} = I_{a1}\angle 240°$ or $I_{a1}\angle -120°$

$I_{c1} = I_{a1}\angle 120°$

Negative sequence components: It consists of three phasors which are equal in magnitude, equally displaced 120° from each other and having the same phase sequence as opposite to *acb*.

Let V_{a2}, V_{b2} and V_{c2} be the negative sequence voltages and I_{a2}, I_{b2} and I_{c2} be the negative sequence currents. It is assumed that the subscript 2 refers to the negative sequence.

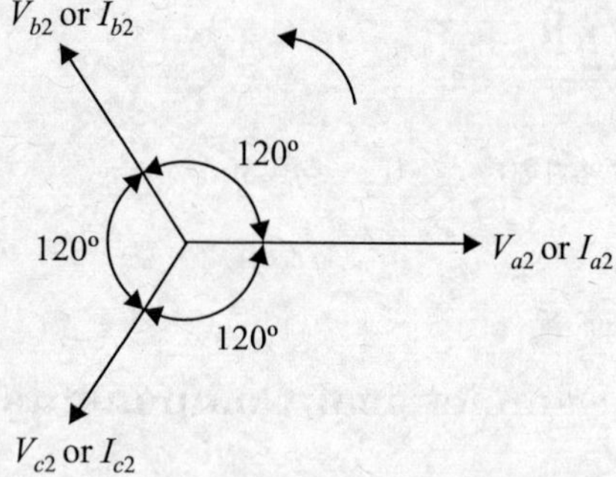

(b) Negative sequence components

$$V_{a2} = V_{a2}\angle 0° \qquad I_{a2} = I_{a2}\angle 0°$$
$$V_{b2} = V_{a2}\angle 120° \qquad I_{b2} = I_{a2}\angle 120°$$
$$V_{c2} = V_{a2}\angle 240° \text{ or } V_{a2}\angle -120° \qquad I_{c2} = I_{a2}\angle 240° \text{ or } I_{a2}\angle -120°$$

Zero sequence components: It consists of three phasors which are equal in magnitude, and zero phase displacement from each other.

Let V_{a0}, V_{b0} and V_{c0} be the zero sequence voltages and I_{a0}, I_{b0} and I_{c0} be the zero sequence currents. It is assumed that the subscript 0 refers to the zero sequence.

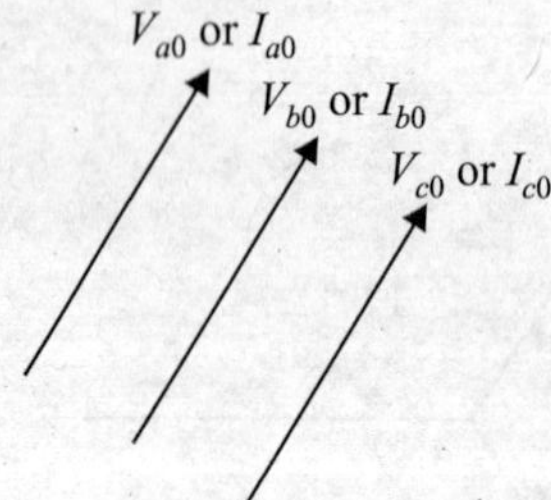

(c) Zero sequence components

Figure 4.1 Phasor diagram of symmetrical components.

$$V_{a0} = V_{b0} = V_{c0} \quad \text{or} \quad I_{a0} = I_{b0} = I_{c0}$$

4.2.3 Determination of Unbalanced Vectors from Their Symmetrical Components

Let V_a, V_b and V_c represent an unbalanced set of voltage phasors. Figure 4.1 (a, b and c) shows three such set of symmetrical components. Since each of the original unbalanced phasors is the sum of its components, the original phasors expressed in terms of their components are

$$V_a = V_{a0} + V_{a1} + V_{a2} \tag{4.1}$$
$$V_b = V_{b0} + V_{b1} + V_{b2} \tag{4.2}$$
$$V_c = V_{c0} + V_{c1} + V_{c2} \tag{4.3}$$

From the phasor diagram shown in the Figure 4.1 (a, b and c), we get

$$V_{a0} = V_{b0} = V_{c0} \tag{4.4}$$

$$V_{b1} = V_{a1}\angle 240° = a^2V_{a1} \qquad V_{b2} = V_{a1}\angle 120° = a^2V_{a2} \tag{4.5}$$

$$V_{c1} = V_{a1}\angle 120° = aV_{a1} \qquad V_{c2} = V_{a1}\angle 240° = a^2V_{a2} \tag{4.6}$$

Repeating Eq. (4.1) and substituting Eqs. (4.4), (4.5) and (4.6) in Eqs. (4.2) and (4.3),

$$V_a = V_{a0} + V_{a1} + V_{a2} \tag{4.7}$$

$$V_b = V_{a0} + a^2V_{a1} + aV_{a2} \tag{4.8}$$

$$V_c = V_{a0} + aV_{a1} + a^2V_{a2} \tag{4.9}$$

In the matrix form

$$\begin{bmatrix} V_a \\ V_b \\ V_c \end{bmatrix} = \begin{bmatrix} 1 & 1 & 1 \\ 1 & a^2 & a \\ 1 & a & a^2 \end{bmatrix} \begin{bmatrix} V_{a0} \\ V_{a1} \\ V_{a2} \end{bmatrix} \tag{4.10}$$

The above equation can be used to calculate the unbalanced voltage vectors from their symmetrical components.

4.2.4 Determination of Symmetrical Components of Unbalanced Vectors

$$\begin{bmatrix} V_a \\ V_b \\ V_c \end{bmatrix} = [A] \begin{bmatrix} V_{a0} \\ V_{a1} \\ V_{a2} \end{bmatrix} \tag{4.11}$$

where,

$$A = \begin{bmatrix} 1 & 1 & 1 \\ 1 & a^2 & a \\ 1 & a & a^2 \end{bmatrix}$$

$$A^{-1} = \frac{1}{3}\begin{bmatrix} 1 & 1 & 1 \\ 1 & a & a^2 \\ 1 & a^2 & a \end{bmatrix}$$

Premultiplying Eq. (4.11) by A^{-1} yields

$$\begin{bmatrix} V_{a0} \\ V_{a1} \\ V_{a2} \end{bmatrix} = [A]^{-1} \begin{bmatrix} V_a \\ V_b \\ V_c \end{bmatrix}$$

$$\begin{bmatrix} V_{a0} \\ V_{a1} \\ V_{a2} \end{bmatrix} = \frac{1}{3}\begin{bmatrix} 1 & 1 & 1 \\ 1 & a & a^2 \\ 1 & a^2 & a \end{bmatrix} \begin{bmatrix} V_a \\ V_b \\ V_c \end{bmatrix} \tag{4.12}$$

As these relations are important, therefore we can write the separate equations in the expanded form

$$V_{a0} = \frac{1}{3}[V_a + V_b + V_c] \tag{4.13}$$

$$V_{a1} = \frac{1}{3}[V_a + aV_b + a^2V_c] \tag{4.14}$$

$$V_{a2} = \frac{1}{3}[V_a + a^2V_b + aV_c] \tag{4.15}$$

The above equations can be used to calculate the symmetrical components of the unbalanced voltages.

The preceding equations could have been written for any set of related phasors, and we might have them currents instead of voltages. They are summarized for currents as follows.

$$I_a = I_{a0} + I_{a1} + I_{a2} \tag{4.16}$$

$$I_b = I_{a0} + a^2I_{a1} + aI_{a2} \tag{4.17}$$

$$I_c = I_{a0} + aI_{a1} + a^2I_{a2} \tag{4.18}$$

In the matrix form

$$\begin{bmatrix} I_a \\ I_b \\ I_c \end{bmatrix} = \begin{bmatrix} 1 & 1 & 1 \\ 1 & a^2 & a \\ 1 & a & a^2 \end{bmatrix} \begin{bmatrix} I_{a0} \\ I_{a1} \\ I_{a2} \end{bmatrix} \tag{4.19}$$

$$I_{a0} = \frac{1}{3}[I_a + I_b + I_c] \tag{4.20}$$

$$I_{a1} = \frac{1}{3}[I_a + aI_b + a^2I_c] \tag{4.21}$$

$$I_{a2} = \frac{1}{3}[I_a + a^2I_b + aI_c] \tag{4.22}$$

In the matrix form

$$\begin{bmatrix} I_{a0} \\ I_{a1} \\ I_{a2} \end{bmatrix} = \frac{1}{3}\begin{bmatrix} 1 & 1 & 1 \\ 1 & a & a^2 \\ 1 & a^2 & a \end{bmatrix} \begin{bmatrix} I_a \\ I_b \\ I_c \end{bmatrix} \tag{4.23}$$

EXAMPLE 4.1 In a 3-phase 4-wire system, the currents in R, Y and B lines under abnormal conditions of loading are as under:

$$I_R = 100\angle 30^\circ \text{ A}; \quad I_Y = 50\angle 300^\circ \text{ A}; \quad I_B = 30\angle 180^\circ \text{ A}$$

Calculate the positive, negative and zero sequence currents in the R line and return current in the neutral wire.

Solution: Let I_{R0}, I_{R1} and I_{R2} be the zero, positive and negative sequence currents respectively of the line current in red line.

$$I_{R0} = \frac{1}{3}[I_R + I_Y + I_B]$$

$$= \frac{1}{3}[100\angle 30° + 50\angle 300° + 30\angle 180°]$$

$$= \frac{1}{3}[(86.60 + j50) + (25 - j43.3) + (-30 + j0)]$$

$$= \frac{1}{3}(81.60 + j6.7) = 27.2 + j2.23 = 27.29\angle 4.68° \text{A}$$

$$I_{R1} = \frac{1}{3}[I_R + aI_Y + a^2 I_B]$$

$$= \frac{1}{3}[100\angle 30° + 1\angle 120° \times 50\angle 300° + 1\angle -120° \times 30\angle 180°]$$

$$= \frac{1}{3}[100\angle 30° + 50\angle 420° + 30\angle 60°]$$

$$= \frac{1}{3}[(86.60 + j50) + (25 + j43.3) + (15 + j25.98)]$$

$$= \frac{1}{3}(126.6 + j119.28) = 42.2 + j39.76 = 57.98\angle 43.3° \text{A}$$

$$I_{R2} = \frac{1}{3}[I_R + a^2 I_Y + aI_B]$$

$$= \frac{1}{3}[100\angle 30° + 1\angle -120° \times 50\angle 300° + 1\angle 120° \times 30\angle 180°]$$

$$= \frac{1}{3}[100\angle 30° + 50\angle 180° + 30\angle 300°]$$

$$= \frac{1}{3}[(86.60 + j50) + (-50 + j0) + (15 - j25.98)]$$

$$= \frac{1}{3}(51.6 + j24.02) = 17.2 + j8.007 = 18.97\angle 24.96° \text{A}$$

EXAMPLE 4.2 The symmetrical components of a set of unbalanced three-phase currents are:

$$I_{a0} = 100 \text{ A}; \quad I_{a1} = 200 - j100 \text{ A}; \quad I_{a2} = -100 \text{ A}$$

Calculate the original unbalanced phasors.

Solution: To find the unbalanced vectors

$$I_a = I_{a0} + I_{a1} + I_{a2}$$

$$= [100 + 200 - j100 - 100]$$

$$= 200 - j100 = 223.6\angle -26.56° \text{ A}$$

$$I_b = I_{a0} + a^2 I_{a1} + aI_{a2}$$

$= [100\angle 0° + 1\angle -120° \times 223.6\angle -26.56° + 1\angle 120° \times 100\angle 180°]$

$= [100\angle 0° + 223.65\angle 213.44° + 100\angle 300°]$

$= -36.58 + j209.8 = 213\angle 99.89°$ A

$I_c = I_{a0} + aI_{a1} + a^2 I_{a2}$

$= [100\angle 0° + 1\angle 120° \times 223.6\angle -26.56° + 1\angle -120° \times 100\angle 180°]$

$= [100\angle 0° + 223.65\angle 93.44° + 100\angle 420°]$

$= 136.6 + j309.8 = 338.57\angle 66.2°$ A

EXAMPLE 4.3 A delta connected balance resistive load is connected across an unbalanced three-phase supply shown in Figure 4.2 with currents in line *a* and *b* specified. Determine the symmetrical components of the currents.

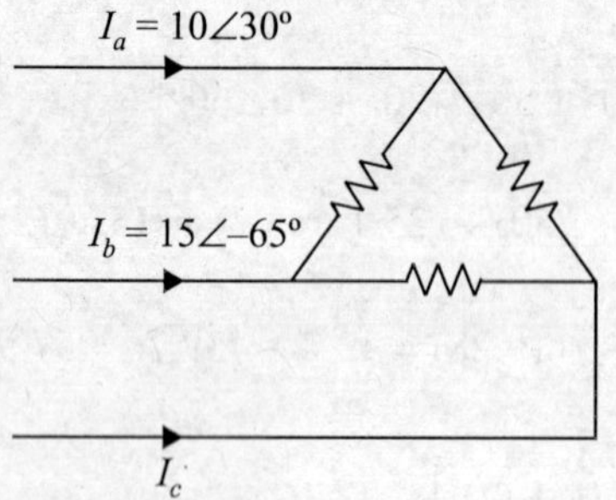

Figure 4.2

Solution:

$$I_a = 10\angle 30°$$
$$I_b = 15\angle -65°$$

In a balanced load

$$I_a + I_b + I_c = 0$$

$$I_c = -I_a - I_b$$

$$I_c = -(10\angle 30°) - (15\angle -65°) = 17.3\angle 150° \text{A}$$

$$I_{a0} = \frac{1}{3}[I_a + I_b + I_c]$$

$$= \frac{1}{3}[10\angle 30° + 15\angle -65° + 17.3\angle 150°]$$

$$= \frac{1}{3}(0) = 0 \text{ A}$$

$$I_{a1} = \frac{1}{3}[I_a + aI_b + a^2 I_c]$$

$$= \frac{1}{3}[10\angle 30° + 1\angle 120° \times 15\angle -65° + 1\angle -120° \times 17.3\angle 150°]$$

$$= \frac{1}{3}(33.38\angle 15°) = 11.13\angle 15° \text{ A}$$

$$I_{a2} = \frac{1}{3}[I_a + a^2 I_b + aI_c]$$

$$= \frac{1}{3}[10\angle 30° + 1\angle{-120°} \times 15\angle{-65°} + 1\angle 120° \times 17.3\angle 150°]$$

$$= \frac{1}{3}(12.66\angle{-119.7°}) = 4.22\angle{-119.7°}\text{A}$$

4.2.5 Power in Symmetrical Components

The symmetrical components of voltages and currents are known, the power in a three-phase circuit can be determined from the symmetrical components. The total complex power flowing into three-phase circuit in all the three-phase lines a, b, c is

$$S = P + jQ = VI^* = V_a I_a^* + V_b I_b^* + V_c I_c^* \tag{4.24}$$

where V_a, V_b, V_c are the phase voltages and I_a, I_b, I_c are the phase currents. The above equation can be written in the matrix form as

$$S = [V_a \quad V_b \quad V_c]\begin{bmatrix} I_a \\ I_b \\ I_c \end{bmatrix}^* = \begin{bmatrix} V_a \\ V_b \\ V_c \end{bmatrix}^T \begin{bmatrix} I_a \\ I_b \\ I_c \end{bmatrix}^* \tag{4.25}$$

Substituting Eqs. (4.10) and (4.19) in the following equation

$$S = [AV]^T\,[AI]^* \tag{4.26}$$

where

$$V = \begin{bmatrix} V_{a0} \\ V_{a1} \\ V_{a2} \end{bmatrix}; \qquad I = \begin{bmatrix} I_{a0} \\ I_{a1} \\ I_{a2} \end{bmatrix}$$

$$S = A^T\,V^T\,A^*\,I^* = V^T\,A^T\,A^*\,I^* \qquad [\because\ A^T = A]$$

$$A = \begin{bmatrix} 1 & 1 & 1 \\ 1 & a^2 & a \\ 1 & a & a^2 \end{bmatrix}$$

$$A^* = \begin{bmatrix} 1 & 1 & 1 \\ 1 & a & a^2 \\ 1 & a^2 & a \end{bmatrix}$$

$$A \cdot A^* = \begin{bmatrix} 1 & 1 & 1 \\ 1 & a^2 & a \\ 1 & a & a^2 \end{bmatrix}\begin{bmatrix} 1 & 1 & 1 \\ 1 & a & a^2 \\ 1 & a^2 & a \end{bmatrix} = 3\begin{bmatrix} 1 & 0 & 0 \\ 0 & 1 & 0 \\ 0 & 0 & 1 \end{bmatrix} = 3[U]$$

$$= 3\ [3 \times 3 \text{ Unit matrix}]$$

The power

$$S = V^T A^T A^* I^* = V^T 3[U]I^*$$

$$S = 3[V]^T[I]^* = 3[V_{a0} \quad V_{a1} \quad V_{a2}]\begin{bmatrix} I_{a0} \\ I_{a1} \\ I_{a2} \end{bmatrix}^*$$

$$S = 3[V_{a0}I_{a0}^* + V_{a1}I_{a1}^* + V_{a2}I_{a2}^*] \tag{4.27}$$

The total unbalanced power can be obtained from the sum of symmetrical components of power.

4.3 Sequence Impedance

Sequence impedance: The sequence impedances are the impedances offered by the power system components or elements to positive, negative and zero sequence currents.

Positive sequence impedance: The impedance of a circuit element when positive sequence currents alone are flowing is called the positive sequence impedance.

Negative sequence impedance: The impedance of a circuit element when negative sequence currents alone are flowing is called the negative sequence impedance.

Zero sequence impedance: The impedance of a circuit element when zero sequence currents alone are flowing is called the zero sequence impedance.

4.4 Sequence Network of Power System Components

The single-phase equivalent circuit of power system consisting of impedances to current of any one sequence only is called sequence network.

4.4.1 Sequence Network of Unloaded Generator

Let us consider three-phase circuit diagram of unloaded generator as shown in Figure 4.3. The neutral of the generator is grounded through impedance.

The positive sequence reactance of a generator may be X_d or X_d' or X_d'' depending upon the condition at which the reactance is calculated with positive sequence voltages applied. When negative sequence currents are impressed on the stator winding, the net flux rotates at twice the synchronous speed relative to the rotor. The negative sequence reactance is approximately given by $X_2 = X_d''$. The zero sequence currents, when they flow, are identical and the spatial distribution of the mmfs is sinusoidal. The resultant air gap flux due to zero sequence currents is zero. Thus, the zero sequence reactance is approximately the same as the leakage flux $X_0 = X$.

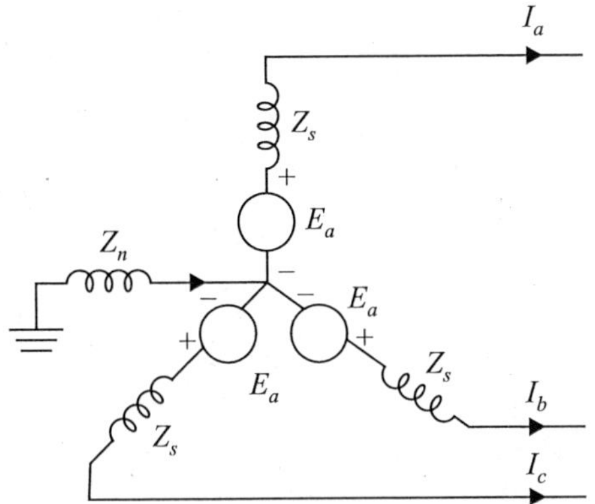

Figure 4.3 Circuit diagram of unloaded generator grounded through impedance.

4.4.2 Sequence Network of Loaded Generator

Figure 4.4 represents a three phase synchronous generator with neutral is grounded through an impedance Z_n. The synchronous generator is supplying a three phase balanced load.

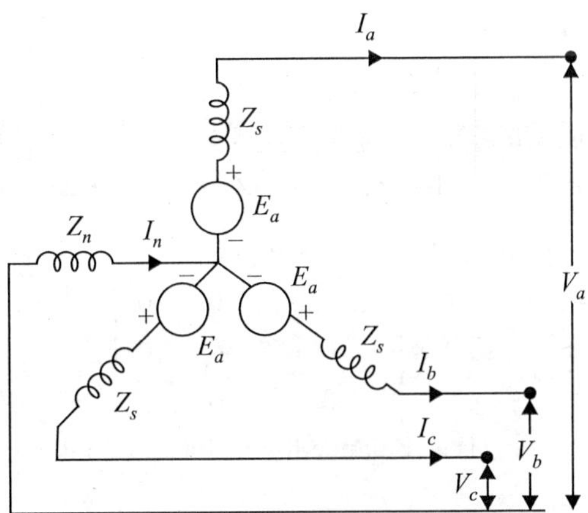

Figure 4.4 Circuit diagram of loaded synchronous generator neutral is grounded through impedance.

$$V_a = E_a - I_a Z_s - I_n Z_n \tag{4.28}$$

$$V_b = E_a - I_b Z_s - I_n Z_n \tag{4.29}$$

$$V_c = E_a - I_c Z_s - I_n Z_n \tag{4.30}$$

$$I_n = I_a + I_b + I_c \tag{4.31}$$

Substituting Eq. (4.31) in Eq. (4.28)

$$V_a = E_a - I_a Z_s - (I_a + I_b + I_c) Z_n$$
$$V_a = E_a - I_a Z_s - I_a Z_n - I_b Z_n - I_c Z_n$$
$$V_a = E_a - I_a(Z_s + Z_n) - (I_b + I_c) Z_n \tag{4.32}$$

Similarly

$$V_b = E_a - I_b(Z_s + Z_n) - (I_a + I_c) Z_n \tag{4.33}$$
$$V_c = E_a - I_c(Z_s + Z_n) - (I_b + I_a) Z_n \tag{4.34}$$

In the matrix form

$$\begin{bmatrix} V_a \\ V_b \\ V_c \end{bmatrix} = \begin{bmatrix} E_a \\ E_a \\ E_a \end{bmatrix} - \begin{bmatrix} Z_s + Z_n & Z_n & Z_n \\ Z_n & Z_s + Z_n & Z_n \\ Z_n & Z_n & Z_s + Z_n \end{bmatrix} \begin{bmatrix} I_a \\ I_b \\ I_c \end{bmatrix} \tag{4.35}$$

$$V^{abc} = E^{abc} - Z^{abc} I^{abc} \tag{4.36}$$

where V^{abc} is the phase terminal voltage vector and I^{abc} is the phase current vector. Converting the terminal voltages and current phasors into their symmetrical components result in

$$[A][V^{012}] = [A][E^{012}] - [A][Z^{abc}][I^{012}]$$
$$[A]^{-1}[A][V^{012}] = [A]^{-1}[A][E^{012}] - [A]^{-1}[A][Z^{abc}]\,[I^{012}]$$
$$V^{012} = E^{012} - Z^{012} I^{012} \tag{4.37}$$

where

$$Z^{012} = A^{-1} Z^{abc} A$$

$$Z^{012} = \frac{1}{3}\begin{bmatrix} 1 & 1 & 1 \\ 1 & a & a^2 \\ 1 & a^2 & a \end{bmatrix} \times \begin{bmatrix} Z_s + Z_n & Z_n & Z_n \\ Z_n & Z_s + Z_n & Z_n \\ Z_n & Z_n & Z_s + Z_n \end{bmatrix} \begin{bmatrix} 1 & 1 & 1 \\ 1 & a^2 & a \\ 1 & a & a^2 \end{bmatrix}$$

Performing the above multiplications, we get

$$Z^{012} = \begin{bmatrix} Z_s + 3Z_n & 0 & 0 \\ 0 & Z_s & 0 \\ 0 & 0 & Z_s \end{bmatrix} \tag{4.38}$$

Since the generated e.m.f is balanced, we have to take only the positive sequence voltage E_a

$$E^{012} = \begin{bmatrix} 0 \\ E_a \\ 0 \end{bmatrix} \tag{4.39}$$

Substituting for Z^{012} and E^{012} in Eq. (4.37)

$$\begin{bmatrix} V_{a0} \\ V_{a1} \\ V_{a2} \end{bmatrix} = \begin{bmatrix} 0 \\ E_a \\ 0 \end{bmatrix} - \begin{bmatrix} Z_s + 3Z_n & 0 & 0 \\ 0 & Z_s & 0 \\ 0 & 0 & Z_s \end{bmatrix} \begin{bmatrix} I_{a0} \\ I_{a1} \\ I_{a2} \end{bmatrix} \tag{4.40}$$

From the above equation

$$V_{a0} = -(Z_s + 3Z_n)I_{a0} \tag{4.41}$$

$$V_{a1} = E_a - (Z_s)I_{a1} \tag{4.42}$$

$$V_{a2} = -(Z_s)I_{a2} \tag{4.43}$$

These may be expressed in the network form as shown in Figures 4.5.

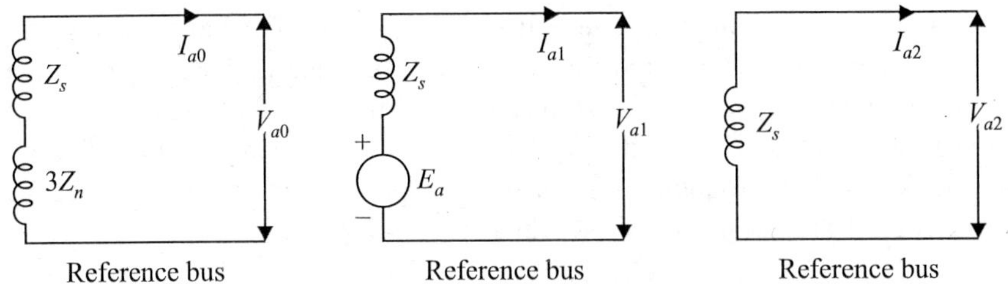

(a) Zero sequence network (b) Positive sequence network (c) Negative sequence network

Figure 4.5 Sequence network of a loaded generator.

4.4.3 Sequence Network of Transmission Line

The conductors of a transmission line, being passive and stationary, do not have an inherent direction. The transmission line (or cable) may be represented by a single reactance in the single-line diagram.

Thus they always have the same positive sequence impedance and negative sequence impedance. However, as the zero sequence paths also involve the earth wire and the earth return path, the zero sequence impedance is higher in value.

The zero, positive and zero sequence impedances of transmission lines are represented as a series impedance in their respective sequence networks as shown in Figure 4.6.

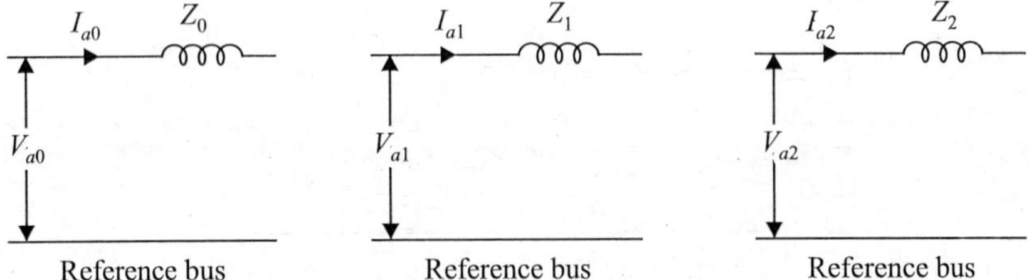

(a) Zero sequence network (b) Positive sequence network (c) Negative sequence network

Figure 4.6 Sequence network of a transmission line.

Typically, the ratio of the zero sequence impedance to the positive sequence impedance would be of the order of 2 for a single circuit transmission line with earth wire, about 3.5 for a single circuit with no earth wire or for a double circuit line.

For a single core cable, the ratio of the zero sequence impedance to the positive sequence impedance would be around 1 to 1.25.

Transmission lines are assumed to be symmetrical in all three phases. However, this assumption would not be valid for long untransposed lines (say, beyond 500 km) as the mutual coupling between the phases would be unequal, and then symmetrical components cannot be used.

4.4.4 Sequence Network of Transformer

The transformer too, being passive and stationary, does not have an inherent direction. Thus it always has the same positive sequence impedance, negative sequence impedance and even the zero sequence impedance. However, the zero sequence paths across the windings of a transformer depend on the winding connections and even grounding impedance. The positive and negative sequence networks of a transformer are shown in Figure 4.7.

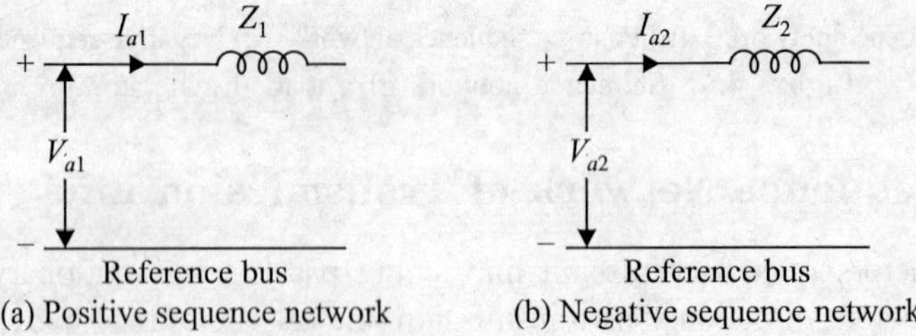

Figure 4.7 Positive and negative sequence networks of a transformer.

Zero sequence network of three phase transformers

However, the zero sequence paths across the windings of transformer depend on the different winding connections and even grounding impedance. The zero sequence network of three-phase transformer can be easily constructed by considering the arrangement as follows.

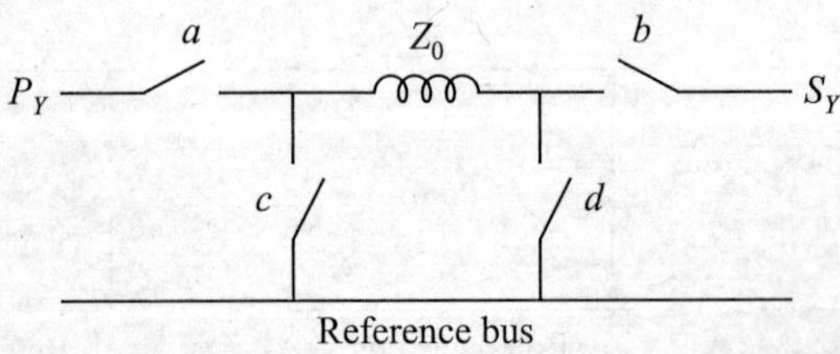

S.No.	*Primary winding* (P_Y)	*Secondary winding* (S_Y)
1.	Grounded star—close '*a*'	Grounded star—close '*b*'
2.	Delta—close '*c*'	Delta—close '*d*'
3.	Ungrounded—open '*a*', '*c*'	Ungrounded—open '*b*', '*d*'

The zero sequence network of three-phase transformers is shown in Figure 4.8.

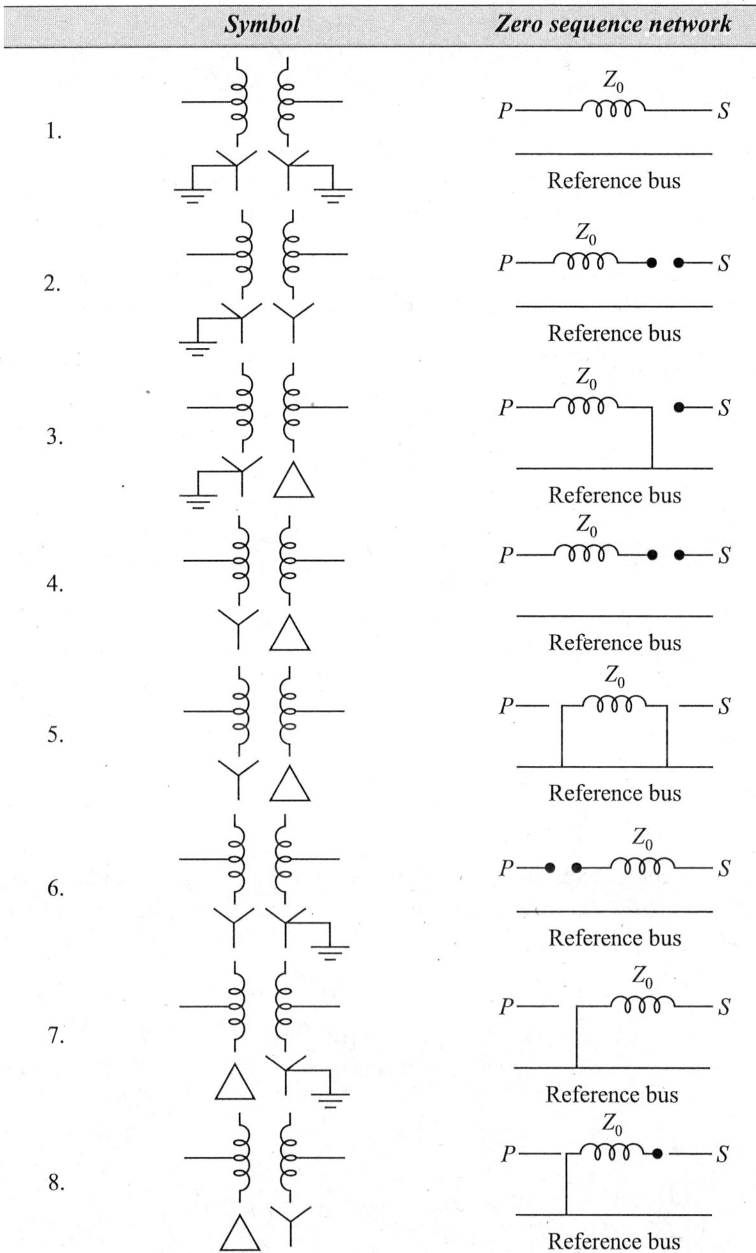

Figure 4.8 Zero sequence network of three-phase transformer.

4.4.5 Sequence Network of Star Connected Load Grounded Through Impedance

A three-phase balanced load with self and mutual elements is shown in Figure 4.9. The load neutral is grounded through an impedance Z_n.

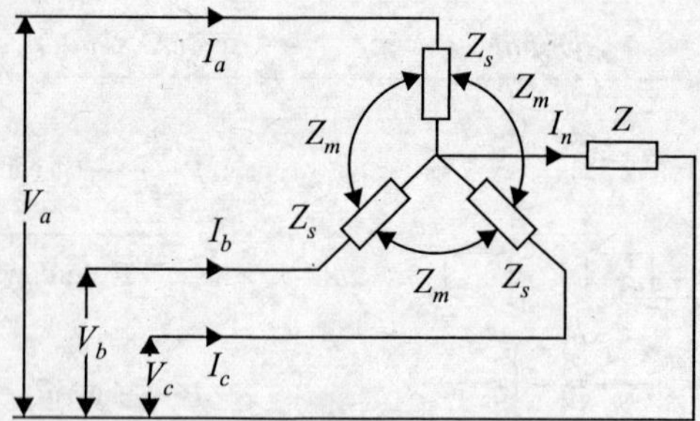

Figure 4.9 Circuit diagram of star connected load grounded through Z_n.

Lines to neutral voltages are

$$V_a = I_a Z_s + I_b Z_m + I_c Z_m + I_n Z_n \tag{4.44}$$

$$V_b = I_a Z_m + I_b Z_s + I_c Z_m + I_n Z_n \tag{4.45}$$

$$V_c = I_a Z_m + I_b Z_m + I_c Z_s + I_n Z_n \tag{4.46}$$

From KCL, we have

$$I_n = I_a + I_b + I_c \tag{4.47}$$

Substituting for I_n from Eq. (4.47) into Eqs. (4.44) to (4.46) and rewriting these equations in matrix form,

$$\begin{bmatrix} V_a \\ V_b \\ V_c \end{bmatrix} = \begin{bmatrix} Z_s + Z_n & Z_m + Z_n & Z_m + Z_n \\ Z_m + Z_n & Z_s + Z_n & Z_m + Z_n \\ Z_m + Z_n & Z_m + Z_s & Z_s + Z_n \end{bmatrix} \begin{bmatrix} I_a \\ I_b \\ I_c \end{bmatrix} \tag{4.48}$$

$$V^{abc} = Z^{abc} I^{abc} \tag{4.49}$$

where V^{abc} is the phase terminal voltage vector and I^{abc} is the phase current vector. Converting the terminal voltages and current phasors into their symmetrical components result in

$$[A][V^{012}] = [A][Z^{abc}][I^{012}]$$

$$[A]^{-1}[A][V^{012}] = [A]^{-1}[A][Z^{abc}][I^{012}]$$

$$V^{012} = Z^{012} I^{012} \tag{4.50}$$

where

$$Z^{012} = A^{-1} Z^{abc} A$$

$$Z^{012} = \frac{1}{3}\begin{bmatrix} 1 & 1 & 1 \\ 1 & a & a^2 \\ 1 & a^2 & a \end{bmatrix} \begin{bmatrix} Z_s + Z_n & Z_m + Z_n & Z_m + Z_n \\ Z_m + Z_n & Z_s + Z_n & Z_m + Z_n \\ Z_m + Z_n & Z_m + Z_n & Z_s + Z_n \end{bmatrix} \begin{bmatrix} 1 & 1 & 1 \\ 1 & a^2 & a \\ 1 & a & a^2 \end{bmatrix}$$

Performing the above multiplications, we get

$$Z^{012} = \begin{bmatrix} Z_s + 3Z_n + 2Z_m & 0 & 0 \\ 0 & Z_s & 0 \\ 0 & 0 & Z_s \end{bmatrix} \tag{4.51}$$

When there is no mutual coupling, $Z_m = 0$. Therefore,

$$Z^{012} = \begin{bmatrix} Z_s + 3Z_n & 0 & 0 \\ 0 & Z_s & 0 \\ 0 & 0 & Z_s \end{bmatrix} \tag{4.52}$$

Substituting for Z^{012} in Eq. (4.50)

$$\begin{bmatrix} V_{a0} \\ V_{a1} \\ V_{a2} \end{bmatrix} = \begin{bmatrix} Z_s + 3Z_n & 0 & 0 \\ 0 & Z_s & 0 \\ 0 & 0 & Z_s \end{bmatrix} \begin{bmatrix} I_{a0} \\ I_{a1} \\ I_{a2} \end{bmatrix} \tag{4.53}$$

From the above equation

$$V_{a0} = (Z_s + 3Z_n)I_{a0} \tag{4.54}$$

$$V_{a1} = Z_s I_{a1} \tag{4.55}$$

$$V_{a2} = Z_s I_{a2} \tag{4.56}$$

These may be expressed in network form as shown in Figure 4.10.

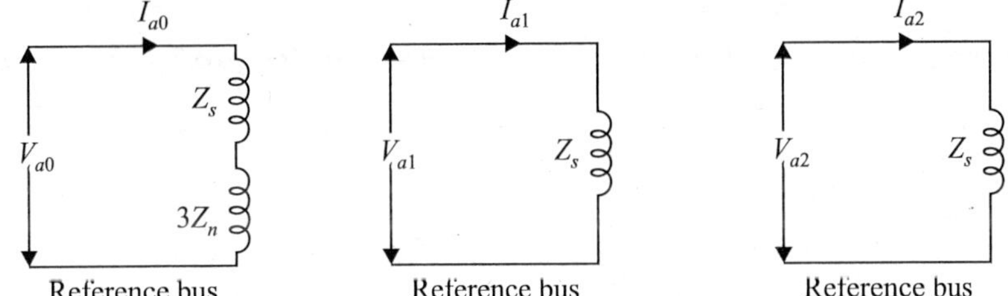

(a) Zero sequence network (b) Positive sequence network (c) Negative sequence network

Figure 4.10 Sequence network of a star connected load grounded through impedance.

Sequence network of three-phase balance star connected load with solid grounded

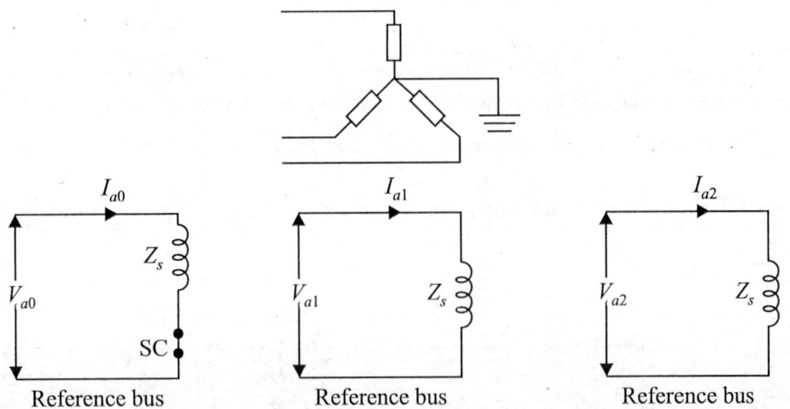

(a) Zero sequence network (b) Positive sequence network (c) Negative sequence network

Figure 4.11 Sequence network of a star connected load with solid grounded.

Sequence network of three-phase balance star connected load ungrounded

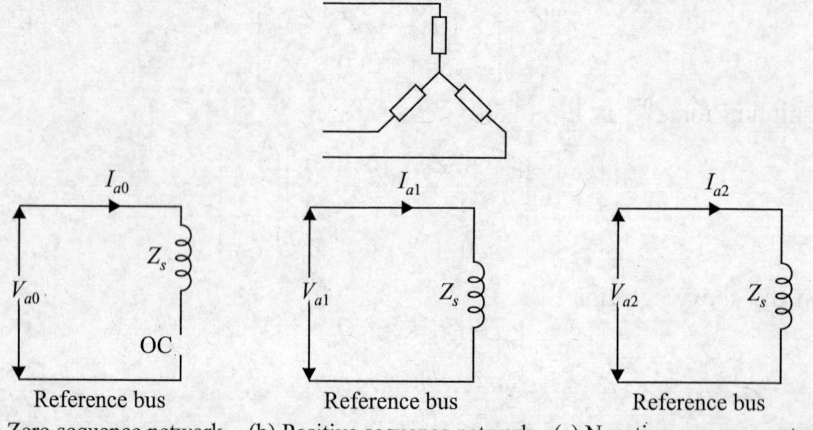

(a) Zero sequence network (b) Positive sequence network (c) Negative sequence network

Figure 4.12 Sequence network of a star connected load ungrounded.

Sequence network of three-phase balance delta connected load

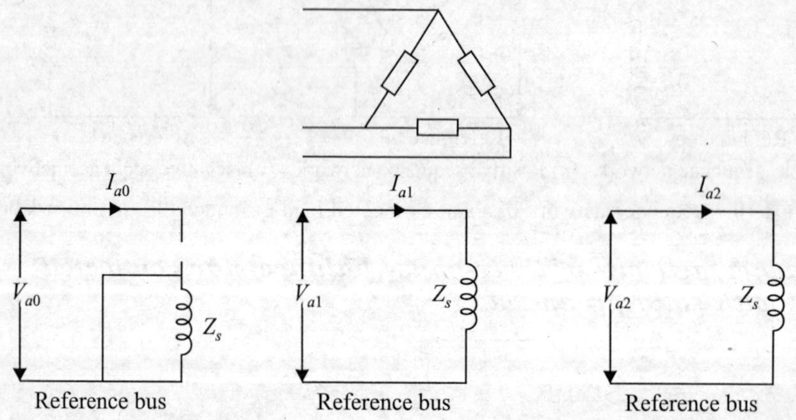

(a) Zero sequence network (b) Positive sequence network (c) Negative sequence network

Figure 4.13 Sequence network of a delta connected load.

EXAMPLE 4.4 Draw the positive, negative and zero sequence impedance diagram.

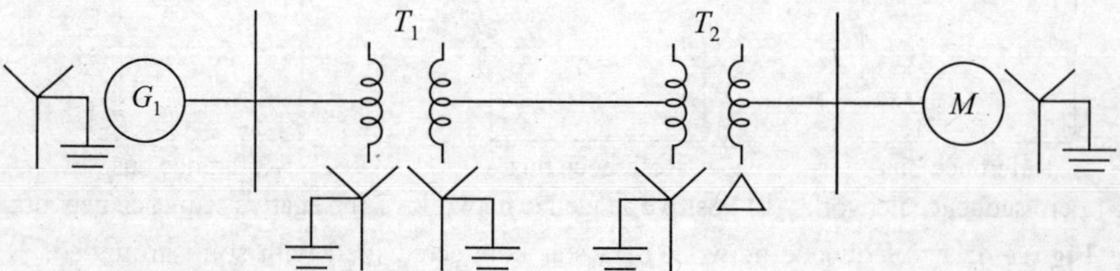

Solution:

Positive sequence impedance diagram

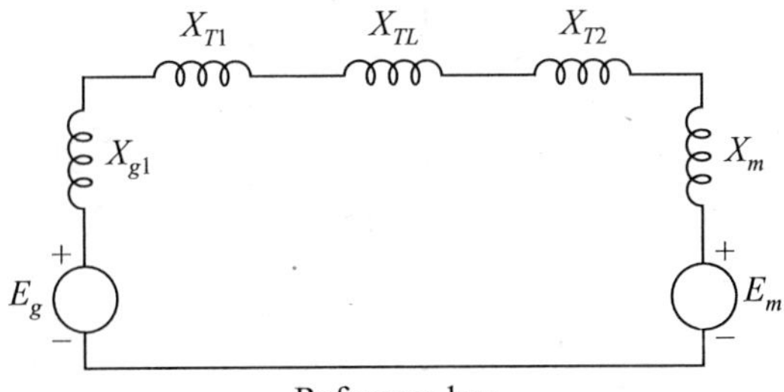

Negative sequence impedance diagram

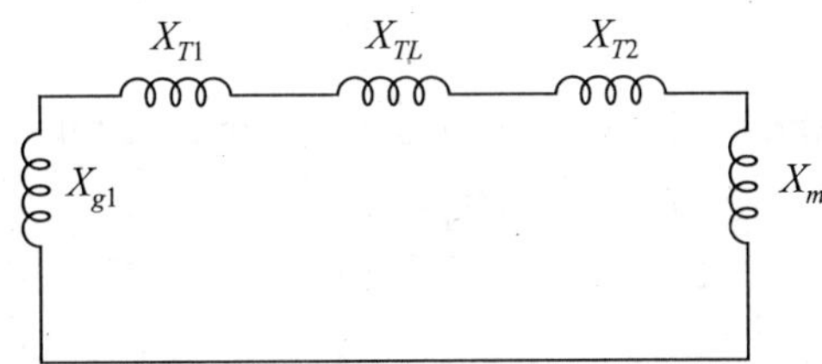

Zero sequence impedance diagram

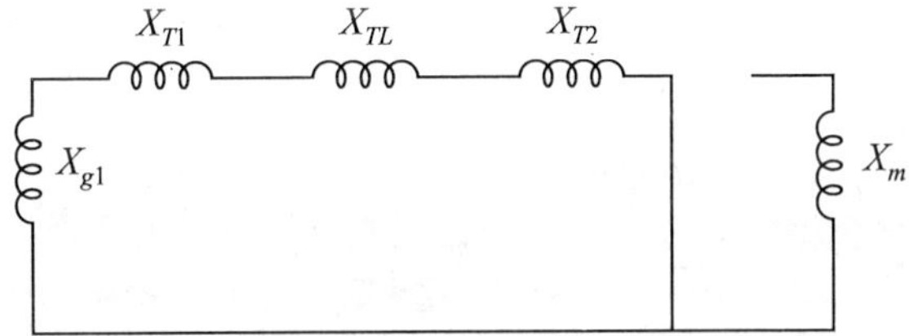

EXAMPLE 4.5 Draw the zero sequence networks for the system.

T_1 G_1 L_1 T_3 G_3 T_2 L_2 G_2

Solution:

Zero sequence impedance diagram

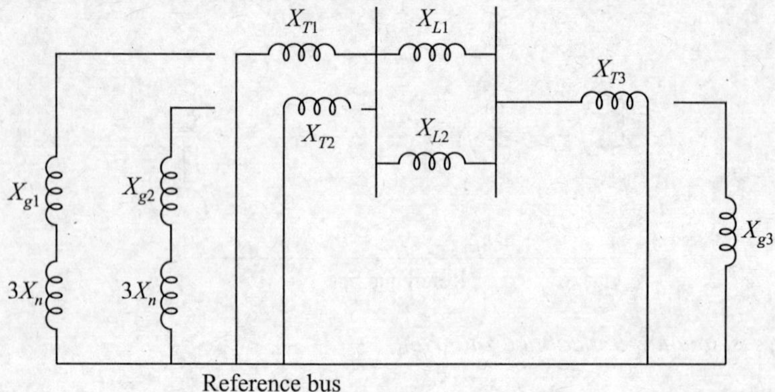

EXAMPLE 4.6 Draw the zero sequence networks for the system.

Solution:

Zero sequence impedance diagram

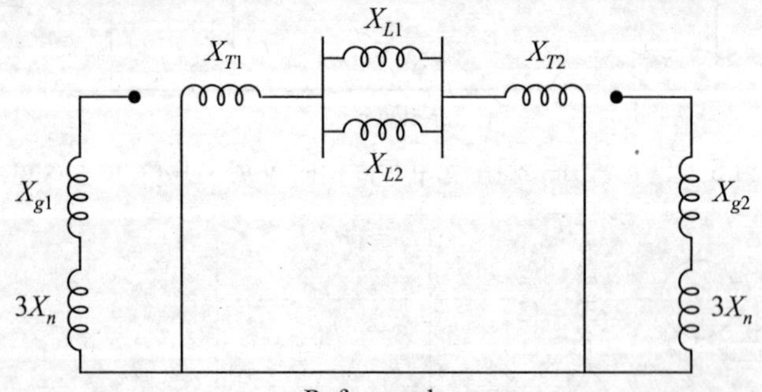

4.5 Unsymmetrical Faults

On the occurrence of a fault, current and voltage conditions become abnormal, the delivery of power to the loads may be unsatisfactory over a considerable area, and if the faulted equipment is not promptly disconnected from the remainder of the system, damage may result to other pieces of operating equipment. Most of the faults that occur on power system are single line to ground faults, line to line faults and double line to ground faults, with and without fault impedance.

While the unbalanced currents are caused by unsymmetrical faults, the method of symmetrical components is used to determine the currents and voltages in all parts of the power system after the occurrence of the fault.

In this topic we shall first discuss faults at the terminals of unloaded synchronous generator with fault impedance. Then we shall consider faults on power system by applying Thevenin's theorem, which allows us to find the fault current by replacing the entire system by a single generator and series impedance.

Important assumptions of power system representation

(i) Power system operates under balanced steady state conditions before the fault occurs. Therefore, the positive, negative and zero sequence networks are uncoupled before the occurrence of the fault. When an unsymmetrical fault occurs, they get interconnected at the point of fault.

(ii) Prefault load current at the point of fault is generally neglected. Positive sequence voltages of all the three phases are equal to the prefault voltage.

(iii) Transformer winding resistances and shunt admittances are neglected.

(iv) Transmission line series resistances and shunt admittances are neglected.

(v) Synchronous machine armature resistance, saliency and saturation are neglected.

(vi) Induction motors are either neglected or represented as synchronous machines.

Types of unsymmetrical faults

1. Single line to ground fault (L–G fault)
2. Line to line fault (L–L fault)
3. Double line to ground fault (L–L–G fault)

4.5.1 Single Line to Ground Fault (L–G Fault)

Let us consider three-phase circuit diagram of unloaded generator shown in Figure 4.14. The neutral of the generator is grounded through impedance.

Suppose a single line to ground fault occurs on phase *a* through impedance Z_f. Assuming the generator is initially on no load, the boundary conditions at the fault point are

(i) $V_a = Z_f I_a$ (4.57)

(ii) $I_b = I_c = 0$ (4.58)

(iii) Fault current $I_f = I_a$ (4.59)

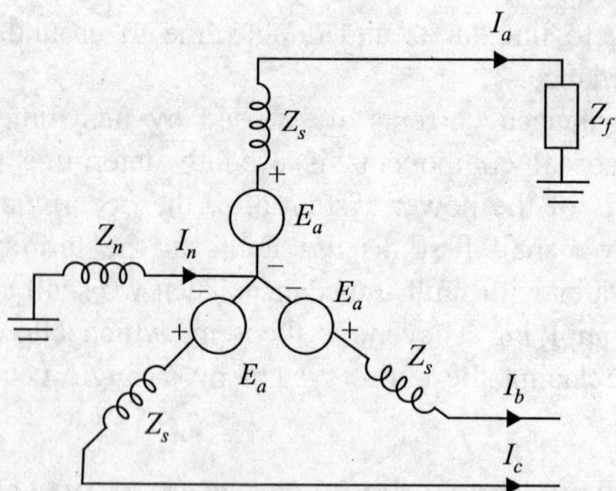

Figure 4.14 Single line to ground fault through Z_f on phase a of unloaded generator.

The symmetrical components of currents from Eq. (4.23) can be rewritten as

$$\begin{bmatrix} I_{a0} \\ I_{a1} \\ I_{a2} \end{bmatrix} = \frac{1}{3}\begin{bmatrix} 1 & 1 & 1 \\ 1 & a & a^2 \\ 1 & a^2 & a \end{bmatrix}\begin{bmatrix} I_a \\ I_b \\ I_c \end{bmatrix} \tag{4.60}$$

Substituting Eq. (4.58) in Eq. (4.60), we get

$$\begin{bmatrix} I_{a0} \\ I_{a1} \\ I_{a2} \end{bmatrix} = \frac{1}{3}\begin{bmatrix} 1 & 1 & 1 \\ 1 & a & a^2 \\ 1 & a^2 & a \end{bmatrix}\begin{bmatrix} I_a \\ 0 \\ 0 \end{bmatrix} \tag{4.61}$$

From the above equation, we find that

$$I_{a0} = I_{a1} = I_{a2} = \frac{1}{3} I_a \tag{4.62}$$

Rewriting Eq. (4.40)

$$\begin{bmatrix} V_{a0} \\ V_{a1} \\ V_{a2} \end{bmatrix} = \begin{bmatrix} 0 \\ E_a \\ 0 \end{bmatrix} - \begin{bmatrix} Z_s + 3Z_n & 0 & 0 \\ 0 & Z_s & 0 \\ 0 & 0 & Z_s \end{bmatrix}\begin{bmatrix} I_{a0} \\ I_{a1} \\ I_{a2} \end{bmatrix} \tag{4.63}$$

where zero sequence impedance, $Z_0 = Z_s + 3Z_n$
positive sequence impedance, $Z_1 = Z_s$
negative sequence impedance, $Z_2 = Z_s$

$$\begin{bmatrix} V_{a0} \\ V_{a1} \\ V_{a2} \end{bmatrix} = \begin{bmatrix} 0 \\ E_a \\ 0 \end{bmatrix} - \begin{bmatrix} Z_0 & 0 & 0 \\ 0 & Z_1 & 0 \\ 0 & 0 & Z_2 \end{bmatrix}\begin{bmatrix} I_{a0} \\ I_{a1} \\ I_{a2} \end{bmatrix} \tag{4.64}$$

From the above equation

$$V_{a0} = -Z_0 I_{a0} \tag{4.65}$$

$$V_{a1} = E_a - Z_1 I_{a1} \tag{4.66}$$
$$V_{a2} = -Z_2 I_{a2} \tag{4.67}$$

Rewriting Eq. (4.10)

$$\begin{bmatrix} V_a \\ V_b \\ V_c \end{bmatrix} = \begin{bmatrix} 1 & 1 & 1 \\ 1 & a^2 & a \\ 1 & a & a^2 \end{bmatrix} \begin{bmatrix} V_{a0} \\ V_{a1} \\ V_{a2} \end{bmatrix} \tag{4.68}$$

From the above equation

$$V_a = V_{a0} + V_{a1} + V_{a2} \tag{4.69}$$

Substituting Eqs. (4.65), (4.66) and (4.67) in Eq. (4.69), we get

$$V_a = -Z_0 I_{a0} + (E_a - Z_1 I_{a1}) - Z_2 I_{a2} \tag{4.70}$$
$$V_a = E_a - (Z_0 I_{a0} + Z_1 I_{a1} + Z_2 I_{a2}) \tag{4.71}$$

Substituting Eq. (4.62) in Eq. (4.71), we get

$$V_a = E_a - \left(Z_0 \frac{I_a}{3} + Z_1 \frac{I_a}{3} + Z_2 \frac{I_a}{3} \right) \tag{4.72}$$

$$V_a = E_a - \frac{I_a}{3}(Z_0 + Z_1 + Z_2) \tag{4.73}$$

From the boundary conditions (i) $V_a = Z_f I_a$

$$E_a - \frac{I_a}{3}(Z_0 + Z_1 + Z_2) = Z_f I_a$$
$$3E_a - I_a(Z_0 + Z_1 + Z_2) = 3Z_f I_a$$

Therefore the fault current

$$I_f = I_a = \frac{3E_a}{Z_0 + Z_1 + Z_2 + 3Z_f} \tag{4.74}$$

or

From Eq. (4.62)

$$I_{a0} = I_{a1} = I_{a2} = \frac{1}{3} I_a$$

$$I_{a0} = I_{a1} = I_{a2} = \frac{E_a}{Z_0 + Z_1 + Z_2 + 3Z_f} \tag{4.75}$$

Suppose the fault impedance $Z_f = 0$ (direct short-circuit)

$$I_f = I_a = \frac{3E_a}{Z_0 + Z_1 + Z_2} \tag{4.76}$$

Equations (4.62) and (4.76) can be represented by connecting the sequence network in series as shown in the equivalent circuit of Figure 4.15. Thus, for line to ground faults, the Thevenin's impedance to the point of fault is obtained from each sequence network, and the three sequence networks are placed in series. In many practical applications, Z_1 and Z_2 are the same. If the neutral of the synchronous generator is solidly grounded, $Z_n = 0$.

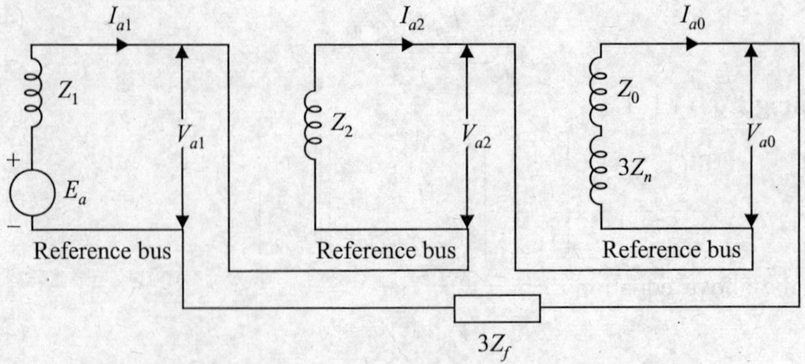

Figure 4.15 Sequence network of single line to ground fault.

EXAMPLE 4.7 A 30 MVA, 11 kV, 3Φ synchronous generator has a direct subtransient reactance of 0.25 p.u. The negative and zero sequence reactance are 0.35 and 0.1 p.u. respectively. The neutral of the generator is solidly grounded. Determine the subtransient current in the generator and the line to line voltages for subtransient conditions when a single line to ground fault occurs at the generator terminals with the generator operating unloaded at rated voltage.

Solution: $E_a = 1$ p.u.

Direct subtransient reactance, $X''_d = Z_1 = j0.25$ p.u.

$$X_2 = Z_2 = j0.35 \text{ p.u.}$$

$$X_0 = Z_0 = j0.1 \text{ p.u.}$$

$$Z_f = 0$$

$$\text{Fault current } I_f = I_a = \frac{3E_a}{Z_0 + Z_1 + Z_2 + 3Z_f}$$

$$= \frac{3 \times 1.0}{j0.1 + j0.25 + j0.35} = -\,j4.2857 \text{ p.u.}$$

$$\text{Base current} = \frac{\text{MVA}_{\text{base}}}{\sqrt{3}\,\text{kV}_b} \times 10^3 = \frac{30}{\sqrt{3} \times 11} \times 10^3 = 1574.59 \text{ A}$$

Fault current in A = Fault current in p.u. (I_f) × base current

Fault current A, $|I_f| = 4.2857 \times 1574.59 = 6748.22$ A

The symmetrical components of the voltages from point a to ground are:

$$I_{a0} = I_{a1} = I_{a2} = \frac{E_a}{Z_0 + Z_1 + Z_2 + 3Z_f} = \frac{1.0}{j0.1 + j0.25 + j0.35} = -\,j1.4286 \text{ p.u.}$$

$$V_{a0} = -Z_0 I_{a0} = -(j0.1)\,(-j1.4286) = -0.143 \text{ p.u.}$$

$$V_{a1} = E_a - Z_1 I_{a1} = 1.0 - (j0.25)\,(-j1.4286) = 0.643 \text{ p.u.}$$

$$V_{a2} = -Z_2 I_{a2} = -(j0.35)\,(-j1.4286) = -0.50 \text{ p.u.}$$

Line to ground voltages are

$$V_a = V_{a0} + V_{a1} + V_{a2} = -0.143 + 0.643 - 0.50 = 0$$

$$V_b = V_{a0} + a^2V_{a1} + aV_{a2}$$

$$= -0.143 + 1\angle{-120°} \times 0.643 + 1\angle 120° \times (-0.50)$$

$$= -0.143 + (-0.5 - j0.866) \times 0.643 + (-0.5 + j0.866) \times (-0.50)$$

$$= -0.215 - j0.989 \text{ p.u.}$$

$$V_c = V_{a0} - aV_{a1} + a^2V_{a2}$$

$$= -0.143 + 1\angle 120° \times 0.643 + 1\angle{-120°} \times (-0.50)$$

$$= -0.143 + (-0.5 + j0.8666) \times 0.643 + (-0.5 - j0.866) \times (-0.50)$$

$$= -0.215 + j0.989 \text{ p.u.}$$

Line to line voltages are

$$V_{ab} = V_a - V_b = 0 - (-0.215 - j0.989) = 0.215 + j0.989$$

$$= 1.012\angle 77.7° \text{ p.u.}$$

$$V_{bc} = V_b - V_c = (-0.215 - j0.989) - (-0.215 + j0.989)$$

$$= 0 - j1.978 = 1.978\angle 270° \text{ p.u.}$$

$$V_{ca} = V_c - V_a = (-0.215 + j0.989) - (0)$$

$$= -0.215 + j0.989 = -1.012\angle 102.3° \text{ p.u.}$$

The above line voltages are expressed in per unit of the base voltage to neutral. Therefore, the post fault line voltages expressed in kV are

$$V_{ab} = 1.012\angle 77.7° \times \frac{11}{\sqrt{3}} = 6.427\ \angle 77.7° \text{ kV}$$

$$V_{bc} = 1.978\angle 270° \times \frac{11}{\sqrt{3}} = 12.562\ \angle 270° \text{ kV}$$

$$V_{ca} = -1.012\angle 102.3° \times \frac{11}{\sqrt{3}} = -\ 6.427\ \angle 102.3° \text{ kV}$$

EXAMPLE 4.8 Determine the fault current and MVA at faulted bus for a line to ground fault at bus 4 as shown in the figure.

G_1 and G_2: 100 MVA, 11 kV, $X^+ = X^- = 15\%$; $X^0 = 5\%$ and $X_n = 6\%$
T_1 and T_2: 100 MVA, 11/220 kV, $X_{\text{leakage}} = 9\%$
L_1 and L_2: $X^+ = X^- = 10\%$; $X^0 = 10\%$ on a base 100 MVA. Consider a fault at a phase.

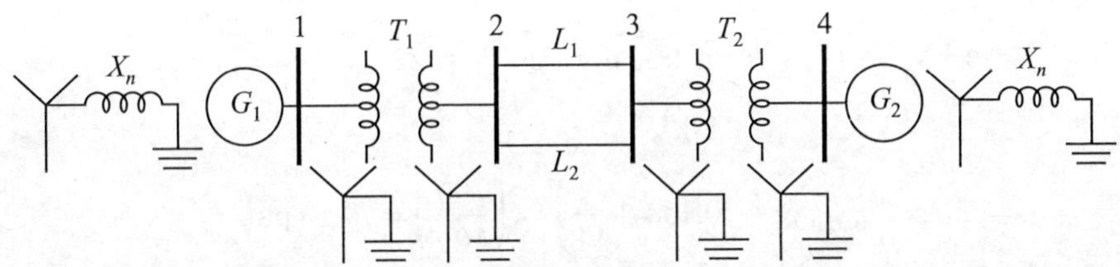

Solution:

Base MVA, $\text{MVA}_{\text{new}} = 100$ MVA

Base kV, $\text{kV}_{\text{new}} = 220$ kV

Positive and negative reactances of transmission lines L_1 and L_2

$X_{\text{p.u.(given)}} = 0.10$ p.u., $\text{MVA}_{\text{given}} = 100$, $\text{MVA}_{\text{new}} = 100$, $\text{kV}_{\text{given}} = 220$, $\text{kV}_{\text{new}} = 220$

$$X_{\text{p.u.(new)}} = X_{\text{p.u.given}} \times \left(\frac{\text{kV}_{\text{given}}}{\text{kV}_{\text{new}}}\right)^2 \times \left(\frac{\text{MVA}_{\text{new}}}{\text{MVA}_{\text{given}}}\right)$$

$$X_{\text{p.u.(new)}} = j0.1 \times \left(\frac{220}{220}\right)^2 \times \left(\frac{100}{100}\right) = j0.1 \text{ p.}$$

Zero reactance of transmission lines L_1 and L_2

$X_{\text{p.u.(given)}} = 0.1$ p.u.

$$X_{\text{p.u.(new)}} = j0.1 \times \left(\frac{220}{220}\right)^2 \times \left(\frac{100}{100}\right) = j0.1 \text{ p.u.}$$

Reactance of transformers T_1 and T_2 (secondary)

$X_{\text{p.u.(given)}} = 0.09$ p.u., $\text{MVA}_{\text{given}} = 100$, $\text{MVA}_{\text{new}} = 100$, $\text{kV}_{\text{given}} = 220$, $\text{kV}_{\text{new}} = 220$

$$X_{\text{p.u.(new)}} = j0.09 \times \left(\frac{220}{220}\right)^2 \times \left(\frac{100}{100}\right) = j0.09 \text{ p.u.}$$

Base kV on LT side of transformer T_1

$$= \text{Base kV on HT side} \times \frac{\text{LT voltage rating}}{\text{HT voltage rating}}$$

$$\text{Base kV on LT side of transformer } T_1 = 220 \times \frac{33}{220} = 33 \text{ kV}$$

$$\text{kV}_{\text{new}} = 33 \text{ kV}$$

Positive and negative reactances of generators G_1 and G_2

$X_{\text{p.u.(given)}} = 0.15$ p.u., $\text{MVA}_{\text{given}} = 100$, $\text{MVA}_{\text{new}} = 100$, $\text{kV}_{\text{given}} = 11$, $\text{kV}_{\text{new}} = ?$

Base kV on LT side of transformer T_1

$$= \text{Base kV on HT side} \times \frac{\text{LT voltage rating}}{\text{HT voltage rating}}$$

$$\text{Base kV on LT side of transformer } T_1 = 220 \times \frac{11}{220} = 11 \text{ kV}$$

$$\text{kV}_{\text{new}} = 11 \text{ kV}$$

$$X_{\text{p.u.(new)}} = j0.15 \times \left(\frac{11}{11}\right)^2 \times \left(\frac{100}{100}\right) = j0.15 \text{ p.u.}$$

Zero reactance of generators G_1 and G_2

$X_{\text{p.u.(given)}} = 0.05$ p.u.

$$X_{\text{p.u.(new)}} = j0.05 \times \left(\frac{11}{11}\right)^2 \times \left(\frac{100}{100}\right) = j0.05 \text{ p.u.}$$

Neutral reactance of generators G_1 and G_2

$X_{\text{p.u.(given)}} = 0.06$ p.u.

$$X_{\text{p.u.(new)}} = j0.06 \times \left(\frac{11}{11}\right)^2 \times \left(\frac{100}{100}\right) = j0.06 \text{ p.u.}$$

Reactance diagram

Positive sequence impedance diagram

Use Thevenin's theorem to find the positive sequence impedance Z_1.

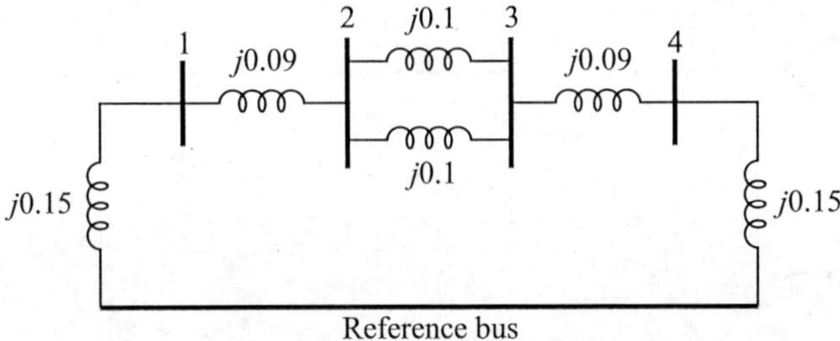

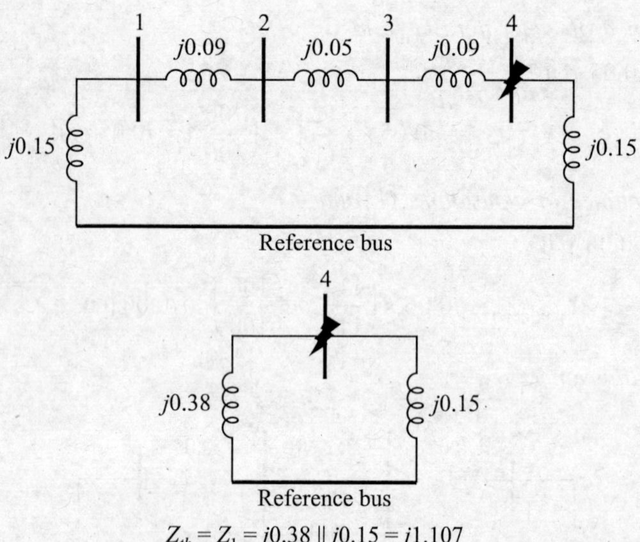

$$Z_{th} = Z_1 = j0.38 \parallel j0.15 = j1.107$$

Negative sequence impedance diagram

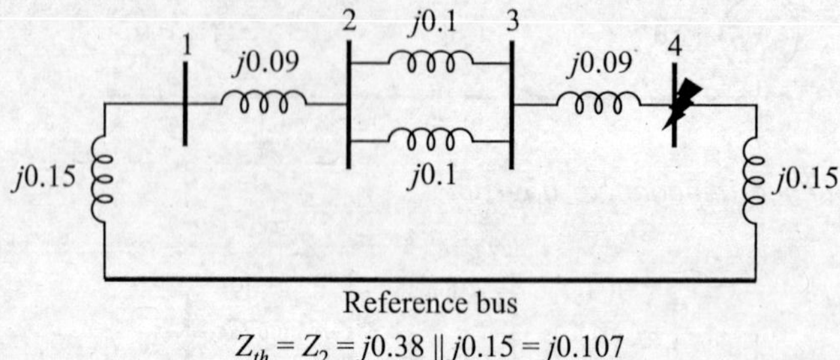

$$Z_{th} = Z_2 = j0.38 \parallel j0.15 = j0.107$$

Zero sequence impedance diagram

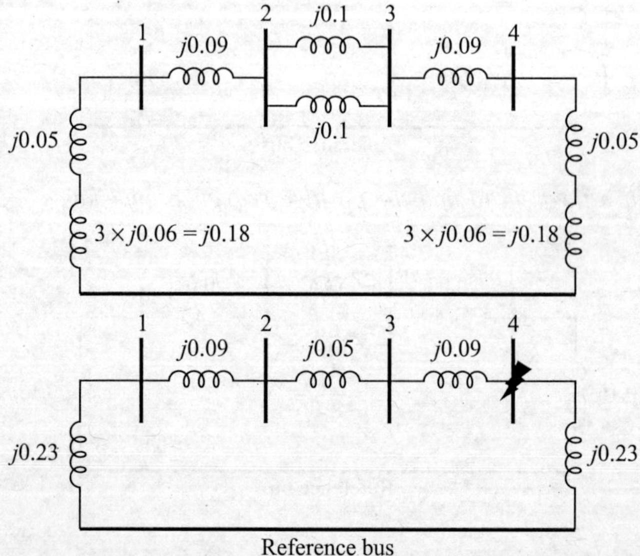

4

$j0.46$ $j0.23$

Reference bus

$$Z_{th} = Z_0 = j0.46 \,||\, j0.23 = j0.1533$$

$$E_a = 1 \text{ p.u.}$$

$$\text{Fault current } I_f = I_a = \frac{3E_a}{Z_0 + Z_1 + Z_2 + 3Z_f}$$

$$= \frac{3 \times 1.0}{j0.1533 + j0.107 + j0.107} = -\,j8.1677 \text{ p.u.}$$

$$\text{Base current at fault point} = \frac{\text{MVA}_{\text{base}}}{\sqrt{3}\text{kV}_\text{b}} \times 10^3 = \frac{100}{\sqrt{3} \times 11} \times 10^3 = 5248.64 \text{ A}$$

Fault current in A = fault current in p.u. (I_f) × base current

Fault current A, $|I_f| = 8.1677 \times 5248.64 = 42.869$ kA

4.5.2 Line to Line Fault (L–L Fault)

Let us consider three-phase circuit diagram of unloaded generator fault through impedance Z_f between phases b and c as shown in Figure 4.16. The neutral of the generator is grounded through impedance. Assume that the generator is initially on no load.

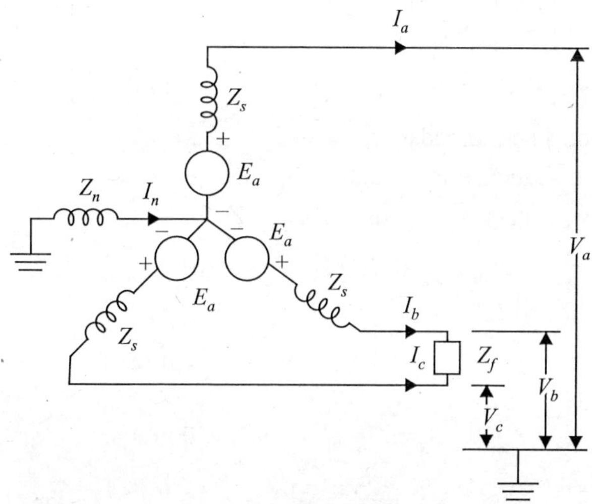

Figure 4.16 Line to line fault between b and c.

The boundary conditions at the fault point are

(i) $V_b - V_c = Z_f I_a$ (4.77)

(ii) $I_b + I_c = 0$ or $I_b = -I_c$ (4.78)

(iii) $I_a = 0$ (4.79)

The symmetrical components of currents from Eq. (4.23) can be rewritten as

$$\begin{bmatrix} I_{a0} \\ I_{a1} \\ I_{a2} \end{bmatrix} = \frac{1}{3}\begin{bmatrix} 1 & 1 & 1 \\ 1 & a & a^2 \\ 1 & a^2 & a \end{bmatrix}\begin{bmatrix} I_a \\ I_b \\ I_c \end{bmatrix} \tag{4.80}$$

Substituting Eqs. (4.78) and (4.79) in Eq. (4.80), we get

$$\begin{bmatrix} I_{a0} \\ I_{a1} \\ I_{a2} \end{bmatrix} = \frac{1}{3}\begin{bmatrix} 1 & 1 & 1 \\ 1 & a & a^2 \\ 1 & a^2 & a \end{bmatrix}\begin{bmatrix} 0 \\ I_b \\ -I_b \end{bmatrix} \tag{4.81}$$

From Eq. (4.81), we find that

$$I_{a0} = 0 \tag{4.82}$$

$$I_{a1} = \frac{1}{3}(a - a^2)I_b \tag{4.83}$$

$$I_{a2} = \frac{1}{3}(a^2 - a)I_b \tag{4.84}$$

Also, from Eqs. (4.83) and (4.84), we get

$$I_{a1} = -I_{a2} \tag{4.85}$$

Rewriting Eq. (4.40)

$$\begin{bmatrix} V_{a0} \\ V_{a1} \\ V_{a2} \end{bmatrix} = \begin{bmatrix} 0 \\ E_a \\ 0 \end{bmatrix} - \begin{bmatrix} Z_s + 3Z_n & 0 & 0 \\ 0 & Z_s & 0 \\ 0 & 0 & Z_s \end{bmatrix}\begin{bmatrix} I_{a0} \\ I_{a1} \\ I_{a2} \end{bmatrix} \tag{4.86}$$

where zero sequence impedance, $Z_0 = Z_s + 3Z_n$

positive sequence impedance, $Z_1 = Z_s$

negative sequence impedance, $Z_2 = Z_s$

$$\begin{bmatrix} V_{a0} \\ V_{a1} \\ V_{a2} \end{bmatrix} = \begin{bmatrix} 0 \\ E_a \\ 0 \end{bmatrix} - \begin{bmatrix} Z_0 & 0 & 0 \\ 0 & Z_1 & 0 \\ 0 & 0 & Z_2 \end{bmatrix}\begin{bmatrix} I_{a0} \\ I_{a1} \\ I_{a2} \end{bmatrix} \tag{4.87}$$

From Eq. (4.87)

$$V_{a0} = -Z_0 I_{a0} = -Z_0 \times 0 = 0 \tag{4.88}$$

$$V_{a1} = E_a - Z_1 I_{a1} \tag{4.89}$$

$$V_{a2} = -Z_2 I_{a2} \tag{4.90}$$

The phase currents are

$$\begin{bmatrix} I_a \\ I_b \\ I_c \end{bmatrix} = \begin{bmatrix} 1 & 1 & 1 \\ 1 & a^2 & a \\ 1 & a & a^2 \end{bmatrix} \begin{bmatrix} I_{a0} \\ I_{a1} \\ I_{a2} \end{bmatrix} \tag{4.91}$$

$$\begin{bmatrix} I_a \\ I_b \\ I_c \end{bmatrix} = \begin{bmatrix} 1 & 1 & 1 \\ 1 & a^2 & a \\ 1 & a & a^2 \end{bmatrix} \begin{bmatrix} 0 \\ I_{a1} \\ -I_{a1} \end{bmatrix} \tag{4.92}$$

From Eq. (4.92)

$$I_a = 0 \tag{4.93}$$

$$I_b = a^2 I_{a1} - aI_{a1} = I_{a1}(a^2 - a) \tag{4.94}$$

$$I_c = aI_{a1} - a^2 I_{a1} = I_{a1}(a - a^2) = -I_b \tag{4.95}$$

Rewriting Eq. (4.10)

$$\begin{bmatrix} V_a \\ V_b \\ V_c \end{bmatrix} = \begin{bmatrix} 1 & 1 & 1 \\ 1 & a^2 & a \\ 1 & a & a^2 \end{bmatrix} \begin{bmatrix} V_{a0} \\ V_{a1} \\ V_{a2} \end{bmatrix} \tag{4.96}$$

Substituting Eq. (4.88) in Eq. (4.96), we get

$$\begin{bmatrix} V_a \\ V_b \\ V_c \end{bmatrix} = \begin{bmatrix} 1 & 1 & 1 \\ 1 & a^2 & a \\ 1 & a & a^2 \end{bmatrix} \begin{bmatrix} 0 \\ V_{a1} \\ V_{a2} \end{bmatrix} \tag{4.97}$$

From Eq. (4.97)

$$V_a = V_{a1} + V_{a2} \tag{4.98}$$

$$V_b = a^2 V_{a1} + aV_{a2} \tag{4.99}$$

$$V_c = aV_{a1} + a^2 V_{a2} \tag{4.100}$$

From the boundary condition (i) $V_b - V_c = Z_f I_a$

Substituting Eqs. (4.99) and (4.100) in the above boundary conditions, we get

$$(a^2 V_{a1} + aV_{a2}) - (aV_{a1} + a^2 V_{a2}) = Z_f I_a$$

$$(a^2 - a)\,(V_{a1} - V_{a2}) = Z_f I_a \tag{4.101}$$

Substituting the Eq. (4.94) in Eq. (4.101), we get

$$(a^2 - a)\,(V_{a1} - V_{a2}) = Z_f (a^2 - a) I_{a1}$$

$$V_{a1} - V_{a2} = Z_f I_{a1} \tag{4.102}$$

Substituting Eqs. (4.89) and (4.90) in Eq. (4.102), we get

$$E_a - Z_1 I_{a1} - (-Z_2 I_{a2}) = Z_f I_{a1}$$

$$E_a = (Z_1 + Z_2 + Z_f) I_{a1}$$

$$I_{a1} = \frac{E_a}{Z_1 + Z_2 + Z_f} \tag{4.103}$$

$$I_{a2} = -I_{a1} \tag{4.104}$$

$$I_{a0} = 0 \tag{4.105}$$

Therefore fault current

$$I_f = I_b = -I_c = I_{a1}(a - a^2)$$

$$I_f = I_b = -I_c = I_{a1}(-j\sqrt{3})$$

Substituting Eq. (4.103) in the above equation, we get

$$I_f = I_b = -I_c = (-j\sqrt{3})\frac{E_a}{Z_1 + Z_2 + Z_f} \tag{4.106}$$

Equations (4.85) and (4.103) can be represented by connecting the positive sequence network in parallel with negative sequence network through fault impedance as shown in the equivalent circuit of Figure 4.17. In many practical applications, Z_1 and Z_2 are the same. For bolted fault, $Z_f = 0$.

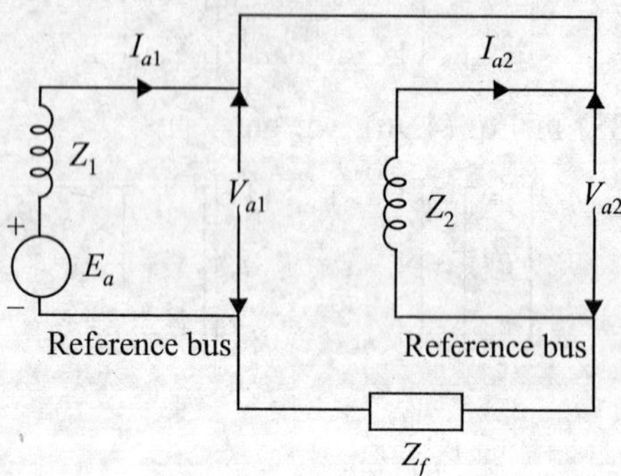

Figure 4.17 Sequence network of line to line fault.

EXAMPLE 4.9 Determine the subtransient current and the line to line voltages at the fault under subtransient conditions when a line to line fault occurs at the terminals of the generator described in Example 4.7. Assume that the generator is unloaded and operating at rated terminal voltage when the fault occurs.

Solution: $E_a = 1$ p.u.

Direct subtransient reactance, $X''_d = Z_1 = j0.25$ p.u.

$$X_2 = Z_2 = j0.35 \text{ p.u.}$$

$$Z_f = 0$$

$$I_f = I_b = -I_c = (-j\sqrt{3})\frac{E_a}{Z_1 + Z_2 + Z_f}$$

$$\text{Fault current, } I_f = I_b = -I_c = (-j\sqrt{3})\frac{1.0}{j0.25 + j0.35} = -2.887 \text{ p.u.}$$

$$\text{Base current} = \frac{\text{MVA}_{\text{base}}}{\sqrt{3}\text{kV}_b} \times 10^3 = \frac{30}{\sqrt{3} \times 11} \times 10^3 = 1574.59 \text{ A}$$

Fault current in A = fault current in p.u. (I_f) × base current

Fault current in A, $|I_f| = 2.887 \times 1574.59 = 4545.84$ A

$$I_{a1} = -I_{a2} = \frac{E_a}{Z_1 + Z_2 + Z_f} = \frac{1.0}{j0.25 + j0.35} = -j1.667 \text{ p.u.}$$

$$I_{a0} = 0$$

$$V_{a0} = -Z_0 I_{a0} = 0 \text{ p.u.}$$

$$V_{a1} = V_{a2} = E_a - Z_1 I_{a1} = 1.0 - (j0.25)(-j1.667) = 0.584 \text{ p.u.}$$

Line to ground voltages are

$$V_a = V_{a0} + V_{a1} + V_{a2} = 0 + 0.584 + 0.584 = 1.168 \text{ p.u.}$$

$$\begin{aligned} V_b &= V_{a0} + a^2 V_{a1} + a V_{a2} \\ &= 0 + 1\angle -120^\circ \times 0.584 + 1\angle 120^\circ \times (0.584) \\ &= 0 + (-0.5 - j0.866) \times 0.584 + (-0.5 + j0.866) \times (0.584) \\ &= -0.584 \text{ p.u.} \end{aligned}$$

$$\begin{aligned} V_c &= V_{a0} - a V_{a1} + a^2 V_{a2} \\ &= 0 + 1\angle 120^\circ \times 0.584 + 1\angle -120^\circ \times (0.584) \\ &= 0 + (-0.5 + j0.866) \times 0.584 + (-0.5 - j0.866) \times (0.584) \\ &= -0.584 \text{ p.u.} \end{aligned}$$

Line to line voltages are

$$\begin{aligned} V_{ab} = V_a - V_b = 1.168 + 0.584 &= 1.752\angle 0^\circ \text{ p.u.} \\ &= 1.752\angle 0^\circ \times \frac{11}{\sqrt{3}} = 11.127\angle 0^\circ \text{ kV} \end{aligned}$$

$$V_{bc} = V_b - V_c = -0.584 + 0.584 = 0 \text{ kV}$$

$$\begin{aligned} V_{ca} = V_c - V_a = -0.584 - 1.168 &= 1.752\angle 180^\circ \text{ p.u.} \\ &= 1.752\angle 180^\circ \times \frac{11}{\sqrt{3}} = 11.127\angle 180^\circ \text{ kV} \end{aligned}$$

EXAMPLE 4.10 Determine the fault current at the faulted bus for a line to line fault which occurs between phases 'b' and 'c' at bus 4 as shown in the figure.

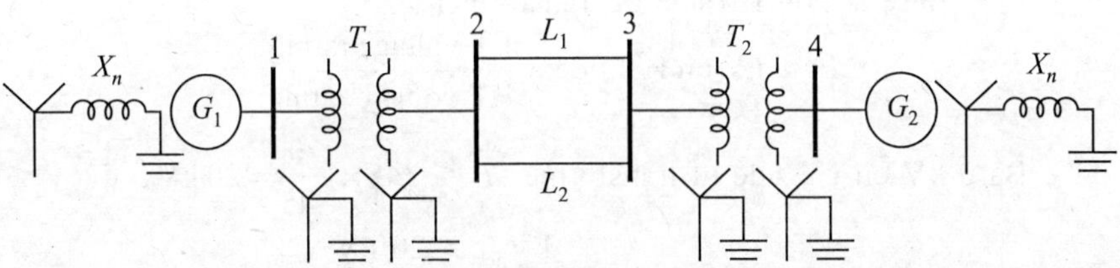

X_n G_1 1 T_1 2 L_1 L_2 3 T_2 4 G_2 X_n

G_1 and G_2 : 100 MVA, 20 kV, $X^+ = X^- = 15\%$; $X^0 = 4\%$ and $X_n = 6\%$
T_1 and T_2 : 100 MVA, 20/345 kV, $X_{\text{leakage}} = 9\%$
L_1 and L_2 : $X^+ = X^- = 10\%$; $X^0 = 40\%$ on a base 100 MVA.

Solution:

Base MVA, $\text{MVA}_{\text{new}} = 100$ MVA
Base kV, $\text{kV}_{\text{new}} = 345$ kV

Positive and negative reactances of transmission lines L_1 and L_2

$X_{\text{p.u.(given)}} = 0.10$ p.u., $\text{MVA}_{\text{given}} = 100$, $\text{MVA}_{\text{new}} = 100$, $\text{kV}_{\text{given}} = 345$, $\text{kV}_{\text{new}} = 345$

$$X_{\text{p.u.(new)}} = X_{\text{p.u.given}} \times \left(\frac{\text{kV}_{\text{given}}}{\text{kV}_{\text{new}}}\right)^2 \times \left(\frac{\text{MVA}_{\text{new}}}{\text{MVA}_{\text{given}}}\right)$$

$$X_{\text{p.u.(new)}} = j0.1 \times \left(\frac{345}{345}\right)^2 \times \left(\frac{100}{100}\right) = j0.1 \text{ p.u.}$$

Zero reactance of transmission lines L_1 and L_2

$X_{\text{p.u.(given)}} = 0.4$ p.u.

$$X_{\text{p.u.(new)}} = j0.4 \times \left(\frac{345}{345}\right)^2 \times \left(\frac{100}{100}\right) = j0.4 \text{ p.u.}$$

Reactance of transformers T_1 and T_2 (secondary)

$X_{\text{p.u.(given)}} = 0.09$ p.u., $\text{MVA}_{\text{given}} = 100$, $\text{MVA}_{\text{new}} = 100$, $\text{kV}_{\text{given}} = 345$
$\text{kV}_{\text{new}} = 345$

$$X_{\text{p.u.(new)}} = j0.09 \times \left(\frac{345}{345}\right)^2 \times \left(\frac{100}{100}\right) = j0.09 \text{ p.u.}$$

Base kV on LT side of transformer T_1

$$= \text{Base kV on HT side} \times \frac{\text{LT voltage rating}}{\text{HT voltage rating}}$$

$$\text{Base kV on LT side of transformer } T_1 = 345 \times \frac{20}{345} = 20 \text{ kV}$$

$$\text{kV}_{\text{new}} = 20 \text{ kV}$$

Positive and negative reactances of generators G_1 and G_2

$X_{\text{p.u.(given)}} = 0.15$ p.u., $\text{MVA}_{\text{given}} = 100$, $\text{MVA}_{\text{new}} = 100$, $\text{kV}_{\text{given}} = 20$, $\text{kV}_{\text{new}} = ?$

Base kV on LT side of transformer T_1

$$= \text{Base kV on HT side} \times \frac{\text{LT voltage rating}}{\text{HT voltage rating}}$$

$$\text{Base kV on LT side of transformer } T_1 = 345 \times \frac{20}{345} = 20 \text{ kV}$$

$$\text{kV}_{\text{new}} = 20 \text{ kV}$$

$$X_{\text{p.u.(new)}} = j0.15 \times \left(\frac{20}{20}\right)^2 \times \left(\frac{100}{100}\right) = j0.15 \text{ p.u.}$$

Zero reactance of generators G_1 and G_2

$X_{\text{p.u.(given)}} = 0.04$ p.u.

$$X_{\text{p.u.(new)}} = j0.04 \times \left(\frac{20}{20}\right)^2 \times \left(\frac{100}{100}\right) = j0.04 \text{ p.u.}$$

Neutral reactance of generators G_1 and G_2

$X_{\text{p.u.(given)}} = 0.06$ p.u.

$$X_{\text{p.u.(new)}} = j0.06 \times \left(\frac{20}{20}\right)^2 \times \left(\frac{100}{100}\right) = j0.06 \text{ p.u.}$$

Reactance diagram

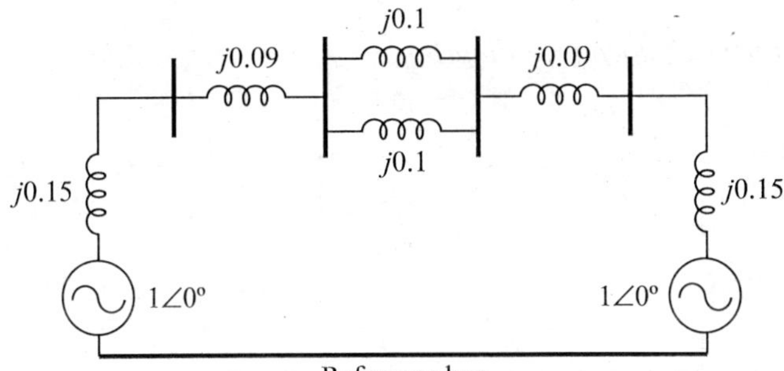

Positive sequence impedance diagram

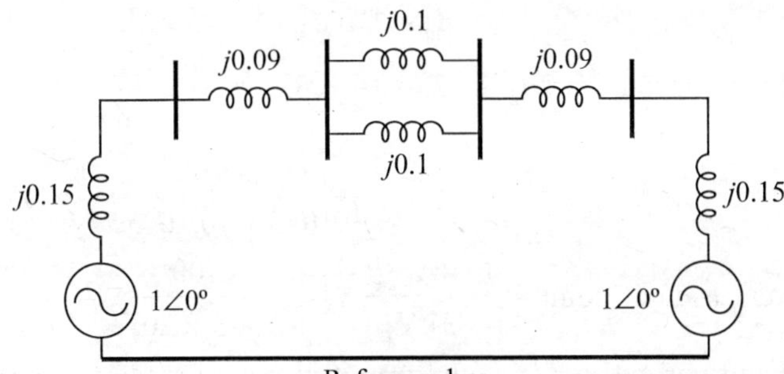

Use Thevenin's theorem to find the positive sequence impedance Z_1.

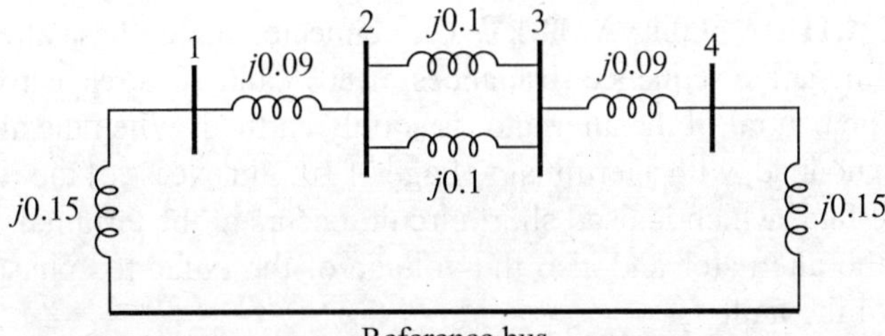

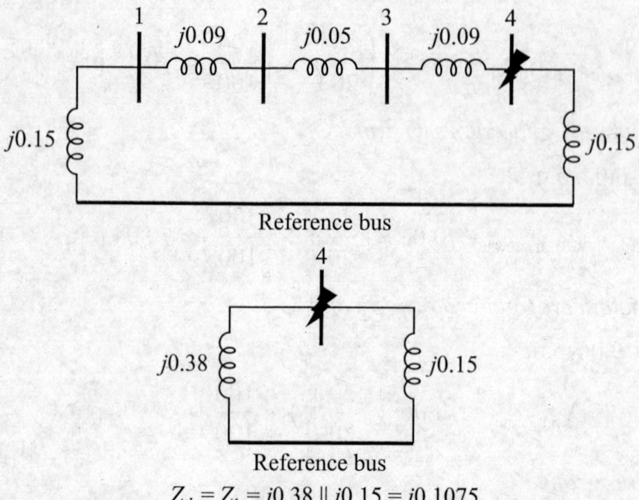

$$Z_{th} = Z_1 = j0.38 \parallel j0.15 = j0.1075$$

Negative sequence impedance diagram

1 2 3 4

j0.09 j0.1 j0.09

j0.1

j0.15 j0.15

Reference bus

$$Z_{th} = Z_2 = j0.38 \parallel j0.15 = j0.1075$$

$$E_a = 1 \text{ p.u.}$$

$$\text{Fault current, } I_f = I_b = -I_c = (-j\sqrt{3})\frac{E_a}{Z_1 + Z_2 + Z_f}$$

$$= \frac{-j\sqrt{3}(1.0)}{j0.1075 + j0.1075} = -8.056 \text{ p.u.}$$

$$\text{Base current at fault point} = \frac{\text{MVA}_{\text{base}}}{\sqrt{3}\text{kV}_b} \times 10^3 = \frac{100}{\sqrt{3} \times 20} \times 10^3 = 2886.75 \text{ A}$$

Fault current in A = fault current in p.u. (I_f) × base current

Fault current in A, $|I_f| = 8.056 \times 2886.75 = 23.254$ kA

EXAMPLE 4.11 A 600 kVA, 11 kV, star connected three-phase alternator has positive and negative sequence reactances of 80% and 40% respectively on its own base. The neutral of the alternator is solidly earthed. When the alternator is operating on no load, with a terminal voltage of 10% in excess of the rated value, a line to line fault which is dead short circuit, occurs at the terminal. First fault currents in the alternator and also the voltage of the unfaulted phase after the occurrence of the fault.

Solution: Referring to Figure 4.16, we shall assume that the fault occurs across the phases b and c, and that the phase 'a' is the unfaulted phase; the generated voltage (on open circuit) of phase a is E_a = 1.1 p.u., taking the rated voltage as 1 p.u.

1 p.u = 11 kV (line to line)

$$\frac{11}{\sqrt{3}} \text{kV per phase}$$

E_a = 1.1 p.u.

$$Z_1 = j0.8;\ Z_2 = j0.4$$

$$\text{Fault current } I_f = I_b = -I_c = \frac{(-j\sqrt{3})E_a}{Z_1 + Z_2} = \frac{(-j\sqrt{3}) \times 1.1}{j0.8 + j0.4} = -1.59 \text{ p.u.}$$

$$\text{Base current at fault point} = \frac{\text{MVA}_{\text{base}}}{\sqrt{3}\text{kV}_b} \times 10^3 = \frac{600}{\sqrt{3} \times 11} \times 10^3 = 31.49 \text{ A}$$

Fault current in A = fault current in p.u. (I_f) × base current

Fault current in A, $|I_f|$ = 1.59 × 31.49 = 50 A

4.5.3 Double Line to Ground Fault (L–L–G Fault)

Figure 4.18 shows the three-phase circuit diagram of unloaded generator with a fault on phases b and c through impedance Z_f to ground. The neutral of the generator is grounded through impedance. Assume the generator is initially on no load.

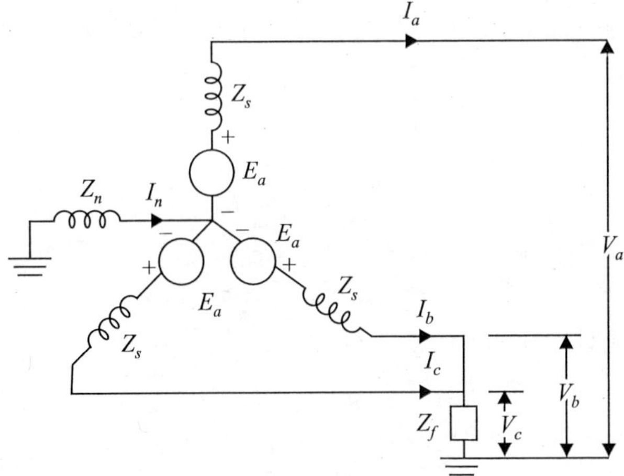

Figure 4.18 Double line to ground fault between b and c.

The boundary conditions at the fault point are

(i) $V_b = V_c = Z_f(I_b + I_c)$ (4.107)

(ii) $I_b + I_c = I_f$ (4.108)

(iii) $I_a = 0$ (4.109)

The symmetrical components of current from Eq. (4.12) can be rewritten as

$$\begin{bmatrix} V_{a0} \\ V_{a1} \\ V_{a2} \end{bmatrix} = \frac{1}{3}\begin{bmatrix} 1 & 1 & 1 \\ 1 & a & a^2 \\ 1 & a^2 & a \end{bmatrix}\begin{bmatrix} V_a \\ V_b \\ V_c \end{bmatrix} \quad (4.110)$$

Substituting $V_b = V_c$ in Eq. (4.110)

$$\begin{bmatrix} V_{a0} \\ V_{a1} \\ V_{a2} \end{bmatrix} = \frac{1}{3}\begin{bmatrix} 1 & 1 & 1 \\ 1 & a & a^2 \\ 1 & a^2 & a \end{bmatrix}\begin{bmatrix} V_a \\ V_b \\ V_b \end{bmatrix}$$

From the above equation we find that

$$V_{a0} = \frac{1}{3}(V_a + V_b + V_b) = \frac{1}{3}(V_a + 2V_b)$$

$$V_{a1} = \frac{1}{3}(V_a + aV_b + a^2V_b) = \frac{1}{3}(V_a + (a + a^2)V_b) = \frac{1}{3}(V_a - V_b)$$

$$V_{a2} = \frac{1}{3}(V_a + a^2V_b + aV_b) = \frac{1}{3}(V_a + (a^2 + a)V_b) = \frac{1}{3}(V_a - V_b)$$

$$V_{a1} = V_{a2} \quad (4.111)$$

The phase currents are

$$\begin{bmatrix} I_a \\ I_b \\ I_c \end{bmatrix} = \begin{bmatrix} 1 & 1 & 1 \\ 1 & a^2 & a \\ 1 & a & a^2 \end{bmatrix}\begin{bmatrix} I_{a0} \\ I_{a1} \\ I_{a2} \end{bmatrix}$$

From the above equation

$$I_a = I_{a0} + I_{a1} + I_{a2}$$

$$I_b = I_{a0} + a^2I_{a1} + aI_{a2}$$

$$I_c = I_{a0} + aI_{a1} + a^2I_{a2}$$

From the boundary condition

$$\begin{aligned} I_f = I_b + I_c &= (I_{a0} + a^2I_{a1} + aI_{a2}) + (I_{a0} + aI_{a1} + a^2I_{a2}) \\ &= 2I_{a0} + (a^2 + a)I_{a1} + (a + a^2)I_{a2} \\ &= 2I_{a0} + (-1)I_{a1} + (-1)I_{a2} \end{aligned}$$

$$I_f = 2I_{a0} - (I_{a1} + I_{a2}) \quad (4.112)$$

From the boundary condition

$$I_a = 0$$

$$I_a = I_{a0} + I_{a1} + I_{a2}$$
$$0 = I_{a0} + I_{a1} + I_{a2}$$

or

$$I_{a1} + I_{a2} = -I_{a0} \tag{4.113}$$

Substituting Eq. (4.112) in Eq. (4.111), we get

$$I_f = I_b + I_c = 2I_{a0} + I_{a0} = 3I_{a0}$$

From the boundary condition

$$V_b = V_c = Z_f(I_b + I_c)$$
$$V_b = V_c = 3Z_f I_{a0} \tag{4.114}$$

Rewriting the Eq. (4.10)

$$\begin{bmatrix} V_a \\ V_b \\ V_c \end{bmatrix} = \begin{bmatrix} 1 & 1 & 1 \\ 1 & a^2 & a \\ 1 & a & a^2 \end{bmatrix} \begin{bmatrix} V_{a0} \\ V_{a1} \\ V_{a2} \end{bmatrix}$$

$$V_a = V_{a0} + V_{a1} + V_{a2}$$
$$V_b = V_{a0} + a^2 V_{a1} + aV_{a2}$$

but $\quad V_{a1} = V_{a2}$

$$V_b = V_{a0} + a^2 V_{a1} + aV_{a1}$$
$$V_b = V_{a0} + (a^2 + a)V_{a1}$$
$$V_b = V_{a0} - V_{a1} \tag{4.115}$$

Equating Eqs. (4.114) and (4.115)

$$V_{a0} - V_{a1} = 3Z_f I_{a0} \tag{4.116}$$

Rewriting Eq. (4.40)

$$\begin{bmatrix} V_{a0} \\ V_{a1} \\ V_{a2} \end{bmatrix} = \begin{bmatrix} 0 \\ E_a \\ 0 \end{bmatrix} - \begin{bmatrix} Z_s + 3Z_n & 0 & 0 \\ 0 & Z_s & 0 \\ 0 & 0 & Z_s \end{bmatrix} \begin{bmatrix} I_{a0} \\ I_{a1} \\ I_{a2} \end{bmatrix}$$

where zero sequence impedance, $Z_0 = Z_s + 3Z_n$
positive sequence impedance, $Z_1 = Z_s$
negative sequence impedance, $Z_2 = Z_s$

$$\begin{bmatrix} V_{a0} \\ V_{a1} \\ V_{a2} \end{bmatrix} = \begin{bmatrix} 0 \\ E_a \\ 0 \end{bmatrix} - \begin{bmatrix} Z_0 & 0 & 0 \\ 0 & Z_1 & 0 \\ 0 & 0 & Z_2 \end{bmatrix} \begin{bmatrix} I_{a0} \\ I_{a1} \\ I_{a2} \end{bmatrix}$$

From the above equation

$$V_{a0} = -Z_0 I_{a0} \tag{4.117}$$

$$V_{a1} = E_a - Z_1 I_{a1} \tag{4.118}$$

$$V_{a2} = -Z_2 I_{a2} \tag{4.119}$$

Substituting Eqs. (4.117) and (4.118) in Eq. (4.116), we get

$$-Z_0 I_{a0} - (E_a - Z_1 I_{a1}) = 3Z_f I_{a0}$$

$$-Z_0 I_{a0} - E_a + Z_1 I_{a1} - 3Z_f I_{a0} = 0$$

$$-I_{a0}(Z_0 + 3Z_f) = E_a - Z_1 I_{a1}$$

$$I_{a0} = \frac{-E_a + Z_1 I_{a1}}{Z_0 + 3Z_f} \tag{4.120}$$

From Eq. (4.111)

$$V_{a1} = V_{a2}$$

$$E_a - Z_1 I_{a1} = -Z_2 I_{a2}$$

$$I_{a2} = \frac{-E_a + Z_1 I_{a1}}{Z_2} \tag{4.121}$$

From Eq. (4.113)

$$I_{a1} = -I_{a0} - I_{a2}$$

$$I_{a1} = -\left(\frac{-E_a + Z_1 I_{a1}}{Z_0 + 3Z_f}\right) - \left(\frac{-E_a + Z_1 I_{a1}}{Z_2}\right)$$

$$I_{a1} = \frac{E_a}{Z_1 + \dfrac{Z_2(Z_0 + 3Z_f)}{Z_2 + Z_0 + 3Z_f}} \tag{4.122}$$

Equations (4.119) to (4.121) can be represented by connecting the positive sequence impedance in series with the parallel combination of negative sequence and zero sequence networks as shown in the equivalent circuit of Figure 4.19. The value of I_{a1} found from Eq. (4.121) is substituted in Eqs. (4.119) and (4.120), and I_{a0} and I_{a2} are found. Finally, the fault current is calculated from

$$I_f = I_b + I_c = 3I_{a0} \tag{4.123}$$

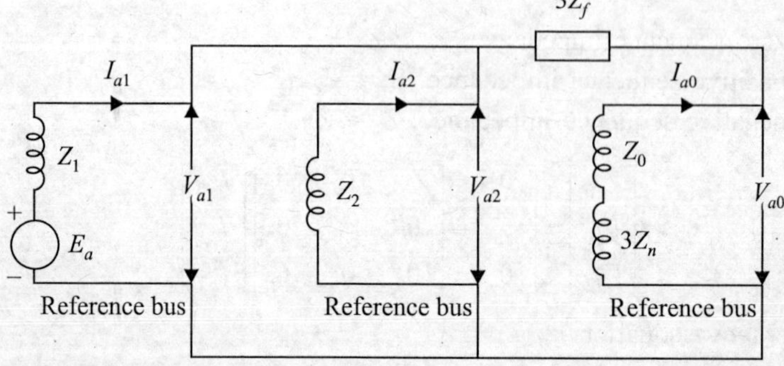

Figure 4.19 Sequence network of double line to ground fault.

EXAMPLE 4.12 Determine the subtransient current and the line to line voltages at the fault under subtransient conditions when double line to ground fault occurs at the terminals of the generator described in Example 4.7. Assume that the generator is unloaded and operating at rated terminal voltage when the fault occurs.

Solution:

$$E_a = 1 \text{ p.u.}$$

Direct subtransient reactance, $X_d'' = Z_1 = j0.25$ p.u.

$$X_2 = Z_2 = j0.35 \text{ p.u.}$$

$$X_0 = Z_0 = j0.1 \text{ p.u.}$$

$$Z_f = 0$$

$$I_{a1} = \frac{E_a}{Z_1 + \dfrac{Z_2(Z_0 + 3Z_f)}{Z_2 + Z_0 + 3Z_f}} = \frac{1.0}{j0.25 + \dfrac{j0.35(j0.1 + 0)}{j0.35 + j0.1 + 0}} = -\,j3.05 \text{ p.u.}$$

$$I_{a2} = \frac{-E_a + Z_1 I_{a1}}{Z_2} = \frac{-1.0 + (j0.25)\,(-j3.05)}{j0.35} = j0.678 \text{ p.u.}$$

$$I_{a0} = \frac{-E_a + Z_1 I_{a1}}{Z_0 + 3Z_f} = \frac{-1.0 + (j0.25)\,(-j3.05)}{j0.1} = j2.375$$

$$I_f = I_b + I_c = 3I_{a0} = 3 \times j2.375 = j7.125 \text{ p.u.}$$

$$\text{Base current} = \frac{\text{MVA}_{\text{base}}}{\sqrt{3}\,\text{kV}_b} \times 10^3 = \frac{30}{\sqrt{3} \times 11} \times 10^3 = 1574.59 \text{ A}$$

Fault current in A = fault current in p.u. (I_f) × base current

Fault current in A, $|I_f| = 7.125 \times 1574.59 = 11.22$ kA

$$I_{a0} = I_{a0} + I_{a1} + I_{a2}$$

$$= j2.37 - j3.05 + j0.68 = 0$$

$$I_b = I_{a0} + a^2 I_{a1} + a I_{a2} = -3.229 + j3.555$$

$$I_c = I_{a0} + a I_{a1} + a^2 I_{a2} = 3.229 + j3.555$$

$$V_{a0} = V_{a1} = V_{a2} = E_a - Z_1 I_{a1} = 1.0 - (j0.25)\,(-j3.05) = 0.237 \text{ p.u.}$$

Line to ground voltages are

$$V_a = V_{a0} + V_{a1} + V_{a2}$$

$$= 0.237 + 0.237 + 0.237 = 0.711 \text{ p.u.}$$

$$V_b = 0$$

$$V_c = 0$$

Line to line voltages are

$$V_{ab} = V_a - V_b = 0.711 \text{ p.u.} = 0.711 \times \frac{11}{\sqrt{3}} = 4.515\angle 0° \text{ kV}$$

$$V_{bc} = V_b - V_c = 0 \text{ kV}$$

$$V_{ca} = V_c - V_a = -0.711 \text{ p.u.} = -0.711 \times \frac{11}{\sqrt{3}} = -4.515\angle 180° \text{ kV}$$

EXAMPLE 4.13 A three-phase generator rated 11 kV, 20 MVA has a solidly grounded neutral. Its positive, negative and zero sequence reactances are 60%, 25% and 15% respectively.

(i) Determine the value of reactance that should be placed in generator neutral such that the current for single line to ground fault does not exceed the rated current.

(ii) What value of resistance in the neutral will serve the same purpose?

Solution:

(i) $E_a = 1$ p.u., $Z_1 = j0.60$ p.u., $Z_2 = j0.25$ p.u., $Z_0 = j0.15$ p.u.

$$I_f = \frac{3E_a}{Z_0 + Z_1 + Z_2 + 3Z_n}$$

$$= \frac{3 \times 1.0}{j0.15 + j0.60 + j0.25 + j3X_n} = \frac{3}{j(1.0 + 3X_n)}$$

$$= \frac{-j3}{1.0 + 3X_n} = \frac{3\angle -90°}{1.0 + 3X_n}$$

where X_n is the reactance connected to the neutral. Since the rated current is 1.0 p.u., therefore, ground fault current is also 1.0 p.u.

$$|I_f| = 1.0 = \frac{3}{1.0 + 3X_n}$$

$$X_n = 0.666 \text{ p.u.}$$

$$X_n \text{ (in Ohm)} = X_n \text{ p.u.} \times \frac{\text{kV}_b^2}{\text{MVA}_b}$$

$$= 0.66 \times \frac{11^2}{20} = 4\,\Omega$$

(ii) To find R_n

$$I_f = \frac{3E_a}{Z_0 + Z_1 + Z_2 + 3R_n}$$

$$= \frac{3 \times 1.0}{j0.15 + j0.60 + j0.25 + 3R_n}$$

$$= \frac{3}{3R_n + j1.0}$$

where R_n is the reactance connected to the neutral. Since the rated current is 1.0 p.u., therefore, ground fault current is also 1.0 p.u.

$$|I_f| = 1.0 = \frac{3}{j1.0 + 3R_n}$$

$$1.0 = \frac{3}{\sqrt{1.0 + 9R_n^2}}$$

$$R_n = 0.9428 \text{ p.u.}$$

$$R_n \text{ (in Ohm)} = R_n \text{ p.u.} \times \frac{\text{kV}_b^2}{\text{MVA}_b}$$

$$= 0.9428 \times \frac{11^2}{20} = 5.7\ \Omega$$

$$R_n = 5.7\ \Omega$$

EXAMPLE 4.14 An alternator of negligible resistance, with solidly grounded neutral having rated voltage at no load condition is subjected to different types of fault at its terminal. The p.u. values of the magnitude of the fault currents are (i) three-phase fault = 4.0 p.u. (ii) line to ground fault = 4.2857 p.u. (iii) line to line fault = 2.8868 p.u. Determine the p.u. values of the sequence reactances of the machine.

Solution:

(i) Three-phase fault, I_f = 4.0 p.u.

$$E_a = E_g' = E_g'' = 1.0 \text{ p.u.}$$

$$|I_f| = \frac{|E_a|}{X_d'}$$

$$X_d' = \frac{|E_a|}{|I_f|} = \frac{1.0}{4.0} = 0.25 \text{ p.u.}$$

$$Z_1 = X_d' = 0.25 \text{ p.u.}$$

(ii) Line to line fault, I_f = 2.8868 p.u.

$$I_f = (-j\sqrt{3}) \frac{E_a}{Z_1 + Z_2}$$

$$I_f = (-j\sqrt{3}) \frac{1.0}{j0.25 + jZ_2}$$

$$|I_f| = \frac{\sqrt{3}}{0.25 + Z_2}$$

$$2.8868 = \frac{\sqrt{3}}{0.25 + Z_2}$$

$$0.25 + Z_2 = \frac{\sqrt{3}}{2.8868}$$

$$0.25 + Z_2 = 0.5999$$

$$Z_2 = 0.5999 - 0.25 = 0.35$$
$$Z_2 = 0.35 \text{ p.u.}$$

(iii) Single line to ground fault, $I_f = 4.2857$ p.u.

$$I_f = \frac{3E_a}{Z_0 + Z_1 + Z_2}$$

$$Z_0 + Z_1 + Z_2 = \frac{|3E_a|}{|I_f|}$$

$$Z_0 + 0.25 + 0.35 = \frac{3}{4.2857}$$

$$Z_0 = 0.7 - 0.25 - 0.35 = 0.1$$
$$Z_0 = 0.1 \text{ p.u.}$$

Review Questions

Part-A

1. What are the symmetrical components of a three-phase system?
2. What are the positive sequence components?
3. What are the negative sequence components?
4. What are the zero sequence components?
5. What is the sequence operator?
6. Write down the equations to convert the symmetrical components into the unbalanced phase currents. (or) How to determine the unbalanced currents from the symmetrical currents?
7. Write down the equations to convert the unbalanced phase currents into symmetrical components. (or) How to determine the symmetrical currents from the unbalanced currents?
8. What are the sequence impedance and sequence network?

Part-B

1. The phase voltages across a certain load are given as follows

$$V_a = 176 - j132 \text{ V}$$
$$V_b = -128 - j96 \text{ V}$$
$$V_c = -160 + j100 \text{ V}$$

Compute the positive, negative and zero sequence components of voltage.

2. A balanced delta connected load is connected to a three-phase system and a current of 15 A is supplied to it. If the fuse of one of the lines melts, compute the symmetrical components of line currents.

3. Draw the zero sequence network of the power system as shown in the figure below.

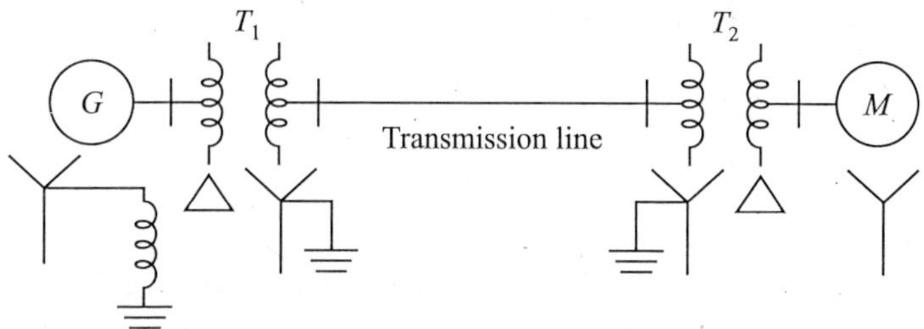

4. Draw the zero sequence network of the power system as shown in the figure below.

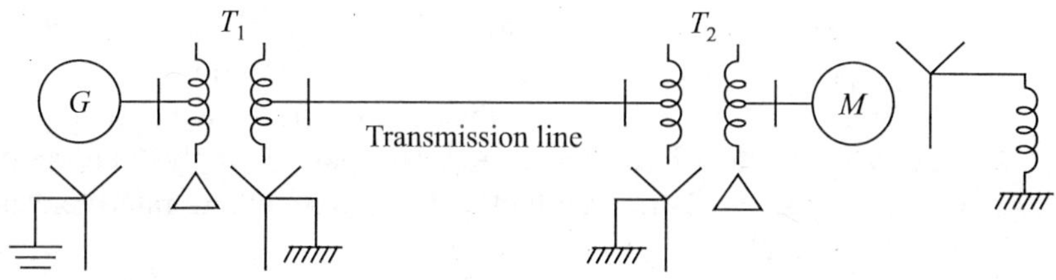

5. Draw the zero sequence network of the power system as shown in the figure below. Data are given below.

G: $X_{g0} = 0.05$ p.u.	M: $X_{m0} = 0.03$ p.u.
T_1: $X_{T1} = 0.12$ p.u.	T_2: $X_{T2} = 0.10$ p.u.
Line 1: $X_{L10} = 0.70$ p.u.	Line 2: $X_{L20} = 0.70$ p.u.

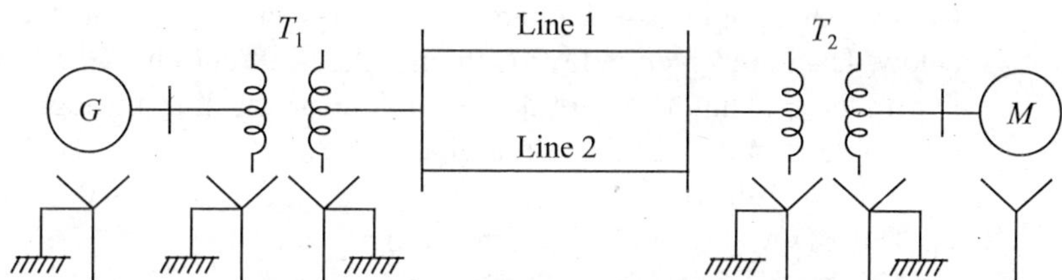

6. A 50 MVA, 11 kV, synchronous generator has a subtransient reactance of 20%. The generator supplies two motors over a transmission line with transformers at both ends as shown in the figure below. The motors have rated inputs of 30 MVA and 15 MVA, both 10 kV, with 25% subtransient reactance. The three-phase transformers are both rated 60 MVA, 10.8/121 kV, with leakage reactance of 10% each. Assume zero sequence reactance for the generator and motors of 6% each. The current limiting reactors of 2.5 Ω each are connected in the neutral of the generator and the motor number is 2. The zero sequence reactance of the transmission line is 300 Ω. The series reactance of the line is 100 Ω. Draw the positive, negative and zero sequence networks.

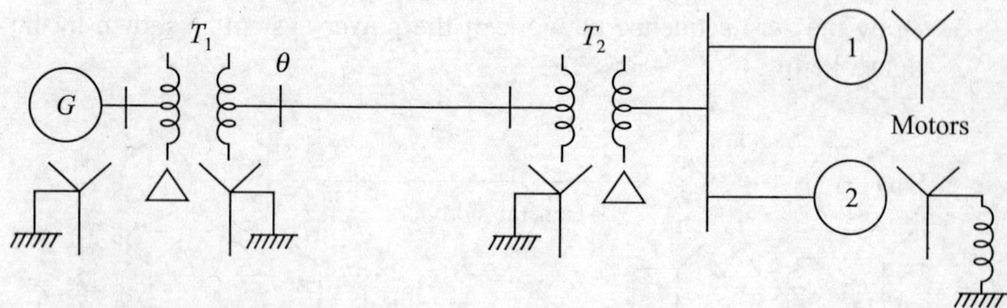

7. A 30 MVA, 13.2 kV synchronous generator has a solidly grounded neutral. Its positive, negative and zero sequence impedances are 0.30, 0.40 and 0.05 p.u. respectively.
   (a) What value of reactance must be placed in the generator neutral so that the fault current for a line to ground fault of zero fault impedance shall not exceed the rated line current?
   (b) What value of resistance in the neutral will serve the same purpose?
   (c) What value of reactance must be placed in the neutral of the generator to restrict the fault current to ground to rated line current for a double line to ground fault?
   (d) What will be the magnitude of the line current when the ground current is restricted as above?
   (e) As the reactance in the neutral is indefinitely increased, what are the limiting values of the line current?

8. Two alternators are operating in parallel and supplying a synchronous motor which is receiving 60 MW power at 0.8 power factor lagging at 6.0 kV. The single line diagram for this system is given in the figure below. Data are given below. Compute the fault current when a single line to ground fault occurs at the middle of the line through a fault resistance of 4.033 Ω. Data are given below.
   G_1 and G_2: 100 MVA, 11 kV, $X^+ = 0.2$ p.u., $X^- = X^\circ = 0.1$ p.u.
   T_1: 180 MVA, 11.5/115 kV, $X = 0.1$ p.u.
   T_2: 170 MVA, 6.6/115 kV, $X = 0.1$ p.u.
   $M = 160$ MVA, 6.3 kV, $X^+ = X^- = 0.3$ p.u., $X^\circ = 0.1$ p.u.
   Line: $X^+ = X^- = 30.25\ \Omega$, $X^\circ = 60.5\ \Omega$

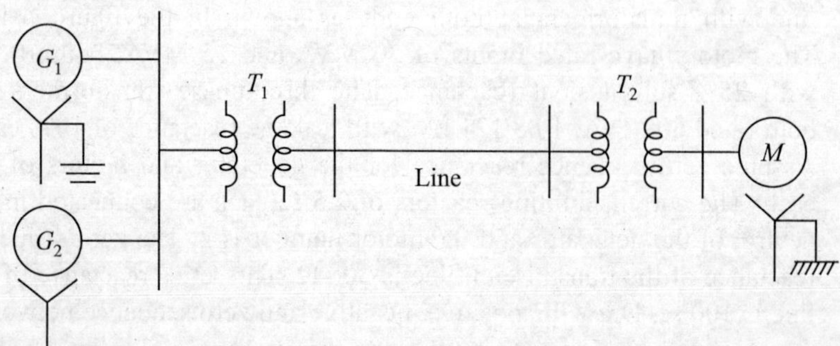

CHAPTER 5

Power System Stability

5.1 Introduction

The present day electric power system network forms a complete, nonlinear dynamical system. Several controls are provided in order to perform the power system into a proper way. During the normal operation, all these controls try to bring the system to an operating equilibrium ensuring the balance of real and reactive powers in the system. Following a disturbance, the balance of real and reactive powers gets disturbed. The dynamical power system network undergoes a transition period and may settle down to an operating equilibrium with the help of the above controls, which may or may not be the same as the predisturbance equilibrium point. The capability of the system to achieve an operating equilibrium, after disturbances, depends on its inherent strength, nature and amount of disturbances. The system becomes unstable if it is not capable of regaining the operating equilibrium. Thus, a general definition of stability is given as follows:

"The stability of a dynamical system is its property or ability to remain in a state of operating equilibrium under normal operating conditions and to regain an acceptable state of equilibrium after being subjected to a disturbance".

During the early part of the 20th century, the concern of the power system engineers was to maximize the real power transfer from the remotely located generating stations to the load centre. The problem of maintaining synchronous operation started when two or more generators were connected in the network to share the system power demand. The difficulty in maintaining the synchronous operations was experienced specifically in the case of severe disturbances such as network faults and outage of large generating plants. This was called the **transient stability** problem. Several practical measures were suggested to improve the transient stability including the fast exciters and protection system. Although these measures helped in improving the synchronizing capability and the transient stability limit, a few of these resulted into deterioration in system damping. With poor damping, the system becomes oscillatory unstable, called

small signal stability problem. Stabilizing controls such as power system stabilizers have been used to improve the system small signal stability, facilitating the transmission system to be utilized close to their maximum power transfer capability. The stressed operation of the power system, due to increased real power transfer capability, makes the transfer of reactive power difficult, giving rise to a new stability phenomenon known as **voltage stability**.

5.2 Classification of Power System Stability

Although the power system stability is one single phenomenon, it has been classified into various types for the ease of analysis and identifying the factors affecting the stability and hence planning the control actions for its enhancement. The classification of power system stability is shown in Figure 5.1. It is broadly classified into two types: 1. angular stability and 2. voltage stability.

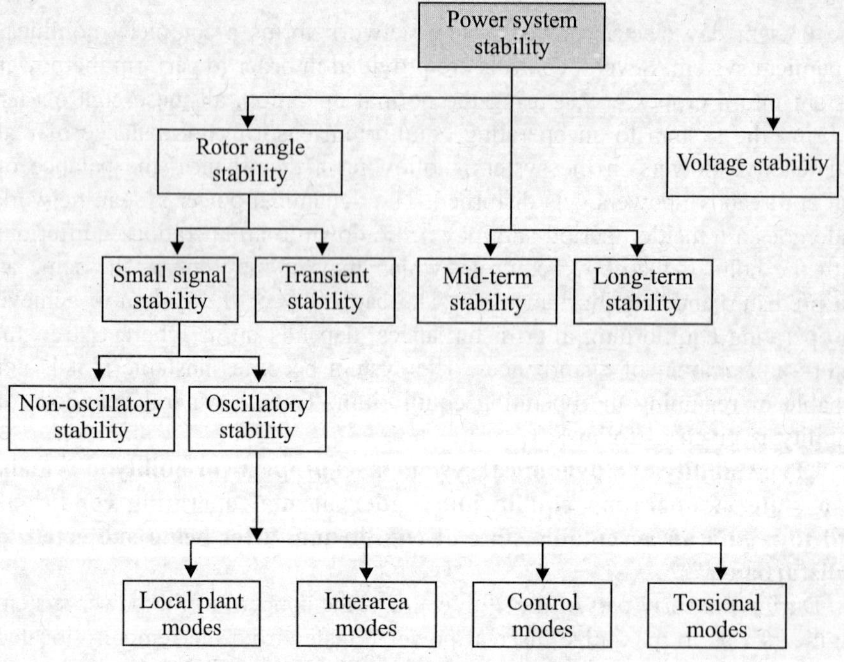

Figure 5.1 Classification of power system.

The (voltage) angle stability is the property of the interconnected power system network to maintain synchronous operation of various generating plants subjected to a disturbance. It is mainly concerned with maintaining real power requirement in the system. The stability problem involves the study of electromechanical oscillations inherent in the power systems. Disturbances in the system can be large or small, gradual or sudden. Depending on the nature of disturbance, the angle stability can be further classified as transient stability or small signal stability.

Transient stability

Transient stability refers to the large disturbances in the system. It can be defined as the **"ability of the system and its generating units to remain in synchronism following a large (severe) and sudden disturbance"**. Faults in the transmission system, sudden change of bulk load, loss of operating units, line switching are the examples of large disturbances. In general, the postdisturbance operating equilibrium is different from the predisturbance equilibrium point in case of such disturbances. Since the severe disturbances involve a large deviation in rotor angles, nonlinear dynamical model of the system is considered for the transient stability studies.

Small signal stability

Small signal stability refers to the **"ability of the system to maintain synchronism under small and sudden disturbances"**. Such disturbances occur continuously in the system due to small variation in loads and generations. Small signal instability can be either due to insufficient synchronizing torque resulting into monotonous increase in the rotor angles or due to insufficient damping torque resulting into undamped angle oscillations in the system. The stability depends on several factors such as initial operating point, transmission system strength, generator excitation and other controls in the system. Since the disturbances are small, linearized dynamical model of the system can be used for analysis. The small signal stability can be further divided into the following types.

(i) Local modes or machine-system mode, due to swinging of a generating plant unit with the rest of the system. The frequency of oscillation may range from 0.7 to 2 Hz.

(ii) Interarea mode, due to swinging of a group of coherent generating units with other group(s) of coherent units. In general, these groups are interconnected with weak tie lines. The frequency of oscillation may range from 0.1 to 0.7 Hz.

(iii) Control mode, due to the poorly tuned controllers in the system such as exciters, speed governors, HVDC converters, SVC, etc.

(iv) Torsional mode, due to interaction of mechanical oscillation of turbine generator shaft system with the oscillations in the electrical circuit, involving various controls and series compensated lines.

Voltage stability

The voltage stability also called load stability refers to the **"ability of the system to maintain load bus voltages within acceptable limit, following some disturbance or change in power demand"**.

The voltage stability can be further classified as follows.

(i) Large disturbance voltage stability, which is the ability of the system to regain voltages at all the buses within the acceptable steady state levels, when subjected to a large disturbance. The study ranges from a few seconds to tens of minutes and requires nonlinear dynamic simulation of load characteristics, and various controls including load tap changer dynamics and generator current limiters.

(ii) Small disturbance voltage stability considers small disturbances such as incremental change in loads. Static analysis is utilized to identify voltage instability conditions, various contributing factors and the stability margin.

An alternate classification of power system transient stability study is based on the time frame considered and the time response of the concerned phenomenon. It is broadly classified into three types.

(i) Short-term for a time period between 0 and 10 seconds
(ii) Mid-term for 10 seconds to a few minutes
(iii) Long-term for a few minutes to tens of minutes.

The modelling details of various power system components depend on the time frame of the phenomenon being studied. For example, the network transient is ignored in mid-term and long-term stability studies. Slow dynamics such as boiler, and on-load tap changer dynamics is required to be considered in the long-term stability study.

5.3 Transient Stability

5.3.1 Introduction

The power system transient stability has been defined as the ability of the synchronous generators in an interconnected network to remain in synchronism after being subjected to a large or severe disturbance. During a steady state operation, the generators run at a constant synchronous speed, with rotor acceleration being zero, maintaining a balance between the mechanical input power (P_m) from the turbine and the electrical power (P_e) output to the electrical network. A disturbance in the electrical network causes the (real power) output of generators to change creating an imbalance with the mechanical power input. Since the mechanical power input from turbine cannot change instantaneously, the change in electrical power requirement is met initially from the stored kinetic energy of the rotors causing the rotors to accelerate or decelerate and also changing the rotor angle position. Severe disturbances may cause a large excursion in the rotor angles. The transient stability requires

(i) the calculation of the electrical power output of generators during prefault, fault and postfault conditions. This involves solution of network power flow equations, which are nonlinear algebraic in nature.

(ii) solving the rotor dynamic equations to study the variation of rotor angle with time. The generator mechanical dynamics is described by the nonlinear differential equation known as swing equation. This requires some numerical integration method for solution.

The system is said to be stable during the postdisturbance period, if the rotors of all the machines achieve constant synchronous speed. To simplify the transient stability analysis, the classical approach has been utilized which is also discussed in this chapter.

5.3.2 Assumptions of Transient Stability Analysis

The classical technique involves the following main assumptions.

1. Mechanical input to the generator remains constant (i.e. speed governing system action is neglected).
2. Machine damping and AVR action are neglected. Synchronous machine is modelled as constant voltage source behind the transient reactance.
3. Network transients are neglected. Thus static model of network can be used.
4. Loads are represented as constant impedance/admittance type.
5. Mechanical angle of each machine rotor coincides with the electrical phase of voltage behind transient reactance.

In addition, the transmission line resistances and saliency of the synchronous machine can also be neglected, which gives conservative results. The static network equations and the machine dynamics can be formulated as given below.

5.4 Power Angle Equation of a Two Machine System

Consider a very simple system as shown in Figure 5.2.

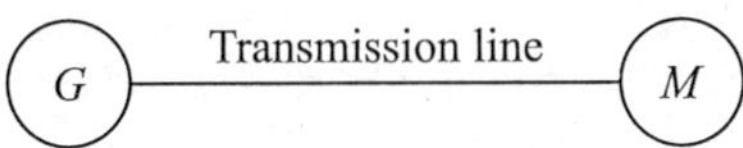

Figure 5.2 Two machine system.

It consists of a synchronous generator supplying power to a synchronous motor through a transmission line.

To draw the reactance diagram, we know that any synchronous machine is represented by a constant voltage source in series with a reactance X. Depending upon the condition under study, the reactance may be subtransient reactance X_d'', transient reactance X_d' or steady state synchronous reactance X_d. Thus the above one line diagram can be drawn in terms of reactance diagram as shown in Figure 5.3.

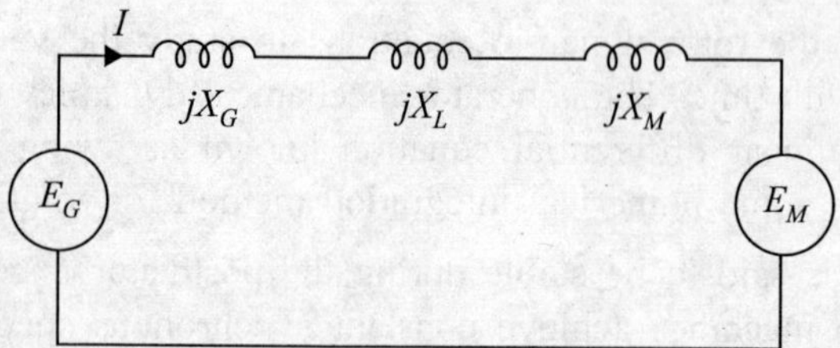

Figure 5.3 Reactance diagram.

In Figure 5.3, the generator is represented by E_G in series with X_G,

the motor is represented by E_M in series with X_M and

the transmission line with leakage reactance is given by X_L.

The total reactance between the machines is given by

$$X = X_G + X_L + X_M \tag{5.1}$$

The internal voltages E_G and E_M are generated by the flux produced by the field windings of the machines, hence their phase difference is the same as the electrical angle between the machine rotors.

The vector diagram is shown in Figure 5.4.

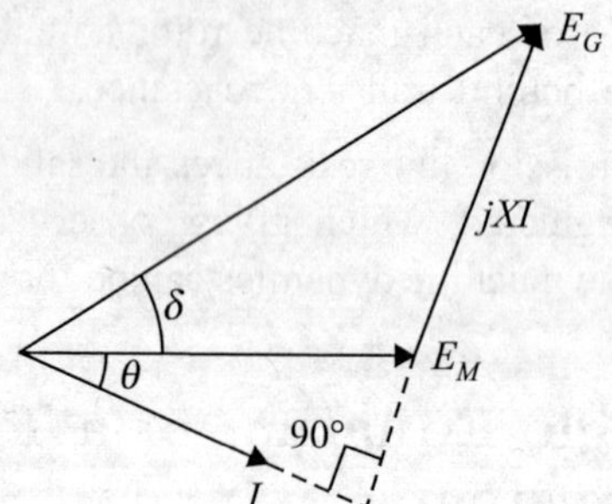

Figure 5.4 Vector diagram.

From the vector diagram,

$$\overline{E_G} = \overline{E_M} + jX\,\bar{I} \tag{5.2}$$

The equation for current is

$$\bar{I} = \frac{\overline{E_G} - \overline{E_M}}{jX} \tag{5.3}$$

Since the resistances of the machines and the transmission lines are neglected, the power output of the generator is also the power input to the motor and is given by

$$P = \text{Real part of } (\overline{E_G}^* \times \bar{I})$$

$$= \text{Re}\left[\overline{E_G}^*\left(\frac{\overline{E_G} - \overline{E_M}}{jX}\right)\right] \tag{5.4}$$

Let $\overline{E_M} = EM\angle 0$, $\overline{E_G} = E_G\angle\delta$,

$\therefore$ $\overline{E_G}^* = E_G\angle -\delta$,

Upon substitution,

$$P = \text{Re}\left[E_G\angle -\delta\left(\frac{E_G\angle\delta - E_M\angle 0}{X\angle 90°}\right)\right]$$

$$= \text{Re}\left[\frac{E_G^2}{X}\angle -90° - \frac{E_G E_M}{X}\angle -90° - \delta\right] \tag{5.5}$$

$\therefore$ Real power P is given by

$$P = -\frac{E_G E_M}{X}\cos(-90° - \delta)$$

$$= -\frac{E_G E_M}{X}\cos(90° + \delta)$$

$$P = \frac{E_G E_M}{X}\sin\delta \tag{5.6}$$

The above equation shows that the power transmitted from the generator to the motor varies with the sine of the displacement angle δ between the two rotors. Hence this equation is called the power angle equation and if the curve δ against P is plotted, it is called the power angle curve as shown in Figure 5.5.

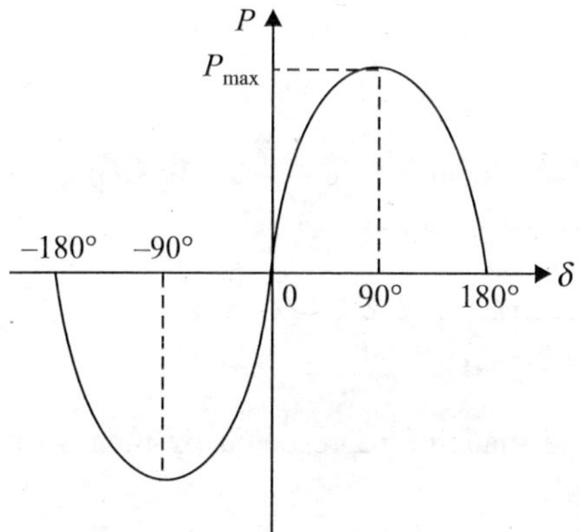

Figure 5.5 Power angle curve.

The maximum power occurs when $\sin\delta = 1$, i.e. $\delta = 90°$.

$\therefore$ $P_{max} = \frac{E_G E_M}{X}$ is the steady state stability limit.

When the slope $dP/d\delta$ is positive ($-90° \leq \delta \leq 90°$), it means that an increase in displacement angle results in an increase in transmitted power and hence the system will be stable. If $dP/d\delta$ is negative, it indicates that the system is unstable.

EXAMPLE 5.1 Two synchronous machines of equal rating have internal voltages of 1.1 + *j*0.5 and 0.8 – *j*0.4 per unit voltages respectively. The machines are connected by a line of 50 km length having only reactance and the second machine receives power of 0.9 per unit. Determine the reactance of the line per km length. Assume that there is no internal reactance for simplification.

Solution:

Given

$$\overline{E_G} = 1.1 + j0.5 = 1.21\angle 24.4°$$

$$\overline{E_M} = 0.8 - j0.4 = 0.89\angle -26.6°$$

$$P = 0.9, \text{ length of transmission line} = 50 \text{ km}$$

$$X_G = X_M = 0$$

$$\delta = 24.4° - (-26.6°) = 51°$$

We know that the power angle equation is

$$P = \frac{E_G E_M}{X} \sin \delta$$

$$0.9 = \frac{1.21 \times 0.89}{X} \sin 51°$$

$$X = \frac{0.8087}{0.9} = 0.8986 \text{ p.u.}$$

Since $X_G = X_M = 0$, X denotes the reactance of the transmission line.

$$X = 0.8986 \text{ p.u}$$

$$X \text{ per km} = \frac{0.8986}{50} = 0.0186 \text{ p.u.}$$

5.5 Power Angle Equation of a Salient Pole Machine

Consider a salient pole machine represented by means of a one line diagram as shown in Figure 5.6.

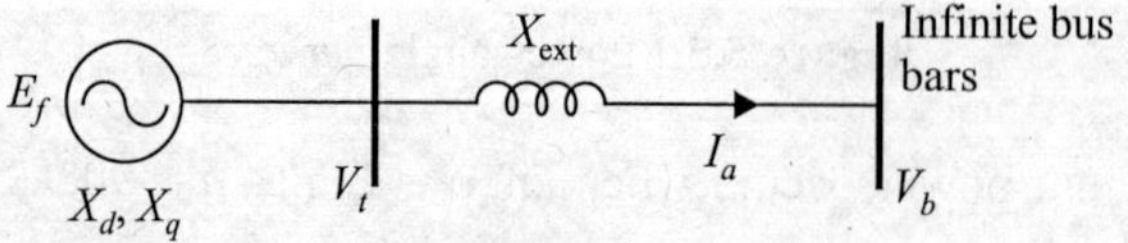

Figure 5.6 Representation of a salient pole machine.

Let E_f be the excitation emf per phase

V_t be the terminal voltage per phase

V_b be the voltage of the infinite bus

X_d be the direct axis synchronous reactance
X_q be the quadrature axis synchronous reactance
X_{ext} be the reactance between generator and infinite bus

The electrical power output of a salient pole generator is given by,

$$P_e = \underset{\text{(Excitation power)}}{\frac{E_f V_b}{X_d} \sin\delta} + \underset{\text{(Reluctance power)}}{\frac{V_b^2 (X_d - X_q)}{2\, X_d X_q} \sin 2\delta} \tag{5.7}$$

The excitation power is the same as the power angle equation of a simple two machine system. The reluctance power varies as $\sin 2\delta$ with the maximum value of $\delta = 45°$. This term is independent of field excitation and would be present even if the field is unexcited. The reluctance component is of the order of 10 to 20 per cent of the excitation component. The reluctance component of power is usually neglected in the steady state stability studies.

For a non-salient pole machine, $X_d = X_q$, we get the original power angle equation of a simple two machine system.

5.6 Swing Equation

The behaviour of a synchronous machine during the transient period is described by the swing equation.

We know that the torque exerted on a rotating body is given by the product of moment of inertia J (kg·m^2) and angular acceleration α (rad/s^2), that is,

$$T_a = J\alpha = J\frac{d^2\theta}{dt^2} \tag{5.8}$$

where θ is the angular position of the rotor in radians at any instant of time, and t is the time in seconds.

It is convenient to measure θ with respect to a reference axis that is rotating at the synchronous speed. If δ is the angular displacement of the rotor in electrical degrees from the synchronously rotating reference axis and ω_s is the synchronous speed in electrical radians, then θ can be expressed as the sum of: (1) time varying angle $\omega_s t$ on the rotating reference axis, and (2) the torque angle δ of the rotor with respect to the rotating reference axis. In other words,

$$\theta = \omega_s t + \delta \qquad \text{electrical radians} \tag{5.9}$$

Differentiating with respect to t, we get

$$\frac{d\theta}{dt} = \omega_s + \frac{d\delta}{dt} \tag{5.10}$$

Differentiating once again with respect to t, we get

$$\frac{d^2\theta}{dt^2} = \frac{d^2\delta}{dt^2} \tag{5.11}$$

∴ Angular acceleration of rotor, $\alpha = \dfrac{d^2\theta}{dt^2}$

$$\alpha = \frac{d^2\delta}{dt^2} \quad \text{electrical radians} \tag{5.12}$$

In a synchronous generator, the accelerating torque T_a is equal to the difference of input shaft torque T_m and the output electromagnetic torque T_e.

$$\therefore \quad T_a = T_m - T_e$$

$$J \cdot \frac{d^2\theta}{dt^2} = J \cdot \frac{d^2\delta}{dt^2} \tag{5.13}$$

$$\therefore \quad T_a = T_m - T_e = J \cdot \frac{d^2\delta}{dt^2}$$

Multiplying both sides by angular velocity, ω, we get

$$\omega T_a = \omega T_m - \omega T_e = J\omega \frac{d^2\delta}{dt^2} \tag{5.14}$$

If P_a, P_m and P_e denote the accelerating power, mechanical power input and electrical power output respectively, we get

$$P_a = P_m - P_e = J\omega \frac{d^2\delta}{dt^2} \tag{5.15}$$

Also, since angular momentum $M = J\omega$, therefore Eq. (5.15) can be written as

$$P_a = P_m - P_e = M \frac{d^2\delta}{dt^2} \tag{5.16}$$

Equation (5.16) is called the swing equation. It is a nonlinear differential equation of the second order.

5.6.1 Swing Curves

The solution of swing equation gives the variation of δ (in electrical radians) with respect to time (in seconds). The graph when plotted is called a swing curve as shown in Figure 5.7. It provides information regarding stability. They show the tendency of δ to oscillate and/or increase beyond the point of return. If δ increases continuously with time, the system is unstable. While if δ starts decreasing after reaching a maximum value, it is inferred that the system will remain stable.

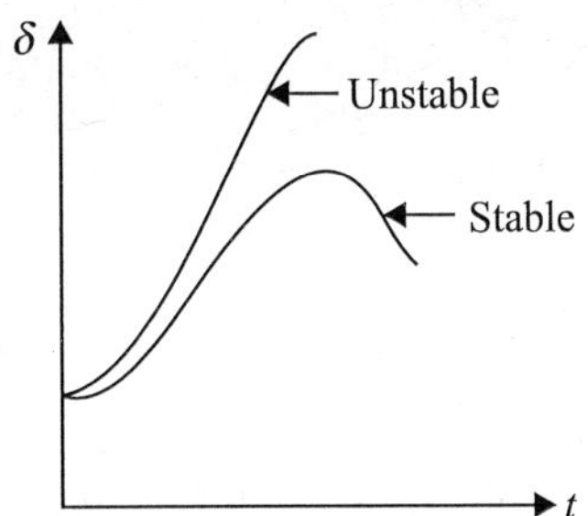

Figure 5.7 Swing curves.

5.6.2 Constants Used in Stability Analysis

Inertia constant, M

From the swing equation $M \dfrac{d^2\delta}{dt^2} = P_a$

If power is in W, δ is in rad and t is in s, then M is in W/rad/s^2 or W·s^2/rad. Since 1 J = 1 W·s, M can have its unit as J·s/rad. If power is in MW, then M is MJ·s/rad.

If δ is specified in electrical degrees, then M has unit as MJ·s/electrical degree.

If power is in pu, then M has pu power s^2/electrical degree. The value of M will be referred to as per unit value of M.

In general, constant M may be defined as the power in MW required to produce unit angular acceleration.

Kinetic energy, N

The kinetic energy of the rotor at synchronous speed denoted by N is given by

$$N = \frac{1}{2} M\omega_s$$

where $\omega_s = 2\pi\, n_s$; mechanical rad/s
$= 2\pi f$; electrical rad/s
$= 360\, f$; electrical degree/s

where n_s is the speed in rps and f is the frequency in Hz.

Normally generators of the same MVA ratings may have different values of kinetic energy and momentum. To express them in a common way, we use a constant H (also called inertia constant).

Inertia constant, H

It is defined as the ratio of stored kinetic energy to volt ampere rating of machine.

$$H = \frac{\text{kinetic energy}}{\text{MVA rating}} \quad \text{MJ/MVA}$$

$$= \frac{N}{S} \quad \text{where } S \text{ is the MVA rating}$$

$$\therefore \quad N = SH$$

Equivalent H constant

Consider a system in which 'n' number of generators are connected in parallel to the same bus bar.

Let $S_1, S_2, S_3, \ldots, S_n$ be the MVA rating of individual machines
$H_1, H_2, H_3, \ldots, H_n$ be the inertia constants of individual machines
$N_1, N_2, N_3, \ldots, N_n$ be the kinetic energy stored in individual machines
S_e be the MVA rating of equivalent machine
H_e be the inertia constant of equivalent machine
N_e be the kinetic energy stored in equivalent machine and S_b be the base MVA.

The energy stored by the equivalent machine is given by the sum of energies stored by individual machines.

$$N = N_1 + N_2 + \cdots + N_n$$

$$S_e H_e = S_1 H_1 + S_2 H_2 + \cdots + S_n H_n$$

where

$$S_e = S_1 + S_2 + \cdots + S_n$$

If the base MVA, S_b, is equal to the combined MVA rating of individual machines S_e, i.e. $S_b = S_e$, we get

$$H_e = H_1\left(\frac{S_1}{S_b}\right) + H_2\left(\frac{S_2}{S_b}\right) + \cdots + H_n\left(\frac{S_n}{S_b}\right)$$

If the machines are identical, we have

$$S_1 = S_2 = \cdots = S_n = S$$

$$H_1 = H_2 = \cdots = H_n = H$$

then

$$H_e = n \times \left(\frac{HS}{nS}\right)$$

With identical machines

$$S_b = S_e = n \times S$$

Substituting S_b, we get

$$H_e = n \times \left(\frac{HS}{nS}\right)$$

$$H_e = H$$

Thus the equivalent H constant of several identical machines operating in parallel is the same as that of any one of the machines.

Equivalent M constant of two machines

Two synchronous machines connected by a reactance can be replaced by one equivalent machine connected through a reactance to an infinite bus as follows. The swing equation of machine 1 is given by

$$M_1 \frac{d^2\delta_1}{dt^2} = P_{m1} - P_{e1} \tag{5.17}$$

The swing equation of machine 2 is given by

$$M_2 \frac{d^2\delta_2}{dt^2} = P_{m2} - P_{e2} \tag{5.18}$$

From Eq. (5.17)

$$\frac{d^2\delta_1}{dt^2} = \frac{P_{m1} - P_{e1}}{M_1} \tag{5.19}$$

From Eq. (5.18)

$$\frac{d^2\delta_2}{dt^2} = \frac{P_{m2} - P_{e2}}{M_2} \tag{5.20}$$

Subtracting Eq. (5.20) from Eq. (5.19), we get

$$\frac{d^2\delta_1}{dt^2} - \frac{d^2\delta_2}{dt^2} = \frac{P_{m1} - P_{e1}}{M_1} - \frac{P_{m2} - P_{e2}}{M_2}$$

We can write

$$\frac{d^2(\delta_1 - \delta_2)}{dt^2} = \frac{M_2(P_{m1} - P_{e1}) - M_1(P_{m2} - P_{e2})}{M_1 M_2} \tag{5.21}$$

If δ is the relative angle between the rotors of the two machines, then $\delta = \delta_1 - \delta_2$. We can write Eq. (5.21) as

$$\frac{d^2\delta}{dt^2} = \frac{M_2 P_{m1} - M_1 P_{m2}}{M_1 M_2} - \frac{M_2 P_{e1} - M_1 P_{e2}}{M_1 M_2} \tag{5.22}$$

Multiplying both sides of the above equation by $M_1 M_2/(M_1 + M_2)$, we get

$$\frac{M_1 M_2}{M_1 + M_2} \frac{d^2\delta}{dt^2} = \frac{M_1 M_2}{M_1 + M_2}\left(\frac{M_2 P_{m1} - M_1 P_{m2}}{M_1 M_2} - \frac{M_2 P_{e1} - M_1 P_{e2}}{M_1 M_2}\right)$$

$$\frac{M_1 M_2}{M_1 + M_2} \frac{d^2\delta}{dt^2} = \frac{M_2 P_{m1} - M_1 P_{m2}}{M_1 + M_2} - \frac{M_2 P_{e1} - M_1 P_{e2}}{M_1 + M_2} \tag{5.23}$$

The swing equation of an equivalent machine is given by

$$M' \frac{d^2\delta}{dt^2} = P'_m - P'_e \tag{5.24}$$

From Eq. (5.24) we can say that the equivalent values of M', P'_m and P'_e are given by

$$M' = \frac{M_1 M_2}{M_1 + M_2}$$

$$P'_m = \frac{M_2 P_{m1} - M_1 P_{m2}}{M_1 + M_2}$$

and $$P'_e = \frac{M_2 P_{e1} - M_1 P_{e2}}{M_1 + M_2}$$

Relationship between inertia constant M and inertia constant H

We have

$$M = \frac{2N}{\omega_s} = \frac{2N}{360f} = \frac{N}{180f}$$

$$= \frac{SH}{180f} \text{ MJ·s/electrical degree} \qquad \text{(since } N = SH\text{)}$$

If the angle is expressed in radians

$$M = \frac{SH}{\pi f} \text{ MJ·s/electrical radian}$$

EXAMPLE 5.2 The moment of inertia of a 4 pole, 100 MVA, 11 kV, 3-ϕ, 0.8 power factor, 50 Hz turbo alternator is 10000 kg·m^2. Calculate H and M.

Solution:

$$J = 10000 \text{ kg·m}^2$$

$$N_s = \frac{120f}{p} = \frac{120 \times 50}{4} = 1500 \text{ rpm}$$

$$n_s = \frac{N_s}{60} = \frac{1500}{60} = 25 \text{ rps}$$

$$\omega_s = 2\pi n_s = 50\pi$$

$$N = \frac{1}{2} J\omega_s^2 = \frac{1}{2} \times 10000 \times (50\pi)^2 = 123.37 \text{ MJ}$$

$$H = \frac{N}{S} = \frac{123.37}{100} = 1.2337 \text{ MJ/MVA}$$

$$M = \frac{SH}{180f} = \frac{100 \times 1.2337}{180 \times 50} = 0.0137 \text{ MJ·s/electrical degree}$$

EXAMPLE 5.3 A 50 Hz, 4 pole, turbo alternator rated 100 MVA, 11 kV has an inertia constant of 8 MJ/MVA. Determine

1. the energy stored in the rotor at synchronous speed.
2. find the rotor acceleration if the mechanical input is suddenly raised to 80 MW for an electric load of 50 MW. (Neglect mechanical and electrical losses).

Solution:

(i) $H = 8$ MJ/MVA; $S = 100$ MVA

We know that

$$N = HS = 800 \text{ MJ}$$

(ii) Swing equation is $M\dfrac{d^2\theta}{dt^2} = P_a = P_m - P_e$

Here for alternator, $P_m = 80$ MW

$P_e = 50$ MW

$\therefore$ $P_a = 30$ MW

$$\text{Also } M = \frac{SH}{180f} = \frac{N}{180f} = \frac{800}{180 \times 50} = 0.0889 \text{ MJ}\cdot\text{s}$$

$$\therefore \text{ Acceleration} = \frac{d^2\delta}{dt^2} = \frac{P_a}{M} = \frac{30}{0.0889} = 337.5 \text{ electrical degree/s}$$

EXAMPLE 5.4 A 50 Hz, 4 pole turbo generator rated 20 MVA, 11 kV has an inertia constant of $H = 9$ kW·s/kVA. Find the kinetic energy stored in the rotor at synchronous speed. Find the acceleration, if the input less the rotational losses is 26800 HP and the electrical power developed is 16 MW.

Solution:

$S = 20$ MVA, 11 kV,

$$H = 9 \text{ kW}\cdot\text{s/kVA} = 9 \text{ kJ/kVA}$$

$$H = 9 \text{ MJ/MVA}$$

$$\text{Kinetic energy} = N = HS = 9 \times 20 = 180 \text{ MJ}$$

$$P_a = P_m - P_e$$

$$P_m = 26800 \times 746 = 19992800 \text{ W} = 19.99 \text{ MW}$$

$$P_a = 19.99 - 16 = 3.99 \text{ MW}$$

$$M = \frac{N}{180f} = \frac{180}{180 \times 50} = 0.02 \text{ MW}\cdot\text{s}^2/\text{electrical degree}$$

We know that

$$M\frac{d^2\delta}{dt^2} = P_a \quad \Rightarrow \quad \frac{d^2\delta}{dt^2} = \frac{P_a}{M} = \frac{3.99}{0.02}$$

$$\text{Acceleration } \frac{d^2\delta}{dt^2} = 199.5 \text{ electrical degree/s}^2$$

EXAMPLE 5.5 A power station with 4 generators each 80 MVA, 8 MJ/MVA is in proximity with another power station having 3 generators each 200 MVA, 3.5 MJ/MVA. Determine the inertia constant of a single equivalent machine for use in stability studies. Assume a base value of 100 MVA.

Solution:

4 generators are each of 80 MVA, 8 MJ/MVA

3 generators are each of 200 MVA, 3.5 MJ/MVA

We know that

$$H_eS_e = H_1S_1 + H_2S_2 + \cdots$$

$$= \sum_{i=1}^{4} H_1S_1 + \sum_{i=1}^{3} H_2S_2$$

$$= (4 \times 80 \times 8) + (3 \times 200 \times 3.5)$$

$$= 2560 + 2100 = 4660 \text{ MJ}$$

$$H_e = \frac{4660}{S_e} = \frac{4660}{100} = 46.6 \text{ MJ/MVA}$$

EXAMPLE 5.6 Two turbo alternators specified below are interconnected using a short line:

Machine 1 : 4 poles, 50 Hz, 125 MVA, 0.8 lag, 25000 kg·m^2

Machine 2 : 4 poles, 50 Hz, 150 MVA, 0.9 lag, 20000 kg·m^2

Determine the inertia constant of the single equivalent machine on a base of 150 MVA.

Solution:

Machine 1

$$M_1 = \frac{N_1}{180f}$$

$$N_1 = \frac{1}{2}J\omega_s^2$$

$$N_s = \frac{120 \times 50}{4} = 1500 \text{ rpm}$$

$$n_s = \frac{1500}{60} = 25 \text{ rps}$$

$\therefore$
$$N_1 = \frac{1}{2} \times 25000 \times \omega_s^2$$

$$\omega_s = 2\pi\, n_s = 157.0796 \text{ rad/s} = 308.425 \text{ MJ}$$

$$M_1 = \frac{N_1}{180f} = 0.03426 \text{ MJ·s/electrical degree}$$

M_1 in p.u. on a base of 150 MVA = 2.2846 × 10^{-4} p.u.

Machine 2

$$n_s = 25 \text{ rps}$$

$$N_2 = \frac{1}{2}J\omega_s^2 = \frac{1}{2} \times 20000 \times (157.0796)^2 = 246.74$$

$$M_2 = \frac{N_2}{180f} = 0.274155 \text{ MJ}\cdot\text{s/electrical degree}$$

M_2 in p.u on a base of 150 MVA = 1.8277×10^{-4} p.u.

$$M = \frac{M_1 M_2}{M_1 + M_2} = 1.01538 \times 10^{-4} \text{ p.u.}$$

EXAMPLE 5.7 A generator A is rated at 50 Hz, 60 MW, 75 MVA, 1500 rpm and has an inertia constant H = 7 MJ/MVA. The corresponding data for another generator B is 50 Hz, 120 MW, 133.3 MVA, 3000 rpm, and 4 MJ/MVA.

(a) If these two generators operate in parallel in a power station, calculate H for the equivalent generator on a base of 100 MVA.

(b) If the power station is connected to another power station which has two of each type of generator, calculate H for the equivalent generator connected to an infinite bus bar.

Solution:

(a) We know that

$$S_e H_e = H_1 S_1 + H_2 S_2$$

$$H_e S_e = (7 \times 75) + (4 \times 133.3)$$

$$H_e = \frac{(7 \times 75) + (4 \times 133.3)}{100} = 10.582 \text{ MJ/MVA}$$

(b) Another power station has two of each type of generator. So the equivalent H_e becomes twice the original H_{e1}.

$$H_{e2} = 2 \times 10.582 = 21.164 \text{ MJ/MVA}$$

When they are connected in parallel, the equivalent machine

$$H_e = \frac{H_{e1} \cdot H_{e2}}{H_{e1} + H_{e2}} = 7.055 \text{ MJ/MVA}$$

EXAMPLE 5.8 Two turbo alternators given below are interconnected using a short line.

Machine 1 : 4 poles, 50 Hz, 75 MVA, 0.8 lag, 30000 kg·m^2
Machine 2 : 2 poles, 50 Hz, 100 MVA, 0.85 lag, and 10000 kg·m^2

Determine the inertia constant of the single equivalent machine on a base of 200 MVA.

Solution:

Machine 1

$$\omega_s = 2\pi\, n_s = 2\pi \times \frac{120f}{4 \times 60} = 157.079$$

$$\text{Kinetic energy} = \frac{1}{2}J\omega_s^2 = \frac{1}{2}\times 30000\times(157.079)^2$$

$$N_1 = 370$$

$$H_1 = \frac{N_1}{S_1} = 4.935 \text{ MJ/MVA}$$

Machine 2

$$\omega_s = 314.159$$

$$N_2 = \frac{1}{2}J\omega_s^2 = \frac{1}{2}\times 10000\times(314.159)^2 = 493.48$$

$$H_2 = \frac{N_2}{S_2} = \frac{493.48}{100} = 4.9348 \text{ MJ/MVA}$$

Equivalent inertia constant

$$M_1 = \frac{SH_1}{180f} = \frac{\frac{75}{200}\times 4.935}{180\times f} = 2.056\times 10^{-4} \text{ p.u.}$$

$$M_2 = \frac{SH_2}{180f} = 2.738\times 10^{-4} \text{ p.u.}$$

$$M = \frac{M_1M_2}{M_1+M_2} = 1.174\times 10^{-4} \text{ p.u.}$$

5.6.3 Determination of Change in Rotor Angle When the Machine is Loaded

The swing equation is given by

$$M\frac{d^2\delta}{dt^2} = P_a$$

$$\therefore \quad \frac{d^2\delta}{dt^2} = \frac{P_a}{M}$$

where P_a/M is a constant.

Multiplying both sides by $2\dfrac{d\delta}{dt}$

$$2\frac{d\delta}{dt}\frac{d^2\delta}{dt^2} = \frac{P_a}{M}\cdot 2\frac{d\delta}{dt}$$

$$= \frac{2P_a}{M}\cdot\frac{d\delta}{dt}$$

$$\frac{d}{dt}\left[\frac{d\delta}{dt}\right]^2 = 2\frac{P_a}{M}\frac{d\delta}{dt}$$

Upon integration,

$$\int d\left(\frac{d\delta}{dt}\right)^2 = 2\frac{P_a}{M}\int d\delta$$

$$\left(\frac{d\delta}{dt}\right)^2 = 2\frac{P_a}{M}\cdot\delta$$

$$\frac{d\delta}{dt} = \sqrt{\frac{2P_a}{M}}\,\delta^{1/2}$$

$$\frac{d\delta}{\delta^{1/2}} = \sqrt{\frac{2P_a}{M}}\cdot dt \tag{5.25}$$

Integrating once again,

$$\int \delta^{-1/2}\,d\delta = \int\sqrt{\frac{2P_a}{M}}\cdot dt$$

$$\frac{\delta^{-1/2+1}}{-\frac{1}{2}+1} = \sqrt{\frac{2P_a}{M}}\cdot t$$

$$\frac{\delta^{1/2}}{\frac{1}{2}} = \sqrt{\frac{2P_a}{M}}\cdot t \tag{5.26}$$

$$\delta^{1/2} = \frac{1}{2}\sqrt{\frac{2P_a}{M}}\cdot t = \sqrt{\frac{P_a}{2M}}\cdot t$$

Substituting Eq. (5.26) in Eq. (5.25), we get

$$\frac{d\delta}{dt} = \sqrt{\frac{2P_a}{M}}\cdot\sqrt{\frac{P_a}{2M}}\cdot t = \sqrt{\frac{2P_a^2}{2M^2}}\cdot t$$

$$\frac{d\delta}{dt} = \left(\frac{P_a}{M}\right)t$$ is the change in rotor angle at anytime

EXAMPLE 5.9 The rotor of an alternator is subjected to an acceleration of 15 electrical rad/s^2. If this acceleration exists constantly, compute the change in rotor angle and the speed in rpm at the end of 5 cycles. H = 5 MJ/MVA. Frequency = 50 Hz. Initially the machine is running at a normal speed without any acceleration. Number of poles = 2.

Solution:

Given the acceleration $\dfrac{d^2\delta}{dt^2}$ = 15 electrical rad/s^2

From swing equation, $\dfrac{d^2\delta}{dt^2} = \dfrac{P_a}{M}$ = 15 electrical rad/s^2

Change in rotor angle $= \dfrac{d\delta}{dt} = \dfrac{P_a}{M} \cdot t$

Time period for five cycles = no. of cycles × time period for the given frequency

$$= 5 \times \frac{1}{50} = 0.1 \text{ s}$$

$\therefore$ Change in rotor angle $= \dfrac{d\delta}{dt} = 15 \times 0.1 = 1.5$ electrical rad/s

$$\frac{d\delta}{dt} = 1.5 \text{ electrical rad/s}$$

Since pole pair $p = 1$, we have $\theta_m = \theta_e$

$$\therefore \quad \frac{d\delta}{dt} = 1.5 \text{ mechanical rad/s} = 2\pi\, n_s$$

$$n_s = \frac{1.5}{2\pi} = 0.2387 \text{ rps}$$

$$\therefore \quad N_s = 0.2387 \times 60 = 14.32 \text{ rpm}$$

Since the machine is subjected to constant acceleration, the speed will increase by 14.32 rpm.

$$\therefore \quad \text{New speed} = \text{synchronous speed} + N_s$$

$$\text{Synchronous speed} = \frac{120 f}{p} = 3000 \text{ rpm}$$

$$\therefore \quad \text{New speed} = 3014.32 \text{ rpm}$$

EXAMPLE 5.10 A 200 MVA, 11 kV, 50 Hz, 4 pole turbo alternator has an inertia constant of 6 MJ/MVA.

(i) Determine the stored energy in the rotor at synchronous speed.

(ii) The machine is operating at a load of 120 MW when the load suddenly increases to 160 MW. Determine the rotor retardation. Neglect losses.

(iii) The retardation calculated above is maintained for 5 cycles. Determine the change in power angle and the rotor speed in rpm at the end of this period.

Solution:

$H = 6$ MJ/MVA, $S = 200$ MVA

(i) $N = HS = 6 \times 200 = 1200$ MJ

(ii) $P_a = 40$ (retardation)

$$M = \frac{N}{180 f} = \frac{1200}{180 \times 50} = 0.1333 \text{ MJ} \cdot \text{s/electrical degree}$$

$$\frac{d^2\delta}{dt^2} = \frac{P_a}{M} = \frac{40}{0.1333} = 300 \text{ electrical degree/s}^2$$

We know that change in rotor angle

$$\frac{d\delta}{dt} = \frac{P_a}{M} \cdot t$$

where t is the time period for acceleration or retardation.

(iii) Here for five cycles $t = 5 \times \frac{1}{50} = 0.1\text{ s}$

$$\therefore \quad \frac{d\delta}{dt} = 300 \times 0.1 = 30 \text{ electrical degree/s}$$

$$= 30 \times \frac{\pi}{180} \text{ electrical rad/s} = 0.5236 \text{ electrical rad/s}$$

$$= \frac{0.5236}{p} \text{ mechanical rad/s}$$

Pole pairs, $p = 2$

$$\therefore \quad \frac{d\delta}{dt} = \frac{0.5236}{2} = 0.2618 \text{ mechancial rad/s } = 2\pi n_s$$

$$n_s = \frac{0.2618}{2\pi} = 0.04167 \text{ rps}$$

$$N_s = n_s \times 60 = 2.5 \text{ rpm}$$

Since the retardation is for 5 cycles,

New speed = synchronous speed – N_s

∴ New speed = 1500 – 2.5 = 1497.5 rpm

5.7 Equal Area Criterion

In a system to determine whether a power system is stable after a disturbance, it is necessary to plot the swing curve. If this curve shows that the angle between any two machines tends to increase without limit, the system is unstable. If after all disturbances, the angle between the two machines reaches the maximum value and thereafter decreasing, thus oscillating with constant amplitude, it is probable although not certain that the system is stable. There is a simple graphical method of determining whether the machines come to rest with respect to each other. This method is known as the equal area criterion for stability.

The principle by which stability under transient conditions is determined without solving the swing equation is called the equal area criterion of stability.

When this method is used, it completely eliminates the need of computing swing curves and hence saves a considerable amount of work. The derivation of the equal area criterion is made for one machine and an infinite bus although the method can be adapted to a two-machine system.

Although not applicable to a multi-machine system, the method helps in understanding how certain factors influence the transient stability of any system.

5.7.1 Assumptions Made in Equal Area Criterion

1. Constant input over the time interval being considered.
2. Damping effect is neglected.
3. Constant voltage behind transient reactance.

In a two-machine system, it is quite likely to be stable, if it survives the first swing.

Validity of the assumptions

1. The assumption of constancy of the input power is justified by the fact that the effect of the action of governors on the input will not be appreciable up to the first swing, and thereafter, it will only tend to restore stability.
2. The effect of damping would be to slightly reduce the amplitude of the first swing and would therefore tend to diminish the amplitude of any subsequent swing.

When a fault occurs in a system, the fault current tends to cause demagnetization of the field due to armature reaction and the field current increases to the extent required to offset this effect so as to keep up the constant flux linkage of the field circuit. If the machine is not provided with a voltage regulator, the field current decreases to its original value, as also the flux linkage. As the time constant may be a few seconds, during the first swing there will not be any appreciable decrease in the flux linkage. Even if a voltage regulator is provided, it will take some time before the regulator and the exciter response becomes effective. During the subsequent swings, however, the voltage regulator will contribute substantially toward the maintenance of stability. It is, therefore, reasonable to assume constant voltage behind transient reactance without any significant error.

5.7.2 Equal Area Criterion Method Applied to a Machine Swinging with Respect to an Infinite Bus

The swing equation of a synchronous machine swinging with respect to an infinite bus is given by

$$M\frac{d^2\delta}{dt^2} = P_a = P_m - P_e$$

$$\frac{d^2\delta}{dt^2} = \frac{P_a}{M}$$

Multiplying both sides by $2\frac{d\delta}{dt}$

$$2\frac{d\delta}{dt}\frac{d^2\delta}{dt^2} = 2\frac{P_a}{M}\frac{d\delta}{dt}$$

$$\frac{d}{dt}\left[\left(\frac{d\delta}{dt}\right)^2\right] = 2\frac{P_a}{M}\frac{d\delta}{dt}$$

$$d\left[\left(\frac{d\delta}{dt}\right)^2\right] = 2\frac{P_a}{M}d\delta$$

Upon integration,

$$\left(\frac{d\delta}{dt}\right)^2 = \int_{\delta_0}^{\delta_t} 2\frac{P_a}{M}d\delta$$

$$= \frac{2}{M}\int_{\delta_0}^{\delta_t} P_a d\delta$$

$$\frac{d\delta}{dt} = \sqrt{\frac{2}{M}\int_{\delta_0}^{\delta_t} P_a d\delta}$$

If $d\delta/dt = \omega$, the velocity of the displacement angle with respect to the infinite bus, then

$$\omega = \frac{d\delta}{dt} = \sqrt{\frac{2}{M}\int_{\delta_0}^{\delta_t} P_a d\delta}$$

If the machine is continuously swinging, then the above equation will be non-zero. The stability is indicated by the zero value, i.e. if the integral vanishes.

i.e. $$\int P_a d\delta = 0$$

$$\int (P_m - P_e) d\delta = 0$$

$$\int P_m d\delta - \int P_e d\delta = 0$$

$\therefore$ $$\int P_m d\delta = \int P_e d\delta$$

Under the steady operating conditions, $P_m = P_e$ as given by the constant input line. The power angle curve is shown in Figure 5.8.

Let us assume that the initial angle be δ_0. The corresponding value of P_e is given by bf.

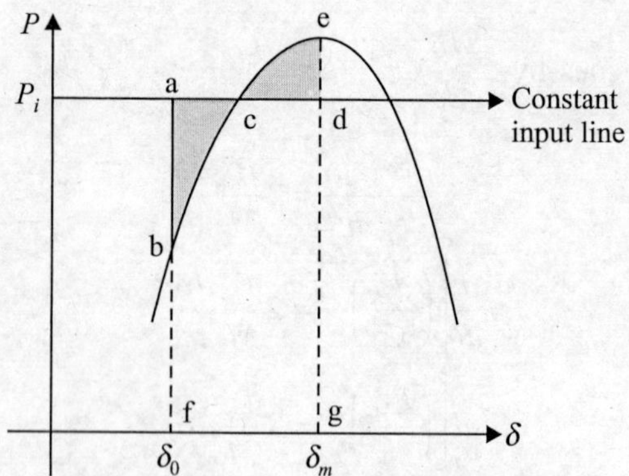

Figure 5.8 Equal area criterion.

For the stability criterion $\int P_m d\delta = \int P_e d\delta$

which is indicated by the equality of the area of the rectangle afgd and the area bcegf.

$$\text{Area afgda} = \text{Area bcedgfb}$$

$$\text{Area abc} + \text{Area bcdgf} = \text{Area ced} + \text{Area bcdgf}$$

$$\text{Area abc} = \text{Area ced}$$

$A_1 = A_2$ which is shown by the dashed line, i.e. the area A_1 below P_m line is equal to the area A_2 above P_m line. Hence this method is called equal area criterion.

From Figure 5.8, 'ab' represents $P_m - P_e \Rightarrow$ accelerating power corresponding to the initial angle δ_0, 'de' represents $P_e - P_m \Rightarrow$ decelerating power and when the accelerating power is equal to the decelerating power, the machine tends to return to the original condition if there is a balance between the two areas at $\delta = \delta_m$.

The system will remain stable only when $A_2 \geq A_1$, i.e. if accelerating area A_1 is greater than the decelerating area A_2, the system will definitely become unstable.

5.7.3 Sudden Change in Mechanical Input

Some of the conditions caused by the sudden increase in the mechanical load on a synchronous motor connected to an infinite bus can be predicted by analyzing Figure 5.9. An infinite bus is considered as a generator with infinite H constant and with constant frequency.

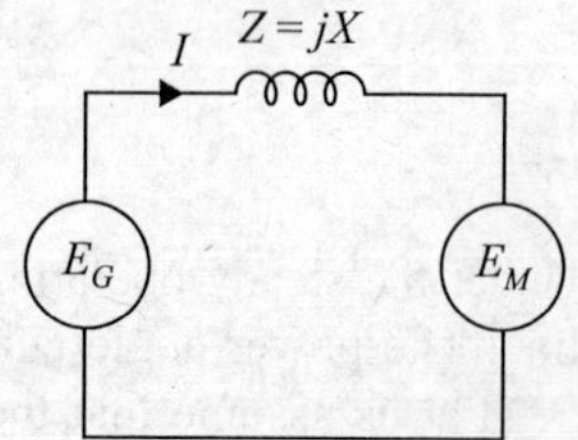

Figure 5.9 Motor connected to infinite bus.

The sinusoidal curve P_e is a plot of the electric power input to the motor with all resistance neglected. The curve P_e is plotted from the equations

$P = (|E_G||E_M|/|X|) \sin \delta$ and $P_{max} = |E_G||E_M|/|X|$, where $|E_M|$ is the voltage of the infinite bus, $|E_G|$ is the voltage behind transient reactance of the motor, and X is determined from the transient reactance of the motor plus the reactance of the transformer and line, if any, between the motor and the infinite bus.

Originally the motor is operating at synchronous speed with a torque angle of δ_0, and the mechanical power output P_0 is equal to the electric power input P_e corresponding to δ_0. When the mechanical load is suddenly increased so that the power output is P_s, which is greater than the electric power input at δ_0, the difference in power must come from the kinetic energy stored in the rotating system. This can be accompanied only by a decrease in speed, which results in an increase in the torque angle δ. As δ increases, the electric power received from the bus increases until $P_e = P_s$ at point "b" in the curve. At this point there is equilibrium of input and output torque so that acceleration is zero, but the motor is running at less than synchronous speed so that δ is increasing. The angle δ continues to increase, but after passing through point "b" the electric power input P_e is greater than P_s, and the difference must be stored in the system through an increase in kinetic energy accompanying an increase in speed. Thus, between points "b" and "c" as δ increases, the speed also increases, until synchronous speed is again reached at point "c", where the torque angle is δ_m. At point "c", P_e is still greater than P_s and speed continues to increase, but δ starts to decrease as soon as the speed of the motor exceeds synchronous speed. The maximum value of δ is δ_m at point "c". As δ decreases, point "b" is reached again with the speed more than the synchronous speed, so that δ continues to decrease until point "b" is reached. The motor is again operating at synchronous speed, and the cycle is repeated.

When the load is suddenly increased from P_0 to P_s, the motor oscillates around the equilibrium torque angle δ_s between δ_0 and δ_m as shown in Figure 5.10. If damping is present, the oscillations decrease, and stable operation results at δ_s. Table 5.1 shows the changes in speed, angle, electric power input, mechanical power output, stored energy and acceleration or deceleration as the machine oscillates. A thorough study of Table 5.1 will lead to a better understanding of transient disturbances.

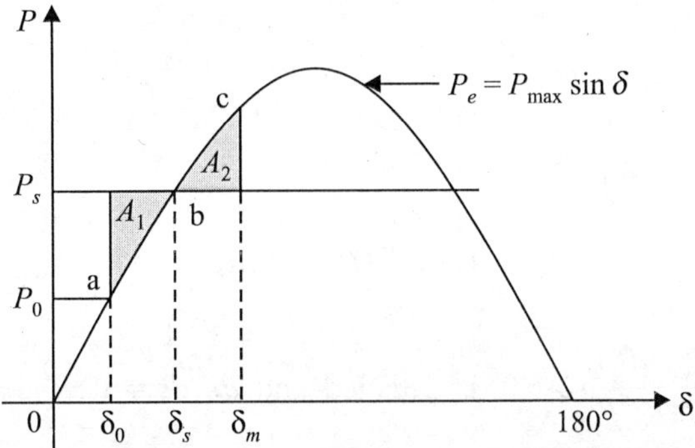

Figure 5.10 Electric power input to a motor as a function of torque angle δ.

Table 5.1 Changing conditions in a synchronous motor swinging with respect to an infinite bus because of a sudden increase in load

Position in cycle	*Motor speed* ω	*Torque angle* δ	*Electric power* P_e	*Stored energy* $1/2\ J\omega_2 = W$	*Rotating system undergoing*
At point a	$\omega = \omega_s$, decreasing	$\delta = \delta_0$, minimum	$P_e < P_s$, minimum	$\omega = \omega_s$, decreasing	Deceleration
From a towards b	$\omega = \omega_s$, decreasing	Increasing	$P_e < P_s$, increasing	$\omega < \omega_s$, decreasing	Deceleration
At point b	$\omega = \omega_s$, minimum	$\delta = \delta_s$, increasing	$P_e = P_s$, increasing	$\omega < \omega_s$, minimum	Acceleration
From b towards c	$\omega = \omega_s$, increasing	Increasing	$P_e > P_s$, increasing	$\omega < \omega_s$, decreasing	
At point c	$\omega = \omega_s$, increasing	$\delta = \delta_m$, maximum	$P_e > P_s$, maximum	$\omega = \omega_s$, increasing	Acceleration
From c towards b	$\omega = \omega_s$, maximum	Decreasing	$P_e > P_s$, decreasing	$\omega > \omega_s$, increasing	
At point b	$\omega = \omega_s$, maximum	$\delta = \delta_s$, decreasing	$P_e = P_s$, decreasing	$\omega > \omega_s$, maximum	Deceleration
From b towards a	$\omega = \omega_s$, decreasing	Decreasing	$P_e < P_s$, minimum	$\omega > \omega_s$, decreasing	

The maximum swing of the motor to a torque angle δ_m can be found by equal area criterion by equating the shaded areas A_1 and A_2.

The shaded area A_1 is given by

$$A_1 = \int_{\delta_0}^{\delta_s} (P_s - P_e)\, d\delta$$

Similarly, the shaded area A_2 is given by

$$A_2 = \int_{\delta_s}^{\delta_m} (P_e - P_s)\, d\delta$$

and

$$A_1 - A_2 = \int_{\delta_0}^{\delta_s} (P_s - P_e)\, d\delta - \int_{\delta_s}^{\delta_m} (P_e - P_s)\, d\delta$$

$$A_1 - A_2 = \int_{\delta_0}^{\delta_m} (P_s - P_e)\, d\delta$$

Equation $\displaystyle\int_{\delta_0}^{\delta} \frac{2(P_s - P_e)}{M} d\delta = 0$ is satisfied and $d\delta/dt = 0$ when $A_1 = A_2$. The maximum torque angle δ_m is located graphically so as to make A_2 equal to A_1.

5.7.4 Estimating Transient Stability Limit

Figure 5.11 shows a suddenly applied load, which is larger than that shown in Figure 5.12. The area A_2 above P_s under the curve P_e is less than A_1 and $d\delta/dt$ is not zero at $\delta = \delta_m$. Therefore δ continues to increase after $\delta = \delta_m$. P_e again becomes less than P_s. The torque angle δ continues to increase beyond δ_m, and restoring forces are not encountered. The system is stable only if an area A_2 located above P_s is equal to A_1. The test of equal areas is called the **equal area criterion**. The maximum allowable increase in the power suddenly taken from the motor originally supplying the power P_0 is shown in Figure 5.12. A suddenly applied load greater than that shown in Figure 5.12 would not permit the torque angle of the motor to stop increasing in magnitude before the input power becomes less than the power required, since the area above P_s would be less than A_1.

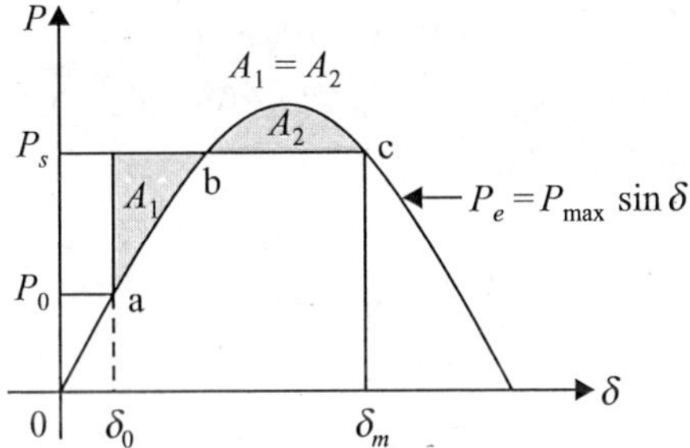

Figure 5.11 Electric power input to a motor as a function of torque angle for a suddenly increased load.

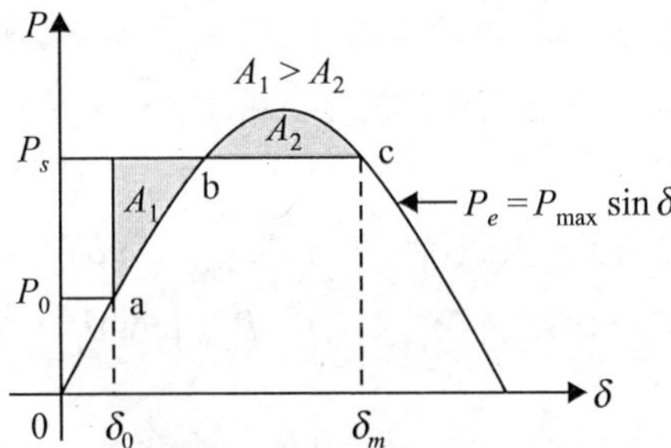

Figure 5.12 Electric power input to a motor as a function of torque angle for the maximum sudden increase of load without loss of stability.

EXAMPLE 5.11 A synchronous motor is receiving 30% of the power which is capable of receiving from an infinite bus. If the load on the motor is doubled, calculate the maximum value of δ during the swinging of the motor around its new equilibrium position.

Solution: The load in the motor is 30% and let the initial operating load angle be δ_0, i.e. $P_e = 0.3P_{max}$.

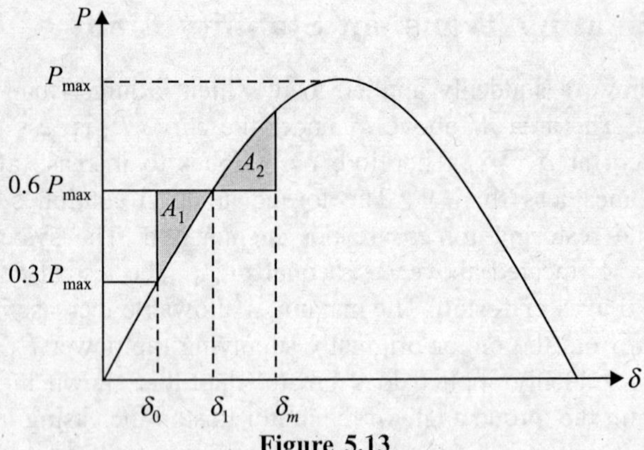

Figure 5.13

Generally,

$$P_{max} \sin \delta_0 = P_e = 0.3P_{max}$$

$$\sin \delta_0 = 0.3$$

$$\delta_0 = 17.46°$$

When the load is doubled (Figure 5.13),

$$P_e = 0.6P_{max}$$

$$\therefore \quad P_{max} \sin \delta_1 = 0.6P_{max}$$

$$\sin \delta_1 = 0.6$$

$$\delta_1 = 36.87°$$

To find the maximum value of $\delta\,(\delta_m)$

Using the equal area criterion, $A_1 = A_2$

$$\text{Area } A_1 = \int_{\delta_0}^{\delta_1} (0.6P_{max} - P_{max} \sin \delta)\, d\delta$$

$$= 0.6P_{max}(\delta_1 - \delta_0) + P_{max}(\cos \delta)_{\delta_0}^{\delta_1}$$

$$= 0.6P_{max}(\delta_1 - \delta_0) + P_{max}(\cos \delta_1 - \cos \delta_0)$$

$$\text{Area } A_2 = \int_{\delta_1}^{\delta_m} (P_{max} \sin \delta - 0.6P_{max})\, d\delta$$

$$= -P_{max}(\cos \delta_m - \cos \delta_1) - 0.6P_{max}(\delta_m - \delta_1)$$

Now $A_1 = A_2$

$$0.6P_{max}(\delta_1 - \delta_0) + P_{max}(\cos \delta_1 - \cos \delta_0) = -P_{max}(\cos \delta_m - \cos \delta_1) - 0.6P_{max}(\delta_m - \delta_1)$$

or $\quad 0.6(\delta_1 - \delta_0) + (\cos \delta_1 - \cos \delta_0) = \cos \delta_1 - \cos \delta_m - 0.6(\delta_m - \delta_1)$

or $\quad -0.6\delta_0 + \cos \delta_1 - \cos \delta_0 = \cos \delta_1 - \cos \delta_m - 0.6\delta_m$

or $\quad \cos \delta_m + 0.6\delta_m = 0.6\delta_0 + \cos \delta_0$

$$\cos\delta_m = \cos\delta_0 + 0.6(\delta_0 - \delta_m) \times \frac{\pi}{180}$$

$$= 0.95393 + 0.1828 - \left(\frac{0.6\,\pi\,\delta_m}{180}\right)$$

$$\cos\delta_m = 1.1368 - 0.01047\delta_m$$

Solving for δ_m by trial and error method, we get

$$\boxed{\delta_m > \delta_1}$$

$$\delta_m = 58.15°$$

5.7.5 Sudden Three Phase Fault at One End of the Transmission Line

Let us consider the three-phase short-circuit fault which occurs at the sending of the transmission line 2 of single machine connected to an infinite system with double circuit transmission line as shown in Figure 5.14.

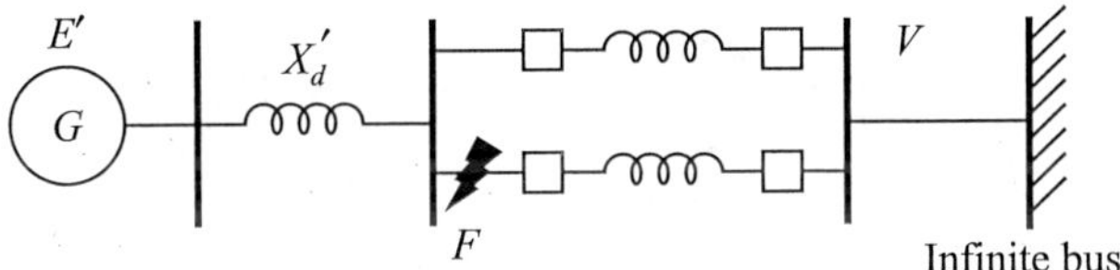

Figure 5.14 Three-phase fault at one end of the transmission line.

Prefault condition: Before the occurrence of a fault, both transmission lines are intact as shown in Figure 5.15. The power angle curve is given by

$$P_{e1} = \frac{|E'||V|}{X_I}\sin\delta = P_{\max 1}\sin\delta$$

where $X_I = X'_d + \left(\frac{X_{TL1} \times X_{TL2}}{X_{TL1} + X_{TL2}}\right)$

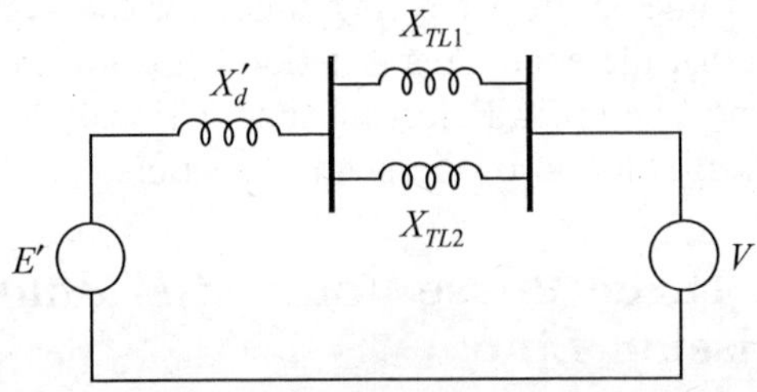

Figure 5.15 Prefault condition.

During fault condition: Upon the occurrence of three phase fault at the sending of the transmission line 2, the generator gets isolated from the power system for the purpose of power flow as shown in Figure 5.16. Thus during the period of fault lasts,

$$P_{e_2} = 0$$

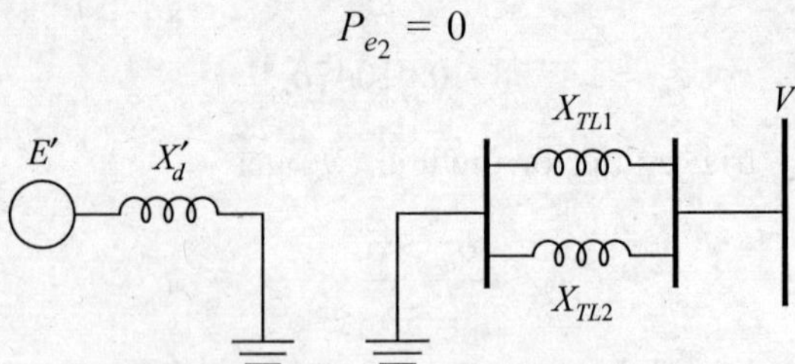

Figure 5.16 During fault condition.

The rotor therefore accelerates and δ angle increases. Synchronism will be lost unless the fault is cleared in time.

Postfault condition: The circuit breakers at the two ends of the faulted line open at time t_c (corresponding to angle δ_c), the clearing time, disconnecting the faulted line as shown in Figure 5.17. The power angle curve is given by

$$P_{e3} = \frac{|E'||V|}{X_{III}} \sin\delta = P_{\max 2} \sin\delta$$

where $X_{III} = X'_d + X_{TL1}$.

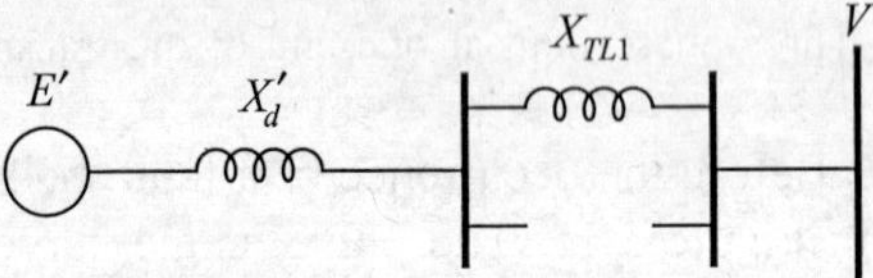

Figure 5.17 Postfault condition.

Obviously, $P_{\max 2} < P_{\max 1}$. The rotor now starts to decelerate as shown in Figure 5.18. The system will be stable if a decelerating area A_2 can be found equal to accelerating area A_1 before δ reaches the maximum allowable value $\delta_{\max}$. As area A_1 depends upon the clearing time t_c, the clearing time must be less than a certain value (critical clearing time) for the system to be stable. It is to be observed that the equal area criterion helps to determine the critical clearing angle and not the critical clearing time. Critical clearing time can be obtained by numerical solution of the swing equation.

5.7.6 Sudden Three Phase Fault at Middle of a Transmission Line

Consider the fault occurs at middle of a transmission line 2 as shown in Figure 5.19.

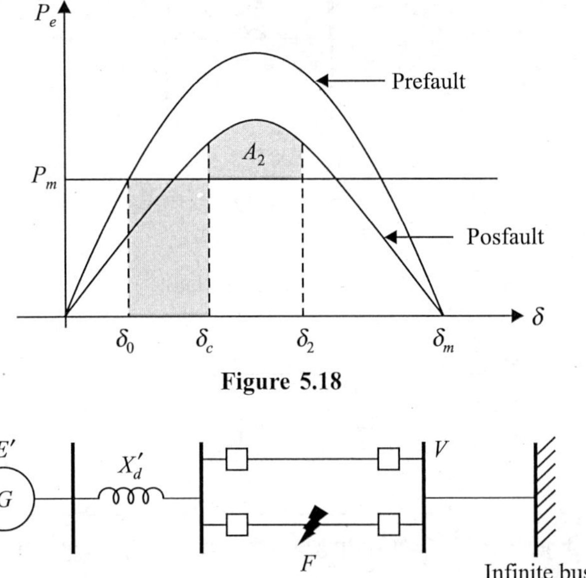

Figure 5.18

Figure 5.19 Fault at middle of transmission line.

Prefault condition: Before the occurrence of a fault, both the lines are connected as shown in Figure 5.20.

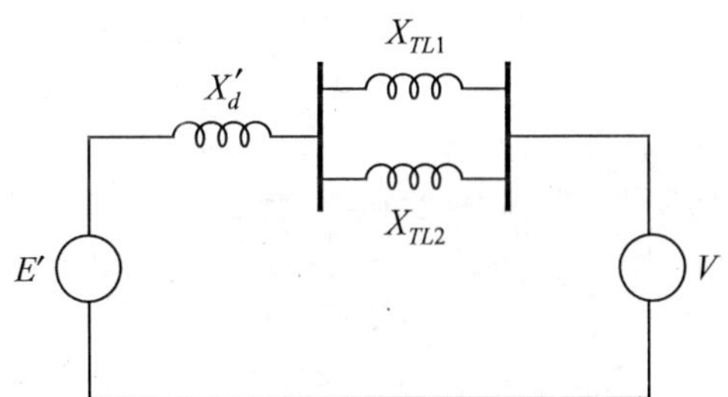

Figure 5.20 Prefault condition.

The power angle curve is given by

$$P_{e1} = \frac{|E'||V|}{X_I} \sin\delta = P_{\max 1} \sin\delta$$

where, $X_I = X'_d + \left(\dfrac{X_{TL1} \times X_{TL2}}{X_{TL1} + X_{TL2}}\right)$

During fault condition: The circuit model of the system during fault is shown in Figure 5.21. This circuit reduces to that of Figure 5.22 through one delta to star and one star to delta conversion.

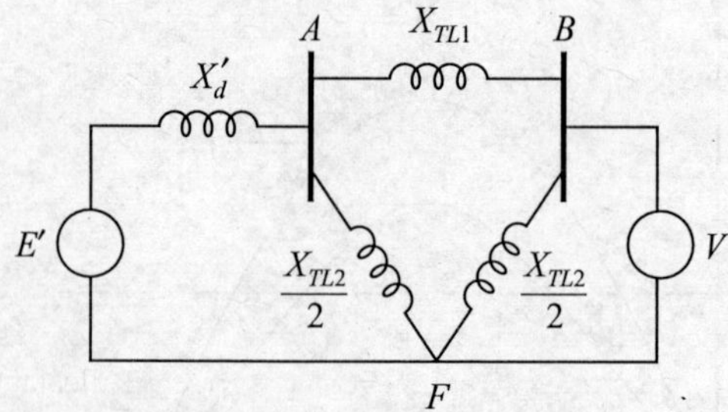

Figure 5.21 During fault.

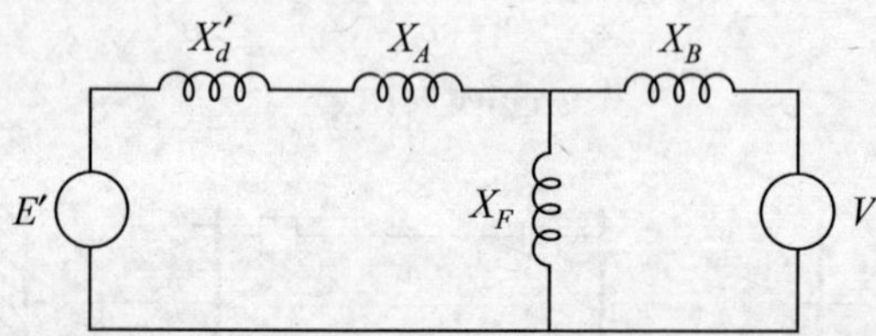

Figure 5.22 Converting reactances from delta to star.

Using delta to star conversion, the circuit becomes as shown in Figure 5.22,

$$X_A = \frac{X_{TL1} \times \dfrac{X_{TL2}}{2}}{X_{TL1} + \dfrac{X_{TL2}}{2} + \dfrac{X_{TL2}}{2}} = X_B$$

$$X_F = \frac{\dfrac{X_{TL2}}{2} \times \dfrac{X_{TL2}}{2}}{X_{TL1} + \dfrac{X_{TL2}}{2} + \dfrac{X_{TL2}}{2}}$$

Convert star connection to delta connection, the circuit becomes as shown in Figure 5.23,

$$X_{II} = \frac{(X'_d + X_A)X_F + X_F X_B + (X'_d + X_A)X_B}{X_F}$$

The power angle curve during fault is given by

$$P_{e2} = \frac{|E'||V|}{X_{II}} \sin\delta = P_{\max 2} \sin\delta$$

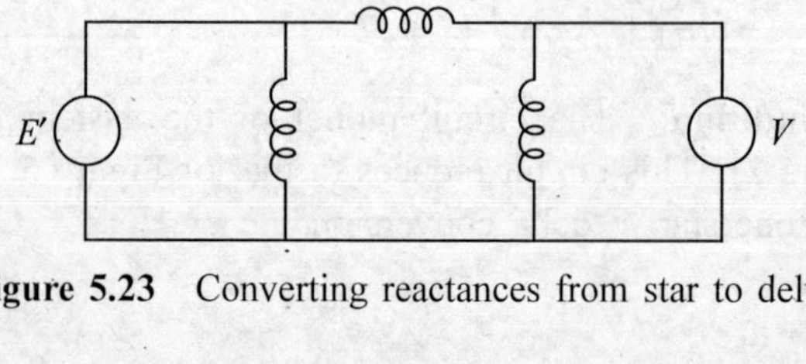

Figure 5.23 Converting reactances from star to delta.

Postfault condition: In this condition, the faulted transmission line 2 is open after fault and the circuit is shown in Figure 5.24.

$$P_{e3} = \frac{|E'||V|}{X_{III}} \sin\delta = P_{\max 3} \sin\delta$$

where $X_{III} = X'_d + X_{TL1}$.

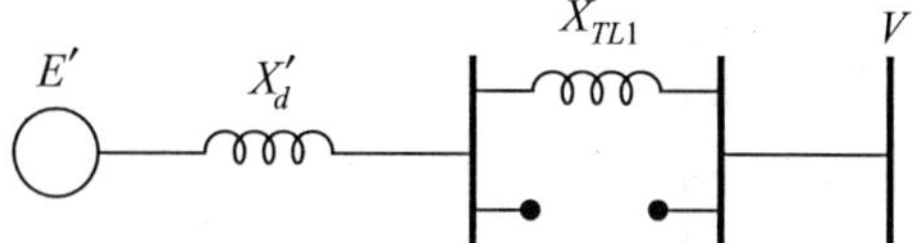

Figure 5.24 Postfault condition.

P_{e1}, P_{e2}, and P_{e3} are plotted in Figure 5.25.

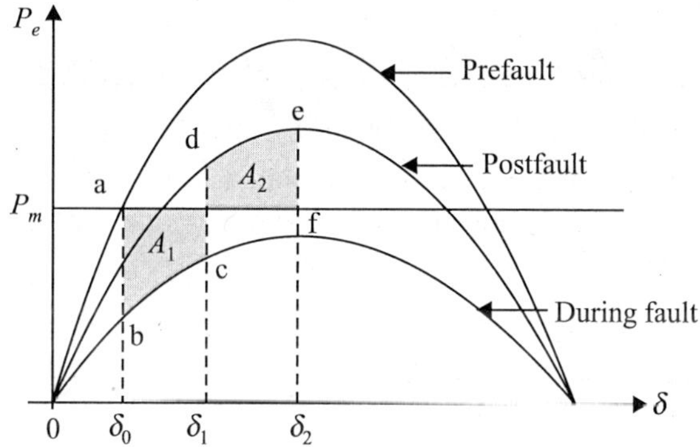

Figure 5.25 Power angle curves.

The accelerating area A_1 corresponding to δ_1 is less than area A_2, giving better chance for the stable operation. It is possible to find an area A_2 equal to area A_1. As δ_1 increases, area A_1 increases.

To find $A_1 = A_2$, δ_1 increases till $\delta_2 = \delta_{\max}$. This case of critical clearing angle is shown in Figure 5.26.

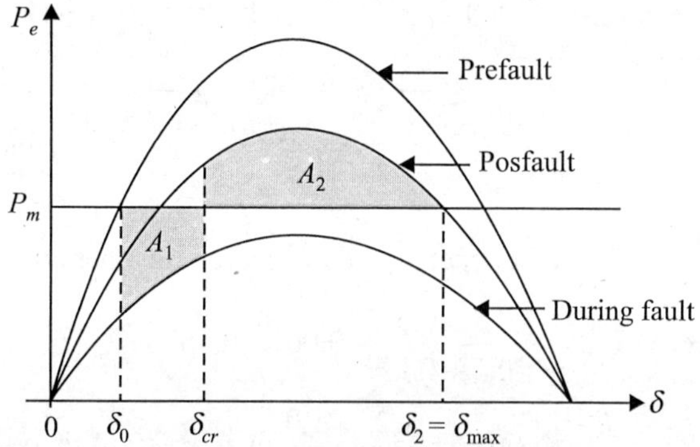

Figure 5.26 Power angle curves.

Applying the equal area criterion, we can write

$$\text{Area } A_1 = \text{Area } A_2$$

$$\int_{\delta_0}^{\delta_{cr}} (P_m - P_{\max 2} \sin\delta)\, d\delta = \int_{\delta_{cr}}^{\delta_{\max}} (P_{\max 3} \sin\delta - P_m)\, d\delta$$

where $\delta_{\max} = \pi - \sin^{-1}\left(\dfrac{P_m}{P_{\max 3}}\right)$

Integrating, we get

$$(P_m\delta + P_{\max 2}\cos\delta)\Big|_{\delta_0}^{\delta_{cr}} + (P_{\max 3}\cos\delta + P_m\delta)\Big|_{\delta_{cr}}^{\delta_{\max}} = 0$$

$$P_m(\delta_{cr} - \delta_0) + P_{\max 2}(\cos\delta_{cr} - \cos\delta_0) + P_m(\delta_{\max} - \delta_{cr}) + P_{\max 3}(\cos\delta_{\max} - \cos\delta_{cr}) = 0$$

$$\cos\delta_{cr} = \frac{P_m(\delta_{\max} - \delta_0) - P_{\max 2}\cos\delta_0 + P_{\max 3}\cos\delta_{\max}}{P_{\max 3} - P_{\max 2}}$$

The critical clearing angle can be calculated from the above equation. The angles in this equation are in radians. The equation modifies as below if the angles are in degrees.

$$\cos\delta_{cr} = \frac{P_m(\delta_{\max} - \delta_0)\dfrac{\pi}{180} - P_{\max 2}\cos\delta_0 + P_{\max 3}\cos\delta_{\max}}{P_{\max 3} - P_{\max 2}}$$

EXAMPLE 5.12 Given the circuit as shown in the figure below where a three-phase fault is applied on one end of a line near circuit breaker CB_4. Find the critical fault clearing angle for clearing the fault with simultaneous opening of breaker CB_2 and CB_4. The generator is delivering 1.0 p.u. MW at the instant preceding the fault. All the p.u. quantities are on the common MVA.

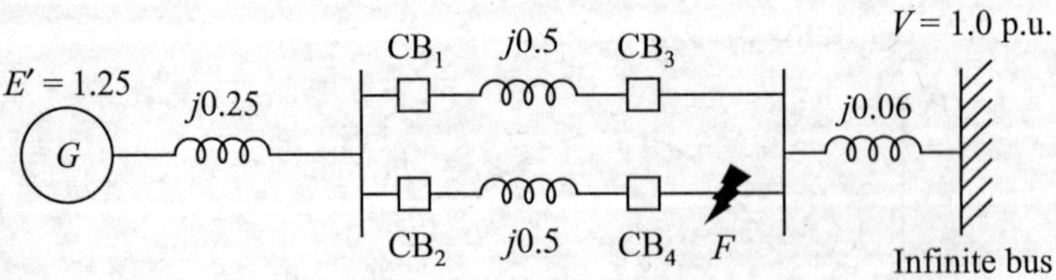

Solution:

Prefault condition Transfer reactance during prefault operation is

$$X_I = 0.25 + \frac{0.5 \times 0.5}{0.5 + 0.5} + 0.06 = 0.56$$

$$P_{e1} = \frac{|E'||V|}{X_I}\sin\delta = \frac{1.25 \times 1.0}{0.56}\sin\delta = 2.232\sin\delta$$

During fault condition The fault occurs at the end of the line 2 or near bus 2. Therefore during the short circuit fault the circuit separates by the circuit breaker for finding the transfer reactance as shown in the Figure below. During the clearing of fault, no power is transferred from the circuit, i.e. $P_{e2} = 0$.

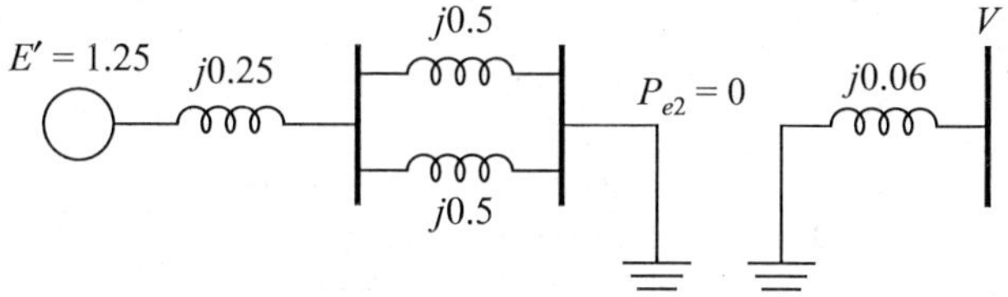

Postfault condition With the opening of the faulted line, say by simultaneous opening of the circuit breakers CB_2 and CB_4, the postfault transfer reactance is

$$X_{III} = 0.25 + 0.5 + 0.06 = 0.81$$

$$P_{e3} = \frac{|E'||V|}{X_{III}} \sin\delta = \frac{1.25 \times 1.0}{0.81} \sin\delta = 1.543 \sin\delta$$

The initial power angle δ_0 is calculated as

$$P_{m0} = P_{e0} = 1.0 = P_{\max 1} \sin\delta_0$$

$$\delta_0 = \sin^{-1}\left(\frac{1.0}{2.232}\right) = 26.32°$$

and

$$\delta_{\max} = 180° - \sin^{-1}\left(\frac{P_{m0}}{P_{\max 3}}\right)$$

$$\delta_{\max} = 180° - \sin^{-1}\left(\frac{1.0}{1.543}\right) = 139.6°$$

$$\cos\delta_{cr} = \frac{P_m(\delta_{\max} - \delta_0)\dfrac{\pi}{180} - P_{\max 2}\cos\delta_0 + P_{\max 3}\cos\delta_{\max}}{P_{\max 3} - P_{\max 2}}$$

$$= \frac{1.0(139.6 - 26.62)\dfrac{\pi}{180} - 0 + 1.543\cos 139.6°}{1.543 - 0} = 0.51640$$

$$\delta_{cr} = 58.9°$$

EXAMPLE 5.13 A 2220 MVA, 24 kV and 60 Hz synchronous machine is connected to an infinite bus through transformer and double circuit transmission line, as shown in the following figure. The infinite bus voltage $V = 1.0$ p.u. The direct axis transient reactance of the machine is 0.30 p.u., the transformer reactance is 0.20 p.u., and the reactance of each transmission line is 0.3 p.u., all to a base of the rating of the synchronous machine. Initially, the machine is delivering 0.8 p.u. real power and reactive power is 0.074 p.u. with a terminal voltage of 1.0 p.u. The inertia constant $H = 5$ MJ/MVA. All resistances are neglected.

(i) A temporary three-phase fault occurs at the sending end of one of the lines. When the fault is cleared, both lines are intact. Determine the critical clearing angle and the critical fault clearing time.

(ii) A three-phase fault occurs at the middle of one of the lines, fault is cleared, and the faulted line is isolated. Determine the critical clearing angle.

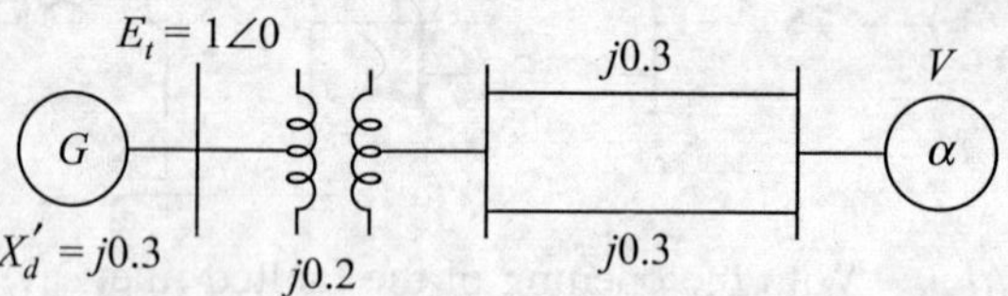

Solution:

Given: infinite bus voltage $V = 1.0$ p.u.

terminal voltage of generator $E_t = 1.0$ p.u.

$X_d' = j0.3$

$P_{m0} = P_{e0} = 0.8$

The current flowing into the infinite bus is

$$I = \frac{S^*}{V^*} = \frac{0.8 - j0.074}{1.0} = 0.8 - j0.074$$

The transfer reactance between the internal voltage and the infinite bus before fault is

$$X_I = 0.3 + 0.2 + \frac{0.3 \times 0.3}{0.3 + 0.3} = 0.65$$

$$E' = V + jX_I I = 1.0 + j(0.65)\,(0.8 - j0.074) = 1.17\angle 26.387°$$

(i) Three-phase fault occurs at the sending end of one of the lines

Prefault condition

$$X_I = 0.3 + 0.2 + \frac{0.3 \times 0.3}{0.3 + 0.3} = 0.65$$

$$P_{e1} = \frac{|E'||V|}{X_I}\sin\delta = \frac{1.17 \times 1.0}{0.65}\sin\delta = 1.8\sin\delta$$

During the fault condition: $P_{e2} = 0$

Postfault condition Since both the lines are intact when the fault is cleared therefore the power angle equation of prefault and postfault are the same.

$$P_{e3} = \frac{|E'||V|}{X_I}\sin\delta = \frac{1.17 \times 1.0}{0.65}\sin\delta = 1.8\sin\delta$$

The initial power angle δ_0 is calculated as

$$P_{m0} = P_{e0} = 0.8 = P_{\max 1}\sin\delta_0$$

$$\delta_0 = \sin^{-1}\left(\frac{0.8}{1.8}\right) = 26.388° = 0.46055 \text{ rad}$$

and

$$\delta_{\max} = 180° - \sin^{-1}\left(\frac{P_{m0}}{P_{\max 3}}\right)$$

$$\delta_{\max} = 180° - \sin^{-1}\left(\frac{0.8}{1.8}\right) = 153.612°$$

$$\cos\delta_{cr} = \frac{P_m(\delta_{\max} - \delta_0)\dfrac{\pi}{180} - P_{\max 2}\cos\delta_0 + P_{\max 3}\cos\delta_{\max}}{P_{\max 3} - P_{\max 2}}$$

$$= \frac{0.8(153.612 - 26.388)\dfrac{\pi}{180} - 0 + 1.8\cos 153.612°}{1.8 - 0} = 1.48 \text{ rad}$$

$$\delta_{cr} = 84.775°$$

The critical clearing time

$$t_c = \sqrt{\frac{2H(\delta_{cr} - \delta_0)}{\pi f P_m}}$$

$$t_c = \sqrt{\frac{2 \times 5(1.48 - 0.46055)}{\pi \times 60 \times 0.8}} = 0.26 \text{ s}$$

(ii) Three-phase fault occurs at the middle of one of the lines

Prefault condition From the reactance diagram,

$$X_T = X_I = 0.3 + 0.2 + \left(\frac{0.3 \times 0.3}{0.3 + 0.3}\right) = 0.65$$

$$P_{e1} = \frac{|E'||V|}{X_I}\sin\delta = \frac{1.17 \times 1.0}{0.65}\sin\delta = 1.8\sin\delta$$

During the fault condition (fault at the middle of the transmission line 2)

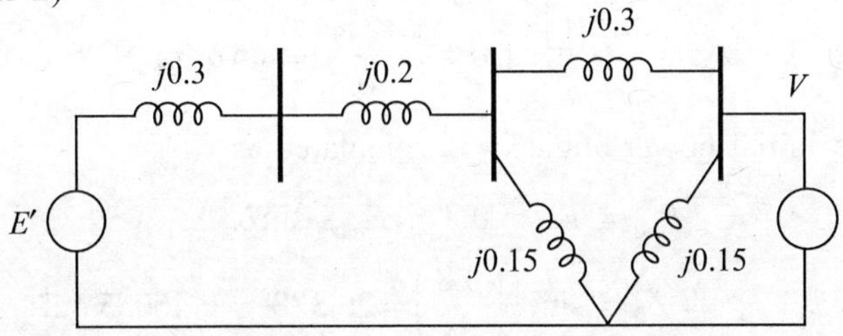

Using delta to star conversion, the circuit becomes

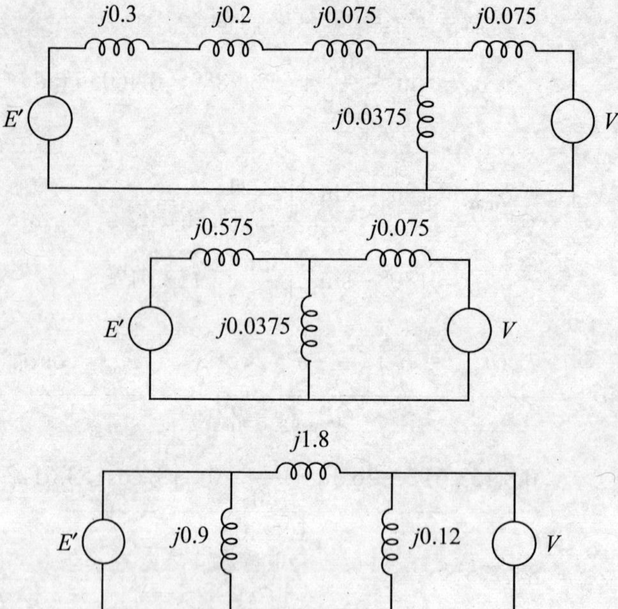

From the reactance diagram,

$$X_T = X_{II} = 1.8$$

$$P_{e2} = \frac{|E'||V|}{X_{II}}\sin\delta = \frac{1.17 \times 1.0}{1.8}\sin\delta = 0.65\sin\delta$$

Postfault condition

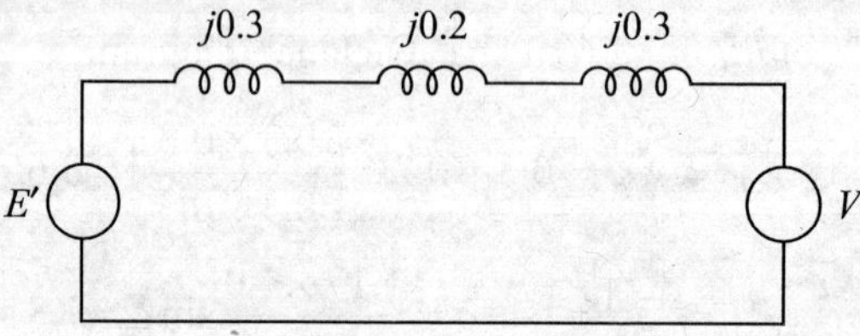

From the reactance diagram,

$$X_T = X_{III} = 0.8$$

$$P_{e3} = \frac{|E'||V|}{X_{III}}\sin\delta = \frac{1.17 \times 1.0}{0.8}\sin\delta = 1.4625\sin\delta$$

The initial power angle δ_0 is calculated as

$$P_{m0} = P_{e0} = 0.8 = P_{\max 1}\sin\delta_0$$

$$\delta_0 = \sin^{-1}\left(\frac{0.8}{1.8}\right) = 26.388° = 0.46055 \text{ rad}$$

and

$$\delta_{max} = 180° - \sin^{-1}\left(\frac{P_{m0}}{P_{max\,3}}\right)$$

$$\delta_{max} = 180° - \sin^{-1}\left(\frac{0.8}{1.4625}\right) = 146.838° = 2.5628 \text{ rad}$$

$$\cos\delta_{cr} = \frac{P_m(\delta_{max} - \delta_0)\dfrac{\pi}{180} - P_{max\,2}\cos\delta_0 + P_{max\,3}\cos\delta_{max}}{P_{max\,3} - P_{max\,2}}$$

$$= \frac{0.8(146.838 - 26.388)\dfrac{\pi}{180} - 0.65\cos 26.388° + 1.4625\cos 146.838°}{1.4625 - 0.65}$$

$$= -0.15356 \text{ rad}$$

$$\delta_{cr} = 98.834°$$

5.8 Solution of Swing Equation

The swing equation, governing the motion of each machine of a system, is

$$M\frac{d^2\delta}{dt^2} = P_a$$

where δ – displacement angle of rotor with respect to a reference axis rotating at normal speed

M – inertia constant of machine

P_a – accelerating power (difference between the mechanical input and output after correcting the losses)

t – time.

The solution of swing equation can be done by applying the following methods.

1. Step by step method.
2. Euler's method.
3. Modified Euler's method.
4. Runge–Kutta method.

The step by step method (point by point method) is the most feasible and widely used way of solving the swing equations. By this method, a good accuracy can be attained and it is also easy to compute δ.

In the step by step method, one or more variables are assumed constant throughout the short interval of time Δt, so that as a result of the assumptions made, the equations can be solved for the changes in the other variables during the same time interval. Then from the values of the other variables at the end of the interval, the new values can be calculated for the variables which were assumed constant. These new values are then used in the next time interval.

5.8.1 Step by Step Method-I

It consists of two processes. These are to be carried out alternately.

1. Assume accelerating power P_a to be constant and compute the angular position and if necessary, the angular velocity (speed) at the end of the time interval from the knowledge of the position and speeds at the beginning of the interval.
2. Then from the angular positions and speed, the accelerating power of each machine is to be calculated. This P_a will be kept constant for the next time interval and the procedure is to be repeated till the required final time is reached.

The swing equation is given by

$$M\frac{d^2\delta}{dt^2} = P_a$$

The above equation is written as,

$$\frac{d^2\delta}{dt^2} = \frac{P_a}{M}$$

Integrating with respect to t,

$$\frac{d\delta}{dt} = \omega = \omega_0 + \frac{P_a}{M}t \tag{5.27}$$

Integrating once again,

$$\delta = \delta + \omega_0 t + \frac{P_a}{M}\cdot\frac{t^2}{2} \tag{5.28}$$

Equations (5.27) and (5.28) respectively provide the speed of the machine (ω) and the angular displacement (δ) of the machine with respect to a reference axis rotating at synchronous speed.

δ_0 and ω_0 are the values of δ and ω at the beginning of the interval. These equations hold for any instant of time t during the interval in which P_a is constant.

We are in the need of δ and ω at the end of the interval.

Let n denote the quantities at the end of the nth interval and $n - 1$ denote the quantities at the end of the $(n - 1)$th interval, which is the beginning of the nth interval. Δt is the length of the interval.

Putting Δt in place of t in Eqs. (5.27) and (5.28) and using the appropriate subscripts, we obtain the speed and angle at the end of the nth interval as

$$\begin{aligned} \omega_n &= \omega_{n-1} + \frac{\Delta t}{M}P_a(n-1) \\ \delta_n &= \delta_{n-1} + \Delta t\,\omega_{n-1} + \frac{\Delta t}{2M}P_a(n-1) \end{aligned} \tag{5.29}$$

The increments of speed and angle during the nth interval are

$$\Delta\omega_n = \omega_n - \omega_{n-1} = \frac{\Delta t}{M} P_a(n-1)$$

$$\Delta\delta_n = \delta_n - \delta_{n-1} = \Delta t\, \omega_{n-1} + \frac{\Delta t^2}{2M} P_a(n-1) \tag{5.30}$$

Equation (5.29) or (5.30) is suitable for step by step calculation.

If we are interested only in the angular position and not in the speed, ω_{n-1} can be eliminated from Eqs. (5.29) and (5.30).

For the preceding interval, we can write

$$\delta_{n-1} = \delta_{n-2} + \Delta t\, \omega_{n-2} + \frac{(\Delta t)^2}{2M} P_{a(n-2)} \tag{5.31}$$

Equation (5.29)–(5.31) gives

$$\delta_n - \delta_{n-1} = \delta_{n-1} - \delta_{n-2} + (\omega_{n-1} - \omega_{n-2})\Delta t + \frac{\Delta t^2}{2M}(P_{a\,(n-1)} - P_{a\,(n-2)})$$

Putting $\Delta\delta_n = \delta_n - \delta_{n-1}$; $\Delta\delta_{n-1} = \delta_{n-1} - \delta_{n-2}$
$\Delta\omega_{n-1} = \omega_{n-1} - \omega_{n-2}$

$$\Delta\delta_n = \Delta\delta_{n-1} + \Delta\omega_{n-1} \cdot \Delta t + \frac{\Delta t^2}{2M}(P_{a\,(n-1)} - P_{a\,(n-2)}) \tag{5.32}$$

But from Eq. (5.30)

$$\Delta\omega_{n-1} = \frac{\Delta t}{M} P_{a\,(n-2)}$$

Substituting in Eq. (5.32)

$$\begin{aligned}\Delta\delta_n &= \Delta\delta_{n-1} + \frac{\Delta t}{M} \cdot P_{a(n-2)} \cdot \Delta t + \frac{\Delta t^2}{2M}(P_{a\,(n-1)} - P_{a\,(n-2)}) \\ &= \Delta\delta_{n-1} + \frac{\Delta t^2}{2M}(P_{a\,(n-1)} - P_{a\,(n-2)})\end{aligned}$$

This equation gives the increment in angle during any interval in terms of the increment for the previous interval.

Time interval Δt should be short enough to give the required accuracy. If it is too short, it will increase the number of calculations to plot a swing curve, and thus it provides accuracy.

Limitations of step by step method-I

The acceleration during each interval of time Δt is constant at the value corresponding to the beginning of the interval.

Figure 5.27 shows the true variation of acceleration (α) as a function of time and the assumed variation of the above method.

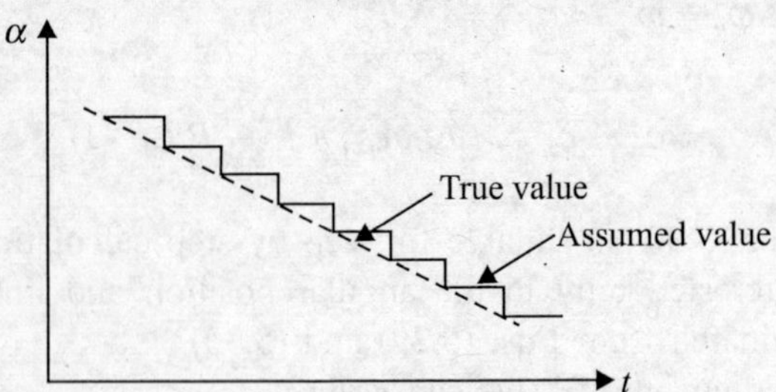

Figure 5.27 Variation of acceleration (α) as a function of time.

EXAMPLE 5.14 Consider a 60 Hz machine for which H = 2.7 MJ/MVA and it is initially operating in steady state with input and output of 1 p.u. and an angular displacement of 45 electrical degree with respect to an infinite bus bar. Upon occurrence of a fault, assume that the input remains constant and the output is given by $P_e = \delta/90°$. Calculate and plot swing curve by step by step method I. Using the time interval Δt = 0.05 s. Up to t = 1 s.

Solution:

Given P_i = 1 p.u.; S = 1 p.u.

$$P_e = \frac{\delta}{90°}$$

Also

$$P_a = P_i - P_e = 1 - \frac{\delta}{90°}$$

$\therefore$

$$P_a = 1 - 0.0111\delta$$

$$M = \frac{SH}{180f} = \frac{2.7}{180 \times 60} = 2.5 \times 10^{-4}$$

We have, by method I

$$\Delta\omega_n = \frac{\Delta t}{M} P_{a(n-1)}$$

$$\Delta\delta_n = \Delta t \cdot \omega_{n-1} + \frac{\Delta t^2}{2M} P_{a(n-1)}$$

Substituting Δt and M in the above two equations

$$\Delta\omega_n = \frac{0.05}{2.5 \times 10^{-4}} P_{a(n-1)}; \qquad \delta_n = \Delta t \cdot \omega_{n-1} + \frac{\Delta t^2}{2M} P_{a\,(n-1)}$$

$$\Delta\omega_n = 200 P_{a\,(n-1)} \qquad \Delta\delta_n = 0.05\,\omega_{n-1} + 5P_{a\,(n-1)}$$

t s	P_e	P_a	$\Delta\omega$	ω	0.05 ω	$5P_a$	$\Delta\delta$ deg.	δ deg.
0+	0.5	0.5	100	0	0	2.5	2.5	45
0.05	0.528	0.472	94.55	100	5	2.36	7.36	47.5
0.1	0.6089	0.391	78.2	194.55	9.7275	1.955	11.6825	54.86
0.15	0.7386	0.2614	52.2757	272.75	13.6375	1.307	14.9445	66.5425
0.2	0.9045	0.0955	19.1	325.0257	16.2513	0.4775	16.7288	81.487
0.25	1.0902	–0.0902	–18.04	344.13	17.21	–0.45	16.76	98.2158
0.3	1.28	–0.28	–55.24	326.09	16.3	–1.4	14.9	114.97
0.35	1.441	–0.44	–88.31	270.85	13.54	–2.2	11.34	129.87
0.4	1.57	–0.57	–113.49	182.54	9.13	–2.85	6.28	141.21
0.45	1.64	–0.64	–127.43	69.05	3.45	–3.2	0.25	147.49
0.5	1.64	–0.64	–127.98	–58.38	–2.92	–3.2	–6.12	147.74
0.55	1.57	–0.57	–114.4	–186.36	–9.32	–2.85	–12.17	141.62
0.6	1.44	–0.44	–88	–300.76	–15.04	–2.2	–17.24	129.45
0.65	1.25	–0.25	–49.11	–388.76	–19.44	–1.25	–20.69	112.21
0.7	1.02	–0.02	–3.17	–437.87	–21.89	–0.1	–21.99	91.52
0.75	0.77	0.23	46	–441.04	–22.05	1.15	–20.9	69.53
0.8	0.54	0.46	92	–395.04	–19.75	2.3	–17.45	48.63
0.85	0.35	0.65	130.75	–303.04	–15.15	3.25	–11.9	31.18
0.9	0.21	0.79	157.2	–172.26	–8.61	3.93	–4.68	19.28
0.95	0.16	0.84	167.59	–15.06	–0.75	4.2	3.45	14.6
1	0.2	0.8	159.94	152.53	7.63	4	11.63	18.05
								29.68

The variation of δ with time t is plotted as shown in the figure below

From the swing curve, we see that the value of δ increases and then decreases, therefore the system is stable. A more accurate approach would be to assume the average value of acceleration over the interval Δt, by using the value of acceleration at the middle of the interval. It is adopted in step by step method II.

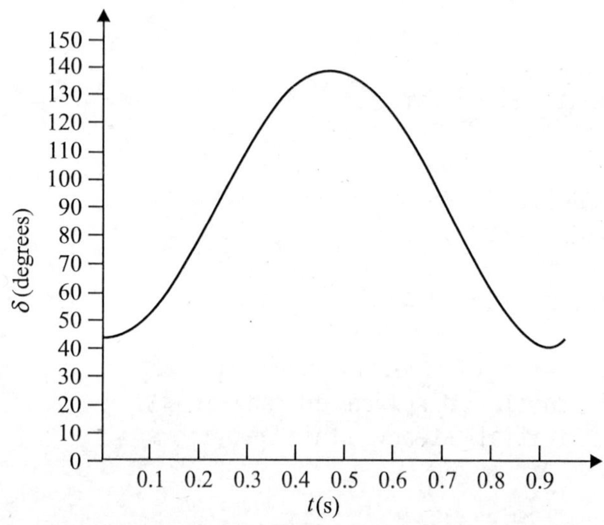

MATLAB program—solution of swing equation using step by step method – I

```
Del_delta=0; i=1;
f=input('Enter the frequency :');
H=input('Enter the value of inertia constant :');
delta=input('Enter initial displacement angle :');
Pi=input('Enter initial steady state power :');
M=H/(180*f); y=0.05/M;yy=0.05^2/(2*M);Pu=delta/90;
del_int=delta*pi/180; Pa=1-Pu;
disp('Time Pe Pa 5*Pa Del_ang Del')
for t=0:.05:1.05
 if t==0
 w=0;
 del_w=y*Pa;
 del_del=0.05*w+yy*Pa;
 fprintf('%g-',t);
 disp([Pi Pa yy*Pa del_del delta]);
 fprintf('%g+',t);
 disp([Pu Pa yy*Pa del_del delta])
 else
 w=w+del_w;
 delta=delta+del_del;
 Pu=delta/90;
 Pa=1-Pu;
 del_w=y*Pa;
 del_del=0.05*w+yy*Pa;
 fprintf('%g',t);
 disp([Pu Pa yy*Pa del_del delta])
 end
 time(i)=t;
 del(i)=delta;
 delta=delta+Del_delta;
 i=i+1;
end
plot(time,del);
title('SWING CURVE');
xlabel('t, sec');
ylabel('delta, elec. deg');
Results:
Enter the value of inertia constant: 2.7
Enter the initial displacement angle: 45
Enter the initial steady state power: 1
```

Time	*Pe*	*Pa*	5**Pa*	Del_ang	Del
0+	0.5	0.5	2.5	2.5	45
0.05	0.52778	0.47222	2.3611	7.3611	47.5
0.1	0.60957	0.39043	1.9522	11.674	54.861
0.15	0.73928	0.26072	1.3036	14.93	66.535
0.2	0.90517	0.09483	0.47413	16.708	81.466
0.25	1.0908	–0.0908	–0.4541	16.728	98.173
0.3	1.2767	–0.2767	–1.3834	14.89	114.9
0.35	1.4421	–0.4421	–2.2107	11.296	129.79
0.4	1.5676	–0.5677	–2.8382	6.2475	141.09
0.45	1.6371	–0.6371	–3.1853	0.22392	147.34
0.5	1.6395	–0.6396	–3.1977	–6.1591	147.56
0.55	1.5711	–0.5711	–2.8556	–12.212	141.4
0.6	1.4354	–0.4354	–2.1771	–17.245	129.19
0.65	1.2438	–0.2438	–1.219	–20.641	111.94
0.7	1.0145	–0.0145	–0.0723	–21.933	91.301
0.75	0.77076	0.22924	1.1462	–20.859	69.369
0.8	0.539	0.461	2.305	–17.408	48.51
0.85	0.34558	0.65442	3.2721	–11.831	31.102
0.9	0.21413	0.78587	3.9293	–4.6291	19.272
0.95	0.1627	0.8373	4.1865	3.4868	14.643
1	0.20144	0.79856	3.9928	11.666	18.13

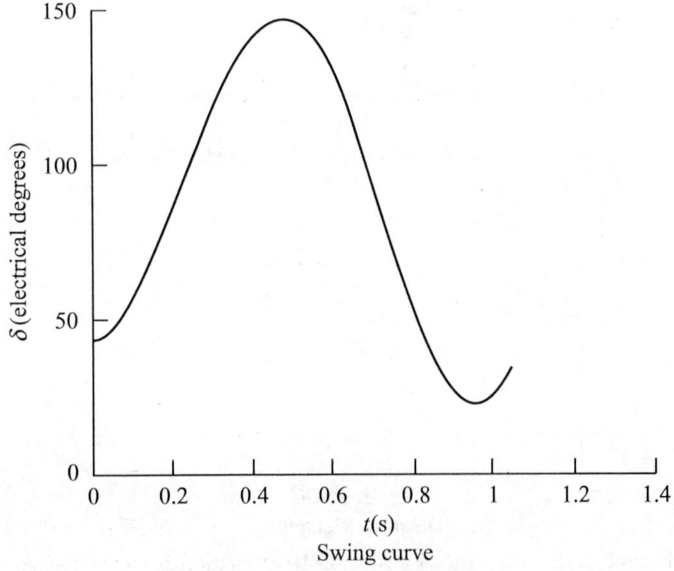

Swing curve

5.8.2 Step by Step Method-II

Acceleration is assumed constant from the middle of one interval to the middle of the next interval.

For example, consider Figure 5.28(a) where α_{n-1} is the equivalent constant value of acceleration from $t = (n - (3/2))\Delta t$ to $t = (n - (1/2))\Delta t$.

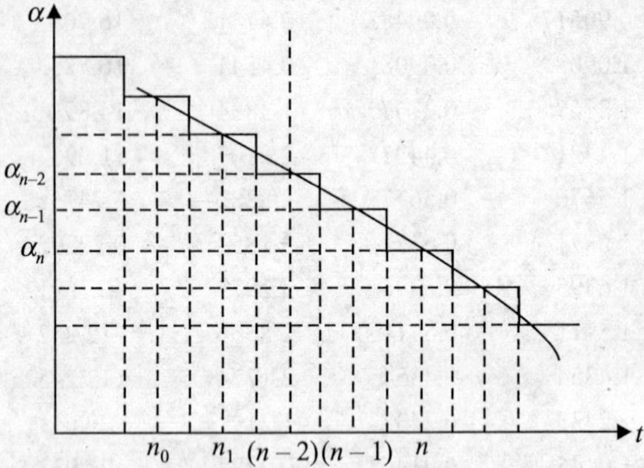

(a) α constant from the middle of one interval to the middle of the next

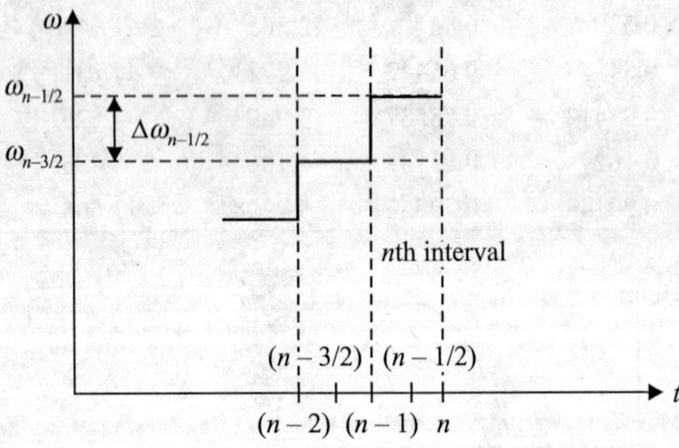

(b) Angular velocity (ω) constant during the interval

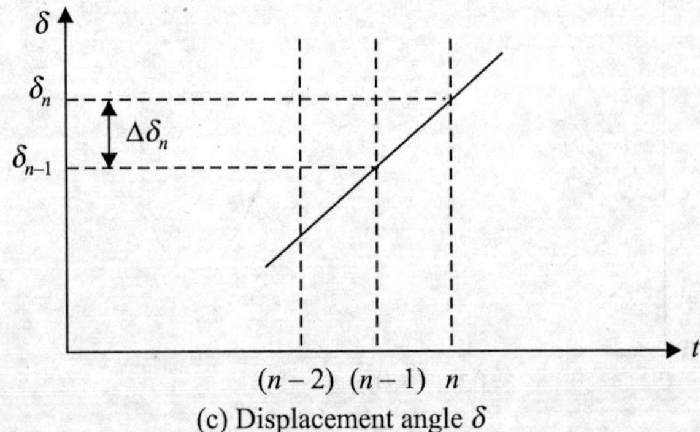

(c) Displacement angle δ

Figure 5.28 Step by step method-II—variation of α, ω and δ.

α_n is constant from $t = (n - (1/2))\Delta t$ to $t = (n + (1/2))\Delta t$ and so on. In the region of constant acceleration α_{n-1}, there is an increment of angular velocity from $\omega_{n-3/2}$ to $\Delta\omega_{n-1/2}$, i.e. [from Figure 5.28(b)]

$$\omega_{n-1/2} = \omega_{n-3/2} + \Delta\omega_{n-1/2} \tag{5.33}$$

where $\Delta\omega_{n-1/2}$ is the increment in angular velocity over a time interval Δt, due to acceleration α_{n-1}.

$$\Delta\omega_{n-1/2} = \alpha_{n-1} \cdot \Delta t \tag{5.34}$$

As
$$\alpha_{n-1} = \frac{d^2\delta_{n-1}}{dt^2} = \frac{P_{a\,(n-1)}}{M}$$

Thus,
$$\Delta\omega_{n-1/2} = \frac{P_{a\,(n-1)}}{M} \cdot \Delta t \tag{5.35}$$

Again, the angular velocity, $\omega_{n-1/2}$ remains constant for $t = (n - 1)\Delta t$, during the nth interval. From Figure 5.28(c), the displacement angle δ_{n-1} increases to δ_n over this interval by an amount $\Delta\delta_n$.

$$\delta_n = \delta_{n-1} + \Delta\delta_n \tag{5.36}$$

$$\Delta\delta_n = \omega_{n-1/2} \cdot \Delta t \tag{5.37}$$

Using Eq. (5.33)

$$\omega_{n-1/2} = \omega_{n-3/2} + \Delta\omega_{n-1/2}$$

Hence

$$\begin{aligned}\Delta\delta_n &= (\omega_{n-3/2} + \Delta\omega_{n-1/2})\Delta t \\ &= \omega_{n-3/2}\,\Delta t + \alpha_{n-1}\,\Delta t^2 \qquad \text{by using Eq. (5.34)}\end{aligned} \tag{5.38}$$

From Eq. (5.37)

$$\Delta\delta_{n-1} = (\omega_{n-3/2})\Delta t \tag{5.39}$$

Substituting Eq. (5.39) in Eq. (5.38), we get

$$\Delta\delta_n = \Delta\delta_{n-1} + \alpha_{n-1}\,\Delta t^2$$

Substituting $\alpha_{n-1} = P_{a(n-1)}/M$, we get

$$\Delta\delta_n = \Delta\delta_{n-1} + \frac{P_{a(n-1)}}{M}\Delta t^2 \tag{5.40}$$

In the method II, it is not necessary to calculate ω, unless it is specifically required.

Using Eq. (5.40), P_a is to be found step by step over a number of intervals of time, from which the increment in displacement angle can be calculated as the inertia constant is known.

To begin with, the power output at $t = 0^-$ and 0^+ are averaged out and the average value of P_a is determined. Then $\Delta\delta$ is calculated from the value during the preceding interval.

EXAMPLE 5.15 Consider a 60 Hz machine for which $H = 2.7$ MJ/MVA and it is initially operating in steady state with input and output of 1 p.u. and an angular displacement of 45 electrical degree with respect to an infinite bus bar. Upon occurrence of a fault, assume that the input remains constant and the output is given by $P_e = \delta/90°$. Calculate and plot the swing curve by the step-by-step method II. Using the time interval $\Delta t = 0.05$ s. Up to $t = 1$ s. Step-by-step method-II using the time interval $\Delta t = 0.05$ s and upto $t = 1$ s.

Solution:

$H = 2.7$ MJ/MVA

At time $t = 0^-$, $P_m = P_e = 1$ p.u.

At time $t = 0^+$, $P_m = 1$ p.u., $P_e = \delta/90°$

$$M = \frac{SH}{180f} = 2.5 \times 10^{-4} \text{ p.u.}$$

$$P_a = 1 - \frac{\delta}{90°}$$

$$\frac{\Delta t^2}{M} = \frac{0.05^2}{2.5 \times 10^{-4}} = 10$$

Now the equation for $\Delta\delta_n$ is given by

$$\Delta\delta_n = \Delta\delta_{n-1} + \frac{\Delta t^2}{M} P_{a\,(n-1)}$$

$$= \Delta\delta_{n-1} + 10P_{a(n-1)}$$

t(s)	P_e	P_a	$10P_a$	$\Delta\delta$ deg.	δ deg.
0^-	1	0	—	—	—
0^+	0.5	0.5	—	—	45°
0_{av}	—	0.25	2.5	—	—
				2.5	
0.05	0.5277	0.472	4.72	—	47.5
				7.22	
0.1	0.608	0.392	3.92	—	54.72
				11.14	
0.15	0.732	0.2682	2.682	—	65.86
				13.822	

(Contd...)

(*Contd...*)

t(s)	P_e	P_a	$10P_a$	$\Delta\delta$ deg.	δ deg.
0.2	0.8854	0.1146	1.1464	—	79.68
				14.9764	
0.25	1.05174	–0.0517	–0.5173	—	94.6564
				14.459	
0.3	1.212	–0.2124	–2.1239	—	109.115
				12.335	
0.35	1.3495	–0.3495	–3.495	—	121.45
				8.84	
0.4	1.448	–0.448	–4.48	—	130.29
				4.36	
0.45	1.496	–0.496	–4.96	—	134.65
				–0.6	
0.5	1.489	–0.489	–4.89	—	134.05
				–5.49	
0.55	1.428	–0.428	–4.28	—	128.56
				–9.77	
0.6	1.32	–0.32	–3.2	—	118.79
				–12.97	
0.65	1.176	–1.1758	–1.757	—	105.82
				–14.727	
0.7	1.012	–0.012	–0.12	—	91.093
				–14.877	
0.75	0.847	0.157	1.53	—	76.216
				–13.347	
0.8	0.699	0.301	3.01	—	62.869
				–10.337	
0.85	0.584	0.416	4.16	—	52.532
				–6.177	
0.9	0.515	0.485	4.85	—	46.355
				–1.327	
0.95	0.5	0.5	5		45.028
				3.673	
1					48.701

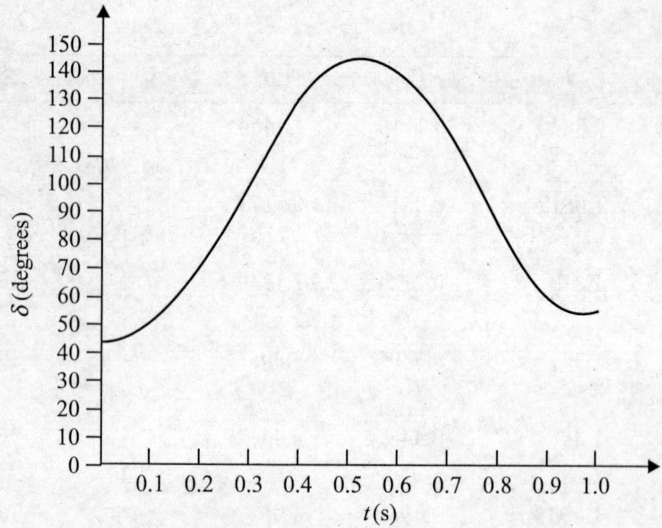

From the swing curve, we see that the value of δ increases and then decreases, which makes the system stable.

Note: In the method-II, the average of the accelerating powers was calculated from the prefault (0^-) and during the fault (0^+) powers, and used in the further iterations. Similarly, if the fault is cleared by some means at any intermediate time t, the same method of calculation of average power is to be adopted for during the fault (t^-) and the postfault (t^+) time periods, and these values are to be used in further calculations.

MATLAB program—Solution of swing equation using step by step method–II

```
Del_delta=0; i=1;
f=input('Enter the frequency :');
H=input('Enter the value of inertia constant :');
delta=input('Enter initial displacement angle :');
Pi=input('Enter initial steady state power :');
M=H/(180*f); y=0.05/M;yy=0.05^2/(M);Pu=delta/90;
del_int=delta*pi/180; Pa=1-Pu;
disp('Time Pe Pa 10*Pa Del_ang Del')
for t=0:.05:1.05
 if t==0
 w=0;
 del_w=y*Pa;
 del_del=0.05*w+yy*Pa;
 fprintf('%g-',t);
 disp([Pi Pa del_w del_del delta]);
 fprintf('%g+',t);
```

```
    disp([Pu Pa del_w del_del delta])
    Pa=Pa/2;
    del_w=y*Pa;
    del_del=0.05*w+yy*Pa;
    fprintf('%gavg',t);
    disp([Pu Pa yy*Pa del_del delta])
  else
    w=w+del_w;
    delta=delta+del_del;
    Pu=delta/90;
    Pa=1-Pu;
    del_w=y*Pa;
    del_del=0.05*w+yy*Pa;
    fprintf('%g',t);
    disp([Pu Pa yy*Pa del_del delta])
  end
  time(i)=t;
  del(i)=delta;
  delta=delta+Del_delta;
  i=i+1;
end
plot(time,del);
title('SWING CURVE');
xlabel('t, sec');
ylabel('delta, elec. deg');
```

Results:

Enter the value of inertia constant : 2.7
Enter the initial displacement angle : 45
Enter the initial steady state power : 1

Time	*Pe*	*Pa*	10**Pa*	Del_ang	Del
0–	1	0.5	—	—	45
0+	0.5	0.5	—	—	45
0avg	—	0.25	2.5	—	45
0.05	0.52778	0.47222	4.7222	7.2222	47.5
0.1	0.60802	0.39198	3.9198	11.142	54.722
0.15	0.73182	0.26818	2.6818	13.824	65.864
0.2	0.88542	0.11458	1.1458	14.97	79.688
0.25	1.0517	–0.0517	–0.5174	14.452	94.657
0.3	1.2123	–0.2123	–2.1233	12.329	109.11
0.35	1.3493	–0.3493	–3.4931	8.8356	121.44
0.4	1.4475	–0.4474	–4.4749	4.3607	130.27

(*Contd...*)

(Contd...)

Time	P_e	P_a	$10*P_a$	Del_ang	Del
0.45	1.4959	–0.4959	–4.9594	–0.5986	134.63
0.5	1.4893	–0.4892	–4.8929	–5.4915	134.04
0.55	1.4283	–0.4282	–4.2827	–9.7742	128.54
0.6	1.3197	–0.3196	–3.1967	–12.971	118.77
0.65	1.1755	–0.1755	–1.7555	–14.726	105.8
0.7	1.0119	–0.0119	–0.1192	–14.846	91.073
0.75	0.84697	0.15303	1.5303	–13.315	76.227
0.8	0.69902	0.30098	3.0098	–10.306	62.912
0.85	0.58452	0.41548	4.1548	–6.1507	52.606
0.9	0.51618	0.48382	4.8382	–1.3124	46.456
0.95	0.50159	0.49841	4.9841	3.6717	45.143
1	0.54239	0.45761	4.5761	8.2478	48.815

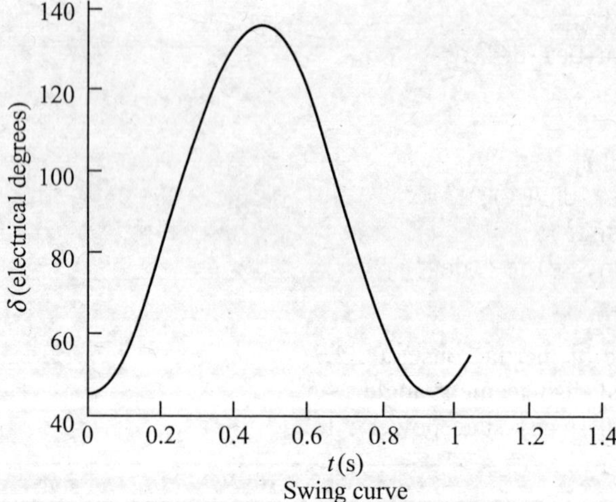

Swing curve

From the swing curve, the value of δ increases and then decreases, which makes the system stable.

EXAMPLE 5.16 A 20 MVA, 3-ϕ, 50 Hz generator delivers rated power at unity power factor via a double circuit transmission line to an infinite bus bar. The generator unit has a kinetic energy of 2.5 MJ/MVA at rated speed. Its $X_d' = 0.3$ p.u. The transformer circuits have negligible resistances and each has a reactance of 0.3 p.u. on a 20 MVA base. The voltage behind the transient reactance is 1.05 p.u. and the voltage of the infinite bus is 1 p.u. A 3-ϕ short circuit occurs at the middle of one of the transformer circuits. It involves ground (a) What is the initial displacement angle of the machine? The fault is cleared in 0.4 s by simultaneous opening of CBs at both ends of the faulted transmission line. (b) Calculate and plot the swing curve for the system and ascertain whether the system is stable or not.

Take $\Delta t = 0.05$ s and $t_{max} = 1$ s.

Solution:

$$M = \frac{SH}{180f} = \frac{1 \times 2.5}{180 \times 50} = 2.778 \times 10^{-4}$$

$$P_i = \frac{\text{MW}}{\text{MVA}} = \frac{20 \times 1}{20} = \frac{20}{20} = 1 \text{ p.u.}$$

The power angle equation for the three conditions should be taken into account.

1. Prefault; 2. During fault; 3. Postfault

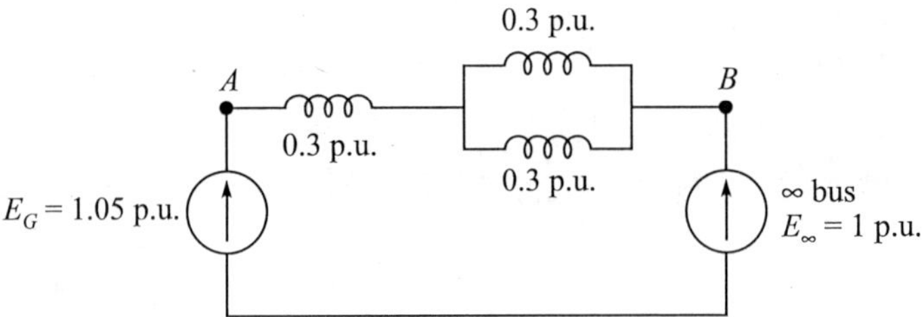

Prefault condition

$$X_1 = X_{AB} = 0.3 + \frac{0.3 \times 0.3}{0.3 + 0.3} = 0.3 + 0.15$$

$$X_1 = 0.45 \text{ p.u.}$$

During fault

$X_2 = X_{AB}$ is obtained by converting the star connection to delta connection.

0.3 p.u.
A 0.3 p.u.
B
N
0.15 p.u. 0.15 p.u.
E_G = 1.05 p.u.
E_∞ = 1 p.u.

$$\therefore \quad X_2 = X_{AB} = 0.3 + 0.3 + \frac{0.3 \times 0.3}{0.15} = 0.6 + 0.6$$

$$X_2 = 1.2 \text{ p.u.}$$

Postfault The faulty transmission line is made out of service by simultaneous opening of the circuit breakers at both ends and hence the faulty line is removed.

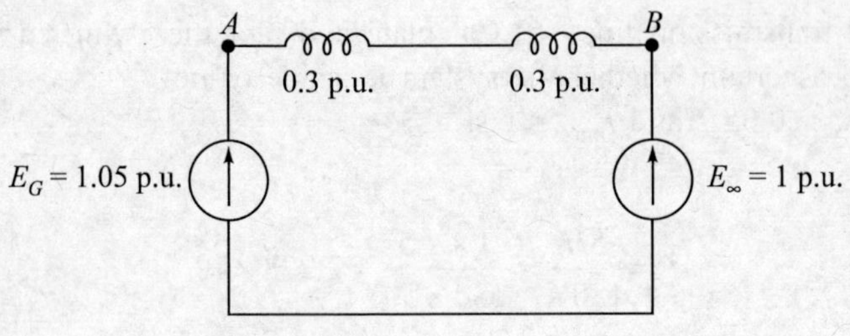

$$X_3 = X_{AB} = 0.3 + 0.3$$
$$= 0.6 \text{ p.u.}$$

Prefault power, $P_{\max 1} = \dfrac{1.05 \times 1}{0.45} = 2.333$ p.u.

During fault power, $P_{\max 2} = \dfrac{1.05 \times 1}{1.2} = 0.875$ p.u.

Postfault power, $P_{\max 3} = \dfrac{1.05 \times 1}{0.6} = 1.75$ p.u.

We know that

$$\Delta\delta_n = \Delta\delta_{n-1} + \frac{\Delta t^2}{M} P_{a(n-1)}$$

$$\therefore \quad \frac{\Delta t^2}{M} = \frac{(0.05)^2}{2.7778 \times 10^{-4}} = 9$$

$$\therefore \quad \Delta\delta_n = \Delta\delta_{n-1} + 9P_{a(n-1)}$$

$$P_i = 1 \text{ p.u.}$$

$$P_a = 1 - P_e$$

In general, $P_e = P_{\max} \sin\delta$

For the prefault condition

$$P_{\max 1} \sin\delta = P_m$$
$$2.333 \sin\delta = 1$$
$$\sin\delta = \frac{1}{2.333} = 0.4286$$
$$\therefore \quad \delta = 25.3808$$

For the during fault condition, $P_e = P_{\max 2} \sin\delta$

For the postfault condition, $P_e = P_{\max 3} \sin\delta$

The calculation of δ versus t is done in the following table.

t (s)	P_{max}	$\sin\delta$	$P_e = P_{max}\sin\delta$	P_a	$9P_a$	$\Delta\delta$ degree	δ degree
0^-	2.333	0.4286	1	—	—	—	25.3808
0^+	0.875	0.4286	0.375	0.625	—	—	25.3808
0_{av}	—	—	—	0.3125	2.8125	—	—
						2.8125	
0.05	0.875	0.4724	0.4134	0.5866	5.2795	—	28.1933
						8.0920	
0.1	0.875	0.5918	0.5178	0.4822	4.3395	—	36.2853
						12.4315	
0.15	0.875	0.7515	0.6575	0.3425	3.0823	—	48.7168
						15.5138	
0.2	0.875	0.9006	0.7880	0.2120	1.9082	—	64.2306
						17.4220	
0.25	0.875	0.9894	0.8657	0.1343	1.2084	—	81.6526
						18.6304	
0.3	0.875	0.9839	0.8609	0.1391	1.2515	—	100.2830
						19.8819	
0.35	0.875	0.8646	0.7565	0.2435	2.1914	—	120.1649
						22.0733	
0.4^-	0.875	0.6124	0.5358	—	—	—	142.2382
0.4^+	1.75	0.6124	1.0717	—	—	—	142.2382
0.4_{av}	—	—	0.8038	0.1962	1.7658	—	
						23.8391	
0.45	1.75	0.2406	0.4211	0.5789	5.2104		166.0773
						29.0495	
0.5	1.75	–0.2610	–0.4567	1.4567	13.1100		195.1268
						42.1595	
0.55	1.75	–0.8414	–1.4724	2.4724	22.2518		237.28
						64.4113	
0.6	1.75	–0.8508	–1.489	2.489	22.4006		301.6976
						86.8119	
0.65	1.75	0.4773	0.8353	0.1647	1.4825		388.5095
						88.2944	
0.7	1.75	0.8926	1.5620	–0.5620	–5.0577		476.8039
						83.2367	
0.75	1.75	–0.3427	–0.5997	1.5997	14.3973		560.0406
						97.634	
0.8	1.75	–0.8856	–1.5498	2.5498	22.9482		657.67
						120.5822	

(Contd...)

(*Contd...*)

t (s)	P_{max}	$\sin\delta$	$P_e = P_{max}\sin\delta$	P_a	$9P_a$	$\Delta\delta$ degree	δ degree
0.85	1.75	0.8504	1.4882	–0.4882	–4.394		778.2568
						116.1882	
0.9	1.75	0.0968	0.1694	0.8306	7.4754		894.445
						123.6636	
0.95	1.75	–0.8821	–1.5436	2.5436	22.8924		1018.1086
						146.556	
1.0	1.75	0.9957	1.7424	–0.7424	–6.6818		1164.6646
						139.8742	
1.05							1304.5388

The variation of δ with time t is plotted as shown below.

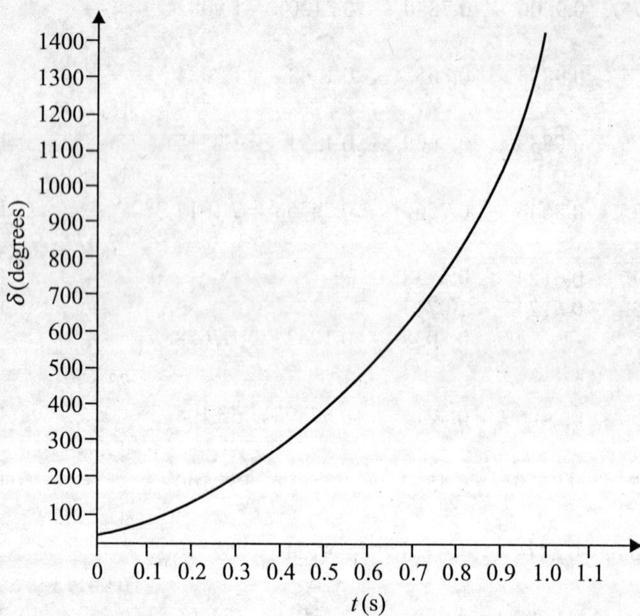

(a) Initial displacement angle δ_0 = 25.3808.

(b) From the swing curve, the displacement angle δ goes on increasing. Hence the system is unstable.

MATLAB program—solution of swing equation by considering critical clearing time using step by step method–II

```
clc;
clear;format short g;
Pm=input('Enter the power limits for prefault,during
fault,postfault conditions :');
Del_delta=0; i=1;
```

```
f=input('Enter the frequency :');
tc=input('Enter the Fault Clearing Time :');
H=input('Enter the value of inertia constant :');
delta=input('Enter initial displacement angle :');
Pi=input('Enter initial steady state power :');
M=H/(180*f); y=0.05^2/M;
k1=Pm(2)/Pm(1);k2=Pm(3)/Pm(1);
del_int=delta*pi/180;
del_max=pi-asin(sin(del_int)/k2);
del_cri=acos(((del_max-del_int)*sin(del_int)-k1*cos(del_
int)+k2*cos(del_max))/(k2-k1));
cri_t=(2*M*(del_cri-del_int)/Pi)^(1/2);
del_cri=(del_cri*180)/pi;
disp('Time P_max Sin(del) Pe Pa 9*Pa Del_ang Delta\n')
for t=0:.05:1.05
 delta=delta*pi/180;
 if t==0
    Paminus=Pi-1;
    Paplus=Pi-Pm(2)*sin(delta);
    Paavg=(Paminus+Paplus)/2;Pma=(Pm(1)+Pm(2))/2;sd=sin(delta);
    Pa=Paavg;delta=(delta*180)/pi;
fprintf('%g-',t);
disp([Pm(1) sd Pi Paminus (y*Paminus) Del_delta delta]);
fprintf('%g+',t);
disp([Pm(2) sd Pm(2)*sd Paplus (y*Paplus) Del_delta delta])
fprintf('%gavg',t);
disp([Pma sd Pma*sd Pa (y*Pa) Del_delta delta])
end
 if t==tc
    Paminus=Pi-Pm(2)*sin(delta);
    Paplus=Pi-Pm(3)*sin(delta);
    Paavg=(Paminus+Paplus)/2;Pma=(Pm(3)+Pm(2))/2;sd=sin(delta);
    Pa=Paavg;delta=(delta*180)/pi;
fprintf('%g-',tc);
disp([Pm(2) sd Pm(2)*sd Paminus (y*Paminus) Del_delta delta])
fprintf('%g+',tc);
disp([Pm(3) sd Pm(3)*sd Paplus (y*Paplus) Del_delta delta])
fprintf('%gavg',tc);
disp([Pma sd Pma*sd Pa (y*Pa) Del_delta delta])
 end
 if t>0 && t<tc
    Pa=Pi-Pm(2)*sin(delta);sd=sin(delta);delta=(delta*180)/pi;
disp([t Pm(2) sd Pm(2)*sd Pa (y*Pa) Del_delta delta])
 end
```

```
  if (t>tc)
     Pa=Pi-Pm(3)*sin(delta);sd=sin(delta);delta=(delta*180)/pi;
 disp([t Pm(3) sd Pm(3)*sd Pa (y*Pa) Del_delta delta])
  end
  Del_delta=Del_delta+(y*Pa);
  time(i)=t;
  del(i)=delta;
  delta=delta+Del_delta;
  i=i+1;
 end
 critical_clearing_angle=del_cri
 critical_clearing_time=cri_t
 plot(time,del);
 title('SWING CURVE');
 xlabel('t, sec');
 ylabel('delta, elec. deg');
```

Results:

Enter the power limits for prefault, during fault, and postfault conditions: [2.333 .875 1.75]
Enter the frequency: 50
Enter the fault clearing time: 0.4
Enter the value of inertia constant: 2.5
Enter the initial displacement angle: 25.3808
Enter the initial steady state power: 1.

Time	*P*_max	sin(del)	*Pe*	*Pa*	9**Pa*	Del_ang	Delta
0–	2.333	0.42863	1	—	—	—	25.381
0+	0.875	0.42863	0.37505	0.62495	—	—	25.381
0avg	—	—	—	0.31247	2.8123	—	—
0.05	0.875	0.47244	0.41339	0.58661	5.2795	2.8123	28.193
0.1	0.875	0.5918	0.51782	0.48218	4.3396	8.0918	36.285
0.15	0.875	0.75145	0.65752	0.34248	3.0823	12.431	48.716
0.2	0.875	0.90055	0.78798	0.21202	1.9082	15.514	64.23
0.25	0.875	0.9894	0.86573	0.13427	1.2084	17.422	81.652
0.3	0.875	0.98394	0.86095	0.13905	1.2515	18.63	100.28
0.35	0.875	0.86459	0.75652	0.24348	2.1913	19.882	120.16
0.4–	0.875	0.6124	0.53585	0.46415	4.1774	22.073	142.24
0.4+	1.75	0.6124	1.0717	–0.0717	–0.6452	22.073	142.24
0.4avg	1.3125	0.6124	0.80377	0.19623	1.7661	22.073	142.24
0.45	1.75	0.24063	0.42111	0.57889	5.21	23.839	166.08
0.5	1.75	–0.26093	–0.4566	1.4566	13.11	29.049	195.13

(Contd...)

(*Contd...*)

Time	*P*_max	sin(del)	*Pe*	*Pa*	9**Pa*	Del_ang	Delta
0.55	1.75	–0.84136	–1.4724	2.4724	22.251	42.159	237.28
0.6	1.75	–0.85086	–1.489	2.489	22.401	64.41	301.69
0.65	1.75	0.47725	0.83519	0.16481	1.4833	86.811	388.51
0.7	1.75	0.89258	1.562	–0.5620	–5.0582	88.295	476.8
0.75	1.75	–0.34263	–0.5996	1.5996	14.396	83.237	560.04
0.8	1.75	–0.88564	–1.5499	2.5499	22.949	97.633	657.67
0.85	1.75	0.85037	1.4881	–0.4881	–4.3933	120.58	778.25
0.9	1.75	0.096883	0.16954	0.83046	7.4741	116.19	894.44
0.95	1.75	–0.8821	–1.5437	2.5437	22.893	123.66	1018.1
1	1.75	0.99566	1.7424	–0.7424	–6.6816	146.56	1164.7
1.05	1.75	–0.70131	–1.2273	2.2273	20.046	139.87	1304.5

critical clearing angle = 98.963
critical clearing time = 0.026711

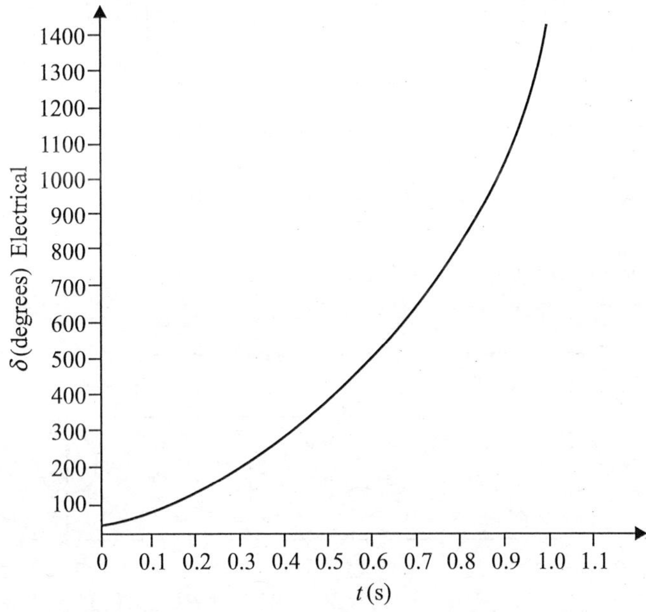

Initial displacement angle, δ_0 = 25.3808.

From the swing curve, the displacement angle δ goes on increasing. Hence the system is unstable.

EXAMPLE 5.17 A 25 MVA, 60 Hz, water wheel generator delivers 20 MW over a double circuit transmission line to a large metropolitan system which may be regarded as an infinite bus. The generating unit has a kinetic energy of 2.76 MJ/MVA at rated speed. The direct axis transient reactance of the generator is 0.3 p.u. The transmission circuits have negligible resistances and each has a reactance of 0.2 p.u. on a 25 MVA base. The voltage behind the transient reactance of the generator is 1.03 p.u. and the voltage of the metropolitan system is 1.0 p.u. A three-phase short circuit occurs at the middle of the transmission line circuit and is cleared in 0.4 s by the simultaneous opening of the circuit breaker at both ends of the line. Calculate and plot the swing curve of the generator for 1 s.

Solution:

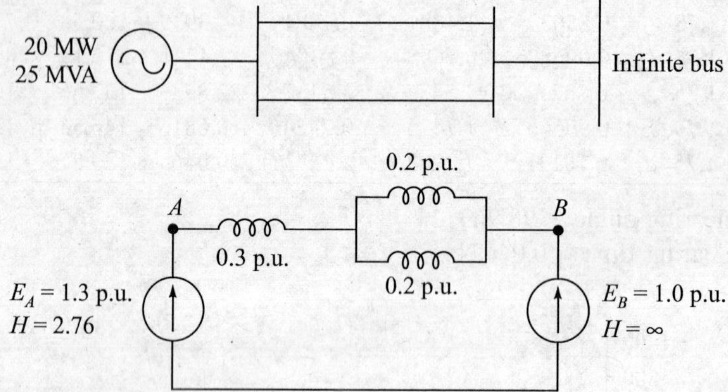

The net reactance for the prefault condition is given by

$$X_1 = X_{AB} = 0.3 + \frac{0.2 \times 0.2}{0.2 + 0.2} = 0.4 \text{ p.u.}$$

During the fault condition

0.2 p.u.
A 0.3 p.u.
B
N
0.1 p.u. 0.1 p.u.
$E_A = 1.03$ p.u.
$E_B = 1$ p.u.

$$X_2 = X_{AB} = \frac{0.3 \times 0.2 + 0.2 \times 0.1 + 0.1 \times 0.3}{0.1}$$

$$= \frac{0.06 + 0.02 + 0.03}{0.1} = 1.1 \text{ p.u.}$$

$$X_2 = 1.1 \text{ p.u.}$$

During the postfault condition

$$X_3 = X_{AB} = 0.3 + 0.2 = 0.5 \text{ p.u.}$$

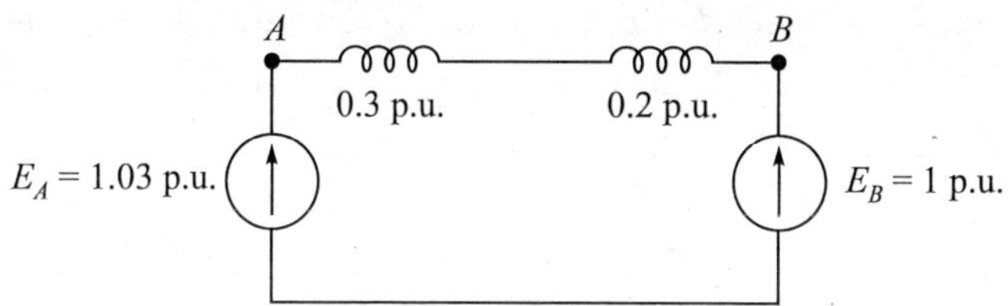

Prefault power, $P_{max\,1} = \dfrac{1.03 \times 1}{0.4} = 2.58$ p.u.

During fault power, $P_{max\,2} = \dfrac{1.03 \times 1}{1.1} = 0.936$ p.u.

Postfault power, $P_{max\,3} = \dfrac{1.03 \times 1}{0.5} = 2.06$ p.u.

$$M = \frac{SH}{180f} = \frac{1 \times 2.76}{180 \times 60} = 2.56 \times 10^{-4}$$

Output, $P_e = \dfrac{20}{25} = 0.8$ p.u.

In general $P_e = P_{max} \sin \delta$

For the prefault condition,

$$P_e = P_{max\,1} \sin \delta$$
$$0.8 = 2.58 \sin \delta$$
$$\sin \delta = \frac{0.8}{2.58}$$
$$\delta = \sin^{-1} \frac{0.8}{2.58} = 18.2°$$

For the during fault condition, $P_e = P_{max2} \sin \delta$

For the postfault condition, $P_e = P_{max3} \sin \delta$

Immediately after the fault, δ remains unchanged momentarily but output changes.

$$P_e = P_{max\,2} \sin \delta = 0.936 \sin 18.2°$$
$$= 0.292 \text{ p.u.}$$

$$\Delta\delta_n = \Delta\delta_{n-1} + \frac{\Delta t^2}{M} P_{a(n-1)}$$
$$= \Delta\delta_{n-1} + \frac{(0.05)^2}{2.564 \times 10^{-4}} P_{a(n-1)}$$
$$= \Delta\delta_{n-1} + 9.76 P_{a\,(n-1)}$$

The calculation of δ versus t is done in the following table.

$$P_a = P_i - P_e = 0.8 - P_e$$

t(s)	P_{max}	$\sin\delta$	P_u	P_a	$9.76P_a$	$\Delta\delta$ degree	δ degree
0^-	2.58	0.31	0.8	0	—	—	18.1
0^+	0.936	0.31	0.29	0.51	—	—	18.1
0_{av}	—	—	—	0.255	2.5	—	—
						2.5	
0.05	0.936	0.352	0.33	0.47	4.6	—	20.6
						7.1	
0.1	0.936	0.465	0.435	0.365	3.562	—	27.7
						10.662	
0.15	0.936	0.621	0.581	0.219	2.138	—	38.362
						12.800	
0.2	0.936	0.779	0.729	0.071	0.692	—	51.162
						13.492	
0.25	0.936	0.904	0.846	–0.046	–0.448	—	64.654
						13.044	
0.3	0.936	0.977	0.915	–0.115	–1.118	—	77.698
						11.926	
0.35	0.936	1.0	0.936	–0.136	–1.327	—	89.624
						10.599	
0.4^-	0.936	0.984	0.921	–0.121	—	—	100.223
0.4^+	2.06	0.983	2.025	–1.125	—	—	100.223
0.4_{av}	—	—	—	–0.623	–6.568	—	—
						4.031	
0.45	2.06	0.969	1.997	–1.197	–11.679	—	104.254
						–7.648	
0.5	2.06	0.993	2.046	–1.246	–12.164	—	96.606
						–19.812	
0.55	2.06	0.974	2.006	–1.206	–11.766	—	76.794
						–31.578	
0.6	2.06	0.710	1.462	–0.662	–6.462	—	45.216
						–38.040	
0.65	2.06	0.125	0.257	0.543	5.297	—	7.176
						–32.743	
0.7	2.06	–0.432	–0.890	1.690	16.494	—	–25.567
						–16.249	
0.75	2.06	–0.667	–1.373	2.173	21.213	—	–41.816
						4.964	

(Contd...)

(*Contd...*)

t(s)	P_{max}	sin δ	P_u	P_a	$9.76P_a$	$\Delta\delta$ degree	δ degree
0.8	2.06	–0.600	–1.235	2.035	19.866	—	–36.852
						24.83	
0.85	2.06	–0.208	–0.429	1.229	11.996		–12.022
						36.826	
0.9	2.06	0.420	0.864	–0.064	–0.627	—	24.804
						36.199	
0.95	2.06	0.875	1.802	–1.002	–9.777	—	61.003
						26.422	
1.0	2.06	0.999	2.058	–1.258	–12.277	—	87.425

The variation of δ with time t is plotted as shown below.

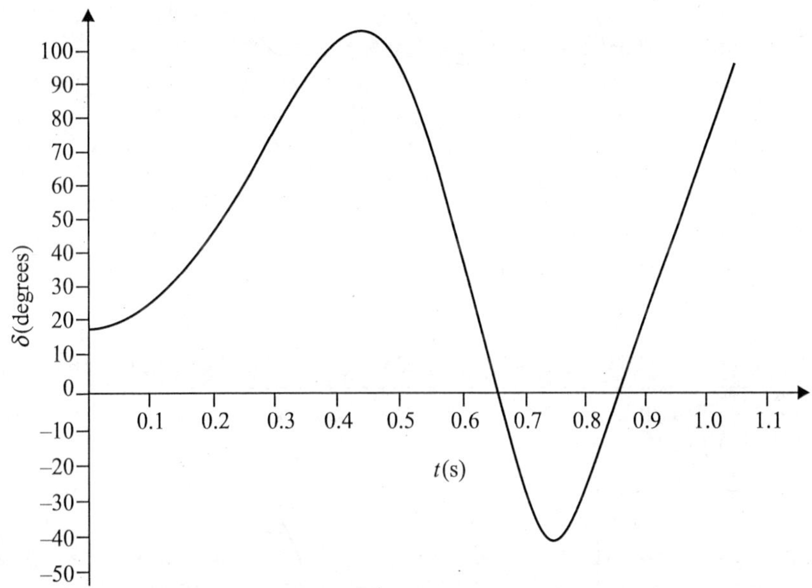

If we plot the swing curve, the value of δ increases and then decreases, this makes the system stable.

Results:

Enter the power limits for prefault, during fault, and postfault conditions: [2.58 .936 2.06]

Enter the frequency: 60

Enter the fault clearing time: 0.4

Enter the value of inertia constant: 2.76

Enter the initial displacement angle: 18.2

Enter the initial steady state power: 0.8.

t(s)	P_{max}	sin δ	Pe	Pa	9*Pa	$\Delta\delta$ degree	δ degree
0–	2.58	0.31233	0.8	0	—	0	18.2
0+	0.936	0.31233	0.29235	0.50765	—	0	18.2
0avg	—	—	—	0.255	2.5	0	18.2
0.05	0.936	0.33717	0.3156	0.4844	4.7387	1.5048	19.705
0.1	0.936	0.43756	0.40956	0.39044	3.8195	6.2436	25.948
0.15	0.936	0.58795	0.55032	0.24968	2.4425	10.063	36.012
0.2	0.936	0.74915	0.70121	0.098792	0.96644	12.506	48.517
0.25	0.936	0.88286	0.82636	–0.02636	–0.2578	13.472	61.989
0.3	0.936	0.96684	0.90496	–0.10496	–1.0268	13.214	75.204
0.35	0.936	0.99896	0.93503	–0.13503	–1.3209	12.187	87.391
0.4^-	0.936	0.98963	0.9263	–0.1263	–1.2355	10.867	98.257
0.4^+	2.06	0.98963	2.0386	–1.2386	–12.117	10.867	98.257
0.4avg	1.498	0.98963	1.4825	–0.68247	–6.6763	10.867	98.257
0.45	2.06	0.97649	2.0116	–1.2116	–11.852	4.1902	102.45
0.5	2.06	0.99651	2.0528	–1.2528	–12.256	–7.6622	94.785
0.55	2.06	0.96532	1.9886	–1.1886	–11.627	–19.918	74.867
0.6	2.06	0.6861	1.4134	–0.61336	–6.0003	–31.545	43.322
0.65	2.06	0.10065	0.20733	0.59267	5.7978	–37.546	5.7764
0.7	2.06	–0.4379	–0.9021	1.7021	16.651	–31.748	–25.971
0.75	2.06	–0.6569	–1.3533	2.1533	21.065	–15.097	–41.068
0.8	2.06	–0.575	–1.1845	1.9845	19.414	5.9685	–35.099
0.85	2.06	–0.1687	–0.3477	1.1477	11.228	25.382	–9.7174
0.9	2.06	0.45231	0.93176	–0.13176	–1.289	36.61	26.892
0.95	2.06	0.88468	1.8225	–1.0225	–10.002	35.321	62.213
1	2.06	0.99907	2.0581	–1.2581	–12.307	25.318	87.531
1.05	2.06	0.98312	2.0252	–1.2252	–11.986	13.011	100.54

critical clearing angle = 137.85
critical clearing time = 0.036526

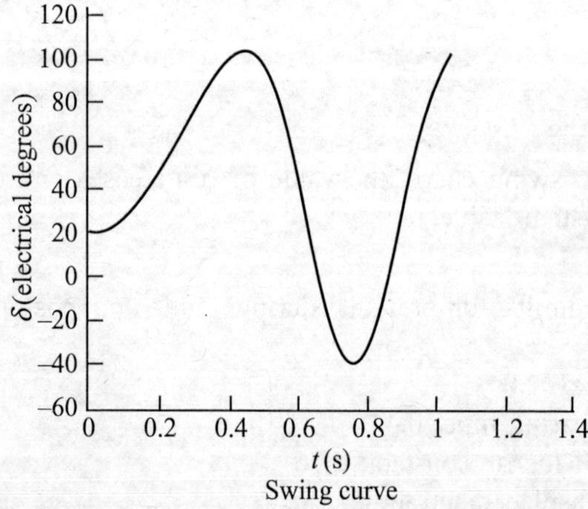

Swing curve

In the swing curve, the value of δ increases and then decreases, this makes the system stable.

5.8.3 Euler's Method

The Euler's method is the simplest and the least accurate of all numerical methods. It is presented here because of its simplicity. By studying this method, we will be able to grasp the basic ideas involved in the numerical solutions of one-dimensional equation (ODE) and can easily understand the comparatively complex method such as the Runge–Kutta procedure.

Let us consider the first order differential equation

$$\frac{dx}{dt} = f(x, t) \tag{5.41}$$

Figure 5.29 illustrate the principles of applying the Euler's method at initial condition $x = x_0$ at $t = t_0$.

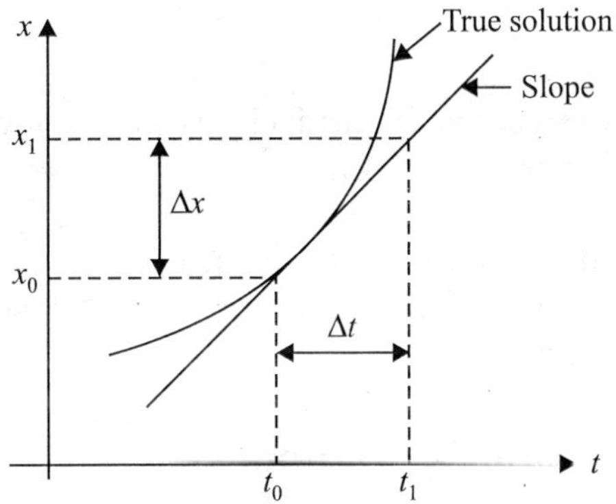

Figure 5.29 Graphical interpretation of Euler's method.

At $x = x_0$, $t = t_0$, we can approximate the curve representing the true solution by its tangent having a slope

$$\left.\frac{dx}{dt}\right|_{x=x_0} = f(x_0, t_0) \tag{5.42}$$

For a small increment in t denoted by Δt, the increment in x is given by Δx Therefore,

$$\Delta x = \left.\frac{dx}{dt}\right|_{x=x_0} \cdot \Delta t \tag{5.43}$$

where $\left.\frac{dx}{dt}\right|_{x=x_0}$ is the slope of the curve at (t_0, x_0), which can be determined from Eq. (5.42).Thus, the value of x at $t = t_1 = t_0 + \Delta t$ is given by

$$x_1 = x_0 + \Delta x = x_0 + \left.\frac{dx}{dt}\right|_{x=x_0} \cdot \Delta t \tag{5.44}$$

The Euler's method is equivalent to using the first two terms of the Taylor series expansion for x around the point (t_0, x_0)

$$x_1 = x_0 + \Delta t(\dot{x}_0) + \frac{\Delta t^2}{2!}(\ddot{x}_0) + \frac{\Delta t^3}{3!}(\dddot{x}_0) + \cdots \tag{5.45}$$

After using the Euler's technique for determining $x = x_1$ corresponding to $t = t_1$, we can take another short time step Δt and determine x_2 corresponding to $t_2 = t_1 + \Delta t$ as follows:

$$x_2 = x_1 + \left.\frac{dx}{dt}\right|_{x=x_1} \cdot \Delta t \tag{5.46}$$

The subsequent values of x can be similarly determined. Hence, the computational algorithm is

$$x_{i+1} = x_i + \left.\frac{dx}{dt}\right|_{x=x_i} \cdot \Delta t \tag{5.47}$$

By applying the above algorithm successively, the values of x can be determined corresponding to different values of t.

The method considers only the first derivative of x and is, therefore, referred to as a first order method. For sufficient accuracy at each step Δt has to be small. This will increase round-off errors, and the computational effort required will be very high.

5.8.4 Modified Euler's Method

The standard Euler's method results in inaccuracies because it uses the derivative at the beginning of the interval though it applied throughout the interval. The slope is constant over the entire interval Δt causing the points to fall below the curve. The above problem is solved by the modified Euler's method. This method can be obtained by calculating the slope both at the beginning and the end of the interval, and then averaging these slopes. This procedure is known as the modified Euler's method.

The modified Euler's method consists of the following steps.

(i) **Predictor step:** By using the derivative at the beginning of the step, the value at the end of the step $(t_1 = t_0 + \Delta t)$ is predicted as

$$x_1^p = x_0 + \left.\frac{dx}{dt}\right|_{x=x_0} \cdot \Delta t \tag{5.48}$$

(ii) **Corrector step:** By using the predicted value of x_1^p, the derivative at the end of the step is computed and the value at the end of the step$(t_1 = t_0 + \Delta t)$ is predicted as

$$\left.\frac{dx}{dt}\right|_{x=x_1^p} = f(x_1^p, t_1) \tag{5.49}$$

Then, the average value of the two derivatives is used to find the corrected value.

$$x_1^c = x_0 + \left(\frac{\left.\frac{dx}{dt}\right|_{x=x_0} + \left.\frac{dx}{dt}\right|_{x=x_1^p}}{2} \right) \cdot \Delta t \tag{5.50}$$

Similarly,

$$x_2^c = x_1 + \left(\frac{\left.\frac{dx}{dt}\right|_{x=x_1} + \left.\frac{dx}{dt}\right|_{x=x_2^p}}{2} \right) \cdot \Delta t \tag{5.51}$$

$$x_{i+}^c = x_i + \left(\frac{\left.\frac{dx}{dt}\right|_{x=x_i} + \left.\frac{dx}{dt}\right|_{x=x_{i+1}^p}}{2} \right) \cdot \Delta t \tag{5.52}$$

This process can be repeated until the successive steps converge with the desired accuracy.

5.8.5 Runge–Kutta (R–K) Method

The Runge–Kutta method approximates the Taylor series solution; however, unlike the formal Taylor series solution, the R–K method does not require explicit evaluation of derivatives higher than the first. The effects of the higher derivatives are included by several evaluations of the first derivative depending on the number of terms effectively retained in the Taylor series, we have R–K method of different orders.

Let us consider the first order differential equation

$$\frac{dx}{dt} = f(x, t) \tag{5.53}$$

Assume the initial condition is x_0, t_0.

Second order R–K method

The second order R–K formula for the value of x at $t = t_0 + \Delta t$ is given by

$$x_1 = x_0 + \Delta x = x_0 + \frac{k_1 + k_2}{2} \tag{5.54}$$

where

k_1 = (slope at the beginning of time step) $\Delta t = f(x_0, t_0)\Delta t$

k_2 = (first approximation to slope at midstep) $\Delta t = f(x_0 + k_1, t_0 + \Delta t)\Delta t$

Fourth order R-K method

The general formula giving the value of x for the $(n + 1)$th step

$$x_{i+1} = x_i + \Delta x = x_i + \frac{1}{6}(k_1 + 2k_2 + 2k_3 + k_4) \quad (5.55)$$

where

k_1 = (slope at the beginning of time step) $\Delta t = f(x_i, t_i)\Delta t$

k_2 = (first approximation to slope at midstep) $\Delta t = f\left(x_i + \frac{k_1}{2}, t_i + \frac{\Delta t}{2}\right)\Delta t$

k_3 = (second approximation to slope at midstep) $\Delta t = f\left(x_i + \frac{k_2}{2}, t_i + \frac{\Delta t}{2}\right)\Delta t$

k_4 = (slope at the end of step) $\Delta t = f(x_i + k_3, t_i + \Delta t)\Delta t$

Thus Δx is the incremental value of x given by the weighted average of estimated based on slopes at the beginning of the mid-point and end of the time step.

EXAMPLE 5.18 A three-phase fault occurs at the point F as shown in the figure is cleared by isolating the faulted circuit simultaneously from both ends. Generator is delivering 0.8 p.u. power at 0.8 p.f lagging. The fault is cleared in 0.1 s. Obtain the numeric solution of the swing equation up to 0.15 s using the (a) modified Euler's method and (b) Runge–Kutta method with step size of Δt = 0.05 s. Take H = 5 MJ/MVA.

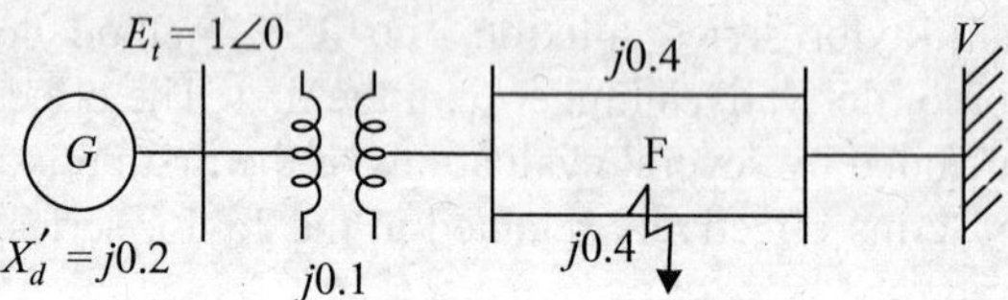

Solution:

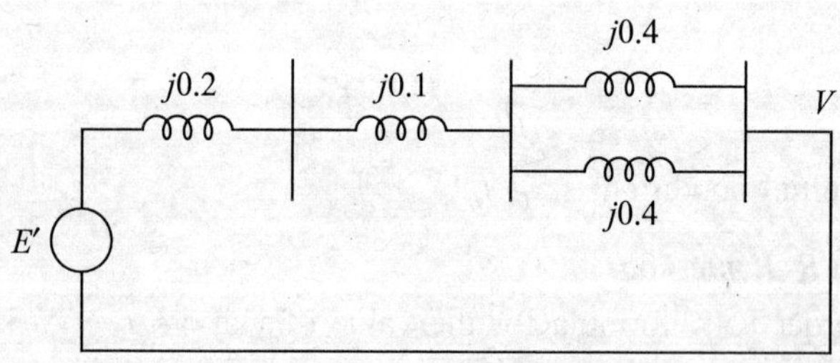

(i) To draw the reactance diagram

$E_t = 1.0\Delta\angle 0°$

$P = 0.8$ p.u.; $\cos\theta = 0.8$; $\theta = \cos^{-1}(0.8) = 36.86° = 0.644$ rad

$Q = P \tan\theta = 0.6$

$$I = \frac{P - jQ}{E_t} = \frac{0.8 - j0.6}{1.0} = 0.8 - j0.6$$

$$E' = E_t + jX'_d I = 1.0 + j0.2(0.8 - j0.6) = 1.13\angle 0.142^\circ$$

$$V = E_t - j(X_{\text{trans}} + X_{t.\text{line}})I = 1.13 + j(0.1 + 0.2)\ (0.8 - j0.6)$$

$$= 0.854\angle{-0.285^\circ}$$

(ii) *Prefault condition* From the reactance diagram,

$$X_T = X_I = 0.2 + 0.1 + \left(\frac{0.4 \times 0.4}{0.4 + 0.4}\right) = 0.5$$

$$P_{e1} = \frac{|E'||V|}{X_t}\sin\delta = \frac{1.13 \times 0.854}{0.5}\sin\delta = 1.93\sin\delta$$

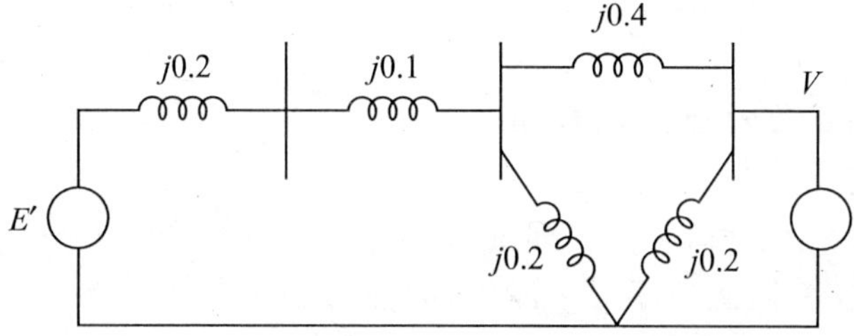

(iii) *During the fault condition* (fault at the middle of the transmission line 2)

Using delta to star conversion, the circuit becomes

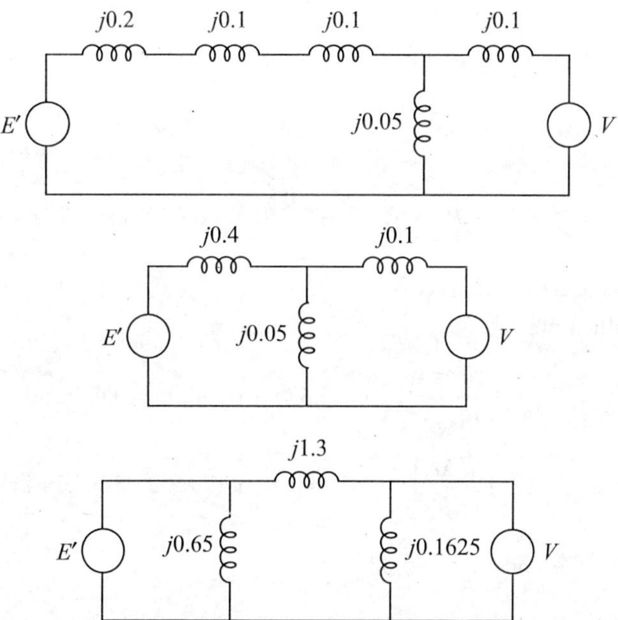

From the reactance diagram, $X_T = X_{II} = 1.3$

$$P_{e2} = \frac{|E'||V|}{X_{II}}\sin\delta = \frac{1.13 \times 0.854}{1.3}\sin\delta = 0.742\sin\delta$$

(iv) *Postfault condition*

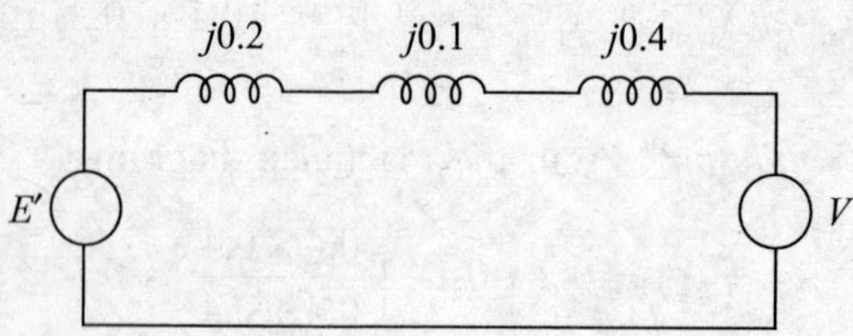

From the reactance diagram, $X_T = X_{III} = j0.7$

$$P_{e3} = \frac{|E'||V|}{X_{III}} \sin\delta = \frac{1.13 \times 0.854}{0.7} \sin\delta = 1.378 \sin\delta$$

(a) Modified Euler's method

During fault,

$$P_e = 0.742 \sin\delta$$

$$P_{e0} = P_{m0} = 0.8 = 1.93 \sin\delta_0$$

$$\delta_0 = \sin^{-1}\left(\frac{0.8}{1.93}\right) = 24.48° = 0.427 \text{ rad}$$

$$\omega_0 = 2\pi f = 2\pi \times 50 = 314.159$$

$$\Delta t = 0.05 \text{ s}$$

Iteration 1: Beginning of the first step at, $t = 0$

$$\left.\frac{d\delta}{dt}\right|_{\Delta\omega_0} = \Delta\omega_0 = \omega_0 - 2\pi f = 314.159 - 314.159 = 0$$

$$\left.\frac{d\Delta\omega}{dt}\right|_{\delta_0} = \frac{\pi f}{H}(P_m - P_e(\delta_0)) = \frac{\pi \times 50}{5}(0.8 - 0.742 \sin 0.427) = 15.479$$

End of the first step, $t = 0.05$
Predicted values are

$$\delta^p_{0.05} = \delta_0 + \left.\frac{d\delta}{dt}\right|_{\Delta\omega_0} \times \Delta t = 0.427 + 0 \times 0.05 = 0.427 \text{ rad}$$

$$\Delta\omega^p_{0.05} = \Delta\omega_0 + \left.\frac{d\Delta\omega}{dt}\right|_{\delta_0} \times \Delta t = 0 + 15.479 \times 0.05 = 0.774 \text{ rad/s}$$

Derivatives at the end of $t = 0.05$

$$t = 0.05, \quad \left.\frac{d\delta}{dt}\right|_{\Delta\omega^p_{0.05}} = \Delta\omega^p_{0.05} = 0.774 \text{ rad/s}$$

$$\left.\frac{d\Delta\omega}{dt}\right|_{\delta^p_{0.05}} = \frac{\pi f}{H}(P_m - P_e(\delta^p_{0.05})) = \frac{\pi \times 50}{5}(0.8 - 0.742 \sin 0.427) = 15.479 \text{ rad/s}$$

The corrected values are

$$\delta_{0.05}^{c} = \delta_0 + \left[\frac{\left.\frac{d\delta}{dt}\right|_{\Delta\omega_0} + \left.\frac{d\delta}{dt}\right|_{\Delta\omega_{0.05}^{p}}}{2}\right] \times \Delta t = 0.427 + \left[\frac{0 + 0.774}{2}\right] \times 0.05 = 0.446 \text{ rad}$$

$$\Delta\omega_{0.05}^{c} = \Delta\omega_0 + \left[\frac{\left.\frac{d\Delta\omega}{dt}\right|_{\delta_0} + \left.\frac{d\Delta\omega}{dt}\right|_{\delta_{0.05}^{p}}}{2}\right] \times \Delta t = 0 + \left[\frac{15.479 + 15.479}{2}\right] \times 0.05$$

$$= 0.774 \text{ rad/s}$$

Iteration 2: Beginning of the first step at $t = 0.05$,

$$\left.\frac{d\delta}{dt}\right|_{\Delta\omega_{0.05}^{c}} = \Delta\omega_{0.05}^{c} = 0.774$$

$$\left.\frac{d\Delta\omega}{dt}\right|_{\delta_{0.05}^{c}} = \frac{\pi f}{H}(P_m - P_e(\delta_{0.05}^{c})) = \frac{\pi \times 50}{5}(0.8 - 0.742 \sin 0.446) = 15.077$$

End of the second step, $t = 0.1$

Predicted values are

$$\delta_{0.1}^{p} = \delta_{0.05}^{c} + \left.\frac{d\delta}{dt}\right|_{\Delta\omega_{0.05}^{c}} \times \Delta t = 0.446 + 0.774 \times 0.05 = 0.485 \text{ rad}$$

$$\Delta\omega_{0.1}^{p} = \Delta\omega_{0.05}^{c} + \left.\frac{d\Delta\omega}{dt}\right|_{\delta_{0.05}^{c}} \times \Delta t - 0.774 + 15.077 \times 0.05 = 1.5278 \text{ rad/s}$$

Derivatives at the end of $t = 0.1$,

$$\left.\frac{d\delta}{dt}\right|_{\Delta\omega_{0.1}^{p}} = \Delta\omega_{0.1}^{p} = 1.5278 \text{ rad/s}$$

$$\left.\frac{d\Delta\omega}{dt}\right|_{\delta_{0.1}^{p}} = \frac{\pi f}{H}(P_m - P_e(\delta_{0.1}^{p})) = \frac{\pi \times 50}{5}(0.8 - 0.742 \sin 0.485) = 14.265 \text{ rad/s}$$

The corrected values are

$$\delta_{0.1}^{c} = \delta_{0.05}^{c} + \left[\frac{\left.\frac{d\delta}{dt}\right|_{\Delta\omega_{0.05}^{c}} + \left.\frac{d\delta}{dt}\right|_{\Delta\omega_{0.1}^{p}}}{2}\right] \times \Delta t = 0.446 + \left[\frac{0.774 + 1.5278}{2}\right] \times 0.05$$

$$= 0.5035 \text{ rad}$$

$$\Delta\omega_{0.1}^{c} = \Delta\omega_{0.05}^{c} + \left[\frac{\left.\frac{d\Delta\omega}{dt}\right|_{\delta_{0.05}^{c}} + \left.\frac{d\Delta\omega}{dt}\right|_{\delta_{0.1}^{p}}}{2}\right] \times \Delta t$$

$$= 0.774 + \left[\frac{15.077 + 14.265}{2}\right] \times 0.05 = 1.5076 \text{ rad/s}$$

The fault is cleared at $t = 0.1$ s and the postfault condition is given by

$$P_e = 1.378 \sin\delta$$

Iteration 3: Beginning of the first step at 0.1 s

$$\left.\frac{d\delta}{dt}\right|_{\Delta\omega_{0.1}^c} = \Delta\omega_{0.1}^c = 1.5076$$

$$\left.\frac{d\Delta\omega}{dt}\right|_{\delta_{0.1}^c} = \frac{\pi f}{H}(P_m - P_e(\delta_{0.1}^c)) = \frac{\pi \times 50}{5}(0.8 - 1.378 \sin 0.5035) = 4.245$$

End of the third step, $t = 0.15$ s
Predicted values are

$$\delta_{0.15}^p = \delta_{0.1}^c + \left.\frac{d\delta}{dt}\right|_{\Delta\omega_{0.1}^c} \times \Delta t = 0.5035 + 1.5076 \times 0.05 = 0.579 \text{ rad}$$

$$\Delta\omega_{0.15}^p = \Delta\omega_{0.1}^c + \left.\frac{d\Delta\omega}{dt}\right|_{\delta_{0.1}^c} \times \Delta t = 1.5076 + 4.245 \times 0.05 = 1.7197 \text{ rad/s}$$

Derivatives at the end of $t = 0.15$ s,

$$\left.\frac{d\delta}{dt}\right|_{\Delta\omega_{0.15}^p} = \Delta\omega_{0.15}^p = 1.7197 \text{ rad/s}$$

$$\left.\frac{d\Delta\omega}{dt}\right|_{\delta_{0.15}^p} = \frac{\pi f}{H}(P_m - P_e(\delta_{0.15}^p)) = \frac{\pi \times 50}{5}(0.8 - 1.378 \sin 0.579) = 1.444 \text{ rad/s}$$

The corrected values are

$$\delta_{0.15}^c = \delta_{0.1}^c + \left[\frac{\left.\frac{d\delta}{dt}\right|_{\Delta\omega_{0.1}^c} + \left.\frac{d\delta}{dt}\right|_{\Delta\omega_{0.15}^p}}{2}\right] \times \Delta t$$

$$= 0.5035 + \left[\frac{1.5076 + 1.7197}{2}\right] \times 0.05 = 0.584 \text{ rad}$$

$$\Delta\omega_{0.15}^c = \Delta\omega_{0.1}^c + \left[\frac{\left.\frac{d\Delta\omega}{dt}\right|_{\delta_{0.1}^c} + \left.\frac{d\Delta\omega}{dt}\right|_{\delta_{0.15}^p}}{2}\right] \times \Delta t$$

$$= 1.5076 + \left[\frac{4.245 + 1.444}{2}\right] \times 0.05 = 1.6498 \text{ rad/s}$$

(b) Runge–Kutta method

$$P_e = 0.742 \sin\delta$$

$$P_{e0} = P_{m0} = 0.8 = 1.93 \sin\delta_0$$

$$\delta_0 = \sin^{-1}\left(\frac{0.8}{1.93}\right) = 24.48° = 0.427 \text{ rad}$$

$$\omega_0 = 2\pi f = 2\pi \times 50 = 314.159$$

$$\Delta t = 0.05 \text{ s}$$

Fourth order method

Iteration 1: at $t = 0$,

Ist estimate: $k_1 = \Delta\omega_0 \times \Delta t = 0 \times 0.05 = 0$

$$l_1 = \frac{\pi f}{H}(P_m - P_e(\delta_0))\Delta t = \frac{\pi \times 50}{5}(0.8 - 0.742 \sin 0.427) \times 0.05 = 0.774$$

IInd estimate: $k_2 = \left(\Delta\omega_0 + \frac{l_1}{2}\right) \times \Delta t = \left(0 + \frac{0.774}{2}\right) \times 0.05 = 0.0194$

$$l_2 = \frac{\pi f}{H}\left(P_m - P_e\left(\delta_0 + \frac{k_1}{2}\right)\right)\Delta t = \frac{\pi \times 50}{5}\left(0.8 - 0.742 \sin\left(0.427 + \frac{0}{2}\right)\right) \times 0.05$$

$$= 0.774$$

IIIrd estimate: $k_3 = \left(\Delta\omega_0 + \frac{l_2}{2}\right) \times \Delta t = \left(0 + \frac{0.774}{2}\right) \times 0.05 = 0.0194$

$$l_3 = \frac{\pi f}{H}\left(P_m - P_e\left(\delta_0 + \frac{k_2}{2}\right)\right)\Delta t = \frac{\pi \times 50}{5}\left(0.8 - 0.742 \sin\left(0.427 + \frac{0.0194}{2}\right)\right) \times 0.05$$

$$= 0.764$$

IVth estimate: $k_4 = (\Delta\omega_0 + l_3) \times \Delta t = (0 + 0.764) \times 0.05 = 0.038$

$$l_4 = \frac{\pi f}{H}(P_m - P_e(\delta_0 + k_3))\Delta t = \frac{\pi \times 50}{5}(0.8 - 0.742 \sin(0.427 + 0.0194)) \times 0.05$$

$$= 0.7535$$

Final estimate:

$$\delta_{0.05} = \delta_0 + \frac{1}{6}(k_1 + 2k_2 + 2k_3 + k_4)$$

$$= 0.427 + \frac{1}{6}(0 + 2 \times 0.0194 + 2 \times 0.0194 + 0.038)$$

$$= 0.446 \text{ rad}$$

$$\Delta\omega_{0.05} = \Delta\omega_0 + \frac{1}{6}(l_1 + 2l_2 + 2l_3 + l_4)$$

$$= 0 + \frac{1}{6}(0.774 + 2 \times 0.774 + 2 \times 0.764 + 0.7535)$$

$$= 0.767 \text{ rad/s}$$

Iteration 2: at $t = 0.05$s,

Ist estimate: $k_1 = \Delta\omega_{0.05} \times \Delta t = 0.767 \times 0.05 = 0.0384$

$$l_1 = \frac{\pi f}{H}(P_m - P_e(\delta_{0.05}))\Delta t = \frac{\pi \times 50}{5}(0.8 - 0.742 \sin 0.446) \times 0.05 = 0.754$$

IInd estimate: $k_2 = \left(\Delta\omega_{0.05} + \frac{l_1}{2}\right) \times \Delta t = \left(0.767 + \frac{0.754}{2}\right) \times 0.05 = 0.0572$

$$l_2 = \frac{\pi f}{H}\left(P_m - P_e\left(\delta_{0.05} + \frac{k_1}{2}\right)\right)\Delta t$$

$$= \frac{\pi \times 50}{5}\left(0.8 - 0.742 \sin\left(0.446 + \frac{0.0384}{2}\right)\right) \times 0.05$$

$$= 0.734$$

IIIrd estimate: $k_3 = \left(\Delta\omega_{0.05} + \frac{l_2}{2}\right) \times \Delta t = \left(0.767 + \frac{0.734}{2}\right) \times 0.05 = 0.0567$

$$l_3 = \frac{\pi f}{H}\left(P_m - P_e\left(\delta_{0.05} + \frac{k_2}{2}\right)\right)\Delta t$$

$$= \frac{\pi \times 50}{5}\left(0.8 - 0.742 \sin\left(0.446 + \frac{0.0572}{2}\right)\right) \times 0.05$$

$$= 0.724$$

IVth estimate: $k_4 = (\Delta\omega_{0.05} + l_3) \times \Delta t = (0.767 + 0.724) \times 0.05 = 0.0746$

$$l_4 = \frac{\pi f}{H}(P_m - P_e(\delta_{0.05} + k_3))\Delta t$$

$$= \frac{\pi \times 50}{5}(0.8 - 0.742 \sin(0.446 + 0.0567)) \times 0.05$$

$$= 0.695$$

Final estimate:

$$\delta_{0.1} = \delta_{0.05} + \frac{1}{6}(k_1 + 2k_2 + 2k_3 + k_4)$$

$$= 0.446 + \frac{1}{6}(0.0384 + 2 \times 0.0572 + 2 \times 0.0567 + 0.0746)$$

$$= 0.503 \text{ rad}$$

$$\Delta\omega_{0.1} = \Delta\omega_{0.05} + \frac{1}{6}(l_1 + 2l_2 + 2l_3 + l_4)$$

$$= 0.767 + \frac{1}{6}(0.754 + 2 \times 0.734 + 2 \times 0.724 + 0.695)$$

$$= 1.495 \text{ rad/s}$$

Fault is cleared at $t = 0.1$

Postfault condition, $P_e = 1.378 \sin\delta$

Iteration 3:

Ist estimate: $k_1 = \Delta\omega_{0.1} \times \Delta t = 1.495 \times 0.05 = 0.0748$

$$l_1 = \frac{\pi f}{H}(P_m - P_e(\delta_{0.1}))\Delta t = \frac{\pi \times 50}{5}(0.8 - 1.378 \sin 0.503) \times 0.05 = 0.213$$

IInd estimate: $k_2 = \left(\Delta\omega_{0.1} + \frac{l_1}{2}\right) \times \Delta t = \left(1.495 + \frac{0.213}{2}\right) \times 0.05 = 0.08$

$$l_2 = \frac{\pi f}{H}\left(P_m - P_e\left(d_{0.1} + \frac{k_1}{2}\right)\right)\Delta t$$

$$= \frac{\pi \times 50}{5}\left(0.8 - 1.378 \sin\left(0.503 + \frac{0.748}{2}\right)\right) \times 0.05$$

$$= 0.143$$

IIIrd estimate: $k_3 = \left(\Delta\omega_{0.1} + \frac{l_2}{2}\right) \times \Delta t = \left(1.495 + \frac{0.143}{2}\right) \times 0.05 = 0.0783$

$$l_3 = \frac{\pi f}{H}\left(P_m - P_e\left(\delta_{0.1} + \frac{k_2}{2}\right)\right)\Delta t$$

$$= \frac{\pi \times 50}{5}\left(0.8 - 1.378 \sin\left(0.503 + \frac{0.08}{2}\right)\right) \times 0.05$$

$$= 0.1382$$

IVth estimate: $k_4 = (\Delta\omega_{0.1} + l_3) \times \Delta t = (1.495 + 0.1382) \times 0.05 = 0.0817$

$$l_4 = \frac{\pi f}{H}(P_m - P_e(\delta_{0.1} + k_3))\Delta t$$

$$= \frac{\pi \times 50}{5}(0.8 - 1.378 \sin(0.503 + 0.0783)) \times 0.05$$

$$= 0.068$$

Final estimate:

$$\delta_{0.15} = \delta_{0.1} + \frac{1}{6}(k_1 + 2k_2 + 2k_3 + k_4)$$

$$= 0.503 + \frac{1}{6}(0.0748 + 2 \times 0.08 + 2 \times 0.0783 + 0.0817)$$

$$= 0.582 \text{ rad}$$

$$\Delta\omega_{0.15} = \Delta\omega_{0.1} + \frac{1}{6}(l_1 + 2l_2 + 2l_3 + l_4)$$

$$= 1.495 + \frac{1}{6}(0.213 + 2 \times 0.143 + 2 \times 0.1382 + 0.068)$$

$$= 1.636 \text{ rad/s}$$

5.9 Multimachine Transient Stability

Transient stability analysis has recently become a major issue in the operation of power system due to the increasing stress on power system networks. This problem requires evaluation of a power system's ability to withstand disturbances while maintaining the quality of service. Many different techniques have been proposed for transient stability analysis in power system, especially for a multi-machine system.

Multi-machine equations can be written similar to the one-machine system connected to the infinite bus. In order to reduce the complexity of the transient stability analysis, similar simplifying assumptions are made as follows.

- Each synchronous machine is represented by a constant voltage source behind the direct axis transient reactance. This representation neglects the effect of saliency and assumes constant flux linkages.
- The actions of the governor are neglected and the input powers are assumed to remain constant during the entire period of simulation.
- Using the prefault bus voltages, all loads are converted to equivalent admittances to ground and are assumed to remain constant.
- Damping or asynchronous powers are ignored.
- The mechanical rotor angle of each machine coincides with the angle of the voltage behind the machine reactance.
- Machines belonging to the same station swing together and are said to be coherent. A group of coherent machines is represented by one equivalent machine.

5.9.1 Mathematical Model of Multimachine Transient Stability Analysis

The first step in the transient stability analysis is to solve the initial load flow and to determine the initial bus voltage magnitudes and phase angles. The machine currents prior to disturbance are calculated from,

$$I_i = \frac{S_i^*}{V_i^*} = \frac{P_i - jQ_i}{V_i^*} \qquad i = 1, 2, ..., m \tag{5.56}$$

where m is the number of generators

V_i is the terminal voltage of the ith generator

P_i and Q_i are the generators of real and reactive powers.

All unknown values are determined from the initial power flow solution. The generator armature resistances are usually neglected and the voltages behind the transient reactance are then obtained as

$$E_i' = V_i + jX_d' I_i \tag{5.57}$$

Next, all loads are converted to equivalent admittances by using the relation

$$y_{i0} = \frac{S_i^*}{|V_i|^2} = \frac{P_i - jQ_i}{|V_i|^2} \tag{5.58}$$

To include voltages behind the transient reactance, m buses are added to the n bus power system network. The equivalent network, with all loads converted to admittances is shown in Figure 5.30.

Nodes $n + 1$, $n + 2$, ..., $n + m$ are the internal machine buses, i.e. the buses behind the transient reactances. The node voltage equation, with node 0 as reference for this network, is

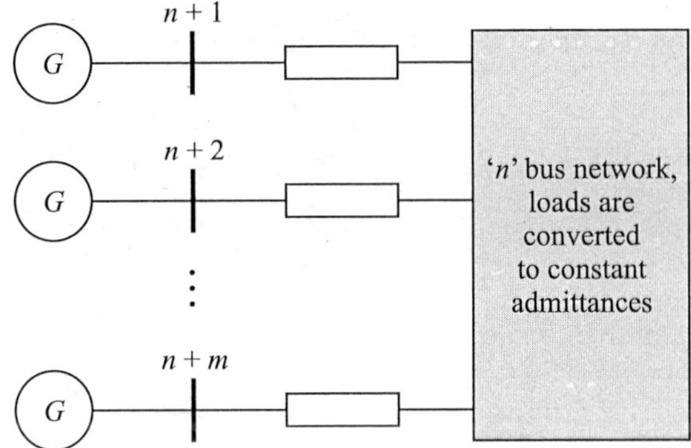

Figure 5.30 Power system representation for transient stability analysis.

$$\begin{bmatrix} I_1 \\ \vdots \\ I_n \\ I_{n+1} \\ \vdots \\ I_{n+m} \end{bmatrix} = \begin{bmatrix} Y_{11} & \cdots & Y_{n1} & Y_{1(n+1)} & \cdots & Y_{1(n+m)} \\ \vdots & \ddots & \vdots & \vdots & \ddots & \vdots \\ Y_{1n} & \cdots & Y_{nm} & Y_{n(n+1)} & \cdots & Y_{n(n+m)} \\ Y_{(n+1)1} & \cdots & Y_{(n+1)n} & Y_{(n+1)(n+1)} & \cdots & Y_{(n+1)(n+m)} \\ \vdots & \ddots & \vdots & \vdots & \ddots & \vdots \\ Y_{(n+m)1} & \cdots & Y_{(n+m)n} & Y_{(n+m)(n+1)} & \cdots & Y_{(n+m)(n+m)} \end{bmatrix} \begin{bmatrix} V_1 \\ \vdots \\ V_n \\ E'_{n+1} \\ \vdots \\ E'_{n+m} \end{bmatrix} \tag{5.59}$$

or

$$I_{bus} = Y_{bus} V_{bus} \tag{5.60}$$

where I_{bus} is the vector of the injected bus currents

V_{bus} is the vector of bus voltages measured from the reference node.

The diagonal elements of the bus admittance matrix are the sum of admittances connected to it, and the off-diagonal elements are equal to the negative of the admittance between the nodes. The reference is that additional nodes are added to include the machine voltages behind transient reactances. Also, the diagonal elements are modified to include the load admittances.

To simplify the analysis, all nodes other than the generator internal nodes are eliminated using Kron's reduction formula. To eliminate the load buses, the bus admittance matrix in Eq. (5.59) is partitioned such that the n buses to be removed are represented in the upper n rows. Since no current enters or leaves the load buses, currents in the n rows is zero. The generator current is denoted by the vector I_m and the generator and load voltages are represented by the vectors E'_m and V_n, respectively. Then, Eq. (5.59), in terms of sub matrices becomes

$$\begin{bmatrix} 0 \\ I_m \end{bmatrix} = \begin{bmatrix} Y_{nn} & Y_{nm} \\ Y_{nm}^t & Y_{mm} \end{bmatrix} \begin{bmatrix} V_n \\ E'_m \end{bmatrix} \tag{5.61}$$

The voltage vector V_n may be eliminated upon substitution as follows.

$$0 = Y_{nn}V_n + Y_{nm}E'_m \tag{5.62}$$

$$I_m = Y_{nm}^t V_n + Y_{mm}E'_m \tag{5.63}$$

From Eq. (5.62)

$$V_n = -Y_{nn}^{-1} + Y_{nm}E'_m \tag{5.64}$$

Now substituting into Eq. (5.63)

$$I_m = [Y_{mm} - Y_{nm}^t Y_{nn}^{-1} Y_{nm}]\, E'_m = Y_{\text{bus}}^{\text{red}} E'_m \tag{5.65}$$

The reduced admittance matrix is

$$Y_{\text{bus}}^{\text{red}} = Y_{mm} - Y_{nm}^t Y_{nn}^{-1} Y_{nm} \tag{5.66}$$

The reduced bus admittance matrix has the dimensions ($m \times m$), where m is the number of generators. The electrical power output of each machine can now be expressed in terms of the machine's internal voltages .

$$S_{ei}^* = E_i'^* I_i$$

or

$$P_{ei} = \text{Re}(E_i'^* I_i) \tag{5.67}$$

where

$$I_i = \sum_{j=1}^{m} E'_j Y_{ij} \tag{5.68}$$

Expressing voltages and admittances in the polar form,

$$E'_i = |E'_i|\angle\delta_i \quad \text{and} \quad Y_{ij} = |Y_{ij}|\angle\theta_{ij}$$

Substituting I_i in Eq. (5.67), we get

$$P_{ei} = \sum_{j=1}^{m} |E'_i||E'_j||Y_{ij}|\cos(\theta_{ij} - \delta_i + \delta_j) \tag{5.69}$$

The above equation is the same as the power flow equation. Prior to disturbance, there is equilibrium between the mechanical power input and the electrical power output, and we have

$$P_{mi} = \sum_{j=1}^{m} |E_i'||E_j'||Y_{ij}| \cos(\theta_{ij} - \delta_i + \delta_j) \tag{5.70}$$

The classical transient stability study is based on the application of a three-phase fault. A solid three-phase fault at bus k in the network results in $V_k = 0$. This is simulated by removing the kth row and column from the prefault bus admittance matrix. The new bus admittance matrix is reduced by eliminating all nodes except the internal generator nodes. The generator excitation voltages during the fault and the postfault modes are assumed to remain constant. The electrical power of the ith generator in terms of the new reduced bus admittance matrices are obtained from Eq. (5.69). The swing equation with damping neglected, for machine i becomes

$$\frac{H_i}{\pi f_0} \frac{d^2\delta_i}{dt^2} = P_{mi} - \sum_{j=1}^{m} |E_i'|| E_j'||Y_{ij}| \cos(\theta_{ij} - \delta_i + \delta_j) \tag{5.71}$$

where, Y_{ij} are the elements of the faulted reduced bus admittance matrix, H_i is the inertia constant of machine i expressed on the common MVA base SB. If H_{Gi} is the inertia constant of machine i expressed on the machine rated MVA S_{Gi}, then H_i is given by

$$H_i = \frac{S_{Gi}}{S_{cb}} H_{Gi} \tag{5.72}$$

Showing the electrical power of the ith generator by P_{ef} and transforming Eq. (5.71) into state variable mode yield

$$\frac{d\delta_i}{dt} = \Delta\omega_i \tag{5.73}$$

$$\frac{d\Delta\omega_i}{dt} = \frac{\pi f_0}{H_i}(P_{mi} - P_{ei}^f) \tag{5.74}$$

In the transient stability analysis problem, we have two state equations for each generator. When the fault is cleared, which may involve the removal of the faulty line, the bus admittance matrix is recomputed to reflect the change in the network. Next the postfault reduced bus admittance matrix is evaluated and the postfault electrical power of the ith generator shown by P_i^{pf} readily determined. Using the postfault power P_i^{pf}, the simulation is continued to determine the system stability, until the plots reveal a definite trend as to stability or instability. Usually the slack generator is selected as the reference machines are plotted. Usually, the solution is carried out for two swings to show that the second swing is not greater than the first one. If the angle differences do not increase, the system is stable. If any of the angle differences increase indefinitely, the system is unstable. The flow chart of transient stability analysis for a multimachine power is given in Figure 5.31.

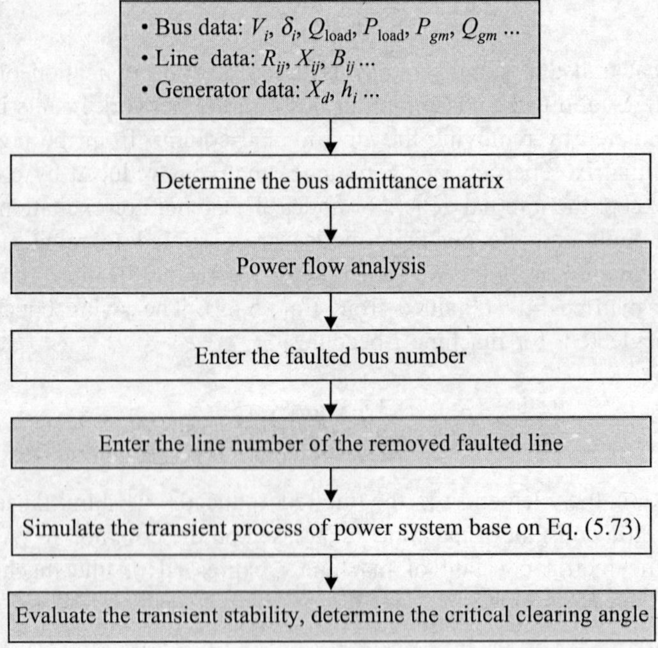

Figure 5.31 Flow chart of transient stability analysis for a multimachine power.

5.10 Factors Influencing Transient Stability

The factors that affect the transient stability are given below.

(i) *The generator inertia.* The higher the inertia, the lower is the rate of change in angle. This reduces the kinetic energy gained during fault.

(ii) *The generator reactance.* A lower reactance increases peak power and reduces initial rotor angle.

(iii) The generator internal voltage magnitude (E'). This depends on the field excitation.

(iv) How heavily the generator is loaded.

(v) The generator output during the fault. This depends upon the fault location and type.

(vi) The fault clearing time.

(vii) The postfault transmission system reactance.

5.11 Techniques for Transient Stability Improvement

(i) Reduction in system transfer reactance

Reducing the series reactance by using the series capacitor is normally economical for lines of length more than 320 km. For lines of length less than 320 km, the objective is achieved by running parallel lines. When parallel lines are used, instead of a single line, some power can be transferred over the healthy line even during a three-phase fault on one of the lines, unless of course when a fault takes place at the paralleling bus when no power can be transferred out of the parallel lines. For other types of faults on more than one line, more power can be transferred during the fault, if there are two lines in parallel, power can be transferred over a single faulted line.

The effect of reducing the series reactance is to increase P_m, which therefore, increases the transient stability of a system.

(ii) Increase of system voltage

From the equation $P_{max} = E_G E_M / X_T$, it is clear that an increase in system voltage results in higher values of power P_{max} that can be transferred between the nodes. Since shaft power $P_e = P_{max} \sin \delta_0$, with higher values of P_{max}, δ_0 is reduced and, therefore, the difference between the critical clearing angle and the initial angle δ_0 is increased. Therefore, increasing P_{max} allows the machine to rotate through large angle before it reaches the critical clearing angle, which results in greater critical clearing time and the probability of maintaining stability.

(iii) Use of high speed reclosing breakers

The quicker a breaker operates, the faster the fault is removed from the system and the better is the tendency of the system to restore to normal operating conditions. The use of high-speed breakers has materially improved the transient stability of the power systems and does not require any other methods for the purpose. The use of reclosing type circuit breakers plays a vital role in improving the transient stability limit.

(iv) HVDC links

A dc link is asynchronous, i.e. the two ac systems at either end do not have to be controlled in phase or even be at exactly the same frequency as they do for an ac link. There is no risk of a fault in one system causing loss of stability in the other system.

(v) Braking resistors

For improving stability, when large load is suddenly lost, a resistive load called a braking resistor is connected at or near the generator bus. This load compensates for at least some of the reduction of load on the generators and so reduces the acceleration. During a fault, the resistors are applied to the terminals of the generators through circuit breakers by means of elaborate control schemes. The control scheme determines the amount of resistance to be applied and its duration.

(vi) Short circuit current limiters

These may be used in long transmission lines to modify favourably the transfer impedance during the fault conditions so that the voltage profile of the system is somewhat improved, thereby raising the system load level during the fault.

(vii) Turbine fast valving or bypass valving

Another recent method of improving the stability of a unit is to decrease the mechanical input power to the turbine. This can be accomplished by means of fast valving, where the difference between the mechanical input and the reduced electrical output of a generator under a fault, as sensed by a control scheme, initiates the closing of a turbine valve to reduce the power input.

(viii) Full load rejection technique

In places where stability is difficult to maintain, the normal procedure is to automatically trip the unit off the line. This, however, causes several hours of delay before the unit can be put back into operation. The loss of a major unit for this length of time can seriously jeopardize the remaining system. To remedy these situations, a full load rejection scheme could be utilized after the unit is separated from the system. To do this, the unit has to be equipped with a large steam bypass system. After the system has recovered from the shock caused by the fault, the unit could be resynchronized and reloaded. The main disadvantage of this method is the extra cost of a large bypass system.

Review Questions

Part-A

1. What is the power system stability?
2. How is the power system stability classified?
3. What is the rotor angle stability?
4. What is the steady state stability?
5. What is the steady state stability limit?
6. What is the transient stability?
7. What is the transient stability limit?
8. What is the dynamic stability?
9. What is the voltage stability?
10. State the causes of voltage instability.
11. Write the power angle equation and draw the power angle curve.
12. Write the expression for the maximum power transfer.
13. Write the swing equation for a SMIB (single machine connected to an infinite bus bar) system.

14. Define the swing curve.
15. In a three machine system having ratings G_1, G_2 and G_3 and inertia constants M_1, M_2 and M_3 what are the inertia constants M and H of the equivalent system.
16. State the assumptions made in stability studies.
17. State equal area criterion.
18. Define the critical clearing angle.
19. List the methods of improving the transient stability limit of a power system.
20. What are the numerical integration methods of power system stability?

Part-B

1. A 400 MVA synchronous machine has H_1 = 4.6 MJ/MVA and a 1200 MVA machine H_2 = 3.0 MJ/MVA. Two machines operate in parallel in a power plant. Find out H_{eq} relative to a 100 MVA base.
2. A 100 MVA, two pole, 50 Hz generator has moment of inertia 40×10^3 kg·m^2. What is the energy stored in the rotor at the rated speed? What is the corresponding angular momentum? Determine the inertia constant H.
3. The sending end and the receiving end voltages of a three-phase transmission line at a 200 MW load are equal at 230 kV. The per phase line impedance is $j14$ Ω. Calculate the maximum steady state power that can be transmitted over the line.
4. A single line diagram of a system is shown in the figure below. All the values are in per unit on a common base. The power delivered into bus 2 is 1.0 p.u. at 0.80 power factor lagging. Obtain the power angle equation and the swing equation for the system. Neglect all losses.

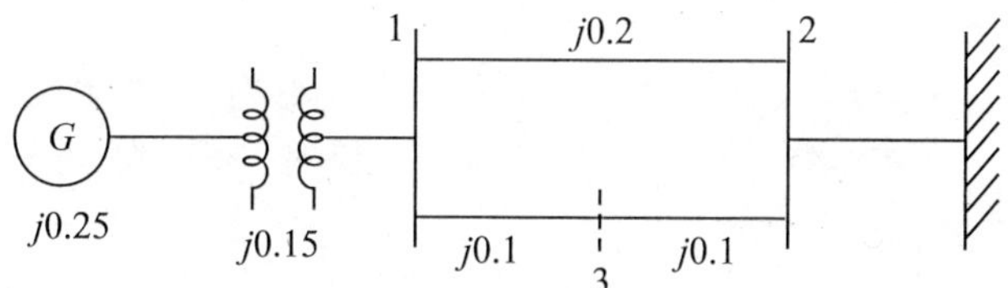

5. A 50 Hz synchronous generator capable of supplying 400 MW of power is connected to a larger power system and is delivering 80 MW when a three-phase fault occurs at its terminals, determine (a) the time in which the fault must be cleared if the maximum power angle is to be –85°, assume H = 7 MJ/MVA on a 100 MVA base and (b) the critical clearing angle.
6. A synchronous generator is connected to a large power system and supplying 0.45 p.u. MW of its maximum power capacity. A three-

phase fault occurs and the effective terminal voltage of the generator becomes 25% of its value before the fault. When the fault is cleared, the generator is delivering 70% of the original maximum value. Determine the critical clearing angle.

7. Determine the critical clearing angle of the power system as shown in the figure below for a three-phase fault at the point F. The generator is supplying 1.0 p.u. MW power under the prefault condition.

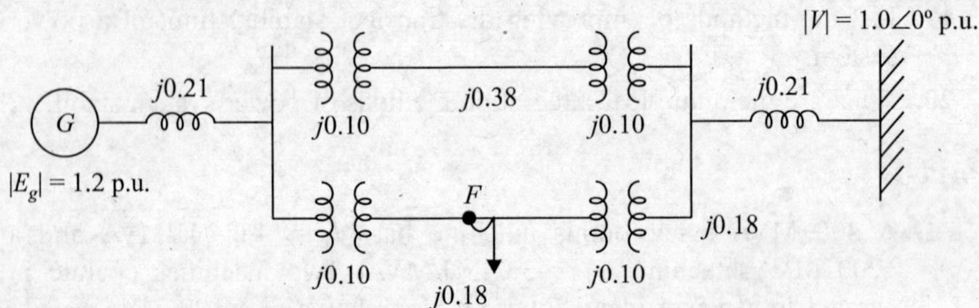

Part II

Power System Security

CHAPTER 6

Operations in Power System Security

6.1 Introduction

Definition

Power system security involves practices designed to keep the system operating when the components fail.

Examples

1. A generating unit may have to be taken off-line because of auxiliary equipment failure.
2. By maintaining the proper amount of spinning reserve, the remaining units on the system can take the deficit without too low a frequency drop or need to shed load.
3. A transmission line may be damaged by a storm and taken out by automatic relaying.

When one failure results in another failure in the system, it is called cascading failure which leads to system blackout.

System security

It is classified into three major functions which are carried out in an operation control centre.

1. System monitoring (SCADA, state estimation).
2. Contingency analysis.
3. Security constrained OPF (SCOPF).

The system monitoring provides the operators of the power system with pertinent up-to-date information on the conditions of the power system. Generally speaking, it is the most important function of the three. From the time that utilities went beyond systems of one unit supplying a group of loads, the effective operation of the system required that critical quantities be measured and the values of the measurements be transmitted to a central location. Such systems of measurement and data transmission, called telemetry systems, have evolved to schemes that can monitor voltages, currents, power flows, and the status of circuit breakers, and switches in every substation in a power system transmission network. In addition, other critical information such as frequency, generator unit outputs and transformer tap positions can also be telemetered. With so much information telemetered simultaneously, no human operator could hope to check all of it in a reasonable time frame. For this reason, digital computers are usually installed in operation control centres to gather the telemetered data, process them, and place them in a database from which operators can display information on large display monitors. More importantly, the computer can check incoming information against prestored limits and alarm the operators in the event of an overload or out-of-limit voltage.

State estimation is often used in such systems to combine telemetered system data with system models to produce the best estimate of the current power system conditions or "state". It is discussed in detail in the other sections.

Such systems are usually combined with supervisory control systems that allow operators to control circuit breakers and disconnect switches and transformer taps remotely. Together, these systems are often referred to as SCADA systems, standing for **S**upervisory **C**ontrol **A**nd **D**ata **A**cquisition system.

The second major security function is the contingency analysis. The results of this type of analysis allow systems to be operated defensively. Many of the problems that occur on a power system can cause serious trouble within such a quick time period that the operator could not take action fast enough. This is often the case with cascading failures. Because of this aspect of system operation, modern operation computers are equipped with contingency analysis programs that model possible system troubles that arise. These programs are based on a model of the power system and are used to study outage events and alarm the operators to any potential overloads or out-of-limit voltages. For example, the simplest form of the contingency analysis can be put together with a standard power-flow program as described in this chapter. Several variations of this type of contingency selection, and automatic initializing of the contingency power flows using the actual system data and the state estimation procedures are discussed in this chapter.

The third method security function is security-constrained optimal power flow. In this function, a contingency analysis is combined with an optimal power flow which seeks to make changes to the optimal dispatch of generation, as well as other adjustments, so that when a security analysis runs, no contingencies result in violation.

To understand the above functions, we shall divide the operating states of the power system into four types:

1. Optimal dispatch
2. Post-contingency
3. Secure dispatch
4. Secure post-contingency

1. Optimal dispatch: It is the state that the power system is in prior to any contingency. It is optimal with respect to economic operation but it may not be secure.

2. Post-contingency: It is the state of the power sytem after contingency has occurred. We shall assume here that this state has a security violation (transmission line or transformer outside its flow limit or bus voltage outside limit).

3. Secure dispatch: It is the state of the power system with no contingency outages but with corrections to the operating parameters to account for security violation.

4. Secure post-contingency: It is the state of the power system when contingency analysis is applied to base operating condition with corrections. It is illustrated with an example. Suppose a trivial power system consisting of two generators, a load and double circuit line with both generators supplying load.

Figure 6.1 shows that the system is in economic dispatch that is 500 MW from unit 1 and 700 MW from unit 2 is in optimal dispatch. Further, the two double circuit lines can carry a maximum of 400 MW so that there is no loading problem with respect to the base operating condition.

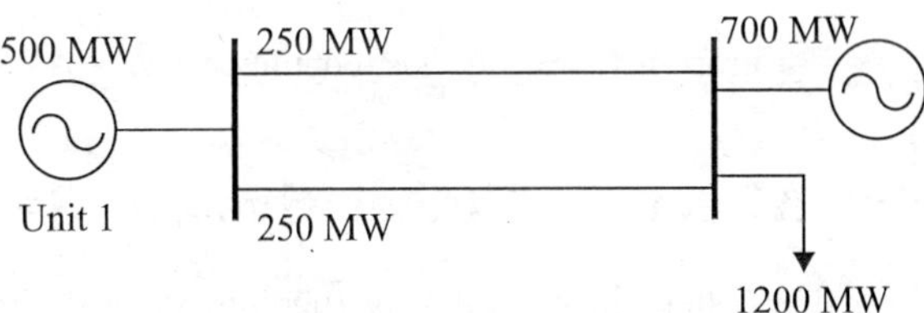

Figure 6.1 Optimal dispatch.

Figure 6.2 shows the post-contingency state. Suppose one of the circuits making double circuit line is opened due to a failure. The circuit will be as shown in figure below. Then there is an overload in the remaining circuit.

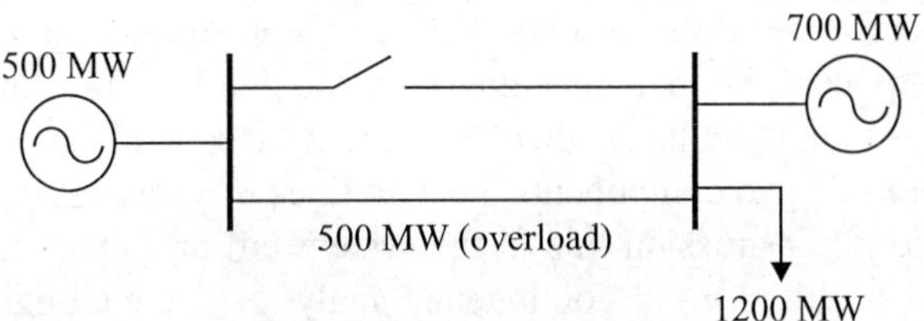

Figure 6.2 Post contingency.

If we don't have this condition to arise and we shall correct this by lowering the generation on unit 1 to 400 MW, then the secure dispatch is as shown in Figure 6.3.

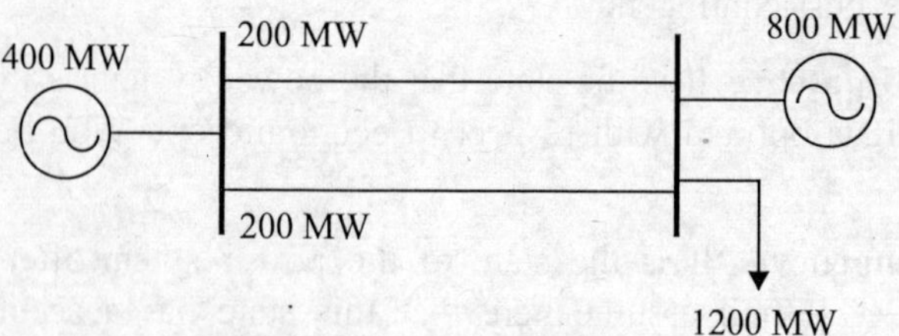

Figure 6.3 Secure dispatch.

Now, if the contingency analysis is done, the secure post-contingency is as shown in Figure 6.4. Thus, by adjusting the generation on unit 1 and unit 2, the post-contingency state is prevented from having an overload. Programs which make control adjustments to the base or pre-contingency condition to prevent violations in post-contingency conditions are called Security Constrained Optimal Power Flow (SCOPF).

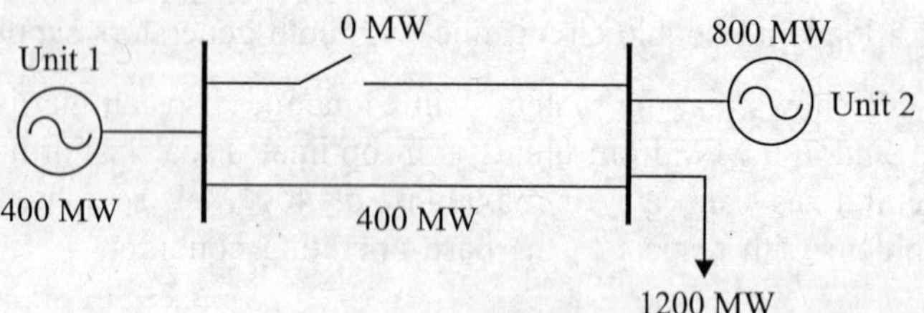

Figure 6.4 Secure post-contingency.

6.2 Factors Affecting Power System Security

1. To operate the system in such a way that power is delivered reliably.
2. Within the constraints placed on the system operation by reliability considerations, the system will be operated most economically.

6.3 Contingency Analysis

Let us consider that n power system components are there in a power system, and if one component, i.e. one generator or a one line in a transmission system fails or outage (single failure), then this event is called $n - 1$ contingency analysis. Whereas if two components, i.e. two lines in a transmission system or, a generator and a transmission line in the system fail or, outage (two failures), then this event is called $n - 2$ contingency analysis. The contingency analysis procedure is given with a flow chart as shown in Figure 6.5.

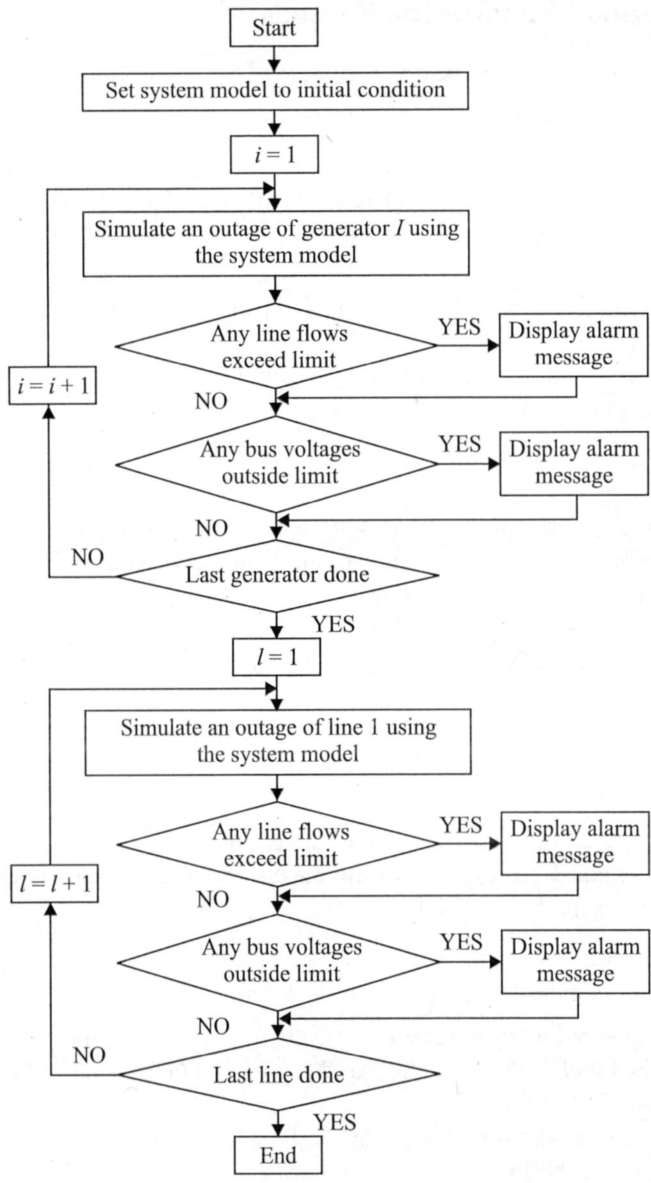

Figure 6.5 Contingency analysis procedure.

6.3.1 Overview of Security Analysis

The problem of studying thousands of possible outages becomes very difficult to solve if it is desired to present the results quickly. One of the easiest ways to provide a quick calculation of possible overloads is to use linear sensitivity factors. These factors show the approximate change in line flows for changes in generation on the network configuration and are derived from the dc load flow.

6.3.2 Linear Sensitivity Factors

There are two factors used in this method:

1. Generation shift sensitivity factor (a_{li})
2. Line outage distribution factor ($d_{l,k}$)

The derivation of these two factors is available in literature.

The determination of the above factors using the dc load flow is explained below.

1. Formulate the sensitivity matrix [x] using the dc load flow equation $\theta = [x]\,[P]$
2. Determine the generation shift sensitivity factor using the following equation

$$a_{li} = \frac{1}{x_l}[X_{ni} - X_{mi}] \tag{6.1}$$

where i corresponds to bus in which the generator is connected, l corresponds to the line under study, i.e. between the buses n and m, x_l is the reactance of the line, X_{ni} and X_{mi} are the corresponding values in the sensitivity matrix.

3. Determine the line outage distribution factor using the following equation

$$d_{l,k} = \frac{\dfrac{x_k}{x_l}[X_{in} - X_{jn} - X_{im} + X_{jm}]}{x_k - [X_{ii} + X_{jj} - 2X_{ij}]} \tag{6.2}$$

where l corresponds to the line under study, i.e. between the buses n and m and k corresponds to the outage of the line which is connected between the buses i and j.

EXAMPLE 6.1 The line reactance of the four-bus system is given in Table 6.1 and assume bus 1 is a slack. Determine

1. the generation shift sensitivity factor of the line connecting between buses 1 and 2, also consider that the outage of the generator is connected to bus 2.
2. the line outage distribution factor for all the lines by performing the outage of the lines 1–2 and 2–3.

Table 6.1 Reactance values

Line	*Reactance* (p.u.)
1–2	0.2
1–4	0.25
2–3	0.15
2–4	0.30
3–4	0.40

Solution:

Step 1: Formation of $[Y_{bus}]$

$$Y_{bus} = \begin{bmatrix} 9 & -5 & 0 & -4 \\ -5 & 15 & -6.667 & -3.33 \\ 0 & -6.667 & 9.1670 & -2.5 \\ -4 & -3.33 & -2.5 & 9.833 \end{bmatrix}$$

Since bus 1 is a slack bus, eliminate the 1st row and the first column and find the inverse.

Step 2: Formation of the sensitivity matrix

$$X = \begin{bmatrix} 0 & 0 & 0 & 0 \\ 0 & 0.1379 & 0.1214 & 0.0776 \\ 0 & 0.1214 & 0.2242 & 0.0981 \\ 0 & 0.0776 & 0.0981 & 0.1529 \end{bmatrix}$$

Step 3: Determination of the generation shift sensitivity factor by performing the outage of the generator connected to bus 2, hence i is selected as 2 and l is the line connected to buses 1 and 2.

$$a_{li} = \frac{1}{x_l}(X_{ni} - X_{mi})$$

$$a_{(1-2)2} = \frac{1}{x_{1-2}}(X_{12} - X_{22})$$

$$= \frac{1}{0.2}(0 - 0.1378) = -0.689$$

Step 4: Determination of the line outage distribution factor by performing the outage of the line connected to bus 1–2, hence i and j refer to 1 and 2 and l is the line connected to buses 1 and 2 and hence n and m refer to 1 and 2.

Outage of line 1–2

$$d_{l,k} = \frac{\dfrac{x_k}{x_l}(X_{in} - X_{jn} - X_{im} + X_{jm})}{x_k - (X_{ii} + X_{jj} - 2X_{ij})}$$

$$d_{1-2,1-2} = \frac{\dfrac{0.2}{0.2}(0 - 0.1379 - 0 + 0.1379)}{0.2 - (0 + 0.1379 - 2(0))} = 0$$

$$d_{1-4,1-2} = \frac{\dfrac{x_{1-2}}{x_{1-4}}(X_{11} - X_{21} - X_{14} + X_{24})}{x_{1-2} - (X_{11} + X_{22} - 2(X_{12}))}$$

$$= \frac{\frac{0.2}{0.25}(0-0-0+0.776)}{0.2-(0+0.1379-2(0))} = 0.9996$$

$$d_{2-3,1-2} = \frac{\frac{x_{1-2}}{x_{2-3}}(X_{12}-X_{22}-X_{13}+X_{23})}{x_{1-2}-(X_{11}+X_{22}-2(X_{12}))}$$

$$= \frac{\frac{0.2}{0.15}(0-0.1379-0+0.1214)}{0.2-(0+0.1379-2(0))} = -0.3542$$

$$d_{2-4,1-2} = \frac{\frac{x_{1-2}}{x_{2-4}}(X_{12}-X_{22}-X_{14}+X_{24})}{x_{1-2}-(X_{11}+X_{22}-2(X_{12}))}$$

$$= \frac{\frac{0.2}{0.30}(0-0.1379-0+0.0776)}{0.2-(0+0.1379-2(0))} = -0.6473$$

$$d_{3-4,1-2} = \frac{\frac{x_{1-2}}{x_{3-4}}(X_{13}-X_{23}-X_{14}+X_{24})}{x_{1-2}-(X_{11}+X_{22}-2(X_{12}))}$$

$$= \frac{\frac{0.2}{0.4}(0-0.1214-0+0.0776)}{0.2-[0.1379]} = -0.3526$$

Outage of line 2–3

$$d_{1-2,2-3} = \frac{\frac{x_{2-3}}{x_{1-2}}(X_{21}-X_{31}-X_{22}+X_{32})}{x_{2-3}-(X_{22}+X_{33}-2(X_{23}))}$$

$$= \frac{\frac{0.15}{0.2}(0-0-0.1379+0.1214)}{0.15-(0.1379+0.2242-2(0.1214))} = -0.4030$$

$$d_{1-4,2-3} = \frac{\frac{x_{2-3}}{x_{1-4}}(X_{21}-X_{31}-X_{24}+X_{34})}{x_{2-3}-(X_{22}+X_{33}-2(X_{23}))}$$

$$= \frac{\frac{0.15}{0.25}(0-0-0.0776+0.0981)}{0.0307} = 0.4006$$

$$d_{2-3,2-3} = 0$$

$$d_{2-4,2-3} = \frac{\frac{x_{2-3}}{x_{2-4}}(X_{22} - X_{32} - X_{24} + X_{34})}{x_{2-3} - (X_{22} + X_{33} - 2(X_{23}))}$$

$$= \frac{\frac{0.15}{0.30}(0.1379 - 0.1214 - 0.0776 + 0.0981)}{0.0307} = 0.6026$$

MATLAB program is written for the computation of generation shift sensitivity factor and the line outage distribution factor. The test system considered for illustration is a six bus sample system, the line data and the bus data are given in this program. The obtained [X] matrix for a six bus sample system together with the generation shift sensitivity factors and the line outage distribution factors is given below.

6.3.3 MATLAB Program

MATLAB programs for computation of generation shift sensitivity factor

```
clear all;
close all;
clc;

% from  to    R     X     Bcap
ld=[1   2    .1    .2    .02
    1   4    .05   .2    .02
    1   5    .08   .3    .03
    2   3    .05   .25   .03
    2   4    .05   .1    .01
    2   5    .1    .3    .02
    2   6    .07   .2    .025
    3   5    .12   .26   .025
    3   6    .02   .1    .01
    4   5    .2    .4    .04
    5   6    .1    .3    .03];

 %      bus.no  type  voltage    Pgen   Pload    Qload
 bd=[     1      0     1.05        0      0        0
          2      1     1.05       .5      0        0
          3      1     1.07       .6      0        0
          4      2     1           0     .7       .7
          5      2     1           0     .7       .7
          6      2     1           0     .7       .7 ];
      nb=length(bd(:,1));
      nl=length(ld(:,1));
```

```
    Y= zeros(nb);
    for i=1:nl
                          Y(ld(i,1),ld(i,2))=-1/(+1i*ld(i,4));
                          Y(ld(i,2),ld(i,1))=-1/(+1i*ld(i,4));
    end;
   for i=1:nb
       Y(i,i)=-sum(Y(i,:));
    end;
    Y1=Y(2:end,2:end);
    X=imag(inv(Y1));
    X1=zeros(nb);
    X1(2:end,2:end)=X1(2:end,2:end)+X;
    genbus=find(bd(:,2)==1)';
    a=zeros(nb,length(genbus));
 for k=1:length(genbus)
for i=1:nl
       a(i,k)=(1/ld(i,4))*(X1(ld(i,1),genbus(k))-
              X1(ld(i,2),genbus(k)));
end;
end;
fprintf('The X matrix is : \n');
disp(X);
fprintf('The Generation Shift Sensitivity Matrix is : ');
fprintf('\n*******************');for i=1:length(genbus)
fprintf('**********');end;fprintf('\n');
fprintf('***    from    ***    to    ***');fprintf('**|  %d
|***',genbus);
fprintf('\n');
fprintf('*******************');for i=1:length(genbus)
fprintf('**********');end;fprintf('\n');
dsp=[ld(:,1) ld(:,2) a];
disp(dsp);
fprintf('*******************');for i=1:length(genbus)
fprintf('**********');end;fprintf('\n');
fprintf('*******************');for i=1:length(genbus)
fprintf('**********');end;fprintf('\n');
The X matrix is:
    0.0941      0.0805      0.0630      0.0643      0.0813
    0.0805      0.1659      0.0590      0.0908      0.1290
    0.0630      0.0590      0.1009      0.0542      0.0592
    0.0643      0.0908      0.0542      0.1222      0.0893
    0.0813      0.1290      0.0592      0.0893      0.1633
```

```
The Generation Shift Sensitivity Matrix is:
****************************************
***   from   ***   to   *****| 2 |*****| 3 |**
****************************************
 1.0000    2.0000   -0.4706   -0.4026
 1.0000    4.0000   -0.3149   -0.2949
 1.0000    5.0000   -0.2145   -0.3026
 2.0000    3.0000    0.0544   -0.3416
 2.0000    4.0000    0.3115    0.2154
 2.0000    5.0000    0.0993   -0.0342
 2.0000    6.0000    0.0642   -0.2422
 3.0000    5.0000    0.0622    0.2890
 3.0000    6.0000   -0.0077    0.3695
 4.0000    5.0000   -0.0034   -0.0795
 5.0000    6.0000   -0.0565   -0.1273
 ****************************************
****************************************
```

MATLAB programs for computation of line outage distribution factor

```
clear all;
close all;
clc;
% from  to    R     X    Bcap
ld=  [1   2    .1    .2   .02
      1   4    .05   .2   .02
      1   5    .08   .3   .03
      2   3    .05   .25  .03
      2   4    .05   .1   .01
      2   5    .1    .3   .02
      2   2    .07   .2   .025
      3   5    .12   .26  .025
      3   6    .02   .1   .01
      4   5    .2    .4   .04
      5   6    .1    .3   .03];
 %    bus.no  type  voltage   Pgen   Pload   Qload
 bd=[   1      0     1.05      0      0       0
        2      1     1.05     .5      0       0
        3      1     1.07     .6      0       0
        4      2     1         0     .7      .7
        5      2     1         0     .7      .7
        6      2     1         0     .7     .7];
```

```
 x=ld(:,4);
 nb=length(bd(:,1));
 nl=length(ld(:,1));
 Y= zeros(nb);

 for i=1:nl
    Y(ld(i,1),ld(i,2))=-1/(+1i*ld(i,4));
    Y(ld(i,2),ld(i,1))=-1/(+1i*ld(i,4));
 end;

 for i=1:nb
    Y(i,i)=-sum(Y(i,:));
 end;
 Y1=Y(2:end,2:end);
 X=imag(inv(Y1));
 X1=zeros(nb);
 X1(2:end,2:end)=X1(2:end,2:end)+X;
 d=zeros(nb);
for k=1:nl
for l=1:nl
 if(l~=k)
  d(l,k)=((x(k)/x(l))*(X1(ld(k,1),ld(l,1))-X1(ld(k,2),ld(l,1))-
X1(ld(k,1),ld(l,2))+X1(ld(k,2),ld(l,2))))/(x(k)-
  (X1(ld(k,1),ld(k,1))+X1(ld(k,2),ld(k,2))-
2*X1(ld(k,1),ld(k,2))));
 end;
end;
end;
fprintf('The Line Outage Distribution Factor Matrix is:
\n\n\n');
disp(d);
```

Line outage distribution factor matrix is:

	$k = 1$	$k = 2$	$k = 3$	$k = 4$	$k = 5$	$k = 6$	$k = 7$	$k = 8$	$k = 9$	$k = 10$	$k = 11$
$l = 1$	0	0.6353	0.5427	–0.1127	–0.5031	–0.2103	–0.1221	–0.1369	0.0135	0.0096	0.1316
$l = 2$	0.5948	0	0.4573	–0.0331	0.6121	–0.0618	–0.0359	–0.0403	0.004	–0.3269	0.0387
$l = 3$	0.4052	0.3647	0	0.1458	–0.109	0.2721	0.158	0.1772	–0.0174	0.3174	–0.1703
$l = 4$	–0.1029	–0.0323	0.1783	0	0.1242	0.2262	0.4662	–0.3995	–0.5253	0.1706	0.132
$l = 5$	–0.5884	0.7647	–0.1708	0.1591	0	0.2969	0.1724	0.1933	–0.019	–0.6731	–0.1858
$l = 6$	–0.1875	–0.0589	0.325	0.2209	0.2264	0	0.2394	0.2685	–0.0264	0.311	–0.258
$l = 7$	–0.1213	–0.0381	0.2102	0.5073	0.1464	0.2667	0	–0.1992	0.5842	0.2011	0.4433
$l = 8$	–0.1175	–0.0369	0.2036	-0.3755	0.1418	0.2583	–0.172	0	0.4747	0.1948	–0.4246
$l = 9$	0.0146	0.0046	–0.0253	-0.6245	–0.0176	–0.0321	0.6382	0.6005	0	–0.0242	0.5567
$l = 10$	0.0065	–0.2353	0.2865	0.1259	–0.3879	0.235	0.1365	0.153	–0.015	0	–0.1471
$l = 11$	0.1067	0.0335	–0.1849	0.1172	–0.1288	–0.2346	0.3618	–0.4013	0.4158	–0.1769	0

MATLAB program for computation of line flow after outage

% MATLAB program for computation of line flow after outage

```
clc;
clear
basemva = 100; accuracy = 0.1; accel = 1.8; maxiter = 10;
% IEEE 6-BUS TEST SYSTEM
% Bus Bus Voltage Angle ---Load---- ----Generator-- Static Mvar
%      No code Mag. Degree MW   Mvar   MW   Mvar Qmin Qmax+Qc/ -Ql
busdata=[1  1  1.05   0.0   0.0   0.0   0.0  0.0    0     0    0
         2  2  1.05   0.0   0.0   0.0  50.0  0.0  -10    80    0
         3  2  1.07   0.0   0.0   0.0  60.0  0.0  -10    95    0
         4  0  0.0    0.0  70.0  70.0   0.0  0.0    0     0    0
         5  0  0.0    0.0  70.0  70.0   0.0  0.0    0     0    0
         6  0  0.0    0.0  70.0  70.0   0.0  0.0    0     0    0
  ];
  %                                  Line code
  %      Bus bus R     X     1/2 B = 1 for lines
  %       nl nr p.u.  p.u.  p.u. > 1 or < 1 tr. tap at
  bus nl
  linedata=[1  2  0.1   0.2   0.002  1
            1  4  0.05  0.2   0.02   1
            1  5  0.08  0.3   0.03   1
            2  3  0.05  0.25  0.03   1
            2  4  0.05  0.1   0.01   1
            2  5  0.1   0.3   0.02   1
            2  6  0.07  0.2   0.025  1
            3  5  0.12  0.26  0.025  1
            3  6  0.02  0.1   0.01   1
            4  5  0.2   0.4   0.04   1
            5  6  0.1   0.3   0.03   1];

  lfybus                    % form the bus admittance matrix
  lfnewton   % Load flow solution by newton raphson method
  busout      % Prints the power flow solution on the screen
  lineflow     % Computes and displays the line flow and losses
  Ybus=abs(Ybus);
  for a = 1:nbus
       for b = 1:nbus
            if a ~= b
                 Ybus(a,b) = -Ybus(a,b);
            end
       end
  end
```

```
Ybusreduced  =  Ybus(2:nbus,2:nbus);
X  =  inv(Ybusreduced);
f=zeros(1,5);
X=[f;X];
e=zeros(6,1);
X=[e X];
fprintf('\n\n\t\tsensitivity  matrix  X\n\n  X  =\n');
disp(X);
n=length(linedata(:,1));
  s=input('\nEnter  the  no.  of  generator  ');
  for  g=1:s
      i=input('\nEnter  the  generator  on  outage  ');
      for  l=1:n
                a(l,i)=(1/linedata(l,4))*(X(linedata(l,1),i)-
                X(linedata(l,2),i));
             %generation  shift  factor  calculation
        end
  end
  l=1;
   %LINE  OUTAGE  DISTRIBUTION  FACTOR  CALCULATION
  for  k=1:n
        for  l=1:n
             if  k~=l
          d(l,k)=((linedata(k,4)/linedata(l,4))*
        (X(linedata(k,1),linedata(l,1))-X(linedata(k,2),
  linedata(l,1))...
          -X(linedata(k,1),linedata(l,2))+X(linedata(k,2),
linedata(l,2))));
         d(l,k)=d(l,k)/(linedata(k,4)-(X(linedata(k,1),
linedata(k,1))+...
          X(linedata(k,2),linedata(k,2))-(2*X(linedata(k,1),
linedata(k,2)))));
             end
        end
  end
  fprintf('\n\t\tGeneration  Shift  Factors\n\n');
  disp(a);
  fprintf('\n\t\tLine  Outage  Distribution  Factors\n\n');
  disp(d);

%CALCULATION OF FLOW ON LINE AFTER OUTAGE OF CERTAIN GENERATION
   q=input('\n\nEnter  the  line  number  in  which  flow  is  to
be  found  out')...
                    ('after  Outage  of  Generator  :   ');
```

```
 if q <= n
       fprintf('\n\nEnter the generator on Outage :   ');
       i=input(' ');
       fprintf('\n\nEnter the base case Generation on bus
%d :   ',i);
       Pi=input('');
         fprintf('\n\nEnter the base case flow on line
%d',linedata(q,1));
       fprintf('to line %d ', line data(q,2));
       flo=input(' ');
       fl=flo+(a(q,i)*(-Pi));
       fprintf('\n\n THE FLOW ON LINE %d',linedata(q,1))...
      fprintf('%dAFTERTHEOUTAGEOFGENERATIONON  BUS
%d=%f',linedata(q,2),i,fl);


 else
 fprintf('\n line number exceed the max no. of lines');
 end
 %CALCULATION OF FLOW ON LINE AFTER OUTAGE OF ANOTHER LINE
 l=input('\n\nEnter the line number in which flow is to be
found out :   ');
 if l <= n
       fprintf('\n\nEnter the Line no. on Outage :   ');
       k=input(' ');
fprintf('\n\nEnter the base case flow on Outage line
%d',linedata(k,1))...
fprintf('to %d: ',linedata(k,2));
fk=input(' ');
fprintf('\n\nEnter the base case flow on Outage line
%d',linedata(l,1))...
fprintf('to %d: ',linedata(l,2));

       flo=input(' ');
       fl=flo+(d(l,k)*(fk));
fprintf('\n\n THE FLOW ON LINE %d to %d',linedata(l,1),
linedata(l,2))...
fprintf('WITH LINE%dto%d ON OUTAGE= %f\n',linedata(k,1),
linedata(k,2),fl);
 else
 fprintf('\n line number exceed the max no. of lines');
 end
```

After determining the generator and the line outage procedures described earlier, one can perform contingency analysis using the sensitivity factors as shown in Figure 6.6. Assume an outage of the generator on bus 3 with all pick up of lost generation coming on the generator at bus 1. To calculate the flow on line 1–4 after the outage of the generator on bus 3, we need

base case flow on line 1–4 = 43.6 MW

base case generation on bus 3 = 60 MW

generation shift distribution factor = $a_{1-4,3} = -0.29$

Then the flow on line 1–4 after generator outage

$$= \text{base case flow}_{1-4} + a_{1-4,3}, \Delta P_{\text{gen3}}$$

$$= 43.6 + (-0.29)\ (-60\ \text{MW}) = 61\ \text{MW}$$

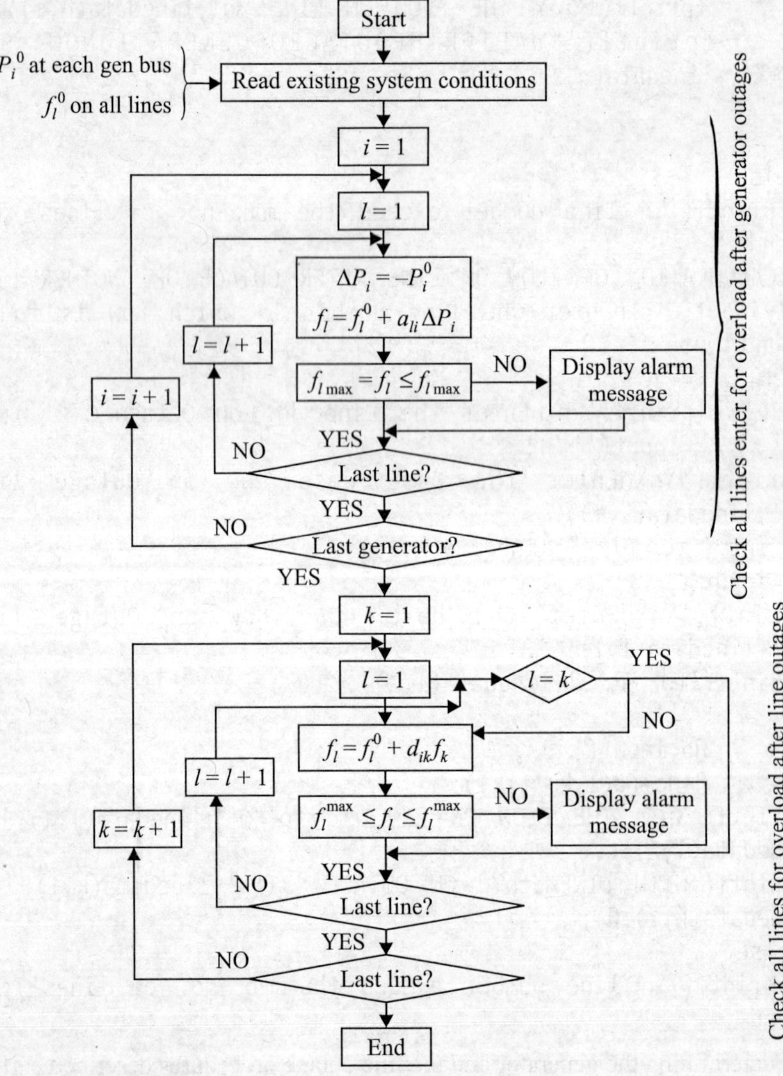

Figure 6.6 Contingency analysis using sensitivity factors.

Assume an outage of line 3–5, then the line flow on line 3–6 with line 3–5 opened using the line outage distribution factor can be calculated as follows:

base case flow on line 3–5 = 19.1 MW
base case flow on line 3–6 = 43.8 MW
line outage distribution factor ($d_{3-6,3-5}$) = 0.60.
Then the flow on line 3–6 after outage

$$= \text{base flow}_{3-6} + d_{3-6,3-5} \times \text{base flow}_{3-5}$$
$$= 43.8 + (0.60) \times (19.1) = 55.26 \text{ MW}$$

6.4 AC Power Flow Security Analysis

The calculations made by the network sensitivity methods are faster than those made by the ac power flow methods and therefore find wide use in operations control systems. However, there are many power systems where voltage magnitudes are the critical factor in assessing contingencies. In addition, there are some systems where VAR flows predominate on some circuits, such as underground cables, and an analysis of only the MW flows will not be adequate to indicate overloads. When such situations present themselves, the network sensitivity methods may not be adequate and the operations control system will have to incorporate a full ac power flow for contingency analysis.

When an ac power flow is to be used to study each contingency case, the speed of solution and the number of cases to be studied are critical. That is, if the contingency alarms come too late for operators to act, they are worthless. Most operations control centres that use an ac power flow program for contingency analysis involve either a Newton–Raphson or the decoupled power flow. These solution algorithms are used because of their speed of solution and the fact that they are reasonably reliable in convergence when solving difficult cases. The decoupled load flow has the further advantage that a matrix alteration formula can be incorporated into it to simulate the outage of transmission lines without reinverting the system Jacobian matrix at each iteration.

The simplest ac security analysis procedure consists of running an ac power flow analysis for each possible generator, transmission line, and the transformer outage as shown in Figure 6.7. This procedure will determine the overloads and voltage limit violations accurately (at least within the accuracy of the power flow program, the accuracy of the model data, and the accuracy with which we have obtained the initial conditions for the power flow). It does suffer a major drawback, however, and that concerns the time such a program takes to execute. If the list of outages has several thousand entries, then the total time to test for all of the outages can be too long.

We are thus confronted with a dilemma. Fast, but inaccurate, methods involving the a and d factors can be used to give rapid analysis of the system, but they cannot give information about MVAR flows and voltages. Slower, full ac power flow methods give full accuracy but take too long.

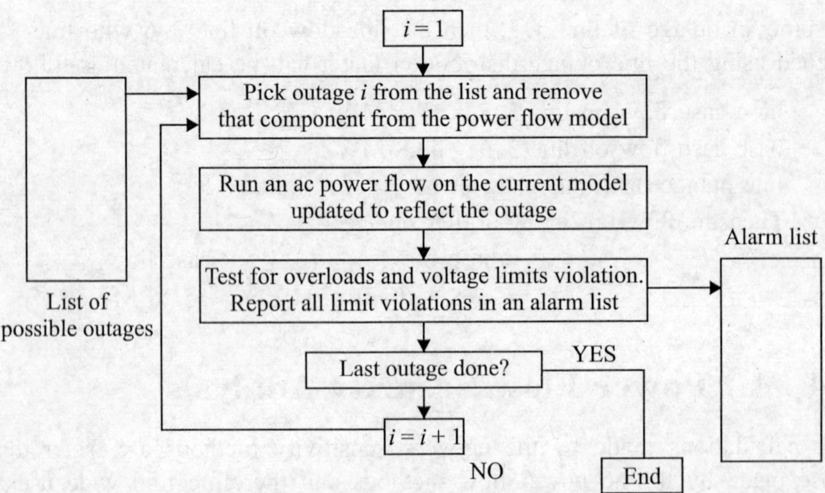

Figure 6.7 AC power flow security analysis.

6.4.1 MATLAB Program for AC Power Flow Security Analysis

% MATLAB programs for formation of bus admittance matrix (lfybus)

```
% This program obtains the Bus Admittance Matrix for power
flow solution
j=sqrt(-1); i = sqrt(-1);
nl = linedata(:,1); nr = linedata(:,2); R = linedata(:,3);
X = linedata(:,4); Bc = j*linedata(:,5); a = linedata(:, 6);
nbr=length(linedata(:,1)); nbus = max(max(nl), max(nr));
Z = R + j*X; y= ones(nbr,1)./Z;              %branch admittance
for n = 1:nbr
if a(n) <= 0  a(n) = 1; else end
Ybus=zeros(nbus,nbus);           % initialize Ybus to zero
                   % formation of the off diagonal elements
for k=1:nbr;
       Ybus(nl(k),nr(k))=Ybus(nl(k),nr(k))-y(k)/a(k);
       Ybus(nr(k),nl(k))=Ybus(nl(k),nr(k));
    end
end
                      % formation of the diagonal elements
for   n=1:nbus
     for k=1:nbr
          if nl(k)==n
          Ybus(n,n) = Ybus(n,n)+y(k)/(a(k)^2) + Bc(k);
          elseif nr(k)==n
          Ybus(n,n) = Ybus(n,n)+y(k) +Bc(k);
```

```
                else, end
        end
end
clear Pgg
```

% MATLAB program for load flow solution by NR method (lfnewton)

```
ns=0; ng=0; Vm=0; delta=0; yload=0; deltad=0;
nbus = length(busdata(:,1));
P=zeros(1,nbus);
Q=zeros(1,nbus);
S=zeros(1,nbus);
for k=1:nbus
n=busdata(k,1);
kb(n)=busdata(k,2); Vm(n)=busdata(k,3); delta(n)=busdata(k, 4);
Pd(n)=busdata(k,5); Qd(n)=busdata(k,6); Pg(n)=busdata(k,7);
Qg(n) = busdata(k,8);
Qmin(n)=busdata(k, 9); Qmax(n)=busdata(k, 10);
Qsh(n)=busdata(k, 11);
      if Vm(n) <= 0  Vm(n) = 1.0; V(n) = 1 + j*0;
      else delta(n) = pi/180*delta(n);
             V(n) = Vm(n)*(cos(delta(n)) + j*sin(delta(n)));
             P(n)=(Pg(n)-Pd(n))/basemva;
             Q(n)=(Qg(n)-Qd(n)+ Qsh(n))/basemva;
             S(n) = P(n) + j*Q(n);
      end
end
for k=1:nbus
if kb(k) == 1, ns = ns+1; else, end
if kb(k) == 2 ng = ng+1; else, end
ngs(k) = ng;
nss(k) = ns;
end
Ym=abs(Ybus); t = angle(Ybus);
m=2*nbus-ng-2*ns;
maxerror = 1; converge=1;
iter = 0;
% Start of iterations
clear A  DC   J  DX
% Test for max. power mismatch
while maxerror >= accuracy & iter <= maxiter
for i=1:m
for k=1:m
    A(i,k)=0;        %Initializing Jacobian matrix
```

```
end, end
iter = iter+1;
for n=1:nbus
nn=n-nss(n);
lm=nbus+n-ngs(n)-nss(n)-ns;
J11=0; J22=0; J33=0; J44=0;
    for i=1:nbr
       if nl(i) == n | nr(i) == n
           if nl(i) == n,   l = nr(i); end
           if nr(i) == n,   l = nl(i); end
           J11=J11+ Vm(n)*Vm(l)*Ym(n,l)*sin(t(n,l)- delta(n)
               + delta(l));
           J33=J33+ Vm(n)*Vm(l)*Ym(n,l)*cos(t(n,l)- delta(n)
               + delta(l));
           if kb(n)~=1
           J22=J22+ Vm(l)*Ym(n,l)*cos(t(n,l)- delta(n) +
               delta(l));
           J44=J44+ Vm(l)*Ym(n,l)*sin(t(n,l)- delta(n) +
               delta(l));
           else, end
           if kb(n)  ~= 1  & kb(l) ~=1
           lk = nbus+l-ngs(l)-nss(l)-ns;
           ll = l -nss(l);
         % off diagonalelements of J1
          A(nn, ll) =-Vm(n)*Vm(l)*Ym(n,l)*sin(t(n,l)- delta(n)
                    + delta(l));
             if kb(l) == 0  % off diagonal elements of J2
          A(nn, lk) =Vm(n)*Ym(n,l)*cos(t(n,l)- delta(n) +
                     delta(l));
                    end
             if kb(n) == 0  % off diagonal elements of J3
          A(lm, ll) =-Vm(n)*Vm(l)*Ym(n,l)*cos(t(n,l)-
                     delta(n)+delta(l));
                    end
                    if kb(n) == 0 & kb(l) == 0 % off
                    diagonal elements of  J4
          A(lm, lk) =-Vm(n)*Ym(n,l)*sin(t(n,l)- delta(n) +
                     delta(l));
                    end
           else end
       else , end
    end
    Pk = Vm(n)^2*Ym(n,n)*cos(t(n,n))+J33;
    Qk = -Vm(n)^2*Ym(n,n)*sin(t(n,n))-J11;
```

```
    if kb(n) == 1 P(n)=Pk; Q(n) = Qk; end    % Swing bus P
       if kb(n) == 2   Q(n)=Qk;
          if Qmax(n) ~= 0
            Qgc = Q(n)*basemva + Qd(n) - Qsh(n);
            if iter <= 7 % Between the 2nd & 6th iterations
             if iter > 2 % the Mvar of generator buses are
           if Qgc < Qmin(n),  % tested. If not within limits
Vm(n)
Vm(n) = Vm(n) + 0.01; %is changed in steps of 0.01 pu to
elseif Qgc> Qmax(n),% bring the generator Mvar within
           Vm(n) = Vm(n) - 0.01;end % the specified limits.
            else, end
          else,end
       else,end
     end
    if kb(n) ~= 1
       A(nn,nn) = J11;  %diagonal elements of J1
       DC(nn) = P(n)-Pk;
    end
    if kb(n) == 0
    A(nn,lm) = 2*Vm(n)*Ym(n,n)*cos(t(n,n))+J22;%diagonal
                elements of J2
    A(lm,nn)= J33;          %diagonal elements of J3
    A(lm,lm) --2*Vm(n)*Ym(n,n)*sin(t(n,n))-J44;%diagonal of
               elements of J4
    DC(lm) = Q(n)-Qk;
  end
 end
DX=A\DC';
for n=1:nbus
   nn=n-nss(n);
   lm=nbus+n-ngs(n)-nss(n)-ns;
      if kb(n) ~= 1
      delta(n) = delta(n)+DX(nn); end
      if kb(n) == 0
      Vm(n)=Vm(n)+DX(lm); end
  end
   maxerror=max(abs(DC));
       if iter == maxiter & maxerror > accuracy
fprintf('\nWARNING: Iterative solution did not converged
      after ')
fprintf('%g', iter), fprintf(' iterations.\n\n')
fprintf('Press Enter to terminate the iterations')
fprintf('and print the results \n')
```

```
      converge = 0; pause, else, end

  end
  if converge ~= 1
      tech= ('       ITERATIVE SOLUTION DID NOT CONVERGE');
  else,
      tech=('       Power Flow Solution by Newton-Raphson
          Method');
  end
  V = Vm.*cos(delta)+j*Vm.*sin(delta);
  deltad=180/pi*delta;
  i=sqrt(-1);
  k=0;
  for n = 1:nbus
         if kb(n) == 1
         k=k+1;
         S(n)= P(n)+j*Q(n);
         Pg(n) = P(n)*basemva + Pd(n);
         Qg(n) = Q(n)*basemva + Qd(n) - Qsh(n);
         Pgg(k)=Pg(n);
         Qgg(k)=Qg(n);
         elseif kb(n) ==2
         k=k+1;
         S(n)=P(n)+j*Q(n);
         Qg(n) = Q(n)*basemva + Qd(n) - Qsh(n);
         Pgg(k)=Pg(n);
         Qgg(k)=Qg(n);
     end
  yload(n) = (Pd(n)- j*Qd(n)+j*Qsh(n))/(basemva*Vm(n)^2);
  end
  busdata(:,3)=Vm'; busdata(:,4)=deltad';
  Pgt = sum(Pg);  Qgt = sum(Qg); Pdt = sum(Pd);
  Qdt = sum(Qd); Qsht = sum(Qsh);
```

% MATLAB program for prints the power flow solution on the screen in a tabulated form (busout)

```
  disp(tech)
  fprintf('          Maximum Power Mismatch = %g \n', maxerror)
  fprintf('                 No. of Iterations = %g \n\n', iter)
  head =['Bus  Voltage Angle ------Load------  ---Generation---
       Injected'
      'No.  Mag.  Degree  MW   Mvar   MW   Mvar     Mvar '     '
  '];
```

```
disp(head)
for  n=1:nbus
    fprintf(' %5g', n), fprintf(' %7.3f', Vm(n)),
    fprintf(' %8.3f', deltad(n)), fprintf(' %9.3f', Pd(n)),
    fprintf(' %9.3f', Qd(n)),  fprintf(' %9.3f', Pg(n)),
    fprintf(' %9.3f ', Qg(n)), fprintf(' %8.3f\n', Qsh(n))
end
  fprintf('      \n'), fprintf('    Total              ')
  fprintf(' %9.3f', Pdt), fprintf(' %9.3f', Qdt),
  fprintf('%9.3f', Pgt),fprintf('%9.3f',Qgt),
  fprintf('%9.3f\n\n', Qsht)
```

% MATLAB program for computes and displays the line flow and losses (lineflow)

```
SLT = 0;
fprintf('\n')
fprintf('                    Line Flow and Losses \n\n')
fprintf('-Line- Power at bus & line flow  -Line loss-
        Transformer\n')
fprintf(' from  to  MW Mvar  MVA   MW    Mvar     tap\n')
for n = 1:nbus
busprt = 0;
    for L = 1:nbr;
     if busprt == 0
  fprintf('\n'), fprintf('%6g',n),
  fprintf(' %9.3f', P(n)*basemva)
  fprintf('%9.3f',Q(n)*basemva),
  fprintf('%9.3f\n', abs(S(n)*basemva))
     busprt = 1;
     else, end
     if nl(L)==n          k = nr(L);
     In = (V(n) - a(L)*V(k))*y(L)/a(L)^2 + Bc(L)/a(L)^2*V(n);
     Ik = (V(k) - V(n)/a(L))*y(L) + Bc(L)*V(k);
     Snk = V(n)*conj(In)*basemva;
     Skn = V(k)*conj(Ik)*basemva;
     SL  = Snk + Skn;
     SLT = SLT + SL;
     elseif nr(L)==n  k = nl(L);
     In = (V(n) - V(k)/a(L))*y(L) + Bc(L)*V(n);
     Ik = (V(k) - a(L)*V(n))*y(L)/a(L)^2 + Bc(L)/a(L)^2*V(k);
     Snk = V(n)*conj(In)*basemva;
     Skn = V(k)*conj(Ik)*basemva;
     SL  = Snk + Skn;
```

```
        SLT  =  SLT  +  SL;
        else,  end
            if  nl(L)==n  |  nr(L)==n
            fprintf('%12g',  k),
            fprintf('%9.3f',  real(Snk)),
            fprintf('%9.3f',  imag(Snk))
            fprintf('%9.3f',  abs(Snk)),
            fprintf('%9.3f',  real(SL)),
            if  nl(L)  ==n  &  a(L)  ~=  1
            fprintf('%9.3f',  imag(SL)),  fprintf('%9.3f\n',  a(L))
            else,  fprintf('%9.3f\n',  imag(SL))
            end
        else,  end
     end
   end
   SLT  =  SLT/2;
   fprintf('   \n'),  fprintf('   Total  loss                              ')
   fprintf('%9.3f',  real(SLT)),  fprintf('%9.3f\n',  imag(SLT))
   clear  Ik  In  SL  SLT  Skn  Snk
```

6.5 AC Power Flow Security Analysis with Contingency Case Selection

Fortunately, there is a way out of this problem. Because of the way the power system is designed and operated, very few of the outages will actually cause trouble. That is, most of the time spent running ac power flows will go for solutions of the power flow model that discover that there are no problems. Only a few of the power flow solutions will, in fact, conclude that an overload or voltage violation exists.

The solution to this problem is to find a way to select contingencies in such a way that only those that are likely to result in an overload or voltage limit violation will actually be studied in detail and the other cases will go unanalyzed. A flow chart is shown in Figure 6.8. Selecting the bad or likely trouble cases from the full outage case list is not an exact procedure and has been the subject of intense research.

We would like to get some measure as to how much a particular outage might affect the power system. The idea of a performance index seems to fulfil this need. The definition of the overload performance index (PI) is as follows:

$$\mathrm{PI} = \sum_{\text{all branches}} \left(\frac{P_{\text{flow}l}}{P_l^{\max}} \right)^{2n} \tag{6.3}$$

If n is a large number, the PI will be a small number if all flows are within limit, and it will be large if one or more lines are overloaded. The problem then is how to use this performance index.

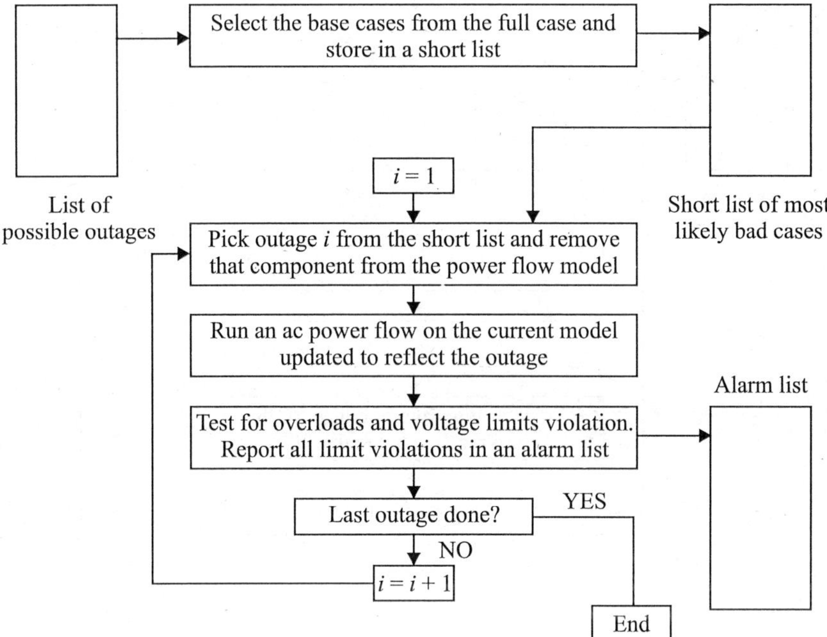

Figure 6.8 The ac power flow security analysis with contingency case selection.

Various techniques have been tried to obtain the value of PI when a branch is taken out. These calculations can be made exactly if $n = 1$; that is, a table of PI values, one for each line in a network, can be calculated quite quickly. The selection procedure then involves ordering the PI table from the largest value to the least. The lines corresponding to the top of the list are then the candidates for the short list. One procedure simply ordered the PI table and then picked the top N_C entries from this list and placed them on a short list.

However when $n = 1$, the PI does not snap from near zero to near infinity as the branch exceeds its limit. Instead, it rises as a quadratic function. A line that is just below its limit contributes to PI almost equal to one that is just over its limit. The result is a PI that may be large when many lines are loaded just below their limit. Thus the PI's ability to distinguish or detect bad cases is limited when $n = 1$. Ordering the PI values when $n = 1$ usually results in a list that is not at all representative of one with the truly bad cases at the top. Trying to develop an algorithm that can quickly calculate PI when $n = 2$ or larger has proven extremely difficult.

One way to perform an outage case selection is to perform what has been called the $1P1Q$ method. Here, a decoupled power flow is used. As shown in Figure 6.9, the solution procedure is interrupted after one iteration (one P-Q

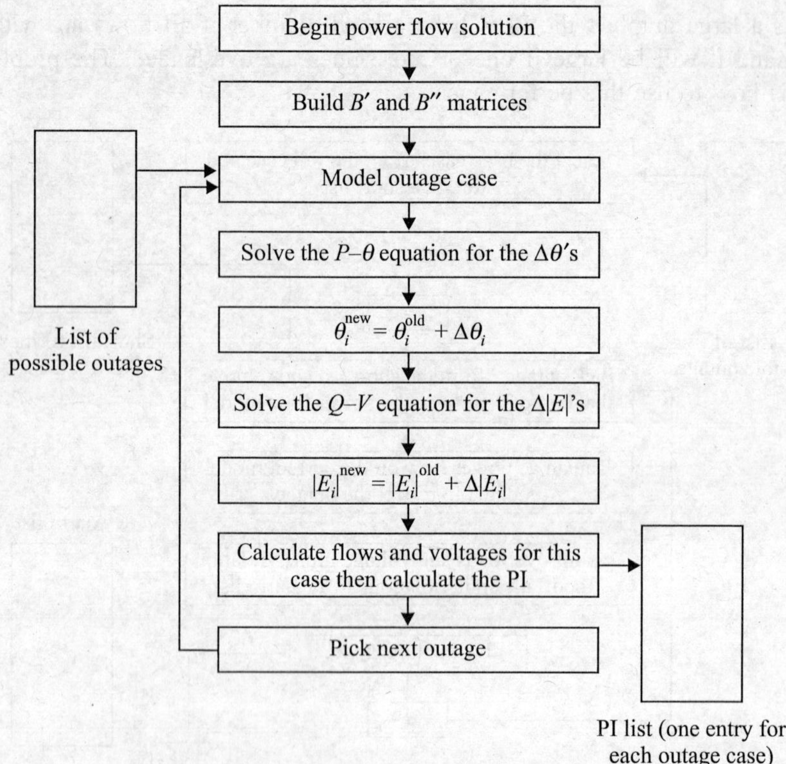

Figure 6.9 $1P1Q$ contingency selection procedure analysis.

calculation and Q-V calculation; thus, the name $1P1Q$). With this procedure, the PI can use as large value an n value as desired, say $n = 5$. There appears to be sufficient information in the solution at the end of the first iteration of the decoupled power flow to give a reasonable PI. Another advantage to this procedure is the fact that the voltages can also be included in the PI. Thus a different PI can be used such as

$$\text{PI} = \sum_{\substack{\text{all branches} \\ i}} \left(\frac{P_{\text{flow}l}}{P_l^{\max}} \right)^{2n} + \sum_{\substack{\text{all buses} \\ i}} \left(\frac{\Delta|E_i|}{\Delta|E|^{\max}} \right)^{2n} \tag{6.4}$$

where $\Delta|E_i|$ is the difference between the voltage magnitude as solved at the end of the $1P1Q$ procedure and the base-case voltage magnitude. $\Delta|E|^{\max}$ is a value set by utility engineers indicating how much they wish to limit a bus voltage from changing on one outage case.

To complete the security analysis, the performance index (PI) list is sorted so that the largest PI appears at the top. The security analysis can then start by executing full power flows with the case which is at the top of the list, then solve the case which is second, and so on down the list. This continues until either a fixed number of cases is solved, or until a predetermined number of cases are solved which do not have any alarms.

6.6 Concentric Relaxation

Another idea to enter the field of security analysis in power systems is that an outage only has a limited geographical effect. The loss of a transmission line does not cause much effect a thousand miles away; in fact, we might hope that it does not cause much trouble beyond 20 miles from the outage, although if the line were a heavy loaded, high-voltage line, its loss will most likely be felt more than 20 miles away.

To realize any benefit from the limited geographical effect of an outage, the power system must be divided into two parts: the affected part and the part that is unaffected. To make this division, the buses at the end of the outaged line are marked as layer zero. The buses that are one transmission line or transformer from layer zero are then labelled layer one. This same process can be carried out, layer by layer until all the buses in the entire network are included. Some arbitrary number of layers is chosen and all the buses included in that layer and lower-numbered layers are solved as a power flow with a outage in place. The buses in the higher-numbered layers are kept as constant voltage and phase angle (i.e., as reference buses).

This procedure can be used in two ways: either the solution of the layers included becomes the final solution of that case and all overloads and voltage violations are determined from this power flow, or the solution simply is used to form a performance index for that outage. Figure 6.10 illustrates this layering procedure.

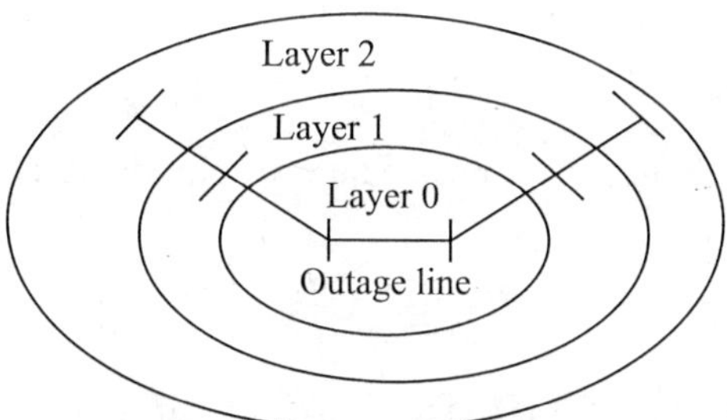

Figure 6.10 Layering of outage effects.

The concentric relaxation procedure was originally proposed by Zaborsky. The trouble with the concentric relaxation technique is that it requires more layers for circuits whose influence is felt further from the outage.

6.7 Bounding Area Method

To perform the analysis in the bounding technique, we shall define the three subsystems of power system as

N_1: the subsystem immediately surrounding the outaged line

N_2: the external subsystem that we shall not solve in detail
N_3: the set of boundary buses that separate N_1 and N_2.

Figure 6.11 shows the three subsystems of power system. The bounding method is based on the fact that we can make assumption about the phase angle spread across the line in N_2, given injections in N_1 and the phase angle appearing across any two buses in N_3. The ΔP_k and ΔP_m injections make the phase angle of buses k and m simulate the outage of the line k-m.

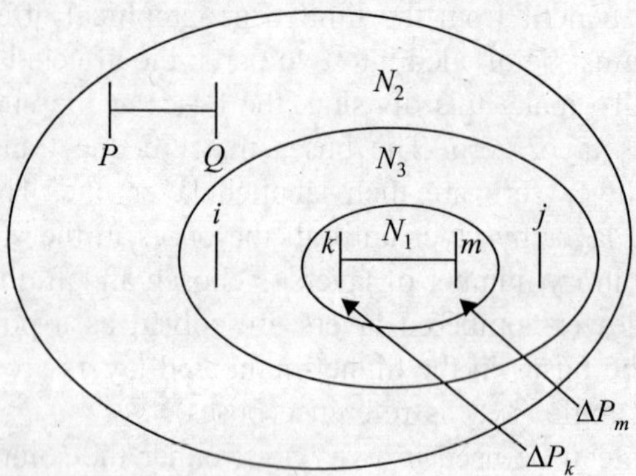

Figure 6.11 Layers used in bounding analysis.

If we are given transmission line in N_2 with a flow f_{pq}^0, then there is a maximum amount that the flow on pq can shift. That is, it can increase from f_{pq}^0 to upper limit or decrease to its lower limit. Then

$$\Delta f_{pq}^{\max} = \text{smaller of } [(f_{pq}^{+} - f_{pq}^{0}), (f_{pq}^{0} - f_{pq}^{-})] \tag{6.5}$$

We shall translate this to maximum change in phase angle difference as

$$f_{pq} = \frac{1}{x_{pq}}(\theta_p - \theta_q) \tag{6.6}$$

$$\Delta f_{pq} = \frac{1}{x_{pq}}(\Delta\theta_p - \Delta\theta_q) \tag{6.7}$$

$$(\Delta\theta_p - \Delta\theta_q)^{\max} = \Delta f_{pq}^{\max}\, x_{pq} \tag{6.8}$$

Thus we define the maximum change in phase angle difference across pq. Then

$$|\Delta\theta_p - \Delta\theta_q| < |\Delta\theta_i - \Delta\theta_j| \tag{6.9}$$

where i and j are the pair of buses in N_2. $\Delta\theta_i$ is the largest $\Delta\theta$ in N_3 and $\Delta\theta_j$ is the smallest $\Delta\theta$ in N_3.

The RHS of Eq. (6.9), that is, $|\Delta\theta_i - \Delta\theta_j|$ provides an upper limit to the maximum change of angular spread across any circuit in N_2.

Figure 6.12 shows the interpretation of the bounding process. The circuit on the top figure will not exceed the limit, whereas the bottom could.

The horizontal line represents the change in flow on circuit pq times its reactance, that is, $\Delta f_{pq}^{max} x_{pq}$. The dotted line $\Delta f_{pq} x_{pq}$ represents a point where the circuit pq goes into overload. Any value of $\Delta f_{pq} x_{pq}$ goes beyond dotted line represents overload. The solid line $|\Delta\theta_i - \Delta\theta_j|$ represents the upper limit on $\Delta f_{pq}^{max} x_{pq}$. If the solid line is below to the left of the dotted line, the circuit will not go into overload. If the solid line is above to the right of the dotted line, the circuit changes in shift to flow due to the outage so as to violate limit.

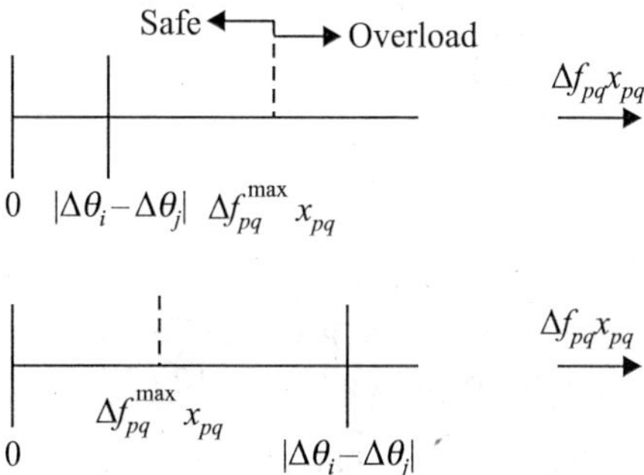

Figure 6.12 Interpretation of bounding.

All circuits of N_2 are safe from overload if the value of $|\Delta\theta_i - \Delta\theta_j|$ is less than the smallest value of $\Delta f_{pq}^{max} x_{pq}$, overall pairs of pq, where pq is the buses at the end of the circuit in N_2. If this fails, N_1 is expanded and the value of $|\Delta\theta_i - \Delta\theta_j|$ becomes smaller and smaller and the new value of $|\Delta\theta_i - \Delta\theta_j|$ is found and rerun the test.

EXAMPLE 6.2 In this example, we shall take the six-bus system used previously and show how the bounding technique works so that not all of the circuits in the system need to be analysed. Note that this is a small system so that the net savings in computer time may not be that great. Nonetheless it demonstrates the principles used in the bounding technique quite well.

Solution: We shall study the outage of transmission line 3–6. The dc power flow will be used throughout and the initial conditions will be those shown in figure. The MW limits on the transmission line are shown in Table 6.2.

In this example, we shall proceed in steps. Step A will analyse the system as if N_1 and N_3 regions consist of only line 3–6 itself, as shown in Figure 6.13. If the bounding criteria is met, no other analysis need to be done as it will establish that no overloads exist anywhere in the system. If the bounding criteria fails, we still proceed to Step B. Step B expands the bounded region from line 3–6 to include all buses which are once removed from buses 3 and 6; that is, it includes buses 2, 3, 5, and 6 as shown in Figure 6.14. and in this case the boundary of the region, N_3, consists of buses 2 and 5.

Table 6.2 Transmission line limits

Line	MW *limit*
1–2	30
1–4	50
1–5	40
2–3	20
2–4	40
2–5	20
2–6	30
3–5	20
3–6	60
4–5	20
5–6	20

To start with we need to calculate $\Delta f_{pq}^{\max}$ and then $\Delta f_{pq}^{\max} x_{pq}$ as given in the equations above. These values are given in Table 6.3 where the flows and flow limits are all converted to per unit on a 100 MVA base.

Table 6.3 Line flows and flow limits

Line	MW *limit* (p.u.)	f_{pq}^{0} (p.u.)	$\Delta f_{pq}^{\max}$	x_{pq}	$\Delta f_{pq}^{\max} x_{pq}$
1–2	0.3	0.253	0.047	0.2	0.0094
1–4	0.5	0.416	0.084	0.2	0.0168
1–5	0.4	0.331	0.069	0.3	0.0207
2–3	0.2	0.018	0.182	0.25	0.0455
2–4	0.4	0.325	0.075	0.1	0.0075
2–5	0.2	0.162	0.038	0.3	0.0114
2–6	0.3	0.248	0.052	0.2	0.0104
3–5	0.2	0.169	0.031	0.26	0.00806
3–6	0.6	0.449	—	—	—
4–5	0.2	0.041	0.159	0.4	0.0636
5–6	0.2	0.003	0.197	0.3	0.0591

For Step A, first calculate $\delta_{3,36}$ and $\delta_{6,36}$ as given by the following equation

$$\delta_{i,nm} = \frac{(X_{in} - X_{im})x_k}{x_k - (X_{nn} + X_{mm} - 2X_{nm})}$$

$$\delta_{3,36} = \frac{(X_{33} - X_{36})x_{36}}{x_{36} - (X_{33} + X_{66} - 2X_{36})} = 0.12865$$

$$\delta_{6,36} = \frac{(X_{63} - X_{66})x_{36}}{x_{36} - (X_{33} + X_{66} - 2X_{36})} = -0.11953$$

then using the equation

$$\delta_{i,nm} = \frac{\Delta\theta_i}{P_{nm}}$$

$$|\Delta\theta_3 - \Delta\theta_6| = 0.111437$$

According to criterion, the value $|\Delta\theta_i - \Delta\theta_j|$ must be less than the smallest value of $|\Delta\theta_p - \Delta\theta_q|$ which equals $\Delta f_{pq}^{\max} x_{pq}$ and is found in Table 6.3 to be at line 2–4. Since $|\Delta\theta_3 - \Delta\theta_6| = 0.111437$ and the minimum $|\Delta\theta_i - \Delta\theta_j|$ is $|\Delta\theta_2 - \Delta\theta_4|$ which has a value of 0.0075, the criteria fails. We must proceed to Step B. Step B requires that we calculate $|\Delta\theta_i - \Delta\theta_j|$ for buses 2 and 5. This value is 0.003564 and the bounding criteria is satisfied. We had used the d factors for the six bus system, we could simply find all the line flows for the 3–6 outage as given in Table 6.4.

Table 6.4 Line flows for the 3–6 outage

Line	MW *limit* (p.u.)	f_{pq}^{0} (p.u.)	$f_{pq}^{3–6\ out}$
1–2	0.3	0.253	0.257
1–4	0.5	0.416	0.416
1–5	0.4	0.331	0.322
2–3	0.2	0.018	**–0.220 (overload)**
2–4	0.4	0.325	0.316
2–5	0.2	0.162	0.148
2–6	0.3	0.248	**0.508 (overload)**
3–5	0.2	0.169	**0.380 (overload)**
3–6	0.6	0.449	—
4–5	0.2	0.041	0.032
5–6	0.2	0.003	0.191

Note that three overloads exist on lines 2–3, 2–6 and 3–5, which are all within the bounded region $N_1 + N_3$ in Figure 6.11.

6.8 Contingency Analysis Using Power World Simulator and PSS/E S/W

6.8.1 Contingency Analysis Using PWS

A six-bus system as per the data given in PWS environment and the single line diagram of the test system is as given in Figure 6.13. The dc power flow

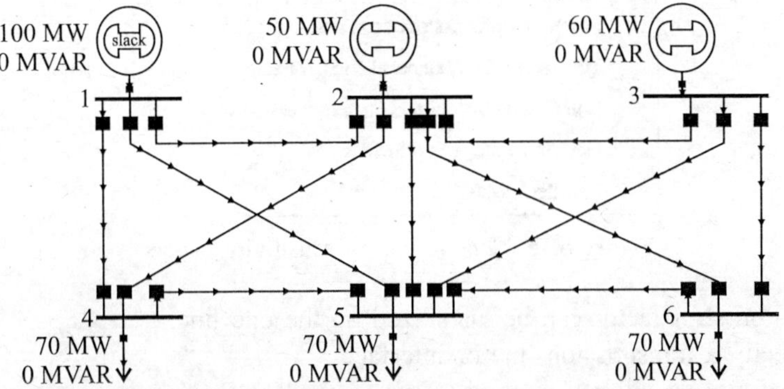

Figure 6.13 Single line diagram of six-bus system.

results are given in Figure 6.14. For example; let us consider the power flow on line 1–4 which is 41.57 MW (indicated in red mark in the figure).

						Bus Flows
BUS	1 1	230.0	MW	% 1.0000	0.00	1 1
GENERATOR 1			100.00			
TO	2 2	1	25.33	0		
TO	4 4	1	41.57	0		
TO	5 5	1	33.10	0		
BUS	2 2	230.0	MW	% 1.0000	-2.90	1 1
GENERATOR 2			50.00			
TO	1 1	1	-25.33	0		
TO	3 3	1	1.85	0		
TO	4 4	1	32.48	0		
TO	5 5	1	16.22	0		
TO	6 6	1	24.78	0		
BUS	3 3	230.0	MW	% 1.0000	-3.17	1 1
GENERATOR 3			60.00			
TO	2 2	1	-1.85	0		
TO	5 5	1	16.93	0		
TO	6 6	1	44.92	0		
BUS	4 4	230.0	MW	% 1.0000	-4.76	1 1
LOAD 1			70.00			
TO	1 1	1	-41.57	0		
TO	2 2	1	-32.48	0		
TO	5 5	1	4.04	0		
BUS	5 5	230.0	MW	% 1.0000	-5.69	1 1
LOAD 1			70.00			
TO	1 1	1	-33.10	0		
TO	2 2	1	-16.22	0		
TO	3 3	1	-16.93	0		
TO	4 4	1	-4.04	0		

Figure 6.14 The dc power flow results of six-bus system.

Now the aim is to consider the outage of the generator at bus 3 and we would like to see the power flow on line 1–4 after the outage of the generator under PWS environment. The step by step procedure of generator outage is given below.

Calculation of generation shift factor

Generation shift factor can be calculated in Simulator by selecting Tools ribbon tab → Sensitivities → TLR Sensitivities/Generation shift factors (Figure 6.15).

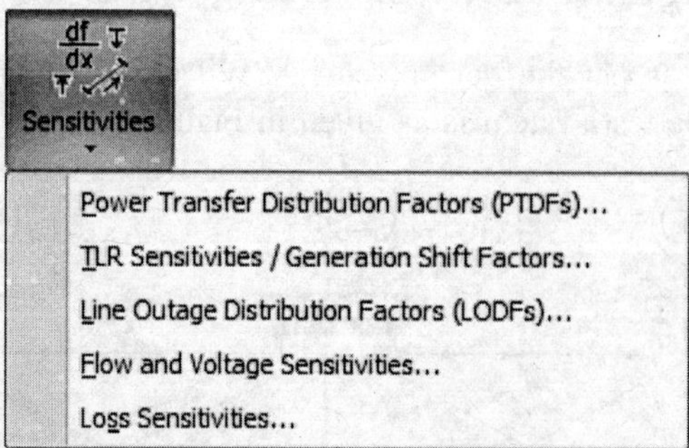

Figure 6.15 Dialog box of sensitivity factors.

Generation shift factor can be visualized on the one line:

Specify a transmission line or interface.

Specify a calculation method (same as for PTDF).

To narrow down the choices for directions, specify one end of the transfer (buyer or seller).

TLR calculates the impact of transferring power between each bus and the specified end of the transfer.

The area sensitivities is just a weighted average of the sensitivities for each generator bus in the area (weighted by Participation Factors).

GSF versus TLR

The generation shift factor calculation is a specific kind of TLR calculation.

GSF implies that the buyer is the slack bus.

From Figure 6.16 it is observed that

base case flow on line 1–4 = 41.57 MW (indicated in red mark in table 1)

base case generation on bus 3 = 60 MW (indicated in blue mark in table 1)

Thus the obtained generation shift distribution factor = –0.091618 (indicated in green mark)

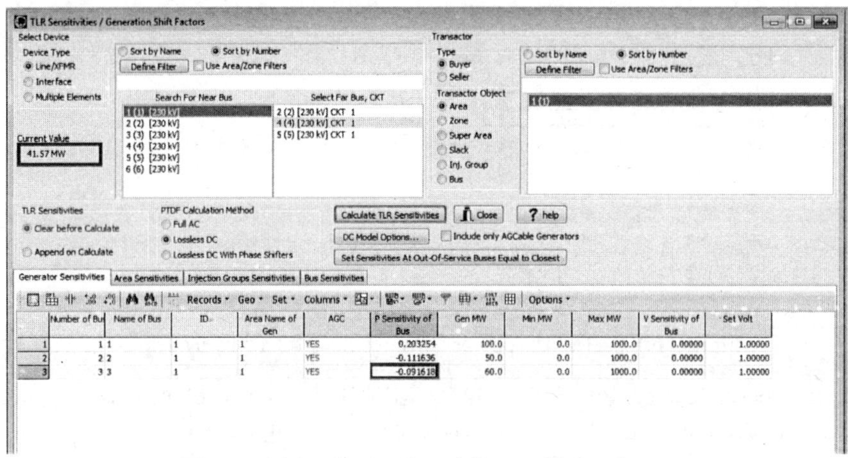

	Number of Bus	Name of Bus	ID	Area Name of Gen	AGC	P Sensitivity of Bus	Gen MW	Min MW	Max MW	V Sensitivity of Bus	Set Volt
1	1	1	1	1	YES	0.203254	100.0	0.0	1000.0	0.00000	1.00000
2	2	2	1	1	YES	-0.111636	50.0	0.0	1000.0	0.00000	1.00000
3	3	3	1	1	YES	-0.091618	60.0	0.0	1000.0	0.00000	1.00000

Figure 6.16 Generation shift sensitivity factor.

Calculation of line outage distribution factors (LODFs)

Let us consider the outage of the line 3–5 and we would like to see the power flow on line 3–6 after the outage of the line under PWS environment.

The step by step procedure of line outage is given below:

- LODFs are another linearized calculation
  - Calculate the impact of opening (outaging) a transmission branch on all the other branches in the case.
  - Also one can calculate the impact of closing a branch (could call this a Line Closure Distribution Factor or LCDF).
- Specify a transmission branch, and the calculation determines what per cent of the flow on that line will appear on all other transmission lines.

— If the branch was initially open, then the LCDF will calculate what per cent of the post-closure flow on the line will appear on other lines.

- Line outage distribution factor can be calculated in Simulator by selecting **Tools ribbon tab → Sensitivities → Line outage distribution factor**.
- Line outage distribution factor can be visualized on the one line.

The dc power flow results of six-bus system, i.e. in more specific with reference to bus 3 is shown in Figure 6.17. From Figure 6.17, it is observed that

base case flow on line 3–5 = 16.93 MW (indicated in red mark)

```
                                                                   Bus Flows
BUS       1 1          230.0   MW   % 1.0000   0.00   1 1
 GENERATOR 1                100.00
 TO       2 2          1     25.33   0
 TO       4 4          1     41.57   0
 TO       5 5          1     33.10   0

BUS       2 2          230.0   MW   % 1.0000  -2.90   1 1
 GENERATOR 2                 50.00
 TO       1 1          1    -25.33   0
 TO       3 3          1      1.85   0
 TO       4 4          1     32.48   0
 TO       5 5          1     16.22   0
 TO       6 6          1     24.78   0

BUS       3 3          230.0   MW   % 1.0000  -3.17   1 1
 GENERATOR 3                 60.00
 TO       2 2          1     -1.85   0
 TO       5 5          1     16.93   0
 TO       6 6          1     44.92   0

BUS       4 4          230.0   MW   % 1.0000  -4.76   1 1
 LOAD 1                      70.00
 TO       1 1          1    -41.57   0
 TO       2 2          1    -32.48   0
 TO       5 5          1      4.04   0

BUS       5 5          230.0   MW   % 1.0000  -5.69   1 1
 LOAD 2                      70.00
 TO       1 1          1    -33.10   0
 TO       2 2          1    -16.22   0
 TO       3 3          1    -16.93   0
 TO       4 4          1     -4.04   0
```

Figure 6.17 The dc power flow results of six bus system.

base case flow on line 3–6 = 44.92 MW (indicated in blue mark).
the line outage disrtibution factor is shown in Figure 6.18.

	From Number	From Name	To Number	To Name	Circuit	% LODF	MW From	MW To	CTG MW From	CTG MW To
1	1	1	2	2	1	-13.7	25.3	-25.3	23.0	-23.0
2	1	1	4	4	1	-4.0	41.6	-41.6	40.9	-40.9
3	1	1	5	5	1	17.7	33.1	-33.1	36.1	-36.1
4	2	2	3	3	1	-40.0	1.9	-1.9	-4.9	4.9
5	2	2	4	4	1	19.3	32.5	-32.5	35.8	-35.8
6	2	2	5	5	1	26.8	16.2	-16.2	20.8	-20.8
7	2	2	6	6	1	-19.9	24.8	-24.8	21.4	-21.4
8	3	3	5	5	1	-100.0	16.9	-16.9	0.0	0.0
9	3	3	6	6	1	60.0	44.9	-44.9	55.1	-55.1
10	4	4	5	5	1	15.3	4.0	-4.0	6.6	-6.6
11	5	5	6	6	1	-40.1	0.3	-0.3	-6.5	6.5

Figure 6.18 Line outage distribution factor dialog box.

Thus the obtained line outage distribution factor = 0.6 or 60% (indicated in green mark).

6.8.2 Contingency Analysis Using PSS/E

A six-bus system as per the data given in PSS/E environment dc power flow results and the single line diagram of the test system are shown in Figures 6.19 and 6.20. For example, let us consider the power flow on line 1–4 is 42.9 MW (as shaded in Figure 6.19).

PTI INTERACTIVE POWER SYSTEM SIMULATOR--PSS®E TUE. APR 26 2011 11:33

FROM BUS BUS#	NAME	BASKV	AREA	BASE ANGLE	CHANGE ANGLE	GEN MW	LOAD MW	TO BUS BUS#	NAME	BASKV	AREA	CKT	BASE CASE MW	BASE CASE %	RATE MVA	CHANGE CASE MW	CHANGE CASE %	DELTA MW
1	SLACK	230.00	1	0.0		103.8	0.0											
								2	PV1	230.00	1	1	26.8					
								4	PQ1	230.00	1	1	42.9					
								5	PQ2	230.00	1	1	34.2					
2	PV1	230.00	1	-3.1		50.0	0.0											
								1	SLACK	230.00	1	1	-26.8					
								3	PV2	230.00	1	1	2.3					
								4	PQ1	230.00	1	1	32.6					
								5	PQ2	230.00	1	1	16.4					
								6	PQ3	230.00	1	1	25.5					
3	PV2	230.00	1	-3.4		60.0	0.0											
								2	PV1	230.00	1	1	-2.3					
								5	PQ2	230.00	1	1	17.1					
								6	PQ3	230.00	1	1	45.3					
4	PQ1	230.00	1	-4.9		0.0	70.0											
								1	SLACK	230.00	1	1	-42.6					
								2	PV1	230.00	1	1	-31.6					
								5	PQ2	230.00	1	1	4.2					
5	PQ2	230.00	1	-5.8		0.0	70.0											
								1	SLACK	230.00	1	1	-34.0					
								2	PV1	230.00	1	1	-16.1					
								3	PV2	230.00	1	1	-16.3					
								4	PQ1	230.00	1	1	-4.2					
								6	PQ3	230.00	1	1	0.6					
6	PQ3	230.00	1	-5.9		0.0	70.0											
								2	PV1	230.00	1	1	-25.1					
								3	PV2	230.00	1	1	-44.3					

Progress Alerts/Warnings Report Report Report Report Report Report Report Report Report Report Report Report Report Report Report Report

Figure 6.19 The dc power flow results of six-bus system.

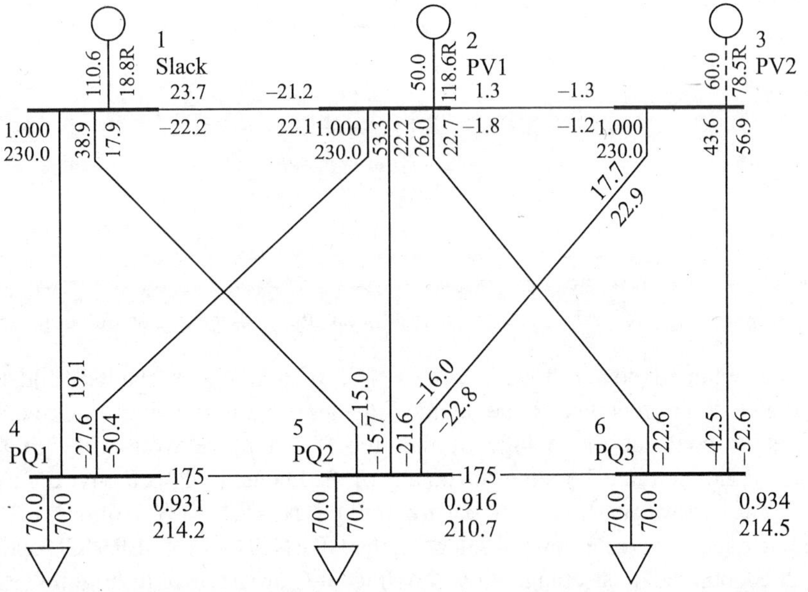

Figure 6.20 Single line diagram of six-bus system.

Let us consider the outage of the generator at bus 3 and we would like to see the power flow on line 1–4 after the outage of the generator under PSS/E environment. The generator outage is created by not selecting the MACHINE → IN SERVICE option and the obtained post outage flow on the line 1–4 are given in Figures 6.21 and 6.22.

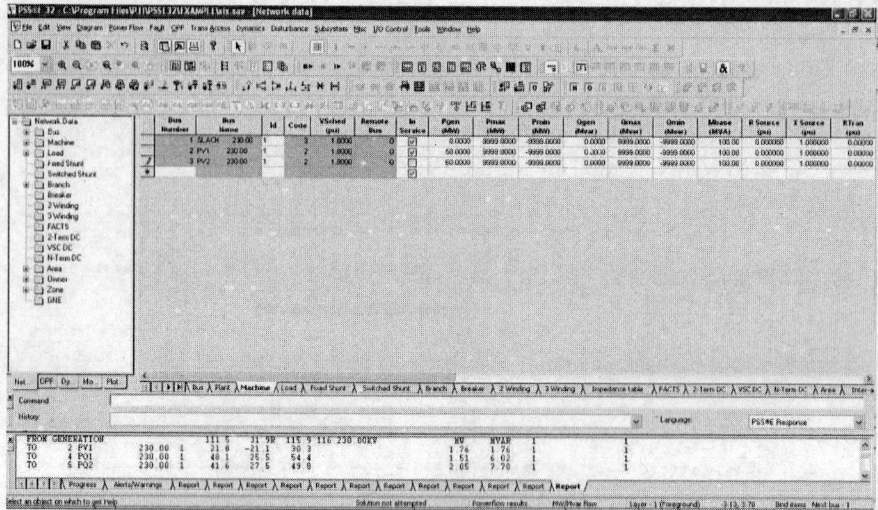

Figure 6.21 Generator outage at bus 3.

```
                 PTI INTERACTIVE POWER SYSTEM SIMULATOR--PSS®E      TUE, APR 26 2011  11:35

X--------- FROM BUS ----------X  BASE CHANGE   GEN.   LOAD X---------- TO BUS -----------X        BASE CASE     RATE   CHANGE CASE   DELTA
 BUS# X-- NAME --X BASKV AREA ANGLE  ANGLE    MW      MW   BUS# X-- NAME --X BASKV AREA CKT      MW    %      MVA     MW    %        MW
   1 SLACK      230.00   1    0.0            163.8    0.0 -------------------------------------------------------------------------
                                                           2 PV1         230.00   1   1      50.9
                                                           4 PQ1         230.00   1   1      60.6
                                                           5 PQ2         230.00   1   1      52.3
   2 PV1        230.00   1   -5.8             50.0    0.0 -------------------------------------------------------------------------
                                                           1 SLACK       230.00   1   1     -50.9
                                                           3 PV2         230.00   1   1      22.8
                                                           4 PQ1         230.00   1   1      19.7
                                                           5 PQ2         230.00   1   1      18.4
                                                           6 PQ3         230.00   1   1      40.0
   3 PV2        230.00   1   -9.1              0.0    0.0 -------------------------------------------------------------------------
                                                           2 PV1         230.00   1   1     -22.8
                                                           5 PQ2         230.00   1   1      -0.3
                                                           6 PQ3         230.00   1   1      23.1
   4 PQ1        230.00   1   -6.9              0.0   70.0 -------------------------------------------------------------------------
                                                           1 SLACK       230.00   1   1     -60.3
                                                           2 PV1         230.00   1   1     -18.7
                                                           5 PQ2         230.00   1   1       9.0
   5 PQ2        230.00   1   -9.0              0.0   70.0 -------------------------------------------------------------------------
                                                           1 SLACK       230.00   1   1     -52.1
                                                           2 PV1         230.00   1   1     -18.2
                                                           3 PV2         230.00   1   1       1.0
                                                           4 PQ1         230.00   1   1      -9.0
                                                           6 PQ3         230.00   1   1       8.2
   6 PQ3        230.00   1  -10.4              0.0   70.0 -------------------------------------------------------------------------
                                                           2 PV1         230.00   1   1     -39.6
                                                           3 PV2         230.00   1   1     -22.1
                                                           5 PQ2         230.00   1   1      -8.2
```

Figure 6.22 The dc power flow results on line 1–4 (generator outage).

The obtained power flow in line 1–4 is 60.6 MW (as shaded) and the single line diagram depicting the outage of generator 2 is shown in Figure 6.23.

Let us consider the outage of the line 3–5 and we would like to see the power flow on line 3–6 after the outage of the line under PSS/E environment. The power flow on line 3–6 before outage is 45.5 MW (Figure 6.19). The line outage is created by not selecting the BRANCH → IN SERVICE option and the obtained post-outage flow on line 3–6 are shown in Figures 6.24 and 6.25.

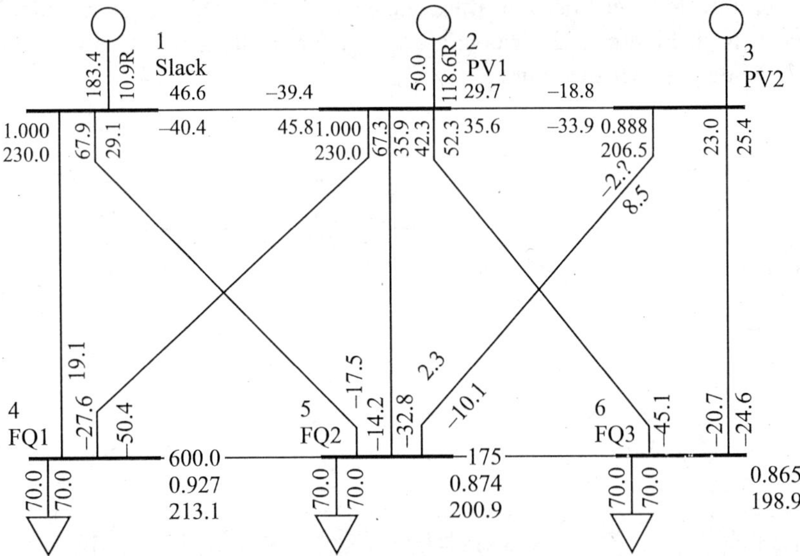

Figure 6.23 Single line diagram-generator outage (dotted).

From Bus Number	From Bus Name		To Bus Number	To Bus Name		Id	Line R (pu)	Line X (pu)	Charging (pu)	In Service	Metered	Rate A (I as MVA)	Rate B (I as MVA)	Rate C (I as MVA)	Line G From (pu)	Line B From (pu)	Line G To (pu)
1	SLACK	230.00	2	PV1	230.00	1	0.200000	0.200000	0.020000	☑	☑ From	0.0	0.0	0.0	0.00000	0.00000	0.00000
1	SLACK	230.00	4	PQ1	230.00	1	0.050000	0.200000	0.020000	☑	☑ From	0.0	0.0	0.0	0.00000	0.00000	0.00000
1	SLACK	230.00	5	PQ2	230.00	1	0.080000	0.300000	0.030000	☑	☑ From	0.0	0.0	0.0	0.00000	0.00000	0.00000
2	PV1	230.00	3	PV2	230.00	1	0.050000	0.250000	0.030000	☑	☑ From	0.0	0.0	0.0	0.00000	0.00000	0.00000
2	PV1	230.00	4	PQ1	230.00	1	0.050000	0.100000	0.010000	☑	☑ From	0.0	0.0	0.0	0.00000	0.00000	0.00000
2	PV1	230.00	5	PQ2	230.00	1	0.100000	0.300000	0.020000	☑	☑ From	0.0	0.0	0.0	0.00000	0.00000	0.00000
2	PV1	230.00	6	PQ3	230.00	1	0.070000	0.200000	0.025000	☑	☑ From	0.0	0.0	0.0	0.00000	0.00000	0.00000
3	PV2	230.00	5	PQ2	230.00	1	0.120000	0.260000	0.025000	☐	☑ From	0.0	0.0	0.0	0.00000	0.00000	0.00000
3	PV2	230.00	6	PQ3	230.00	1	0.020000	0.100000	0.010000	☑	☑ From	0.0	0.0	0.0	0.00000	0.00000	0.00000
4	PQ1	230.00	5	PQ2	230.00	1	0.200000	0.400000	0.040000	☑	☑ From	0.0	0.0	0.0	0.00000	0.00000	0.00000
5	PQ2	230.00	6	PQ3	230.00	1	0.100000	0.300000	0.030000	☑	☑ From	0.0	0.0	0.0	0.00000	0.00000	0.00000

Figure 6.24 Outage of line 3–5.

PTI INTERACTIVE POWER SYSTEM SIMULATOR--PSS®E TUE, APR 26 2011 11:38

FROM BUS#	X-- NAME --X	BASKV	AREA	BASE ANGLE	CHANGE ANGLE	GEN MW	LOAD MW	TO BUS#	X-- NAME --X	BASKV	AREA	CKT	BASE CASE MW	%	RATE MVA	CHANGE CASE MW	%	DELTA MW
1	SLACK	230.00	1	0.0		103.1	0.0	2	PV1	230.00	1	1	24.2					
								4	PQ1	230.00	1	1	42.0					
								5	PQ2	230.00	1	1	36.9					
2	PV1	230.00	1	−2.8		50.0	0.0	1	SLACK	230.00	1	1	−24.2					
								3	PV2	230.00	1	1	−4.5					
								4	PQ1	230.00	1	1	36.0					
								5	PQ2	230.00	1	1	20.8					
								6	PQ3	230.00	1	1	22.0					
3	PV2	230.00	1	−2.1		60.0	0.0	2	PV1	230.00	1	1	4.5					
								6	PQ3	230.00	1	1	55.5					
4	PQ1	230.00	1	−4.8		0.0	70.0	1	SLACK	230.00	1	1	−41.7					
								2	PV1	230.00	1	1	−35.0					
								5	PQ2	230.00	1	1	6.7					
5	PQ2	230.00	1	−6.3		0.0	70.0	1	SLACK	230.00	1	1	−36.7					
								2	PV1	230.00	1	1	−20.5					
								4	PQ1	230.00	1	1	−6.7					
								6	PQ3	230.00	1	1	−6.1					
6	PQ3	230.00	1	−5.3		0.0	70.0	2	PV1	230.00	1	1	−21.6					
								3	PV2	230.00	1	1	−54.5					
								5	PQ2	230.00	1	1	6.1					

Figure 6.25 The dc power flow results on line 3–6 (line outage 3–5).

Thus the flow on line 3–6 after outage is 55.5 MW as represented in a shaded way in Figure 6.25. The single line diagram depicting the line outage of 3–5 is also shown in Figure 6.26.

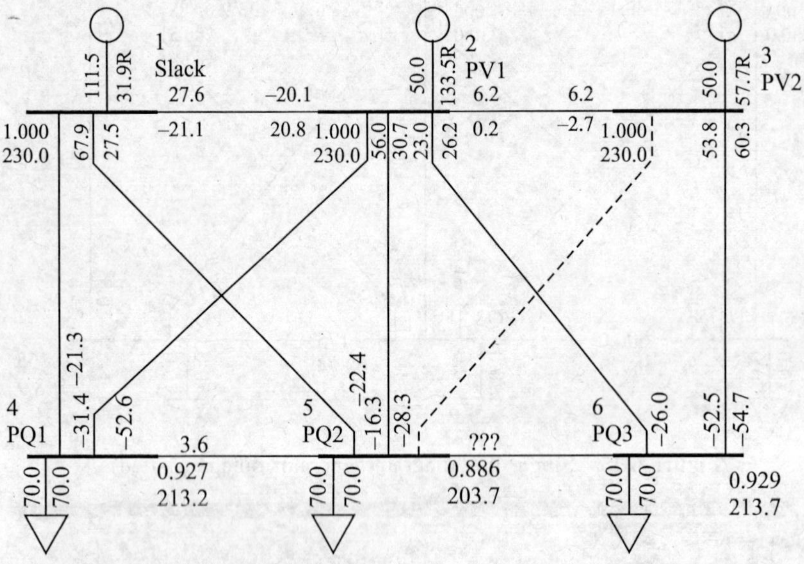

Figure 6.26 One line diagram depicting the outage of the line 3–5.

Review Questions

Part-A

1. List the factors affecting the power system security.
2. Distinguish between security assessment and enhancement.
3. What are the different operating states of a power system?
4. What is SCADA?
5. What is meant by system blockout?
6. Define contingency.
7. Write the dc power flow equation.
8. How to enhance the security level when the system is operating in emergency condition?
9. What is the aim of system monitoring in a power system?

Part-B

1. What are the major functions that are carried out in an operations control centre for system security?
2. (a) State the applications of sensitivity factors for the securit enhancement.

   (b) How do you enhance the steady state security of a power system?

3. Explain the network sensitivity method of calculating line outage distribution factor.
4. Explain generation and line outage contingency analysis of a power system with a flow chart. How is contingency analysis useful in operating the power system efficiently?
5. Explain the four operating states such as optimal dispatch, post-contingency, secure dispatch and secure post-contingency with suitable examples.
6. For a given system data calculate the line outage sensitivity factors for outages on lines 1–2 and 2–3.

Line data		*Bus data*	
Line	***Reactance (p.u.)***	***Bus load (MW)***	***Generation (MW)***
1–2	0.2	1 (slack)	150
1–4	0.25	2 —	350
2–3	0.15	3 220	—
2–4	0.30	4 280	—
3–4	0.40		

7. For a given system data calculate the line outage sensitivity factors for outages on lines 1–2 and also post outage line flow

Line data		*Bus data*	
Line	***Reactance (p.u.)***	***Bus load (MW)***	***Generation (MW)***
1–2	0.04	1 (slack)	100
1–5	0.2	2 15	50
2–3	0.2	3 45	—
3–4	0.06	4 40	—
3–5	0.40	5 50	—
4–5	0.04		

8. Discuss in detail the factors affecting the power system security.
9. The figure below shows a four-bus power system. The impedances, data for transmission lines of the system as well as the generation and load values are also given below.

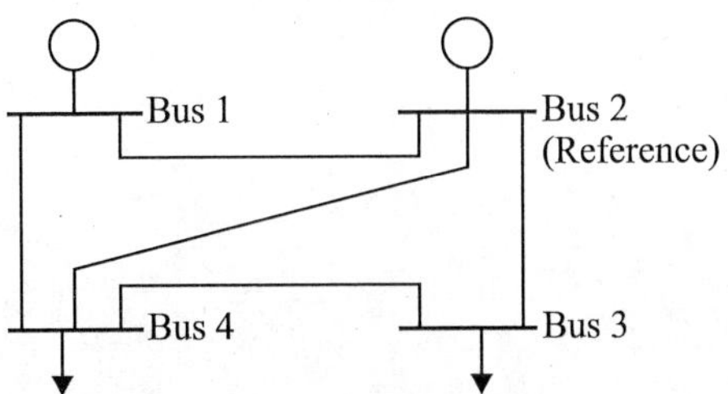

Line data		*Bus data*	
Line	*Reactance* (p.u.)	*Bus load* (MW)	*Generation* (MW)
1–2	0.2	1 (slack)	150
1–4	0.25	2 —	350
2–3	0.15	3 220	—
2–4	0.30	4 280	—
3–4	0.40		

Calculate the line outage sensitivity factors for outages on line 1–2, 1–4, and 2–3.

11. Explain the bounding algorithm in the contingency analysis with suitable examples.

12. Using the flow chart explain the ac power flow security analysis with contingency case selection.

13. Discuss the contingency ranking procedure using a simple example and a flow chart.

CHAPTER 7

State Estimation

7.1 Introduction

In recent years, methods have been developed using measurements from the network to calculate the state of the network–voltage magnitude and phase angle at every bus. These methods are called state estimators because they are essentially weighted least squares techniques to find the best state vector to fit a scatter of data. The scatter of data is due to imperfect measurements of rapidly changing voltage or currents on the network in addition to errors in the assumed values, and variations in the transmission line models, line charging, and so on. The first source of errors, imperfect measurements due to signal noise, metering accuracy, and analog-to-digital conversion, is treated in this chapter. The network topology and parameters are assumed as known until they are "fitted" to the data in parameter estimation.

The power system is assumed to be operating in steady state condition with fixed voltages, currents, and power flow. The remote terminal units (RTUs) which sample network analog variables and convert the signals to digital form are periodically interrogated for the latest values of the signals. For example, in Figure 7.1, the RTUs are sequentially interrogated causing a "time skew" in the data from unit 1 compared to unit M not only due to the time when the unit was scanned, but also due to the time when the actual analog signal was sampled. The set of M measurements is called a snapshot of the power system, even though the data may have as much as 2 s of time skew.

The data collected by the RTUs are often redundant, there may be voltage sensing by step down transformers on each phase—a, b, c—of the transmission line, whereas only one is needed for the balanced operation. In addition, each transmission line voltage to the substation may be monitored on the line side of a circuit breaker, introducing redundancy when all lines are in service. There may be single phase watts and var meters in addition to current measurements on all phase. The state estimator should incorporate all measurements to obtain the greatest possible accuracy.

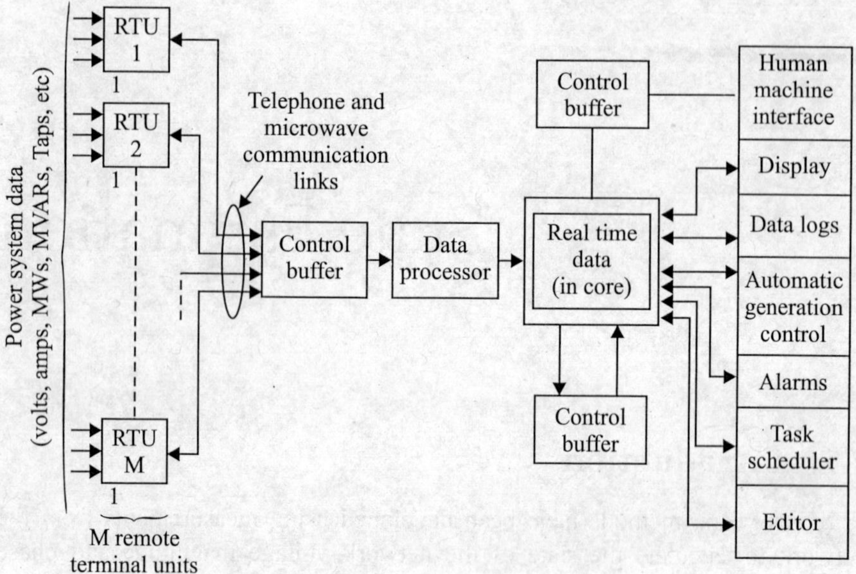

Figure 7.1 Data collection from the power system.

Because the power system data are redundant, the state estimator may be used with statistical methods to detect bad or grossly incorrect data. For example, if all current transformers near a bus, except one, agree on the current flows into and out of the bus, and the exception shows 50% error, the 50% value is far beyond a 2% metering accuracy specified for the current transducers, so this measurements is considered bad, it is removed from the subsequent state estimates until it can be physically checked. The operator of the system is usually alarmed of this action. The establishment of acceptable error limits based on the number, types, and accuracy of all measurements is an important design aspect of state estimators.

The another purpose of a state estimator is to detect changes in network configuration. If a transmission line has one phase abruptly open circuited, the average power flow on the intact phases is far less than a value given by the last estimate. The operator is alerted as to this condition at the first data scan. As of this data, the corrective action by the control computer is not automatic, but may be implemented in the future through "remedial action" programs.

Finally, the other purpose of a state estimator is to complete a set of measurements in order to replace faulty or missing data. It is possible to estimate power flows and voltages at a bus whose measurements are lost due to a communication line failure or RTU failure. Significant problems in this regard are to determine the minimum number of measurements in order to calculate the state, often called ***observability***, and how to improve the state estimates by additional measurements.

The selective monitoring of the generation and transmission system has been providing the data needed for economic dispatch and load frequency control. More recently, however, the interconnected power networks have become more complex and the task of securely operating the system has become more difficult. To help avoid the major system failures and the regional power blackouts, electric utilities have installed more extensive supervisory control and data acquisition (SCADA) throughout the network to support computer-based systems at the energy control centre. The databank created is intended for a number of application programs, some to ensure economic system operation and others to assess how secure the system would be if equipment failures and transmission-line outages were to occur.

Before any security assessment can be made or control actions taken, a reliable estimate of the existing state of the system must be determined. For this purpose, the number of physical measurements cannot be restricted to only those quantities required to support conventional power-flow program are confined to the P,Q injections at load buses and P, $|V|$ values at voltage controlled buses. If even one of these inputs is unavailable, the conventional power-flow solution cannot be obtained. Moreover, the gross error which is one or more of the input quantities can cause the power flow results to become useless. In practice, other conveniently measured quantities such as P, Q line flows are available, but they cannot be used in conventional power flow calculations. These limitations can be removed by state estimation based on weighted least-squares calculations.

The techniques developed in this chapter provide an estimate of the system state and a quantitative measure of how good the estimate is before it is used for real-time power flow calculations or on-line system security assessment. Besides, the inputs required for conventional power-flow analysis, additional measurements are made which usually include MW and MVAR flow in the transmission lines of the system. The unavoidable errors of the measurements are assigned statistical properties and the estimates of the states are subjected to statistical testing before being accepted as satisfactory. Thus, the gross errors detected in the course of state estimation are automatically filtered out.

7.2 Methods of Least Squares

The electric power transmission system uses wattmeters, varmeters, voltmeters, and current meters to measure real power, reactive power, voltages, and currents respectively. These continuous or analog quantities are monitored by current and potential transformers installed on the lines and on transformers and buses of the power plants and substations of the system. The analog quantities pass through transducers and analog-to-digital converters, and the digital outputs are then telemetered to the energy control centre over various communication links. The data received at the energy control centre is processed by computer to inform the system operators of the present state of the system. The acquired data always contains inaccuracies which are unavoidable since physical measurements (as opposed to numerical calculations) cannot be entirely free of random errors or noise. These errors can be quantified in a statistical sense and the estimated values of the quantities being measured are then either accepted as reasonable or rejected if certain measures of accuracy are exceeded.

Because of noise, the true values of physical quantities are never known and we have to consider how to calculate the best possible estimates of the unknown quantities. The method of least squares is often used to "best fit" measured data relating two or more quantities. Here we apply the method to a simple set of dc measurements which contain errors. The best estimates are chosen as those which minimize the weighted sum of the squares of the measurement errors.

7.2.1 Simple DC Circuit Example with Suitable Derivation

Consider the simple dc circuit of Figure 7.2 with five resistances of 1 Ω each and two voltage sources V_1 and V_2 of unknown values which are to be estimated. The measurement set consists of ammeter readings z_1 and z_2 and voltmeter readings z_3 and z_4. The symbol z is normally used for measurements regardless of the physical quantity being measured, and likewise, the symbol x regardless of the physical quantity being measured, applies to quantities being estimated. The system model based on elementary circuit analysis expresses the true values of the measured quantities in terms of the network parameters and the true (but unknown) source voltages $x_1 = V_1$ and $x_2 = V_2$. Then, measurement equations characterizing the meter readings are found by adding error terms to the system model.

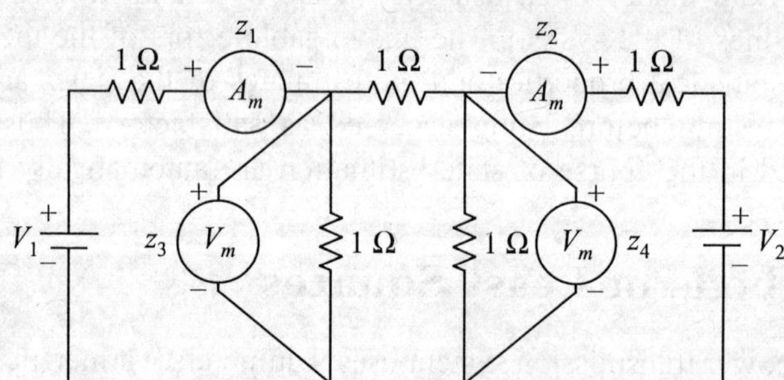

Figure 7.2 Simple dc circuit.

$$z_1 = \frac{5}{8}x_1 - \frac{1}{8}x_2 + e_1 \tag{7.1}$$

$$z_2 = -\frac{1}{8}x_1 + \frac{5}{8}x_2 + e_2 \tag{7.2}$$

$$z_3 = \frac{3}{8}x_1 + \frac{1}{8}x_2 + e_3 \tag{7.3}$$

$$\underbrace{z_4}_{\text{Measurements}} = \underbrace{\frac{1}{8}x_1 + \frac{3}{8}x_2}_{\substack{\text{True values}\\ \text{from system model}}} + \underbrace{e_4}_{\text{Errors}} \tag{7.4}$$

The numerical coefficients are determined by the circuit resistances and the terms e_1, e_2, e_3 and e_4 represent errors in measuring the two currents z_1 and z_2 and the two voltages z_3 and z_4. Sometimes the term residuals is used instead of errors, so we have used both terms interchangeably.

If e_1, e_2, e_3 and e_4 were zero (the ideal case), then any two of the meter readings would give exact and consistent readings from which the true values x_1 and x_2 of V_1 and V_2 could be determined. But in any measurement scheme there are unknown errors which generally follow a statistical pattern. Labelling the coefficients of Eqs. (7.1) through (7.4) in an obvious way, we obtain

$$z_1 = h_{11}x_1 + h_{12}x_2 + e_1 = z_{1,\text{true}} + e_1 \tag{7.5}$$

$$z_2 = h_{21}x_1 + h_{22}x_2 + e_2 = z_{2,\text{true}} + e_2 \tag{7.6}$$

$$z_3 = h_{31}x_1 + h_{32}x_2 + e_3 = z_{3,\text{true}} + e_3 \tag{7.7}$$

$$z_4 = h_{41}x_1 + h_{42}x_2 + e_4 = z_{4,\text{true}} + e_4 \tag{7.8}$$

where $z_{j,\text{true}}$ denotes the true value of the measured quantity z_j. We now rearrange Eqs. (7.5) through (7.8) into the vector-matrix form

$$\begin{bmatrix} e_1 \\ e_2 \\ e_3 \\ e_4 \end{bmatrix} = \begin{bmatrix} z_1 \\ z_2 \\ z_3 \\ z_4 \end{bmatrix} - \begin{bmatrix} z_{1,\text{true}} \\ z_{2,\text{true}} \\ z_{3,\text{true}} \\ z_{4,\text{true}} \end{bmatrix} = \begin{bmatrix} z_1 \\ z_2 \\ z_3 \\ z_4 \end{bmatrix} - \begin{bmatrix} h_{11} & h_{12} \\ h_{21} & h_{22} \\ h_{31} & h_{32} \\ h_{41} & h_{42} \end{bmatrix} \begin{bmatrix} x_1 \\ x_2 \end{bmatrix} \tag{7.9}$$

In more compact notation Eq. (7.9) can be written as

$$e = z - z_{\text{true}} = z - H_X \tag{7.10}$$

which represents the errors between the actual measurements z and the true (but unknown) values $z_{\text{true}} \triangleq HX$ of the measured quantities. The true values of x_1 and x_2 cannot be determined. But we can calculate estimates x_1 and x_2 as we shall soon see. Substituting these estimates in Eq. (7.9) we get the estimated values of the errors in the form

$$\underbrace{\begin{bmatrix} \hat{e}_1 \\ \hat{e}_2 \\ \hat{e}_3 \\ \hat{e}_4 \end{bmatrix}}_{\text{Estimated errors}} = \underbrace{\begin{bmatrix} z_1 \\ z_2 \\ z_3 \\ z_4 \end{bmatrix}}_{\text{Measurements}} - \underbrace{\begin{bmatrix} h_{11} & h_{12} \\ h_{21} & h_{22} \\ h_{31} & h_{32} \\ h_{41} & h_{42} \end{bmatrix} \begin{bmatrix} \hat{x}_1 \\ \hat{x}_2 \end{bmatrix}}_{\text{Estimates of } z_j} \tag{7.11}$$

Quantities with hats, such as $\hat{e}_j$ and $\hat{x}_i$, are the estimates of the corresponding quantities without hats. In Eq. (7.11), the left-hand vector is $\hat{e}$, which represents the differences between the actual measurements z and their estimated values $\hat{z} \triangleq H\hat{x}$, so that we can write

$$\hat{e} = z - \hat{z} = z - H\hat{x} = e - H(\hat{x} - x) \tag{7.12}$$

We must now decide upon a criterion for calculating the estimates $\hat{x}_1$ and $\hat{x}_2$ from which $\hat{e} = [\hat{e}_1 \quad \hat{e}_2 \quad \hat{e}_3 \quad \hat{e}_4]$ and $\hat{z} = [\hat{z}_1 \quad \hat{z}_2 \quad \hat{z}_3 \quad \hat{z}_4]^T$ are to be computed. It is not desirable to choose the algebraic sum of the errors to be minimized since positive and negative errors could then offset one another and the estimates would not necessarily be acceptable. It is preferable to minimize the direct sum of the squares of the errors. However, to ensure that measurements from meters of known greater accuracy are treated more favourably than less accurate measurements, each term in the sum of squares is multiplied by an appropriate weighting factor w to give the objective function.

$$f = \sum_{j=1}^{4} w_j e_j^2 = w_1 e_1^2 + w_2 e_2^2 + w_3 e_3^2 + w_4 e_4^2 \tag{7.13}$$

We select the best estimates of the state variables as those values $\hat{x}_1$ and $\hat{x}_2$ which cause the objective function f to take on its minimum value. According to the usual necessary conditions for minimizing, the estimates x_1 and x_2 are those usual values of x_1 and x_2 which satisfy the equations.

$$\left.\frac{\partial f}{\partial x_1}\right|_{\hat{x}} = 2\left[w_1 e_1 \frac{\partial e_1}{\partial x_1} + w_2 e_2 \frac{\partial e_2}{\partial x_1} + w_3 e_3 \frac{\partial e_3}{\partial x_1} + w_4 e_4 \frac{\partial e_4}{\partial x_1}\right]_{\hat{x}} = 0 \tag{7.14}$$

$$\left.\frac{\partial f}{\partial x_2}\right|_{\hat{x}} = 2\left[w_1 e_1 \frac{\partial e_1}{\partial x_2} + w_2 e_2 \frac{\partial e_2}{\partial x_2} + w_3 e_3 \frac{\partial e_3}{\partial x_2} + w_4 e_4 \frac{\partial e_4}{\partial x_2}\right]_{\hat{x}} = 0 \tag{7.15}$$

The notation $\hat{x}$ indicates that the equations have to be evaluated from the state estimates $\hat{x} = [\hat{x}_1 \hat{x}_2]$ since the true values of the states are not known. The unknown actual errors e_j are then replaced by the estimated errors $\hat{e}_j$, which can be calculated once the state estimates $\hat{x}_j$ are known. Equations (7.14) and (7.15) in vector matrix form become

$$\begin{bmatrix} \dfrac{\partial e_1}{\partial x_1} & \dfrac{\partial e_2}{\partial x_1} & \dfrac{\partial e_3}{\partial x_1} & \dfrac{\partial e_4}{\partial x_1} \\[2ex] \dfrac{\partial e_1}{\partial x_2} & \dfrac{\partial e_2}{\partial x_2} & \dfrac{\partial e_3}{\partial x_2} & \dfrac{\partial e_4}{\partial x_2} \end{bmatrix}_{\hat{x}} \underbrace{\begin{bmatrix} w_1 & \cdot & \cdot & \cdot \\ \cdot & w_2 & \cdot & \cdot \\ \cdot & \cdot & w_3 & \cdot \\ \cdot & \cdot & \cdot & w_4 \end{bmatrix}}_{W} \begin{bmatrix} \hat{e}_1 \\ \hat{e}_2 \\ \hat{e}_3 \\ \hat{e}_4 \end{bmatrix} = \begin{bmatrix} 0 \\ 0 \end{bmatrix} \tag{7.16}$$

where W is the diagonal matrix of weighting factors which have a special significance. The partial derivatives for substitution in Eq. (7.16) are found from Eqs. (7.5) through (7.8) to be the constants given by the elements of H, and so we obtain

$$\begin{bmatrix} h_{11} & h_{21} & h_{31} & h_{41} \\ h_{12} & h_{22} & h_{32} & h_{42} \end{bmatrix} \begin{bmatrix} w_1 & \cdot & \cdot & \cdot \\ \cdot & w_2 & \cdot & \cdot \\ \cdot & \cdot & w_3 & \cdot \\ \cdot & \cdot & \cdot & w_4 \end{bmatrix} \begin{bmatrix} \hat{e}_1 \\ \hat{e}_2 \\ \hat{e}_3 \\ \hat{e}_4 \end{bmatrix} = \begin{bmatrix} 0 \\ 0 \end{bmatrix} \tag{7.17}$$

Using the compact notations of Eq. (7.12) in Eq. (7.17), yields we have

$$H^T W \hat{e} = H^T W (z - H\hat{X}) = 0 \tag{7.18}$$

Multiplying through in this equation and solving for $\hat{X} = [\hat{x}_1 \hat{x}_2]^T$, we get

$$\hat{X} = \begin{bmatrix} \hat{x}_1 \\ \hat{x}_2 \end{bmatrix} = \underbrace{(H^T WH)}_{G}^{-1} H^T Wz = G^{-1} H^T Wz \tag{7.19}$$

where $\hat{x}_1$ and $\hat{x}_2$ are the weighted least squares estimates of the state variables. Because H is rectangular, the symmetrical matrix $H^T\ WH$ (often called the gain matrix G) must be inverted as a single entity to yield $G^{-1} = (H^T WH)^{-1}$, which is also symmetrical.

EXAMPLE 7.1 The measurement set and system model matrix is given as

$$[9.01\text{ A},\ 3.02\text{ A},\ 6.98\text{ V},\ 5.01\text{ V}] \qquad \begin{bmatrix} 0.625 & -0.125 \\ -0.125 & 0.625 \\ 0.375 & 0.125 \\ 0.125 & 0.375 \end{bmatrix}$$

Let us assign the measurement weights $w_1 = 100$ $w_2 = 100$, $w_3 = 50$ and $w_4 = 50$ respectively.

Compute the weighted least square estimates of the state variables.

$$\hat{X}_{\text{est}} = [H^T WH]^{-1} H^T WZ$$

Solution:

$$H^T W = \begin{bmatrix} 0.625 & -0.125 & 0.375 & 0.125 \\ -0.125 & 0.625 & 0.125 & 0.375 \end{bmatrix} \begin{bmatrix} 100 & 0 & 0 & 0 \\ 0 & 100 & 0 & 0 \\ 0 & 0 & 50 & 0 \\ 0 & 0 & 0 & 50 \end{bmatrix}$$

$$H^T W = \begin{bmatrix} 62.5 & -12.5 & 18.75 & 6.25 \\ -12.5 & 62.5 & 6.25 & 18.75 \end{bmatrix}$$

$$H^T WH = \begin{bmatrix} 62.5 & -12.5 & 18.75 & 6.25 \\ -12.5 & 62.5 & 6.25 & 18.75 \end{bmatrix} \begin{bmatrix} 0.625 & -0.125 \\ -0.125 & 0.625 \\ 0.375 & 0.125 \\ 0.125 & 0.375 \end{bmatrix}$$

$$H^T WH = \begin{bmatrix} 48.4375 & -10.9375 \\ -10.9375 & 48.4375 \end{bmatrix}$$

$$G^{-1} = (H^T WH)^{-1} = \begin{bmatrix} 48.4375 & -10.9375 \\ -10.9375 & 48.4375 \end{bmatrix}^{-1} = \begin{bmatrix} 0.02175 & 0.00491 \\ 0.00491 & 0.02175 \end{bmatrix}$$

$$H^T WZ = \begin{bmatrix} 62.5 & -12.5 & 18.75 & 6.25 \\ -12.5 & 62.5 & 6.25 & 18.75 \end{bmatrix} \begin{bmatrix} 9.01 \\ 3.02 \\ 6.98 \\ 5.01 \end{bmatrix}$$

$$\hat{X} = G^{-1}(H^T WZ) = \begin{bmatrix} 16.0072 \text{ V} \\ 8.0261 \text{ V} \end{bmatrix}$$

$$\hat{Z} = H\hat{X} = \begin{bmatrix} 0.625 & -0.125 \\ -0.125 & 0.625 \\ 0.375 & 0.125 \\ 0.125 & 0.375 \end{bmatrix} \begin{bmatrix} 16.0072 \text{ V} \\ 8.0261 \text{ V} \end{bmatrix} = \begin{bmatrix} 9.00123 \text{ A} \\ 3.01544 \text{ A} \\ 7.00596 \text{ V} \\ 5.01070 \text{ V} \end{bmatrix}$$

$$\hat{e} = z - \hat{z} = \begin{bmatrix} 9.01 \\ 3.02 \\ 6.98 \\ 5.01 \end{bmatrix} - \begin{bmatrix} 9.00123 \\ 3.01544 \\ 7.00596 \\ 5.01070 \end{bmatrix} = \begin{bmatrix} 0.00877 \text{ A} \\ 0.00456 \text{ A} \\ -0.02596 \text{ V} \\ -0.00070 \text{ V} \end{bmatrix}$$

EXAMPLE 7.2 Three meters are installed on the three-bus system of Figure 7.3 to measure line real power flows where

$x_{12} = 0.2$ p.u; $\quad M_{12} = 0.6$ p.u.
$x_{13} = 0.4$ p.u.; $\quad M_{13} = 0.4$ p.u.
$x_{23} = 0.25$ p.u.; $\quad M_{32} = 0.405$ p.u.

And the variances are the same, $\sigma = 0.01$ p.u.

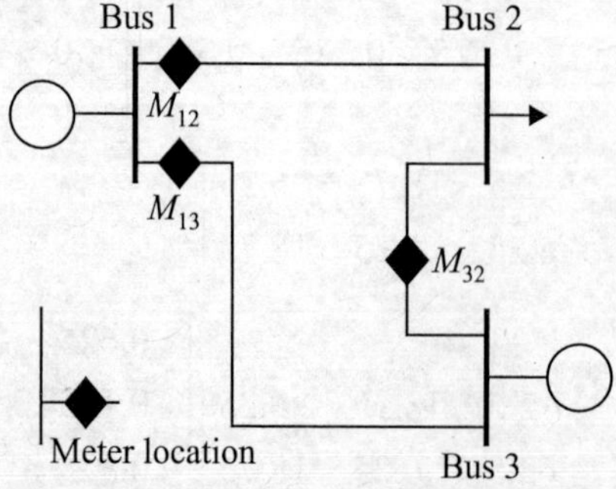

Figure 7.3 Three-bus system.

Compare the weighted least square estimates of the phase angles with bus 3 as the reference.

Solution: Given bus 3 as the reference, hence $\theta_3 = 0$

$$f_{12} = \frac{1}{x_{12}}(\theta_1 - \theta_2) = \frac{1}{0.2}(\theta_1 - \theta_2) = 5(\theta_1 - \theta_2)$$

$$f_{13} = \frac{1}{x_{13}}(\theta_1 - \theta_3) = \frac{1}{0.4}(\theta_1 - 0) = 2.5(\theta_1)$$

$$f_{32} = \frac{1}{x_{32}}(\theta_3 - \theta_2) = \frac{1}{0.25}(0 - \theta_2) = -4(\theta_2)$$

$$\begin{bmatrix} f_{12} \\ f_{13} \\ f_{32} \end{bmatrix} = \begin{bmatrix} 5 & -5 \\ 2.5 & 0 \\ 0 & -4 \end{bmatrix} \begin{bmatrix} \theta_1 \\ \theta_2 \end{bmatrix}$$

$$H = \begin{bmatrix} 5 & -5 \\ 2.5 & 0 \\ 0 & -4 \end{bmatrix}$$

$R = \sigma^2 = (0.01)^2 = 10^{-4}$; $W = R^{-1} = 10^4$

$\hat{X} = G^{-1}(H^T WZ)$, where $G = H^T WH$

$$H^T WH = \begin{bmatrix} 5 & 2.5 & 0 \\ -5 & 0 & -4 \end{bmatrix} \begin{bmatrix} 10^4 & 0 & 0 \\ 0 & 10^4 & 0 \\ 0 & 0 & 10^4 \end{bmatrix} \begin{bmatrix} 5 & -5 \\ 2.5 & 0 \\ 0 & -4 \end{bmatrix}$$

$$= \begin{bmatrix} 0.3125 \times 10^6 & -0.25 \times 10^6 \\ -0.25 \times 10^6 & 0.41 \times 10^6 \end{bmatrix}$$

$$G^{-1} = \begin{bmatrix} 6.2476 \times 10^{-6} & 3.8095 \times 10^{-6} \\ 3.8095 \times 10^{-6} & 4.7619 \times 10^{-6} \end{bmatrix}$$

$$H^T WZ = \begin{bmatrix} 5 & 2.5 & 0 \\ -5 & 0 & -4 \end{bmatrix} \begin{bmatrix} 10^4 & 0 & 0 \\ 0 & 10^4 & 0 \\ 0 & 0 & 10^4 \end{bmatrix} \begin{bmatrix} 0.6 \\ 0.4 \\ 0.405 \end{bmatrix} = \begin{bmatrix} 0.04 \times 10^6 \\ -0.0462 \times 10^6 \end{bmatrix}$$

$$\hat{X} = G^{-1}(H^T WZ) = \begin{bmatrix} 6.2476 \times 10^{-6} & 3.8095 \times 10^{-6} \\ 3.8095 \times 10^{-6} & 4.7619 \times 10^{-6} \end{bmatrix} \begin{bmatrix} 0.04 \times 10^6 \\ -0.0462 \times 10^6 \end{bmatrix}$$

$$= \begin{bmatrix} 0.073904 \\ -0.067619 \end{bmatrix}$$

7.3 Maximum Likelihood Weighted Least-Squares Estimation

Statistical estimation refers to a procedure where one uses samples to calculate the value of one or more unknown parameters in a system. Since the samples (or measurements) are inexact, the estimate obtained for the unknown parameter is also inexact. This leads to the problem of how to formulate a "best" estimate of the unknown parameters given the available measurements.

The development of the notions of state estimation may proceed along several lines, depending on the statistical criterion selected. Of the many criteria that have been examined and used in various applications, the following three are perhaps the most commonly encountered.

1. The maximum likelihood criterion, where the objective is to maximize the probability that the estimate of the state variable, $\hat{X}$, is the true value of the state variable vector, X (i.e. maximize $P(\hat{X}) = X$).
2. The weighted least-squares criterion, where the objective is to minimize the sum of the squares of the weighted deviations of the estimated measurements, $\hat{Z}$, from the actual measurements, Z.
3. The minimum variance criterion, where the object is to minimize the expected value of the sum of the squares of the deviations of the estimated components of the state variable vector from the corresponding components of the true state variable vector.

When normally distributed, unbiased meter error distributions are assumed, each of these approaches results in identical estimators. This chapter will utilize the maximum likelihood approach because the method introduces the measurement error weighting matrix $[R]$ in a straightforward manner.

The maximum likelihood procedure asks the following question: "What is the probability (or likelihood) that I will get the measurements I have obtained?" This probability depends on the random error in the measuring device (transducer) as well as the unknown parameters to be estimated. Therefore, a reasonable procedure would be one that simply chose the estimate as the value that maximizes this probability. As we will see shortly, the maximum likelihood estimator assumes that we know the probability density function (PDF) of the random errors in the measurement. Other estimation schemes could also be used. The "least-squares" estimator does not require that we know the probability density function for the sample or measurement errors. However, if we assume that the probability density function for the sample or measurement error is a normal (Gaussian) distribution, we will end up with the state estimation formula using the maximum likelihood criterion assuming normal distributions for measurement errors. The result will be a "least-squares" or more precisely the formulation using the maximum likelihood criteria. We will illustrate this method with a simple electrical circuit and show how the maximum likelihood estimate can be made.

First, we introduce the concept of random measurement error. Note that we have dropped the term "sample" since the concept of a measurement is much more appropriate to our discussion. The measurements are assumed to be in error: that is, the value obtained from the measurement device is close to the true value of the parameter being measured but differs by an unknown error. Mathematically, this can be modelled as follows.

Let Z^{meas} be the value of a measurement as received from a measurement device. Let Z^{true} be the true value of the quantity being measured. Finally, let η be the random measurement error. We can then represent our measured values.

The random number, η, serves to model the uncertainty in the measurements. If the measurement error is unbiased, the probability density function of η is usually chosen as a normal distribution with zero mean. Note that other measurement probability density functions will also work in the maximum likelihood method as well. The probability density function of η is

$$\text{PDF}(\eta) = \frac{1}{\sigma\sqrt{2\pi}} \exp\left(\frac{-\eta^2}{2\sigma^2}\right) \tag{7.20}$$

where σ is called the standard deviation and σ^2 is called the variance of the random number. PDF(η) describes the behaviour of η. A plot of PDF(η) is shown in Figure 7.4. Note that σ, the standard deviation, provides a way to model the seriousness of the random measurement error. If σ is large, the measurement is relatively inaccurate (i.e., a higher-quality measurement device). The normal distribution is commonly used for modelling measurement errors since it is the distribution that will result when many factors contribute to the overall error.

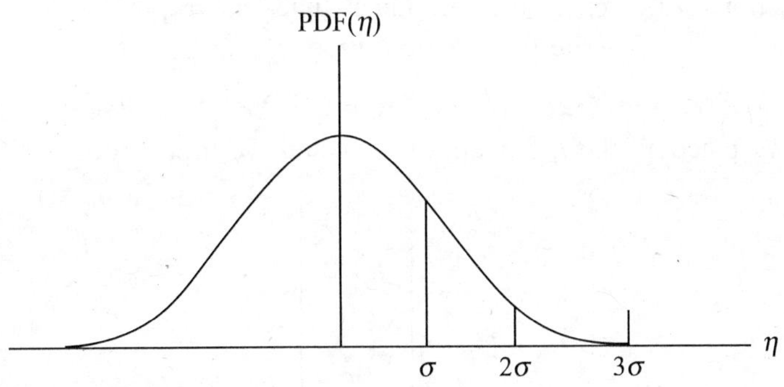

Figure 7.4 Normal distribution.

We see that the maximum likelihood estimate of our unknown parameter is always expressed as that value of the parameter that gives the minimum of the sum of the squares of the difference between each measured value and the true value being measured (expressed as a function of our unknown parameter) with each squared difference divided or "weighted" by the variance of the meter error. Thus, if we are estimating a single parameter, x, using N_M measurements, we would write the expression

$$\min_x J(x) = \sum_{i=1}^{N_M} \frac{[Z_i^{\text{meas}} - f_i(x)]^2}{\sigma_i^2} \tag{7.21}$$

where f_i = function that is used to calculate the value being measured by the ith measurement

σ_i^2 = variance for the ith measurement

$J(x)$ = measurement residual

N_M = number of independent measurements

Z_i^{meas} = i^{th} measured quantity

Note that Eq. (7.21) may be expressed in per unit or in physical units such as in MW, MVAR, or kV.

If we were to try to estimate N_S unknown parameters using N_M measurements, we would write

$$\min_{\{x_1, x_2, ..., x_{N_S}\}} J(x_1, x_2, ..., x_{N_S}) = \sum_{i=1}^{N_M} \frac{[Z_i - f_i(x_1, x_2, ..., x_{N_S})]^2}{\sigma_i^2} \tag{7.22}$$

The estimation calculation shown is known as a weighted least-squares estimator, which, as we have shown earlier, is equivalent to a maximum likelihood estimator if the measurement errors are modelled as random numbers having a normal distribution.

7.3.1 Matrix Formulation

If the functions $f_i(x_1, x_2, ..., x_{N_S})$ are linear functions, Eq. (7.22) has a closed form solution. Let us write the function $f_i(x_1, x_2, ..., x_{N_S})$ as

$$f_1(x_1, x_2, ..., x_{N_S}) = f_i(X) = hi_1x_1 + hi_2x_2 + \cdots + hi_{N_S} x_{N_S}$$

Then, if we place all the f_i function in a vector, we may write

$$f(x) = \begin{bmatrix} f_1(x) \\ f_2(x) \\ \cdot \\ \cdot \\ \cdot \\ f_{N_M}(x) \end{bmatrix} \tag{7.23}$$

where $[H]$ = any matrix containing the coefficients of the linear functions

N_M = number of measurements

N_S = number of unknown parameters in a vector

Placing the measurements in a vector

$$Z^{\text{meas}} = \begin{bmatrix} z_1^{\text{meas}} \\ z_2^{\text{meas}} \\ \cdot \\ \cdot \\ \cdot \\ z_{N_M}^{\text{meas}} \end{bmatrix} \tag{7.24}$$

We may then write Eq. (7.24) in a very compact form as

$$\min_x J(x) = [Z^{\text{meas}} - f(x)]^T [Z^{\text{meas}} - f(x)] \tag{7.24a}$$

where

$$[R] = \begin{bmatrix} \sigma_1^2 & & & & \\ & \sigma_2^2 & & & \\ & & \cdot & & \\ & & & \cdot & \\ & & & & \cdot \\ & & & & & \sigma_{NM}^2 \end{bmatrix} \tag{7.25}$$

$[R]$ is called the covariance matrix of the measurement errors. To obtain the general expression for the minimum in Eq. (7.24a), expand the expression and substitute $[H]X$ for $f(X)$ from

$$\min_x J(X) = \{Z^{\text{meas}^T} [R^{-1}]Z^{\text{meas}} - X^T[H]^T[R^{-1}]Z^{\text{meas}} - Z^{\text{meas}}[R^{-1}][H]X + X^T[H]^T[R^{-1}][H]X\} \tag{7.26}$$

Similar to the procedures of Chapter 3, the minimum of $J(X)$ is found $\partial J(X)/\partial x_i = 0$, for $i = 1, \ldots, N_S$ when this is identical to stating that the gradient of $J(X)$ and $\nabla J(X)$ is exactly zero.

The gradient of $J(X)$ is

$$\nabla J(X) = -2[H]^T [R^{-1}]Z^{\text{meas}} + 2[H]^T [R^{-1}] [H]X \tag{7.26}$$

Then $\nabla J(X) = 0$ gives

$$X^{\text{est}} = [[H]^T [R^{-1}] [H]]^{-1} [H]^T [R^{-1}]Z^{\text{meas}} \tag{7.27}$$

Note that Eq. (7.27) holds when $N_S < N_M$; that is, when the number of parameters being estimated is less than the number of measurements being made.

When $N_S = N_M$, our estimation problem reduces to

$$X^{\text{est}} = [H]^{-1} Z^{\text{meas}} \tag{7.28}$$

There is also a closed form solution to the problem when $N_S > N_M$, although in this case we are not estimating x to maximize a likelihood function since

$N_S > N_M$ usually implies that many different values for X^{est} can be found that cause to equal $i = 1, \ldots, N_M$ exactly.

Rather, the objective is to find X^{est} such that the sum of the squares of X_i^{est} is minimized. That is

$$\min_x \sum_{i=1}^{N_M} x_i^2 = X^T X \tag{7.29}$$

subject to the condition that $Z^{\text{meas}} = [H]X$. The closed form solution for this case is

$$X^{\text{est}} = [H]^T \, [[H] \, [H]^T]^{-1} \, Z^{\text{meas}} \tag{7.30}$$

In the power system state estimation, the underdetermined problems (i.e. where $N_S > N_M$) are not solved. Rather "pseudo-measurements" are added to the measurement set to give a completely determined or overdetermined problem.

Table 7.1 Estimation formulae

Case	*Description*	*Solution*	*Comment*
$N_S < N_M$	Overdetermined	$X^{\text{est}} = [[H]^T [R^{-1}[H]]^{-1} [H]^T [R^{-1}] Z^{\text{meas}}$	X^{est} is the maximum likelihood estimate of X given the measurements
$N_S = N_M$	Completely determined	$X^{\text{est}} = [H]^{-1} Z^{\text{meas}}$	X^{est} fits the measured quantities to the measurements Z^{meas} exactly
$N_S > N_M$	Underdetermined	$X^{\text{est}} = [H]^T[[H]\,[H]^T]^{-1} \, Z^{\text{meas}}$	X^{est} is the vector of minimum norm that fits the measured quantities to the measurements exactly. (The norm of a vector is equal to the sum of the squares of its components)

7.4 State Estimation by Orthogonal Decomposition

One problem with the standard least squares method presented earlier in the chapter is the numerical difficulties encountered with some special state estimation problems. One of these comes about when we wish to derive a state estimator solution to match its measurement almost exactly. This is the case when we have a circuit such as shown in Figure 7.5. All the actual flows and injections are shown in Figure 7.5 along with the values assumed for the measurements.

In this sample system, the measurement of power at bus 1 will be assumed to be 0 MW. If the value is dictated by the fact that the bus had no load or generation attached to it, then we know this value of 0 MW with certainty and the concept of an error in its "measured" value is meaningless. Nonetheless,

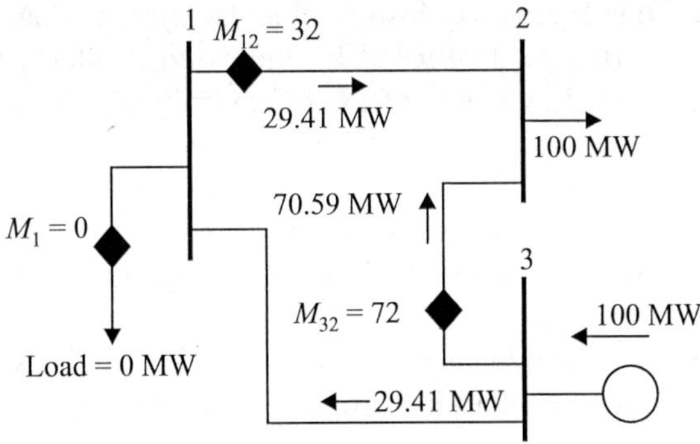

Figure 7.5 Zero injection system example.

we proceed by setting up the standard state estimator equations and specifying the value of the measurement σ for M_1 as : $\sigma_{M1} = 10^{-2}$. This results in the following solution when using the state estimator equations

$$P_{\text{flow}} \text{ estimate on line 1–2} = 30.76 \text{ MW}$$

$$P_{\text{flow}} \text{ estimate on line 3–2} = 72.52 \text{ MW}$$

$$\text{Injection estimate on bus 1} = 0.82 \text{ MW}$$

The estimator has not forced the bus injection to be exactly zero; instead, it reads 0.82 MW. This may not seem like such a big error. However, if there are many such buses (say 100) and they all have errors of this magnitude, then the estimator will have a large amount of load allocated to the buses that are known to be zero.

At first, the solution to this dilemma may seem to be simply forcing the σ value to a very small number for the zero injection buses and rerun the estimator. The problem with this is as follows. Suppose we had changed the zero injection σ to $\sigma_{M1} = 10^{-10}$. Hopefully, this would the estimator to make the zero injection so dominant that it would result in the correct zero value coming out of the estimator calculation. In this case, the $[H^T R^{-1} H]$ matrix used in the standard least-squares method would look like this for the sample system:

$$[H] = \begin{bmatrix} 5.0 & -5.0 \\ 0 & -4.0 \\ 7.5 & -5.0 \end{bmatrix}$$

$$[R] = \begin{bmatrix} 10^{-4} & & \\ & 10^{-4} & \\ & & 10^{-20} \end{bmatrix}$$

then

$$[H^T R^{-1} H] = \begin{bmatrix} 56.25 \times 10^{20} & -37.5 \times 10^{20} \\ -37.5 \times 10^{20} & 25.0 \times 10^{20} \end{bmatrix}$$

Unfortunately, this matrix is close to singular matrix. The reason is that the terms in the matrix are dominated by those terms which are multiplied by the 10^{20} terms from the inverse of the [R] matrix, and the other terms are so small by comparison that they are lost from the computer (unless one is using an extraordinary long word length or extra double precision). When the above is presented to a standard matrix inversion routine or run into a Gaussian elimination solution routine, an error message results and garbage comes out of the estimator.

The solution to this dilemma is to use another algorithm for the least squares solution. This algorithm is called the orthogonal decomposition algorithm and work as follows.

7.4.1 Orthogonal Decomposition Algorithm

This algorithm goes under several different names in texts on linear algebra. It is often called the QR algorithm or the Gram–Schmidt decomposition. The idea is to take the state estimation least squares equation and eliminate the [R^{-1}] matrix as follows. Let

$$[R^{-1}] = R^{-1/2}R^{-1/2} \tag{7.31}$$

where

$$[R^{-1/2}] = \begin{bmatrix} \dfrac{1}{\sigma_{m1}} & & \\ & \dfrac{1}{\sigma_{m2}} & \\ & & \dfrac{1}{\sigma_{m3}} \end{bmatrix} \tag{7.32}$$

then

$$[H^T R^{-1} H]^{-1} = [H^T R^{-1/2} R^{-1/2} H]^{-1} = [H'^T H'] \tag{7.33}$$

with

$$[H'] = [R^{-1/2}]\,[H] \tag{7.34}$$

Finally, Eq. (7.30) becomes

$$X^{\text{est}} = [H'^T H']^{-1}\,[H'^T] Z'^{\text{meas}} \tag{7.35}$$

where

$$Z'^{\text{meas}} = [R^{-1/2}] Z^{\text{meas}} \tag{7.36}$$

The idea of the orthogonal decomposition algorithm is to find a matrix [Q] such that:

$$[H'] = [Q][U] \tag{7.37}$$

(Note that in most linear algebra textbooks, this factorization would be written as [H'] = [Q] [U]; however, we shall use [Q][U] so as not to confuse the identity of the [R] matrix.)

The matrix $[Q]$ has special properties. It is called an orthogonal matrix so that

$$[Q^T][Q] = [I] \tag{7.38}$$

where $[I]$ is the identity matrix, which is to say that the transpose of $[Q]$ is its inverse. The matrix $[U]$ is now upper triangular in structure, although, since the $[H]$ matrix may not be square, $[U]$ will not be square either. Thus,

$$[H'] = \begin{bmatrix} h'_{11} & h'_{12} \\ h'_{21} & h'_{22} \\ h'_{31} & h'_{32} \end{bmatrix} = [Q][U] = \begin{bmatrix} q_{11} & q_{12} & q_{13} \\ q_{21} & q_{22} & q_{23} \\ q_{31} & q_{32} & q_{33} \end{bmatrix} \begin{bmatrix} u_{11} & u_{12} \\ 0 & u_{22} \\ 0 & 0 \end{bmatrix} \tag{7.39}$$

Now, we substitute $[Q]\,[U]$ for $[H']$ in the state estimation equation:

$$X^{\text{est}} = [U^T Q^T Q U]^{-1}\ [U^T]\ [Q^T]Z' \tag{7.40}$$

or

$$X^{\text{est}} = [U^T U]^{-1}\ U^T Z' \tag{7.41}$$

since

$$[Q^T Q] = \text{I} \tag{7.42}$$

and

$$\hat{Z} = [Q^T]Z' \tag{7.43}$$

Then, by rearranging we get

$$[U^T U]X^{\text{est}} = [U^T]\,\hat{Z}$$

and we can eliminate U^T from both sides so that we are left with

$$[U]X^{\text{est}} = \hat{Z} \tag{7.44}$$

or

$$\begin{bmatrix} u_{11} & u_{12} \\ 0 & u_{22} \\ 0 & 0 \end{bmatrix} \begin{bmatrix} x_1^{\text{est}} \\ x_2^{\text{est}} \end{bmatrix} = \begin{bmatrix} \hat{z}_1 \\ \hat{z}_2 \\ \hat{z}_3 \end{bmatrix} \tag{7.45}$$

This can be solved directly since U is upper triangular:

$$x_2^{\text{est}} = \frac{\hat{z}_2}{u_{22}} \tag{7.46}$$

and

$$x_1^{\text{est}} = \frac{1}{u_{11}}(\hat{z}_1 - u_{12}x_2^{\text{est}}) \tag{7.47}$$

The Q matrix and the U matrix are obtained, for our simple two-state-three-measurement problem here, using the Givens rotation method.

For the Givens rotation method, we start out to define the steps necessary to solve:

$$[Q^T][H] = [U] \tag{7.48}$$

where $[H]$ is a 2 × 2 matrix:

$$\begin{bmatrix} h_{11} & h_{12} \\ h_{21} & h_{22} \end{bmatrix} \tag{7.49}$$

and $[U]$ is

$$\begin{bmatrix} u_{11} & u_{12} \\ 0 & u_{22} \end{bmatrix} \tag{7.50}$$

The $[Q]$ matrix must be orthogonal, and when it is multiplied $[H]$, times it eliminates the h_{21} term. The terms in the $[Q]$ matrix are simply

$$\begin{bmatrix} c & s \\ -s & c \end{bmatrix} \tag{7.51}$$

where

$$c = \frac{h_{11}}{\sqrt{h_{11}^2 + h_{21}^2}} \tag{7.52}$$

and

$$s = \frac{h_{21}}{\sqrt{h_{11}^2 + h_{21}^2}} \tag{7.53}$$

The reader can easily verify that the $[Q]$ matrix is indeed orthogonal and that:

$$\begin{bmatrix} u_{11} & u_{12} \\ 0 & u_{22} \end{bmatrix} = \begin{bmatrix} 1 & (ch_{12} + sh_{22}) \\ 0 & (-sh_{12} + ch_{22}) \end{bmatrix} \tag{7.54}$$

When we solve the 3 × 2 $[H]$ matrix in our three-measurement-two-state sample problem, we apply the Givens rotation three times to eliminate h_{21}, h_{31}, and h_{32}. That is, we need to solve

$$[Q^T] = \begin{bmatrix} h_{11} & h_{12} \\ h_{21} & h_{22} \\ h_{31} & h_{32} \end{bmatrix} = \begin{bmatrix} u_{11} & u_{12} \\ 0 & u_{22} \\ 0 & 0 \end{bmatrix} \tag{7.55}$$

We will carry this out in three distinct steps, where each step can be represented as a Givens rotation. The result is that we represent $[Q^T]$ as the product of three matrices:

$$[Q^T] = [N_3]\,[N_2]\,[N_1] \tag{7.56}$$

These matrices are numbered as shown to indicate the order of application. In the case of 3 × 2 $[H]$ matrix,

$$[N_1] = \begin{bmatrix} c & s & 0 \\ -s & c & 0 \\ 0 & 0 & 1 \end{bmatrix} \tag{7.57}$$

where c and s are defined exactly as before. Next, $[N_2]$ must be calculated so as to eliminate the 31 term which results from $[N_1]$ $[H]$. The actual procedure loads $[H]$ into $[U]$ and then determines each $[N]$ based on the current contents of $[U]$. The $[N_2]$ matrix will have terms such as

$$[N_2] = \begin{bmatrix} c' & 0 & s' \\ 0 & 1 & 0 \\ -s' & 0 & c' \end{bmatrix} \tag{7.58}$$

where c' and s' are determined from $[N_1]$ $[H]$. Similarly for $[N_3]$:

$$[N_3] = \begin{bmatrix} 1 & 0 & 0 \\ 0 & c'' & s'' \\ 0 & -s'' & c'' \end{bmatrix} \tag{7.59}$$

For our zero injection example, we start with the $[H]$ and $[R]$ matrices as shown before:

$$[H] = \begin{bmatrix} 5.0 & -5.0 \\ 0 & -4.0 \\ 7.5 & -5.0 \end{bmatrix} \tag{7.60}$$

and

$$[R] = \begin{bmatrix} 10^{-4} & & \\ & 10^{-4} & \\ & & 10^{-20} \end{bmatrix} \tag{7.61}$$

Then, the $[H']$ matrix is

$$[H'] = \begin{bmatrix} 5.0 \times 10^2 & -5.0 \times 10^2 \\ 0 & -4.0 \times 10^2 \\ 7.5 \times 10^{10} & -5.0 \times 10^{10} \end{bmatrix} \tag{7.62}$$

And the measurement vector is

$$\hat{Z} = \begin{bmatrix} 32 \\ 72 \\ 0 \end{bmatrix} \tag{7.63}$$

The resulting state estimate is shown in Figure 7.6. Note particularly that the injection at bus 1 is estimated to be zero, as we desired.

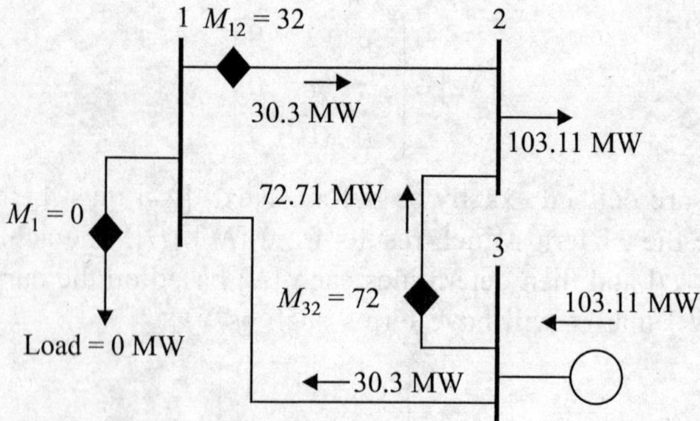

Figure 7.6 State estimate resulting from orthogonal decomposition algorithm.

The orthogonal decomposition algorithm has the advantage that measurement weights can be adjusted to the extreme values as demonstrated by the numerical example shown. As such, its robust numerical advantages have made it a useful algorithm for power system state estimators.

7.5 Detection and Identification of Bad Measurements

The ability to detect and identify bad measurements is extremely valuable to a power system's operations department. Transducers may have been wired incorrectly or the transducer itself may be malfunctioning so that it simply no longer gives accurate readings. The statistical theory required understanding and analyzing bad measurement detection and identification is straightforward but lengthy. We are going to open the door to the subject in this chapter.

To detect the presence of bad measurements, we will rely on the intuitive notion that for a given configuration, the residual, $J(x)$, calculated after the state estimator algorithm converges, will be the smallest if there are no bad measurements. When $J(x)$ is small, a vector x (i.e. voltages and phase angles) has been found that causes all calculated flows, loads, generations, and so forth to closely match all the measurements. Generally, the presence of a bad measurement value will cause the converged value of $J(x)$ to be larger than expected with $x = x^{est}$.

What magnitude of $J(x)$ indicates the presence of bad instruments?

The measurement errors are random numbers so that the value of $J(x)$ is also a random number. If we assume that all the errors are described by their respective normal probability density functions, then we can show that $J(x)$ has a probability density function known as a chi-squared distribution, which is written as $\chi^2(k)$. The parameter k is called the degrees of freedom of the chi-squared distribution. This parameter is defined as follows:

$$k = N_m - N_s \tag{7.64}$$

where N_m = number of measurements (note that $P + jQ$ measurement counts as two measurements)

N_s = number of state variables

Using the tabulated values of $X^2_{k,\alpha}$ given in Table 7.2, for example, choosing $\alpha = 0.01$ and $k = (N_m - N_s) = 2$, we can conclude that the calculated value of $\hat{f}$ is less than the critical value of 9.21 with probability (1–0.01) or 99% confidence since $X^2_{2,0.01} = 9.21$ in Table 7.2. Thus, the chi-squared distribution of $\hat{f}$ provides a test for detection of bad measurements.

Table 7.2 Chi-square distribution table

k	α			
	0.05	**0.025**	**0.01**	**0.005**
1	3.84	5.02	6.64	7.88
2	5.99	7.38	9.21	10.6
3	7.82	9.35	11.35	12.84
4	9.49	11.14	13.28	14.86
5	11.07	12.83	15.09	16.75
6	12.59	14.45	16.81	18.55
7	14.07	16.01	18.48	20.28
8	15.51	17.54	20.09	21.96
9	16.92	19.02	21.67	23.59
10	18.31	20.48	23.21	25.19

The procedure is as follows:

- Use the raw measurements Z_j from the system to determine the weighted least squares estimates $\hat{X}_i$ of the system states.
- Substitute the estimates $\hat{X}_i$ in the equation $\hat{Z} = H\hat{X}$ to calculate the estimated values $\hat{Z}_j$ of the measurements and hence the estimated errors.
- Evaluate the weighted sum of squares $\hat{f} = \sum_{j=1} N_m \frac{\hat{e}_j^2}{\sigma_j^2}$.
- For the appropriate number of degrees of freedom $k = (N_m - N_s)$ and a specified probability α, determine whether or not the values of $\hat{f}$ is less than the critical value corresponding to α. In practice, this means we check that the inequality is satisfied.

$$\hat{f} < X^2_{k,\alpha} \tag{7.65}$$

If it is, then the measured raw data and the state estimates are accepted as being accurate.

When the requirement of inequality is not met, there is reason to suspect the presence of at least one bad measurement. Upon such detection omit the measurement corresponding to the largest standardized error, namely, and reevaluate the state estimates along with the sum of squares $\hat{f}$. If the new value of $\hat{f}$ satisfies the chi-square test of inequality, then the omitted measurements has been successfully identified as the bad data point.

The sum of squares of the estimated errors will be large when bad measurements are present. Thus, detection of bad data points is readily accomplished by the chi-squared test. The identification of the particular bad data is not so easily undertaken. In practical power system applications the number of degrees of freedom is large, which allows discarding groups of measurements corresponding to the standardized errors always indicate the bad measurements, the problem of identifying the gross errors is thereby eased.

EXAMPLE 7.3 The measurement set and system model matrix is given as

$$[9.01\text{ A},\ 3.02\text{ A},\ 6.98\text{ V},\ 4.40\text{ V}] \begin{bmatrix} 0.625 & -0.125 \\ -0.125 & 0.625 \\ 0.375 & 0.125 \\ 0.125 & 0.375 \end{bmatrix}$$

Let us assign the measurement weights $w_1 = 100$, $w_2 = 100$, $w_3 = 50$ and $w_4 = 50$ respectively.

(a) Compute the weighted least square estimates of the state variables.
(b) Compute the chi-square test for $\alpha = 0.01$, identify the bad measurement if present.

Solution: $\hat{X}^{\text{est}} = [H^T WH]^{-1} H^T WZ$

$$H^T W = \begin{bmatrix} 0.625 & -0.125 & 0.375 & 0.125 \\ -0.125 & 0.625 & 0.125 & 0.375 \end{bmatrix} \begin{bmatrix} 100 & 0 & 0 & 0 \\ 0 & 100 & 0 & 0 \\ 0 & 0 & 50 & 0 \\ 0 & 0 & 0 & 50 \end{bmatrix}$$

$$= \begin{bmatrix} 62.5 & -12.5 & 18.75 & 6.25 \\ -12.5 & 62.5 & 6.25 & 18.75 \end{bmatrix}.$$

$$H^T WH = \begin{bmatrix} 62.5 & -12.5 & 18.75 & 6.25 \\ -12.5 & 62.5 & 6.25 & 18.75 \end{bmatrix} \begin{bmatrix} 0.625 & -0.125 \\ -0.125 & 0.625 \\ 0.375 & 0.125 \\ 0.125 & 0.375 \end{bmatrix}$$

$$= \begin{bmatrix} 48.4375 & -10.9375 \\ -10.9375 & 48.4375 \end{bmatrix}$$

$$G^{-1} = (H^T WH)^{-1} = \begin{bmatrix} 48.4375 & -10.9375 \\ -10.9375 & 48.4375 \end{bmatrix}^{-1} = \begin{bmatrix} 0.02175 & 0.00491 \\ 0.00491 & 0.02175 \end{bmatrix}$$

$$H^T WZ = \begin{bmatrix} 62.5 & -12.5 & 18.75 & 6.25 \\ -12.5 & 62.5 & 6.25 & 18.75 \end{bmatrix} = \begin{bmatrix} 9.01 \\ 3.02 \\ 6.98 \\ 4.40 \end{bmatrix} = \begin{bmatrix} 683.75 \\ 202.25 \end{bmatrix}$$

$$\hat{X} = G^{-1}(H^T WZ) = \begin{bmatrix} 0.02175 & 0.00491 \\ 0.00491 & 0.02175 \end{bmatrix} \begin{bmatrix} 683.75 \\ 202.25 \end{bmatrix} = \begin{bmatrix} 15.8680 \\ 7.7585 \end{bmatrix}$$

$$\hat{Z} = H\hat{X} = \begin{bmatrix} 0.625 & -0.125 \\ -0.125 & 0.625 \\ 0.375 & 0.125 \\ 0.125 & 0.375 \end{bmatrix} \begin{bmatrix} 15.8680 \\ 7.7585 \end{bmatrix} = \begin{bmatrix} 8.9476 \\ 2.8655 \\ 6.9203 \\ 4.8929 \end{bmatrix}$$

$$\hat{e} = z - \hat{z} = \begin{bmatrix} 9.01 \\ 3.02 \\ 6.98 \\ 4.4 \end{bmatrix} - \begin{bmatrix} 8.9476 \\ 2.8655 \\ 6.9203 \\ 4.8929 \end{bmatrix} = \begin{bmatrix} 0.0624 \\ 0.1545 \\ 0.0597 \\ -0.4929 \end{bmatrix}$$

chi square test for $\alpha = 0.01$
$N_m = 4; N_s = 2; k = N_m - N_s = 2$

$$\begin{aligned} f &= w_1 e_1^2 + w_2 e_2^2 + w_3 e_3^2 + w_4 e_4^2 \\ &= 100(0.0624)^2 + 100(0.1545)^2 + 50(0.0597)^2 + 50(-0.4929)^2 \\ &= 15.1021 \end{aligned}$$

The value of

$$15.1021 > (\eta(2, 0.01) = 9.21)$$

Hence we found that there is a presence of bad data.

Next, the fourth measurement error estimate is quite higher, i.e. 0.4929 and we eliminate it and the above steps have to be evaluated further

$$H = \begin{bmatrix} 0.625 & -0.125 \\ -0.125 & 0.625 \\ 0.375 & 0.125 \\ 0.125 & 0.375 \end{bmatrix}; \quad Z = \begin{bmatrix} 9.01 \\ 3.02 \\ 6.98 \end{bmatrix}$$

$$W = \begin{bmatrix} 100 & 0 & 0 \\ 0 & 100 & 0 \\ 0 & 0 & 50 \end{bmatrix}$$

$$H^T W = \begin{bmatrix} 0.625 & -0.125 & 0.375 \\ -0.125 & 0.625 & 0.125 \end{bmatrix} \begin{bmatrix} 100 & 0 & 0 \\ 0 & 100 & 0 \\ 0 & 0 & 50 \\ 0 & 0 & 0 \end{bmatrix}$$

$$= \begin{bmatrix} 62.5 & -12.5 & 18.75 \\ -12.5 & 62.5 & 6.25 \end{bmatrix}$$

$$H^T WH = \begin{bmatrix} 62.5 & -12.5 & 18.75 \\ -12.5 & 62.5 & 6.25 \end{bmatrix} \begin{bmatrix} 0.625 & -0.125 \\ -0.125 & 0.625 \\ 0.375 & 0.125 \end{bmatrix} = \begin{bmatrix} 47.656 & -13.281 \\ -13.281 & 41.406 \end{bmatrix}$$

$$G^{-1} = (H^T WH)^{-1} = \begin{bmatrix} 47.656 & -13.281 \\ -13.281 & 41.406 \end{bmatrix}^{-1} = \begin{bmatrix} 0.02304 & 0.00739 \\ 0.00739 & 0.02605 \end{bmatrix}$$

$$H^T WZ = \begin{bmatrix} 62.5 & -12.5 & 18.75 \\ -12.5 & 62.5 & 6.25 \end{bmatrix} \begin{bmatrix} 9.01 \\ 3.02 \\ 6.98 \end{bmatrix} = \begin{bmatrix} 656.25 \\ 119.75 \end{bmatrix}$$

$$\hat{X} = G^{-1}(H^T WZ) = \begin{bmatrix} 0.02304 & 0.00739 \\ 0.00739 & 0.02605 \end{bmatrix} \begin{bmatrix} 656.25 \\ 119.75 \end{bmatrix} = \begin{bmatrix} 16.0049 \\ 8.0230 \end{bmatrix}$$

$$\hat{Z} = H\hat{X} = \begin{bmatrix} 0.625 & -0.125 \\ -0.125 & 0.625 \\ 0.375 & 0.125 \end{bmatrix} \begin{bmatrix} 16.0049 \\ 8.0230 \end{bmatrix} = \begin{bmatrix} 9.0002 \\ 3.0137 \\ 7.0047 \end{bmatrix}$$

$$\hat{e} = z - \hat{z} = \begin{bmatrix} 9.01 \\ 3.02 \\ 6.98 \end{bmatrix} - \begin{bmatrix} 9.0002 \\ 3.0137 \\ 7.0047 \end{bmatrix} = \begin{bmatrix} 0.00978 \\ 0.00620 \\ -0.02474 \end{bmatrix}$$

$$f = w_1 e_1^2 + w_2 e_2^2 + w_3 e_3^2 + w_4 e_4^2$$

$$f = 100(0.00978)^2 + 100(0.00620)^2 + 50(-0.02414)^2$$

$$f = 0.0440$$

$N_m = 3$; $N_s = 2$; $k = N_m - N_s = 1$

The value of

$$0.0440 < (\eta(1, 0.01) = 6.64)$$

Hence it is confirmed that the three measurements are good data, whereas fourth measurement is a bad data.

EXAMPLE 7.4 Five meters are installed on the four-bus system of Figure 7.7 to measure line real power flows where

$x_{12} = 0.05$ p.u. $\qquad z_1 = P_{12} = 0.34$ p.u

$x_{13} = 0.1$ p.u. $\qquad z_2 = P_{13} = 0.26$ p.u.

$x_{23} = 0.04$ p.u. $\qquad z_3 = P_{23} = 0.17$ p.u.

$x_{24} = 0.0625$ p.u. $\qquad z_4 = P_{24} = -0.24$ p.u.

$x_{34} = 0.08$ p.u. $\qquad z_5 = P_{34} = -0.22$ p.u.

and the variances are the same, $\sigma = 0.01$ p.u.

(a) Compute the weighted least square estimates of the phase angle with bus 1 as the reference.

(b) Using chi square test as $\alpha = 0.01$, identify the bad measurement.

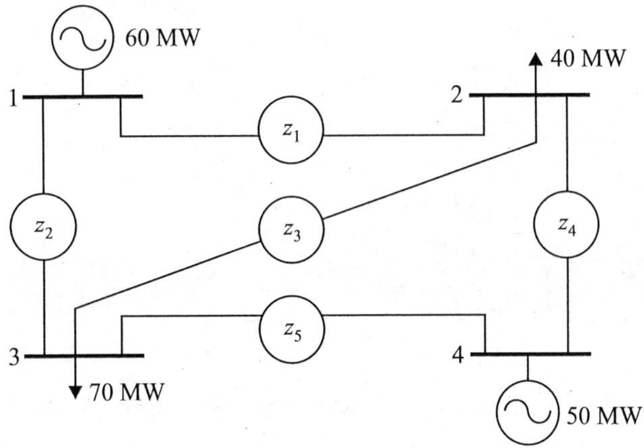

Figure 7.7 Four-bus system.

Solution:

$$P_{12} = \frac{1}{x_{12}}(\theta_1 - \theta_2) = \frac{1}{0.05}(\theta_1 - \theta_2) = -20\theta_2$$

$$P_{13} = \frac{1}{x_{13}}(\theta_1 - \theta_3) = \frac{1}{0.1}(\theta_1 - \theta_3) = -10\theta_3$$

$$P_{23} = \frac{1}{x_{23}}(\theta_2 - \theta_3) = \frac{1}{0.04}(\theta_2 - \theta_3) = 25\theta_2 - 25\theta_3$$

$$P_{24} = \frac{1}{x_{24}}(\theta_2 - \theta_4) = \frac{1}{0.0625}(\theta_2 - \theta_4) = 16\theta_2 - 16\theta_4$$

$$P_{34} = \frac{1}{x_{34}}(\theta_3 - \theta_4) = \frac{1}{0.08}(\theta_3 - \theta_4) = 12.5\theta_3 - 12.5\theta_4$$

$$\begin{bmatrix} P_{12} \\ P_{13} \\ P_{23} \\ P_{24} \\ P_{34} \end{bmatrix} = \begin{bmatrix} -20 & 0 & 0 \\ 0 & -10 & 0 \\ 25 & -25 & 0 \\ 16 & 0 & -16 \\ 0 & 12.5 & -12.5 \end{bmatrix} \begin{bmatrix} \theta_2 \\ \theta_3 \\ \theta_4 \end{bmatrix}$$

$$\hat{X}^{\text{est}} = (H^T WH)^{-1} (H^T WZ)$$

$$W = R^{-1}$$

$$R = \sigma^2 = (0.01)^2 = 10^{-4}$$

$$W = \begin{bmatrix} 10^4 & 0 & 0 & 0 & 0 \\ 0 & 10^4 & 0 & 0 & 0 \\ 0 & 0 & 10^4 & 0 & 0 \\ 0 & 0 & 0 & 10^4 & 0 \\ 0 & 0 & 0 & 0 & 10^4 \end{bmatrix}$$

$$Z = \begin{bmatrix} 0.34 \\ 0.26 \\ 0.17 \\ -0.24 \\ -0.22 \end{bmatrix}$$

$$H^T WH = \begin{bmatrix} 1281 \times 10^4 & -625 \times 10^4 & -256 \times 10^4 \\ -625 \times 10^4 & 881.25 \times 10^4 & -156.25 \times 10^4 \\ -256 \times 10^4 & -156.25 \times 10^4 & 412.25 \times 10^4 \end{bmatrix}$$

$$H^T WZ = \begin{bmatrix} -6.39 \times 10^4 \\ -9.6 \times 10^4 \\ 6.59 \times 10^4 \end{bmatrix}$$

$$\hat{X}^{\text{est}} = \begin{bmatrix} -0.01738 \\ -0.02443 \\ -2.3898 \times 10^{-3} \end{bmatrix}$$

$$\hat{e}^{\text{est}} = Z - H\hat{X} = \begin{bmatrix} -9.6 \times 10^{-3} \\ 0.01 \\ -7 \times 10^{-3} \\ -0.024 \\ 0.0302 \end{bmatrix}$$

$$f = w_1 e_1^2 + w_2 e_2^2 + w_3 e_3^2 + w_4 e_4^2 + w_5 e_5^2$$

$$= 10^4(-9.6 \times 10^{-3})^2 + 10^4(0.01)^2 + 10^4(-7 \times 10^{-3})^2 + 10^4(-0.024)^2 + 10^4(0.0302)^2$$

$$= 17.292 > \chi^2_{(2,0.01)}, \text{ i.e. } 17.292 > 11.35$$

As it is greater, therefore there is a presence of bad data. So eliminate the 5th element and proceed the above steps.

$$H^T WH = \begin{bmatrix} 1281\times10^4 & -625\times10^4 & -256\times10^4 \\ -625\times10^4 & 725\times10^4 & 0 \\ -256\times10^4 & 0 & 256\times10^4 \end{bmatrix}$$

$$H^T WZ = \begin{bmatrix} -6.39\times10^4 \\ -6.85\times10^4 \\ 3.84\times10^4 \end{bmatrix}$$

$$\hat{X}^{\text{est}} = \begin{bmatrix} -0.01748 \\ -0.024 \\ -3.979\times10^{-3} \end{bmatrix}$$

$$\hat{e}^{\text{est}} = Z - H\hat{X} = \begin{bmatrix} -7.6\times10^{-3} \\ 0.0157 \\ -6.2\times10^{-3} \\ -2\times10^{-4} \end{bmatrix}$$

$$\begin{aligned} f &= w_1 e_1^2 + w_2 e_2^2 + w_3 e_3^2 + w_4 e_4^2 \\ &= 10^4(-7.6 \times 10^{-3})^2 + 10^4(0.0157)^2 + 10^4(-6.2 \times 10^{-3})^2 + 10^4(-2 \times 10^{-4})^2 \\ &= 3.4273 > \chi^2_{(1,0.01)},\ \text{i.e. } 3.4273 < 6.6 \end{aligned}$$

Hence it is confirmed that the four measurements are good data, whereas the fifth measurement is bad data.

7.6 Network Observability and Pseudo-measurements

What happens if we continue to lose telemetry so that fewer and fewer measurements are available? Eventually, the state estimation procedure breaks down completely. Mathematically, the matrix

$$[[H]^T\ [R^{-1}]\ [H]] \tag{7.66}$$

becomes singular and cannot be inverted. There is also a very interesting engineering interpretation of this phenomenon that allows us to alter the situation so that the state estimation procedure is not completely disabled.

If we take the three-bus example used in the beginning, we note that when all three measurements are used, we have a redundant set and we can use a least-squares fit to the measurement values. If one of the measurements is lost, we have just enough measurements to calculate the states. If, however, two measurements are lost, we are in trouble. For example, suppose M_{13} and M_{32}

were lost leaving only M_{12}. If we now apply Eq. (7.27) in a straightforward manner, we get

$$M_{12} = f_{12} = \frac{1}{0.2}(\theta_1 - \theta_2) = 5\theta_1 - 5\theta_2 \quad (7.67)$$

Then

$$[H] = [5 \quad -5] \quad (7.68)$$

$$[R] = [\sigma^2_{M12}] = [0.0001]$$

and

$$\begin{bmatrix} \theta_1^{est} \\ \theta_2^{est} \end{bmatrix} = \left[\begin{bmatrix} 5 \\ -5 \end{bmatrix} [0.0001]^{-1} [5 \quad -5]\right]^{-1} [5 \quad -5][0.0001]^{-1} (0.55) \quad (7.69)$$

$$= \begin{bmatrix} 2500 & -2500 \\ -2500 & 2500 \end{bmatrix}^{-1} [5 \quad -5][0.0001]^{-1} (0.55) \quad (7.70)$$

The matrix to be inverted in Eq. (7.70) is clearly singular and, therefore, we have no way of solving for θ_1^{est} and θ_2^{est}. Why is this? The reasons become quite obvious when we look at the one-line diagram of this network as shown in Figure 7.8. With only M_{12} available, all we can say about the network is that the phase angle across line 1–2 must be 0.11 rad, but with no other information available, we cannot tell what relationship θ_1 or θ_2 has to θ_3, which is assumed to be 0 rad. If we write down the equations for the net injected power at buses 1 and 2, we have

$$P_1 = 7.5\theta_1 - 5\theta_2 \quad (7.71)$$

$$P_2 = -5\theta_1 + 9\theta_2 \quad (7.72)$$

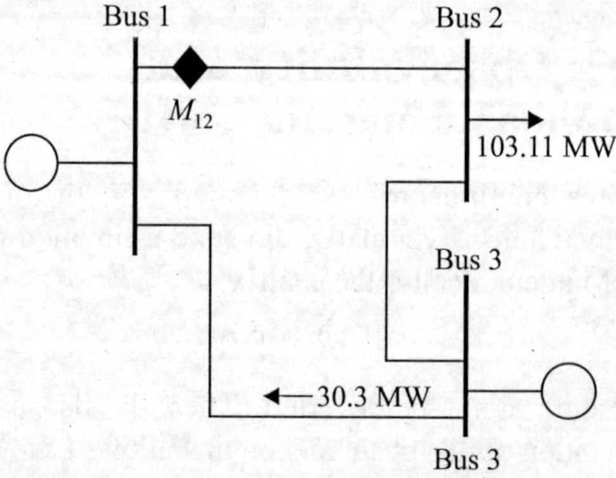

Figure 7.8 Unobservable measurement set.

If measurement M_{12} is reading 55 MW (0.55 p.u.), we have

$$\theta_1 - \theta_2 = 0.11 \quad (7.73)$$

And by substituting Eq. (7.72) and eliminating θ_1, we obtain

$$P_2 = 1.6P_1 - 1.87 \quad (7.74)$$

Furthermore,

$$P_3 = -P_1 - P_2 = -0.6P_1 + 1.87 \tag{7.75}$$

Equations (7.74) and (7.75) give a relationship between P_1, P_2, and P_3, but we still do not know their correct values. The technical term for this phenomenon is to say that the network is unobservable; that is, with only M_{12} available, we cannot observe (calculate) the state of the system.

It is very desirable to be able to circumvent this problem. Often a large power system network will have missing data that render the network unobservable. Rather than just stop the calculations, a procedure is used that allows the estimator calculation to continue. The procedure involves the use of pseudo-measurements. If we look at Eqs. (7.73)–(7.75) it is obvious that θ_1 and θ_2 could be estimated if the value of any one of the bus injections (i.e., P_1, P_2, or P_3) could be determined by some means other than the direct measurement. This value, the pseudo-measurement, is used in the state estimator just as if it were an actual measured value.

To determine the value of an injection without measuring it, we must have some knowledge about the power system beyond the measurements currently being made. For example, it is customary to have access to the generated MW and MVAR values at generating stations through telemetry channels (i.e. the generated MW and MVAR would normally be measurements available to the state estimator). If these channels are out and we must have this measurement for observability, we can probably communicate with the operators in the plant control room by telephone and ask for the MW and MVAR values and enter them into the state estimator calculation manually. Similarly, if we needed a load-bus MW and MVAR for a pseudo-measurement, we could use the historical records that show the relationship between an individual load and the the total system load. We can estimate the total system load fairly accurately by knowing the total power being generated and estimating the network losses. Finally, if we have just experienced a telemetry failure, we could use the most recently estimated values from the estimator (assuming that it is run periodically) as pseudo-measurements. Therefore, if needed, we can provide the state estimator with a reasonable value to use as pseudo-measurement at any bus in the system.

The three-bus sample system in Figure 7.9 requires one pseudo-measurement. Measurement M_{12} allows us to eliminate the voltage magnitude and phase angle at bus 2 (bus 1's voltage magnitude is measured and its phase angle is assumed

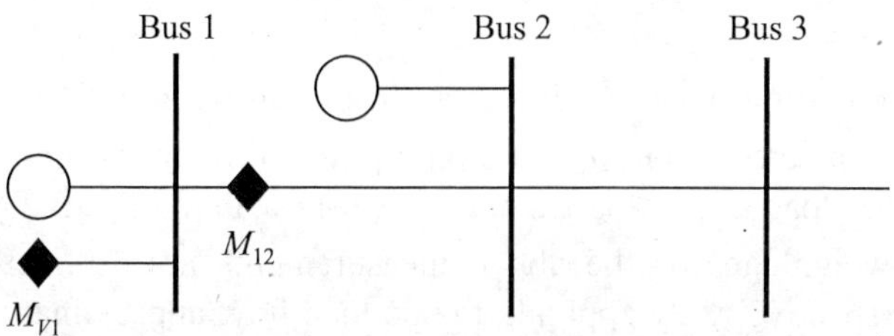

Figure 7.9 Unobservable system showing importance of location of pseudo-measurement.

to be zero). But without knowing the generation output at the generator unit on bus 2 or the load on bus 3, we cannot tell what voltage magnitude and phase angle to place on bus 3; hence, the network is unobservable. We can make this three-bus system observable by adding a pseudo-measurement of the net bus injected MW and MVAR at bus 2 or bus 3, but not bus 1. That is, a pseudo-measurement at bus 1 will do no good at all because it tells nothing about the relationship of the phase angles between bus 2 and bus 3.

When adding a pseudo-measurement to a network, we simply write the equation for the pseudo-measurement injected power as a function of bus voltage magnitudes and phase angles as if it were actually measured. However, we do not wish to have the estimator treat the pseudo-measurement the same as a legitimate measurement, since it is often quite inaccurate and is little better than a guess. To circumvent this difficulty, we assign a large standard deviation to this measurement. The large standard deviation allows the estimator algorithm to treat the pseudo-measurement as if it were a measurement from a very poor quality metering device.

Review Questions

Part-A

1. What is meant by the state estimation?
2. How do you define the network observability?
3. What are the three estimation formulas used in the state estimation?
4. What is meant by number of degrees of freedom?
5. Write the formula to determine the degrees of freedom.
6. What are the three formulas used in the state estimation based on the number of state variables and number of measurements?
7. What is the orthogonal decomposition algorithm?
8. What is the relationship between weighting matrix and covariance matrix?
9. What are the three different criteria used in the state estimation?
10. What are the bad measurements with respect to state estimation?

Part-B

1. A sample power system is shown in the figure as following.

   Power injected at bus 1 is 1.2 p.u.; power flow in the line 1–2, P_{12}, is 1.0 p.u.; load at bus 2 is 1.2 p.u.; power flow in the 3–2 is P_{32} is 0.1 p.u.

   The weightage for the above measurements are 1.0, 0.9, 0.95 and 0.2 respectively. By applying the dc load flow approximation, estimate the state of the system. Use the weighted least square method. Line reactance is marked in the figure in p.u.

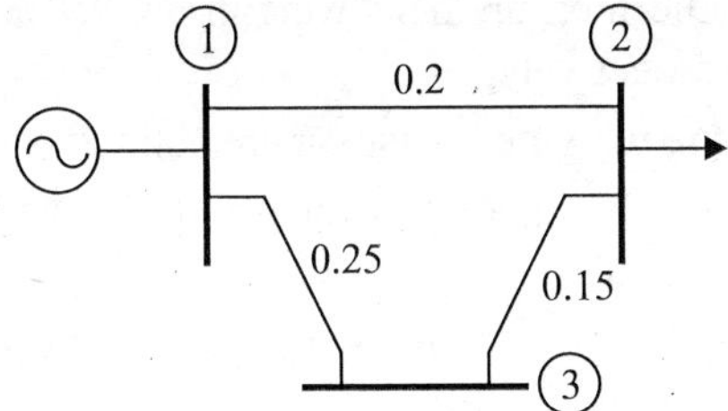

2. What is the importance of bad measurements and describe how the detection and the identification of bad measurements are done in the state estimation?
3. Explain the solution procedure for the state estimation using the weighted least square method with a suitable example.
4. Three meters are installed on the three-bus system as shown in the figure below to measure line real power flows

$X_{12} = 0.2$ p.u.;	$M_{12} = 0.6$ p.u.
$X_{13} = 0.4$ p.u.;	$M_{13} = 0.4$ p.u.
$X_{23} = 0.25$ p.u.;	$M_{23} = 0.405$ p.u.

And the variances are the same $\sigma = 0.01$ p.u.

(a) Compare the weighted least square estimates of the phase angles with bus 3 as the reference.

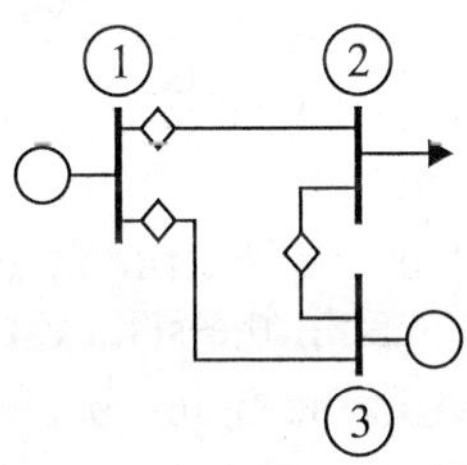

(b) Using the chi square test for $\alpha = 0.01$, identify the bad measurement, if present and use the following table:

k	$\alpha = 0.01$
1	6.64
2	9.21
3	11.35
4	13.28

5. Explain the method of least square in the state estimation problem with a suitable example.
6. The measurement set and system model matrix is given as

$$[9.01\text{ A},\ 3.02\text{ A},\ 6.98\text{ V},\ 4.40\text{ V}]\begin{bmatrix} 0.625 & -0.125 \\ -0.125 & 0.625 \\ 0.625 & 0.125 \\ 0.125 & 0.375 \end{bmatrix}$$

Let us assign the measurement weights $w_1 = 100$, $w_2 = 100$, $w_3 = 50$ and $w_4 = 50$ respectively.

(a) Compute the weighted least square estimates of the state variables.

(b) Compute the chi-square test for $\alpha = 0.01$, identify the bad measurement, if present?

7. Using the three-bus sample network assume that the three meters have the following characteristics

Meter	*Full-scale* (MW)	*Accuracy* (MW)	(p.u.)
M_{12}	100	+6	0.02
M_{13}	100	+3	0.01
M_{32}	100	+0.6	0.002

(a) Calculate the best estimate for the phase angles θ_1 and θ_2 given the following measurements.

Meter	*Measured value* (MW)
M_{12}	60.0
M_{13}	4.0
M_{32}	40.5

(b) Calculate the residual $J(X)$. For a significance level of 0.01, does $J(X)$ indicates the presence of bad data? Explain.

8. With an example explain the determination of performance of index for weighed measurements in the state estimation.

9. For the network shown in the figure below, determine

(a) the phase angles which result in a best fit to the measured values

(b) value of residual function J and

(c) estimated generators output and line flow. Assume 100 MVA base and use dc power flow model with line reactance of $X_{13} = 0.1$ p.u. and $X_{23} = 0.25$ p.u. The meters are all of the same type with a standard deviation of $\sigma = 0.01$ p.u. for each. The measured values are $M_3 = 105$ MW, $M_{32} = 98$ MW, $M_{23} = 135$ MW, $M_2 = 49$ MW and $M_{21} = 148$ MW.

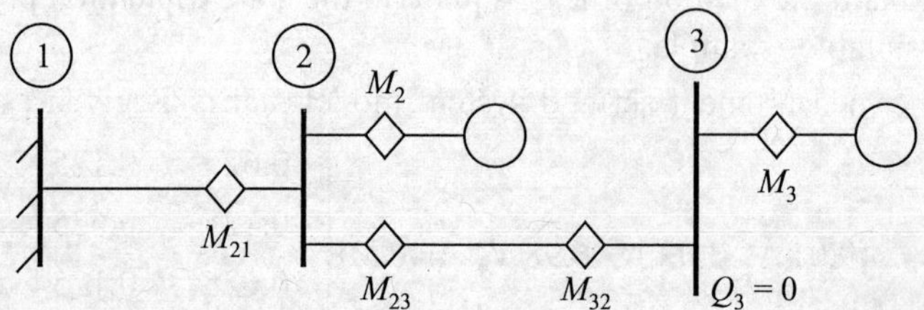

CHAPTER 8

Optimal Power Flow

8.1 Introduction

Conventionally the optimal operation and planning of power system networks have been on economic criterion. Economic load dispatch (ELD) has been utilized for this purpose and widely accepted by most of the utilities and implemented in their computer aided dispatch centres. However, the growing concerns to maintain system security, power quality and clean environment have forced to consider new objectives in the optimal operation of power system such as improvement of system voltage profile, minimum emission dispatch and security constrained dispatch. All these form the subproblems of the optimal power flow, which was first introduced by Carpentier in 1962. A large number of research efforts, since then, made in this area have followed the developments in optimization techniques and computer technology.

The optimal power flow has found two major applications.

(i) As a tool for taking planning decisions such as unit commitment, generation expansion planning and reactive power planning in the system.
(ii) As a power dispatching tool forming part of energy management system.

As a dispatching tool, the OPF has been mostly adopted by utilities for operator guidance to take off-line optimal operating decisions. However, despite number of research efforts in this area, it has found very limited application in closed loop dispatching control. Some of the reasons are the time extensive nature of existing models making them unsuitable for on-line applications and inability to consider many physical system constraints and implementation aspects.

Recently most of the power utilities, worldwide, are undergoing a major restructuring. The deregulation of electricity has introduced new open market pricing structure forcing the optimal operation philosophy of generation and transmission network to change. The OPF is finding extensive applications in the restructured market operation and bid management.

8.2 OPF Formulation

In general, the optimal power flow can be formulated as a nonlinear optimization problem used to minimize the objective function(s)

$$\text{Min. } f(\bar{X}, \bar{U}) \tag{8.1}$$

subject to system equality constraints (usually the power balance equations)

$$h(\bar{X}, \bar{U}) = 0 \tag{8.2}$$

and set of inequality constraints

$$g(\bar{X}, \bar{U}) \le 0 \tag{8.3}$$

where $\bar{X}$ is the set of state variables, $\bar{U}$ is the control variables.

The conventional OPF is solved for given measured or forecasted values of the disturbance variables, which are usually the system real and reactive power loads and these values are assumed constant during the optimization. The OPF results provide the optimum settings of the control variables. Based on the decoupling of real reactive power controls, the OPF can be classified into two broad categories.

(i) Real power (P) optimization subproblem.
(ii) Reactive power (Q) optimization subproblem.

Some of the objectives, control variables and constraints used in these two subproblems are listed in Table 8.1. Both these decoupled subproblems can be

Table 8.1 Active and reactive power subproblems of OPF

Subproblem	*Objective function*	*Controls*	*Constraints*
Active power optimization subproblem	Minimization of – Fuel cost of thermal plant – Emission of pollutants such as SO_2, NO_x, CO_x – Control shift and number of controls rescheduled.	– Generators real power output – Setting of phase angle shifters – Tie line power interchange – HVDC line power flow – Real power load shedding.	– System real power balance – Real power output limits of generators – Phase shifter angle limits – Line flow (real power) transfer limit – Turbine response rate or ramp rate – Emission limits – Contingency constraints or security limits

(*Contd...*)

Table 8.1 Active and reactive power subproblems of OPF (*Contd...*)

Subproblem	*Objective function*	*Controls*	*Constraints*
Reactive power optimization subproblem	Minimization of – Real power transmission loss – Bus voltage deviation – Control shift and number of controls rescheduled.	– Generators terminal settings voltage reactive power output – Reactive power output shunt capacitors, reactors and SVC – Transformer OLTC setting – Reactive power load shedding	– System reactive power balance – Limits on reactive power outputs of generations, SVC, shunt capacitors and reactors – Bus voltage limits – Transformer OLTC limits – Line MVAR or MVA flow limits – Security constraints (voltage security limit)

solved simultaneously as coupled OPF problem or can be solved separately or sequentially as problems. Coupled or full OPF simultaneously determines scheduling of all active and reactive power controls to minimize a global objective. This may be required in some abnormal operations or heavily stressed scenario where cross coupling of the two types of controls cannot be ignored. However, for normal operating conditions, that the decoupled formulations produce solutions that are close to the full OPF solutions. The decoupled approach offers the advantages of computational efficiency. Further it is possible to use different optimization techniques and optimization cycles for each subproblems.

A more common classification of the OPF subproblems has been based on the objective and set of controls considered. Some of these are given below.

8.2.1 Economic Load Dispatch (ELD)

A common objective utilized for ELD is the minimization of total fuel cost (F_T) of thermal power generation, i.e.

$$\text{Min. } F_T = \sum_{i=1}^{N_g} f_i(P_{Gi}) \tag{8.4}$$

where N_g = total number of thermal plants in the system and f_i is the cost characteristics of each plant expressed as function of its real power output P_{Gi}. Generally the cost characteristics of most of the plants are nonlinear, continuously nondifferentiable. However, for ease of ELD solution, it is approximated by a quadratic function given as

$$f_i = \frac{1}{2} a_i P_{Gi}^2 + biP_{Gi} + c_i \tag{8.5}$$

where a_i and b_i and c_i are the cost coefficients obtained from some regression analysis of the actual cost. The above cost minimization is subject to the equality constraints representing real power balance equation written as

$$\sum_{i=1}^{N_g} P_{Gi} - P_L - P_D = 0 \tag{8.6}$$

P_D is the total real power demand and P_L is the total system real power loss. Several loss formula are there such as B-loss formula, etc. The operating limits impose the limit on real power output of generators as well as real power flow on each or selected critical lines.

$$P_{Gi\min} \le P_{Gi} \le P_{Gi\max} \qquad i = 1, ..., N_g \tag{8.7}$$

$$F_1 \le F_{1\max} \qquad l \in \text{All line} \tag{8.8}$$

To express line flows as function of real power output of generators, distribution factors have been used.

EXAMPLE 8.1 Generation company owns three generation units that have the following cost functions:

Unit A: $15 + 1.4P_A + 0.04P_A^2$ \$/h

Unit B: $25 + 1.6P_B + 0.05P_B^2$ \$/h

Unit C: $20 + 1.8P_C + 0.02P_C^2$ \$/h

How should these units be dispatched if generation company must supply a load of 350 MW at a minimum cost?

Solution:

$$F_A = 1.5 + 1.4P_A + 0.04P_A^2$$

$$\frac{dF_A}{dP_A} = \lambda = 1.4 + 0.08P_A \tag{i}$$

$$F_B = 25 + 1.6P_B + 0.05P_B^2$$

$$\frac{dF_B}{dP_B} = \lambda = 1.6 + 0.1P_B \tag{ii}$$

$$F_C = 20 + 1.8P_C + 0.02P_C^2$$

$$\frac{dF_C}{dP_C} = \lambda = 1.8 + 0.04P_C \tag{iii}$$

$$P_A + P_B + P_C = 350 \tag{iv}$$

Equating (i), (ii) and (iii), we get

$$1.4 + 0.08P_A = 1.6 + 0.1P_B = 1.8 + 0.04P_C$$

$$P_B = \frac{0.08P_A - 0.2}{0.1} = 0.8P_A - 2$$

$$P_C = \frac{0.08P_A - 0.4}{0.04} = 2P_A - 10$$

Substituting in (iv), we get

$$P_A + 0.8P_A - 2 + 2P_A - 10 = 350$$
$$P_A = 95.3 \text{ MW}$$

Substituting P_A, we get P_B and P_C as

$$P_B = 0.8P_A - 2 = 74.2 \text{ MW}$$
$$P_C = 2P_A - 10 = 180.5 \text{ MW}$$
$$F_A = 1.5 + 1.4P_A + 0.04P_A^2 = 511.7 \text{ \$/h}$$
$$F_B = 25 + 1.6P_B + 0.05P_B^2 = 419.0 \text{ \$/h}$$
$$F_C = 20 + 1.8P_C + 0.02P_C^2 = 996.5 \text{ \$/h}$$
$$\text{Total hourly cost} = 1927.2 \text{ \$/h}$$

EXAMPLE 8.2 Consider the three-bus power system as shown in Figure 8.1. Table 8.2 below shows the data about the generators connected to the system. Calculate the unconstrained economic dispatch and the nodal prices for the loading conditions as shown in Figure 8.1.

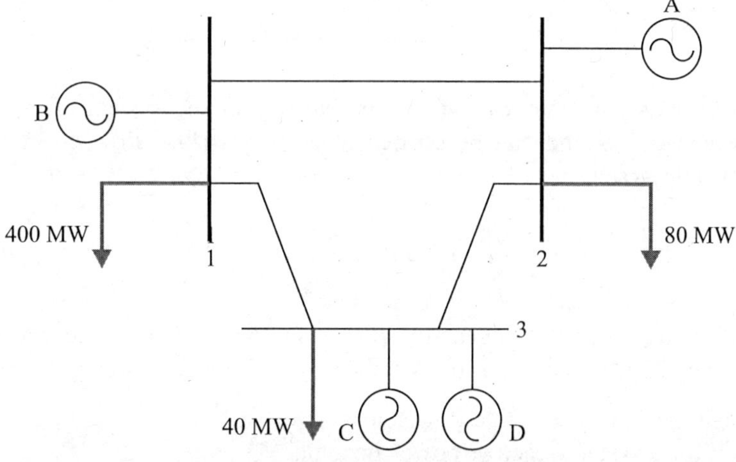

Figure 8.1 Three bus system.

Table 8.2 Generator rating with cost

Generator	*Capacity* (MW)	*Marginal cost* ($/MWh)
A	150	12
B	200	15
C	150	10
D	400	8

Solution:

Total load = 400 + 80 + 40 = 520 MW

Economic dispatch based on marginal costs

P_D = 400 MW; P_C = 120 MW; P_B = 0 MW; P_A = 0 MW.

Nodal prices for the above loading condition

$$\pi_1 = \pi_2 = \pi_3 = \pi_4 = 10 \text{ \$/MWh}$$

8.2.2 Optimal Reactive Power Dispatch (ORPD)

ORPD has recently assumed more importance due to the growing concern of utilities to power qualities in terms of acceptable voltage profile, voltage security and voltage stability of the system. Conventionally, ORPD is used to determine the optimal settings of generator voltage or its reactive output, outputs of synchronous condensers, shunt capacitor banks, transformer on load tap changer (OLTC) settings. The commonly used objectives are the minimization of total system real power loss (P_L) or the voltage deviation from its target or desired values specially at load buses, i.e.

$$\text{Min. } f_1 = P_L \tag{8.9}$$

or

$$f_2 = \sum_i (V_i - V_i \text{ des})^2 \qquad i \in \text{all load buses} \tag{8.10}$$

Subject to satisfying the reactive power balance in the system. This forms equality constraints and can be written at each bus (load flow equation) or for the whole system as

$$\sum_{i=1}^{N_q} Q_{Gi} - Q_L - Q_D = 0 \tag{8.11}$$

where N_q = total number of reactive power sources including capacitors and synchronous condensers (Q_G), transformer taps (t) and bus voltages.

Q_L = total system reactive power loss
Q_D = total system reactive power demand

The operating limits (inequality constraints) are imposed on reactive power output of sources

$$Q_{Gi\min} \le Q_{gi} \le Q_{Gi\max} \qquad i = 1, ..., N_q \tag{8.12}$$

$$V_{i\min} \le V_i \le V_{i\max} \qquad i \in \text{all buses} \tag{8.13}$$

$$t_{i\min} \le t_i \le t_{i\max} \qquad i \in \text{all transformers} \tag{8.14}$$

In addition limits on reactive power flow or total MVA flow on lines can be imposed.

Apart from real time application of ORPD, it is widely used for planning the additional reactive power sources in the system. For planning, the additional objectives such as minimization of cost of new reactive power devices and associated constraints are added in the above formulation. The reactive power planning is based on two approaches.

1. Preventive planning approach, which does not utilize rescheduling of available controls.
2. Corrective planning approach, which considers the effect of rescheduling of available reactive power sources and compensating devices before planning new sources.

8.2.3 Economic Emission Dispatch (EED)

Recently the environmental concerns have assumed a global dimension due to the effect of pollution and wasteful exploitation of natural resources seen in the form of climate change, sea-level rise, depletion of ozone layer (Greenhouse gas effect) and loss of biodiversity. Electricity production from fossil fuels is one of the major contributors to the environmental pollution. In developing countries, specially in Asia, the electricity production is increasing at a faster rate approximately 10 per cent per year in the past two decades. Fossil fuel provide about 64% of the global electricity product, with coal alone accounting for about 40%. A world bank report estimates that, under an 'unchanged practice' scenario, i.e. one in which control technologies are not widely implemented, emission of pollutants from fossil fuel generation of electric power will increase fourfold in the next 20 years and tenfold in the next 40 years.

The use of fossil fuel in thermal power plants emits CO_2, NO_x and SO_2 pollutants, fly ash and the particulates. To control pollution from generating plants, apart from some hard measure such as using precipitators, desulphurization and gas cleaning plants, optimal dispatching controls of generators can provide an economical solution. Economic emission dispatch is a real power optimization subproblem of OPF, combined with ELD formulation given in the previous section. If E_j represents total emission of a type-j given as

$$E_j = \sum_{i=1}^{N_q} E_{ji}(Q_{Gj}) \tag{8.15}$$

The objective function used in EED formulation with only one type of emission is considered as

$$\text{Min. } f = W.F + (1 - W)E_j \tag{8.16}$$

where W is some weighting factor varying between 0 and 1. A trade-off curve between total cost and emission can be obtained. If more than one emission type is considered, the combined objective can be defined as

$$\text{Min. } f' = F_T = W_j \cdot E_j + W_k \cdot E_k + W_m \cdot E_m \tag{8.17}$$

The NO_X, SO_2 and CO_2 emission characteristics of each plant is generally derived from its heat rate curve and depends on the type of fuel(s) used, its combustion characteristics, etc. For the sake of simplicity, many works have considered these as quadratic function of real power output of generator (similar to the cost characteristics)

$$E_i = \alpha_i + \beta_i P_{Gi} + \frac{1}{2}\gamma P_{Gi}^2 \tag{8.18}$$

where α, β, γ are the emission coefficients. A more accurate modelling can be achieved by using third or higher order polynomial fit or exponential terms such as for NO_X modelling used.

$$E_i = \alpha_i + \beta_i P_{Gi} + \frac{1}{2}\gamma P_{Gi}^2 + k_i \exp.(m_i \cdot P_{Gi}) \tag{8.19}$$

where k_i and m_i are the additional coefficients.

In order to limit the pollution from individual plants and their cumulative value in a region, certain countries are imposing regulations, such as U.S. Clean Air Act amendment of 1990. In order to meet such requirements through EED, additional constraint can be included in the model. For example, total emission of type-j can be limited to maximum value $E_{j\max}$ by the following constraint.

$$E_j = \sum_{i=1}^{N_q} E_{ji}(Q_{Gj}) \quad \le E_{j\max} \tag{8.20}$$

8.2.4 Security Constrained OPF (SCOPF)

The traditional notion of security has been based on preventive control. Full SCOPF tries to find optimal feasible solution not only for a base configuration but also for all credible contingencies. For example, security constrained ELD should utilize equations to be solved for each post contingency conditions. Such a contingency constrained OPF involves the following steps.

1. Solve base case OPF without any contingency constraint.
2. Perform contingency screening to identify the critical contingencies.
3. For each critical contingency, perform ac power flow and identify the contingency constraints.
4. Run off including all contingency constraints.
5. Repeat steps 3 and 4 till convergence is achieved.

From the above it can be observed that full SCOPF is extremely time consuming and achieving its solution in real time is still a challenge. Moreover, full SCOPF results sacrifice the main economic criteria. Sometimes the SCOPF solution may become infeasible specially for the most severe contingencies. Many improved methods have been suggested to reduce computational time. Since full SCOPF formulation is very conservative and allows no room for post-contingency corrective actions, it is suggested that system should operate in 'Correctively Secure' state utilizing corrective control actions only when contingency takes place to satisfy the contingency constraints.

8.3 OPF Solution Technique

The optimal power flow is a very large and very difficult mathematical programming problem. Almost every mathematical programming approach that can be applied to this problem has been attempted and it has taken developers many decades to develop computer codes that will solve the OPF problem reliably.

The optimal power flow is essentially a nonlinear optimization problem. Various optimization techniques utilized to solve the OPF and its subproblems can be grouped as follows.

1. Nonlinear programming (NLP) methods: There are several methods for the solution of nonlinear programs. Indeed, even within a particular method, variations exist which make an algorithm more efficient, or particularly suited, for a class of problems. It is not possible to describe all the methods and their variations in a book where the emphasis is on the practical use of algorithms and software. Therefore, it is sufficient to say that methods are classified into two broad categories: direct methods and indirect methods. Indirect methods, by themselves, are many, including the penalty function methods. Among the penalty function methods, the Lagrangian multiplier method is widely used and discussed in this chapter.
2. Linear programming (LP) methods: It is one of the fully developed methods now in common use which easily handles inequality constraints. Nonlinear objective functions and constraints are handled by linearization.
3. Interior point (IP) methods: It is the another fully developed and widely used methods for OPF which easily handles inequality constraints.

8.4 Lagrange Multiplier Method

Consider the following minimization problem.
Select an m vector x to

$$\text{Minimize } f(x) \tag{8.21}$$

subject to n inequality conditions

$$g_i(x) \le k_i \qquad i = 1, 2, ..., n \tag{8.22}$$

where k_i is a constant, $-\infty \le k_i \le \infty$, and $i = 1, 2, ..., n$ and p equality conditions

$$h_j(x) = 0 \qquad j = 1, 2, ..., p \tag{8.23}$$

1. The inequality constraints can be transformed to

$$g_i(x) \le 0 \qquad i = 1, 2, ..., n \text{ by transferring } k \text{ to the left-hand side.} \tag{8.24}$$

2. We convert all constraints to equalities by adding nonnegative slack variable z_i^2

$$g_i(x, z) = g_i(x) + z_i^2 = 0 \qquad i = 1, 2, ..., n \tag{8.25}$$

In the vector form representation

$$g(x, z) = g(x) + z^2 = 0 \tag{8.26}$$

Applying Kuhn–Tucker conditions

Consider the problem of finding the m vector x which minimizes $f(x)$, subject to n inequalities and p equalities expressed as $h_k(x)$, $k = 1, 2, ..., n + p$, where p inequalities have been converted to equalitites by adding variables z.

The Lagrange function corresponding to this problem is given by

$$L = f(x) + \sum_{k=1}^{n+p} \lambda_k h_k(x) \tag{8.27}$$

where λ_k is the Lagrange multiplier of the kth constraint.

The Kuhn–Tucker necessary conditions give

$$\nabla L = \nabla f(x) + \sum_{k=1}^{n+p} \lambda_k \nabla h_k(x) = 0 \tag{8.28}$$

and

$$h_k(x) = 0 \qquad k = 1, ..., n + p \tag{8.29}$$

The above equation can be written as $\nabla f + |G|^T \lambda = 0$ (8.30)
where G is a $m\ x(n + p)$ matrix whose ith column denotes the gradient of the ith constraint h_i. The above equations represent $m + n + p$ nonlinear equations in $m + n + p$ unknowns (x_i, $i = 1, 2, ..., m$ and λ_k, $k = 1, 2, ..., n + p$). These nonlinear equations can be solved using the Jacobian matrix method and written in more compact form as

$$F(z) = 0$$

$$F = \begin{Bmatrix} \nabla L \\ h \end{Bmatrix}_{(m+n+p)} \qquad z = \begin{Bmatrix} x \\ \lambda \end{Bmatrix}_{(m+n+p)} \qquad 0 = \begin{Bmatrix} 0 \\ 0 \end{Bmatrix}_{(m+n+p)} \tag{8.31}$$

with the dimensions of vectors indicated by subscripts.

Starting from an assumed value of $z^{(j)}$ in iteration j, corrections $\Delta z^{(j)}$ to obtain $z^{(j+1)}$ are obtained by using the Jacobian matrix method as follows. The corrections $\Delta z^{(j)}$ in

$$z^{(j+1)} = z^{(j)} + \Delta z^{(j)} \tag{8.32}$$

are given by

$$j\Delta z^{(j)} = \text{error} = 0 - F(z^{(j)}) \tag{8.33}$$

Since $J = [\nabla F]^T$, from the above, we get

$$[\nabla F]_j^T \Delta z^{(j)} = -F(z^{(j)}) \tag{8.34}$$

where $[\nabla F] = [\nabla F(z^{(j)})]$ is the Jacobian matrix of the nonlinear equations whose ith column represents the gradient of the ith nonlinear equation $F_i(z)$ with respect to the $(m + n + p)$ vector z. A substitution of the above equations into the previous equation yields

$$\begin{bmatrix} [\nabla^2 L] & [G] \\ [G]^T & [0] \end{bmatrix}^{(i)} \begin{bmatrix} \Delta x^{(j)} \\ \Delta \lambda^{(j)} \end{bmatrix} = -\begin{bmatrix} \nabla L \\ h \end{bmatrix}^{(j)} \tag{8.35}$$

where $[\nabla^2 L]_{m+n}$ is the Hessian matrix of the Lagrange function with m design variables and n variables z_n^2 arising from n inequalities. The algorithm to obtain the successive iterates of x and the Lagrange multiplier λ is

$$x^{(j+1)} = x^{(j)} + \Delta x^{(j)}$$

$$\lambda^{(j+1)} = \lambda^{(j)} + \Delta \lambda^{(j)}$$

Note: See Appendix for MATLAB program for Lagrange Multiplier Method (Section A.1).

The following example will clarify the procedure.

EXAMPLE 8.3 Minimize

$$f(x_1, x_2) = 0.25x_1^2 + x_2^2$$

subject to

$$h_1(x_1, x_2) = 5 - x_1 - x_2 = 0$$

and

$$g(x_1, x_2) = x_1 + 0.2x_2 - 3 \le 0$$

Solution: We transform all constraints to equalities by adding slack variable x_3^2 as

$$h_1(x_1, x_2) = 5 - x_1 - x_2 = 0$$

and

$$h_2(x_1, x_2) = g(x_1, x_2) = x_1 + 0.2x_2 - 3 + x_3^2 = 0$$

We now solve for x_1, x_2, x_3, λ_1 and λ_2 as follows.

Since

$$L = 0.25x_1^2 + x_2^2 + \lambda_1[5 - x_1 - x_2] + \lambda_2[x_1 + 0.2x_2 - 3 + x_3^2]$$

We have

$$\nabla L = \begin{bmatrix} 0.5x_1 - \lambda_1 + \lambda_2 \\ 2x_2 - \lambda_1 + 0.2\lambda_2 \\ 2\lambda_2 x_3 \end{bmatrix} = \nabla f + G\lambda$$

$$\nabla^2 L = \begin{bmatrix} 0.5 & 0 & 0 \\ 0 & 2 & 0 \\ 0 & 0 & 2\lambda_2 \end{bmatrix}$$

and G as

$$G = \begin{bmatrix} -1 & 1 \\ -1 & 0.2 \\ 0 & 2x_3 \end{bmatrix}$$

$$\begin{bmatrix} [\nabla^2 L] & [G] \\ [G]^T & [0] \end{bmatrix}^{(j)} \begin{bmatrix} \Delta x^{(j)} \\ \lambda^{(j+i)} \end{bmatrix} = -\begin{bmatrix} \Delta L \\ h \end{bmatrix}^{(j)}$$

$$J = \begin{bmatrix} [\nabla^2 L] & [G] \\ [G]^T & [0] \end{bmatrix}^{(j)}$$

Initial point assume all the values (x_1, x_2, x_3, λ_1, λ_2) as 1.

Iteration 1:

$$\nabla f = \begin{bmatrix} 0.5\times 1 & 0 & 0 \\ 0 & 2\times 2 & 0 \\ 0 & 0 & 0 \end{bmatrix} = \begin{bmatrix} 0.5 & 0 & 0 \\ 0 & 2 & 0 \\ 0 & 0 & 0 \end{bmatrix}$$

$$G = \begin{bmatrix} -1 & 1 \\ -1 & 0.2 \\ 0 & 2 \end{bmatrix}$$

$$\nabla L = \begin{bmatrix} 0.5 \\ 1.2 \\ 2 \end{bmatrix}; \qquad h = \begin{bmatrix} 3 \\ -0.8 \end{bmatrix}$$

$$\text{Jacobian matrix } J = \begin{bmatrix} 0.5 & 0 & 0 & -1 & 1 \\ 0 & 2 & 0 & -1 & 0.2 \\ 0 & 0 & 2 & 0 & 2 \\ -1 & -1 & 0 & 0 & 0 \\ 1 & 0.2 & 2 & 0 & 0 \end{bmatrix}$$

The inverse of the Jacobian matrix is given below

$$\begin{bmatrix} 0.35461 & -0.35461 & -0.14184 & -0.68085 & 0.14184 \\ -0.35461 & 0.35461 & 0.14184 & -0.31915 & -0.14184 \\ -0.14184 & 0.14184 & 0.05674 & 0.37234 & 0.44326 \\ -0.68085 & -0.31915 & 0.37234 & -0.71277 & -0.37234 \\ 0.14184 & -0.14184 & 0.44326 & -0.37234 & -0.44326 \end{bmatrix}$$

Δx and $\Delta \lambda$ at the end of iteration 1

$$\begin{bmatrix} 2.68794 \\ 0.31206 \\ -0.97518 \\ 1.81915 \\ -0.02482 \end{bmatrix}$$

After four iterations

$$x_1 = 2.5$$
$$x_2 = 2.5$$
$$x_3 = 2.03 \times 10^{-6}$$
$$\lambda_1 = 5.9375$$
$$\lambda_2 = 4.6875$$

EXAMPLE 8.4 Minimise $f(x_1, x_2, x_3) = 4x_1^2 + 3x_2^2 + 5x_3^2 - 6x_1x_2 + x_1x_3 + 15$. Subject to one inequality ($n = 1$) and two equalities ($p = 2$) as follows.

$$g(x) = x_1^2 + x_3^2 - 30 \le 0$$
$$h_2(x) = 2x_1 + 3x_2^2 + x_3 - 8 = 0$$
$$h_3(x) = 4x_1 + 5x_2 - x_3^3 - 9 = 0$$

Solution: We first add a nonnegative slack variable x_4^2 to the inequality to convert it to an equality constraint $h_1(x) = x_1^2 + x_3^2 - 30 + x_4^2 = 0$

Lagrangian is given by

$$L = [4x_1^2 + 3x_2^2 + 5x_3^2 - 6x_1x_2 + x_1x_3 + 15] + \lambda_1[x_1^2 + x_3^2 - 30 + x_4^2]$$
$$+ \lambda_2[2x_1 + 3x_2^3 + x_3 - 8] + \lambda_3[4x_1 + 5x_2 - x_3^3 - 9]$$

Kuhn–Tucker necessary condition requires that the gradient of the Lagrangain with respect to four choice variables $x_1, \ldots, x_4$ is zero

$$\nabla L = \begin{bmatrix} 8x_1 - 6x_2 + x_3 + 2\lambda_1 x_1 + 2\lambda_2 + 4\lambda_3 \\ 6x_2 - 6x_1 + 6x_2\lambda_2 + 5\lambda_3 \\ 10x_3 + x_1 + 2\lambda_1 x_3 + \lambda_2 - 3\lambda_3 x_3^2 \\ 2\lambda_1 x_4 \end{bmatrix} = 0$$

The above equation can be written as

$$\nabla f + [G]\lambda = 0$$

$$\nabla f = \begin{bmatrix} 8x_1 - 6x_2 + x_3 \\ 6x_2 - 6x_1 \\ 10x_3 + x_1 \end{bmatrix}$$

$$G = \begin{bmatrix} \frac{\partial h_1}{\partial x_1} & \frac{\partial h_2}{\partial x_1} & \frac{\partial h_3}{\partial x_1} \\ \frac{\partial h_1}{\partial x_2} & \frac{\partial h_2}{\partial x_2} & \frac{\partial h_3}{\partial x_2} \\ \frac{\partial h_1}{\partial x_3} & \frac{\partial h_2}{\partial x_3} & \frac{\partial h_3}{\partial x_3} \\ \frac{\partial h_1}{\partial x_4} & \frac{\partial h_2}{\partial x_4} & \frac{\partial h_3}{\partial x_4} \end{bmatrix} = \begin{bmatrix} 2x_1 & 2 & 4 \\ 0 & 6x_2 & 5 \\ 2x_3 & 1 & -3x_3^2 \\ 2x_4 & 0 & 0 \end{bmatrix}$$

$$J = \begin{bmatrix} [\nabla^2 L] & [G] \\ [G]^T & [0] \end{bmatrix}^{(j)}$$

$$J = \begin{bmatrix} 8+2\lambda_1 & -6 & 1 & 0 & 2x_1 & 2 & 4 \\ -6 & 6+6\lambda_2 & 0 & 0 & 0 & 6x_2 & 5 \\ 1 & 0 & 10+2\lambda_2 - 6\lambda_3 x_3 & 0 & 2x_3 & 1 & -3x_3^2 \\ 0 & 0 & 0 & 2\lambda_1 & 2x_4 & 0 & 0 \\ 2x_1 & 0 & 2x_3 & 2x_4 & 0 & 0 & 0 \\ 2 & 6x_2 & 1 & 0 & 0 & 0 & 0 \\ 4 & 5 & -3x_3^2 & 0 & 0 & 0 & 0 \end{bmatrix}$$

Initial point assume all the values (x_1, x_2, x_3, x_4, λ_1, λ_2, λ_3) as 1.

Iteration 1:

$$\begin{bmatrix} 10 & -6 & 1 & 0 & 2 & 2 & 4 \\ -6 & 12 & 0 & 0 & 0 & 6 & 5 \\ 1 & 0 & 6 & 0 & 2 & 1 & -3 \\ 0 & 0 & 0 & 2 & 2 & 0 & 0 \\ 2 & 0 & 2 & 2 & 0 & 0 & 0 \\ 2 & 6 & 1 & 0 & 0 & 0 & 0 \\ 4 & 5 & -3 & 0 & 0 & 0 & 0 \end{bmatrix} \begin{bmatrix} \Delta x \\ \Delta\lambda \end{bmatrix} = -\begin{bmatrix} 11 \\ 11 \\ 11 \\ 2 \\ -27 \\ -2 \\ -1 \end{bmatrix}$$

Δx and $\Delta\lambda$ at the end of iteration 1

$$\begin{bmatrix} 1.3709 \\ -0.2917 \\ 1.0084 \\ 11.1207 \\ -12.1207 \\ 1.3599 \\ -1.4867 \end{bmatrix}$$

After 8 iteration the outputs are

$$x_1 = 0.3304, \quad x_2 = 1.5384, \quad x_3 = 0.2391, \quad x_4 = 5.4620,$$
$$\lambda_1 = 3.87 \times 10^{-7}, \quad \lambda_2 = -2.2559, \quad \lambda_3 = 2.7150$$

8.5 Linear Programming OPF (LPOPF)

The gradient and Newton methods of solving an OPF suffer from the difficulty in handling inequality constraints. Linear programming, however, is very adept at handling inequality constraints, as long as the problem to be solved is such that it can be linearized without loss of accuracy.

Figure 8.2 shows the type of strategy used to create an OPF using linear programming. The power flow equations could be for the dc representation,

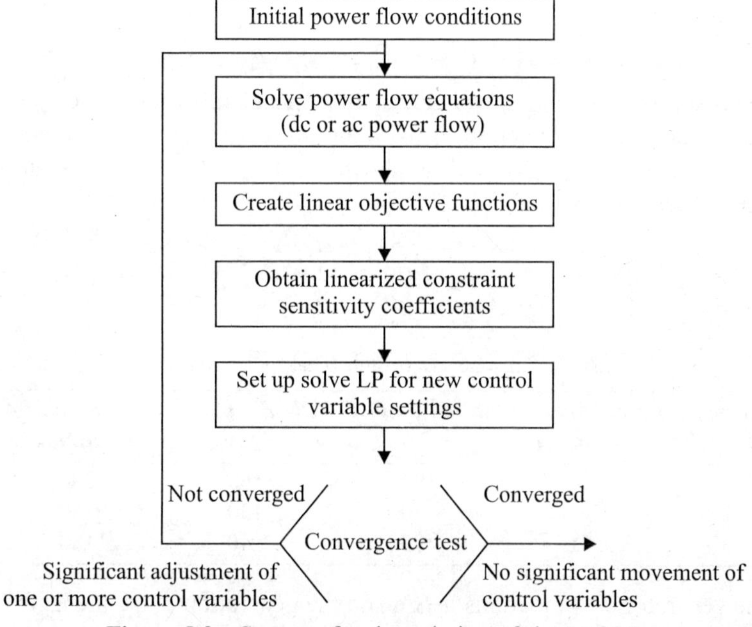

Figure 8.2 Strategy for the solution of the LPOPF.

the decoupled set of ac equations, or the full ac power flow equations. The choice will affect the difficulty of obtaining the linearized sensitivity coefficients and the convergence test used.

In the formulation below, we show how the OPF can be structured as linear programming. First, we tackle the problem of expressing the nonlinear input–output or cost functions as a set of linear functions. Let the constant function be $F_i(P_i)$ as shown in Figure 8.3.

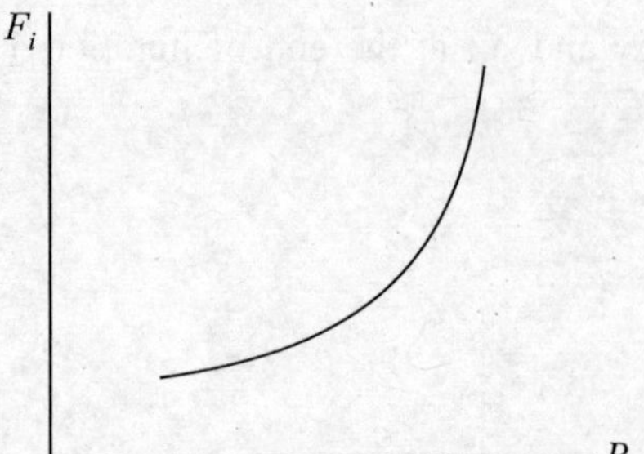

Figure 8.3 A nonlinear cost function characteristic.

We can approximate this nonlinear function as a series of straight line segments as shown in Figure 8.4. The three segments shown will be represented as P_{i1}, P_{i2}, P_{i3} and each segment will have a slope designated: S_{i1}, S_{i2}, S_{i3}. Then the cost function itself is

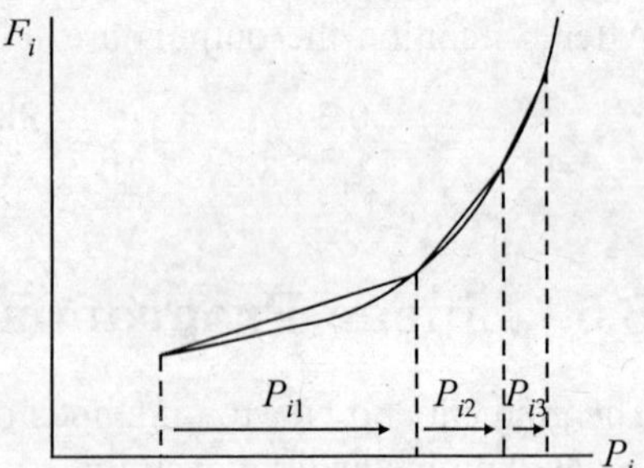

Figure 8.4 A linearized cost function.

$$F_i(P_i) = F_i(P_i^{\min}) + S_{i1}P_{i1} + S_{i2}P_{i2} + S_{i3}P_{i3} \tag{8.36}$$

and

$$0 \le P_{ik} \le P_{ik}^{+} \quad \text{for } k = 1, 2, 3 \tag{8.37}$$

and finally

$$P_i = P_i^{\min} + P_{i1} + P_{i2} + P_{i3} \tag{8.38}$$

The cost function is *m* is now made up of a linear expression in the P_{ik} values.

The generators cost functions broken into three straight line segments such that the break points are located as shown in Table 8.3. The generator cost function slopes are computed as follows.

$$S_{if} = \frac{F_i(P_{ij}^{+}) - F_i(P_{ij}^{-})}{P_{ij}^{+} - P_{ij}^{-}} \tag{8.39}$$

Table 8.3 Generator unit break point MWs

Unit	*Break point 1 (unit min.)*	*Break point 2*	*Break point 3*	*Break point 4 (unit max.)*
1	50	100	160	200
2	37.5	70	130	150
3	45	90	140	180

The generator cost functions in \$/h and the generation limits are as follows:

$$F_1(P_1) = 0.00533P_1^2 + 11.669P_1 + 213.1; \quad 50 \text{ MW} \le P_1 \le 200 \text{ MW}$$

$$F_2(P_2) = 0.00889P_2^2 + 10.333P_2 + 200; \quad 37.5 \text{ MW} \le P_2 \le 150 \text{ MW}$$

$$F_3(P_3) = 0.00741P_3^2 + 10.833P_3 + 240; \quad 45 \text{ MW} \le P_3 \le 180 \text{ MW}$$

The generator cost curve segments are obtained using the above equations and given in Table 8.4.

Table 8.4 Generator cost curve segment slope

Generator	S_{i1}	S_{i2}	S_{i3}
1	12.4685	13.0548	13.5875
2	11.2887	12.1110	12.8222
3	11.8333	12.5373	13.2042

The LP cost function is

$$\begin{aligned}[F_1(P_1^{\min}) + 12.4685P_{11} + 13.0548P_{12} + 13.5875P_{13}]\\ + [F_2(P_2^{\min}) + 11.2887P_{21} + 12.1110P_{22} + 12.8222P_{23}]\\ + [F_3(P_3^{\min}) + 11.8333P_{31} + 12.5373P_{32} + 13.2042P_{33}]\end{aligned}$$

Since the $F_i(P_i^{\min})$ terms are constant, we can drop them in the LP. Then the cost function becomes

$$\begin{aligned}[12.4685P_{11} + 13.0548P_{12} + 13.5875P_{13}] + [11.2887P_{21} + 12.1110P_{22}\\ + 12.8222P_{23}] + [11.8333P_{31} + 12.5373P_{32} + 13.2042P_{33}]\end{aligned}$$

The generation, load and losses equality constraint is

$$P_1 + P_2 + P_3 = P_{\text{load}} + P_{\text{losses}}$$

The load is 210 MW and the losses from the initial power flow are 7.87 MW. Substituting the equivalent expression for each generator output in terms of its three linear segments, we obtain:

$$\begin{aligned}P_1^{\min} + P_{11} + P_{12} + P_{13} + P_2^{\min} + P_{21} + P_{22} + P_{23} + P_3^{\min} + P_{31} + P_{32} + P_{33}\\ = P_{\text{load}} + P_{\text{losses}}\end{aligned}$$

This results in the following after $P_1^{\min}$, P_{load} and P_{losses} values are substituted:

$$\begin{aligned}P_{11} + P_{12} + P_{13} + P_{21} + P_{22} + P_{23} + P_{31} + P_{32} + P_{33}\\ = 210 + 7.87 - 50 - 37.5 - 45 = 85.37\end{aligned}$$

We now solve the LP with the cost function and equality constraint given above, and with the six variables representing the generator outputs. The solution to the LP is shown in Table 8.5.

The total generation on each generator is

$$P_i = P_i^{\min} + P_{i1} + P_{i2} + P_{i3}$$

then the generator optimal outputs are $P_1 = 50$ MW, $P_2 = 77.87$ MW and $P_3 = 90$ MW.

Table 8.5 LP solution

Variable	*Min.* MW	*Solution* MW	*Max.* MW
P_{11}	0	0	50
P_{12}	0	0	60
P_{13}	0	0	40
P_{21}	0	32.5	32.5
P_{22}	0	7.87	60
P_{23}	0	0	20
P_{31}	0	45	45
P_{32}	0	0	50
P_{33}	0	0	40

8.6 Interior Point Method

The new projective scaling algorithm for linear programming developed by N. Karmarker has caused quite stir in the optimization community partly because the speed advantage gained by this method (for large problem) is reported to be as much as 50:1 when compared to the simplex method. This Interior Point method (Karmarker algorithm) has a polynomial bound on worst case running time that is better than ellipsoid algorithms.

Karmarker's algorithm is significantly different from George Dantzig's simplex method that solves a linear programming problem starting with one extreme point along the boundary of the feasible region and skips to a better neighbouring extreme point along the boundary, finally stopping at an optimal extreme point. Karmarker's interior point rarely visits very many points before an optimal point is found. The IP method stays in the interior of the polytope and tries to position a current solution as the "centre of the universe" in finding a better direction for the next move. By properly choosing the step lengths, an optimal solution is achieved after a number of iterations. Although this IP approach requires more computational time in finding a moving direction than the traditional simplex method, a better moving direction is achieved resulting in fever iterations. Therefore, the IP approach has become a major rival of the simplex method and is attracting in the optimization community.

Figure 8.5 illustrates how the two methods approach an optimal solution. In this problem, the projective scaling algorithm requires approximately the same amount of iterations as the simplex method. However, for a large problem, this method only requires a fraction of the number of iterations that the simplex method would require.

A major theoretical attraction of the projective scaling method is its superior worst case running time. Assume that the size of a problem is defined as the number of bits N required to represent the problem in a computer. If an algorithm's running time on a computer is never greater than some fixed

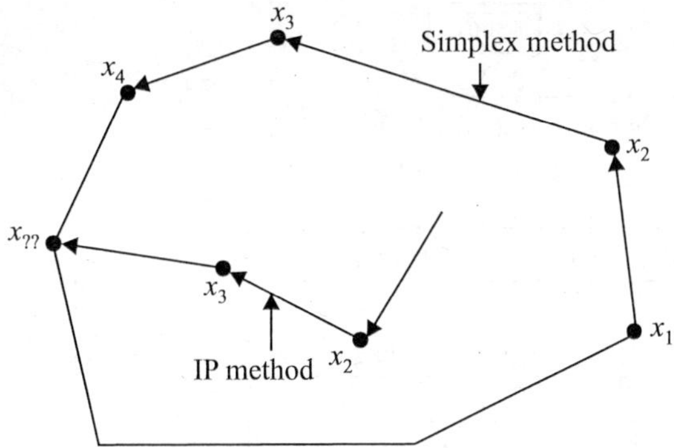

Figure 8.5 Illustration of interior point method.

power of N, no matter what problem is solved, the algorithm is said to have polynomial worst case running time. The new projective scaling method is such an algorithm.

Due to results of, several variants of interior points have been proposed such as the affine scaling method which is discussed in this chapter. Affine scaling methods have no known polynomial time complexity, and can require an exponential number of iterations if they are started close to the boundary of the feasible region. It has also been shown that these methods can make it difficult to recover dual solutions and prove optimality when there is degeneracy. However, these methods do work well in practice. Very recently, a polynomial time bound for a primal-dual affine method has been obtained.

As mentioned above, since Karmarker's discovery of the interior point method and its reported speed advantage obtained over other traditionally used methods, many variants of the IP method have evolved in an attempt to solve the above posed problems. Of these the projective scaling, the dual and primal affine methods, and the barrier function method are the most popular. An algorithm for the IP method is given with a flow chart as shown in Figure 8.6.

Note: See Appendix for MATLAB program for interior point method (Section A.2.)

EXAMPLE 8.5 Solve the constrained problem using the interior point method Maximize

$$Z = x_1 + 2x_2$$

Subject to:

$$x_1 + x_2 + x_3 \leq 8$$
$$x_j \geq 0$$

Solution: Based on the above flow chart, we can say that $Z = x_1 + 2x_2 = C^t x \Rightarrow C^t = [1 \;\; 2 \;\; 0]$ as $x = [x_1, x_2, x_3]^t$

Subject to:

$$Ax = b \quad \Rightarrow \quad A = [1 \quad 1 \quad 1]$$

We are going to take $\alpha = 0.7$, $\varepsilon = 0.1$.

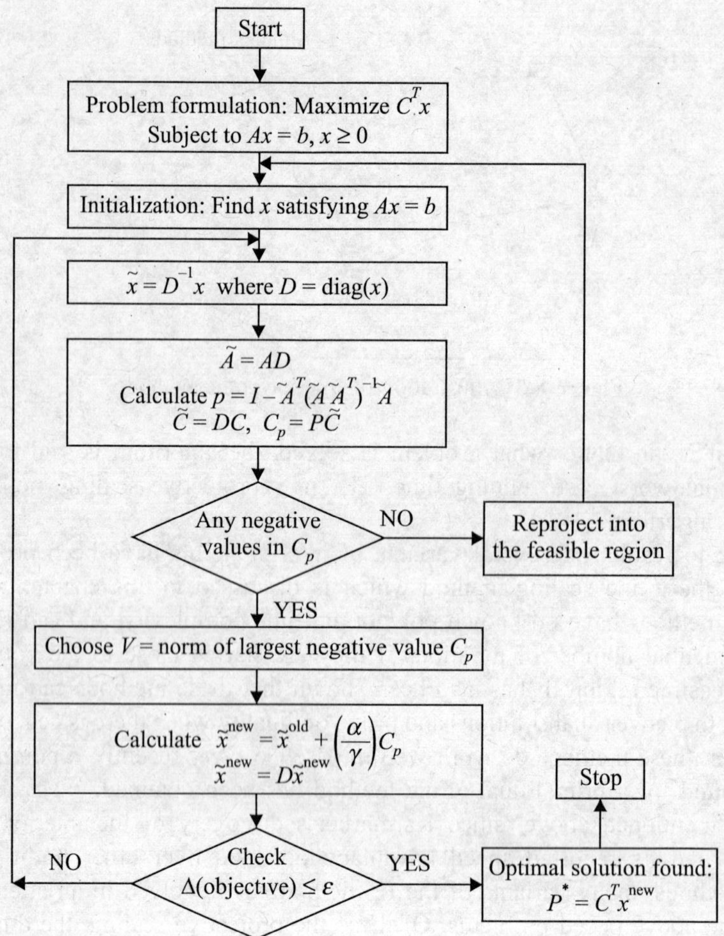

Figure 8.6 Algorithm for the interior point method.

First iteration: As an initial point, we start by $x = [1, 1, 2]^t$. Substitute in the objective function,

$$Z = C^t x = [1 \;\; 2 \;\; 0]\begin{bmatrix} 1 \\ 1 \\ 2 \end{bmatrix} = 3.0$$

$$D = \text{diag}(x) = \begin{bmatrix} 1 & 0 & 0 \\ 0 & 1 & 0 \\ 0 & 0 & 2 \end{bmatrix}$$

$$\tilde{x} = D^{-1}x = \begin{bmatrix} 1 & 0 & 0 \\ 0 & 1 & 0 \\ 0 & 0 & 2 \end{bmatrix}^{-1}\begin{bmatrix} 1 \\ 1 \\ 2 \end{bmatrix} = \begin{bmatrix} 1 & 0 & 0 \\ 0 & 1 & 0 \\ 0 & 0 & 0.5 \end{bmatrix}\begin{bmatrix} 1 \\ 1 \\ 2 \end{bmatrix} = \begin{bmatrix} 1 \\ 1 \\ 1 \end{bmatrix}$$

$$\tilde{A} = AD = [1 \ \ 1 \ \ 1]\begin{bmatrix} 1 & 0 & 0 \\ 0 & 1 & 0 \\ 0 & 0 & 2 \end{bmatrix} = [1 \ \ 1 \ \ 2]$$

The projection area P,

$$P = I - \tilde{A}^t(\tilde{A}\tilde{A}^t)^{-1}\tilde{A} = \begin{bmatrix} 0.833 & -0.1667 & -0.333 \\ -0.1667 & 0.833 & -0.333 \\ -0.333 & -0.333 & 0.333 \end{bmatrix}$$

$$\tilde{C} = DC = \begin{bmatrix} 1 & 0 & 0 \\ 0 & 1 & 0 \\ 0 & 0 & 2 \end{bmatrix}\begin{bmatrix} 1 \\ 2 \\ 0 \end{bmatrix} = \begin{bmatrix} 1 \\ 2 \\ 0 \end{bmatrix}$$

$$C_p = P\tilde{C} = \begin{bmatrix} 0.5 \\ 1.5 \\ -1 \end{bmatrix}$$

Then we can get the value of $\gamma = 1$.

$$\tilde{x}^{\text{new}} = \tilde{x}^{\text{old}} + \left(\frac{\alpha}{\gamma}\right)C_p = \begin{bmatrix} 1.35 \\ 2.05 \\ 0.3 \end{bmatrix}$$

$$x^{\text{new}} = D\tilde{x}^{\text{new}} = \begin{bmatrix} 1.35 \\ 2.05 \\ 0.6 \end{bmatrix}$$

$$Z^{\text{new}} = C'x^{\text{new}} = [1 \ \ 2 \ \ 0]\begin{bmatrix} 2.35 \\ 2.05 \\ 0.6 \end{bmatrix} = 5.45$$

$$\Delta\text{objective} = Z^{\text{new}} - Z^{\text{old}} = 5.45 - 3.0 = 2.45 > \varepsilon$$

Then we go to the second iteration.

Second iteration:

$$x = [1.35, \ \ 2.05, \ \ 0.6]^t$$

$$D = \text{diag}\,(x) = \begin{bmatrix} 1.35 & 0 & 0 \\ 0 & 2.05 & 0 \\ 0 & 0 & 0.6 \end{bmatrix}$$

$$\tilde{x} = D^{-1}x = \begin{bmatrix} 1.35 & 0 & 0 \\ 0 & 2.05 & 0 \\ 0 & 0 & 0.6 \end{bmatrix}^{-1}\begin{bmatrix} 1.35 \\ 2.05 \\ 0.6 \end{bmatrix}$$

$$= \begin{bmatrix} \left(\frac{1}{1.35}\right) & 0 & 0 \\ 0 & \left(\frac{1}{2.05}\right) & 0 \\ 0 & 0 & \left(\frac{1}{0.6}\right) \end{bmatrix} \begin{bmatrix} 1.35 \\ 2.05 \\ 0.6 \end{bmatrix} = \begin{bmatrix} 1 \\ 1 \\ 1 \end{bmatrix}$$

$$\tilde{A} = AD = [1 \ 1 \ 1] \begin{bmatrix} 1.35 & 0 & 0 \\ 0 & 2.05 & 0 \\ 0 & 0 & 0.6 \end{bmatrix} = [1.35 \ 2.05 \ 0.6]$$

The projection area P,

$$P = I - \tilde{A}^t(\tilde{A}\tilde{A}^t)^{-1}\tilde{A} = \begin{bmatrix} 0.7146 & -0.4334 & -0.1269 \\ -0.4334 & 0.3148 & -0.1926 \\ -0.1296 & -0.1926 & 0.9436 \end{bmatrix}$$

$$\tilde{C} = DC = \begin{bmatrix} 1.35 & 0 & 0 \\ 0 & 2.05 & 0 \\ 0 & 0 & 0.6 \end{bmatrix} \begin{bmatrix} 1 \\ 2 \\ 0 \end{bmatrix} = \begin{bmatrix} 1.335 \\ 4.1 \\ 0 \end{bmatrix}$$

$$C_p = P\tilde{C} = \begin{bmatrix} -0.8124 \\ 0.8163 \\ -0.9611 \end{bmatrix}$$

Then we get the value of $\gamma = 0.9611$.

$$\tilde{x}^{\text{new}} = \tilde{x}^{\text{old}} + \left(\frac{\alpha}{\gamma}\right) C_p = \begin{bmatrix} 0.4083 \\ 1.5945 \\ 0.3 \end{bmatrix}$$

$$x^{\text{new}} = D\tilde{x}^{\text{new}} = \begin{bmatrix} 0.5512 \\ 3.2688 \\ 0.18 \end{bmatrix}$$

$$Z^{\text{new}} = C^t x^{\text{new}} = [1 \ 2 \ 0] \begin{bmatrix} 0.5512 \\ 3.2688 \\ 0.18 \end{bmatrix} = 7.0888$$

$$\Delta\text{objective} = Z^{\text{new}} - Z^{\text{old}} = 7.0888 - 5.45 = 1.6388 > \varepsilon.$$

Then we go to the third iteration.

Third iteration:

$$x = \begin{bmatrix} 0.5512 \\ 3.2688 \\ 0.18 \end{bmatrix} \quad \gamma = 0.5328$$

$$x^{\text{new}} = \begin{bmatrix} 0.1654 \\ 3.7383 \\ 0.0963 \end{bmatrix} \qquad Z = 7.6421$$

$$\Delta\text{objective} = Z^{\text{new}} - Z^{\text{old}} = 7.6421 - 7.0888 = 0.5533 > \varepsilon.$$

Then we go to the fourth iteration.

Fourth iteration:

$$x = \begin{bmatrix} 0.1654 \\ 3.7383 \\ 0.0963 \end{bmatrix} \qquad \gamma = 0.1923$$

$$x^{\text{new}} = \begin{bmatrix} 0.0661 \\ 3.905 \\ 0.0289 \end{bmatrix} \qquad Z = 7.9577$$

$$\Delta\text{objective} = Z^{\text{new}} - Z^{\text{old}} = 7.9577 - 7.6421 = 0.0816 > \varepsilon.$$

Then we can stop here with a result

$$x_1 = 0.0661, \quad x_2 = 3.905, \quad x_3 = 0.0289, \quad \text{and} \quad Z = 7.9577.$$

EXAMPLE 8.6 Consider the following problem

Maximize

$$Z = 3x_1 + x_2$$

Subject to:

$$x_1 + x_2 \leq 4$$
$$x_j \geq 0$$

Starting from the initial point (1, 2), solve the problem using the interior point algorithm.

Solution:

$$Z = 3x_1 + x_2 = C^t x \quad \Rightarrow \quad C^t = [3 \quad 1] \text{ as } x = [x_1, \; x_2]^t$$

Subject to:

$$Ax = b \quad \Rightarrow \quad A = [1 \quad 1]$$

We are going to take $\alpha = 0.7$, $\varepsilon = 0.1$.

First iteration: As an initial point, we start by $x = [1, 2]^t$. Substituting in the objective function,

$$Z = C^t x = [3 \quad 1] \begin{bmatrix} 1 \\ 2 \end{bmatrix} = 5.0$$

$$D = \text{diag}(x) = \begin{bmatrix} 1 & 0 \\ 0 & 2 \end{bmatrix}$$

$$\tilde{x} = D^{-1}x = \begin{bmatrix} 1 & 0 \\ 0 & 2 \end{bmatrix}^{-1} \begin{bmatrix} 1 \\ 2 \end{bmatrix} = \begin{bmatrix} 1 & 0 \\ 0 & 0.5 \end{bmatrix} \begin{bmatrix} 1 \\ 2 \end{bmatrix} = \begin{bmatrix} 1 \\ 1 \end{bmatrix}$$

$$\bar{A} = AD = [1 \;\; 1] \begin{bmatrix} 1 & 0 \\ 0 & 2 \end{bmatrix} = [1 \;\; 2].$$

The projection area P,

$$P = I - \tilde{A}^t (\tilde{A}\tilde{A}^t)^{-1} \tilde{A} = \begin{bmatrix} 0.8 & -0.4 \\ -0.4 & 0.2 \end{bmatrix}$$

$$\tilde{C} = DC = \begin{bmatrix} 1 & 0 \\ 0 & 2 \end{bmatrix} \begin{bmatrix} 3 \\ 1 \end{bmatrix} = \begin{bmatrix} 3 \\ 2 \end{bmatrix}$$

$$C_p = P\tilde{C} = \begin{bmatrix} 1.6 \\ -0.8 \end{bmatrix}$$

Then we can get the value of $\gamma = 0.8$

$$\tilde{x}^{\text{new}} = \tilde{x}^{\text{old}} + \left(\frac{\alpha}{\gamma}\right) C_p = \begin{bmatrix} 2.4 \\ 0.3 \end{bmatrix}$$

$$x^{\text{new}} = D\tilde{x}^{\text{new}} = \begin{bmatrix} 2.4 \\ 0.6 \end{bmatrix}$$

$$Z^{\text{new}} = C'x^{\text{new}} = [3 \;\; 1] \begin{bmatrix} 2.4 \\ 0.6 \end{bmatrix} = 7.8$$

$$\Delta\text{objective} = Z^{\text{new}} - Z^{\text{old}} = 7.8 - 5.0 = 2.8 > \varepsilon$$

Then we go to the second iteration.

Second iteration:

$$x = [2.4, \;\; 0.6]^t$$

$$D = \text{diag}(x) = \begin{bmatrix} 2.4 & 0 \\ 0 & 0.6 \end{bmatrix}$$

$$\tilde{x} = D^{-1}x = \begin{bmatrix} 2.4 & 0 \\ 0 & 0.6 \end{bmatrix}^{-1} \begin{bmatrix} 2.4 \\ 0.6 \end{bmatrix} = \begin{bmatrix} 1 \\ 1 \end{bmatrix}$$

$$\tilde{A} = AD = [1 \;\; 1] \begin{bmatrix} 2.4 & 0 \\ 0 & 0.6 \end{bmatrix} = [2.4 \;\; 0.6]$$

The projection area P,

$$P = I - \tilde{A}^t (\tilde{A}\tilde{A}^t)^{-1} \tilde{A} = \begin{bmatrix} 0.0588 & -0.2353 \\ -0.2353 & 0.9412 \end{bmatrix}$$

$$\tilde{C} = DC = \begin{bmatrix} 7.2 \\ 0.6 \end{bmatrix}$$

$$C_p = P\tilde{C} = \begin{bmatrix} 0.2824 \\ -1.1294 \end{bmatrix}$$

Then we get the value of $\gamma = 1.1294$.

$$\tilde{x}^{\text{new}} = \tilde{x}^{\text{old}} + \left(\frac{\alpha}{\gamma}\right)C_p = \begin{bmatrix} 1.175 \\ 0.3 \end{bmatrix}$$

$$x^{\text{new}} = D\tilde{x}^{\text{new}} = \begin{bmatrix} 2.82 \\ 0.18 \end{bmatrix}$$

$$Z^{\text{new}} = C^t x^{\text{new}} = [3 \;\; 1]\begin{bmatrix} 2.82 \\ 0.18 \end{bmatrix} = 8.64$$

$$\Delta\text{objective} = Z^{\text{new}} - Z^{\text{old}} = 8.64 - 7.8 = 0.84 > \varepsilon.$$

Then we go to the third iteration.

Third iteration:

$$x = [2.82, \;\; 0.18]^t$$

$$D = \text{diag}(x) = \begin{bmatrix} 2.82 & 0 \\ 0 & 0.18 \end{bmatrix}$$

$$\tilde{x} = D^{-1}x = \begin{bmatrix} 1 \\ 1 \end{bmatrix}$$

$$\tilde{A} = AD = [2.82 \;\; 0.18]$$

The projection area P,

$$P = I - \tilde{A}^t(\tilde{A}\tilde{A}^t)^{-1}\tilde{A} = \begin{bmatrix} 0.0041 & -0.00636 \\ -0.00636 & 0.9959 \end{bmatrix}$$

$$\tilde{C} = DC = \begin{bmatrix} 8.9788 \\ 0.0071 \end{bmatrix}\begin{bmatrix} 8.46 \\ 0.18 \end{bmatrix}$$

$$C_p = P\tilde{C} = \begin{bmatrix} 0.0 \\ -0.0142 \end{bmatrix}\begin{bmatrix} 0.0229 \\ -0.3585 \end{bmatrix}$$

Then we get the value of $\gamma = 0.3585$

$$\tilde{x}^{\text{new}} = \tilde{x}^{\text{old}} + \left(\frac{\alpha}{\gamma}\right)C_p = \begin{bmatrix} 1.0447 \\ 0.3 \end{bmatrix}$$

$$x^{\text{new}} = D\tilde{x}^{\text{new}} = \begin{bmatrix} 2.9929 \\ 0.0021 \end{bmatrix}\begin{bmatrix} 2.9460 \\ 0.0540 \end{bmatrix}$$

$$Z^{\text{new}} = C^t x^{\text{new}} [3 \ \ 1] \begin{bmatrix} 2.9929 \\ 0.0021 \end{bmatrix} = 8.8920$$

$$\Delta\text{objective} = Z^{\text{new}} - Z^{\text{old}} = 8.8920 - 8.64 = 0.2520 > \varepsilon.$$

At the end of fourth iteration

$$x_1 = 2.9838, \quad x_2 = 0.0162 \quad \text{and} \quad Z = 8.9676$$

8.7 Unit Commitment

The unit commitment (UC) problem is a somewhat longer term scheduling problem usually covering a time range from 24 hours (1 day) to 168 hours (1 week) ahead, and is handled by the operator in the pre-dispatch stage. In this problem, the operator needs to take decisions on how to commit or de-commit (i.e. keep running or shutdown) its available units over the week, or over the next day. The input to the operator is the demand forecast for the next week or next day, as the case may be, aggregated for the whole system.

In the same way, the ELD problem is formulated, the operator seeks to minimize its system costs over the planning horizon in a UC problem, while meeting the forecast demand to decide upon the unit up/down status for every hour.

This planning activity is essential due to the fact that the system load varies over a day or even over a weekly period and hence it is not economical to keep all the units on-line for the entire duration. A proper schedule for starting up, or shutting down the units can save costs significantly.

The UC problems are much more complex to solve, compared to the ELD problem discussed earlier, due to the presence of binary decision variables on unit status (on/off). Depending upon the need of the system and computational facilities, the utilities choose to use UC models that suit their requirements.

In the following sub-sections, we first discuss the basic structure of an UC model and subsequently some of those additional issues addressed within the UC set up by various researchers.

8.7.1 Objective Function

As mentioned earlier, the operator's objective function, while solving the UC problem still remains the same, i.e. to minimize the system costs. However, due to the longer, time-scale of the problem, the total system cost will be affected by the start-up and shutdown decisions of generating units, effected within the planning period. These are explained below.

Fuel cost: There have been two different approaches to represent fuel costs in UC models. The first and the most common approach has been to use a cost characteristics derived from the heart-rate characteristics and represented by a polynomial function, which is usually quadratic, and can be written as follows,

$$C_i = a_i P_i^2 + b_i P_i + c_i \tag{8.40}$$

The other approach has been to represent the generator cost as a constant, which is derived from the generator's average full load cost.

Start up cost: This component appears in the UC objective function to take into account the cost incurred during a generator start-up operation. This is often modelled as a function of the time for which the unit was off-line.

$$ST_i = \alpha_i + \beta_i(1 - e^{-T_i^{\text{OFF}}/\tau_i}) \tag{8.41}$$

α is a fixed cost associated with the unit start-up, β is the cost involved in a cold start-up, T^{off} is the time for which the unit has been off and τ is a time-constant representing the cooling speed of the unit.

Another approach has been to use a constant cost representation, which is included in the objective function when the unit is on start-up.

Shutdown cost: Usually this component of cost is not considered in UC models since it is not very significant compared to other costs. However, a constant cost representation has been used, and is included when the unit undergoes a shutdown.

The composite objective function for the UC problem can be constructed using the above as follows:

$$J = \sum_{k=t}^{T} [C_{i,k}\,(P_{i,k}) \cdot W_{i,k} + \text{ST}_{i,k} \cdot \text{UST}_{i,k} + \text{SD}_{i,k} \cdot \text{USD}_{i,k}] \tag{8.42}$$

UST< USD and W are integer decision variables denoting the status of the unit at hour h. W denotes the unit status (1 = running, 0 = off); UST denotes the unit start-up (1 = start-up, 0 = no shutdown).

8.7.2 Constraints in Unit Commitment

Demand–supply balance and spinning reserves: This constraint ensures that the operator has scheduled enough capacity for a particular hour so that the demand at that hour is met. This can also include any pre-decided import or export contracts with other utilities, and a certain amount of reserve capacity. A typical demand–supply balance constraint is given as follows.

$$\sum_{i=1}^{NG} P_{i,k} \cdot W_{i,k} + (I_k - E_k) \geq \text{PD}_k + \text{RESV}_k \tag{8.43}$$

The term RESV denotes the spinning reserve in the system, which is a reserve available to the operator from its spinning units, i.e. from the generators already running. Therefore, this reserve is available almost instantaneously to the operator in case of need. The operator has the very important responsibility of maintaining adequate spinning reserves in the system, not only on a total-MW basis, but he also needs to take care of the location aspect of this reserve, taking into account transmission capacities available in the system.

The operator generally uses his experience or certain rules for determining this reserve to be maintained in his system. As mentioned, the RESV component could typically comprise a base component, a fraction of the load requirement and a fraction of the high operating limit of the largest on-line unit.

Minimum up and down time constraints on thermal units: These constraints ensure the minimum number of hours a unit must be on, before it can be shutdown (minimum up-time) or the minimum number of hours a unit must be off-line before it can be brought on-line again (minimum down-time). These constraints are usually applicable to large thermal units.

$$\sum_{n=1}^{\text{MUT}} \text{USD}_{th,k-n+1} \leq 1; \qquad \forall\ k \geq \text{MUT} \tag{8.44}$$

$$\sum_{m=1}^{\text{MUT}} \text{UST}_{th,k-m+1} \leq 1; \qquad \forall\ k \geq \text{MDT} \tag{8.45}$$

MUT is the minimum time in hours the unit should be running before shutdown; MDT is the minimum time in hours the unit should remain shutdown before start-up.

Generation limit: This constraint describes the allowable range of generation available for scheduling, as defined by the maximum and minimum limits of the unit.

$$P_i^{\min} \leq P_{i,k} \cdot W_{i,k} \leq P_i^{\max} \tag{8.46}$$

Must-run units: Some units such as large coal-based units or nuclear units cannot be start up or shutdown on a day-to-day basis following the daily variations because they involve very high start-up costs and other technical constraints. Such units need to be assigned a must-run status.

$$W_{i,k} = 1; \qquad \forall\ i \in \text{MR} \tag{8.47}$$

Crew constraints: These constraints pertain to the number of units that can be started at the time in a particular plant.

8.8 Unit Commitment Solution Methods

The techniques for solving unit commitment problem discussed in this chapter are priority list scheme and dynamic programming method.

8.8.1 Priority List Method

This method consists of creating a priority list of units and it is obtained by an exhaustive enumeration of all unit combinations at each load level or determining the full-load average production cost (FLAPC) of each unit, where FLAPC is simply the net heat rate at full load multiplied by the fuel cost.

EXAMPLE 8.7 Create a unit commitment using the priority list method for the following three units.

The fuel cost equations are as follows:

Unit 1: $F_1(P_1) = 561 + 7.92\ P_1 + 0.001562\ P_1^2$ $\quad 150 \le P_1 \le 600$
Unit 2: $F_2(P_2) = 310 + 7.85\ P_2 + 0.00194\ P_2^2$ $\quad 100 \le P_2 \le 400$
Unit 3: $F_3(P_3) = 93.6 + 9.56\ P_3 + 0.005784\ P_3^2$ $\quad 50 \le P_3 \le 200$

Solution:

Step 1: Determine the full-load average production cost (FLAPC)

Unit 1: $F_1(600)/600 = 9.7922$
Unit 2: $F_2(400)/400 = 9.4010$
Unit 3: $F_3(200)/200 = 11.1848$

Step 2: From the above units, the first unit going to commit is selected based on the lower FLAPC value and hence unit 2 is committed first then unit 1 and unit 3.

Step 3: Ignoring the minimum up/down time, start-up cost, etc., we have the combination of commitment scheme as given in Table 8.6.

Table 8.6 Unit commitment using priority list method

Combination	*Minimum MW*	*Maximum MW*
2+1+3	300	1200
2+1	250	1000
2	100	400

The disadvantage of the method is that ranking is based on the maximum output power of each unit, i.e. all the units are not always operating at full load conditions. Generally the loading pattern does not match the maximum output power of each unit or all the units.

8.8.2 Dynamic Programming Method

In a practical problem, the UC table is to be arrived at for the complete load cycle. If the load is assumed to increase in small but finite size steps, dynamic programming (DP) is to be used for computing the UC table, wherein it is not necessary to solve the coordination equations; while at the same time the unit combinations to be tried are much reduced in number. For these reasons, only the DP approach will be advanced here.

The total number of units available, their individual cost characteristics and the load cycle on the station are assumed to be known a priori. Further, it shall be assumed that the load on each unit of combination of units changes in suitably small but uniform steps of size ΔMW (e.g. 1 MW).

Starting arbitrarily with any two units, the most economical combination is determined for all discrete load levels of the combined output of the two units. At each load level the most economic answer may be to run either unit or both units with a certain load sharing between the two. The most economical cost curve in discrete form for the two units thus obtained, can be viewed as the cost curve of a single equivalent unit. The third unit is now added and the procedure repeated to find the cost curve of the three combined units. It may be noted that in this procedure the operating combinations of third and first, also third and second are not required to be worked out resulting in considerable saving in computational effort. The process is repeated, till all available units are exhausted. The advantage of this approach is that having obtained the optimal way of loading k units, it is quite easy to determine the optimal manner of loading $(k + 1)$ units.

Let a cost function $F_N(x)$ be defined as follows:

$F_N(x)$ = the minimum cost in ₹/h of generating x MW by N units
$F_N(y)$ = the cost of generating y MW by the Nth unit
$F_{N-1}(x - y)$ = the minimum cost of generating $(x - y)$ MW by the remaining $(N - 1)$ units

Now the application of DP results in the following recursive relation

$$F_N(x) = \min_{y}\{f_N(y) + F_{N-1}(x - y)\} \tag{8.48}$$

Using the above recursive relation, we can easily determine the combination of units, yielding minimum operating costs for loads ranging in convenient steps from the minimum permissible load of the smallest unit to the sum of the capacities of all available units. In this process the total minimum operating cost and the load shared by each unit of the optimal combination are automatically determined for each load level.

The use of DP for solving the UC problem is illustrated by means of an example. Consider a sample system having four thermal generating units with parameters listed in Table 8.7. It is required to determine the most economical units to be committed for a load of 9 MW. Let the load can be changed in steps of 1 MW.

Table 8.7 Generating unit parameters for the sample system

Unit no.	*Capacity* (MW)		*Fuel cost coefficients*	
	Min.	*Max.*	*a* (₹/MW^2)	*b* (₹/MW)
1	1.0	12.0	0.77	23.5
2	1.0	12.0	1.60	26.5
3	1.0	12.0	2.00	30.0
4	1.0	12.0	2.50	32.0

Now

$$F_1(x) = f_1(x)$$

$$F_1(9) = f_1(9) = \frac{1}{2}a_1P_{G1}^2 + b_1P_{G1}$$

$$= 0.385 \times 9^2 + 23.5 \times 9 = 242.685 \text{ ₹/h}$$

From the recursive relation, computation is made for $F_2(0)$, $F_2(1)$, $F_2(2)$, ..., $F_2(9)$. Of these

$$F_2(9) = \min\{[f_2(0) + F_1(9)],\ [f_2(1) + F_1(9)]$$
$$[f_2(2) + F_1(7)],\ [f_2(3) + F_1(6)],\ [f_2(4) + F_1(5)],$$
$$[f_2(5) + F_1(4)],\ [f_2(6) + F_1(3)],\ [f_2(7) + F_1(2)],$$
$$[f_2(8) + F_1(1)],\ [f_2(9) + F_1(0)]\}$$

On computing term-by-term and comparing, we get

$$F_2(9) = [f_2(2) + F_1(7)] = 239.565 \text{ ₹/h}$$

Similarly, we can calculate $F_2(8)$, $F_2(7)$, ..., $F_2(1)$, $F_2(0)$.

Using the recursive relation (7.12), we now compute $F_3(0)$, $F_3(1)$, ..., $F_3(9)$. Of these

$$F_3(9) = \min\{[f_3(0) + F_2(9)], [f_3(1) + F_2(8)], ..., [f_3(9) + F_2(0)]\}$$
$$= [f_3(0) + F_2(9)] = 239.565 \text{ ₹/h}$$

Proceeding similarly, we get

$$F_4(9) = [f_4(0) + F_3(9)] = 239.565 \text{ ₹/h}$$

Examination of $F_1(9)$, $F_2(9)$, $F_3(9)$ and $F_4(9)$ leads to the conclusion that optimum units to be committed for a 9 MW load are 1 and 2 sharing the load as 7 MW and 2 MW respectively with a minimum operating cost of 239.565 ₹/h.

It must be pointed out here that the optimal UC table is independent of the numbering of units, which could be completely arbitrary. To verify, the reader may solve the above problem once again by choosing a different unit numbering scheme. If a higher accuracy is desired, the step size could be reduced (e.g. ½ MW), with a considerable increase in computation time and the required storage capacity.

The effect of step size could be altogether eliminated, if the branch and bound technique is employed. The answer to the above problem using branch and bound is the same in terms of units to be committed, i.e. units 1 and 2, but with a load sharing of 7.34 MW and 1.66 MW, respectively and a total operating cost of ₹ 239.2175/h. In fact the best scheme is to restrict the use of the DP method to obtain the UC table for various discrete load levels; while the load sharing among committed units is then decided by use of the coordination.

For example, the UC table is prepared in steps of 1 MW. By combining the load range over which the unit commitment does not change, the overall result can be represented in the form of a table as Table 8.8.

Table 8.8 Status of units for minimum operating cost

Load range	*Unit number*			
	1	2	3	4
1–15	1	0	0	0
6–13	1	1	0	0
14–18	1	1	1	0
19–48	1	1	1	1

The UC table is prepared once and for all for a given set of units. As the load cycle on the station changes, it would only mean changes in starting and stopping of units with the basic UC table remaining unchanged.

Review Questions

Part-A

1. What do you mean by SCOPF?
2. Indicate the various methods to solve OPF problems.
3. What is the significance of security constrained economic dispatch problem?
4. What are the applications of optimal power flow?
5. How is the optimal flow represented as nonlinear optimization problem?

Part-B

1. Solve the given problems up to the first iteration using the Lagrange multiplier method assuming all the starting point variables are one
   Minimum $f = 0.25\,X_1^2 + X_2^2$
   Subject to $5 - X_1 - X_3 = 0$
   $X_1 + 0.2X_2 - 3 <= 0$
2. Solve the given problem up to the first iteration using the interior point method
   Maximize $Z = X_1 + 2X_2$
   Subject to $X_1 + X_2 + X_3 <= 8$
   Assume the initial starting point [1,1,2]
   $\alpha = 0.7$ $\varepsilon = 0.1$, $\gamma = 1$

3. Determine X_1 and X_2 to minimize the function
   $f = 0.25\ X_1^2 + X_2^2$
   Subject to the constraints
   $5 - X_1 - X_2 = 0$
   $X_1 + 0.2X_2 - 3 <= 0$ using the Lagrange multiplier method for one iteration.
4. Solve the given problem up to the first iteration using the interior point method
   Maximize $Z = X_1 + 2X_2$
   Subject to $X_1 + X_2 + X_3 <= 8$
5. Explain any one method to solve the nonlinear OPF problem.
6. Formulate the LPOPF problem for the data given below.
   Unit 1: $F(P) = 600 + 6P + 0.002P^2$
   $70 <= P_1 <= 250$ MW
   Unit 2: $F(P) = 220 + 7.3P + 0.003P^2$
   $55 <= P_2 <= 135$ MW
   Unit 3: $F(P) = 100 + 8P + 0.004P^2$
   $70 <= P_3 <= 160$ MW
   Three straight line segments with break points as below:
   Unit 1: Break points at 70, 130, 180, 250 MW
   Unit 2: Break points at 55, 76, 95, 135 MW
   Unit 3: Break points at 70, 80, 120, 160 MW
7. With an example explain the procedure for solving security constrained economic dispatch problem using the LP method.

Part III

DEREGULATION

CHAPTER 9

Power System Restructuring
An Overview

This chapter provides an overview of the need for restructuring, benefits of restructuring and various entities and model of restructured power market. A glimpse of restructuring processes taken place in international scenario and time line factor about the Indian power sector—major milestone before and after independence has been discussed.

9.1 Introduction

The existing rules of the monopolistic electricity market authorize a single utility to generate, transfer, distribute and sell electricity in a region, state or a country. Utilities have to operate according to the government policies, guidelines and regulations. They are also assured of fair returns without bearing any risk. In most part of the world, this has led to incompetence and lethargic attitude in the industry as they lack motivation for technical innovation, managerial inefficiency and customer focus. In order to dispense with these adversities of the monopolistic market, most of the utilities are undergoing restructuring.

Restructuring of the power industry aims at abolishing the monopoly in the generation and trading sectors, thereby, introducing competition at various levels wherever it is possible. Generating companies may enter into contracts to supply the generated power to the power dealers/distributors or bulk consumers or sell the power in a pool in which the power brokers and customers also participate. In a power exchange, the buyers can bid for their demands along with their willingness to pay. Power generation and trading will, thus, become free from the conventional regulations and become competitive.

Electricity sector restructuring, also popularly known as deregulation, is expected to draw private investment, increase efficiency, promote technical growth and improve customer satisfaction as different parties compete with each other to win their market share and remain in business. As per

L. Phillipson and H.L. Willis, "Deregulation is a restructuring of the rules and economic incentives that governing authority sets up to control and drive the electric power industry". The power system deregulation is expected to offer the benefit of lower electricity price, better consumer service and improved system efficiency. However, it poses several technical challenges with respect to its conceptualization and integrated operation. The complexity is more in such arrangement.

The power system restructuring is expected to offer a wide range of benefits to the consumers. However, it poses several technical challenges with respect to its conceptualization and integrated operation. Basic issues of ensuring economical, secured and stable operation of the power system which can deliver the power at desired quality, have to be addressed carefully in a deregulated market.

Restructured power market is also called in different names, viz. re-regulated market, open power market, competitive power market, vertically unbundled power system, open access, etc. The commonly used terms in power system are:

Competition: In competition, two or more entities are vying for the same business or opportunity. Competition can be introduced in generation and distribution businesses.

Deregulation: The suitable word is re-regulation which creates changes to encourage competition wherever it is possible. In power system, deregulation is more frequently used, however, re-regulation is very common in economics and regulatory aspects. Deregulation is a restructuring of the rules and economic incentives that government set up to control and drives the electric supply industries.

Restructuring: In electric supply industries, it is disassembly of the original structure and re-assembly into another form for better efficiency and performance.

Open access: A common way for a government to encourage competition in electric supply industries is an open access of wire business (transmission and distribution) which provides a way for competing generators to reach customers.

9.2 Motivation for Restructuring of Power System

The electricity supply industry has been undergoing drastic change right from 1980s. A significant feature of these changes is to allow for competition among generators and to create market conditions in the industry, which are necessary to reduce the costs of energy production and distribution, eliminate certain inefficiencies, shed manpower and increase customer choice and benefits. In a nutshell, restructuring refers to breaking the vertically integrated system as shown in Figure 9.1 into three distinct businesses (generation, transmission and distribution) by separating vertically (cutting horizontally) to provide competition in generation and distribution businesses. For effective competition, there should

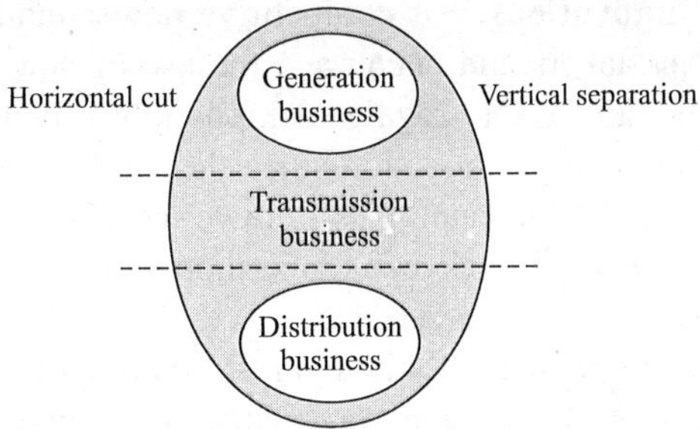

Figure 9.1 Vertically integrated electricity market.

be a large number of participants and therefore generation and distribution businesses are separated horizontally (cutting vertically) as shown in Figure 9.2.

After unbundling and creating competition, the regulated cost based generation becomes the unregulated price based generation.

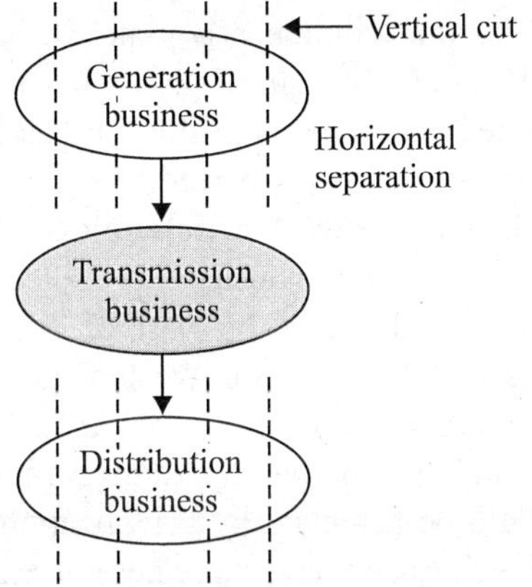

Figure 9.2 Vertically unbundled electricity market.

The reasons for deregulation are different in different countries. Many countries made the changes as a result of the failure of the state to adequately manage electricity companies. In other countries, the force behind this has been the lack of public resources to finance the required investment for the development. World Bank initiated to give loans to the utilities with a condition to start deregulation processes.

The following points provide justification for transforming the power industry.

1. **High tariffs:** The electricity price in several countries/states is much more and it was expected that price will drop after deregulation. Service may improve as a result of the restructuring, but there is also a serious concern in many countries about falling maintenance standards. Competition breeds innovation, efficiency, and lowers costs but also leads to shot-termism.

2. **Encourage innovations:** A competitive power industry will provide rewards to risk takers and encourage the use of new technologies and business approaches. The regulated monopoly scheme was unable to provide incentives for innovation since the utility had little motivation to use new ideas and technologies to lower costs under a regulated rate of return framework. Lack of competition also gave electric utilities little incentive to improve service.
3. **Better customer choice:** Although restructuring of the power industry inevitably results in some new problems, governments and consumers in many countries believed that the benefits of the restructuring would outweigh potential problems. Consumers will have more choice and benefits out of restructuring.
4. **Change in generation economies of scale:** The change in generation economies of scale that occurred throughout the 1980's was an important stimulus to industry restructuring. Advances in gas turbine technology led to more efficient small turbines and generators. As a result, smaller generators could nearly match the efficiency of very large units, particularly if run on natural gas rather than coal. The price of natural gas declined and the prohibition on gas burning for electricity generation was removed in this period.
5. **Improvement in managerial efficiencies:** Restructuring of the government-owned electricity industry encouraged privatization, although privatization does not have to be part of a restructuring effort. In the 1980s and early 1990s several Western governments were of the view that private organizations could do a better job of running the power industry, and that higher operating efficiencies and reduction of manpower could be achieved by privatization. Private utilities also refuse to subsidize rates and have a greater interest in eliminating power thefts and managerial or workplace inefficiencies. In other countries either ownership or responsibility for various functions was transferred to co-operative or to private organizations, or to new types of public corporations or quasi-governmental entities that could act like market sensitive economic agents. Ownership and functional restructuring has therefore taken many different forms. Incremental involvement of private capital, which has played an important role in Asia, can be considered as private sector participation rather than privatization.
6. **Better experience of other deregulated market:** The industries such as oil and gas, airlines, banking, auto-manufacturing, etc. had already showed very good performance because of restructuring. Although the electricity is a different type of commodity which cannot be stored in bulk quantity and also related to the interconnected grid management, it is expected the electric supply industries will also show the good results as other deregulated industries.

7. **Pressure from financial institutions:** The electricity supply industries in the developing courtiers are in red and require huge financial assistance/loan from foreign financial institutions such as World Bank, Asian Development Bank, etc. Knowing the situation of electric supply industries that is difficult to get the loans back from these industries, financial institutions are providing the loans/assistance with condition. These conditions are nothing but to restructure their operational and managerial structures.
8. **Lack of public resources for future development:** As the economic development of developing countries is faster than the other developed countries, the resource require is also enormous. The governments are unable to concentrate much on electric sectors as there are several other sectors where much attention is required. Due to limited resource, electricity sector is now open to private investors which required some regulation to be changed. Restructuring gave opportunity to the private investors to build, own and operate in the electricity business.
9. **Need for regulation changed:** The basic need of regulation was to provide risk free investment to build infrastructure which is no more important. Now power system grid which comprises of generation, transmission and distribution is in mature state. The network is expanded to reach each customer. The revenue obtained from the existing setup can be used for future extension and development of the systems. Now technology is almost matured and there is only incremental addition in system. Therefore there is a little risk in the investment.

Some other forces behind the restructuring are:

- Global economic crises
- Overstaffing in the regulated electric industry
- Political and ideological changes
- Rise in environmentalism factor

9.3 Electricity Market Entities and Model

The deregulation of the electric utility industry allows many independent power producers (IPP) to be connected across the transmission system. Power producers (sellers) and dealers/customers (buyers) have to share a common transmission network for wheeling the power from the point of generation to the point of consumption. Thus, interconnected transmission system is considered to be a natural monopoly so as to avoid the duplicity, the problem of right-of-the-way, huge investment for new infrastructure, and to take the advantage of the interconnected network, viz. reduced installed capacity, increased system reliability and improved system performance.

The power flow patterns in a deregulated environment are likely to be different from those in the existing regulated environment. All parties will try to get the benefits of cheaper source and greater profit margins, which may lead overloading and congestion of certain transmission corridors. This may well exceed the thermal, voltage and stability limits, thereby undermining the system security. Further, some players may try to exercise the market power by exploiting the system limitations.

Thus, there is a need of System Operator (SO) or a Grid Operator (GRIDCO) to manage the transmission network, its operation, security, and reliability while ensuring its open access to all the market entities in free and transparent manner. A brief introduction of different electricity market entities and model of the restructured electricity market is given in this section.

The restructuring of electricity has changed the role of traditional entities of the vertically integrated utility and created new entities that can function independently. The structural components representing various entities of the deregulated electricity market are Generation Companies (GENCOs), Distribution Companies (DISCOs), Scheduling Coordinators (SCs), Transmission Companies (TRANSCOs), an Independent System Operator (ISO), Power Exchange (PX), etc. Figure 9.3 depicts the typical structure of vertically integrated electric utility with money, energy and information flow arrangement. Figure 9.4 shows the typical structure of deregulated electricity system with information about all such flows.

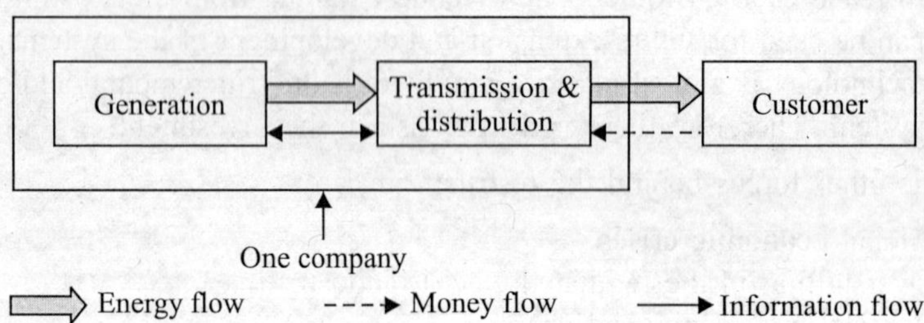

Figure 9.3 Typical structure of vertically integrated electric utility.

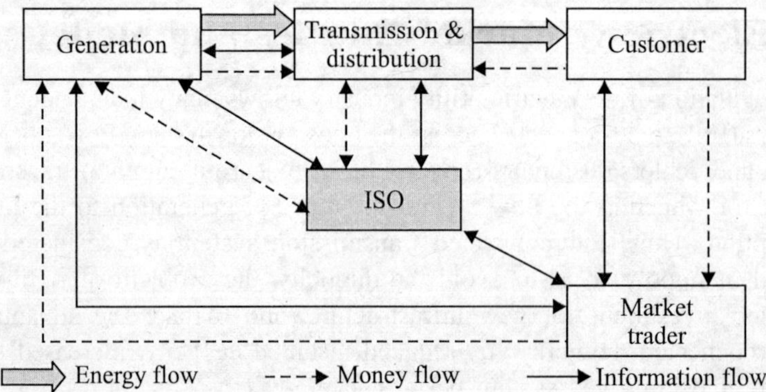

Figure 9.4 Typical structure of a deregulated electric system.

A brief introduction to various market participants are given below:

Generating Companies (GENCOs): GENCOs generate electricity and have the opportunity to sell the electricity to entities with which they have negotiated sales contracts. GENCOs are more often a group of generating units within a single company ownership structure with the sole objective of producing power. In addition to real power, GENCOs may also sell reactive power and operating reserves.

Transmission Companies (TRANSCOs): TRANSCOs transport electricity using a high voltage, bulk transmission system from GENCOs to distribution companies (DISCOs)/retailers for delivering power to consumers. A TRANSCO has role of building, owning, maintaining and operating the transmission system in a certain geographical region to provide services for maintaining the overall reliability of the electrical systems and provides open access of transmission wires to all market entities in the system. The investment and operating costs of transmission facilities are recovered using access charges, which are usually paid by every user within the area/region, and transmission usage charges based on line flows contributed by each user.

Distribution Companies (DISCOs): DISCOs distribute the electricity, through its facilities, to customers in certain geographical region. They buy wholesale electricity either through the spot markets or through direct contracts with GENCOs and supply electricity to the end-use customers. A DISCO is a regulated utility that constructs and maintains distribution wires connecting the transmission grid to the end use customers. A DISCO is responsible for building and operating its electric system to maintain a desired degree of reliability and availability.

Customers: A customer is the end user of electricity with certain facilities connected to the distribution system in the case of small customers, and connected to the transmission system in the case of bulk customers. In a restructure system, customers are no longer obligated to purchase electricity from their local utility company and have several options to buy electricity. They may choose to buy electricity from spot market by bidding for purchase or through direct contracts with GENCOs or even from the local distribution company with the best overall value.

Market operator: A market operator is an entity responsible for operation of electricity market trading. It receives bids from the market participants and determines the market price based on certain criteria in accordance with the market structure. The markets may have different trading schemes such as hourly trading for the next day or trading in future weeks, months, or years ahead.

System operator (ISO): A competitive market would necessitate an independent operation and control of the grid, which is guaranteed establishing a system operator (ISO). ISO or SO is an entity, which is entrusted with the responsibility of ensuring the reliability, security and efficient operation of an open access transmission system. It administers transmission tariff, maintains the system security, coordinate maintenance scheduling, and has a role in coordinating long-term planning. It is an independent supreme entity and does not participate in the electricity market trades. The SO has the authority to commit and redispatch the system resources and to curtail loads for maintaining the system security, i.e. to remove the transmission violations, balance supply and demand, and maintain the acceptable system frequency. This responsibility of SO forms the basis for the functionality of the Transmission Dispatch and Congestion Management System (TDCMS). SO can procure various ancillary services such as supply of emergency reserves, or reactive power from other entities in the system to maintain reliability. The basic requirement of an SO is disassociation from all market participants and absence from any financial interest in the generation and distribution business.

In general, there are two possible structure of SO and the choice of the structure depends on the SO's objective and authority. These structures are:

- Min SO
- Max SO

Min SO is mainly concerned with maintaining transmission security in the operation of the power market to the extent that SO is able to schedule power transfers in a constrained transmission system. This structure is based on coordinated multilateral traders and has no role in the market administration. California independent system operator is an example of this structure.

Max SO includes a power exchange, which is an independent non-government and non-profit entity that ensures a competitive market place for electricity rules. It performs the functions such as deciding and posting of market clearing price (MCP). The Pennsylvania New Jersy Marryland (PJM) SO and National Grid Company (NGC) are the examples of this structure.

Some other market entities which has come up in the restructured electricity market are as follows.

Aggregators: An aggregator is an entity or a firm that combines customers into a buying group. The group buys large blocks of power and other services at cheaper prices. The aggregator may act as an agent between customers and retailers.

Brokers: A broker of electric energy services is an entity or firm that acts like a middleman in a market place in which these services are priced, purchased and traded. A broker does not take a title on available transactions, generate, purchase, or sell electric energy, but facilitate transactions between buyer and seller. A broker may act as an agent between GENCOs and DISCOs.

Retail Companies (RETAILCOs): A RETAILCO obtains legal approval to sell retail electricity. A retailer buys electric energy and other necessary services to provide electricity to its customers and may combine electricity products and services in various packages for sale. A retailer may deal indirectly with end-use customers through aggregators.

Power Exchange (PX): The PX handles the electric power pool, which provides a forum to match electric energy supply and demand based on bid prices.

Scheduling Coordinators (SCs): Scheduling Coordinators aggregate participants in the energy trade and are free to use protocols that may differ from pool rules. In other words, market participants may enter an SC's market under the SC's rules and this could give rise to different market strategies. In some markets such as England & Wales, SCs are not allowed to operate. In many new countries such as California, SCs are an integral component of the market.

9.4 Benefits of Deregulation

Transformation in the electricity sector is an important step put forth to increase the efficiency of power generation and thereby to benefit consumers at large. The competitive electricity market offers customers and industry participants a range of benefits.

Cheaper electricity: This is a prime factor and it induces to set up more industries and business opportunities in a region thus paving the way for economic growth.

Efficient capacity expansion planning: Through greater knowledge of demand–supply conditions prevailing, generating companies will eagerly come forward to set up new plants at appropriate locations as there is greater hope for surety of returns. New participants are encouraged to enter the various competitive sectors of the power industry.

Pricing is cost reflective rather than a set tariff: Price signals drive the competitive market, encouraging industry participants to minimize the cost of supplying electricity to consumers. There will be always healthy competition among the power producers which will in turn benefit the consumers.

Cost minimization: Results from the pressure on industry participants because of increased competition in selected sectors, third party access arrangements and independent economic regulation of the natural monopoly functions.

More choice: Customers will have more choice in this deregulated environment since the retailers will offer more range of options for buying electricity.

Better service: Retailers have to be more competitive in terms of better price and quality service.

Employment: Due to greater business and industry investment, employment opportunities are enhanced. The beneficiaries are not only skilled power engineers but also peoples such as finance personnel, bankers, market traders, etc.

9.5 Basic Terminologies

The important terminologies used in restructured market have been explained in the following section.

Wheeling: Wheeling is the transmission of power from a seller to a buyer through a third party network. Wheeling is defined as, "the use of transmission or distribution facilities of a system to transmit power of and for another entity or entities". It may be also defined as, 'Wheeling is the use of some party's (or parties) transmission system(s) for the benefit of the other parties".

Bilateral Wheeling Transaction: It is a bilateral exchange of power between a buying and selling entity. The exchange may be a proposed, scheduled or actual one.

Multilateral Wheeling Transaction: Multilateral transactions are an extension of bilateral transactions. In a multilateral transaction, power is injected at different buses and taken out at some other different buses simultaneously, such that the sum of all generations is equal to all loads in the transaction, excluding losses. This trade is arranged by energy brokers and involves more than two parties.

Transmission Open Access (TOA): Because of transmission open access, entities that did not own transmission lines were granted the right to use the transmission system. The aim of TOA is to introduce competition into the traditional regulated utilities without giving up the existing regulating structure.

Restructuring: Restructuring of regulated power sector is to separate the functions of power generation, transmission, distribution and electricity supply to consumers.

Deregulation: It is changing the existing monopoly franchise rule or other regulations of regulated industry, that affect how electric companies do business, and how customers may buy electric power and services.

Available Transfer Capability (ATC): The ATC is a measure of the transfer capability remaining in the physical transmission network for further commercial activity over and above already committed uses.

Total Transfer Capability (TTC): It is defined as the amount of electric power that can be transferred over the interconnected transmission network or particular path or interface in a reliable manner, while meeting all of a well-defined pre- and post-contingency system conditions from a specified set.

Transmission Reliability Margin (TRM): It is defined as that amount of transmission transfer capability necessary to ensure that the interconnected transmission network is secured under a reasonable range of uncertainties in the system.

Capacity Benefit Margin (CBM): It is defined as the amount of transmission transfer capability reserved for load serving entities on the host transmission system to ensure access to generation from interconnected systems to meet generation reliability requirements.

Transmission System Congestion: In a competitive electricity market, congestion refers to the overloading of lines or transformers due to market settlement. The changes of congestion in the deregulated market are quite high as compared to the monopolistic market, as the customers would like to purchase electricity from the cheapest available sources. The congestion is undesirable in the system and should be alleviated for the secure operation of the system.

9.6 Deregulation—International Scenario

Restructuring of Electric Supply Industries (ESI) is taking place all over the world, in different rates and shapes. A broad classification of the world countries is made into developed countries and developing countries. USA, Europe, Australia and New Zealand belong to developed countries category and India comes under the category of developing country.

In the USA, PURPA (Public Utility Regulation Policy Act) is enacted in the year 1978. Accordingly non-utility generators should participate in the market. Based on this act, 42,000 MW and 98,000 MW are introduced in the year 1989 and 1998 respectively. Hence it is noticed that there is a hike of 200% generation during the decade. Then, Energy policy act is enforced in the year 1992. The first commission to be formulated is Federal Energy Regulatory Commission (FERC). The Commission has coined several new technical terms associated with deregulation involved in it. Open Transmission Access (OTA) policy and Regional Transmission Organization (RTO) is introduced in the year 1996 and 1999 respectively.

Next one is of European Union (EU) in the year 1999. The two power pools functioning in EU are UK Power Pool (British Power Pool) and Nord Power Pool. The purpose of European Transmission System Operator (ETSO) is to implement the efficient European Electricity Market. National Grid Company (NGC) and Central Electricity Generating Board (CEGB) is functioning in the UK Power Pool. Nordic countries such as Norway and Sweden, Finland and Denmark are functioning in the Nord Power Pool from the year 1996, 1998 and 1999 onwards. In Sweden till 1991, the sector was dominated by Vatten fall, i.e. 50 % of total generation and 400 kV and 200 kV transmission lines are under its control. In 1991 onwards, Swedish government decided to remove transmission activities from Vattenfall and create the state owned transmission company Svenska Kraftnet, to manage the national transmission network. In the year 1995, a new transmission tariff is introduced based on the point of connection, which aimed at promoting competitions on the electricity market. In Norway, entire generation is based on hydro plants. A largest player, namely Statkraft is having 35% generation in addition to transmission network. National Electricity Market Management Company (NEMMCO), Australia starts to operate in the year 1994 onwards. Similarly in New Zealand, New Zealand Energy Market (NZEM) and Trans Power are responsible for power market from the year 1996.

The following shortcomings are noticed in the developing countries before going to implement the deregulation:

1. Inefficiency in production (generation shortage), transmission (high transmission losses), distribution (energy theft, improper use of agriculture) and use (not efficient metering).
2. Irrational pricing policies (non-uniformity in different customers such as industrial, domestic, agriculture, commercial and electric traction.
3. Underutilization and poor technological advancements.

Thus a competition has been introduced in power systems based on the premise that it will increase the efficiency of this industrial sector and reduce the cost of electrical energy of consumers.

9.7 Milestones of Deregulation in the World

From 1980 onwards, a major transformation took place throughout the electric power industry in South America. Chile was the first nation to restructure its electricity sector. The year wise milestones of restructuring are given below:

1982: Chile
1990: United Kingdom
1992: Argentina, Sweden and Norway
1993: Bolivia and Colombia
1994: Australia
1996: New Zealand
1997: Panama, Costa Rica, Honduras, Guatemala and El Salvador
1998: California, USA and others

9.8 Indian Power Sector—Past and Present Status

This topic gives an overview of the Indian power sector, starting from the past history to the current status. The major players in the sector in various areas such as generation, transmission, distribution, regulation, research and professional bodies are briefly discussed.

India is the second largest country in the world in terms of population (over 1 billion) and the seventh largest in terms of geographical area

(3.3 million sq. km.). India achieved freedom from British colonial rule in 1947 and soon embarked on a massive infrastructure building exercise. Power (electricity), being one of the most critical infrastructures of a modern industrial economy, received high priority and allocation of resources both in terms of personnel and finance. India has twenty eight states (and seven union territories) and the Constitution of India clearly demarcates the authority and responsibilities of state governments and of the central or federal government.

As per the Indian Constitution, the power sector is the joint responsibility of the state and central governments. Till the enactment of the Electricity Act 2003, the Indian power sector was governed by three principal Acts namely, the Indian Electricity Act, 1910; the Electricity (supply) Act, 1948 and the Electricity Regulatory Commissions Act, 1998. The Indian Electricity Act (1910) deals with the functioning and regulation of the private licensees whereas the Indian Electricity (supply) Act mainly deals with the establishment and functioning of the state government owned integrated monopoly utilities (within the state) called State Electricity Boards (SEBs). The more recent electricity Regulatory Commissions Act provides for establishment of state level and central level Electricity Regulatory Commissions (ERCs) for regulating the functioning of private licensees as well as the SEBs. Figure 9.5 depicts the institutional structure of the power sector in India before the evolution of Independent Power Producers (IPPs) and Independent Regulatory Commissions.

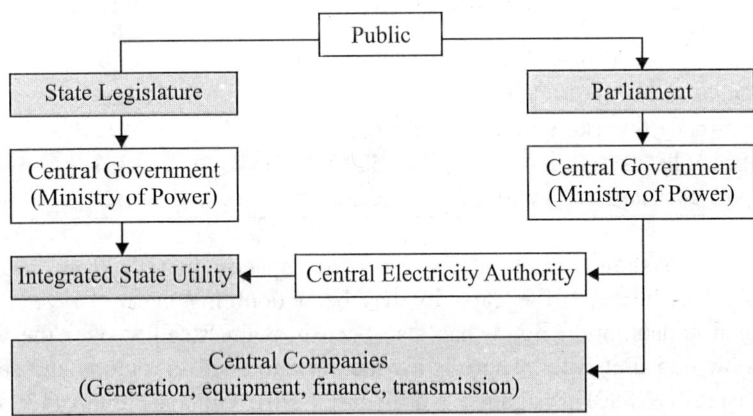

Figure 9.5 Institutional structure of Indian power sector before reforms.

The Indian Electricity (Supply) Act led to the evolution of state owned State Electricity Boards (SEBs), which were formed in the 1960s and soon took over numerous small private generation and distribution utilities in the respective states. SEBs is integrated utilities with monopoly over generation, transmission and distribution of power within the state. Except for a few urban-based private distribution licensees in cities such as Mumbai, Kolkata and Ahmedabad, the entire distribution was in the hands of SEBs.

In the late1970s, the central government established the National Themal Power Corporation (NTPC) for generation of power from large coal thermal generating stations. Currently, NTPC accounts for around 20% of India's total installed capacity and sells power to various state utilities (i.e. SEBs). Apart from NTPC, the central government also established companies such as Bharat Heavy Electricals Limited (BHEL) and Power Grid Corporation of India Limited (PGCIL) to manufacture electrical equipment (turbines, transformers, boilers, etc.) and erect and maintain interstate transmission lines respectively. The central government also regulates investments in the power sector through its agencies such as the Central Electricity Authority (CEA), which was created as per the Indian Electricity Act, 1948. All generation or distribution schemes above a particular size require the approval of the CEA. Until 1991, the power sector was mainly under government ownership (>95% distribution and ~98% generation) under various state and central government owned utilities.

9.8.1 Growth of Power Sector in India—An Overview

Table 9.1 highlights the growth of the Indian power sector since independence.

Table 9.1 Growth of the Indian power sector

Parameter	**2005** *status*	*Growth since independence (times)*
Installed capacity (GW)	11	87
No. of consumers (Crores)	13.4	89
Agricultural connections (Crores)	1.4	665
T&D network (`000 ckt. km)	635	216
Electrified Villages (`000)	508	333
Per captial consumption (kWh)′	625	42

Figure 9.6 shows graph of the installed capacity in GW from 1951 to 2005. As can be seen, the capacity has been doubling every 10 year. The per-capital consumption figure has also been growing steadily over the years and is now 625 units/year. There is a wide variation across regions and states: Western region (880) as against North-East (220); Gujarat/Punjab (1300) as against Bihar (75). Looking at international figures, India's per-capita electricity consumption is about half the value for China, is equal to the Asia average and is about one-fourth the world average. An important point to note is the recent change in the method of calculating the per capital consumption figure. Until 2001, the total consumption was divided by the population to arrive at the per capital consumption figure. Currently, as per United Nations guidelines, it is calculated by dividing the gross generation (at the generator terminals) by the population. Thus, per capital consumption is jumped from 366 units/year in 2001 to 559 units/year in 2002.

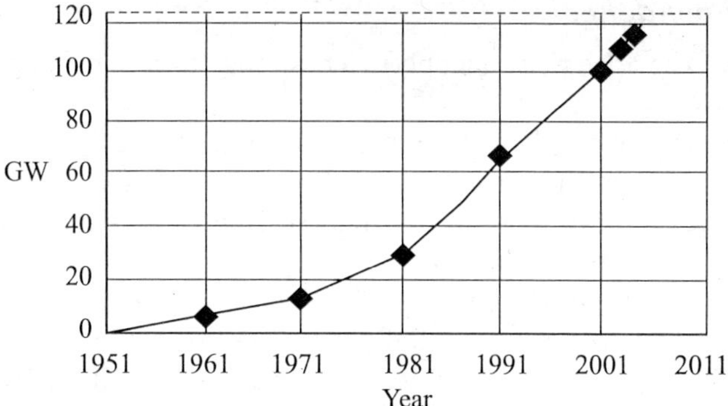

Figure 9.6 Growth of installed capacity.

The remarkable growth of physical infrastructure was facilitated by four main policies, viz

1. centralized supply and grid expansion
2. large support from government budgets in the form of long term, concessional
3. interest loans
4. development of the sector based on indigenous resources
5. cross-subsidy, i.e. charging industrial and commercial consumers above the cost of supply, and charging agricultural and domestic consumers below the cost of supply.

9.8.2 A Time Line of the Indian Power Sector

The major milestones occurred in the Indian power sector before and after independence have been provided below:

Before independence

1. 1879: Electric lighting demonstrated in Calcutta
2. 1897: First generating station set up near Darjeeling. A 130 kW hydroelectric station
3. 1899: The first thermal generating station set up in Calcutta
4. 1899: with electric lights, fans, Calcutta is the first electrified city in India. (New York in 1882 and London 1888)
5. 1900–1920: Generating stations at Khopoli, Maharashtra (set up by Tatas to supply Bombay), Sivasamudram, Mysore (power to Kolar gold fields), Mettur dam, Madras (power to Madras city), etc. Distribution by private companies.
6. 1910: The Indian Electricity (supply) Act
7. 1947: Installed capacity of 1363 MW (74% with the government), around 10 lakh consumers in 1500 locations (80% distribution in private hands).

After Independence

1. 1948: The Electricity (supply) Act, similar to a corresponding act in the UK.
2. 1956: Industry Policy Resolution. Generation and Distribution to be undertaken by the government. CEA to co-ordinate the sector. SEBs to be set up. Five private distribution licences remain.
3. 1960–90: SEBs set up, River Valley Corporations (DVC, BBMB), NLC (Lignite based power), DAE (Nuclear Power), REC to give thrust to rural electrification, central generating companies (NTPC, NHPC, NEEPCO), central transmission company (POWERGRID), external funding for generation and big transmission projects.
4. 1980s: Flat rate tariff for power for agriculture announced in many states (Tamil Nadu, Punjab, Andhra Pradesh, etc.).
5. 1990–2002: Economic liberalization (1991), private generation—IPPs (1991 onwards), Electricity Regulatory Commission Act (1998), CERC and State RCs set up. External funding for reforms. A few SEBs unbundled. Distribution Privatised in Orissa and Delhi.
6. 2003: Electricity Act 2003.

There is generally a correlation between the growth of Gross Domestic Product (GDP) of a country and the electricity consumption. It is a good sign that with improving efficiency of electricity use, this correlation has been reducing in India. This is indicated by the elasticity of electricity consumption with respect to GDP, which has gone down over the years. While consumption went up by 3.14% for every 1% growth in GDP in the first five-year plan period (1951–56), it went up by only 0.97% in the eighth plan period (1992–97).

While all this must be appreciated, it must also be realized that neither the growth of the sector has been balanced nor has it been sufficiently reflected in the equitable development of the country. Only about 56% of households have access to electricity, with the rural access being 42% and urban access about 82% in 2001. (In 1991, rural access was 30% and urban was 75%.)

Another issue is investment in the power sector. It has been pointed out that the plan outlay for the power sector has been heavily biased towards generation. It is generally said that for every 1 rupee invested in generation, 1 rupee should be invested in transmission and distribution. (This is as per the Rajadhyaksha committee report-1980, which mentions the proportion of 4:2:1:1 for Generation: Transmission: Distribution: Rural electrification). This proportion was 3:1 in 1993 and has improved to 1.3:1 in the Ninth plan period (1997–02). This welcome shift has been due to the (somewhat late) realization of the anomaly, and also due to the fact that the state is not investing much in generation now. Another shocking fact is that almost 50–60% of the energy sold is not metered. As much as 30–50% of the energy generated is lost in transmission and distribution. For the year 2004, the all India T&D loss figure is 32.53% and the Aggregate Technical & Commercial loss 39.22%. The revenue collection arrears are also quite high—anything between 30% and 200% of the annual revenue of the utility. Almost all the SEBs make losses (the total loss being nearly 20,500 Crores in 2004) and power shortages continue. The peak power shortage in the country was 11.7% and the energy shortage 7.3% (2005).

9.8.3 Players in the Indian Power Sector

The government dominates the electricity sector in India. In 2005, the government controlled nearly 89% of the generation, 100% of transmission and 90% of distribution of the power. Governments at the centre and state share the responsibility of the power sector. At the central level, the Ministry of Power (MoP) co-ordinates the sector. Central generating utilities, transmission utilities, policy bodies and research institutions help the MoP. The non-conventional energy sector is managed by the Ministry of Non-Conventional Energy Sources (MNES), and Nuclear Power by the Department of Atomic Energy (DAE). Organizations that supply fuel-coal, oil, natural gas are also managed by the central government under different ministries. Reliance Industries Limited is a major private sector player in the petrochemical area. State governments control water resources and coordinate water release for hydro power.

At the state level, there is a ministry, department and a state electricity board in states where restructuring has not taken place. The SEB is a vertically integrated utility with generation, transmission and distribution functions. SEBs were structured to operate without the direct control of state governments, but even though there is no formal mechanisms of control, SEBs are actually under state control through budget provisions and top level appointments which are decided by the state.

In states where restructuring has taken place, there are separate companies for generation, transmission and distribution functions. The private sector has started participating in generation and distribution in a big way since 1990s. In addition, there is a well-established electrical engineering and manufacturing industry in India. There are also many consultants, industry organizations and Civil Society Institutions that play an active role in the sector.

Generation

Power is generated by central generating utilities, state utilities and private utilities. Of the total installed capacity in 2005, central utilities accounted for 33%, state 56% and private utilities 11%. Tables 9.2 and 9.3 give details of installed capacity and energy generated by ownership and fuel used.

Table 9.2 Installed generation capacity: ownershipwise

Owner	*Installed* MW	*Capacity* %	*Annual* MU	*Generation* %
State	65941	56	240300	41
Central	38790	33	296401	50
Private	13688	11	50665	9
Total	**118419**	**100**	**587366**	**100**

Table 9.3 Installed generation capacity: fuelwise

Owner	*Installed* MW	*Capacity %*	*Annual* MU	*Generation %*
Thermal	84714	71.5	486031	83
Hydel	30935	26	84497	14
Nuclear	2770	2.5	16838	3
Total	**118419**	**100**	**587366**	**100**

Central generating utilities include the National Thermal Power Corporation (NTPC), the biggest thermal generation utility in India, set up in 1975. It has 23 plants, coal and gas based, spread all over the country with a total capacity of nearly 24,000 MW (about 20% of the total capacity of nearly in 2005). The National Hydroelectric Power Corporation (NHPC) was also set up in 1975. NHPC has an installed capacity of about 3755 MW from 11 plants. The Nuclear power Corporation has six plants with a total capacity of about 3000 MW. Other central generating utilities are: Neyveli Lignite Corporation (NLC) which has a Coal (Lignite) based thermal power project at Neyveli (2490 MW); North Eastern Electric Power Corporation (NEEPCO), set up in 1976 for generation and transmission systems in north-east; Bhakra Beas Management Board (BBMB), set up in 1976 to manage the generation and transmission systems of the dams on the Bhakra and Pong rivers; the Damodar Valley Corporation (DVC), set up in 1948 with generation and transmission systems in Bihar and Bengal; Tehri Hydro Development Corporation (THDC) set up in 1988 (joint venture of GoI and GoUP) to manage the Bhagirathi-Bilangna valley projects on the Tehri river in Uttaranchal; Nathpa Jhakri Power Corporation (NJPC), set up in 1988 (joint venture of GoI and GoHP) to manage the hydro projects in the Satluj river in Himachal Pradesh (NJPC has been recently renamed as Satluj Jal Vidyut Nigam).

SEBs own several generating units (thermal and hydel) and many states have separate generation corporations. Private generation was limited to a few Tata Power stations in Maharashtra, CESC stations in Kolkata, AEC in Gujarat and industry captives till 1990s. With the opening up of generation to private companies in the 1990s, many Independent Power Producers (IPPs) have come forward to set up generating stations. In 2005, there were about 30 private generating stations with a total capacity of 14,000 MW. Captive generating stations with industry add up to about 20,000 MW, out of which, about 15,000 MW was connected to the grid.

MNES and the Indian Renewable Energy Development Agency Ltd (IREDA) support renewable power generation efforts. These include solar, wind co-generation, and small hydro projects.

Independent power producers (IPPs)

In 1991, in response to a severe foreign exchange crisis and lack of capital for expanding power generation capacity, the central government opened up power generation for foreign and Indian private investment. The Government of India offered concessions such as 100% foreign ownership, long-term purchase agreement, and assured profits (as high as 32% post tax return on equity every year in the currency of investment). In the initial period state governments and SEBs were allowed to enter into negotiated contracts with IPPs without competitive bidding.

The initial response to this was enormous. During the three-year period when such non-competitive contracts were allowed, SEBs signed 243 contracts (MoUs) for a capacity addition of over 90,000 MW (more than the national installed capacity at that time), amounting to contracts of nearly 90 MW per working day. In their zeal to sign as many IPP contracts as possible, states and SEBs virtually gave a go-by to even elementary norms of power planning including proper demand forecasts and evolution of least-cost plans based on comparative costing of different options for sites and fuels. Only a handful of these contracts are likely to result in actual capacity addition.

After 1995, the central government enforced the competitive bidding route for acquiring new capacity (i.e. IPPs). Some projects have gone ahead through this route too. According to the IPP Report 2001, published by Power Line Research, since the opening up in 1991, only 3,200 MW of power generated by IPPs has come online and another 2,700 MW have achieved financial closure. These figures include the projects that started after competitive bidding was introduced.

The major reasons for this failure to add capacity were the weak financial situation of the SEBs, and the lack of demand. IPPs found it difficult to achieve financial closure, because of the lack of creditworthiness of the sole buyer, i.e. the SEBs. SEBs were making huge financial losses mainly due to huge transmission and distribution losses (including theft), and highly subsidized tariff to agricultural and domestic consumers. Some IPPs could progress beyond the initial stage due to credit enhancement through guarantees from state and central government as allocation of escrow facility. Many of these projects are planned using gas or imported coal. Many of them are not into the overall generation plan of the states. All this has created many problems in many states.

Transmission

Power Grid Corporation is the main central transmission utility. It was set up in 1989 to mange the regional and national power grids. For convenience of operation, the whole country is divided into five regional power grids, namely Northern, Eastern, North-Eastern, Southern and Western. Power Grid operated nearly 50,000 circuit km of EHVAC (765 kV to 132 kV) and HVDC (+/– 500 kV), with about 85 substations and 50,000 MVA transformation capacity (2005). These play a crucial role towards setting up the National Power Grid (connecting all the 5 regions), which is expected to be fully operational by 2012. Power Grid has also set up Regional Load Dispatch and communication facilities in all the five regions. Similar National load dispatch system at the national level is expected to be set up shortly.

The Power Trading Corporation (PTC) was set up in 1999, promoted by NTPC, Power Grid and PFC. PTC is to engage in trading electric power, especially in case of multi-state power projects. It was fully state in it. Transmission has been opened up to the private sector in 2001. The Tala transmission system has been set up by a joint venture of Power Grid and Tata Power and more joint ventures are being planned.

SEBs has their own transmission system and the restructured states have separate transmission corporations. It is expected that the transmission system will continue to remain largely in the hands of the state sector.

Distribution

The central government is not involved in distribution of power. State governments owned 90% of the distribution system in India in 2001. Until recently, BSES in Mumbai, CESC in Calcutta, AEC in Ahmedabad and Surat Electricity Company in Surat were the only private sector distribution system. BEST, Mumbai was a body of the Municipal Corporation of Mumbai and managed the distribution in some parts handled by BSES and AES since 1999, in NOIDA by NOIDA Power Corporation since 2000 and in the state of Delhi by BSES and Tata Power from July 2002. As a part of the reform process, more privatization is expected in this area. In state where SEBs has been un-bundled, one to four companies have been set up in each state to handle distribution.

Regulation

Regulatory Commissions (RCs) are new actors in the power sector in India. RCs are quasi judicial in nature and are set up to make regulation independent of the state and make it more transparent and participative. RCs control the functioning of transmission and distribution utilities through regulations and a public consultative process. The Orissa Electricity Regulatory Commission (OERC) was the first to be set up in 1996. The Central Electricity Regulatory Commission (CERC) was set up in 1998, and as of March 2005, 24 of the 28 states have State Electricity Regulatory Commissions. Until the Electricity Act 2003 was passed, appeals on the orders of the RC could be filed at the respective state high courts or the Supreme Court. (The Electricity Act has set up an Appellate Tribunal for Electricity [ATE] at the national level, which is to accept appeals on decisions made by any RC. Appeals on decisions of ATE are to be filed in the Supreme Court.) In the last few years of functioning, there have been many such appeals. In some states, appeals can only be on procedural grounds.

Fuel supply

The fuel used can be coal, petroleum products, nuclear or in case of hydroelectric stations, flowing water. Coal has to be mined, washed (in case of coal with high ash content) and transported (by rail or ship) to the coal yard of the station. Today, central government companies manage most of these functions

(Coal India Limited, Neyveli Lignite Corporation, Indian Railways, Shipping Corporation of India). Some states (Gujarat, Karnataka) import coal for their power plants. Petroleum fuels include Liquefied Natural Gas (LNG), naphtha, and diesel in small captive stations. These are produced in the refineries and transported over long pipelines or rails. LNG terminals have been set up to import from other countries. Both government and private companies are engaged in these activities. (Government companies: ONGC, GAIL, IOC, HP, and BPCL, private companies: Reliance.) The Department of Atomic Energy (DAE) is managing nuclear fuel production and distribution. In the case of hydro stations, irrigation also has to be taken into account while planning power generation. Many of the dams have irrigation canals originating from the dam reservoir.

9.8.4 Research and Professional Bodies

There are many research and training institutions both with the government and outside it. The Central Power Research Institute (CPRI) is a research facility with the MoP. The Central Board of Irrigation and Power (CBIP) is involved in some standardization initiatives. The Bureau of Energy Efficiency (BEE) works on policy framework and directions for the national energy conservation activities. BEE is a recent initiative (2002) and has USAID and Indo German Energy Efficiency Project (IGEEP) as Partners. The National Power Training Institute (NPTI) and the Engineering Staff College of India (ESCI) are training facilities for working engineers. ASTRA and SUTRA in the IISc, Bangalore have done significant work on alternative energy technologies. IITs, IIMs XLRI (Bhubaneswar), IPE (Hyderabad), ASCI (Hyderabad) and some engineering colleges are involved in some of the consultancy projects.

The Energy and Resources Institute (TERI), known as Tata Energy Resources Institute (TERI, known as Tata Energy Research Institute till 2003) is one of the leading private research-cum-consultancy agencies working on energy issues. There are many organizations working in the area of renewable energy like Tata BP Solar, CEL, BHEL, Exide, Ankur, Winrock, etc.

The professional bodies include the BIS involved in standardization efforts, the Institution of Engineers–India (Electrical Chapter), Institution of Electrical and Electronics Engineers (IEEE) USA–India Chapter, Institution of Electrical Engineers (IEE) UK–India Chapter. These have regular publications and organize seminars and conferences on technical issues. There are also portals and discussion groups on the Internet. Portals showcase products and services in the sector and are a good marketing medium. The discussion groups are used to debate issues and share ideas. India Power Systems Group (inpowerg) hosted by IIT-Bombay is an Indian Discussion group. Power globe, hosted by the University of North Dakota, USA, is a well known international group.

Review Questions

Part-A

1. Give any two ISO websites related to Indian power system restructuring environment.
2. What are the countries involved in the Nordic deregulation process?
3. State any two benefits in the competitive restructuring environment.
4. Define electricity regulation.
5. Mention some of the benefits of deregulation.
6. Define power wheeling.
7. What are the advantages of deregulation?
8. Give some of the countries that have already employed deregulation in power sector.
9. What is the role of PURPA act in the US?
10. Give any two ISO operator websites in abroad.
11. What is the role of the website ID http: // cercind.org?
12. What are the reasons for restructuring of electric supply industries?
13. What are the different companies in deregulated electric market?
14. What is meant by bilateral and multilateral transactions?
15. What are the issues in developing countries going for restructuring?
16. Give any two websites related to ISO in restructured electricity market.
17. Give any two websites related to power system restructuring environment.
18. Give any two websites related to electricity deregulation process in International and Indian scenarios and describe the information available in it.

Part-B

1. Explain the structure of a deregulated electricity market with necessary diagram.
2. What are the different entries in a deregulated market? Explain them in brief.
3. Explain how vertically integrated electricity market is transformed in the deregulation process and also give yearwise milestones of deregulation.
4. Discuss about the international scenario in deregulation of power industry.

CHAPTER 10

Operations in Power Market

10.1 Introduction

Based on the role of Independent System Operator (ISO), the two broad classifications in the power market are power pool and open access. The first and the more common one is the pool structure in which the ISO is responsible for both market settlement and including scheduling and dispatch and transmission system management, i.e. transmission pricing and security aspects. This power pool model exists in the UK, Australia and some of the US markets. The second one is of open access. It is dominated by bilateral contracts and can be found in Nordic countries. ISO has no role in generation scheduling or dispatch and is only responsible for system operation. Market operation is carried out by a separate entity. Generally the two types of mechanism employed in power pool are single auction power pool and double auction power pool. In the case of single auction power pool, the generating companies submit their bids that are then stacked in the increasing order of prices. The highest priced bid to intersect with the system demand forecast determined the market price. In the case of double auction power pool, both supply and demand bids are invited from participants in the markets. The system price is obtained by stacking the supply bids in increasing order of prices and the demand bids in decreasing order of prices. The system price and the amount of energy cleared for trading is obtained from the crossing point of these curves. The explanation of power pool auctions with suitable examples is given in the next section.

10.2 Power Pools

In the early days of the introduction of competition in the electrical energy trading, the bilateral trading was seen as too big a departure from the existing practice. Since electrical energy is pooled as it flows from the generators to the loads, it was felt that trading might as well be done in a centralized manner and involve all producers and consumers. Competitive electricity pools were thus created. Pools are a very unusual form of commodity trading but they have well-established roots in the operation of large power systems. In fact, some of the competitive electricity pools created by monopoly utility companies with adjacent service territories.

Rather than relying on repeated interactions between suppliers and consumers to reach the market equilibrium, a pool provides a mechanism for determining this equilibrium in a systematic way. While there are many possible variations, a pool essentially operates as follows:

1. Generating companies submit bids to supply a certain amount of electrical energy at a certain price for the period under consideration. These bids are ranked in order of increasing price. From this ranking, a curve showing the bid price as function of the cumulative bid quantity can be built. This curve is deemed to be the supply curve of the market.
2. Similarly, the demand curve of the market can be established by asking consumers to submit offers specifiying quantity and price and ranking these offers in decreasing order of price. Since the demand for electricity is highly inelastic, this step is sometimes omitted and the demand is set at a value determined using a forecast of the load. In other words, the demand curve is assumed to be a vertical line at the value of the load forecast.
3. The intersection of these "constructed" supply and demand curves represents the market equilibrium. All the bids submitted at a price lower than or equal to the market clearing price are accepted and generators are instructed to produce the amount of energy corresponding to their accepted bids. Similarly, all the offers submitted at a price greater than or equal to the market clearing price are accepted and the consumers are informed of the amount of energy that they are allowed to draw from the system.
4. The market clearing price represents the price of one additional megawatt-hour or energy and is therefore called the system marginal price of SMP. Generators are paid this SMP for every megawatt-hour that they produce, whereas consumers pay the SMP for every megawatt-hour that they consume, irrespective of the bids and offers that they submitted.

10.2.1 Single Auction Power Pool Example

EXAMPLE 10.1 The operator of a centralized market for electrical energy has received the bids shown in Table 10.1 for the supply of electrical energy during a given period.

Table 10.1 Company bid pattern

Company	*Amount* (MWh)	*Price* ($/MWh)
Red	100	12.5
Red	100	14.0
Red	50	18.0
Blue	200	10.5
Blue	200	13.0
Blue	100	15.0
Green	50	13.5
Green	50	14.5
Green	50	15.5

(a) Build the supply curve.

(b) Assume that this market operates unilaterally, that is, that the demand does not bid and is represented by a forecast. Calculate the market price, the quantity produced by each company and the revenue of each company for each of the following loads: 400 MW, 600 MW, 875 MW.

(c) Suppose that instead of being treated as constant, the load is represented by the inverse demand curve, which is assumed to have the following form: $D = L - 4.0\ \pi$, where D is the demand, L is the forecasted load and π is the price. Calculate the effect that this price sensitivity of demand has on the market price and the quantity traded.

Solution: (a)

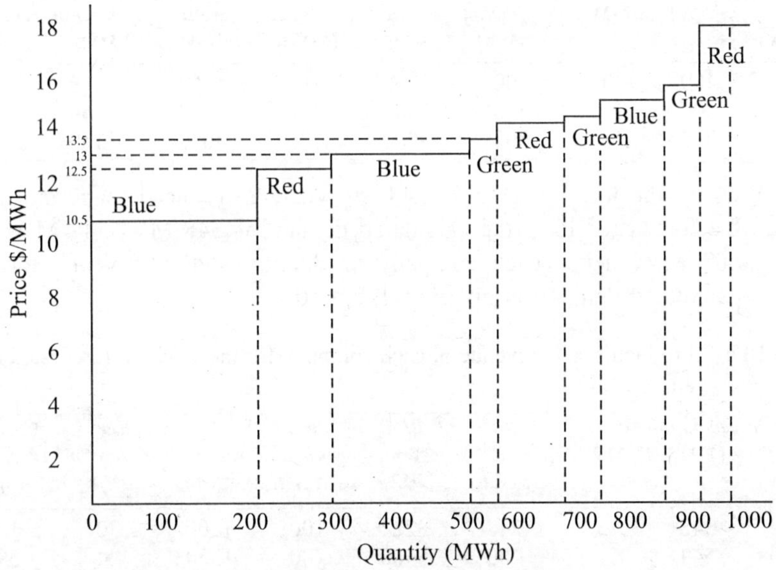

Figure 10.1 Supply curve.

The supply curve shown in Figure 10.1 is piecewise constant and in tabular form it is as follows Table 10.2.

Table 10.2 Representation of supply curve bid

Company	*Amount* (MWh)	*Cumulative amount* (MWh)	*Price* ($/MWh)
Blue	200	(0–200)	10.5
Red	100	(200–300)	12.5
Blue	200	(300–500)	13
Green	50	(500–550)	13.5
Red	100	(550–650)	14
Green	50	(650–700)	14.5
Blue	100	(700–800)	15
Green	50	(800–850)	15.5
Red	50	(850–900)	18

(b) Here, we make an assumption that forecasted load and demand are the same.

(i) 400 MW Blue supplies at the rate of $ 13/MWh
(ii) 600 MW Red supplies at the rate of $ 14/MWh
(iii) 875 MW Red supplies at the rate of $ 18/MWh

Each company production and its revenue for the given demand is given in Table 10.3.

Table 10.3 Production and revenue of each company for the same forecasted load and demand

Forecast load (MW)	*Demand* (MW)	*Price* ($/MWh)	*Blue production* (MWh)	*Blue revenue* ($)	*Red production* (MWh)	*Red revenue* ($)	*Green production* (MWh)	*Green revenue* ($)
400	400	13	300	3900	100	1300	0	0
600	600	14	400	5600	150	2100	50	700
875	875	18	500	9000	225	4050	150	2700

(c) Using the formula $D = L - 4.0\ \pi$, where D is the demand and L is the forecasted load, the calculated demand is 348 MW, 544 MW and 803 MW, hence each company production and its revenue for the calculated demand is given in Table 10.4.

Table 10.4 Production and revenue of each company for the different forecasted load and demand

Forecast load (MW)	*Demand* (MW)	*Price* ($/MWh)	*Blue production* (MWh)	*Blue revenue* ($)	*Red production* (MWh)	*Red revenue* ($)	*Green production* (MWh)	*Green revenue* ($)
400	348	13	248	3224	100	1300	0	0
600	544	13.5	400	5400	100	1350	44	594
875	803	15.5	500	7750	200	3100	103	1596.5

10.2.2 Double Auction Power Pool Example

EXAMPLE 10.2 The electricity pool of one company has received the bids and offers shown in Table 10.5 for the period between 9 a.m. and 10 a.m. on a particular day. Determine the system marginal price.

Table 10.5 Company bid and offer

Bids	*Company*	*Quantity* (MWh)	*Price* ($/MWh)
Supply	Red	200	12.00
	Red	50	15.00
	Red	50	20.00
	Green	150	16.00
	Green	50	17.00
	Blue	100	13.00
	Blue	50	18.00
Demand	Yellow	50	13.00
	Yellow	100	23.00
	Purple	50	11.00
	Purple	150	22.00
	Orange	50	10.00
	Orange	200	25.00

Solution: Figure 10.2 shows how these bids and offers stack up to form the supply and demand curves respectively. From the intersection of these two curves, we conclude that for the particular period the SMP will be set at $16/MWh and that 450 MWh will be traded through the pool. Table 10.6 shows how much energy each generator will be instructed to produce and how much energy each consumer will be allowed to draw. It also shows the revenues and expenses for each company.

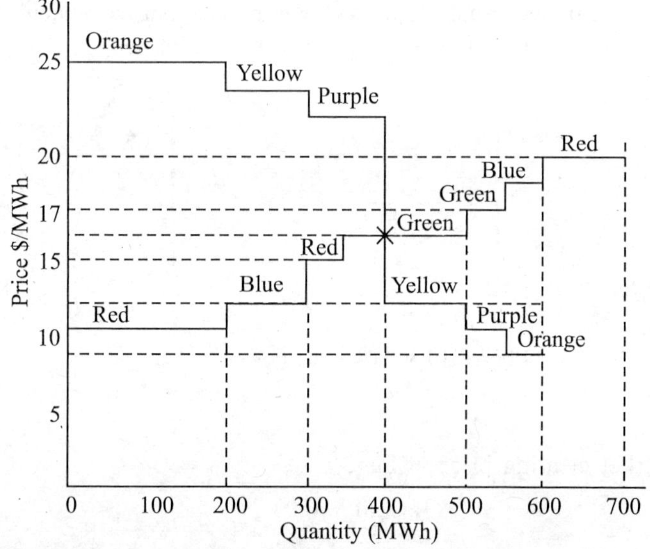

Figure 10.2 Stacks of bids and offers of one company.

Table 10.6 Revenues and expenses for each company

Company	*Production* (MWh)	*Consumption* (MWh)	*Revenue* ($)	*Expense* ($)
Red	250		4000	
Blue	100		1600	
Green	100		1600	
Orange		200		3200
Yellow		100		1600
Purple		150		2400
Total	450	450	7200	7200

EXAMPLE 10.3 Consider the two-bus power system as shown in Figure 10.3. The marginal cost of production of the generators connected to buses A and B are given respectively by the following expressions: $MC_A = 20 + 0.03\ P_A$ \$/MWh, $MC_B = 15 + 0.02\ P_B$ \$/MWh.

Assume that the demand is constant and insensitive to price, that energy is sold at its marginal cost of production and that there are no limits on the output of the generators. Calculate the price of electricity at each bus, the production of each generator and the flow on the line for the following cases:

(a) The line between buses A and B is disconnected.
(b) The line between buses A and B is in service and has an unlimited capacity.
(c) The line between buses A and B is in service and has an unlimited capacity, but the maximum output of generator B is 1500 MW.
(d) The line between buses A and B is in service and has an unlimited capacity, but the maximum output of generator A is 900 MW. The output of generator B is unlimited.
(e) The line between buses A and B is in service but its capacity is limited to 600 MW. The output of generators is unlimited.

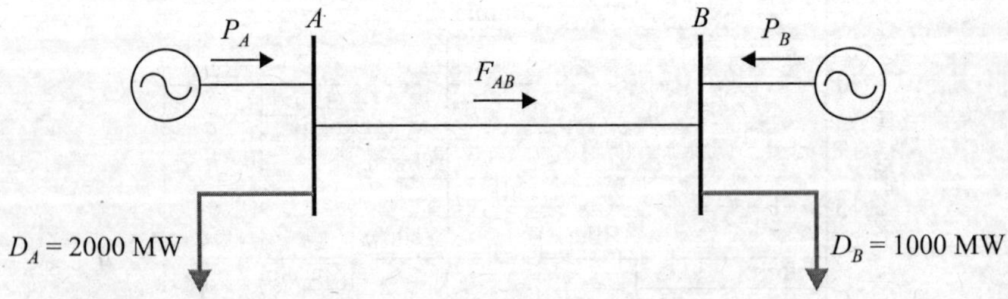

Figure 10.3 Two-bus power system.

Solution:

(a) Market clearing price at bus A

$$MC_A = 20 + 0.03\ P_A$$

Since $\quad P_A = 2000 \text{ MW} = \text{Demand}$

Then $\quad \text{Cost} = 20 + 0.03\ (2000)$

$\text{Cost} = \$\ 80 \text{ for } A$

Market clearing price at bus B,

$$MC_B = 15 + 0.02\ P_B$$

Since $\quad P_B = 1000 \text{ MW}$

Then $\quad \text{Cost} = 15 + 0.02\ (1000)$

$\text{Cost} = \$\ 35 \text{ for } B$

Therefore, the flow on the line is nil because buses A and B are disconnected.

(b) The line is in service.

$$20 + 0.03\ P_A = MC_B = 15 + 0.02\ P_B$$

$$0.03\ P_A - 0.02\ P_B = -5$$

$$P_A + P_B = 2000 + 1000 = 3000 \text{ MW}$$

Now solving the above equations

$$P_A = 1100 \text{ MW}; \quad P_B = 1900 \text{ MW}$$

$$\text{Total system cost} = \$\ 53$$

Flow on the transmission line, $F_{BA} = 900$ MW

(c) The line is in service and has unlimited capacity but the maximum output of generator B is 1500 MW.

$$P_B = 1500 \text{ MW}$$

$$P_A = 1500 \text{ MW}$$

$$\text{Cost} = \$\ 65 \text{ for } A$$

$$\text{Cost} = \$\ 45 \text{ for } B$$

Flow on the transmission line, $F_{BA} = 500$ MW

(d) The line between buses A and B is in service and has an unlimited capacity, but the maximum output of generator A is 900 MW. The output of generator B is unlimited.

$$P_A = 900 \text{ MW}$$

$$P_B = 2100 \text{ MW}$$

$$\text{Cost} = \$\ 47 \text{ for } A$$

$$\text{Cost} = \$\ 57 \text{ for } B$$

Flow on the transmission line, $F_{BA} = 1100$ MW

(e) The line between buses A and B is in service but its capacity is limited to 600 MW. The output of generators is unlimited.

$$\text{Total demand} = 3000 \text{ MW}$$

$$P_B = 1000 + 600 = 1600 \text{ MW}$$

$$P_A = 1400 \text{ MW}$$

$$\text{Cost} = \$\ 62 \text{ for A}$$
$$\text{Cost} = \$\ 47 \text{ for B}$$

Flow on the transmission line, $F_{BA} = 600$ MW

EXAMPLE 10.4 Consider a four utility joint dispatch as shown in Figure 10.4. The generation capacity and composite cost functions are given in Table 10.7. Find the system cost reductions when the utilities operate through a joint dispatch as compared to when they operate independently.

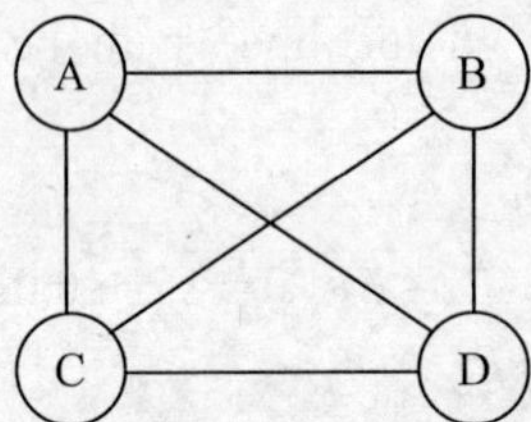

Figure 10.4 Four utility joint dispatch model.

Table 10.7 Multi-utility power interchange system

Utility	a_0 (\$/MWh)	b_0 (\$/MWh)	c_0 (\$/MWh)	P_{max} (MW)	P_{min} (MW)	P_D (MW)
A	1.8	10.5	0.5	150	20	120
B	2.8	24.5	0.8	250	30	200
C	3.0	15.6	0.4	230	40	180
D	1.5	20.1	0.6	125	25	75

Solution:

(i) Separate Market:

$$F_1 = (1.8P_1^2 + 10.5P_1 + 0.5) + (2.8P_2^2 + 24.5P_2 + 0.8)$$
$$+ (3P_3^2 + 15.6P_3 + 0.4) + \lambda(P_1 + P_2 - 575)$$

$$P_1 + P_2 - 575 = 0$$
$$P_1 + P_2 = 575$$

Area A:

$$1.8P_i^2 + 10.5P_i + 0.5 = \$\ 27180.5$$
$$= 3.6P_i + 10.5 = \$\ 442.5\ /\text{MWh}$$

Area B:

$$\text{System cost} = 2.8P_i^2 + 24.5P_i + 0.8$$
$$= 2.8(200)^2 + 24.5(200) + 0.8$$
$$= \$116900.8$$
$$\lambda = 5.6P_i + 24.5 = 5.6(200) + 24.5$$
$$\lambda = \$1144.5/\text{MWh}$$

Area C:

$$\text{System cost} = 3P_i^2 + 15.6P_i + 0.4$$
$$= 3(180)^2 + 15.6(180) + 0.4$$
$$= \$\,100008.4$$
$$\lambda = 6P_i + 15.6 = 6(180) + 15.6$$
$$\lambda = \$\,1095.6/\text{MWh}$$

Area D:

$$\text{System cost} = 1.5P_i^2 + 20.1P_i + 0.6$$
$$= 1.5(75)^2 + 20.1(75) + 0.6 = \$9945.6$$
$$\lambda = 3P_i + 20.1$$
$$\lambda = \$\,245.1/\text{MWh}$$

Table 10.8 Data for Example 10.4

Utility	*P* **(MW)**	λ **(\$/MWh)**	*System cost* **(\$)**
A	120	442.5	27180.5
B	200	1144.5	116900.8
C	180	1095.6	100008.4
D	75	245.1	9945.6
			Σ = 254035.5

(ii) Single Market:

$$\lambda_A = \lambda_B = \lambda_C = \lambda_D$$

$$P_A + P_B + P_C + P_D = 575$$

$$3.6\,P_A + 10.5 = 5.6\,P_B + 24.5 = 6\,P_C + 15.6$$
$$= 3P_D + 20.1$$

$$3.6P_A + 10.5 = 5.6P_B + 24.5$$

$$P_B = \frac{3.6P_A - 14}{5.6}$$

$$3.6P_A + 10.5 = 6P_C + 15.6$$

$$P_C = \frac{3.6P_A - 5.1}{6}$$

$$3.6P_A + 10.5 = 3P_D + 20.1$$

$$P_D = \frac{3.6P_A - 9.6}{3}$$

$$P_A + \left(\frac{3.6P_A - 14}{5.6}\right) + \left(\frac{3.6P_A - 5.1}{6}\right) + \left(\frac{3.6P_A - 9.6}{3}\right) = 575$$

On solving the above equations, we get

$$P_A = 168.83 \text{ MW}$$
$$P_B = 106.03 \text{ MW}$$
$$P_C = 100.447 \text{ MW}$$
$$P_D = 199.394 \text{ MW}$$

Hence the model, when it is operated as a single entity the obtained generations, the cost of generation of each utility and the total system cost are as given in Table 10.9.

Table 10.9 Total system cost

Utility	*P* (MW)	λ ($/MWh)	*System cost* ($)
A	168.83	618.29	53079.64
B	106.03	618.29	34077.15
C	100.447	618.29	1156493.3
D	199.394	618.29	585852.02
			Σ = 1829502.1

From Tables 10.8 and 10.9 it is inferred that if all the utilities are operating as a single entity, then the system cost is reduced less than the operating as a separate entity. Based on the least cost of generation of particular utility, more power is produced and it is transferred to higher cost of generation of other utilities by means of transmission line. Suppose there is a limitation in the transfer of power in the transmission line between each utility, hence a study is made to assume a transfer of power between each utility is 1 MW to 10 MW in steps of 1 MW.

(iii) Single market with transfer of power between each utility:

(a) 1 MW

Utility	*P* (MW)	λ ($/MWh)	*System cost* ($)
A	121	446	27624.8
B	197	1127.7	113492.5
C	179	1089.6	98915.8
D	78	254	10694.4
			Σ = 250727.5

(b) 2 MW

Utility	*P* (MW)	λ ($/MWh)	*System cost* ($)
A	122	449.7	28072.7
B	194	1110.9	110134.6
C	178	1083.6	97829.2
D	81	263.1	11470.2
			Σ = 247506.7

(c) 3 MW

Utility	*P* (MW)	λ ($/MWh)	*System cost* ($)
A	123	453.3	28524.2
B	191	1094.1	106827.1
C	177	1077.6	96748.6
D	84	272.1	11894.8
			Σ = 243994.7

(d) 4 MW

Utility	*P* (MW)	λ ($/MWh)	*System cost* ($)
A	124	456.9	28979.3
B	188	1077.3	103570
C	176	1071.6	95674
D	87	281.1	13102.8
			Σ = 241326.1

(e) 5 MW

Utility	*P* (MW)	λ ($/MWh)	*System cost* ($)
A	125	460.5	29438
B	185	1060.5	100363.3
C	175	1065.6	94605.4
D	90	281.1	13959.6
			Σ = 238366.3

(f) 6 MW

Utility	*P* (MW)	λ ($/MWh)	*System cost* ($)
A	126	464.1	29900.3
B	182	1043.7	97207
C	174	1059.6	95542.8
D	93	299.1	14843.4
			Σ = 235493.5

(g) 7 MW

Utility	*P* (MW)	λ ($/MWh)	*System cost* ($)
A	127	467.7	30366.2
B	179	1026.9	94101.1
C	173	1053.6	92486.2
D	96	308.1	15754.2
			Σ = 232707.7

(h) 8 MW

Utility	*P* (MW)	λ ($/MWh)	*System cost* ($)
A	128	471.3	30835.7
B	173	993.3	88040.5
C	171	1041.6	90391
D	102	326.1	17656.8
			Σ = 227397.1

(i) 9 MW

Utility	*P* (MW)	λ ($/MWh)	*System cost* ($)
A	129	474.5	31308.8
B	176	1010.1	91045.6
C	172	1047.6	91435.6
D	99	317.1	16692
			Σ = 229408.9

(j) 10 MW

Utility	*P* (MW)	λ ($/MWh)	*System cost* ($)
A	130	478.5	31785.5
B	170	976.5	85085.8
C	170	1035.5	89352.4
D	105	335.1	18648.6
			Σ = 224872.3

From the above cases it is observed that the total system cost is reduced in the case of 10 MW. Then a question is if we can increase the transfer of power between the utilities from 10 MW, then there is a reduction in the total system cost. Still if you can increase the transfer of power between each utility then you can observe at one stage that there is no change in total system cost. This is a task for the readers to visualize!

10.3 Transmission Networks and Electricity Markets

In a decentralised or bilateral trading system, all transactions for electrical energy involve only two parties: a buyer and a seller. These two parties agree on a quantity, a price and any other condition that they may want to attach to the trade. The system operator does not get involved in these transactions and does not set the prices at which transaction take place. Its role is limited to maintaining the balance and the security of the system. This involves the following:

1. Buying or selling energy to balance the load and the generation. Under normal circumstances, the amounts involved in these balancing transactions should be small.
2. Limiting the amount of power that generators can inject at some nodes of the system if security cannot be maintained through other means.

Let us consider the two-bus power system as shown in Figure 10.5 in which trading in electrical energy operates on a bilateral basis. Let us suppose that generator G_1 signed a contract for the delivery of 300 MW to load L_1 and that generator G_2 has agreed to deliver 200 MW to load L_2. Since these transactions are bilateral, the agreed prices are a private matter between the buyer and the seller. On the other hand, the amount of power to be transmitted must be reported to the system operator because this power flows on the transmission system that is open to all parties. The system operator must check that the system will remain secure when all these transactions are implemented. In this case, security is not a problem as long as the capacity of the transmission lines connecting buses A and B is at least 500 MW even under contingency conditions. If the amount of power that can be securely be transmitted between buses A and B is less than 500 MW, the system operator has to intervene. Some of the bilateral transactions that were concluded between generators at bus A and loads at bus B must be curtailed.

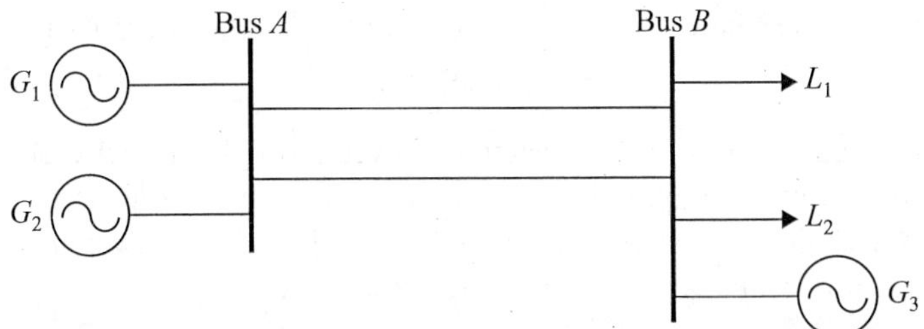

Figure 10.5 Bilateral trading in a two-bus power system.

For example, let us suppose that generator G_1 and load L_1 of Figure 10.5 have agreed on price of \$ 30/MWh, while generator G_2 and load L_2 have agreed on \$ 32/MWh. At the same time, generator G_3 offers energy at \$ 35/MWh. Load L_2 should therefore not agree to pay more than \$ 3/MWh for transmission rights because this would make the energy it purchases from G_1 more expensive than the energy it could purchase from G_3. The price of transmission rights would have to rise above \$ 5/MWh before L_1 reaches the same conclusion. The cost of transmission rights is also an argument that the consumers can use in their negotiations with the generators at bus B to convince them to lower their prices.

The power flows through the network is determined by physical laws and not by the wishes of market participants. Let us explain with the following example.

In the simple example as shown in Figure 10.6, a current $\overline{I}$ can flow from node 1 to node 2 along two parallel paths of impedances z_A and z_B. The voltage difference between the two nodes is thus

$$\overline{V}_{12} = z_A \overline{I}_A = z_B \overline{I}_B \tag{10.1}$$

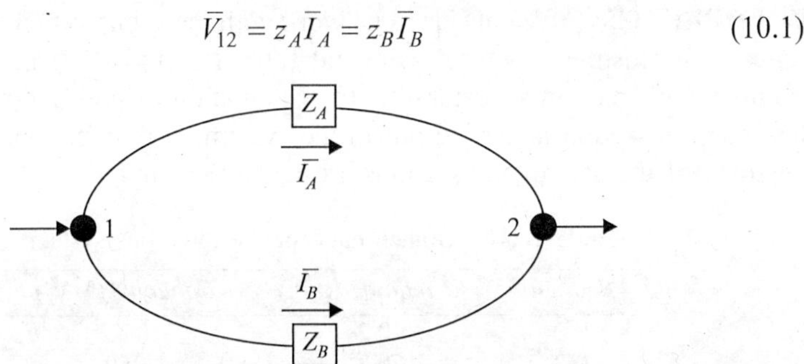

Figure 10.6 Illustration of Kirchhoff's voltage law.

Since $\overline{I} = \overline{I}_A + \overline{I}_B$, we have

$$\overline{I}_A = \frac{z_B}{z_A + z_B}\overline{I} \tag{10.2}$$

$$\overline{I}_B = \frac{z_A}{z_A + z_B}\overline{I} \tag{10.3}$$

Currents in parallel paths therefore divide themselves in inverse proportion of the impedance of each path. To simplify the following discussion, we will assume that the resistance of any branch is much smaller than its reactance.

$$Z = R + jX \approx jX \tag{10.4}$$

We also neglect the flow of reactive power through the network and the losses. Under these assumptions, the system of figure can be depicted in terms of active power flows as shown in Figure 10.7. The active power flows in the parallel path are related by the following expressions:

$$F^A = \frac{x_B}{x_A + x_B}P \tag{10.5}$$

$$F^B = \frac{x_A}{x_A + x_B}P \tag{10.6}$$

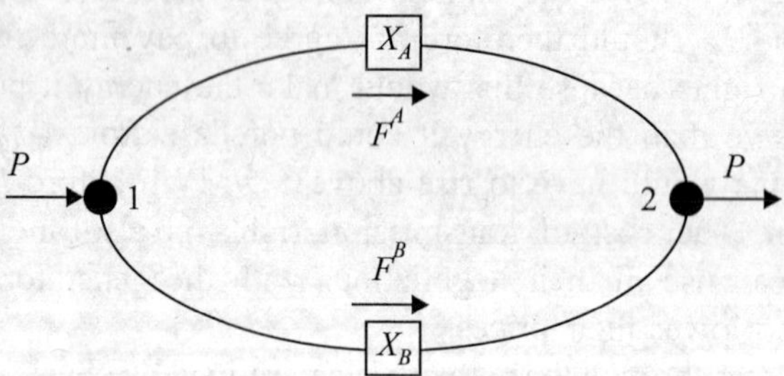

Figure 10.7 Active power flows on parallel paths.

The factors relating the active power injections and the branch flows are called power transfer distribution factors (PTDF).

EXAMPLE 10.5: We consider a network with three-bus system and one loop. Figure 10.8 illustrates such a system and Table 10.10 gives its parameters. This example explains how to determine the calculation of power flow when more than one transaction is carried out in the system. It is important to know that the some of the sets of transactions are feasible or not.

Table 10.10 Branch data for the three-bus system

Branch	*Reactance* (p.u.)	*Capacity* (MW)
1–2	0.2	126
1–3	0.2	250
2–3	0.1	130

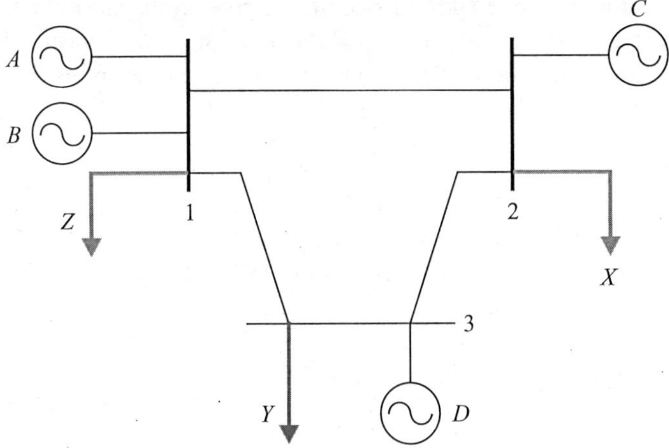

Figure 10.8 A simple three-bus system.

Solution: Let us suppose that generator B and load Y want to sign a contract for the delivery of 400 MW. If generator B injects these 400 MW at bus 1 and load Y extracts them at bus 3, this power flows along the two paths shown in Figure 10.9. The amount of power flowing along paths I and II are given by

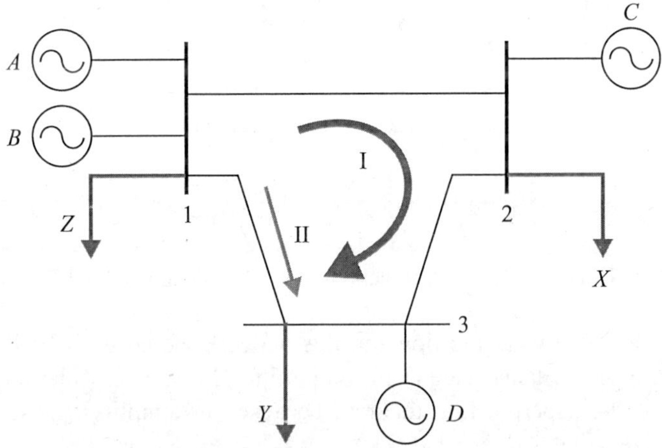

Figure 10.9 Paths for transaction between generator B and load Y.

$$F^{I} = \frac{0.2}{0.2+0.3} \times 400 = 160 \text{ MW}$$

$$F^{II} = \frac{0.3}{0.2+0.3} \times 400 = 240 \text{ MW}$$

To guarantee that this transaction can actually take place, the parties therefore need to secure 240 MW of transmission rights on line 1–3 as well as 160 MW of transmission rights on line 1–2 and 2–3. This is clearly not possible if this transaction is the only one taking place in this network because the maximum capacity of lines 1–2 and 2–3 are 126 MW and 130 MW respectively. In the absence of any other transactions, since the most constraining limitation is the capacity of line 1–2, the maximum amount that *A* and *Y* can trade is thus

$$P_{max} = \frac{0.5}{0.2} \times 126 = 315 \text{ MW}$$

However, suppose that load *Z* would like to purchase 200 MW from generator *D*. This power would flow in the following proportions along the paths shown in Figure 10.10.

$$F^{III} = \frac{0.2}{0.2+0.3} \times 200 = 80 \text{ MW}$$

$$F^{IV} = \frac{0.3}{0.2+0.3} \times 200 = 120 \text{ MW}$$

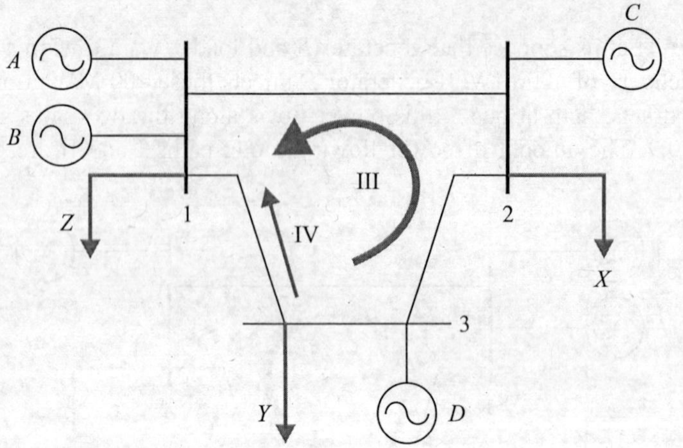

Figure 10.10 Paths for transaction between generator *D* and load *Z*.

Let us calculate what the flows in this network would be if both of these transactions were to take place at the same time. For this calculation, we can make use of the superposition theorem because our simplifying assumptions have linearized the relations between flows and injections. The flows in the various line are thus given by

$$F_{12} = F_{23} = F^{I} - F^{III} = 160 - 80 = 80 \text{ MW}$$

$$F_{13} = F^{II} - F^{IV} = 240 - 120 = 120 \text{ MW}$$

The transaction between generator *D* and load *Z* thus creates a counterflow that increases the power that generator *D* and load *Y* can trade.

EXAMPLE 10.6 Consider the power system as shown in Figure 10.11, assuming that the only limitations imposed by the network are imposed by the thermal capacity of the transmission lines and that the reactive power flows are negligible, check that the following sets of transactions are simultaneously feasible.

	Seller	*Buyer*	*Amount*
Set 1	B	X	200
	A	Z	400
	C	Y	300
Set 2	B	Z	600
	A	X	300
	A	Y	200
	A	Z	200
Set 3	A	Y	400
	B	Z	300
	C	X	1000
	A	Z	200
	A	Z	100

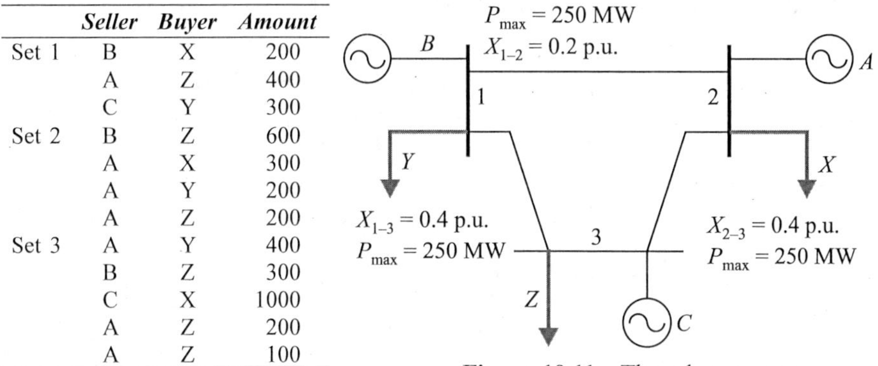

Figure 10.11 Three-bus system.

Solution:

Set 1: Let us consider the transaction $B \to X$ (200 MW)

$$F_1^A = \frac{X_1^B}{X_1^A + X_1^B} \cdot P = \frac{0.8}{1} \times 200$$

$$F_1^A = 160 \text{ MW}$$

$$F_1^B = \frac{X_1^A}{X_1^A + X_1^B} \text{ or } \frac{X_1^A}{X_1^A + X_1^B} \cdot P = \frac{0.2}{1} \times 200$$

$$F_1^B = 40 \text{ MW}$$

Transaction $A \to Z$ (400 MW)

$$F_2^A = \frac{X_2^B}{X_2^A + X_2^B} \cdot P = \frac{0.4}{1} \times 400 = 160 \text{ MW}$$

$$F_2^B = \frac{X_2^A}{X_2^A + X_2^B} \cdot P = \frac{0.6}{1} \times 400 = 240 \text{ MW}$$

Transaction $C \to Y$ (300 MW)

$$F_3^A = \frac{X_3^B}{X_3^A + X_3^B} \cdot P = \frac{0.4}{1} \times 300 = 120 \text{ MW}$$

$$F_3^B = \frac{X_3^A}{X_3^A + X_3^B} \cdot P = \frac{0.6}{1} \times 300 = 180 \text{ MW}$$

By applying the superposition theorem,

$$F_{12} = F_1^A - F_2^A - F_3^A = 160 - 160 - 120 = -120 \text{ MW}$$

$$F_{13} = F_1^B + F_2^A - F_3^B = 40 + 160 - 180 = 20 \text{ MW}$$
$$F_{23} = -F_1^B + F_2^B - F_3^A = -40 + 240 - 120 = 80 \text{ MW}$$

All the line flows are within the thermal limits. Thus this is a feasible transaction.

Set 2: Let us consider the transaction $B \to Z$ (600 MW)

$$F_1^A = \frac{0.4}{1} \times 600 = 240 \text{ MW}$$

$$F_1^B = \frac{0.6}{1} \times 600 = 360 \text{ MW}$$

Transaction $A \to X$ (300 MW)

$$F_2^A = F_2^B = 0$$

Transaction $A \to Y$ (200 MW)

$$F_3^A = \frac{0.8}{1} \times 200 = 160 \text{ MW}$$

$$F_3^B = \frac{0.2}{1} \times 200 = 40 \text{ MW}$$

Transaction $A \to Z$ (200 MW)

$$F_4^A = \frac{0.4}{1} \times 200 = 80 \text{ MW}$$

$$F_4^B = \frac{0.6}{1} \times 200 = 120 \text{ MW}$$

By applying the superposition theorem,

$$F_{12} = F_1^A - F_3^A - F_4^A = 240 - 160 - 80 = 0 \text{ MW}$$
$$F_{13} = F_1^B - F_3^B + F_4^A = 360 - 40 + 80 = 400 \text{ MW}$$
$$F_{23} = F_1^A + F_3^B + F_4^B = 240 + 40 + 120 = 400 \text{ MW}$$

This is not a feasible transaction as line thermal limits are violated.

Set 3: Let us consider the transaction $A \to Y$ (400 MW)

$$F_1^A = \frac{0.8}{1} \times 400 = 320 \text{ MW}$$

$$F_1^B = \frac{0.2}{1} \times 400 = 80 \text{ MW}$$

Transaction $B \to Z$ (300 MW)

$$F_2^A = \frac{0.4}{1} \times 300 = 120 \text{ MW}$$

$$F_2^B = \frac{0.6}{1} \times 300 = 180 \text{ MW}$$

Transaction $C \to X$ (1000 MW)

$$F_3^A = \frac{0.4}{1} \times 1000 = 400 \text{ MW}$$

$$F_3^B = \frac{0.6}{1} \times 1000 = 600 \text{ MW}$$

Transaction $A \to Z$ (200 MW)

$$F_4^A = \frac{0.4}{1} \times 200 = 80 \text{ MW}$$

$$F_4^B = \frac{0.6}{1} \times 200 = 120 \text{ MW}$$

Transaction $A \to Z$ (100 MW)

$$F_5^A = \frac{0.4}{1} \times 100 = 40 \text{ MW}$$

$$F_5^B = \frac{0.6}{1} \times 100 = 60 \text{ MW}$$

By applying the superposition theorem,

$$F_{12} = -F_1^A + F_2^A + F_3^A - F_4^A - F_5^A = -320 + 120 + 400 - 80 - 40$$
$$= 80 \text{ MW}$$

$$F_{13} = -F_1^B + F_2^B - F_3^A + F_4^A + F_5^A = -80 + 180 - 400 + 80 + 40$$
$$= -180 \text{ MW}$$

$$F_{23} = F_1^B + F_2^A - F_3^B + F_4^B + F_5^B = 80 + 120 - 600 + 120 + 60$$
$$= -220 \text{ MW}$$

As line flows are within the limits, this is a feasible transaction.

10.4 Operations in Power Market Using Power World Simulator

Let us explain the power market operations of the three area system as shown in Figure 10.12 using PWS. The names of the three areas are given as top, left and right. Now the study is to find out how the total system cost is reducing when the transactions are carried between the neighbouring areas. Hence the five cases are considered in the study for better understanding of the concept using PWS.

Case 1: Independent operation of each area, i.e. no transaction is carried out.
Case 2: Assuming a transaction of T_1 (top to left) is 40 MW.
Case 3: Assuming a transaction of T_2 (top to right) is 40 MW.
Case 4: Assuming a simultaneous bilateral transaction of T_1 (top to left) is 30 MW and T_2 (top to right) is 40 MW.

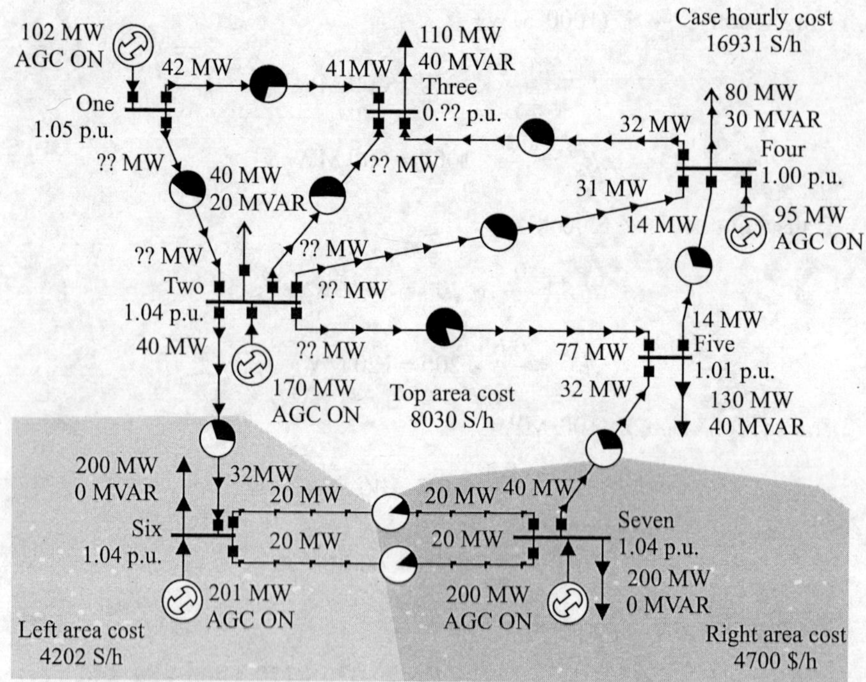

Figure 10.12 Three area system in PWS environment.

Case 5: Assuming a simultaneous bilateral transaction of T_1 (top to left) is 40 MW and T_2 (top to right) is 40 MW.

Case 1: Independent operation of each area, i.e. no transaction is carried out.

All the three areas are operating independently and there is no transaction between the areas, then the system cost for each area and the total system cost is 16931 $/ h. Each area system generation, load and system cost are given in separate figures (Figures 10.13, 10.14 and 10.15) and are as follows:

Area summary totals

	MW	MVAR
Load	360.0	130.0
Generation	366.6	58.5
Fixed bus shunts	0.0	0.0
Switched bus shunts		
Line shunts	0.0	0.0
Losses	6.98	–13.49
Interchange	–0.3	–58.0
Hourly cost ($/hr)	8036	

Figure 10.13 Top area summary.

Area summary totals

	MW	MVAR
Load	200.0	0.0
Generation	201.0	–6.5
Fixed bus shunts	0.0	0.0
Switched bus shunts		
Line shunts	0.0	0.0
Losses	0.32	–4.44
Interchange	0.7	–2.4
Hourly cost ($/hr)	4202	

Figure 10.14 Left area summary.

Area summary totals

	MW	MVAR
Load	200.0	0.0
Generation	200.0	51.6
Fixed bus shunts	0.0	0.0
Switched bus shunts		
Line shunts	0.0	0.0
Losses	0.66	–8.82
Interchange	–0.7	60.4
Hourly cost ($/hr)	4700	

Figure 10.15 Right area summary.

Case 2: Assuming a transaction of T_1 (top to left) is 40 MW.

Considering a transaction of top to left, the areawise cost and system cost for the particular transaction is given in Table 10.11. The three area system in PWS environment for case 2 is shown in Figure 10.16.

Table 10.11 Areawise cost and system cost for case 2

Area	*Cost* ($/h)	*System cost* ($/h)
Top	8690	
Left	3530	16924
Right	4710	

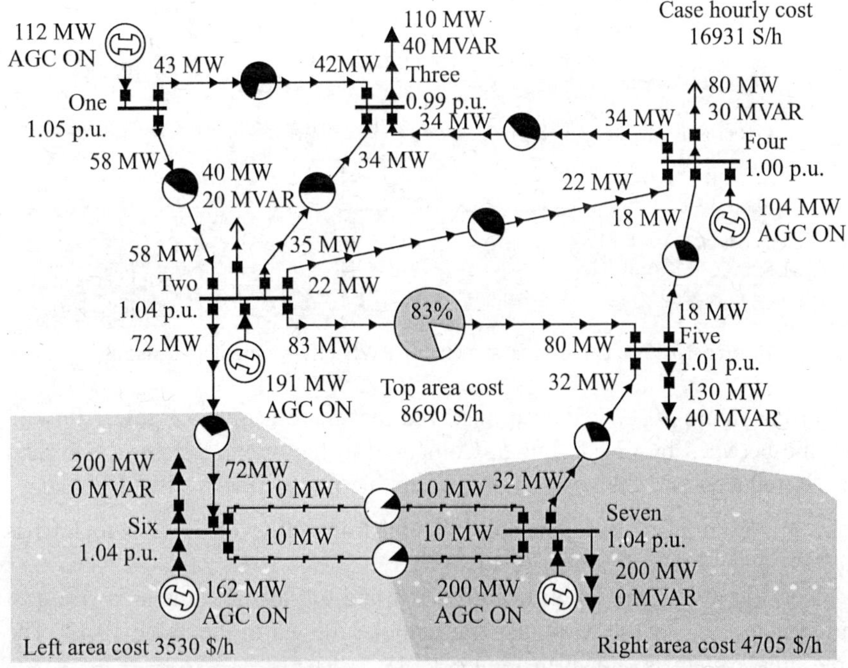

Figure 10.16 Three area system in PWS environment for case 2.

From Figure 10.16 it is also observed that there is 83% of power flow in the line between bus 2 and bus 5. Compared to the previous case, the system cost is reduced and the power flow under this transaction is also depicted.

Case 3: Assuming a transaction of T_2 (top to right) is 40 MW.

Considering a transaction of top to right, the areawise cost and system cost for the particular transaction is given in the Table 10.12. The three area system is as shown in Figure 10.17.

Table 10.12 Areawise cost and system cost for case 3

Area	*Cost* (\$/h)	*System cost* (\$/h)
Top	8703	
Left	4181	16777
Right	3892	

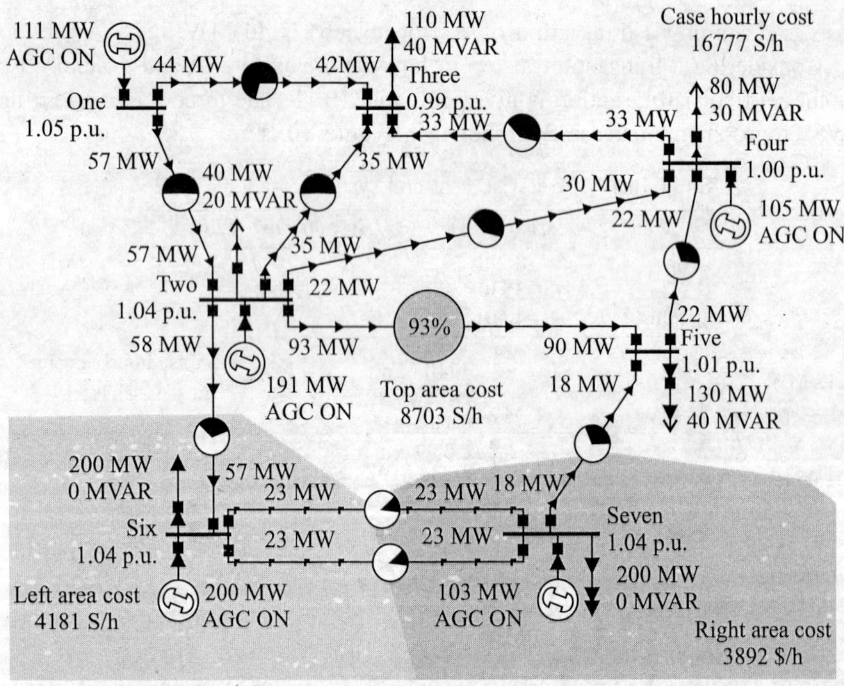

Figure 10.17 Three area system in PWS environment for case 3.

From Figure 10.17 it is also observed that there is 93% of power flow in the line between bus 2 and bus 5. Compared to the previous case, the system cost is reduced and the power flow under this transaction is also depicted.

Case 4: Assuming a simultaneous bilateral transaction of T_1 (top to left) is 30 MW and T_2 (top to right) is 40 MW.

Considering a transaction of top to left and top to right, the areawise cost and system cost for the particular transaction is given in the Table 10.13. The three area system is shown in Figure 10.18.

Table 10.13 Areawise cost and system cost for case 4

Area	*Cost* (\$/h)	*System cost* (\$/h)
Top	9211	
Left	3702	16765
Right	3853	

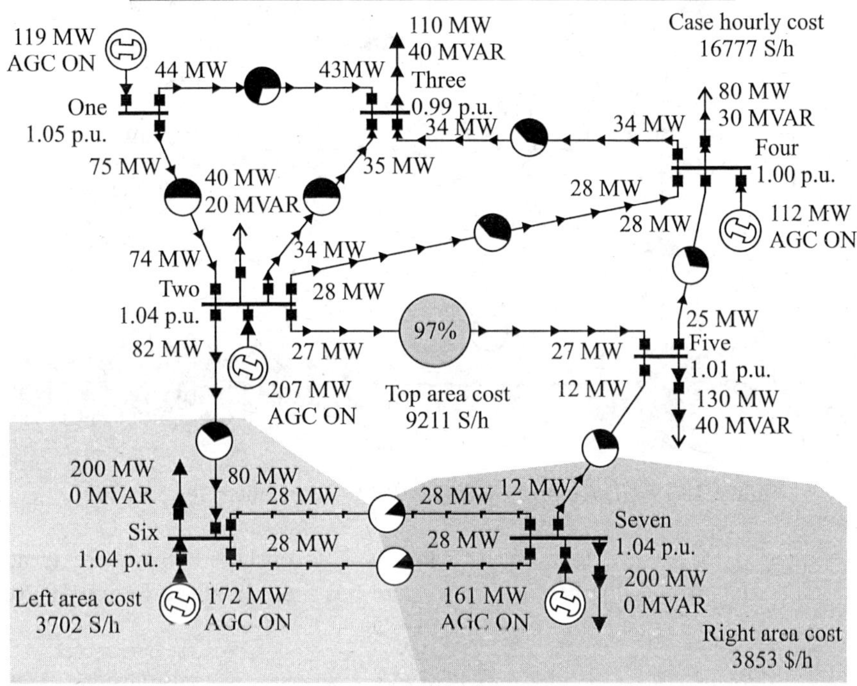

Figure 10.18 Three area system in PWS environment for case 4.

From Figure 10.18 it is also observed that there is 97% of power flow in the line between bus 2 and bus 5. Compared to the previous case, the system cost is reduced and the power flow under this transaction is also depicted.

Case 5: Assuming a simultaneous bilateral transaction of T_1 (top to left) is 40 MW and T_2 (top to right) is 40 MW.

Considering a transaction of top to left and top to right, the areawise cost and system cost for the particular transaction is given in Table 10.14. The three area system is shown in Figure 10.19.

From Figure 10.19 it is also observed that there is 98% of power flow in the line between bus 2 and bus 5. Compared to the previous case, the system cost is reduced and the power flow under this transaction is also depicted.

Table 10.14 Areawise cost and system cost for case 5

Area	*Cost* (\$/h)	*System cost* (\$/h)
Top	9211	
Left	3702	16765
Right	3853	

Suppose if we assume the simultaneous bilateral transaction of T_1 (top to left) is 50 MW and T_2 (top to right) is 50 MW, it is found that there is a reduction in the system cost (\$ 16733/h)

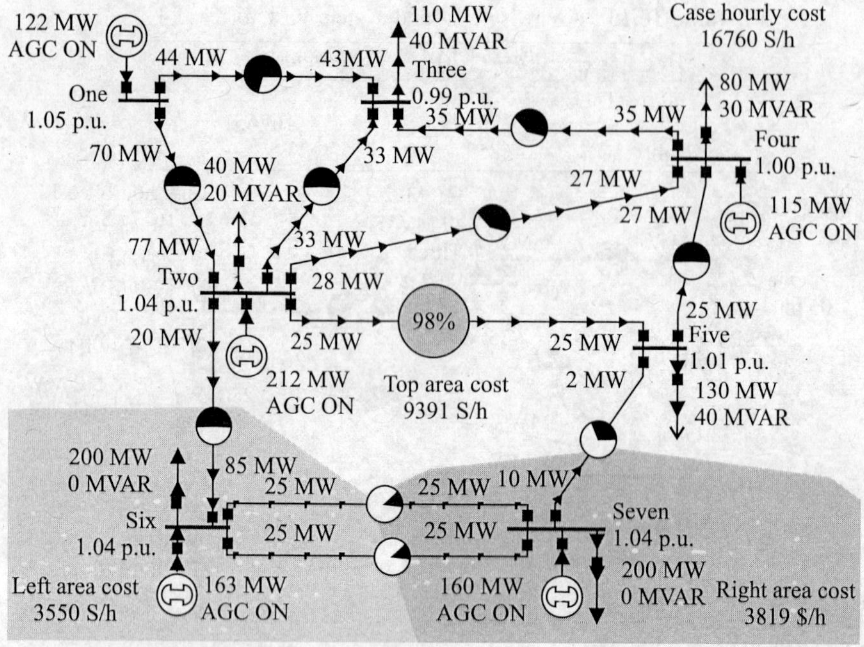

Figure 10.19 Three area system in PWS environment for case 5.

as compared to the previous cases, whereas it is observed that there is an overload exists in the line between bus 2 and bus 5 as shown in Figure 10.20.

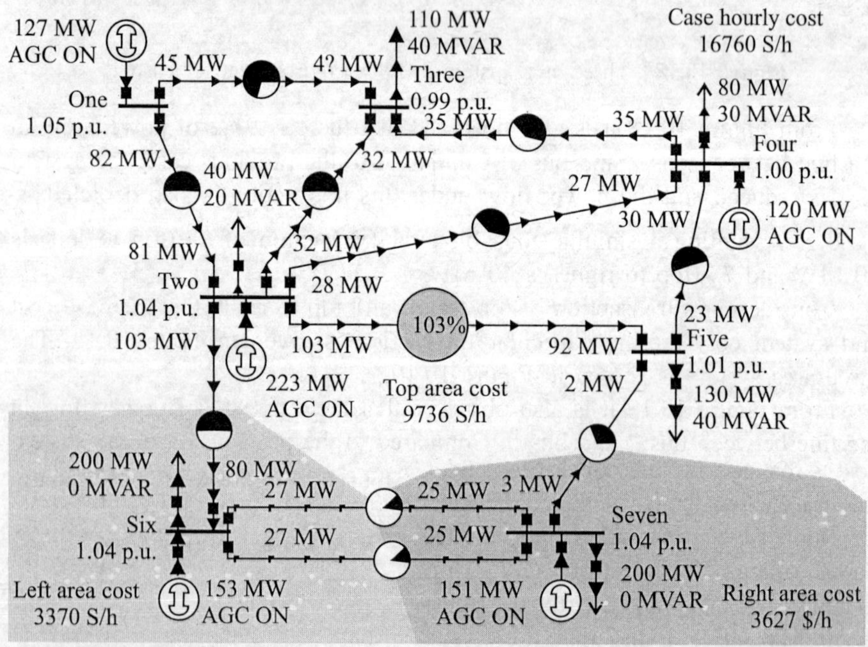

Figure 10.20 Three area system depicting an overload in PWS environment.

Review Questions

Part-A

1. Draw the figure which represents the single auction power pool.
2. Draw the figure which represents the double auction power pool.
3. What are the various structures of power pools?
4. How are the energy interchange schedules cleared in energy brokerage system?
5. Tabulate the comparison between the open access and the pool structure.
6. What is meant by the single auction power pool?
7. What is the double auction power pool?
8. What is meant by the joint dispatch?
9. What are the three types of power pools?
10. What is a power pool?
11. What are the two types of market settlement adopted by the market operator?
12. Define the system marginal price.

Part-B

1. Give the comparison of two different market structures with respect to ISO and also explain any one market structure in detail.
2. Explain the multi-area joint dispatch problem with a suitable example.
3. Consider a four utility joint dispatch as shown in the figure below. The generation capacity and composite cost functions are given in the table. Find the system cost reductions when the utilities operate through a joint dispatch as compared to when they operate independently. Take T_{KM} = 18MW

Table Multi-utility power interchange system

Utility	a_0 (\$/MWh)	b_0 (\$/MWh)	c_0 (\$/MWh)	P_{max} (MW)	P_{min} (MW)	P_D (MW)
A	1.8	10.5	0.5	150	20	120
B	2.8	24.5	0.8	250	30	200
C	3.0	15.6	0.4	230	40	180
D	1.5	20.1	0.6	125	25	75

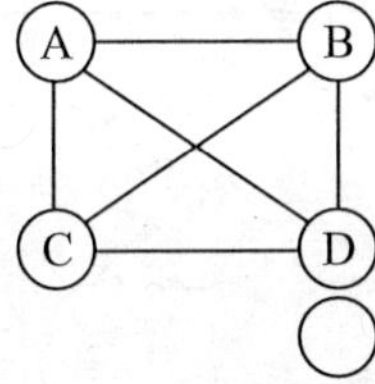

Figure A four utility joint dispatch model.

4. Explain the activities of ISO in pool markets.
5. Consider the four utilities joined together for dispatch. The generation capacity and cost function are given in the following table.

Utility	a_0 ($/MWh)	b_0 ($/MWh)	c_0 ($/MWh)	P_{max} (MW)	P_{min} (MW)	P_D (MW)
A	1.8	10.5	0.5	150	20	120
B	2.8	24.5	0.8	250	30	200
C	3.0	15.6	0.4	230	40	180
D	1.5	20.1	0.6	125	25	75

Let each transmission line has a power carrying capacity of 15 MW. Explain the optimum interchange schedule obtained through joint dispatch.
6. Explain the operation and the need of power pools with a suitable example.
7. Explain the single auction market settlement with a suitable example.
8. What are the two types of market structure? Explain the role of ISO in any one market structure.
9. Explain the multi-area joint dispatch problem with a suitable example.
10. The operator of a centralized market for electrical energy has received the bids as shown in the following table for the supply of electrical energy during a given period. Build the supply curve and assume that this market operates unilaterally, that is, the demand does not bid and is represented by a forecast. Calculate the market price, and the revenue of each of the following loads: 400 MW, 600 MW.

Company	*Amount* (MWh)	*Price* ($/MWh)
Red	200	12.5
Red	50	14.0
Red	50	18.0
Blue	150	10.5
Blue	50	13.0
Blue	100	15.0
Green	50	13.5
Green	50	14.5
Green	50	15.5

CHAPTER 11

Available Transfer Capability

11.1 Introduction

Since 1980s, the electricity supply industry has been undergoing rapid and irreversible changes reshaping the industry that is remarkably stable and served the public well. A significant feature of these changes is that it allows for competition among generators and creates market conditions in the industry, which are seen as necessary to reduce costs of energy production and distribution, eliminate certain inefficiencies, shed manpower and increase customer choice.

South American countries, such as Argentina and Chile, were the first few to introduce deregulated market of electricity in the mid-eighties followed by the UK, Scandivinian countries and the USA in the 1990s, where it is now fully operational. Some of the Asian countries, including India, have already taken initial steps in this direction. Many factors such as technology advances, changes in political and ideological attitudes, regulatory failures, high tariffs, managerial inadequacy, global financial drives, the rise of environmentalism, and the shortage of public resources for investment in developing countries contributed to the worldwide trend towards deregulation.

There are many variations in the deregulated scenarios for electric power systems around the world. Accordingly, there exist different schemes for operation and regulating access to transmission systems. The difference may be due to historical, political, geographical or economic factors, specific to each country or area. However, each deregulated scheme must address the fundamental technical issue associated with the properly operating open transmission network. One such technical problem that has to be handled carefully is the Available Transfer Capability (ATC).

11.2 Definitions

According to NERC Report–ATC is a measure of the transfer capability remaining in the physical transmission network for further commercial activity over and above already committed uses. The term capability here refers to the ability of the line(s) to reliably transfer power from one bus/area to another. It is different from the transfer capacity in the sense that capacity implies the rating of the specified line(s) and that accounts for the thermal limits only. Mathematically, ATC is defined as:

$$\text{ATC} = \text{TTC} - \text{TRM} - \{\text{ETC} + \text{CBM}\} \tag{11.1}$$

where TTC refers to total transfer capability, TRM refers to transmission reliability margin, ETC stands for existing transfer commitments and CBM indicates capacity benefit margin.

The ATC between two specific areas/buses gives the upper limit of additional power flow between them for a specified time period under given conditions. The terms associated with the definition of ATC are described below in Figure 11.1.

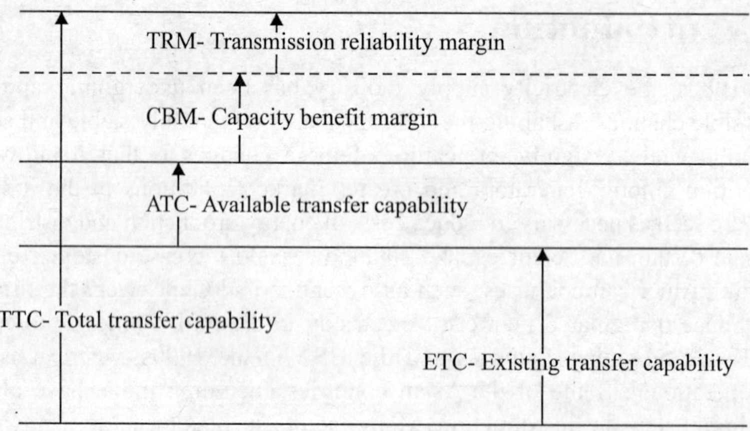

Figure 11.1 Basic definition of ATC.

Total transfer capability (TTC): It is the amount of electric power that can be transferred over the interconnected transmission network in a reliable manner under a reasonable range of uncertainties and contingencies. In the process of determining TTC, system conditions, system limits, contingencies, parallel path flows and effects of non-simultaneous and simultaneous transfers are to be considered.

Transmission reliability margin (TRM): It is defined as the amount of transmission transfer capability necessary to ensure that the interconnected network is secure under a reasonable range of uncertainties in the system conditions.

Capacity benefit margin (CBM): It is the amount of transmission transfer capability reserved by the load serving entitles to ensure access to generation from interconnected systems to meet generation reliability requirements. It also helps to reduce the installed capacity of the plant.

Existing transfer commitments (ETC): It refers to the power transfer capability that must be reserved for already committed transactions.

A general method for determination of ATC, TRM and CBM is given in the NERC report. However, the service providers is free to choose any appropriate method that gives the loadability of the system according to the security and reliability requirements. A high value of ATC will promote the commercial transaction opportunities but it will undermine the system security, while a low value will unnecessarily limit the commercial transactions. Usually, TRM and CBM are decided by the utilities according to their operating guidelines and reliability requirements.

In the literatures pertaining the methods for determining ATC, a more simplified definition of ATC is considered. As per Gravener and Nwankpa, 'The ATC is the limiting transfer value between two control areas (source and sink) that is available without any violation of power system operating properties, e.g. thermal overload and voltage limits'. The inclusion of TRM and CBM in the value of ATC as defined above is implied. The ISO or the TRANSCO has to set aside correct margins from the ATC. CBM may be treated by the generating entities to ensure their own reliability.

The information of ATC, as an important indicator of the system performance, is useful in restructured energy market in the following ways:

1. It provides the knowledge of power system capability about the present system condition.
2. Running the system under the ATC limits also ensures system security and reliability to some extent, since the calculation of ATC is based on the security constraints with the consideration of critical contingencies that can lead the system normal state to alert state.
3. The ATC is required in making decisions for the transactions between the market participants after checking the power contracts between themselves.
4. The ATC is also useful in enhancing the system capability. With the knowledge of the limiting condition for the ATC, the system operator can take some operating or planning decision to avoid this limiting condition and thus enhance the system capability.
5. The ATC value can also serve as an indicator of power congestion through transmission lines.
6. The ATC is useful in transmission costing function. The ISO can put more transmission cost for the transaction through transmission path having a low value of ATC. This extra transmission cost can be used in increasing the transmission capabilities for the transmission path.

11.3 Principles of ATC Determination

ATC of a transmission network is its unutilized transfer capacity that is available for further transactions to the market participants. Power transaction between a specific seller bus/area and a buyer bus/area can be committed only when sufficient ATC is available for that interface to ensure the system security. The information about the ATC is to be continuously updated and made available to the market participants through the internet based system such as open access same time information system (OASIS).

The basic objective behind the determination of ATC is to tell market entities about the system limitations, beforehand, in terms of additional amount of power that can be transferred from one area to another. Since private parties are interested only in commercial aspects, it is the responsibility of the SO to determine, update and post the current value of ATC. Following are the governing principles for ATC determination.

1. ATC calculation must produce commercially viable results. ATC provided by the calculations must give a reasonable and dependable indication of transfer capabilities available to the power market.
2. ATC calculations must recognize time-variant power flow conditions on the entire inter-connected transmission network.
3. ATC calculations must recognize the dependency of ATC on points of electric power injection, the directions of transfers across the interconnected transmission network, and the points of power extraction.
4. Regional and wide-area co-ordination is necessary to develop and post the information that reflects the ATC of the inter-connected transmission network.
5. ATC calculations must conform to regulatory guidelines in the specific country (such as NERC in the US), regional, sub-regional, power pool, and individual system reliability and operating policies, criteria or guidelines.
6. The determination of ATC must accommodate reasonable uncertainties in the system conditions and provide operating flexibility to ensure the secure operation of the interconnected network.

The ETC determines the base case operating point for the specified time interval. In general, without considering the TRM and CBM, the ATC can be defined as:

$$\text{ATC} = \text{TTC} - \text{ETC} \tag{11.2}$$

It shows the direct relationship between TTC and ATC. Hence, all the constraints applicable to TTC are also applicable to ATC and vice-versa. The static limits considered for the calculation of static ATC or TTC may be broadly classified as:

Line flow limits: The line flow limits have been defined as the maximum real power transfer capability of a line obtained from its thermal and stability limit considerations.

Bus voltage limits: The bus voltage limits are imposed to ensure secure and satisfactory operation of the electric devices in the system. Most of the electric devices fail to operate properly at under-voltage while over voltages stress the insulation and may be destructive. Therefore, it is common practice to limit the bus voltages within narrow range around the nominal voltage. Usually it lies between ±5% and ±10% from its nominal value.

Steady state stability limit: When the generation and loadings in a power system is gradually increased such that power balance is maintained, a limit is reached at which the load-flow fails to converge. This is known as the steady state stability limit of the transmission system and is the maximum power that the transmission network can transfer in steady state. If the load admittance is further increased in an attempt to increase the load, the voltage instability may occur and the power delivered to the load will decrease. At the steady state stability limit, which is also characterized by non-convergence of the load flow equations, one of the eigenvalues of the load flow Jacobian becomes zero. This also corresponds to Saddle node bifurcation in the system.

11.4 Methods of Static ATC Determination

The methods used for the ATC determination can be classified under three categories, namely

(i) Method based on multiple load flow and continuation power flow
(ii) Method based on optimization power flow
(iii) Method based on linear sensitivity factors

11.4.1 ATC Determination Using Multiple Load Flow and Continuation Power Flow

This method runs ac load flow for each increment of transaction between an interface and checks whether any of the operating conditions such as line flow limit or bus voltage limit is violated. For the increment of transaction, continuation power flow (CPF) is also run to find out the maximum loadability or voltage instability point. The minimum out of the two critical transaction values is taken as the TTC for the system intact condition. This is repeated for each outage case and the worst case is used to declare the TTC and ATC values. A procedure to calculate ATC based on this concept is given in Figure 11.2.

The selected base case condition and the transmission path are used as an input data to the methods for further calculation of the transfer capability. TC11 is the transfer capability of the transmission line with all elements present in the system considering thermal limit, bus voltage limit and generator real and reactive power limit. TC12 is the transfer capability of the transmission path with all elements present in the system considering voltage instability condition determined from the CPF. TC1 gives the transfer capability of the transmission path with all elements present in the system. It is calculated as, TC1 = Minimum {TC11, TC12}.

For each contingency condition transfer capability is calculated using repetitive power flow with incremental increase of power transfer through

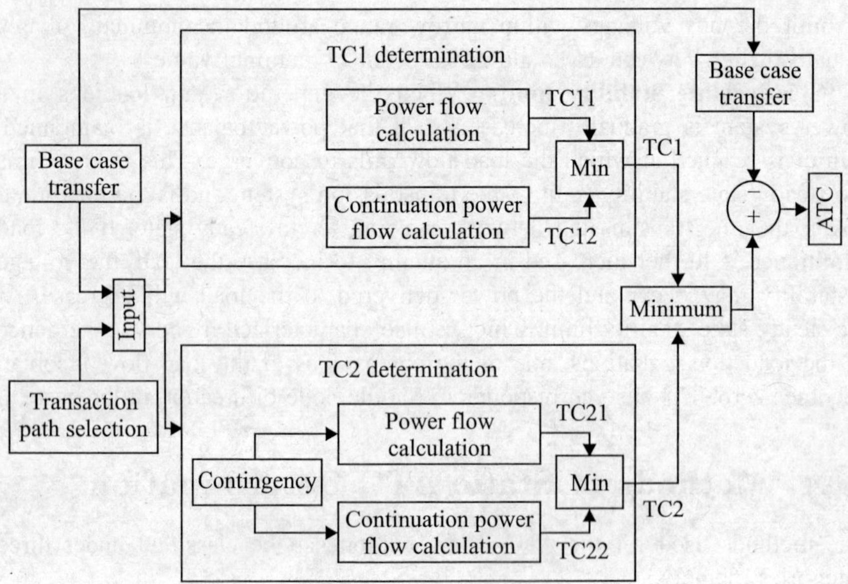

Figure 11.2 Flow chart for ATC determination.

the selected transmission path. The minimum of these transfer capabilities is taken as TC21. TC22 is the minimum of the transfer capability calculated for different contingency conditions considering the voltage instability criteria. TC2 gives the transfer capability of the transmission path considering different contingency conditions. It is calculated as TC2 = Minimum {TC21, TC22}.

Total transfer capability (TTC) of the transmission path is calculated as

$$\text{TTC} = \text{Minimum } \{\text{TC1, TC2}\}$$

Then, ATC for the transmission path is given as

$$\text{ATC} = \text{TTC} - \text{base case power transfer on transmission path}$$

11.4.2 Optimization Based Method

The ATC determination can be formulated as an optimization problem which finds out the maximum value of the transaction between given interface while satisfying the network power balance (equality constraints) and security constraints such as line flow, voltage limits and voltage instability or SNB conditions. G. Hamoud proposed an optimization-based method using dc load-flow. A large fictitious load and a large fictitious generator with very high cost-function were assumed to be connected at the buyer bus and a large but cheap generator connected to the seller bus. The generation at the seller bus was maximized through economic load dispatch. ATC was computed from the optimal output of the fictitious generator at the seller bus.

11.4.3 ATC Determination Using Linear Sensitivity Factors

Linear sensitivity factors offer a great potential for real time calculation of ATC. Use of these factors offers an approximate but extremely fast model for the static ATC determination. Christe et al. and Ejebe et al. have discussed the use of dc power transfer distribution factors (DCPTDFs) and line outage distribution factors for the ATC determination. But these factors are derived based on dc load flow assumptions and hence provides less accurate results. Ashwani et al. have proposed a new set of ac power transfer distribution factors (ACPTDFs), voltage distribution factors (VDFs) and outage distribution factors to determine static ATC more precisely.

The coefficient of linear relationship between the amount of a transaction and the flow on a line has been termed power transfer distribution factor (PTDF). PTDFs determine the linear impact of a transfer (or changes in power injection) on the elements of the power system. These values provide a linearized approximation of how the flow on the transmission lines and interfaces change in response to transaction between the seller and the buyer.

(a) DC power transfer distribution factors (DCPTDFs): A transaction is a specific amount of power that is injected into the system at a bus by a generating company and consumed at another bus by a consumer. The linearity property of the dc power flow model has been used to find the transaction amount that would give rise to a specific power flow, such as an interface limit. The PTDF defined from dc load flow relationship is being called DCPTDF. $\text{PTDF}_{ij,\,mn}$ is the fraction of the amount of a transaction from bus m to bus n that flows over a transmission line connecting bus i and bus j.

Using dc power flow, the real power flow (P_{ij}) in a line between buses i and j can be computed as:

$$P_{ij} = \frac{1}{x_{ij}}(\delta_i - \delta_j) \tag{11.3}$$

where x_{ij} is the series reactance of the line, δ_i and δ_j are the voltage angles at buses i and j respectively. Voltage magnitudes at all the buses are assumed to be one per unit. For a given real power injection vector $[P]$, the dc load flow can be used to solve the bus angle vector $[\delta]$ as given below,

$$[\delta] = [X]\,[P] \tag{11.4}$$

If X_{pq} denotes pqth element of the matrix $[X]$, the DCPTDF for a transaction between buses m and n and flow in line-ij can be expressed as,

$$\text{DCPTDF}_{ij,mn} = \frac{X_{im} - X_{jm} - X_{in} + X_{jn}}{x_{ij}} \tag{11.5}$$

The change in the line flow ($\Delta P_{ij}^{\text{new}}$) associated with a new transaction ($\Delta P_{mn}^{\text{new}}$) is given by the following equation,

$$\Delta P_{ij}^{\text{new}} = \text{DCPTDF}_{ij,mn} * P_{mn}^{\text{new}} \tag{11.6}$$

Since, the PTDFs define a linear relationship, for a multilateral transaction case, the new real power flows in the lines can be determined by superimposing those corresponding to the individual transactions.

(b) ACPTDF formulation: The ac power transfer distribution factors proposed for calculation of ATC were used to find various transmission system quantities for a change in MW transaction at different operating conditions.

Consider a bilateral transaction t_k between a seller bus m and a buyer bus n. Line 1 carries the part of the transacted power and is connected between buses i and j. For a change in real power, transaction among the above buyer and seller by Δt_k MW, if the change in a transmission line quantity q_1 is Δq_1, power transfer distribution factors can be defined as,

$$\text{ACPTDF}_{ij,mn} = \frac{\Delta q_l}{\Delta t_k} \tag{11.7}$$

The transmission quantity q_l can be either real power flow from bus i to j (P_{ij}) (or) real power flow from bus j to bus i (P_{ji}). The above factors have been proposed to compute at a base case load flow with results using sensitivity properties of NRLF Jacobian. Consider full Jacobian in polar coordinates $[J_T]$, defined to include all the buses except slack (including ΔQ-ΔV equations also for PV buses).

$$\begin{bmatrix} \Delta\delta \\ \Delta V \end{bmatrix} = \begin{bmatrix} \dfrac{\partial P}{\partial \delta} & \dfrac{\partial P}{\partial V} \\ \dfrac{\partial Q}{\partial \delta} & \dfrac{\partial Q}{\partial V} \end{bmatrix}^{-1} \begin{bmatrix} \Delta P \\ \Delta Q \end{bmatrix} = [J_T]^{-1} \begin{bmatrix} \Delta P \\ \Delta Q \end{bmatrix} \tag{11.8}$$

In Eq. (11.8), the change in active power flow of line i–j with respect to changes in state variables is determined as

$$\frac{\partial P_{ij}}{\partial \delta_e} = \begin{Bmatrix} 0 & \text{for } e \neq i, j \\ -V_i V_j Y_{ij} \sin(\delta_i - \delta_j - \theta_{ij}) & \text{for } e = i \\ V_i V_j Y_{ij} \sin(\delta_i - \delta_j - \theta_{ij}) & \text{for } e = j \end{Bmatrix}$$

$$\frac{\partial P_{ij}}{\partial V_e} = \begin{Bmatrix} 0 & \text{for } e \neq i, j \\ 2V_i Y_{ij} \cos\theta_{ij} + V_j Y_{ij} \cos(\delta_i - \delta_j - \theta_{ij}) & \text{for } e = i \\ V_j Y_{ij} \cos(\delta_i - \delta_j - \theta_{ij}) & \text{for } e = j \end{Bmatrix}$$

In a base case load flow, if only one of the kth bilateral transactions is changed by Δt_k MW, only the following two entries in the mismatch vector on RHS of Eq. (11.8) will be non-zero.

$$\Delta P_m = \Delta t_k; \quad \Delta P_n = -\Delta t_k \tag{11.9}$$

With the above mismatch vector elements, the change in voltage angle and magnitude at all buses can be computed from Eqs. (11.8) and (11.9) and, hence, the new voltage profile can be calculated. These can be utilized to compute all the transmission quantities q_l and hence the corresponding quantities Δq_l from the base case. Once the Δq_l for all the lines corresponding to a change in transaction Δt_k is known, PTDFs can be obtained from Eq. (11.7). These ACPTDFs, which are computed at a base load flow condition, have been utilized for computing change in transmission quantities at other operating conditions as well.

ACPTDF is also calculated for multilateral transaction in which a group of sellers have a bilateral contract with a group of buyers. The change in multilateral transaction can be assumed to be shared equally by each of the sellers and buyers. However, the transaction amount can be shared in any pre-decided ratio in a deregulated environment. The mismatch vector for the multilateral transactions will have non-zero entries corresponding to the buyer and seller buses. The rest of the procedure for the calculation of ACPTDF will be the same as outlined above for the bilateral transaction case.

(c) Formulation of ACPTDFs for multilateral transactions: The ACPTDFs can also be calculated for multilateral transactions in which a group of sellers have bilateral contract with a group of buyers. In the present study, a change in the multilateral transaction is assumed to be shared equally amongst each of the buyers. However, the transaction amount can be shared in any pre-decided ratio in a deregulated market. The mismatch vector for the multilateral transactions will have non-zero entries corresponding to the buyer and seller buses between which the transactions are taking place. With this mismatch vector, change in the voltage angle and voltage magnitude at all the buses can be computed using Eq. (11.8), and hence the new voltage profile can be obtained. These can be utilized to compute MW values of all the transmission quantities q_l and hence the corresponding changes in these quantities Δq_l from the base case. Once the Δq_l for all the lines corresponding to a change in transaction Δt_k is known, ACPTDFs can be obtained from Eq. (11.7).

These ACPTDFs, which are computed at a base-case load flow condition, have been utilized for computing change in transmission quantities at other operating conditions too.

ATC at base case, between buses m and n using the line flow limit (thermal limit) criterion is mathematically formulated using PTDF as,

$$\text{ATC}_{mn} = \min\{T_{ij,mn}\},\ ij \in N_L \tag{11.10}$$

where $T_{ij,mn}$ denotes the transfer limit values for each line in the system. It is given by

$$T_{ij,mn} = \begin{cases} \dfrac{(P_{ij}^{\max} - P_{ij}^{0})}{\text{PTDF}_{ij,mn}}; & \text{PTDF}_{ij,mn} > 0 \\ \alpha\,(\text{infinite}); & \text{PTDF}_{ij,mn} = 0 \\ \dfrac{(-P_{ij}^{\max} - P_{ij}^{0})}{\text{PTDF}_{ij,mn}}; & \text{PTDF}_{ij,mn} < 0 \end{cases} \tag{11.11}$$

where $P_{ij}^{\max}$ is the MW power limit of a line between buses i and j, P_{ij}^{0} is the base case power flow in line between buses i and j, $\text{PTDF}_{ij,mn}$ is the power transfer distribution factor for the line between buses i and j when a transaction is taking place between buses m and n and N_L is the total number of lines.

The PTDF may be either DCPTDF or ACPTDF and it depends on the method of formulation.

11.5 ATC Determination Considering the Effect of Contingency Analysis

ATC determination for line outage contingency mode and generator outage contingency mode are discussed below. Formulation of line outage power transfer distribution factor (LOPTDF) and outage transfer distribution factor (OTDF) are necessary for the determination of ATC under line outage contingency. The most sensitive line can be found out using one index termed real power line flow performance index (PI). The severity of the system loading under normal and contingency cases in an area or between areas can be described by index PI as given below.

$$\text{PI} = \sum_{m=1}^{N_l} \frac{w_m}{2n} \left[\frac{P_{lm}}{P_{lm}^{\max}} \right]^{2n} \tag{11.12}$$

where P_{lm} is the real power flow and $P_{lm}^{\max}$ is the rated capacity of the line l–m, n is the exponent and w_m is a real non-negative weighing coefficient which may be used to reflect the importance of lines. PI will be small when all the lines are within their limits and reach a high value when there are overloads.

Formulation of generator outage distribution factor (GODF) is necessary for determining ATC under generator outage contingency condition. The procedure adopted for formulating GODF is similar to PTDF in all aspects.

Line outage power transfer distribution factor (LOPTDF) is a sensitivity measure of how a change in a line's status affects the flows on other lines in the system. On an energized line, the LOPTDF calculation determines the percentage of the present line flow that will be show up on other transmission lines after the outage of the line. When calculating PTDF values for interfaces that include contingent lines, the PTDF values calculated are actually called an outage transfer distribution factor (OTDF). An OTDF is similar to PTDF, except an OTDF provides a linearized approximation of the post-outage change in flow on a transmission line in response to a transaction between the seller and the buyer. The OTDF value is a function of PTDF values and LOPTDF values.

Consider the outage of a line connected between buses r and s having preoutage real power flow P_{rs}^0 and P_{sr}^0 from bus r to bus s and bus s to bus r respectively. Let $P_{ij,\,rs}$ be the post-outage flow in a line connected between buses i and j. The change in the line flows can be written as,

$$\Delta P_{ij,rs} = P_{ij,rs} - P_{ij}^0 \tag{11.13}$$

The line outage power transfer distribution factor (LOPTDF) can be defined as the ratio of $P_{ij,\,rs}$ to the real power flow transmitted in the line taken for outage and connected between the buses r and s.

$$\text{LOPTDF}_{ij,rs} = \Delta P_{ij,rs} / P_{rs}^0 \tag{11.14}$$

The OTDF value for line i-j during outage of line r-s is

$$\text{OTDF}_{ij,rs} = \text{PTDF}_{ij,mn} + \text{LOPTDF}_{ij,rs} \times \text{PTDF}_{rs,mn} \tag{11.15}$$

Then, for each line during each contingency, determine another transfer limit value

$$T_{ij,rs} = \begin{Bmatrix} \dfrac{(P_{ij}^{\max} - P_{ij,rs})}{\text{OTDF}_{ij,rs}}; & \text{OTDF}_{ij,rs} > 0 \\ \alpha\,(\text{infinite}); & \text{OTDF}_{ij,rs} = 0 \\ \dfrac{(-P_{ij}^{\max} - P_{ij,rs})}{\text{OTDF}_{ij,\,rs}}; & \text{OTDF}_{ij,rs} < 0 \end{Bmatrix} \tag{11.16}$$

ATC under a line outage condition, for the transaction between m and n, taking the line flow limit criteria into account can be determined as

$$\text{ATC}_{mn,rs} = \min\{T_{ij,mn}, T_{ij,rs}\}, \quad ij \in N_L \quad \text{and} \quad rs \in N_{LC} \tag{11.17}$$

where N_{LC} is the total number of line outage contingencies, $P_{ij,\,rs}$ is the power flow on line i-j after outage of the line r-s, $\text{LOPTDF}_{ij,\,rs}$ are the line outage power transfer distribution factor for line i-j when line r-s is out, $\text{PTDF}_{ij,\,mn}$ are the power transfer distribution factor for line i-j when transaction is taking place between bus m and bus n, $\text{PTDF}_{rs,\,mn}$ is power transfer distribution factor for line r-s outage and for transaction between bus m and bus n.

The outage of generator is equivalent to a transfer of $-P_k^0$ from the generator bus to the contingency assumed sink. Hence it is correct to assume that GODF's are equal to PTDF's of this transfer. For dc power flow method, generation shift sensitivity factor $a_{ij,\,k}$ are calculated and denotes the sensitivity of the MW power flow on line i-j to a change or outage of generation occurring at bus k.

It is assumed that, the change in generation, ΔP_k is exactly compensated by an opposite change in generation at the reference bus, and that all other generators remain fixed. Using the pre-calculated set of 'a' factors, the change in power flow on each line due to the generator outage is given by

$$\Delta P_{ij,k} = a_{ij,k} \times \Delta P_k \tag{11.18}$$

where $\Delta P_k = -P_k^0$ and the outage generator was generating P_k^0 before outage. The resultant power flow on each line due to generator outage is,

$$P_{ij,k} = P_{ij}^0 + \Delta P_{ij,k} \qquad ij \in N_L \text{ and } k \in N_{GC} \tag{11.19}$$

where P_{ij}^0 is the pre-outage power flow and N_{GC} represents total number of generator outage contingencies.

For ac power flow method, the network sensitivity methods may not be adequate and the operation of control system will have to incorporate full ac power flow for each generator outage contingency analysis.

For each generator outage contingency, determine the transfer limit value as

$$T_{ij,k} = \begin{cases} \dfrac{(P_{ij}^{\max} - P_{ij,k})}{\text{GODF}_{ij,k}}; & \text{GODF}_{ij,k} > 0 \\ \alpha\,(\text{infinite}); & \text{GODF}_{ij,k} = 0 \\ \dfrac{(-P_{ij}^{\max} - P_{ij,k})}{\text{GODF}_{ij,k}}; & \text{GODF}_{ij,k} < 0 \end{cases} \tag{11.20}$$

where $\text{GODF}_{ij,k}$ is the generator outage distribution factors for line i-j due to outage of generator k for the transaction taking place between bus m and bus n.

ATC under generator outage condition, for the transaction between m and n, taking the line flow limit criteria into account can be determined as,

$$\text{ATC}_{mn,k} = \min\{T_{ij,mn}, T_{ij,k}\} \qquad ij \in N_L \text{ and } k \in N_{GC} \tag{11.21}$$

11.6 ATC Calculation Using MATLAB

11.6.1 Algorithm for Static ATC Determination

The basic steps used for computing ATC using ACPTDFs for each transaction are as follows:

Step 1: Read the system input data.

Step 2: Run base case load flow and determine the optimal settings of the generators.

Step 3: Consider wheeling transactions (t_k).

Step 4: Compute ac power transfer distribution factors as per Eq. (11.7).

Step 5: Take transactions as variables, line flow, real and reactive power limits of generators as constraints and compute the feasible wheeling transactions.

Step 6: Dispatch the possible transactions and determine the ATC as per Eq. (11.10).

Step 7: If any line outage contingency analysis is performed, then perform contingency analysis as per Eq. (11.12) and then proceed, otherwise go to step 12.

Step 8: Calculate LOPTDF and OTDF as per Eqs. (11.14) and (11.15).

Step 9: Calculate ATC for line outage contingency case as per Eq. (11.17).

Step 10: If any generator outage contingency is performed, then proceed otherwise go to step 12.

Step 11: Calculate ATC for generator outage contingency using GODF case as per Eq. (11.21).

Step 12: If any other transaction is carried out, then consider the next transaction and go to step 4, otherwise proceed.

Step 13: Print the value ATC.

Example

ATC determination with AC power transfer distribution factors using MATLAB environment is shown for a sample six-bus system (Figure 11.3). This system has 3 generators and 11 lines. Generator at bus 1 is considered as slack bus. The simulation studies were carried out on Intel Pentium Dual Core, 2.40 GHz system in MATLAB 7.3 environment. Bus data and line data for the system are provided in the program data sheet.

ATC is determined for both normal mode operation, i.e. base case and line outage contingency mode operation. The steps starting with Y-bus formation, Newton-Raphson load flow, line flow results, ac power transfer distribution factor formulation and ATC determination are dealt separately. The limiting line for the considered transaction is also specified.

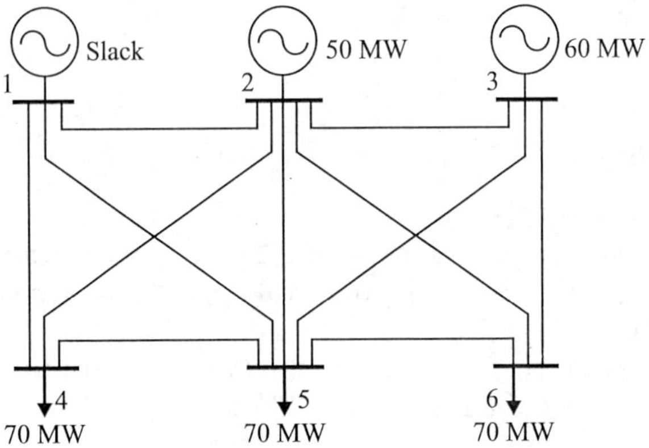

Figure 11.3 Sample six-bus system.

The program can be used for determining ATC for the simultaneous bilateral and multilateral transactions. The given coding shows the procedure for calculating ATC for the considered bilateral transaction between buses 3 (seller bus) and 6 (buyer bus). The thermal limit of each line is considered as a constraint and reactive power demand at load buses has been taken as constant.

Base Case ATC Calculation

Bus Datas and Line Datas of Sample Six-Bus System

```
basemva = 100; accuracy = 0.001; accel = 1.8; maxiter = 100;G=3;
% 0 Load Bus 1 Slack Bus 2 -Pv Bus
% Bus Bus Voltage Angle ---Load---- ----Generator---- Static Mvar
%   No code Mag.     Degree MW Mvar MW     Mvar Qmin Qmax +Qc/-Ql
busdata=    [1 1 1.05 0.0    0  0    0.0   0.0  0.0  0.0  0
             2 2 1.05  0.0    0  0    69.36 0.0  0.0  0.0  0
             3 2 1.07  0.0    0  0    77.47 0.0  0.0  0.0  0
             4 0 1.0   0.0    70 70   0.0   0.0  0.0  0.0  0
             5 0 1.0   0.0    70 70   0     0.0  0.0  0.0  0
             6 0 1.0   0.0    70 70   0     0.0  0.0  0.0  0];

%          Bus bus R X 1/2 B = 1 for lines
%            nl nr p.u. p.u. p.u. tr. tap, thermal limit
linedata=[1  2  0.1   0.2  0.02    1      40
          1  4  0.05  0.2  0.02    1      80
          1  5  0.08  0.3  0.030   1      60
          2  3  0.05  0.25 0.030   1      40
          2  4  0.05  0.10 0.01    1      60
          2  5  0.1   0.3  0.020   1      30
          2  6  0.07  0.20 0.025   1      90
          3  5  0.12  0.26 0.025   1      70
          3  6  0.02  0.10 0.01    1      100
          4  5  0.2   0.40 0.04    1      20
          5  6  0.1   0.30 0.03    1      40];
```

Y Bus Formation

```
j=sqrt(-1); i = sqrt(-1);
nl = linedata(:,1); nr = linedata(:,2); R = linedata(:,3);
X = linedata(:,4); Bc = j*linedata(:,5); a = linedata(:, 6);
limit=linedata(:,7);
nbr=length(linedata(:,1)); nbus = max(max(nl), max(nr));
Z = R + j*X; y= ones(nbr,1)./Z;   %branch admittance
for n = 1:nbr
if a(n) <= 0 a(n) = 1; else end
Ybus=zeros(nbus,nbus); % initialize Ybus to zero
  % formation of the off diagonal elements
for k=1:nbr;
```

```
    Ybus(nl(k),nr(k))=Ybus(nl(k),nr(k))-y(k)/a(k);
    Ybus(nr(k),nl(k))=Ybus(nl(k),nr(k));
  end
end
  % formation of the diagonal elements
for n=1:nbus
  for k=1:nbr
    if nl(k)==n
    Ybus(n,n) = Ybus(n,n)+y(k)/(a(k)^2) + Bc(k);
    elseif nr(k)==n
    Ybus(n,n) = Ybus(n,n)+y(k) +Bc(k);
    else, end
  end
end
%clear Pgg
Ybus;
```

Newton-Raphson Load Flow

```
ns=0; ng=0; Vm=0; delta=0; yload=0; deltad=0;
nbus = length(busdata(:,1));
for k=1:nbus
n=busdata(k,1);
kb(n)=busdata(k,2); Vm(n)=busdata(k,3); delta(n)=busdata(k, 4);
Pd(n)=busdata(k,5); Qd(n)=busdata(k,6); Pg(n)=busdata(k,7); Qg(n)
= busdata(k,8);
Qmin(n)=busdata(k, 9); Qmax(n)=busdata(k, 10);
Qsh(n)=busdata(k, 11);
  if Vm(n) <= 0 Vm(n) = 1.0; V(n) = 1 + j*0;
  else delta(n) = pi/180*delta(n);
    V(n) = Vm(n)*(cos(delta(n)) + j*sin(delta(n)));
    P(n)=(Pg(n)-Pd(n))/basemva;
    Q(n)=(Qg(n)-Qd(n)+ Qsh(n))/basemva;
    S(n) = P(n) + j*Q(n);
  end
end
for k=1:nbus
if kb(k) == 1, ns = ns+1; else, end
if kb(k) == 2 ng = ng+1; else, end
ngs(k) = ng;
nss(k) = ns;
end
Ym=abs(Ybus); t = angle(Ybus);
m=2*nbus-ng-2*ns;
maxerror = 1; converge=1;
```

```
iter = 0;
% Start of iterations
clear A DC J DX
while maxerror >= accuracy & iter <= maxiter % Test for max. power
mismatch
for i=1:m
for k=1:m
  A(i,k)=0; %Initializing Jacobian matrix
end, end
iter = iter+1;
for n=1:nbus
nn=n-nss(n);
lm=nbus+n-ngs(n)-nss(n)-ns;
J11=0; J22=0; J33=0; J44=0;
  for i=1:nbr
    if nl(i) == n | nr(i) == n
      if nl(i) == n, l = nr(i); end
      if nr(i) == n, l = nl(i); end
      J11=J11+ Vm(n)*Vm(l)*Ym(n,l)*sin(t(n,l)- delta(n) +
delta(l));
      J33=J33+ Vm(n)*Vm(l)*Ym(n,l)*cos(t(n,l)- delta(n) +
delta(l));
      if kb(n)~=1
      J22=J22+ Vm(l)*Ym(n,l)*cos(t(n,l)- delta(n) + delta(l));
      J44=J44+ Vm(l)*Ym(n,l)*sin(t(n,l)- delta(n) + delta(l));
      else, end
      if kb(n) ~= 1 & kb(l) ~=1
      lk = nbus+l-ngs(l)-nss(l)-ns;
      ll = l -nss(l);
    % off diagonalelements of J1
  A(nn, ll) =-Vm(n)*Vm(l)*Ym(n,l)*sin(t(n,l)- delta(n) + delta(l));
      if kb(l) == 0 % off diagonal elements of J2
      A(nn, lk) =Vm(n)*Ym(n,l)*cos(t(n,l)- delta(n) + delta(l));end
      if kb(n) == 0 % off diagonal elements of J3
      A(lm, ll) =-Vm(n)*Vm(l)*Ym(n,l)*cos(t(n,l)-
delta(n)+delta(l)); end
     if kb(n) == 0 & kb(l) == 0 % off diagonal elements of J4
     A(lm, lk) =-Vm(n)*Ym(n,l)*sin(t(n,l)- delta(n) + delta(l));end
  else end
 else , end
end
Pk = Vm(n)^2*Ym(n,n)*cos(t(n,n))+J33;
Qk = -Vm(n)^2*Ym(n,n)*sin(t(n,n))-J11;
if kb(n) == 1 P(n)=Pk; Q(n) = Qk; end % Swing bus P
```

```
  if kb(n) == 2 Q(n)=Qk;
    if Qmax(n) ~= 0
    Qgc = Q(n)*basemva + Qd(n) - Qsh(n);
      if Qgc < Qmin(n), % tested. If not within limits Vm(n)
      Vm(n) = Vm(n) + 0.01; % is changed in steps of 0.01 pu to
      elseif Qgc > Qmax(n), % bring the generator Mvar within
      Vm(n) = Vm(n) - 0.01;end % the specified limits.
  else,end
end
if kb(n) ~= 1
  A(nn,nn) = J11; %diagonal elements of J1
  DC(nn) = P(n)-Pk;
  end
  if kb(n) == 0
    A(nn,lm) = 2*Vm(n)*Ym(n,n)*cos(t(n,n))+J22; %diagonal elements
of J2
  A(lm,nn)= J33; %diagonal elements of J3
  A(lm,lm)  =-2*Vm(n)*Ym(n,n)*sin(t(n,n))-J44; %diagonal  of
elements of J4
  DC(lm) = Q(n)-Qk;
 end
end
DX=A\DC';
for n=1:nbus
  nn=n-nss(n);
  lm=nbus+n-ngs(n)-nss(n)-ns;
  if kb(n) ~= 1
  delta(n) = delta(n)+DX(nn); end
  if kb(n) == 0
  Vm(n)=Vm(n)+DX(lm); end
end
 maxerror=max(abs(DC));
  if iter == maxiter & maxerror > accuracy
 fprintf('\nWARNING: Iterative solution did not converged after ')
 fprintf('%g', iter), fprintf(' iterations.\n\n')
 fprintf('Press Enter to terminate the iterations and print the
results \n')
 converge = 0; pause, else, end
 end
if converge ~= 1
  tech= (' ITERATIVE SOLUTION DID NOT CONVERGE'); else,
  tech=(' Power Flow Solution by Newton-Raphson Method');
end
V = Vm.*cos(delta)+j*Vm.*sin(delta);
```

```
deltad=180/pi*delta;
i=sqrt(-1);
k=0;
for n = 1:nbus
   if kb(n) == 1
   k=k+1;
   S(n)= P(n)+j*Q(n);
   Pg(n) = P(n)*basemva + Pd(n);
   Qg(n) = Q(n)*basemva + Qd(n) - Qsh(n);
   Pgg(k)=Pg(n);
   Qgg(k)=Qg(n); %june 97
   elseif kb(n) ==2
   k=k+1;
   S(n)=P(n)+j*Q(n);
   Qg(n) = Q(n)*basemva + Qd(n) - Qsh(n);
   Pgg(k)=Pg(n);
   Qgg(k)=Qg(n); % June 1997
 end
yload(n) = (Pd(n)- j*Qd(n)+j*Qsh(n))/(basemva*Vm(n)^2);
end
busdata(:,3)=Vm'; busdata(:,4)=deltad';
Pgt = sum(Pg); Qgt = sum(Qg); Pdt = sum(Pd); Qdt = sum(Qd); Qsht
= sum(Qsh);
```

Line Flow Results

```
SLT = 0;SL=0;linef=0;linel=0;
fprintf('\n')
fprintf(' Line Flow and Losses \n\n')
fprintf(' --Line-- Power at bus & line flow --Line loss--
Transformer\n')
fprintf(' from to MW Mvar MVA MW Mvar tap\n')

for n = 1:nbus
busprt = 0;
   for L = 1:nbr;
      if busprt == 0
      fprintf(' \n'), fprintf('%6g', n), fprintf(' %9.5f',
P(n)*basemva)
      fprintf('%9.5f', Q(n)*basemva), fprintf('%9.5f\n',
abs(S(n)*basemva))

      busprt = 1;
      else, end
      if nl(L)==n k = nr(L);
```

```
    In = (V(n) - a(L)*V(k))*y(L)/a(L)^2 + Bc(L)/a(L)^2*V(n);
    Ik = (V(k) - V(n)/a(L))*y(L) + Bc(L)*V(k);
    Snk = V(n)*conj(In)*basemva;
    Skn = V(k)*conj(Ik)*basemva;
    SL = Snk + Skn;
    SLT = SLT + SL;
    elseif nr(L)==n k = nl(L);
    In = (V(n) - V(k)/a(L))*y(L) + Bc(L)*V(n);
    Ik = (V(k) - a(L)*V(n))*y(L)/a(L)^2 + Bc(L)/a(L)^2*V(k);
    Snk = V(n)*conj(In)*basemva;
    Skn = V(k)*conj(Ik)*basemva;
    SL = Snk + Skn;
    SLL(L)=imag(SL);
    SLL1(L)=imag(Snk);
    SLT = SLT + SL;
    else, end
      if nl(L)==n | nr(L)==n
      fprintf('%12g', k),
      fprintf('%9.5f', real(Snk)), fprintf('%9.5f', imag(Snk))
      fprintf('%9.5f', abs(Snk)),
      fprintf('%9.5f', real(SL)),
      linef(n,k)=Snk;linel(n,k)=SL;
        if nl(L) ==n & a(L) ~= 1
        fprintf('%9.5f', imag(SL)), fprintf('%9.5f\n', a(L))
        else, fprintf('%9.5f\n', imag(SL))
        end
      else, end
  end
end
SLT = SLT/2;
fprintf(' \n'), fprintf(' Total loss ')
fprintf('%9.5f', real(SLT)), fprintf('%9.5f\n', imag(SLT))
clear Ik In SL SLT Skn Snk
if nbr==11
  pre_flow=real(linef);
else
  post_flow=real(linef);
end
gen_pre_flow=real(linef);
```

ACPTDF Formulation

```
Y=abs(Ybus);
theta=angle(Ybus);
V=abs(V);
```

```
% P - powerflow; A-jacobian matrix;
% slack always bus 1; N - no. of buses; G - no. of pq bus;
PTDF=zeros(6,6);
Pt=[0;1;0;0;-1;0;0;0]; % TRANSACTION Between bus 3 and bus 6
  for n=1:nbus
    for k=1:nbus
      col=1;
      for x=2:nbus
        if(x==n)
          M(1,col)=V(n)*V(k)*Y(n,k)*sin(delta(n)-delta(k)-
theta(n,k));
        elseif(x==k)
          M(1,col)=-(V(n)*V(k)*Y(n,k)*sin(delta(n)-delta(k)-
theta(n,k)));
        else
          M(1,col)=0;
        end
        col=col+1;
      end
      for x=G+1:nbus
        if(x==n) & (nl(col)==n) & (nr(col)==k)
          M(1,col)=  2*V(n)*Y(n,k)*cos(theta(n,k))  -
(V(k)*Y(n,k)*cos(delta(n)-delta(k)-theta(n,k)));
        elseif (x==k)
          M(1,col)=  -(V(n)*Y(n,k)*cos(delta(n)-delta(k)-
theta(n,k)));
        else
          M(1,col)=0;
        end
        col=col+1;
      end
      M;
      D=M*inv(A);
      PTDF(n,k)=D*Pt;
    end
end
PTDF=PTDF
```

ATC Determination

```
for i=1:nbr
    if PTDF(nl(i),nr(i))>0
      atc(i)  =  (limit(i)-(real(linef(nl(i),nr(i)))))/
PTDF(nl(i),nr(i));
    else
```

```
      atc(i) = (-limit(i)-(real(linef(nl(i),nr(i)))))/
PTDF(nl(i),nr(i));
    end
  end
atc
[P_tr_max,ele]=sort(atc)
ATC=P_tr_max(1) % BASE CASE ATC VALUE
Limiting_element=[nl(ele(1)) nr(ele(1))] %LIMITING LINE
```

ATC Determination for the Line Outage Contingency Mode

Bus Datas and Line Datas for Contingency Analysis

```
clear all
basemva = 100; accuracy = 0.001; accel = 1.8; maxiter =
100;G=3;format short
%    0 Load Bus 1 Slack Bus 2 -Pv Bus
%    Bus Bus Voltage Angle ---Load---- ---Generator--- Static Mvar
%    No code Mag. Degree MW   Mvar MW     Mvar Qmin Qmax +Qc/-Ql
busdata=[1  1 1.05 0.0     0    0    0.0    0.0  0.0    0.0   0
         2  2 1.05 0.0     0    0    69.36  0.0  0.0    0.0   0
         3  2 1.07 0.0     0    0    77.47  0.0  0.0    0.0   0
         4  0 1.0  0.0     70   70   0.0    0.0  0.0    0.0   0
         5  0 1.0  0.0     70   70   0      0.0  0.0    0.0   0
         6  0 1.0  0.0     70   70   0      0.0  0.0    0.0   0];
out_max=[ 1 2
  1 4
  1 5
  2 3
  2 4
  2 5
  2 6
  3 5
  3 6
  4 5
  5 6];
cc=out_max(:,1);dd=out_max(:,2);nnn=length(out_max);kk=1;clear
contt;clear vilate;
for ii=1:nnn
%        Bus bus  R     X     1/2 B = 1 for lines
%        nl  nr   p.u.  p.u.  p.u. tr. tap, thermal limit
linedata=[1  2    0.1   0.2   0.02       1          40
          1  4    0.05  0.2   0.02       1          80
          1  5    0.08  0.3   0.030      1          60
          2  3    0.05  0.25  0.030      1          40
          2  4    0.05  0.10  0.01       1          60
```

```
           2   5   0.1   0.3  0.020    1        30
           2   6   0.07  0.20 0.025    1        90
           3   5   0.12  0.26 0.025    1        70
           3   6   0.02  0.10 0.01     1        100
           4   5   0.2   0.40 0.04     1        20
           5   6   0.1   0.30 0.03     1        40];
   c=linedata(:,1); d=linedata(:,2);ele=[c d];
  for j=1:nnn
    if cc(ii)==c(j) & dd(ii)==d(j)
      linedata(ii,:)=[ ];
    end
  end
linedata;
Pmaxx=linedata(:, 7);
Lfybus;
Lfnewton;
Lineflow1;
% (real(linef))
% Pmaxx
     for i=1:nbr
       temp(i)=abs(real(linef(nl(i),nr(i)))/Pmaxx(i));
   end
   for i=1:nbr
     if temp(i)>1
       contt(kk,:)=ele(ii,:);
       vilate(kk,:)=ele(i,:);

       kk=kk+1;
     end
    end
   temp;
   PI(ii)=sum(temp);
end
[PII,pos]=sort(PI)
value=PII(1)
element_selection=[nl(pos(1)) nr(pos(1))]
contt'
vilate'
   lf1;  %CALLING BUS DATA & LINEDATA PROGRAM
   linedata(pos(1),:)=[]
   Lfybus;  %CALLING YBUS PROGRAM
   Lfnewton; ;  %CALLING NR LOADFLOW PROGRAM
   Lineflow; ;  %CALLING LINEFLOW PROGRAM
```

LOPTDF and OTDF Formulation

```
Y=abs(Ybus);
theta=angle(Ybus);
V=abs(V);
% P - powerflow; A-jacobian matrix;
% slack always bus 1; N - no. of buses; G - no. of pq bus;
PTDF=zeros(6,6);
Pt=[0;1;0;0;-1;0;0;0]; % TRANSACTION B/W 3 TO 6
for n=1:nbus
  for k=1:nbus
    col=1;
    for x=2:nbus
      if(x==n)
        M(1,col)=V(n)*V(k)*Y(n,k)*sin(delta(n)-delta(k)-
theta(n,k));
      elseif(x==k)
        M(1,col)=-(V(n)*V(k)*Y(n,k)*sin(delta(n)-delta(k)-
theta(n,k)));
      else
        M(1,col)=0;
      end
      col=col+1;
    end
    for x=G+1:nbus
      if(x==n) & (nl(col)==n) & (nr(col)==k)
        M(1,col)=  2*V(n)*Y(n,k)*cos(theta(n,k))  -
(V(k)*Y(n,k)*cos(delta(n)-delta(k)-theta(n,k)));
    elseif (x==k)
        M(1,col)=  -(V(n)*Y(n,k)*cos(delta(n)-delta(k)-
theta(n,k)));
    else
      M(1,col)=0;
    end
    col=col+1;
  end
  M;
  D=M*inv(A);
  PTDF(n,k)=D*Pt;
  end
end
LODF=(post_flow-pre_flow)./pre_flow(nl(pos(1)),nr(pos(1))) % LINE
OUTAGE DISTRIBUTION FACTOR
OTDF=PTDF+LODF*PTDF(nl(pos(1)),nr(pos(1))) % OUTAGE TRANSFER
```

```
DISTRIBUTION FACTOR
OMW=pre_flow+LODF*pre_flow(nl(pos(1)),nr(pos(1)))
```

ATC Calculation for Contingency Analysis

```
for i=1:nbr
    if OTDF(nl(i),nr(i))>0
      atc(i) = (limit(i)-(pre_flow(nl(i),nr(i))))/
OTDF(nl(i),nr(i));
    elseif OTDF(nl(i),nr(i))<0
      atc(i) = (limit(i)-(pre_flow(nl(i),nr(i))))/
OTDF(nl(i),nr(i));
    else
      atc(i)=inf;
    end
end
[iii,jjj]=sort(abs(atc))
By_OTDF_ATC_contn=iii(1) % CONTINGENCY CASE ATC
Lt_Element=[nl(jjj(1)) nr(jjj(1))] %LIMITING LINE
Base_case_ATC=ATC
Lt_Element=Limiting_element
OTDF_Value_in_Percentage=OTDF(Lt_Element(1),Lt_Element(2))*100 %
OTDF VALUE
```

11.7 ATC Determination Using Power World Simulator (PWS)

The assessment of ATC using PTDF methods has been illustrated on IEEE 30 bus system for normal mode operation and line outage contingency mode operation. Thermal limit of each line is considered as a constraint and reactive power demand at load buses has been taken as constant. ATC determination is carried out for the simultaneous bilateral and multilateral transactions. The simulation studies are carried out on Intel Pentium IV, 2.66 GHz system in MATLAB environment. The results are compared with Power World Simulator (PWS) package. The limiting elements are also given for each transaction. Some of the results are not possible to verify because of the limitation of PWS package. (For example, multilateral transactions are not possible to perform using Power World Simulator.)

IEEE 30 bus system contains six generators and forty-one transmission lines. The bus data, line data and generator data are taken from http: //www.washington.edu.in. Two simultaneous bilateral transactions T_1 and T_2 and a multilateral transaction T_3 are considered. Transaction T_1 is considered between buses 2 and 28. Transaction T_2 is between bus 5 and bus 23. Multilateral transaction T_3 is taking place between seller bus group, i.e. buses 2 and 11 and buyer bus group, i.e. buses 28 and 26. Case A refers to normal mode

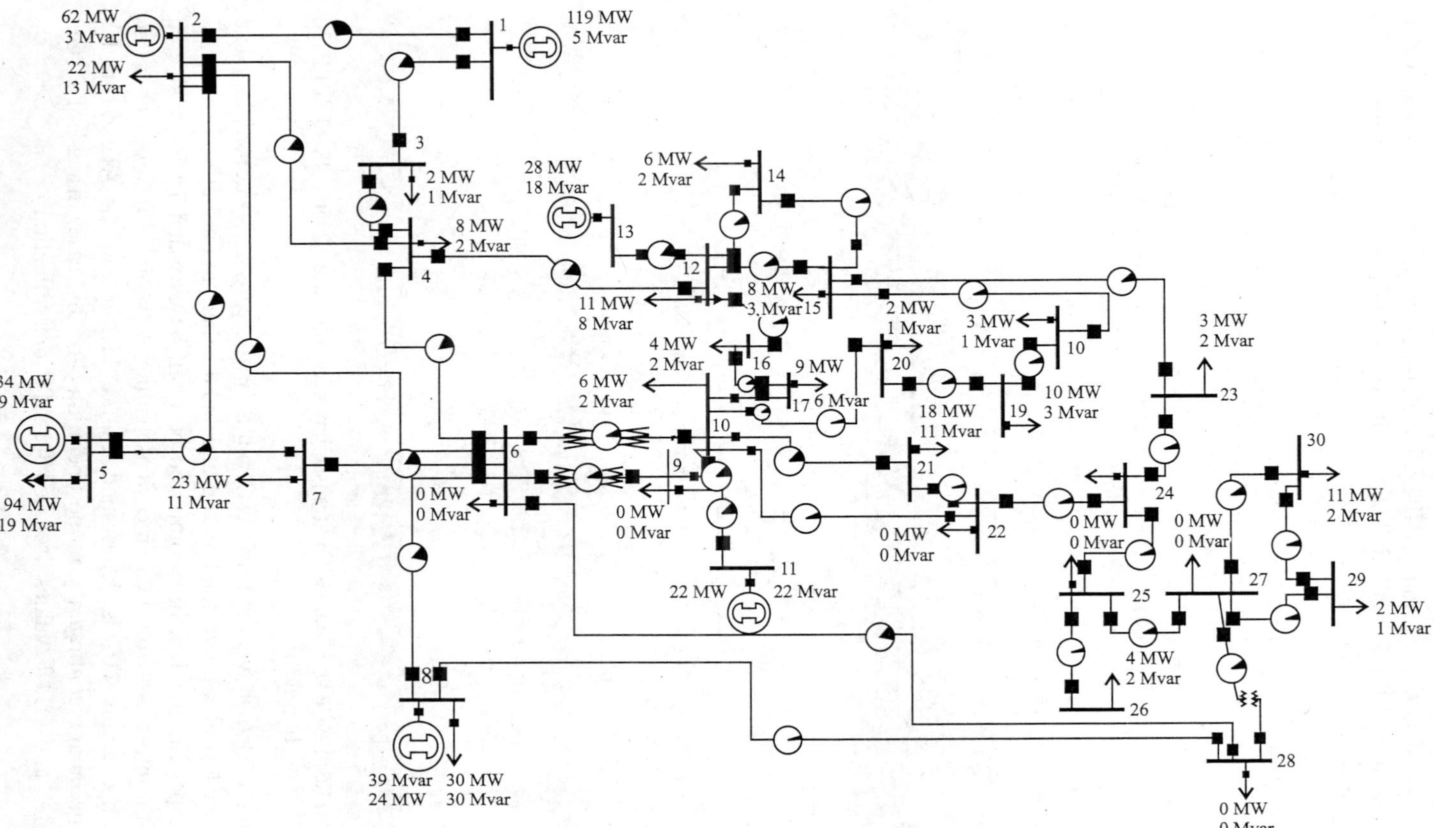

Figure 11.4 Power flows due to transaction between buses 2 and 28 of IEEE 30 bus system.

operation and case B denotes line outage contingency mode operation. From the results, it is evident that, ACPTDF method is giving accurate ATC value compared to DCPTDF method. The validity of the results is also verified using PWS package. By comparing with PWS package, a small deviation in the ATC results using ACPTDF is found since the linearized ac method is not used for ATC determination in the PWS tool.

Figure 11.4 shows the power flows due to transaction between bus 2 (seller bus) and bus 28 (buyer bus) which is obtained from Power World Simulator package.

In this example problem, ATC is determined using both dc power transfer distribution factors and ac power transfer distribution factors. Figure 11.5 shows the ac power transfer distribution factors value for the considered bilateral transaction between buses 2 and 28.

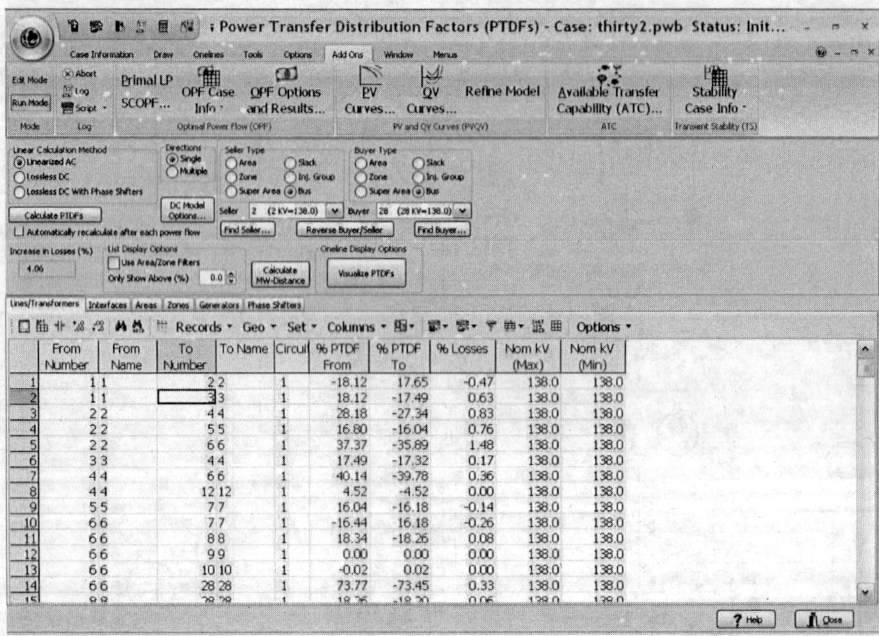

	From Number	From Name	To Number	To Name	Circuit	% PTDF From	% PTDF To	% Losses	Nom kV (Max)	Nom kV (Min)
1	1 1		2 2		1	-18.12	17.65	-0.47	138.0	138.0
2	1 1		3 3		1	18.12	-17.49	0.63	138.0	138.0
3	2 2		4 4		1	28.18	-27.34	0.83	138.0	138.0
4	2 2		5 5		1	16.80	-16.04	0.76	138.0	138.0
5	2 2		6 6		1	37.37	-35.89	1.48	138.0	138.0
6	3 3		4 4		1	17.49	-17.32	0.17	138.0	138.0
7	4 4		6 6		1	40.14	-39.78	0.36	138.0	138.0
8	4 4		12 12		1	4.52	-4.52	0.00	138.0	138.0
9	5 5		7 7		1	16.04	-16.18	-0.14	138.0	138.0
10	6 6		7 7		1	-16.44	16.18	-0.26	138.0	138.0
11	6 6		8 8		1	18.34	-18.26	0.08	138.0	138.0
12	6 6		9 9		1	0.00	0.00	0.00	138.0	138.0
13	6 6		10 10		1	-0.02	0.02	0.00	138.0	138.0
14	6 6		28 28		1	73.77	-73.45	0.33	138.0	138.0

Figure 11.5 ACPTDF values for transaction between buses 2 and 28 of IEEE 30 bus system.

Figure 11.6 shows the final ATC value for the considered transaction. The PWS window also shows the limiting line and the thermal limit used for the line.

As per Eq. (11.12), line connected between buses 9 and 10 is considered to be the most sensitive line since it is having very high PI value. This line is taken out and ATC is determined. Figure 11.7 shows the ATC value for this line outage contingency mode operation. For this case, instead of PTDF, LOPTDF and OTDF values are used for ATC determination.

Available Transfer Capability

Options | Analysis | Result

Records ▾ Set ▾ Columns ▾ Options ▾

All Limiters | Branch Limiters | Interface Limiters | Nomogram Interface Limiters

	Trans Lim	Limiting Element	Limiting CTG	% OTDF	Pre-Tra Est	Limit Used
1	24.87	Branch 6 (6) TO 28 (28) CKT 1 [138.00 - 1:	Base Case	73.77	13.65	32.00
2	77.42	Branch 2 (2) TO 6 (6) CKT 1 [138.00 - 138.	Base Case	37.37	36.07	65.00
3	130.10	Branch 6 (6) TO 8 (8) CKT 1 [138.00 - 138.	Base Case	18.34	8.14	32.00
4	131.72	Branch 4 (4) TO 6 (6) CKT 1 [138.00 - 138.	Base Case	40.14	37.12	90.00
5	132.23	Branch 2 (2) TO 4 (4) CKT 1 [138.00 - 138.	Base Case	28.18	27.74	65.00

Figure 11.6 ATC value for transaction between buses 2 and 28 of IEEE 30 bus system.

Available Transfer Capability

Options | Analysis | Result

Records ▾ Set ▾ Columns ▾ Options ▾

All Limiters | Branch Limiters | Interface Limiters | Nomogram Interface Limiters

	Trans Lim	Limiting Element	Limiting CTG	% OTDF	Pre-Tra Est	Limit Used
1	24.87	Branch 6 (6) TO 28 (28) CKT 1 [138.00 - 1:	Base Case	73.77	13.65	32.00
2	77.42	Branch 2 (2) TO 6 (6) CKT 1 [138.00 - 138.	Base Case	37.37	36.07	65.00
3	130.10	Branch 6 (6) TO 8 (8) CKT 1 [138.00 - 138.	Base Case	18.34	8.14	32.00
4	131.72	Branch 4 (4) TO 6 (6) CKT 1 [138.00 - 138.	Base Case	40.14	37.12	90.00
5	132.23	Branch 2 (2) TO 4 (4) CKT 1 [138.00 - 138.	Base Case	28.18	27.74	65.00

Figure 11.7 ATC value for line outage contingency mode for transaction between buses 2 and 28 of IEEE 30 bus system.

For the two bilateral and one multilateral transactions considered for this test system, the ATC values using MATLAB and Power World Simulator are shown in Table 11.1. Case A refers to normal mode operation and case B denotes line outage contingency mode operation. From the results, it is evident that,

Table 11.1 ATC in MW-IEEE 30 bus system

Transaction	*Case*	*Normal mode using* **DCPTDF** *method*		*Limiting element for* **DCPTDF**	*Normal mode using* **ACPTDF** *method*		*Line outage mode using* **LOPTDF** *method*		*Limiting element for* **ACPTDF**
		MATLAB	**PWS**		**MATLAB**	**PWS**	**MATLAB**	**PWS**	
T_1 (2–28)	A	23.65	23.78	6–28	24.82	24.87	–	–	6–28
	B	18.26	18.04		–	–	18.83	19.08	
T_2 (5–23)	A	16.25	17.36	15–23	19.35	17.53	–	–	15–23
	B	12.16	13.53		–	–	14.18	12.25	
T_3 (2, 11 –28, 26)	A	15.56	–	6–28	16.95	–	–	–	6–28
	B	11.35	–		–	–	12.23	–	

ACPTDF method is giving accurate ATC value compared to DCPTDF method. The validity of the results is also verified using PWS package. By comparing with PWS package, a small deviation in the ATC results using ACPTDF is found since the linearized ac method is not used for ATC determination in the PWS tool.

In contingency mode operation, as per Eq. (11.12) outage of line 9–10 is considered for IEEE 30 bus system. The ATC values obtained for contingency case are lesser than the base case ATC. The limiting element of the transactions is found to be same with PWS package. In the case of contingency studies, LOPTDF method is more suitable than ACPTDF method for all transactions.

11.8 Sensitivity of Network Uncertainties on ATC Determination

11.8.1 Introduction

In a restructured power system, ATC indicates the unutilized transfer capability of the transmission network that is available for further transaction by the market entities. Any power transactions can be carried out only when sufficient ATC is available in the system. Normally, ATC is calculated under a particular system operating point. For the changes in operating point and network uncertainties, the calculated ATC values may also vary. So, it is necessary to determine the effect of varying the operating conditions or assumptions based on this determined ATC. Sensitivity computations can be used to estimate the effects of varying assumptions on the transfer capability.

The sensitivity methods could contribute to the rapid update of transfer capabilities when operating conditions or other transfers change and for the computation of transfer reserve margin. Market participants could utilize these factors as a means to:

1. Forecast the effect of a target area load variation on the ATC that is under consideration for commercial activity.
2. Knowledge of the effect of simultaneous transfers on a commercial path ATC could provide an idea of when curtailment could be expected.
3. The effect of generators re-dispatches based on geographical nature are illustrated on areawise transactions.
4. Effect on areawise transfer capabilities based on variations of voltage set point at a generator are explained.
5. Many network variables or uncertainties affected ATC based on its geographical location of limiting lines.

The transfer capability depends mainly on the network topology, generation dispatch, system load demand, power transactions and change in voltage set points. So the first order sensitivity formulae are derived utilizing base case single area ATC and multi area ATC values in order to estimate corresponding

ATC values in the above said network uncertainties. The proposed formulae have been tested and validated on IEEE 30 bus and Indian utility 69 bus systems by considering various uncertainties such as changes in generation dispatch, system load demand, power transactions and voltage set points.

11.8.2 Overview of Network Uncertainties

There are several network parameters that needs to be varied in power system under various operating conditions. Some examples of network parameters are as follows:

Generation Dispatch: It is useful to know how the transfer capability depends on the assumed generator dispatch. The sensitivity of the transfer capability to the generator dispatch yields information on how the generator dispatch can be changed to the best in order to increase the transfer capability.

System Load Demand: The effect on transfer capability can be estimated by varying the assumptions of the power system load.

Simultaneous Power Transfers: The sensitivity of the transfer capability can be estimated due to the other simultaneous power transfers on the system. This could be used to update the transfer capability quickly when another transfer is executed.

Voltage Set Point: The change in regulated voltage set point under the considered power system indicates the greatest effect on the transfer margin.

The following assumptions have been established for the computation of initial transfer margin:

1. A secure, solved base case consistent with the study operating horizon.
2. Specification of transfer direction including source, sink and loss assumptions.
3. A solved transfer-limited case and a binding security limit. The binding security limit can be a limit on line flow, voltage magnitude, voltage collapse or other operating constraint. Further transfer in the specified direction would cause the violation of the binding limit and compromise system security.
4. The transfer margin is the difference between the transfer at base case and limiting case.

Once the transfer capability, corresponding binding limit and solved base case have been computed, the first order sensitivity of this transfer capability can be quickly computed over a wide range of parameters. These first order sensitivities can contribute to the rapid update of transfer capabilities when operating conditions or other transfers change. Moreover, the sensitivities can be used to select operator actions to increase or decrease transfer capability.

11.8.3 First Order Sensitivity of Network Uncertainties on ATC Determination

Since various network uncertainties such as generation dispatch, system load demand, power transactions and change in voltage set point have to be considered, the ATC parameter becomes a random variable. An understanding of the effect of network uncertainties on transfer capability is critical to the system operator and market participants. Due to these uncertainties in network parameters, there is a necessity to predict ATC accurately values before posting on OASIS. In general, the effects of the network variable (NV) using first order approximation is given as

$$\text{ATC}_{(n+1)} = \text{ATC}_{(n)} + \left[\left. \frac{d\,\text{ATC}}{d\,\text{NV}} \right|_{\text{ATC}_{(n)}} \times \Delta\text{NV} \right] \qquad (11.22)$$

where $\frac{d\,\text{ATC}}{d\,\text{NV}}$ is the fraction of incremental change in ATC of certain path to the incremental change in a specific network variable, such as generation dispatch or load.

These sensitivity factors could be utilized by market participants to forecast the new ATC owing the effect of changes in network variables within an area or between areas. These sensitivities can contribute to the quick update of transfer capability for the change in the operating conditions also.

Sensitivity to Load Variation

The load variation could have a small or large impact on the available transfer capability and it depends largely on the geographical location of load with regard to the transactions considered. The sensitivity estimates for the change in ATC as a function of load variation is determined by Eq. (11.23). The estimates are then compared with actual ATC values computed by AC repetitive load flow method.

$$\text{Areawise ATC}(n+1) = \text{Areawise ATC}(n) + \left[\begin{array}{r} \left. \dfrac{d\,\text{Areawise ATC}}{d\,\text{Area-load}} \right|_{\text{ATC}(n)} \\ \times \Delta\,\text{Area-load} \end{array} \right] \qquad (11.23)$$

where, $\frac{d\,\text{Areawise ATC}}{d\,\text{Area-load}}$ is the ratio between the incremental change in areawise ATC and the incremental change in a particular area-load.

The effect on ATC values with respect to load variation is estimated by Eq. (11.23). In the Indian utility 69 bus system, transaction between two areas, i.e., area 1 – area 3 is considered for analyzing the effect of sensitivity to load variation on ATC. The load variation is effected from –1% to +11% for loads in various areas.

As per Eq. (11.23), the first order approximation of ATC for the variation of loads located in area 1 is given in Table 11.2. During the total base load of 1169 MW in area 1, the ATC is 101.366 MW. The ATC value is decreased by 91.2239 MW by increasing area 1 load to 1297.6 MW, i.e., by 11%. The average incremental $\dfrac{d\,\text{Areawise ATC}}{d\,\text{Area - load}}$ factor is –0.0781. So, the impact of area 1 load variation is very less on ATC calculated for the transaction between area 1 and area 3. The deviation between estimated ATC and actual ATC is very less and its maximum error value is 0.0823% only. The negative sensitivity values indicate that the ATC is decreased by the increment of loads in the selected areas.

Table 11.2 Effect of sensitivity to area 1 load variation

Area 1 load variation (%)	*Area 1 load* (MW)	*ATC* (MW)	*Incremental* $\dfrac{dAreawise\ ATC}{dArea-load}$	*First order approximation of ATC* (MW)	*Error* (%)
–3	1133.9	104.031	–	–	–
–2	1145.6	103.096	–0.0803	–	–
–1	1157.31	102.232	–0.0731	102.15	0.0823
0	1169.0	101.366	–0.0742	101.378	–0.0119
1	1180.7	100.489	–0.0749	100.498	–0.0087
2	1192.4	99.6039	–0.0756	99.6128	–0.0088
3	1204.1	98.7094	–0.0764	98.7184	–0.0091
4	1215.8	97.8059	–0.0772	97.8149	–0.0092
5	1227.5	96.8934	–0.0781	96.9025	–0.0093
6	1239.1	95.9717	–0.0794	95.9808	–0.0095
7	1250.8	95.0408	–0.0795	95.0501	–0.0096
8	1262.5	94.1007	–0.0803	94.1099	–0.0098
9	1274.2	93.1512	–0.0811	93.1605	–0.0101
10	1285.9	92.1923	–0.0819	92.2017	–0.0102
11	1297.6	91.2239	–0.0827	91.2333	–0.0104

The effect of load variation in area 2 on ATC values by the above transaction is analyzed. The incremental sensitivity values and first order approximation of ATC values are given in Table 11.3. For this area 2 load variation, the rate of average incremental ATC value by its incremental load is –0.01037. This incremental $\dfrac{d\,\text{Areawise ATC}}{d\,\text{Area- Load}}$ value is also negative and low. Therefore, variation of loads in area 2 will have only minor impact in ATC value for the transaction considered and ATC is reduced for the increment of loads.

Table 11.3 Effect of sensitivity to area 2 load variation

Area 2 load variation (%)	*Area 2 load* (MW)	*ATC* (MW)	*Incremental* $\frac{dAreawise\ ATC}{dArea-load}$	*First order approximation of ATC* (MW)	*Error* (%)
–3	1777.0	101.411	–	–	–
–2	1795.4	101.380	–0.0016	–	–
–1	1813.7	101.347	–0.0017	101.349	–0.0014
0	1832.0	101.366	0.0011	101.315	0.0501
1	1850.3	101.361	–0.0002	101.384	–0.0225
2	1868.6	101.334	–0.0015	101.357	–0.0227
3	1887.0	101.283	–0.0027	101.307	–0.0229
4	1905.3	101.209	–0.0040	101.233	–0.0231
5	1923.6	101.111	–0.0053	101.135	–0.0234
6	1941.9	100.990	–0.0066	101.013	–0.0237
7	1960.2	100.844	–0.0079	100.868	–0.0239
8	1978.6	100.673	–0.0092	100.698	–0.0242
9	1996.9	100.478	–0.0106	100.503	–0.0246
10	2015.2	100.258	–0.0120	100.283	–0.0249
11	2033.5	98.7512	–0.0823	100.038	–1.3031

For the same transaction, i.e., area 1 – area 3, variation of loads located in area 3 has yielded a different sensitivity pattern (Table 11.4). The sensitivity

Table 11.4 Effect of sensitivity to area 3 load variation

Area 3 load variation (%)	*Area 3 load* (MW)	*ATC* (MW)	*Incremental* $\frac{d\ Areawise\ ATC}{d\ Area-load}$	*First order approximation of ATC* (MW)	*Error* (%)
–3	1853.7	98.475	–	–	–
–2	1872.8	99.441	0.0505	–	–
–1	1891.9	100.385	0.0494	100.407	–0.0219
0	1911.0	101.366	0.0513	101.328	0.0368
1	1930.1	102.315	0.0496	102.347	–0.0314
2	1949.2	103.232	0.0480	103.264	–0.0308
3	1968.3	104.118	0.0463	104.150	–0.0301
4	1987.4	104.973	0.0447	105.004	–0.0295
5	2006.5	105.771	0.0417	105.828	–0.0536
6	2025.7	90.0929	–0.8165	106.569	–1.2818
7	2044.8	74.7596	–0.8027	74.4145	0.4615
8	2063.9	59.8188	–0.7822	59.4262	0.6562
9	2083.0	45.3222	–0.7589	44.8780	0.9800
10	2102.1	31.3256	–0.7328	30.8256	1.5961
11	2121.2	17.8891	–0.7034	17.3290	3.1307

factor is 0.04768 for variation of load from –1% to 5% and it is –0.7661 for load variation from 6% to 11%. The first portion of load variation has produced negligible impact on ATC value and the influence is very high for the second portion of load variation. This is because, the limiting line for the first portion of load variation is the line between buses 61–62 which is present in area 2 and the transaction considered is in between area 1 and area 3. For the second portion of load variation, the limiting line is the line connected between buses 32–43 which belongs to area 3 itself. The overall effects on ATC values due to respective areas for the load variations are clearly depicted in Figure 11.8. The ATC results estimated by the first order sensitivity are quite closer to the actual ATC values.

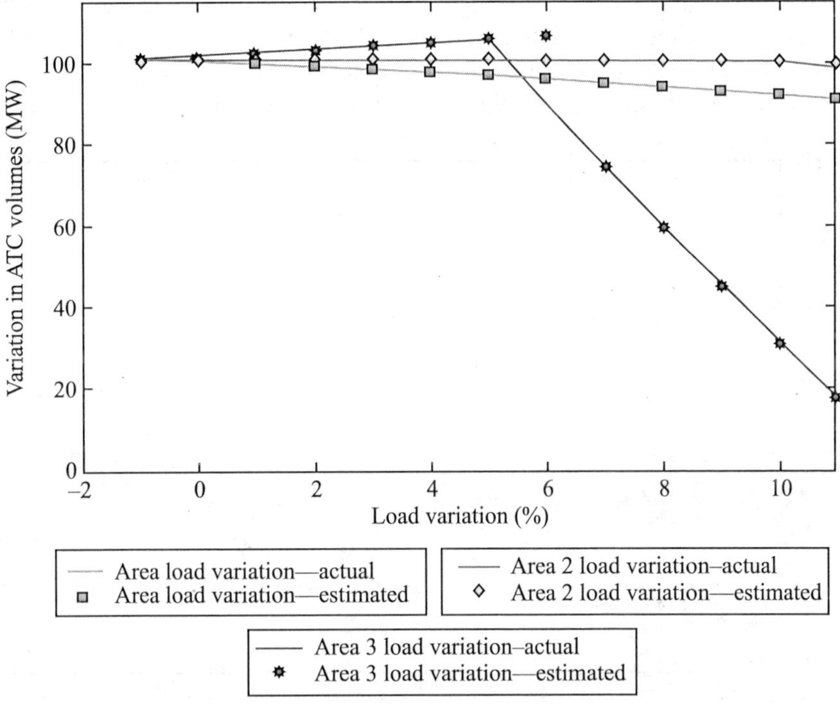

Figure 11.8 Effect of load variation on ATC for area 1–Area 3 transaction.

Sensitivity to simultaneous transfers

Since the existence of multiple transactions is a reality in the market structure, the effect of other simultaneous transaction(s) on the computed ATC while considering a particular transaction is discussed in this section. The effect of sensitivity to simultaneous transfers is estimated by Eq. (11.24).

$$\text{Areawise ATC}(n+1) = \text{Areawise ATC}(n) + \left[\left. \frac{d\,\text{Areawise ATC}}{d\,\text{Transfer}} \right|_{\text{ATC}(n)} \times \Delta\text{Transfer} \right] \tag{11.24}$$

where, $\dfrac{d\,\text{Areawise ATC}}{d\,\text{Transfer}}$ is the ratio of incremental change in areawise ATC to the incremental change in simultaneous transactions. Once the capability for one transfer direction has been determined, it is useful to estimate the effect on the transfer capability of adjusting simultaneous transfers and of modifying the assumptions used for the initial transfer capability determination.

This study is performed on the standard IEEE 30 bus test system and transaction between area 2 and Area 1 is considered. Three simultaneous bilateral transactions, i.e., BT_1 between buses (2–28), BT_2 between buses (5–23) and BT_3 between buses (8–18); and one multilateral transaction, i.e., MT between buses (11, 13–26, 19, 30) have been considered. Figure 11.9 depicts the change in ATC value of transaction between area 2 and area 1 due to the addition of bilateral and multilateral transactions in different combinations like BT_1 separately, MT separately, combining BT_1 and BT_2, combining three bilateral transactions and combining all bilateral and multilateral transactions.

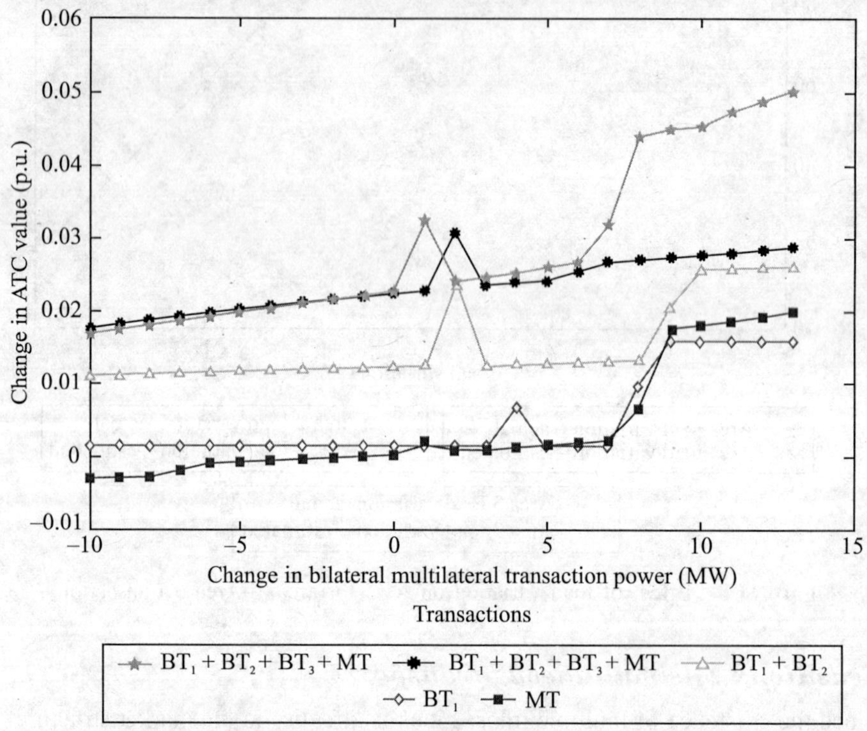

Figure 11.9 Effect of simultaneous transactions on ATC.

From the results, it is observed that the impact on the ATC values for the combination of three bilateral transactions and one multilateral transaction is higher than the combination of all bilateral transactions. The effect of combining all three bilateral transactions is higher than combining the transactions BT_1

and BT_2. The impact of transaction BT_1 and MT individually on the ATC value of transaction considered is very low. Any change in the transfer values due to these transactions would have negligible effect on the ATC value of the transaction considered. This nature of sensitivity analysis on simultaneous transfers is deemed to be more important as it offers the system operators an index to evaluate new areawise transaction that could be allocated among the existing transactions of the system.

Sensitivity to generation dispatch

It is true that the generation redispatch between any two generators will have an effect on the power transfer capability thus leading to a change in calculated ATC values. The effect of sensitivity to generation dispatch is estimated by Eq. (11.25).

$$\text{Areawise ATC}(n+1) = \text{Areawise ATC}(n) + \left[\left.\frac{d\,\text{Areawise ATC}}{d\,\text{Generation dispatch}}\right|_{\text{ATC}(n)} \times \Delta\text{Generation dispatch} \right] \tag{11.25}$$

where, $\dfrac{d\,\text{Areawise ATC}}{d\,\text{Generation dispatch}}$ is the ratio between incremental change in areawise ATC and the incremental change in generation dispatch. Assumptions concerning which generators back off or increase output to satisfy transfers can influence the transfer capability computation.

The impact is analyzed with a sensitivity factor for the areawise transaction of Indian utility 69 bus system. Transactions are considered between area 1 and area 3, area 2 and area 1, and area 2 and area 3. For this study, the generators at buses 14 and 21 in area 1, generators at buses 13 and 60 in area 2 and generators connected to buses 39 and 52 in area 3 are redispatched. The other generators are kept at base case value. In each area, for the specified two generators, if generation in one generator is increased by ΔP_g from base case, then in the other generator, generation is decreased by ΔP_g simultaneously. The results are clearly depicted in Figures 11.10, 11.11, 11.12 and 11.13.

For area 1– area 3 transaction, the $\dfrac{d\,\text{Areawise ATC}}{d\,\text{Generation dispatch}}$ value is 0.08732 for redispatch of area 1 generators and it is 0.00489 and 0.00272 for

re-dispatching area 2 and area 3 generators. The impact on ATC value will be very high for redispatching generators in area 1 since the limiting line (67–65) for the transaction considered is present in area 1. Since the limiting line is geographically located nearer to area 2 as shown in Figure 11.10, the redispatch of generation in area 2 will have more impact than redispatch of generation in area 3.

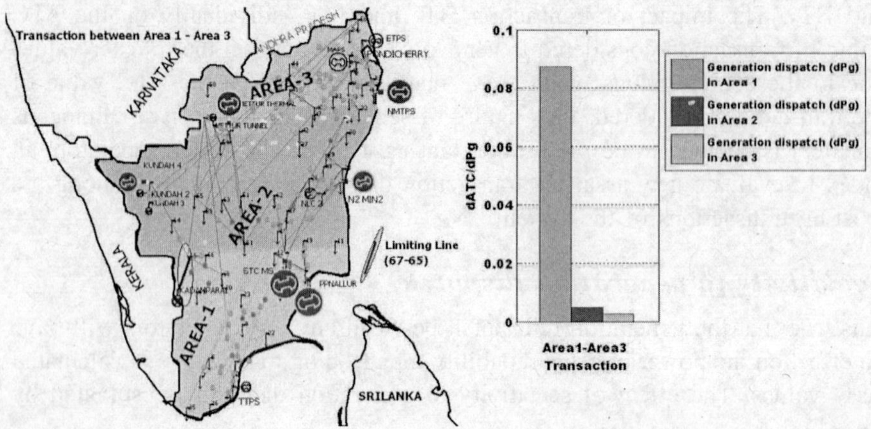

Figure 11.10 Effect of generation dispatch on areas 1–3 ATC.

Similarly, for the transaction between area 2 and area 1, the limiting line (24–26) is present in area 2 and located nearer to area 3. Therefore, re-dispatching of generators in area 2 will have significant effect on computed ATC value and redispatching of generators in area 3 will have more impact than redispatching area 1 generators.

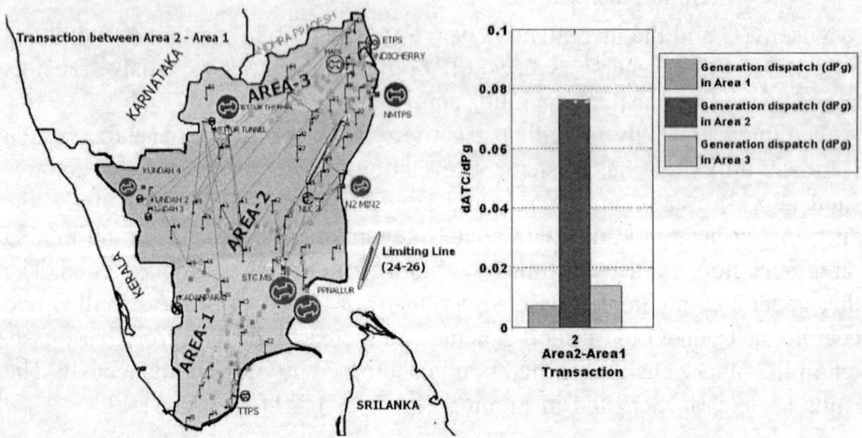

Figure 11.11 Effect of generation dispatch on areas 2–1 ATC.

For the transaction taking place between area 2 and area 3, limiting line (62–61) is located in area 2 and nearer to area 1 boundary. Therefore, re-dispatching of generators in area 2 will have more effect on the calculated ATC value than redispatching generators of area 1 and area 3. The overall impacts on ATC for the generation dispatches are clearly depicted in Figure 11.13.

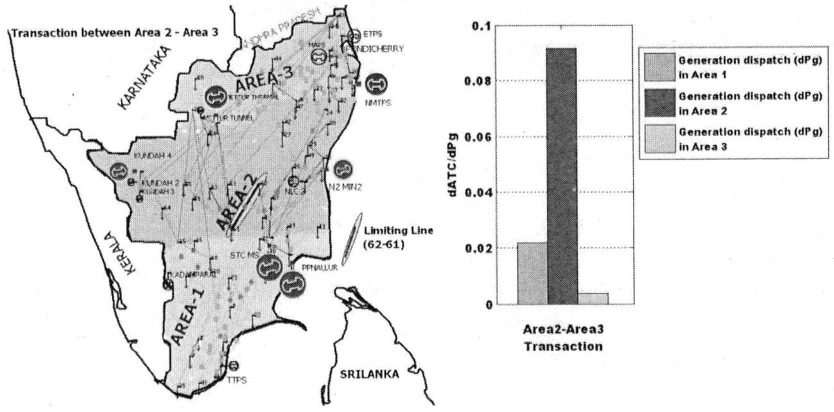

Figure 11.12 Effect of generation dispatch on area 2–3 ATC.

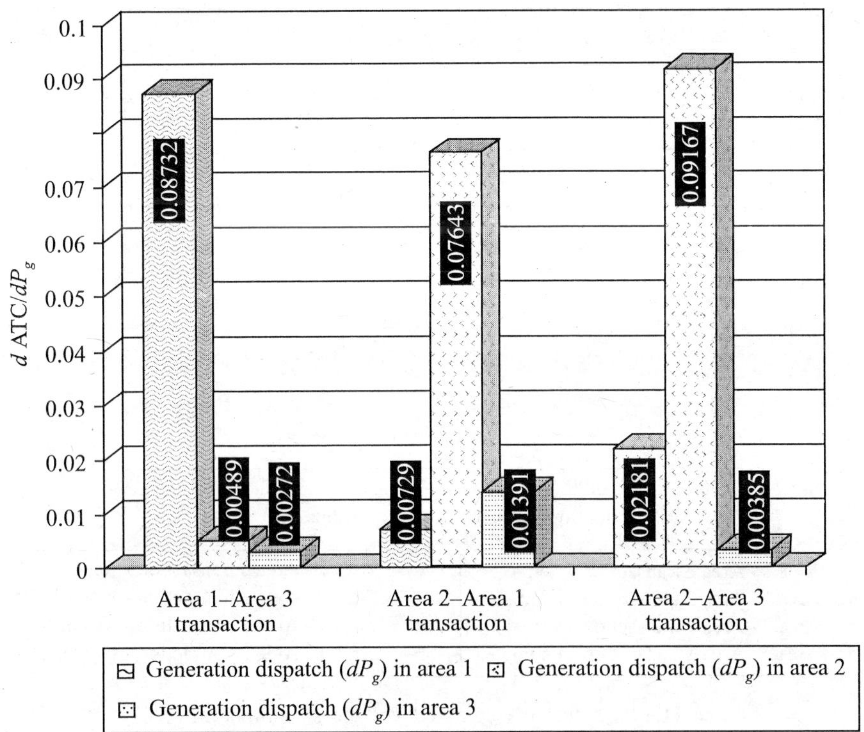

Figure 11.13 Comparison of generation dispatch.

Sensitivity to voltage set points variation

The sensitivity of transfer margins to the variations in voltage set point is obtained using Eq. (11.26). These estimates are compared with actual values computed by ac load flow analysis.

$$\text{Areawise ATC}(n+1) = \text{Areawise ATC}(n) + \left[\left. \frac{d \text{ Areawise ATC}}{d \text{ Voltage setpoint}} \right|_{\text{ATC}(n)} \times \Delta \text{ Voltage setpoint} \right] \tag{11.26}$$

where, $\dfrac{d \text{ Areawise ATC}}{d \text{ Voltage setpoint}}$ is the fraction of incremental change in areawise ATC to the incremental change in voltage set point.

Figure 11.14 shows the linear estimate of the variation in ATC to the voltage limit as a function of the voltage set point at the Kadamparai generator (bus no. 67) of Indian utility 69 bus system. Interestingly, Kadamparai station belongs to pumped storage type which operates daily during peak loads only. Since this bus is more influential on the system, it is considered for this study. The results are obtained by incrementing the voltage set point and adopting the procedure for ATC calculation.

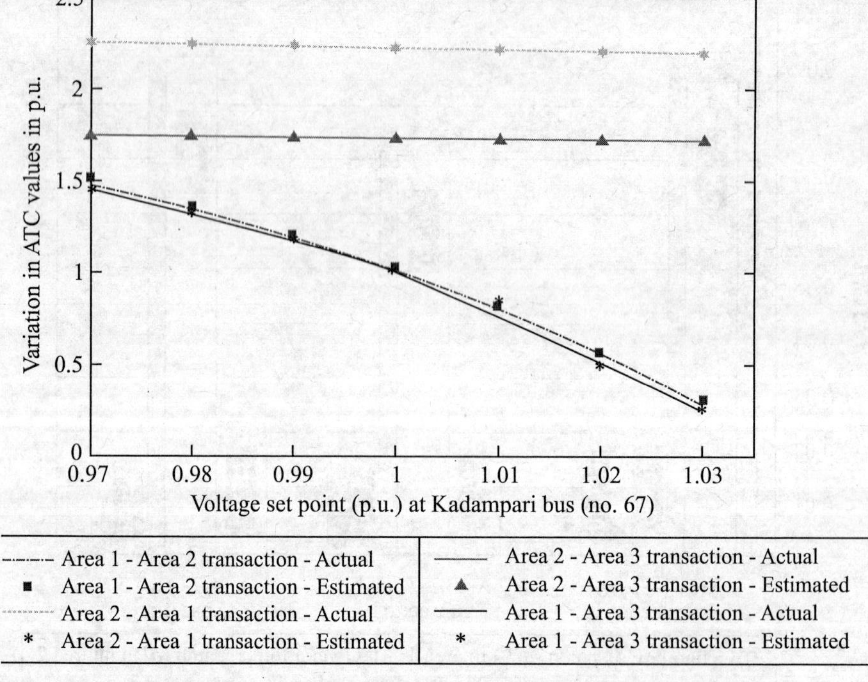

Figure 11.14 Effect of regulated voltage set points on ATC.

Four transactions are considered. For the transaction between area 1 and area 2, high variations in ATC results are obtained due to variation in voltage set points. Similarly, for the transaction between Area 1 and area 3, high variations are noticed. For these two transactions, the limiting element is 67–65 which is located in area 1 itself. The limiting lines for the other transactions, i.e., area 2 – area 1 and area 2 – area 3, are line 24–26 and line 62–61 respectively.

Although these two limiting lines belong to seller area 2, the effect of regulating voltage set point has produced negligible impact on ATC values and such type of information is vital for realistic operation of restructured system.

Review Questions

Part-A

1. Define ATC and explain the terms associated with it.
2. What are the different methods of ATC determination and how is it useful in the restructured electricity market?
3. Define OASIS. What is meant by electronic trading?
4. Mention the methods of static ATC determination.
5. What is the significance of security in constrained economic dispatch problem?
6. What are the principles for TC determination?
7. List the various network uncertainties.
8. Write the formula used for finding first order sensitivity of network uncertainties on ATC calculation.
9. What is meant by pumped storage power plant?

Part-B

1. Explain with a necessary diagram how ATC determination is made using the continuation power flow method.
2. Explain with a necessary diagram how ATC determination is made using the sensitivity factor method.
3. Explain the accurate method of ATC calculations with relevant equations. Draw a flow chart for the computation of ATC.
4. Explain ATC determination using DCPTDF method with a flow chart.
5. Explain static ATC determination using multiple load flow and continuation power flow with a neat flow chart.
6. Explain the impact on areawise ATC values for system load variation.
7. Demonstrate the sensitivity of ATC values on simultaneous power transaction considered.
8. Illustrate the impact of generation dispatch on ATC values.

CHAPTER 12

Transmission Open Access and Pricing

12.1 Introduction

Transmission pricing is necessary to recover costs of transmission network, and its operation, provide assured open access (i.e. equitable treatment and opportunity) for all users, and encourage investment in transmission and a simple and understandable price structure. The transmission sector, by providing open access to different players in the market, is the part of the industry essential for all these structural changes and thus has a significant disproportional to its relative share in the industry's either revenue or total capital investment.

Transmission is the only part of the power industry that needs to be regulated to provide open access and a fair competitive environment for all participants in the power market. On the other hand, unbundling of the different sectors of the power system from transmission has posed questions and created many worries regarding the availability and adequacy of the revenue for the transmission industry, in order to operate, maintain, and expand.

At the transmission level of the power system, the primary service is to move the power from the production point to the point of use. Therefore, the establishment of rules for operating the transmission network (technical issues) and for pricing transmission services (economic issues) is the real challenge. This task is highly complex since the technical and economic issues are intermingled with political and legal issues.

12.2 Transmission Open Access

Today transmission open access is the key to a free and fair electricity market. It is the transmission tariff, which shapes the level of competition in the electricity market. As per the IEEE task force on transmission access, the term 'transmission access' refers to the requirement that the transmission network owners make their systems available to the other players in the system.

"Open Access" means the non-discriminatory provision for the use of transmission lines or distribution system or associated facilities with such lines or system by any licensee or consumer or a person engaged in generation in accordance with the regulations specified by the Commission. The US Energy Policy Act of 1992 has laid the basic stone for the provision of open access. In India, the enactment of Electricity Act 2003 lays down the guidelines towards "transmission open access" for inter- and intra-state transmission.

12.2.1 Types of Transmission Services in Open Access

In a competitive market environment, a transmission transaction refers to the transmission components of the service provided by an electric utility, e.g. the transmission services associated with a power sale, and a power purchase, etc. There are various types of transmission transactions, and several categories to which the type of transmission transaction may belong.

The transmission services can be classified into:

(a) Point-to-point services
(b) Network services.

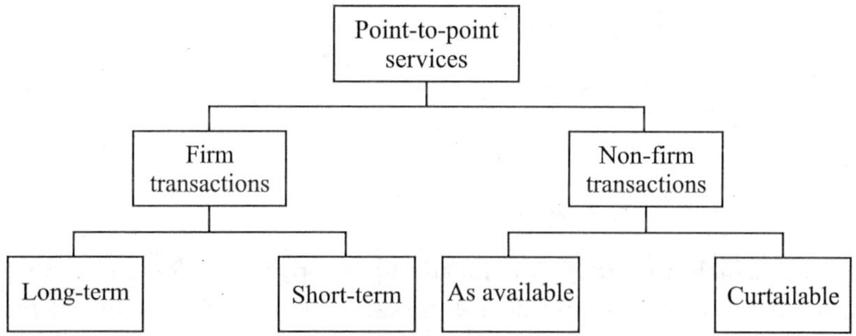

Figure 12.1 Classification of point-to-point services.

Point-to-point transaction

This service is for the receipt of capacity and energy at designated point(s) of receipt and the transmission of such capacity and energy to designated point(s) of delivery.

(i) Firm point-to-point transaction service

Customers that elect to purchase "firm" transmission service for a bilateral transaction commit to pay a transmission usage charge that may include congestion charges. Their schedules will not be cut except for system reliability reasons. These could either be on a **long-term** basis, in the order of years, in which case the charges for such transactions can be designed to incorporate capacity investment needs of the network, or on **short-term** contracts (up to one year).

(ii) Non-firm point-to-point transaction service

Non-firm point-to-point transmission service shall be available when there is no congestion between the point(s) of receipt and the point(s) of delivery for the transaction. The **'as–available'** transactions are basically isolated contracts on a short-term basis as per availability of transmission capacity, whereas **'curtailments'** will be made on a non-discriminatory basis to the transaction(s) that effectively relieve the constraint.

Network service

The ISO will provide firm transmission service over the transmission system to the network customer for the delivery of energy from its designated network resources to serve its network loads on a basis that is comparable to a transmission owner's use of the transmission system to reliably serve its native load customers. Such energy shall be transmitted, on an as-available basis (i.e. when there is no congestion between the non-network resource and the network load), at no additional charge.

12.3 Cost Components of Transmission System

12.3.1 Operating Cost

This includes the variable cost mainly due to generator rescheduling, maintaining system voltages, reactive power support and line flow limits.

12.3.2 Loss of Opportunity Cost

It is a cost which transmission company (Transco) has to forego to meet the transactions such as it could not use cheaper generation or could not realize revenue from firm contracts due to line flow reaching the limits.

12.3.3 Reinforcement Cost

This cost is charged to only firm transactions and includes capital cost of the new facilities required to meet the transaction.

12.3.4 Existing Cost

This includes capital cost of the existing facilities and need to be allocated to various transactions on some rational basis.

12.4 Transmission Pricing Methods

The objective of any transmission pricing method is to allocate all or part of the existing and the new cost of transmission system to the customers. However, tariffs for transmission services are more often set by government regulations, and are based on its policy directives. The pricing of transmission services should be carried out to achieve the following goals.

(a) It recovers the capital and operating costs

The tariff charged for the use of transmission services must produce enough revenue to cover all the expenses made in investment, operation and maintenance of the transmission network, as well as to provide a small (regulated) level of profit for the owners.

(b) It encourages efficiency of use and investment

The price structure should give incentives for using the transmission system efficiently. Efficient use could mean ensuring both, economic efficiency by maximizing social benefits and technical efficiency by minimizing losses. Also, the price structure and the way money is paid to the owners should provide an incentive for investment in new facilities, when and where they are needed.

(c) It provides equal opportunity to all users

The pricing method must be fair and equitable to all users.

(d) It offers a simple and understandable price structure

All users must be able to understand the pricing structure more clearly.

(e) It is easily implementable

The pricing scheme should be easily implementable in the actual system.

The transmission prices are imposed to recover the cost of wheeling the power through the transmission system. As per PURA (1978) USA, 'Wheeling refers to transmission of Real & Reactive Power from a seller to buyer involving transmission network of a third party. Wheeling cost is due to transmission losses and re-dispatching of generators resulting in loss opportunity'.

The wheeling can be broadly classified into four categories which are as follows:

1. Bulk power wheeling that involves transaction of two fully regulated utilities using network of a third utility.
2. Customer wheeling in which an independent customer purchases power from an utility using network of another party.
3. Supplier wheeling in which an independent GENCO sells power to an utility using network of another party.
4. Supplier-to-customer wheeling in which an independent GENCO sells power to an independent customer using network of a third party.

In general, the following three pricing schemes are employed for transmission services:

- **Embedded cost based pricing:** This method is based on recovering, on pro rata basis, the embedded capital cost, average annuals operating cost, replacement cost considering service life and depreciation.

- **Incremental cost based pricing:** This method employs economic load dispatch formulation to compute short-run marginal cost (SRMC) and long-run marginal cost (LRMC). In case of SRMC, the revenue reconciliation is required to recover the capital cost.
- Combination of the above two.

12.4.1 Postage Stamp Method

The name of this scheme has evolved from the basis on which postage stamps are priced, i.e. the customer only pays according to the weight of the package, not on the basis of distance of delivery point, or how the package will contribute to the postal transport requirement, etc.

This transmission pricing methodology allocates transmission charges (existing or rolled-in) based on the magnitude of the transacted power. The magnitude of the transacted power for a particular transmission transaction is usually measured at the time of system peak load condition.

$$R_t = TC \times \frac{P_t}{P_{\text{peak}}} \tag{12.1}$$

where R_t is the transmission price for transaction t, TC is the total transmission charges and P_t and P_{peak} are transaction t load and the entire system load at the time of system peak load condition respectively.

The main justification for using this pricing methodology has been that the entire transmission system is considered as a centrally operated integrated system. The simplicity of this approach is also one of its strongest selling points.

Since this methodology ignores the actual system operation, it is likely to send incorrect economic signal to transmission customers. As a result, a wheeling transaction that may require extensive and costly system upgrades can still take place because the wheeling customer will be responsible for only a fraction of the transmission related cost caused by the transaction. This drawback also applies when the postage stamp methodology is used in conjunction with composite embedded/incremental pricing paradigm for allocating the existing system costs. Under these circumstances, the short distance wheeling customers may bypass the system due to high transmission prices causing all remaining customers to pay more for using the same service.

12.4.2 Contract Path Method

Contract path-pricing calls for transmission from point A to point B based on the cost of single identified path. The price includes a capacity charge to cover the capital costs, and energy charges based on losses and other operating costs. Suppose two parties want to move 400 MW of power between two points, and choose a transmission line as "contract path" between the two points, then even knowing that the power will actually move on different parallel paths between the two stations, they calculate the costs to be paid based on this "contract path". This method requires the identification of the supply and the receipt point for a bilateral transaction and a "contract path" between the two nodes. This method directs the amount of contracted capacity as well as the distance associated with the contract path. In this method the network charges are allocated to individual transaction.

The contract path is fiction path method. The physical load flow of a single transaction may be different from the contractual load flow, particularly in the meshed electricity network. Transmission pricing becomes complex when electricity does not flow over the contracted path. The problems associated with this method are the direction of the load flow, congestion management, allocation of charges for ancillary services and system control for single transactions. The problem related to the contract path due to parallel path flow can be understood by the following example.

In Figure 12.2, the points A and D are the points of supply and demand respectively. If the path A-B-D is nominated as a contract path for the transaction, it carries only some of the contracted capacity and the remaining are flowing in the parallel path A-C-D. If the impedance of path A-C-D is lower than that of contracted path A-B-D, the former carries a greater part of the contracted capacity. While the path A-C-D is not a contracted path so C is not paid for this transaction. This example shows why the contract path is unfair.

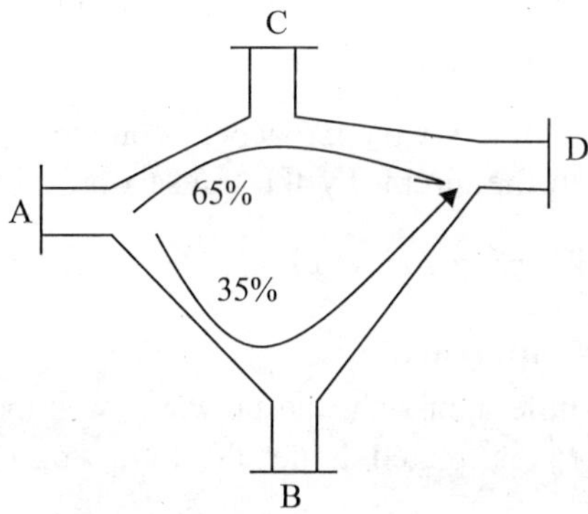

Figure 12.2 Contract path method.

The other problems associated with the contract path include:

1. Fixed cost of transmission network is not recovered
2. Pricing manipulation
3. Difference between short-term and long-term prices
4. Calculation of available transfer capacity is difficult
5. Transmission affects the other parallel paths in the electricity meshed networks. Power can flow on different paths depending upon the generation schedule.

12.4.3 MW-Mile Method

The existing regional postage stamp method of transmission pricing does not consider the effect of circuit loading, hence it is quite unfair. So, depending on the direction of power flow, the three methods of MW-mile method have been discussed. The MW-mile method calculates the flow at each circuit caused by the generation/load pattern of each agent based on a power flow model. Costs are then allocated in proportion to ratio of power flow and circuit capacity. According to this method, the embedded cost of transmission facility is allocated based on the changes in power flow caused by a transaction in a transmission line and length of the line. This method is also called line-by-line method. Depending on the direction of power flow, MW-mile method can be described as, dominant and reverse approaches. Generally, for MW mile method, the cost allocated to each individual transaction is given by

$$TC_k = \sum_{i=1}^{n} \frac{L_{ij} F_{ij} P_{ij}^k}{P_{ij}^{\max}} \tag{12.2}$$

where,

TC_k is the transmission pricing for the transaction k

L_{ij} is the length of the line i–j

F_{ij} is the cost of the line i–j

P_{ij}^k is the power flow of line i–j due to the transaction k

$P_{ij}^{\max}$ is the thermal limit of line i–j

The main difference in the two approaches is on the treatment of the power flow that is imposed on the circuit by the transaction.

Approaches of MW-mile method

- **Dominant MW-mile approach**

In the dominant MW-mile approach, the power flow imposed on the line i, j by the transaction k, P_{ij}^k is treated as per the following condition,

$$\begin{aligned} P_{ij}^k &= |P_{ij}^k| \quad \text{for direct flows} \\ &= 0 \quad \text{for reverse flows} \end{aligned} \tag{12.3}$$

- **Reverse MW-mile approach**

The reverse MW-mile approach takes into account the power flows that are in reverse direction and the charge for each line is based on the net flows. The reason is that the reverse power flows reduce the burden on the line. Power flow imposed on the line i, j by transaction k, P_{ij}^k is treated as per the following condition,

$$P_{ij}^k = P_{ij}^k \quad \text{for direct flows}$$
$$= -P_{ij}^k \quad \text{for reverse flows} \tag{12.4}$$

In dominant MW-mile approach, network users are only charged on the basis of direct power flow imposed on each line. Reverse power flows are not counted, so users responsible for the reverse power flows do not receive a credit like reverse MW-mile approach and do not pay any charge like dominant MW-mile approach.

12.4.4 Marginal Participation (MP) Method

Normally, the cost allocation method used to identify the contribution of individual generators and loads to line flows and the real power transfer between individual generators and loads is another important issue in wheeling transaction since it reflects the way the cost of transmission services satisfactorily allocated among the trading parties. The marginal participation method is based on the load flow studies indicating the use of the system. Transmission charges determined using this method is found to have better economic and technical properties as compared to other methods. This method analyses how the flows in the grid are modified when minor changes are introduced in the buyer m and seller n, with the relationship of the flow through line i–j. This method computes the relative use of each network branch by buyer m and seller n. It provides clear signal locational signals to generation and demand customers. The steps for the calculation of transmission price using the MP method is:

1. Assume length and cost of each line.
2. Calculate the line flows for base case using Newton–Raphson load flow method.
3. Consider a transaction with t_k MW between GENCO m and DISCO n and then calculate line flows using Newton–Raphson load flow studies.
4. Calculate the difference in line power flows:

$$\Delta P_{ij,mn} = (P_{ij,mn} - P_{ij}^0) \tag{12.5}$$

   where,

   $\Delta P_{ij,mn}$ is the difference in line power flows

   $P_{ij,mn}$ is the loading of line i–j due to t_k MW transaction

   P_{ij}^0 is the loading of line i–j under base case.

5. Compute the total change in line flows, i.e. multiply change in line flows with total MW injected

$$\Delta P_{g(ij,mn)} = (P_{ij,mn} - P_{ij}^0) * P_n \tag{12.6}$$

   where, P_n is the power generation at bus m under transaction case.

6. The change in line power flows based on transaction k is considered by the following approaches:

   (a) Dominant MP approach

$$\begin{aligned} P_{ij}^k &= |P_{ij}^k| && \text{for direct flows} \\ &= 0 && \text{for reverse flows} \end{aligned} \tag{12.7}$$

   (b) Reverse MP approach

$$\begin{aligned} P_{ij}^k &= P_{ij}^k && \text{for direct flows} \\ &= -P_{ij}^k && \text{for reverse flows} \end{aligned} \tag{12.8}$$

7. Find the marginal participation factor of generation/demand at each bus.

$$\text{MP Factor} = \frac{\Delta P_{g(ij,mn)}}{\sum_{ij} \Delta P_{g(ij,mn)}} \tag{12.9}$$

8. Compute the transmission charges at each node and then compute overall cost for transaction.

$$TC_{mn} = \frac{L_{ij} C_{ij} \Delta P_{g(ij,mn)}}{\sum_{ij} \Delta P_{g(ij,mn)}} \tag{12.10}$$

   where,

   TC_{mn} is the transmission pricing between buying bus m and selling bus n
   L_{ij} is the length of line i–j
   C_{ij} is the cost of power in the line i–j
   $\Delta P_{ij,mn}$ is the power flow due to line i–j due to transactions m, n.

12.5 PSS/E Interface with Python

PSS/E software is used to simulate and study power systems, which stands for Power System Simulator for Engineers. The main functions of this PSS/E are:

- Power flow and related network analysis functions.
- Balanced and unbalanced fault analysis.
- Network equivalent construction.
- Dynamic simulation.

PSS/E software is used to simulate power flow problems and network analysis functions. There are six automation processors in PSS/E. PSS/E contains an embedded Python interpreter. PSS/E allows to execute Python files and commands. When the PSS/E GUI is started, it initializes the Python interpreter and executes a few initial commands. Python is an OSI certified freely available, object-oriented, interpreted programming language.

The bus data and line data values of standard system are entered in PSS/E. The Python scripts are written in a notepad to execute load flow program and the cost of transacted power is calculated. Interfacing of PSS/E with Python is done since PSS/E displays only the final result and the intermediate values in all iterations can only be known with the help of Python. Psspy module is used for interface of PSS/E with Python.

Power flow is obtained from PSS/E by entering the bus data, load data, branch data. PSS/E does not support for the calculation of transmission pricing, so PSS/E is interfaced with Python. For interfacing, I/O control option is used. I/O control option will link the obtained power flow in PSS/E to Python. Using power flow in Python, the Python code is written to calculate the transmission price. Figure 12.3 shows the interfacing of PSS/E with Python.

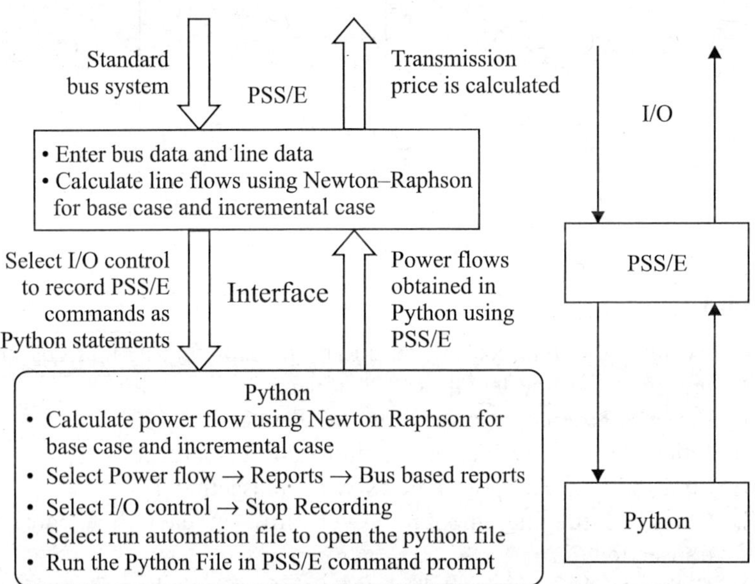

Figure 12.3 Interfacing of PSS/E with Python.

EXAMPLE 12.1 Consider a six-bus system comprising bus 1 as slack and buses 2 and 3 as generator buses and three load buses, namely 4, 5 and 6 are 75 MW each. The generation power at buses 2 and 3 are 50 MW and 60 MW respectively. There are two transactions from seller to buyer:

T_1: From bus 2 to bus 5 of 30 MW
T_2: From bus 3 to bus 6 of 20 MW

The total system demand is 210 MW. Transmission network parameters are given in Table 12.1.

Table 12.1 Line reactance values

Line	1–2	1–4	1–5	2–3	2–4	2–5	2–6	3–5	3–6	4–5	5–6
***X*(p.u.)**	0.2	0.2	0.3	0.25	0.1	0.3	0.2	0.26	0.1	0.4	0.3

Line reactances are in p.u. on a base of 100 MVA. Assume the distance of all the lines as 100 miles and unit cost of the line is 100 \$/MW mile. Calculate the proportional cost of 2 transactions using the MW mile method.

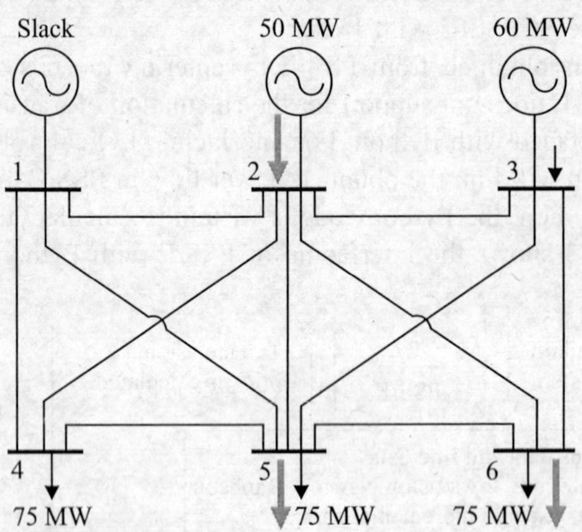

Figure 12.4 One line diagram.

Procedure

Step A: Evaluate the total cost of the line by multiplying the unit cost of the line with the line length as 100 miles.

Step B: Find the base case power flow on all lines.

Step C: Calculate the new line power flows due to transaction T_1.

Step D: Find the new line power flows with transaction T_2.

Step E: Calculate the incremental power flow on each line caused by transaction T_1.

Step F: Calculate the incremental power flow on each line caused by the transaction T_2.

Step G: Calculate each line usage due to transaction T_1 and hence find the total transmission usage by T_1.

Step H: Calculate each line usage due to transaction T_2 and hence find the total transmission usage by T_2.

Step I: Calculate the total transmission system usage by T_1 and T_2 for proportional allocation of the costs.

Step J: Calculate the proportional allocation of cost to transaction T_1.

Step K: Calculate the proportional allocation of cost to transaction T_2.

Solution:

Base case load flow

Take bus 1 as reference.

The formula for dc power flow is given by

$$P_{ij} = \frac{1}{x_{ij}}(\theta_i - \theta_j) \tag{12.11}$$

where

$$\theta = [X]*[P]$$

$$[X] = [Y_{bus}]^{-1}$$

Step 1: Calculate $[Y_{bus}]$ using the line information. Neglect 1st row and 1st column as bus 1 is the slack bus. It is given in Eq. (12.11)

$$Y_{bus} = \begin{bmatrix} 27.333 & -4 & -10 & -3.333 & -5 \\ -4 & 17.846 & 0 & -3.8462 & -10 \\ -10 & 0 & 17.5 & -2.5 & 0 \\ -3.333 & -3.846 & -2.5 & 16.346 & -3.333 \\ -5 & -10 & 0 & -3.333 & 18.333 \end{bmatrix}$$

Step 2: Calculate X.

$$[X] = \begin{bmatrix} 0.0941 & 0.0804 & 0.0629 & 0.0643 & 0.0812 \\ 0.0804 & 0.1658 & 0.0589 & 0.0907 & 0.1288 \\ 0.0629 & 0.0589 & 0.1008 & 0.0542 & 0.0591 \\ 0.0643 & 0.0907 & 0.0542 & 0.1220 & 0.0891 \\ 0.0812 & 0.1288 & 0.0591 & 0.0891 & 0.1632 \end{bmatrix}$$

The bus power flows are in p.u.

$$[P] = \begin{bmatrix} 0.5 \\ 0.6 \\ -0.75 \\ -0.75 \\ -0.75 \end{bmatrix}$$

Now the voltage angle is

$$\theta = [X][P]$$

$$\begin{bmatrix} \theta_2 \\ \theta_3 \\ \theta_4 \\ \theta_5 \\ \theta_6 \end{bmatrix} = \begin{bmatrix} -0.06095 \\ -0.06912 \\ -0.09378 \\ -0.11241 \\ -0.11586 \end{bmatrix}$$

Now the line flows are calculated as

$$P_{12} = \frac{1}{x_{12}}[\theta_1 - \theta_2] = \frac{1}{0.2}[0 + 0.06095] = 0.305 \text{ p.u.}$$

$$P_{14} = \frac{1}{x_{14}}[\theta_1 - \theta_4] = \frac{1}{0.2}[0 + 0.09378] = 0.469 \text{ p.u.}$$

$$P_{15} = 0.375 \text{ p.u.}$$
$$P_{23} = 0.033 \text{ p.u.}$$
$$P_{24} = 0.328 \text{ p.u.}$$
$$P_{25} = 0.172 \text{ p.u.}$$
$$P_{26} = 0.275 \text{ p.u.}$$
$$P_{35} = 0.166 \text{ p.u.}$$
$$P_{36} = 0.467 \text{ p.u.}$$
$$P_{45} = 0.047 \text{ p.u.}$$
$$P_{56} = 0.012 \text{ p.u.}$$

Consider transaction T_1.

T_1: From bus 2 to bus 5 of 30 MW

So the bus powers are changed as

$\therefore \quad P_2 = (0.5 + 0.3) \text{ p.u.} = 0.8 \text{ p.u.}$

$\therefore \quad P_5 = (-0.75 - 0.3) \text{ p.u.} = -1.05 \text{ p.u.}$

$$P = \begin{bmatrix} 0.8 \\ 0.6 \\ -0.75 \\ -1.05 \\ -0.75 \end{bmatrix}$$

Now, using Eq. (12.11),

$$\begin{bmatrix} \theta_2 \\ \theta_3 \\ \theta_4 \\ \theta_5 \\ \theta_6 \end{bmatrix} = \begin{bmatrix} -0.052 \\ -0.072 \\ -0.091 \\ -0.13 \\ -0.118 \end{bmatrix}$$

Now the line flows are calculated for transaction T_1,

$$P_{12} = \frac{1}{x_{12}}[\theta_1 - \theta_2] = \frac{1}{0.2}[0 + 0.052] = 0.26 \text{ p.u.}$$

$$P_{14} = \frac{1}{x_{14}}[\theta_1 - \theta_4] = \frac{1}{0.2}[0 + 0.091] = 0.455 \text{ p.u.}$$

$$P_{15} = 0.433 \text{ p.u.}$$
$$P_{23} = 0.08 \text{ p.u.}$$
$$P_{24} = 0.39 \text{ p.u.}$$
$$P_{25} = 0.26 \text{ p.u.}$$
$$P_{26} = 0.33 \text{ p.u.}$$
$$P_{35} = 0.223 \text{ p.u.}$$
$$P_{36} = 0.46 \text{ p.u.}$$
$$P_{45} = 0.098 \text{ p.u.}$$
$$P_{56} = -0.04 \text{ p.u.}$$

Consider transaction T_2

T_2: From bus 3 to bus 6 of 20 MW

$\therefore$ $P_3 = (0.6 + 0.2) \text{ p.u.} = 0.8 \text{ p.u.}$

$\therefore$ $P_5 = (-0.75 - 0.2) \text{ p.u.} = -0.95 \text{ p.u.}$

$$P = \begin{bmatrix} 0.5 \\ 0.8 \\ -0.75 \\ -0.75 \\ -0.95 \end{bmatrix}$$

Now, using Eq. (12.11),

$$\begin{bmatrix} \theta_2 \\ \theta_3 \\ \theta_4 \\ \theta_5 \\ \theta_6 \end{bmatrix} = \begin{bmatrix} -0.061 \\ -0.062 \\ -0.094 \\ -0.112 \\ -0.123 \end{bmatrix}$$

$$P_{12} = \frac{1}{x_{12}}[\theta_1 - \theta_2] = \frac{1}{0.2}[0 + 0.061] = 0.305 \text{ p.u.}$$

$$P_{14} = \frac{1}{x_{14}}[\theta_1 - \theta_4] = \frac{1}{0.2}[0 + 0.094] = 0.47 \text{ p.u.}$$

$$P_{15} = 0.373 \text{ p.u.}$$
$$P_{23} = 0.004 \text{ p.u.}$$
$$P_{24} = 0.33 \text{ p.u.}$$
$$P_{25} = 0.17 \text{ p.u.}$$

$$P_{26} = 0.31 \text{ p.u.}$$
$$P_{35} = 0.192 \text{ p.u.}$$
$$P_{36} = 0.61 \text{ p.u.}$$
$$P_{45} = 0.045 \text{ p.u.}$$
$$P_{56} = -0.037 \text{ p.u.}$$

As per Table 12.2, the transaction T_1 should pay 65.7% of the total costs while the transaction T_2 should pay for the remaining 34.3%.

EXAMPLE 12.2 Consider a six-bus system, having three generator buses and three load buses with the total demand of 210 MW. The length of each line is shown in Figure 12.5.

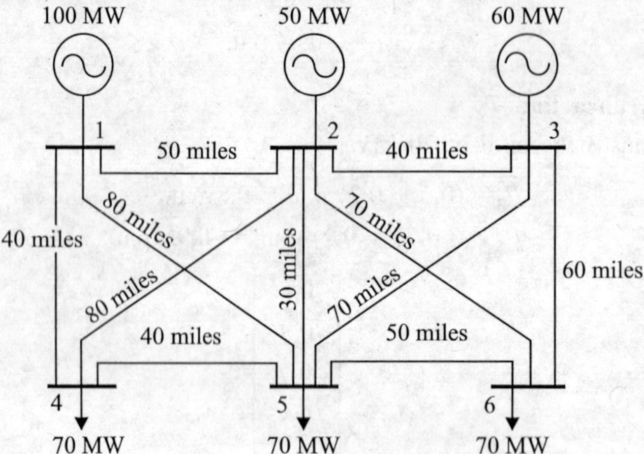

Figure 12.5 One line diagram.

Four transactions are carried out as T_1, T_2, T_3 and T_4.

Transaction T_1: Seller bus 2 to buyer bus 4 for 10 MW transaction.
Transaction T_2: Seller bus 2 to buyer bus 5 for 10 MW transaction.
Transaction T_3: Seller bus 3 to buyer bus 4 for 10 MW transaction.
Transaction T_4: Seller bus 3 to buyer bus 5 for 10 MW transaction.

Calculate and compare the cost of transactions by MW-mile and MP methods using MATLAB and PSS/E software.

Solution:

MATLAB

MW-mile method

Step 1: Read the bus data, line data and cost and length of lines.

Step 2: Run Newton–Raphson power flow to get the power flow details of all lines.

Step 3: Using Eq. (12.3) to modify the line power flows for dominant MW-mile approach.

Table 12.2 Transaction cost

Steps	Line, i–j	1–2	1–4	1–3	2–3	2–4	2–5	2–6	3–5	3–6	4–5	4–6	Total
A	$L^*_{ij} c_{i,j}$	10000	10000	10000	10000	10000	10000	10000	10000	10000	10000	10000	—
B	$P_{ij\text{base}}$	0.305	0.469	0.375	0.033	0.328	0.172	0.275	0.166	0.467	0.047	0.012	—
C	$P_{ij\text{ due}}$ to T_1	0.26	0.455	0.433	0.08	0.39	0.26	0.33	0.223	0.46	0.098	0.04	—
D	$P_{ij\text{ due}}$ to T_2	0.305	0.47	0.373	0.004	0.33	0.17	0.31	0.192	0.61	0.045	0.037	—
E	$F_{j\text{ due}}$ to T_1	0.045	0.014	0.058	0.047	0.062	0.088	0.055	0.057	0.007	0.051	0.028	—
F	$F_{j\text{ due}}$ to T_2	0	0.001	0.002	0.029	0.002	0.002	0.035	0.026	0.143	0.002	0.025	—
G	$A * E$	450	140	580	470	620	880	550	570	70	510	280	5120
H	$A * F$	0	10	20	290	20	20	350	260	1430	20	250	2670
I	$G_{\text{total}} + H_{\text{total}}$						—						7790
J	G_{total}/I						—						**0.657**
K	H_{total}/I						—						**0.343**

Step 4: Using Eq. (12.4) to modify the line power flows for reverse MW-mile approach.

Step 5: Find the transaction cost using Eq. (12.2).

Step 6: Repeat the procedure for other transactions.

Marginal participation method

The step by step procedure is explained from Eq. (12.5) to Eq. (12.10) in section 12.4.4. The same procedure is repeated for other transactions.

PSS/E

The programs are written for MW-mile and MP methods using Python scripts and it is interfaced with PSS/E software. The line power flows are calculated using PSS/E software and these values are passed to the Python. The outputs are obtained by Python and they are shown in Figures 12.6 and 12.7.

```
PSS®E-32 Command Prompt

 BUS       1 SLACK         230.00 CKT      MW      MVAR      MVA   PU     0.00  X--- LO
SSES ---X X---- AREA -----X X---- ZONE -----X         1
  FROM GENERATION                          79.1    35.4R    86.7  87 230.00KV
     MW      MVAR     1                      1
  TO       2 PV1           230.00  1       10.7   -11.3     15.5
    0.44     0.44     1                      1
  TO       4 PQ1           230.00  1       38.3    27.1     46.9
    1.13     4.51     1                      1
  TO       5 PQ2           230.00  1       30.1    19.6     35.9
    1.08     4.06     1                      1

 BUS       2 PV1           230.00 CKT      MW      MVAR      MVA   PU    -2.40  X--- LO
SSES ---X X---- AREA -----X X---- ZONE -----X         2
  FROM GENERATION                          90.0    99.3R   134.0 134 230.00KV
     MW      MVAR     1                      1
  TO       1 SLACK         230.00  1      -10.3     9.7     14.1
    0.44     0.44     1                      1
  TO       3 PV2           230.00  1        4.0    -2.3      4.6
    0.01     0.04     1                      1
  TO       4 PQ1           230.00  1       48.4    48.8     68.7
    2.39     4.77     1                      1
  TO       5 PQ2           230.00  1       19.0    21.1     28.4
    0.85     2.55     1                      1
  TO       6 PQ3           230.00  1       28.8    22.0     36.3
    0.96     2.75     1                      1

 BUS       3 PV2           230.00 CKT      MW      MVAR      MVA   PU    -2.99  X--- LO
SSES ---X X---- AREA -----X X---- ZONE -----X         3
  FROM GENERATION                          60.0    78.4R    98.7  99 230.00KV
     MW      MVAR     1                      1
  TO       2 PV1           230.00  1       -3.9    -0.7      4.0
    0.01     0.04     1                      1
  TO       5 PQ2           230.00  1       20.6    21.9     30.1
    1.15     2.50     1                      1
  TO LOAD-PQ                               80.0    70.0    106.3
  TO       1 SLACK         230.00  1      -37.2   -24.4     44.5
    1.13     4.51     1                      1
  TO       2 PV1           230.00  1      -46.0   -44.9     64.3
    2.39     4.77     1                      1
  TO       5 PQ2           230.00  1        3.2    -0.7      3.3
    0.03     0.05     1                      1

 BUS       5 PQ2           230.00 CKT      MW      MVAR      MVA   PU    -4.60  X--- LO
SSES ---X X---- AREA -----X X---- ZONE -----X         5
                                                                     210.55KV
     MW      MVAR     1                      1
  TO LOAD-PQ                               70.0    70.0     99.0
  TO       1 SLACK         230.00  1      -29.0   -18.3     34.3
    1.08     4.06     1                      1
  TO       2 PV1           230.00  1      -18.2   -20.3     27.3
    0.85     2.55     1                      1
  TO       3 PV2           230.00  1      -19.4   -21.7     29.1
    1.15     2.50     1                      1
  TO       4 PQ1           230.00  1       -3.2    -2.7      4.2
    0.03     0.05     1                      1
  TO       6 PQ3           230.00  1       -0.2    -6.9      6.9
    0.04     0.12     1                      1

 BUS       6 PQ3           230.00 CKT      MW      MVAR      MVA   PU    -4.94  X--- LO
SSES ---X X---- AREA -----X X---- ZONE -----X         6
                                                                     214.87KV
     MW      MVAR     1                      1
  TO LOAD-PQ                               70.0    70.0     99.0
  TO       2 PV1           230.00  1      -27.9   -21.6     35.3
    0.96     2.75     1                      1
  TO       3 PV2           230.00  1      -42.3   -52.9     67.7
    1.04     5.20     1                      1
  TO       5 PQ2           230.00  1        0.2     4.5      4.5
    0.04     0.12     1                      1
```

Figure 12.6 Line flows due to transaction T_2.

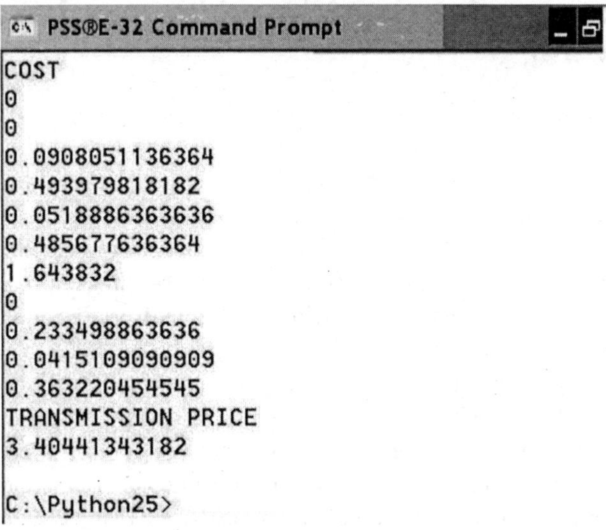

Figure 12.7 Output window for T_2 in Python.

The transmission prices for the above four transactions are calculated using MP method and MW-mile method. The transmission cost for transaction T_1 using dominant MP method is 1.8515 \$/MWhr, whereas 2.3241 \$/MWhr for dominant MW-mile method. The results for other transactions are given in Table 12.3. Based on the results, reverse MW-mile and reverse marginal participation methods take into account the reverse flows, and the transmission price is the lowest, so it is pessimistic. The transmission pricing obtained using marginal participation method is less compared to MW-mile method. For dominant MW-mile and dominant marginal participation method, the transmission price is charged only for direct flows so it is an exact method. The transmission pricing obtained using the marginal participation method is less compared to MW-mile method and the transmission pricing obtained by MP method is less compared to the existing method.

Table 12.3 Transaction costs

Transaction	*Transmission price using* MATLAB (\$/MWhr)				*Transmission price using* PSS/E (\$/MWhr)	
	MW-*mile method*		MP *method*		MW-*mile method*	MP *method*
	Dominant MW-*mile method*	*Reverse* MW-*mile method*	*Dominant* MP *method*	*Reverse* MP *method*	*Dominant* MW-*mile method*	*Dominant* MP *method*
T_1	2.3241	1.5785	1.8515	0.5425	2.2129	1.8215
T_2	3.5022	2.7217	3.0661	2.3964	3.4533	3.0028
T_3	3.0503	0.2467	2.0786	–3.6626	2.9868	1.8830
T_4	3.5071	1.3847	2.8370	1.8466	2.8876	2.6007

12.6 Incremental Cost Based Transmission Pricing

This incremental cost based pricing methodology assigns part or all the incremental cost of accommodating transmission transactions directly to that transaction. They are mainly used with the incremental transmission pricing paradigm to determine the price of a transmission transaction. Incremental pricing methodologies are also used with the composite embedded/incremental pricing paradigm for determining a component of transmission prices.

Two major points are associated with incremental pricing methodologies. The first one deals with the costs that should be included in the price, i.e. short-run versus long-run costs. The second major point deals with whether prices should be based on marginal or incremental costs. The major difference between the marginal and incremental costs is in the way they are evaluated. Incremental costs of a transaction are evaluated by all comparing the transmission system costs with and without the entire transaction. However, the marginal approach would multiply the cost for a unit of additional transaction by the size of that transaction. There may be a large gap between the incremental and the marginal costs of a transaction.

12.6.1 Short-Run Incremental Cost (SRIC) Pricing

This SRIC pricing method deals with evaluating and assigning the operating costs associated with a new transaction. The transaction operating costs can be estimated using an optimal power flow (OPF) model that accounts for all operating constraints including transmission system (static or dynamic security) constraints and generation scheduling constraints. The short-run incremental cost of a transmission transaction can also be negative.

There are several concerns associated with the SRIC pricing methodology in addition to technical challenges involved in accurately evaluating the operating costs. First, in order to provide timely economic signals to transmission customers, this pricing methodology should forecast operating costs. It requires forecasting future operating scenarios which can become less and less accurate as the forecast time horizon extends-of farther into the future. The second concern is related to the allocation of the short-run incremental cost among several transactions that are collectively responsible for changes in operating costs. The third concern deals with volatility of transmission prices determined using this methodology for long-term transactions. These factors would make it difficult to make efficient economic decision for the long-term transmission transaction based on the short-run incremental cost prices.

Since revenues collected through this pricing methodology only compensate for the operating cost incurred by a transaction, SRIC pricing could discourage host utilities from expanding their transmission system.

12.6.2 Long-Run Incremental Cost (LRIC) Pricing

This pricing methodology evaluates all long-run costs such as operating and reinforcement costs necessary to accommodate a transmission transaction and assigning such costs to that transaction. The operating cost component may be determined as explained under SRIC pricing methodology.

The reinforcement cost component of a transmission transaction can be evaluated based on the changes caused in the long-term transmission plans due to the transmission transaction. Similar to the operating costs, reinforcement costs could be negative indicating that the transaction have resulted in the deferral of planned transmission reinforcements.

Although the concept of reinforcement cost is simple and straightforward, its evaluation is very difficult since it involves solving the least cost transmission expansion problem. Again, there are concerns related to allocation of the reinforcement costs among multiple transactions that collectively cause such costs.

12.6.3 Short-Run Marginal Cost (SRMC) Pricing

In this SRMC pricing methodology, the marginal operating cost of the power system due to a transmission transaction is calculated first. The marginal operating cost is the cost of accommodating a marginal increase in the transacted power. The marginal operating cost per MW of transacted power can be estimated as the difference in the optimal cost of power at all points of delivery and receipt of that transaction. The marginal operating cost is then multiplied by the magnitude of the transacted power to obtain the short-run marginal cost (SRMC) for the transmission transaction.

$$\text{SRMC}_t = \sum_{i \in B_t} \text{BMC}_i \times P_{i,t} \tag{12.12}$$

where, BMC_i is the i bus marginal cost,

P_{it} is the injected power at bus i due to transaction t,

B_t is the set of transmission buses involved in the transaction t.

The bus marginal cost of power can be calculated using OPF sensitivity methods. SRMC prices for a transmission transaction can be also negative.

The SRMC prices for a transmission transaction are normally calculated with the transaction included in the base case. As a result, the SRMC prices are higher than the actual operating cost of accommodating the transaction. It has been proposed that this extra "profit" be accumulated by the wheeling utility to fund future transmission expansions.

The challenges for SRMC pricing are similar to SRIC pricing methodology. In addition, the SRMC prices may not closely follow a transmission transaction actual operating cost if the magnitude of the transacted power is large compared to the magnitude of native load in the transmission system. Finally, "profits" collected through this pricing methodology generally very low when compared with the cost of lumpy transmission reinforcements. Hence, the SRMC prices may discourage the host utility from expanding its transmission system. In fact, if the host utility make any expansion in its transmission system, the SRMC prices will decrease dramatically reducing the possibility of recovering transmissions reinforcement costs.

12.6.4 Long-Run Marginal Cost (LRMC) Pricing

In this pricing methodology, the marginal operating and reinforcement costs of the power system are used to evaluate the prices for a transmission transaction. The marginal operating cost determination is explained under SRMC pricing and the calculation of the marginal reinforcement cost is discussed below.

Over a "long" time horizon of several years, all transmission expansion projects are identified and cost is estimated. This cost is then divided over the total power magnitude of all new planned transactions to calculate the marginal reinforcement cost. Similar to all other incremental pricing methodologies, the LRMC prices may be negative. The concerns associated and discussed with the LRIC pricing are also applicable to LRMC pricing.

Review Questions

Part-A

1. Define transmission access.
2. What are the goals of transmission pricing strategy?
3. What are the cost components involved in transmission services?
4. What are the different pricing schemes of transmission?
5. What are the cost components in pricing?
6. What are the two methods used under the embedded cost transmission pricing?
7. What is meant by firm transaction?
8. Which organization will be responsible for TSO operation in Indian restructuring environment?
9. What is the disadvantage in postage stamp method of transmission pricing?

Part-B

1. Explain the procedure of MW-mile method of calculation of transmission pricing in deregulated environment.
2. Write short notes on (i) types of transmission services in open access, and (ii) pricing of power transmission.

3. Explain the transmission access and pricing mechanisms in various countries.
4. Explain the MW-mile method of transmission pricing with a suitable example.
5. Explain the pricing mechanism employed in Sweden with necessary diagrams.
6. Explain the short-run marginal cost based pricing with a suitable example.
7. Explain any one method of incremental cost based transmission pricing scheme and give the advantage involved in it.
8. What are the different types of transmission services in open access? Explain them in detail.
9. Consider a six-bus system comprising bus 1 as slack and buses 2 and 3 are generator buses and three load buses, namely 4, 5 and 6 and of 70 MW each. Generator power at buses 2 and 3 are 50 and 60 MW respectively. There are two transactions (seller to buyer) to the existing system. (i) T_1 2–5 30 MW, (ii) T_2 3–6 20 MW.

   The total system demand is 210 MW. The transmission network parameters are given in the following table. The line reactance is unit on a base of 100 MVA.

1–2	1–4	1–5	2–3	2–5	2–6	3–5	3–6	4–5	5–6
0.2	0.2	0.3	0.25	0.3	0.2	0.26	0.1	0.4	0.3

   Assume the distance of all the lines is 100 miles and the unit cost of the lines is 100 \$/MW · mile. Calculate the proportional cost of two transactions using MW · mile method.

CHAPTER 13

Transmission Congestion Management

13.1 Introduction

Power system security has been one among the major concerns of system operators (SOs) and the restructuring has laid further emphasis on it. The transmission networks are often driven close to or even beyond their thermal limits in order to satisfy the increased electric power consumption and trades due to increase of the unplanned power exchanges. If the exchanges were not controlled, some lines located on particular paths may become overloaded, this phenomenon is called *congestion*. The congestion in the system cannot be allowed to persist for a long time, as it can cause sudden rise in the electricity price and threaten system security and reliability. The management of congestion is more complex in deregulated power markets and leads to several disputes. Congestion management is one of the major tasks performed by SOs to ensure the operation of transmission system within operating limits. The methods generally adopted to manage congestion include rescheduling generator outputs, supplying reactive power support or physically curtail transactions. Mostly, first option is being used by the system operators. In different types of market, the method of tackling the transmission congestion differs.

13.2 Congestion

Whenever the physical or operational constraints in a transmission network become active, the system is said to be in a state of congestion. The possible limits that may be hit in case of congestion are: line thermal limits, transformer emergency ratings, bus voltage limits, transient or oscillatory stability, etc. These limits constrain the amount of electric power that can be transmitted between two locations through a transmission network. Flows should not be allowed to increase to levels where a contingency would cause the network to collapse because of voltage instability, etc.

A sample system shown in Figure 13.1 is considered for an example. This system has four Generating Companies (GENCOs) (TTPS, KKNP, Kayathar

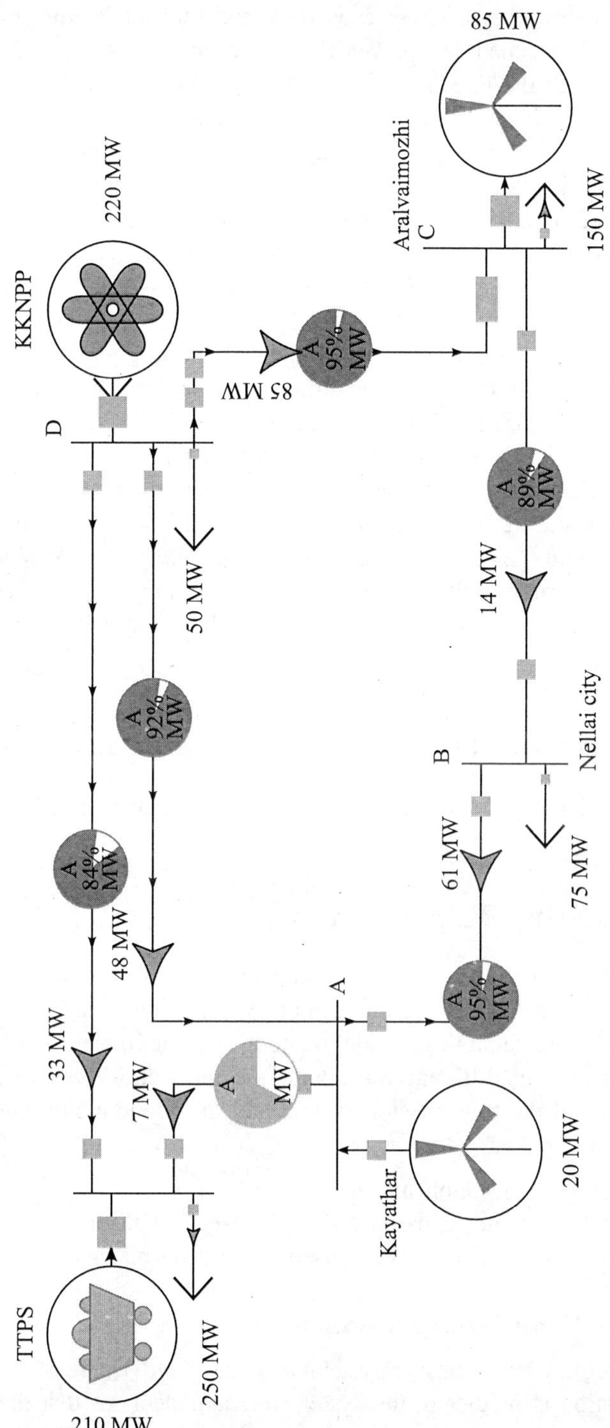

Figure 13.1 A sample.

and Aralvaimozhi) with different capacities, and four loads with total demand of 525 MW. The scheduled power flow in each line is calculated and the power flows in all the lines are within the limit. This implies that there is no congestion occurs in any line. The two transmission lines A-B and C-D are loaded up to 95%. Among the two lines, line A-B is to be congested when changing the schedule.

When load demand at Nellai city is increased from 75 MW to 85 MW. The power flow in the transmission line A-B is 68 MW, which exceeds its thermal limit (65 MW). So that congestion occurs in A-B line. It is represented in Figure 13.2.

To relieve congestion from the system explained in Figure 13.1, congestion management is carried out by rescheduling of generators. Here, rescheduling is done in two GENCOS, i.e., TTPS and Aralvaimozhi. The dispatched amounts for these two GENCOs are 228 MW and 80 MW respectively. The remaining GENCOs are dispatched to the same amount what it had before rescheduling.

After rescheduling the power flow in each line is within its thermal limit. The power flow in the congested line after rescheduling is 61 MW which does not exceed its thermal limit. So the congestion is completely relieved from the system. Figure 13.3 represents the congestion relieved system after congestion management taken place.

13.3 Classification of Congestion Management

Congestion relief techniques are classified based on cost of relief action and existing market survey.

13.3.1 Existing Market Survey

The form of deregulated electric power industry differs in each country and among various regions in the United States. Three main forms can be identified, although details vary widely among specific implementations. These three models deal in different ways with the interaction between properties and limitations of the transmission system and the economic efficiency of the energy market. They are:

1. Price area congestion management
2. Available transfer capability (ATC) based congestion management
3. Optimal power flow (OPF) based congestion management

Price Area Congestion Management

In Nordic Pool, which consists of Norway, Sweden, Denmark and Finland when congestion is predicted, the system operator declares that the system is split into price areas at predicted congestion bottlenecks. Spot market bidders must submit bids for each price area in which they have generation or loads.

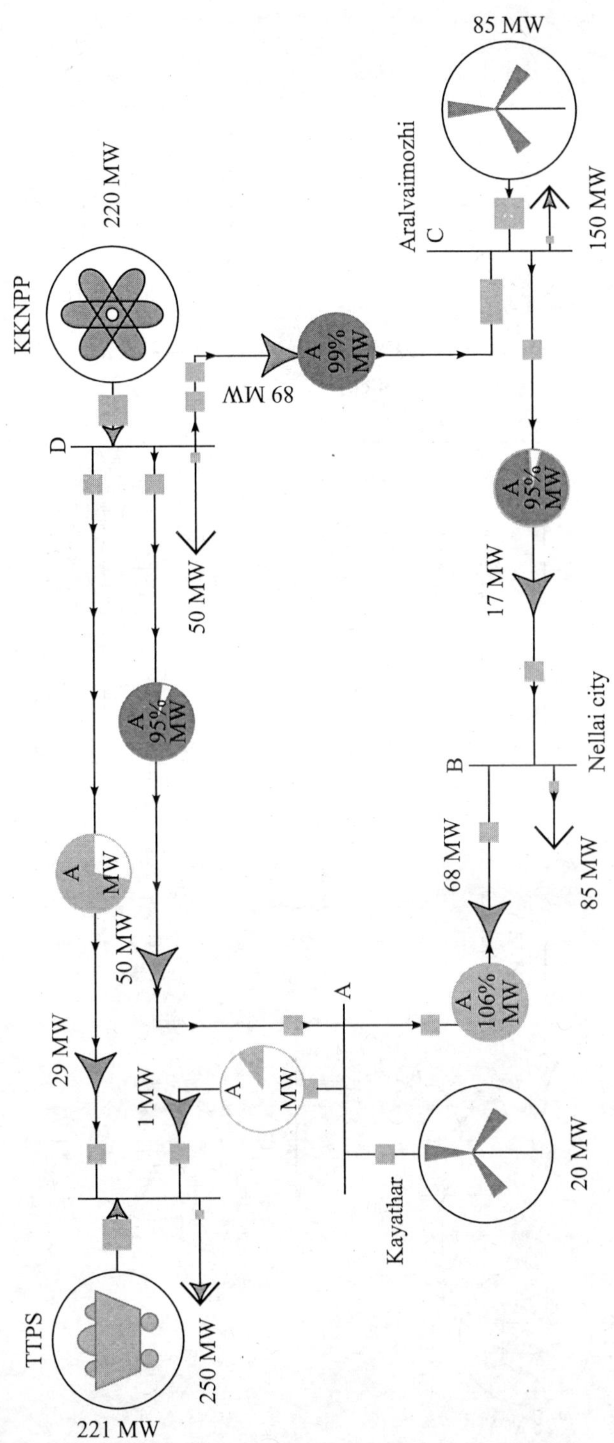

Figure 13.2 Congested system.

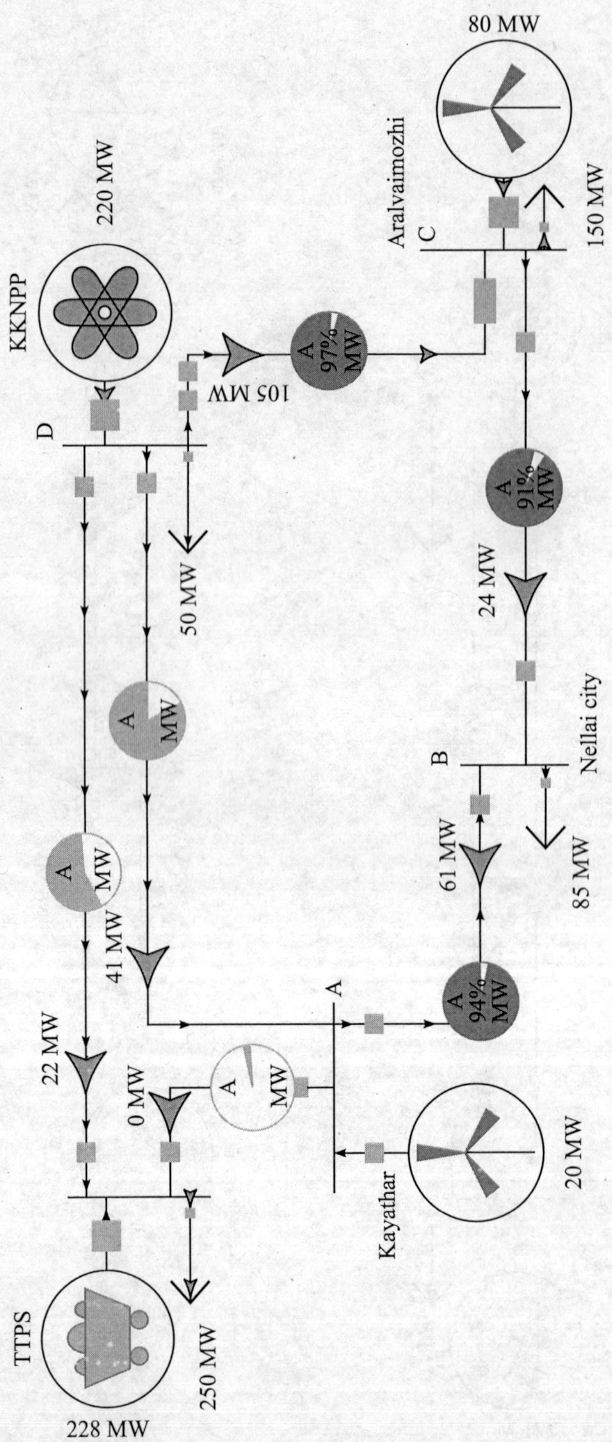

Figure 13.3 Congestion relieved system.

In case of no congestion, the price areas are separated and settled at price that satisfies transmission constraints. Area with excess generation will have lower price and those with excess loads will have higher prices.

Available Transfer Capability (ATC) Based Congestion Management

The US Federal Energy Regulatory Commission (FERC) established a system, where each system operator (SO) would be responsible for monitoring its own regional transmission system and calculating its ATC for potentially congested paths entering, leaving and inside its network. The ATC values for next hour and for each hour in the future are replaced on a website known as *open access same-time information system* (OASIS), by the system operator (SO). Anyone wishing to do transaction would access OASIS web pages and use ATC information available there to determine whether the system could accommodate transaction.

Optimal Power Flow (OPF) Based Congestion Management

In this method, optimal power flow is performed to minimize generator's operating costs subject to set constraints that represents a model of the transmission system within which the generator can operate. Here in case of no congestion, the generators are paid the same price as the loads pay, and when there is congestion, the generators and loads will have different payments.

13.3.2 Cost of Relief Action

Congestion management methods are classified based on the cost incurred for relieving congestion. This classification is as follows:

1. Cost free means
2. Non-cost free means

Cost free means

Cost free means of congestion management is nothing but using the already installed devices. It includes the operations such as changing transformer tap positions and operating FACTS devices. This method does not cause change in cost during congestion relief and hence the name. Though it is free of cost, it fails to provide real time solution many times.

Non-cost free means

Non-cost free means of congestion management includes re-dispatch of generation and load curtailment. As the name implies, these methods involve in cost for congestion relief. In congestion relief process, these basic ways are implemented in the following priority order:

(a) Carry out rescheduling in the non-firm contract without disturbing firm contract.

(b) If not enough introduce new contracts or curtail some of the loads, which is possible.
(c) If it is still not enough, reschedule the firm contracts.

The congestion management by rescheduling the generation and if needed and possible, load curtailment is also performed in the subsequent topics.

13.4 Cluster/Zone Based Approach

A congestion clusters based method identifies the group of system users that have a similar effect on a transmission constraint of interest. These clusters/zones are obtained using transmission congestion distribution factors (TCDFs). These clusters are termed as of types 1, 2 and higher, where type 1 cluster represents users with the strongest and non-uniform effects on transmission constraint on interest. This clustering based approach has been used to create an efficient congestion management where the transactions in the most sensitive cluster can help in eliminating congestion.

13.4.1 Transmission Congestion Distribution Factors (TCDFs)

Transmission congestion distribution factors (TCDFs) are defined as the change in real power flow (ΔP_{ij}) in a transmission line k, connected between bus i and bus j due to unit change in the power injection (ΔP_j) at bus j. Mathematically, the TCDF for the line k can be written as:

$$\text{TCDF}_j^k = \Delta P_{ij} / \Delta P_i \tag{13.1}$$

TCDF_j^k denotes how much active power flow over a transmission line connecting bus i and bus j would change due to active power injection at bus n. Since TCDF involves with bus power and line flow, it can be obtained using either dc load flow or ac load flow method.

13.4.2 DC Load Flow Based Approach (DC Method)

In dc load flow based approach, transmission congestion distribution factor (TCDF) is determined for real power flows in a line connected between bus i and bus j is given as follows:

$$P_{ij} = \frac{\delta_i - \delta_j}{x_{ij}} = b_{ij}(\delta_i - \delta_j) \tag{13.2}$$

where, x_{ij} and b_{ij} are the series reactance and susceptance of the transmission line, and δ_i is the phase angle of voltage at bus i.

Equation (13.2) can be rewritten in the vector form as:

$$\left[P_{ij}\right] = \left[L_{ij}\right]^T [\delta] \tag{13.3}$$

where, $[L_{ij}]$ is a sensitivity vector of the line power flow with respect to bus voltage phase angle. All the elements of $[L_{ij}]$ are zero except ith and jth elements, which are b_{ij} and $-b_{ij}$ respectively. $[\delta]$ is a vector of the voltage phase angles at all the buses. The dc load flow equation, describing the relationship between the bus voltage angle vector $[\delta]$ and real power injection vector $[P]$ for a N_B bus system, is given as follows:

$$[P]=[B][\delta] \tag{13.4}$$

where, $[B]$ is the $N_B \times N_B$ susceptance matrix, whose entries are:

$$B_{ij} = -b_{ij} \qquad \forall \; i \neq j$$

$$B_{ii} = \sum_{j=1}^{N_B} b_{ij} \qquad i = 1,2....N_B \tag{13.5}$$

Selecting bus n to be reference bus, the row and column of the $[B]$ matrix corresponding to the reference bus can be eliminated. The voltage at other buses relative to this bus can be solved in terms of $[P]$ as:

$$[\delta_{-n}]=[B_{-n}]^{-1}[P_{-n}] \tag{13.6}$$

Where, $(.)_{-n}$ represents a vector without nth row and column or a matrix with corresponding nth row and column eliminated. The actual phase angle can be rewritten by simply adding the relative phase angle and the phase angles of the reference bus.

$$[\delta]=\begin{bmatrix}\delta_{-n}\\ 0\end{bmatrix}+\delta_n\{1\} \tag{13.7}$$

$$[\delta]=\begin{bmatrix}[B_{-n}]^{-1} & 0\\ 0 & 0\end{bmatrix}[P]+\delta_n\{1\} \tag{13.8}$$

where, δ_n is the phase angle of bus n. $\{1\}$ is an x_1 unity vector. Combining Eq. (13.3) and Eq. (13.8), the power flow in the line connected between buses i and j, can be expressed in terms of real power injections as:

$$[P_{ij}]=[L_{ij}]^T\begin{bmatrix}[B_{-n}]^{-1} & 0\\ 0 & 0\end{bmatrix}[P]+\delta_n[L_{ij}]^T\{1\} \tag{13.9}$$

$$[P_{ij}]=[D_n^{ij}][P] \tag{13.10}$$

The second term of Eq. (13.9) is equal to zero because $[L_{ij}]^T\ \{1\} = 0$. Thus, the distribution factor $[D_n^{ij}]$, with bus n as a reference bus is obtained as:

$$[D_{-n}^{ij}]=\begin{bmatrix}[B_{-n}]^{-1} & 0\\ 0 & 0\end{bmatrix}[L_{ij}] \tag{13.11}$$

The nth element corresponding to slack bus in Eq. (13.11) is zero. To obtain the fairness in the competitive environment, the line flow sensitivity at the slack bus should not be zero corresponding to the injections at the slack bus. To attain this, a shift factor has been defined as:

$$\left[\beta_{ij}\right] = -\left[\frac{D_n^{ij}(i) + D_n^{ij}(j)}{2}\right] \tag{13.12}$$

The proposed congestion distribution factors (CDFs) for the transmission line connected between buses i and j can be obtained as:

$$\text{TCDF}_n^{ij} = D_n^{ij} + \beta_{ij} \tag{13.13}$$

These distribution factors derived from dc load flow model have been termed as dc *transmission congestion distribution factors* (DCTCDFs).

13.4.3 AC Load Flow Based Approach (AC Method)

In order to overcome the drawbacks of the existing dc load flow based methods, ac load flow based methods have been used. The TCDFs have been derived utilizing the sensitivity properties of the Newton-Raphson Load Flow (NRLF) Jacobian as given below:

The real power flow (P_{ij}) in a line k, connected between buses i and j, can be written as:

$$P_{ij} = V_i V_j Y_{ij} \cos(\theta_{ij} + \delta_j - \delta_i) - V_i^2 Y_{ij} \cos\theta_{ij} \tag{13.14}$$

where, V_i and δ_i are the voltage magnitude and angle at bus i. Y_{ij} and θ_{ij} are magnitude and angle of ijth element of $[Y_{\text{bus}}]$.

Using Taylor's series approximation and ignoring higher order terms, Eq. (13.14) can be written as:

$$\Delta P_{ij} = \frac{\partial P_{ij}}{\partial \delta_i}\Delta\delta_i + \frac{\partial P_{ij}}{\partial \delta_j}\Delta\delta_j + \frac{\partial P_{ij}}{\partial V_i}\Delta V_i + \frac{\partial P_{ij}}{\partial V_i}\Delta V_j \tag{13.15}$$

Equation (13.15) can be rewritten as:

$$\Delta P_{ij} = a_{ij}\Delta\delta_i + b_{ij}\Delta\delta_j + c_{ij}\Delta V_i + d_{ij}\Delta V_j \tag{13.16}$$

The coefficients appearing in Eq. (13.16) can be obtained using the partial derivatives of real power flow Eq. (13.14) with respect to variables δ and V as:

$$a_{ij} = \frac{\partial P_{ij}}{\partial \delta_i} = V_i V_j Y_{ij} \sin(\theta_{ij} + \delta_j - \delta_i) \tag{13.17}$$

$$b_{ij} = \frac{\partial P_{ij}}{\partial \delta_j} = -V_i V_j Y_{ij} \sin(\theta_{ij} + \delta_j - \delta_i) \tag{13.18}$$

$$c_{ij} = \frac{\partial P_{ij}}{\partial V_i} = V_j Y_{ij} \cos(\theta_{ij} + \delta_j - \delta_i) - 2V_i Y_{ij} \cos\theta_{ij} \tag{13.19}$$

$$d_{ij} = \frac{\partial P_{ij}}{\partial V_j} = V_i Y_{ij} \cos(\theta_{ij} + \delta_j - \delta_i) \tag{13.20}$$

There are two different methods for determination of real power TCDFs using NRLF Jacobian relationship in polar coordinates.

$$\begin{bmatrix} \Delta P \\ \Delta Q \end{bmatrix} = [J] \begin{bmatrix} \Delta\delta \\ \Delta V \end{bmatrix} = \begin{bmatrix} J_{11} & J_{12} \\ J_{21} & J_{22} \end{bmatrix} \begin{bmatrix} \Delta\delta \\ \Delta V \end{bmatrix} \tag{13.21}$$

In this chapter, the coupling between ΔP-$\Delta\delta$ is considered, i.e., J_{11} only.

$$\Delta P = [J_{11}][\Delta\delta] \tag{13.22}$$

$$\Delta Q = [J_{12}][\Delta V] \tag{13.23}$$

From Eq. (13.22), we get

$$\Delta\delta = [J_{11}]^{-1}[\Delta P] = [M][\Delta P] \tag{13.24}$$

Equation (13.22) can be written in the form:

$$\Delta\delta_i = \sum_{l=1}^{N_B} m_{il} \Delta P_i \qquad i = 1, 2, ...N_B, i \neq s \tag{13.25}$$

where, N_B is the number of buses in the system and s is the slack bus.

It is assumed that the impact of change in the voltage magnitude on real power flow is negligible and therefore, Eq. (13.16) can be written as:

$$\Delta P_{ij} = a_{ij}\Delta\delta_i + b_{ij}\Delta\delta_j \tag{13.26}$$

Substituting Eq. (13.25) into Eq. (13.26), we get

$$\Delta P_{ij} = a_{ij}\sum_{l=1}^{N_B} m_{il}\Delta P_l + b_{ij}\sum_{l=1}^{N_B} m_{jl}\Delta P_l \tag{13.27}$$

$$\Delta P_{ij} = (a_{ij}m_{i1} + b_{ij}m_{j1})\Delta P_1 + (a_{ij}m_{i2} + b_{ij}m_{j2})\Delta P_2 + \ldots + (a_{ij}m_{in} + b_{ij}m_{jn})\Delta P_n \tag{13.28}$$

Therefore, the change in real power flow can be written as:

$$\Delta P_{ij} = \text{TCDF}_1^k\, \Delta P_1 + \text{TCDF}_2^k\, \Delta P_2 + \ldots + \text{TCDF}_n^k\, \Delta P_n \tag{13.29}$$

where, $\text{TCDF}_n^k = a_{ij}m_{in} + b_{ij}m_{jn}$ are the transmission congestion distribution factors corresponding to bus n and line k, connecting buses i and j.

The Jacobian used in the determination of ACTCDFs is with a specified reference bus. Therefore, the power flow sensitivities for any line connected between buses i and j will be zero for the element with respect to change in injected power at the reference bus. It means that the reference bus will not have impact on any transmission line flows.

To attain the fairness in the competitive market environment, the power flow sensitivities with respect to the reference bus should not be zero. A shift factor corresponding to real power flow is defined as:

$$P_{\text{shift factor}} = -\frac{\left(\dfrac{\partial P_{ij}}{\partial P_i} + \dfrac{\partial P_{ij}}{\partial P_j}\right)}{2} \tag{13.30}$$

This shift factor has been added to the TCDFs, given in Eq. (13.29), to account for the non-zero element with respect to the reference bus.

13.5 Cluster/Zone Based Transmission Congestion Management

Among the broad methods for congestion management in a deregulated market, the approach based on readjustment of transactions is considered. Congestion zones are nothing but cluster of buses, selected based on sensitivity of flow in the congested line.

The TCDFs obtained based on the methodology discussed above have been utilized for identifying congestion clusters (zones) for a given system. The congestion cluster/zone of type 1 has been defined as zone having large and non-uniform TCDFs, and the congestion zones of type 2 and higher have been defined as those having small and similar TCDfs. Therefore, the transactions in the congestion zone 1 have critical and unequal impact on the line flow. The congestion zones of types 2, 3 and higher are farther from the congested line of interest. Therefore, any transaction outside the most sensitive zone 1 will contribute very little to the line flow. Thus, the identification of congestion zones will reduce the computational burden considerably in both re-dispatching and physical curtailments necessary for the transmission loading relief (TLR) in case of emergency and the adjustment of system users themselves under normal conditions.

The congestion cluster/zonal based approach is also applicable if more than one transmission line congestion conditions are present in the system. The congestion clusters/zones for a multi-congestion case can be obtained by superimposing the clusters/zones corresponding to the individual line congestion.

13.5.1 Re-dispatch

To manage congestion in real time, re-dispatch of generation is performed after the bids are received from GENCOs. In cluster/zone based approach, re-dispatch is carried out at GENCOs in the sensitive zone only. This approach results in economic and efficient relief for congestion.

After the bids from GENCOs are received, the optimal re-dispatch problem has been formulated with an objective to minimize the cost for rescheduling subject to the power flow equations, ramp rates of GENCOs and line flow constraints. The optimization problem has been formulated as follows:

Objective Function—Cost Minimization

The optimal rescheduling of generation with an objective of minimizing the rescheduling cost is formulated subject to the power flow equations, ramp rates of generators and line flow constraints. It is given as:

$$\text{Minimize} \sum_{\substack{i=1 \\ \neq s}}^{N_G} C_i(\Delta P_i)\Delta P_i \quad 13.31)$$

Subject to

$$\sum_{\substack{i=1 \\ \neq s}}^{N_G} [(\text{TCDF}_i^k)\Delta P_i] + F_k^0 \le F_k^{\max} \quad k = 1, 2....N_l \quad (13.32)$$

$$\Delta P_i^{\min} \le \Delta P_i \le \Delta P_i^{\max} \quad i = 1, 2....N_G, i \ne s \quad (13.33)$$

$$P_i^{\min} \le P_i + \Delta P_i \le P_i^{\max} \quad i = 1, 2....N_G, i \ne s \quad (13.34)$$

$$P_{Gm} - P_{Dn} = 0 \quad (13.35)$$

$$\sum_m P_{Gm}^t - \sum_n P_{Dn}^t = 0 \quad t = 1, 2....N_t \quad (13.36)$$

where, $C_i(\Delta P_i)$ is the incremental or decremental bid submitted by GENCO-*i*. ΔP_i is the real power adjustment at GENCO-*i*. N_G represents the number of GENCOs in the sensitive zone. Equation (13.32) denotes line flow constraint formed using TCDF for congested lines. F_k^0 is the power flow caused by all contracts previously settled on line *k*. $F_k^{\max}$ is the line flow limit of line *k* connecting buses *i* and *j*. N_l and N_t represent total number of lines and total transactions considered respectively. Equation (13.33) represents ramp limits for GENCOs. Equation (13.34) limits the output of each GENCO within its maximum and minimum limits. Equation (13.35) and Eq. (13.36) are power flow equations for bilateral and multilateral contracts between *m* and *n* buses respectively.

Objective Function—Loss Minimization

The objective function for congestion management with loss minimization is given as:

$$\text{Minimize } P_L = \sum_{\substack{i=1 \\ i \neq s}}^{N_G} \sum_{\substack{j=1, \\ j \neq i}}^{N_G} (2B_{ij}P_j + B_{io})\Delta P_i \quad (13.37)$$

where, P_L is the overall system loss. B_{ij} and B_{io} are the elements of B loss matrix. Subject to the same constraints listed above, i.e., Eq. (13.32) to Eq. (13.36). The above rescheduling problems formulated for congestion management are non-linear programming problems and it can be solved by using any swarm intelligent techniques.

13.5.2 Load Curtailment

If congestion exists even after rescheduling of generation as per the method outlined above, load curtailment option is introduced. A strategy to decide who will be the most likely volunteer to lower its consumption of electricity when transmission congestion occurs and how much load can be curtailed is to be found out based on simple load curtailment indices. A very brief discussion on these indices is given as follows:

(a) Sensitivity index: Using the sensitivity factor, the expected change of power flow on the target branch k, due to a change in load power at bus j is given as:

$$\Delta P_k = T_{kj} \Delta P_j \tag{13.38}$$

where, $T_{kj} = (X_{mj} - X_{nj})/x_{mn}$ and k is line joining buses m and n. The sensitivity factors of different locations (j) of the system are ranked by the following index:

$$\mu_{Tj} = \frac{T_{kj} - T^{\min}}{T^{\max} - T^{\min}} \text{ for } (T^{\min} \le T_{kj} \le T^{\max}) \tag{13.39}$$

$T^{\max}$ is the maximum sensitivity in the system. $T^{\min}$ is the smallest sensitivity and it gives a dead band below which loads with smaller sensitivity will be neglected. The index μ_T is highest at '1' and if sensitivity is below $T^{\min}$, the index is zero, reflecting no effect on congestion relief.

(b) Customer load curtailment index: If the minimum reduction of power flow on the congested branch is given by ΔP_d, the required amount of adjustment at bus j will be given as:

$$u_{Lj}^* = \Delta P_d / T_{kj} \tag{13.40}$$

Generally, the higher the sensitivity, the smaller the amount of curtailment needed. The customer is supposed to expresses the acceptable range of curtailment by $u^{\max}$ and $u^{\min}$. The acceptable level is measured by the index as:

$$\mu_{Lj} = \begin{cases} 1 & (u_{Lj} \le u^{\min}) \\ \dfrac{u^{\max} - u_{Lj}}{u^{\max} - u^{\min}} & (u^{\min} \le u_{Lj} \le u^{\max}) \\ 0 & (u_{Lj} \ge u^{\min}) \end{cases} \tag{13.41}$$

If the index μ_{Lj} is '1', then the required amount of load curtailment is within the acceptable range of the customer. If μ_{Lj} is '0', then the required amount of load curtailment is higher than the acceptable range and it is not permitted by the customer.

(c) Incentive cost index: High price is an incentive to curtail load. Customer will be happy to curtail load if the incentive price is maximum. The index μ_{Cj} measures the level of customer incentive to curtail load and it is taken as '1'.

(d) Overall index: The overall index for possible load management is then given as:

$$\omega_{Lj} = \mu_{Tj} \cdot \mu_{Lj} \cdot \mu_{Cj} \tag{13.42}$$

Since all the individual indices are scaled between 0 and 1, the overall index also falls between 0 and 1. By calculating the same index for all buses, the feasibility of congestion management options by load curtailment can be measured.

13.5.3 Rescheduling Cost

It is the cost involved in re-dispatching the generation schedule based on the objective selected. The objective is either to minimize the rescheduling cost or minimizing real power loss. The cost of rescheduling is determined from the increment and decrement bid submitted by each GENCO. It is assumed that the bid for increment and decrement are same. The incremental or decremental bid cost function for each generator is $C_i(\Delta P_i)$. This is given by the first order derivative of cost function evaluated at generation before rescheduling. The bid cost function of each generator is given by:

$$\frac{dC_i}{dP_i} = 2a_i \times P_i + b_i \qquad \$/\text{MW-h} \tag{13.43}$$

After obtaining the rescheduling of generation required relieving congestion, the rescheduling cost is calculated using Eq. (13.44).

$$\text{Rescheduling cost} = \sum_{\substack{i=1 \\ \neq s}}^{N_G} C_i(\Delta P_i)\Delta P_i \qquad \$/\text{h} \tag{13.44}$$

Exceeding power flow limit of one or more lines and outage of some important elements are termed as congestion in a power system. For explaining congestion management concept, there are two different standard systems considered. In sample 6 bus system, this concept is demonstrated due to unexpected increase of loads with bilateral transaction. Congestion due to outage of transmission line and its relieving procedure is discussed in IEEE 30 bus system.

13.6 Sample 6 Bus System

In this power system, bilateral transaction is carried out between bus 3 (seller) and bus 6 (buyer). Repeated ac load flow shows that transaction of 7.5 MW between bus 3 and bus 6 is in safer operation. During normal operation, if the loading of buses 4 and 5 are increased by 2 MW, congestion occurs. This load increase has resulted in the violation of line flow limits in two lines, i.e., 1–2 and 3–5. In the line 1–2, line flow is 30.1231 MW against its limit of 30 MW and in the line 3–5, it is 20.2220 MW against its limit of 20 MW.

13.6.1 Cluster/Zone Formation

TCDFs are determined for the congestion in transmission lines 1–2 and 3–5 using Eq. (13.1). Based on the TCDF values, congestion clusters/zones are formed and it is given in Table 13.1.

Table 13.1 Congestion clusters for sample 6 bus system

Congestion of line 1–2				*Congestion of line 3–5*			
Zone 1		*Zone 2*		*Zone 1*		*Zone 2*	
Bus	*TCDF (p.u.)*	*Bus*	*TCDF (p.u.)*	*Bus*	*TCDF (p.u.)*	*Bus*	*TCDF (p.u.)*
1	0.2396	4	–0.0694	2	–0.0051	1	–0.0717
2	–0.2396	5	–0.0917	3	0.1948	4	–0.0505
3	–0.1778	–	–	5	–0.1948	6	0.0809
6	–0.1872	–	–	–	–	–	–

13.6.2 Rescheduling Cost Minimization

As per the cluster/zone based approach, rescheduling is carried out in the most sensitive zone only, i.e., zone 1. In the case of above mentioned two-line congestion, the most sensitive zone is obtained by superimposing two zones 1s based on TCDF values. It has resulted in generators 1, 2 and 3. Therefore, rescheduling is done on generators at buses 2 and 3 only since generator 1 is slack bus. Considering the first objective of rescheduling cost minimization, the rescheduling problem is formulated using Eq. (13.31) to Eq. (13.36) and this minimization problem can be solved using evolutionary computation techniques to find out the amount of rescheduling required to relieve congestion.

Table 13.2 gives the generation rescheduling details for generators 1, 2 and 3 and the corresponding rescheduling cost calculated using Eq. (13.44). The system losses are also calculated. With this amount of generation rescheduling, congestion is completely relieved from the two congested lines. The power flow in the line 1–2 is 29.9214 MW and it is only 19.8976 MW in the line 3–5. Now the flows are within the line flow limits specified in the two congested lines.

Table 13.2 Cost minimization results—6 bus system

GENCOs	*During congestion* — *Generation (P_i) (MW)*	*During congestion* — *Loss (MW)*	*Rescheduling details* — *Change in Generation (ΔP_i) (MW)*	*Rescheduling details* — *Cost (\$/h)*		*After congestion relief* — *Generation (P_i) (MW)*	*After congestion relief* — *Loss (MW)*
2	50		+1.6697	17.278		51.6697	
3	60	8.357	–1.2153	13.176	35.847	58.7847	8.370
1	112.3487		–0.4621	5.393		111.8866	

13.6.3 Loss Minimization

Considering another objective of real power loss minimization, the rescheduling problem is formulated using Eq. (13.37) subject to the constraints given by Eq. (13.32) to Eq. (13.36) and can be solved using any evolutionary computing technique. Table 13.3 gives the generation rescheduling details and the corresponding rescheduling cost and losses for before congestion and after congestion relief. With this amount of generation rescheduling, congestion is completely relieved from the two congested lines. The flow in the line 1–2 is 29.7380 MW and it is only 19.9821 MW in the line 3–5.

Table 13.3 Loss minimization results—6 bus system

GENCOs	*During congestion* — *Generation (P_i) (MW)*	*During congestion* — *Loss (MW)*	*Rescheduling details* — *Change in generation (ΔP_i) (MW)*	*Rescheduling details* — *Cost (\$/h)*		*After congestion relief* — *Generation (P_i) (MW)*	*After congestion relief* — *Loss (MW)*
2	50		+1.7641	18.256		51.764	
3	60	8.357	–1.0965	11.887	38.185	58.904	8.348
1	112.3487		+0.6889	8.041		113.04	

13.6.4 Comparison—Simple 6 Bus System

Table 13.4 gives the comparison of generation rescheduling results for relieving congestion based on the above two objective functions. For the first objective of rescheduling cost minimization, even though there is decrease in rescheduling cost, there is marginal rise in system losses. For the second objective, although the objective of loss minimization is achieved, there is an increase in rescheduling cost. Also, for each objective, the rescheduling of generation required to relieve congestion is specified. In the rescheduling of generation required column, '+' sign indicates increase in generation required and '–' sign denotes decrease in generation required to relieve congestion. From Table 13.4, it is clear that, one objective is achieved at the expense of the other. If rescheduling cost is minimized, there is increase in losses and if losses are minimized, rescheduling cost is increased.

Table 13.4 Comparison—sample 6 bus system

Type of objective	*Rescheduling details*	*System loss* (MW)	*Rescheduling cost* ($/h)	*Rescheduling of generation required* (MW)
Rescheduling cost minimization	Before rescheduling	8.357	**35.847**	G_2 = + 1.6697 G_3 = – 1.2153 G_1 = – 0.4621
	After rescheduling	8.370		
Loss minimization	Before rescheduling	8.357	38.1855	G_2 = + 1.7641 G_3 = – 1.0965 G_1 = + 0.6889
	After rescheduling	**8.348**		

13.7 IEEE 30 Bus System

There are 6 generators and 41 lines in IEEE 30 bus system. Generator connected to bus 1 is considered as slack. In this IEEE test system, congestion due to outage of an element is considered. An outage of line 4–6 in the system causes congestion on lines 1–2 and 2–6. In the line 1–2, line flow is 132.8875 MW against its limit of 130 MW and in the line 2–6, it is 69.5312 MW against its limit of 65 MW.

13.7.1 Rescheduling Cost Minimization

Based on the TCDF values, congestion clusters/zones are formed for the two congested lines first. Rescheduling is carried out in the most sensitive zone only. Zone 1 is the most sensitive zone. Figure 13.4 and Figure 13.5 show the zone's classification for congested lines 1–2 and 2–6 separately. For each congested line, zone 1, zone 2, zone 3 and zone 4 are shown separately.

After superimposing two zones 1s, the generators connected to buses 1, 2, 5 and 8 are identified for rescheduling process. Among these generators, rescheduling is done on generators at buses 2, 5 and 8 only. The generator at bus 1 is slack and it will support for the change in system loss and hence it is not subjected to rescheduling process. The rescheduling problem is formulated using Eq. (13.31) to Eq. (13.36) for rescheduling cost minimization objective.

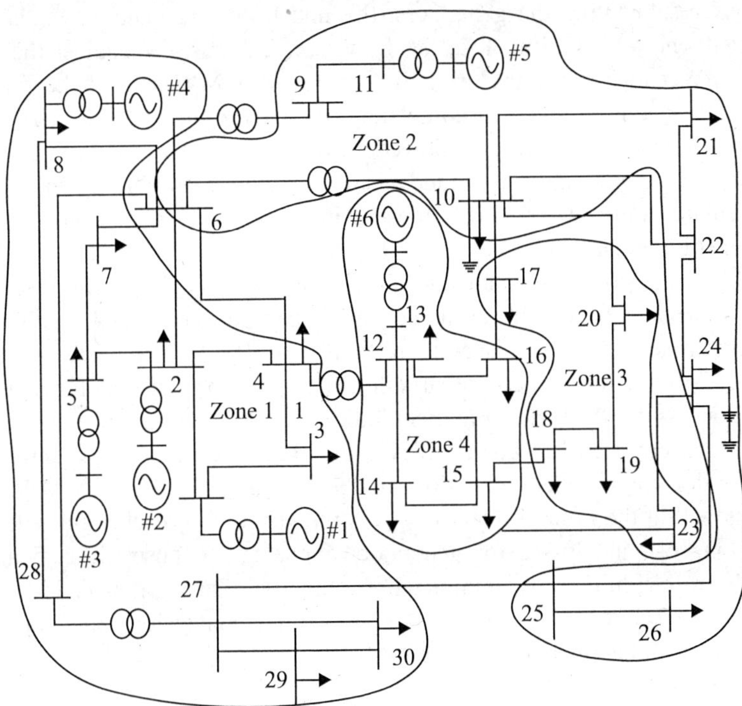

Figure 13.4 Clusters for congestion of line 1–2.

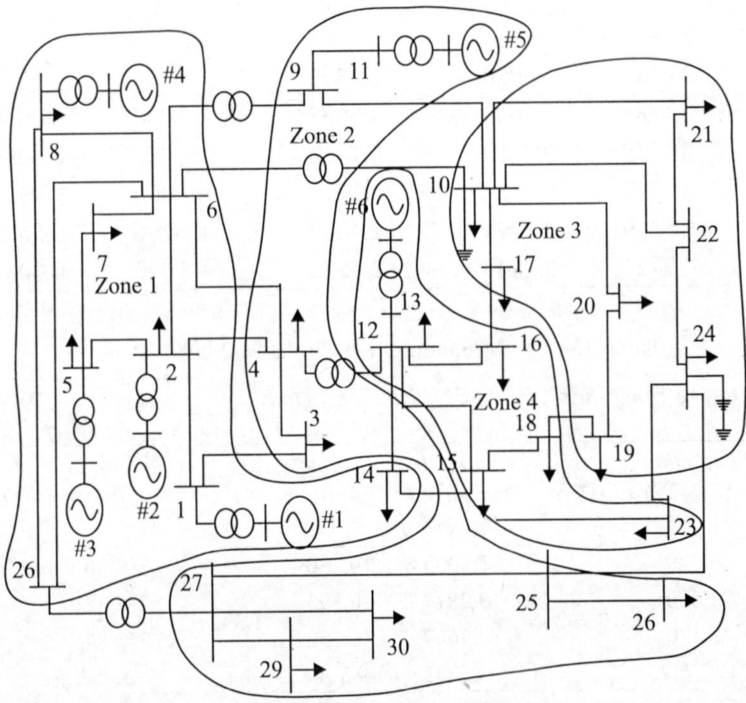

Figure 13.5 Clusters for congestion of line 2–6.

After rescheduling the generators, the line flows are checked in the two congested lines. In the line 1–2, the flow is 131.7130 MW against the limit of 130 MW and in the line 2–6, it is only 64.9941 MW against the limit of 65 MW. Still congestion is not completely removed in the line 1–2. Therefore, load curtailment procedure is followed in order to relieve congestion in the line. As a computational time reducing measure, the load curtailment indices are calculated only for the loads present in the zone 1, since zone 1 is the most sensitive zone.

Table 13.5 gives the load curtailment indices calculated for the loads present in zone 1 only. All the indices are scaled between 0 and 1 and if the load curtailment index and overall index is close to 1, it indicates that, the customer is most likely to accept curtailment of some part of load for relieving congestion. As per the load curtailment indices calculated, curtailment of 2.3613 MW at load connected to bus 5 relieves the congestion more efficiently.

After load curtailment, the flow in the line 1–2 is 129.5125 MW only which is within the limit. Table 13.6 gives the generation rescheduling details, generation cost and losses for generators connected to buses 1, 2, 5 and 8 using the rescheduling cost minimization objective. During congestion in the system, the system loss is 10.992 MW. But, after congestion relief measure, the system loss has increased to 11.116 MW.

Table 13.5 Load curtailment indices

Load bus	*Sensitivity T*	*Sensitivity index, μ_T*	*Load curtailment magnitude, μ_T^* (MW)*	*Load curtailment index, μ_T*	*Overall index, ω_L*
2	0.8637	1.0000	2.2875	0.6306	0.6306
3	0.4389	0.0000	4.5008	0.0000	0.0000
4	0.5288	0.2115	3.7362	0.0000	0.0000
5	0.8367	0.9364	2.3613	1.0000	0.9364
7	0.8209	0.8993	2.4067	0.6296	0.5622
30	0.7723	0.7848	2.5582	0.0000	0.0000

Table 13.6 Cost minimization results—30 bus system

GENCOs	*During congestion*		*Rescheduling details*		*After congestion relief*	
	Generation (P_i) (MW)	*Loss (MW)*	*Change in generation (ΔP_i) (MW)*	*Cost (\$/h)*	*Generation (P_i) (MW)*	*Loss (MW)*
2	48.790	10.992	–10.000	19.250	38.790	11.116
5	21.500		+7.2817	10.595	28.782	
8	22.120		+3.7637	12.350	25.884	
1	177.742		–4.5591	9.196	173.183	
				51.392		

13.7.2 Loss Minimization

For the loss minimization objective, Eq. (13.37) is to be solved subject to the constraints given by Eq. (13.32) to Eq. (13.36). Table 13.7 gives the generation rescheduling details and the corresponding rescheduling cost and losses for the loss minimization objective. The flows in the congested lines are checked once more. The flows in the two congested lines are: in line 1–2, it is 127.18 MW and in line 2–6, it is 63.19 MW. Therefore, congestion is completely relieved. The positive aspect with this proposed objective is that, congestion is completely removed without the need for load curtailment.

The system loss during congestion is 10.992 MW and after congestion relief, it has decreased to 9.946 MW. The objective of minimizing losses is met, but there is a sharp rise in the rescheduling cost. For the objective of rescheduling cost minimization, the rescheduling cost is 51.392 \$/h only. But for the objective of loss reduction, it has increased to 57.235 \$/h.

Table 13.7 Loss minimization results—30 bus system

GENCOs	*During congestion*		*Rescheduling details*		*After congestion relief*	
	Generation (P_i) (MW)	*Loss* (MW)	*Change in generation* (ΔP_i) (MW)	*Cost* (\$/h)	*Generation* (P_i) (MW)	*Loss* (MW)
2	48.790	10.99	– 4.426	8.089	44.364	9.946
5	21.500		+0.776	0.814	22.276	
8	22.120		+10.00	33.33	32.120	
1	177.742		– 7.396	14.99	170.346	
				57.23		

13.7.3 Comparison—IEEE 30 Bus System

Table 13.8 gives the comparison of rescheduling cost and losses for relieving congestion based on two objectives. The rescheduling of generation details is also specified for comparison. From Table 13.8, it is clear that one objective

Table 13.8 Comparison—IEEE 30 bus system

Type of objective	*Rescheduling details*	*System loss* (MW)	*Rescheduling cost* (\$/h)	*Rescheduling of generation required* (MW)
Rescheduling cost minimization	Before rescheduling	10.992	**51.3920**	G_2 = – 10.000 G_5 = + 7.2817
	After rescheduling	10.116		G_8 = + 3.7637 G_1 = + 4.5591
Loss minimization	Before rescheduling	10.992	57.235	G_2 = – 4.4264 G_5 = + 0.7764
	After rescheduling	**9.946**		G_8 = + 10.000 G_1 = – 7.3962

is achieved at the expense of other. If rescheduling cost is minimized, there is increase in losses and if losses are minimized, rescheduling cost is increased.

13.8 MATLAB Programs

TCDF formulation based on DC power flow method

```
%finding congested line & forming DCTCDF
j=input('enter number of congested lines: ');
for co_li=1:j
    s=input('congested line starting end: ');
ter=input('congested line terminating end: ');
cdfs(co_li)=s;
cdft(co_li)=ter;
end
for i=1:nbr
    s=nl(i);ter=nr(i);
iflineflow(s,ter)<0
        s=nr(i);ter=nl(i);end
iflineflow(s,ter)>limit(i)
fprintf('line %d-%d gets congested ',s,ter);
  j=j+1;
conbr=i;
cdfs(j)=s;
cdft(j)=ter;
end
end
end
r=1;
for i=1:nbus
if kb(i)==1
     r=i;
end
end
Z =  X;                   %branch impedance
% y = ones(nbr,1)/Z;      %branch admittance
ybus=zeros(nbus,nbus); % initialize ybus to zero
for k = 1:nbr;            % formation of the off diagonal elements
ifnl(k) > 0 & nr(k) > 0
ybus(nl(k),nr(k)) = ybus(nl(k),nr(k)) - (1/X(k));
ybus(nr(k),nl(k)) = ybus(nl(k),nr(k));
end
end
for n = 1:nbus            % formation of the diagonal elements
```

```
for k = 1:nbr
if nl(k) == n | nr(k) == n
ybus(n,n) = ybus(n,n) + (1/X(k));
else, end
end
end
ybus1=ybus;
ybus(:,r)=[];
ybus(r,:)=[];
ybus;   %B without reference
z=zeros(nbus,1);
z1=zeros(1,nbus-1);
ybusinv=vertcat(z1,inv(ybus));
ybusinv=horzcat(z,ybusinv);
ybus;
ybusinv;
DCTCDF=zeros(nbus,1);
conline=j;
clear j;
BETA=zeros(nbus,1);tcdf=zeros(nbus,conline);
%TCDF determination
for l=1:conline
b=0;
L=zeros(nbus,1);
i=cdfs(l);j=cdft(l);
b=ybus1(i,j);
L(i,1)=-b;
L(j,1)=-L(i,1);
D=ybusinv*L;
beta=-(D(i,1)+D(j,1))/2;
foryy=1:nbus
tcdf(yy,l)=D(yy,1)+beta; % tcdf=D+BETA;
end
fprintf('the DCTCDF for congestion of line:%d-%d is: ',i,j);
tcdf(:,l)
end
```

TCDF formation based on AC power flow method

```
% ACTCDF
J=zeros(nbus-ns);
J=A(1:nbus-ns,1:nbus-ns);
ACTCDF=zeros(nbus,1);
j1=inv(J);
z=zeros(nbus,1);
```

```
z1=zeros(1,nbus-1);
j11=vertcat(z1,j1);j11=horzcat(z,j11);
clearcdfscdft ac bc
j=input('enter number of congested lines: ');
forco_li=1:j
    s=input('congested line starting end: ');
ter=input('congested line terminating end: ');
cdfs(co_li)=s;
cdft(co_li)=ter;
end
j=0;
for i=1:nbr
    s=nl(i);ter=nr(i);
iflineflow(s,ter)<0
      s=nr(i);ter=nl(i);end
iflineflow(s,ter)>limit(i) & (lineflow(s,ter)-limit(i))>0.02
fprintf('line %d   %d-%d gets congested ',i,s,ter);
      j=j+1;
conbr(j)=i;
cdfs(j)=s;
cdft(j)=ter;
end
end
end
tcdf=zeros(nbus,j);
forconline=1:j
    c1=cdfs(conline);
    c2=cdft(conline);
    ac(conline)=Vm(c1)*Vm(c2)*Ym(c1,c2)*sin(t(c1,c2)+delta(c2)-
delta(c1));
    bc(conline)=-Vm(c1)*Vm(c2)*Ym(c1,c2)*sin(t(c1,c2)+delta(c2)-
delta(c1));
for i=1:nbus
if kb(i)~=1
tcdf(i,conline)=ac(conline)*j11(c1,i)+bc(conline)*j11(c2,i);
end
end
tcdf;
beta=0;
beta=-(tcdf(c1,conline)+tcdf(c2,conline))/2;
for i=1:nbus
tcdf(i,conline)=tcdf(i,conline)+beta;
end
fprintf('\n ACTCDF for line congestion of %d-%d is ',c1,c2);
tcdf
```

Review Questions

Part-A

1. Name any two way of reducing congestion management.
2. Write the role of SOs.
3. Define congestion.
4. What is meant by congestion management?
5. Define rescheduling cost.
6. What is meant by customer load curtailment index?
7. Write the cost minimization objective function.
8. Mention about cost free means.
9. What is meant by OPF based congestion management?
10. Define TCDF.

Part-B

1. Explain the concept of cluster/zone based method to relieve the congestion takes place in the power system with the suitable equations.
2. Explain the concept of load curtailment to relieve the congestion takes place in the power system with the suitable equations.
3. Demonstrate the procedure to formulate objective functions for managing power line congestion with simple power system.

Appendix

A.1 Matlab Program for Lagrange Multiplier Method

```
clc;
clear all;
c=[1;1;1;1;1];
for i=1:4
    display('ITERATION NO:');  disp(i);
    x1=c(1);x2=c(2);x3=c(3);  l1=c(4);l2=c(5);
     j=[0.5 0 0 -1 1;0 2 0 -1 0.2;0 0 2*l2 0 2*x3; -1 -1 0 0 0;
     1 0.2 2*x3 0 0];
    display('J:');  disp(j);
    p=inv(j); display('J inverse matrix:');  disp(p);
    b=[(-0.5*x1)+l1-l2;(-2*x2)+l1-(0.2*l2);(-2*l2*x3);-5+x1+x2;
    -x1-(0.2*x2)+3-(x3*x3)];  ch=p*b;
    display('Change in variables:');  disp(ch);
    c=c+ch;display('Variable value matrix:');
    disp(c);
end
```

Output

Iteration No. 1

J:

0.5000	0	0	–1.0000	1.0000
0	2.0000	0	–1.0000	0.2000
0	0	2.0000	0	2.0000
–1.0000	–1.0000	0	0	0
1.0000	0.2000	2.0000	0	0

J inverse matrix:

0.3546	–0.3546	–0.1418	–0.6809	0.1418
–0.3546	0.3546	0.1418	–0.3191	–0.1418
–0.1418	0.1418	0.0567	0.3723	0.4433
–0.6809	–0.3191	0.3723	–0.7128	–0.3723
0.1418	–0.1418	0.4433	–0.3723	–0.4433

Change in variables:

2.6879
0.3121
–0.9752
1.8191
–0.0248

Variable value matrix:

3.6879
1.3121
0.0248
2.8191
0.9752

Iteration No. 2

J:

0.5000	0	0	–1.0000	1.0000
0	2.0000	0	–1.0000	0.2000
0	0	1.9504	0	0.0496
–1.0000	–1.0000	0	0	0
1.0000	0.2000	0.0496	0	0

J inverse matrix:

0.0020	–0.0020	–0.0317	0.2448	1.2439
–0.0020	0.0020	0.0317	–1.2448	–1.2439
–0.0317	0.0317	0.5102	0.0831	0.0989
0.2448	–1.2448	0.0831	–3.1427	–3.2651
1.2439	–1.2439	0.0989	–3.2651	–3.8871

Change in variables:

–1.1813
1.1813
–0.1188
3.1010
3.6917

Variable value matrix:

2.5066
2.4934
–0.0940
5.9202
4.6669

Iteration No. 3

J:

0.5000	0	0	–1.0000	1.0000
0	2.0000	0	–1.0000	0.2000
0	0	9.3337	0	–0.1879
–1.0000	–1.0000	0	0	0
1.0000	0.2000	–0.1879	0	0

J inverse matrix:

0.0058	–0.0058	0.0248	0.2347	1.2318
–0.0058	0.0058	–0.0248	–1.2347	–1.2318
0.0248	–0.0248	0.1056	–0.0651	–0.0775
0.2347	–1.2347	–0.0651	–3.1161	–3.2335
1.2318	–1.2318	–0.0775	–3.2335	–3.8493

Change in variables:

0.0044
–0.0044
0.0937
–0.0115
–0.0137

Variable value matrix:

2.5110
2.4890
–0.0003
5.9087
4.6532

Iteration No. 4

J:

0.5000	0	0	–1.0000	1.0000
0	2.0000	0	–1.0000	0.2000
0	0	9.3064	0	–0.0006
–1.0000	–1.0000	0	0	0
1.0000	0.2000	–0.0006	0	0

J inverse matrix:

0.0000	–0.0000	0.0001	0.2500	1.2500
–0.0000	0.0000	–0.0001	–1.2500	–1.2500
0.0001	–0.0001	0.1075	–0.0002	–0.0002
0.2500	–1.2500	–0.0002	–3.1562	–3.2812
1.2500	–1.2500	–0.0002	–3.2812	–3.9062

Change in variables:

–0.0110
0.0110
0.0003
0.0288
0.0343

Variable value matrix:

2.5000
2.5000
0.0000
5.9375
4.6875

A.2 Matlab Program For Interior Point Method

```
clc;
clear;
A=[1 1 1];
Ct=[1 2 0];
alpha=0.7;
epsilon=0.1;
iteration=4;
X=[1;1;2];
for i=1:iteration
    Z=Ct*X;
    if(i==1)
      Zold=Z;
    end
    D=diag(X);
    Xcap=inv(D)*X;
    Acap=A*D;
    P=(eye(3)-(Acap'*(inv(Acap*Acap'))*Acap));
    Ccap=D*Ct';
    Cp=P*Ccap;
    gamma=norm(min(Cp));
```

```
    Xcapnew=Xcap+(alpha/gamma)*Cp;
    Xnew=D*Xcapnew;
    Znew=Ct*Xnew;
    delZ=Znew-Zold;
    if delZ>epsilon
      X=Xnew;
      Zold=Znew;
    elseif delZ<=epsilon
      break;
    end
end
if delZ>epsilon
    disp('Iteration not enough to find Optimal Solution');
    disp('X')
    disp(Xnew);
    disp('Z');
    disp(Znew);
    disp('delZ');
    disp(delZ);
elseif delZ<=epsilon
    disp('Optimal Solution Z');
    disp(Znew);
    disp('Iteration Required');
    disp(i);
end
```

Bibliography

A. Kumar, S.C. Srivastava and S.N. Singh, "A zonal congestion management approach using real and reactive power rescheduling", *IEEE Transactions on Power Systems*, Vol. 19, No. 1, pp. 554–562, 2004c.

A QIP course *Proceedings on Power System Operation and Control*, October 4–8, 2004, IIT Bombay.

A QIP short-term course on analysis of modern power systems, February 6–10, 2006, IISc, Bangalore.

A short term course Proceedings on Electric Power System Operation and Management in Restructured Environment, July 21–25, 2003, IIT Kanpur.

Bhattacharya, K., M.H.J. Bollen and J.K. Dadder, *Operation of Restructured Power Systems*, Kluwer Academic Publishers, USA, 2001.

Chao, H.P. and H.G. Huntington, *Designing Competitive Electricity Markets*, Kluwer Academic Publishers, 1998.

Charles Raja, S., P. Venkatesh, B.V. Manikandan and S.C. Srivastava, "Available Transfer Capability Determination Incorporating Reactive Power Flows and Network Uncertainties under a Deregulated Environment", *International Journal of Electric Power Components and Systems*, Vol. 40, Issue 11, pp. 1246–1265, August 2012.

Charles Raja, S., P. Venkatesh and B.V. Manikandan, "Transmission Congestion Management in restructured power systems," *2011 IEEE International Conference on Emerging Trends in Electrical and Computer Technology*, Tamil Nadu, pp. 23–28, 2011.

Denny, F.I. and D.E. Dismuks, *Power System Operations and Electricity Markets*, CRC Press, 2002.

doi: 10.1109/ICETECT.2011.5760085

Einhorn, M. and R. Siddiqi, *Electricity Transmission Pricing and Technology*, Kluwer Academic Publishers, 1996.

Gangadhar, K.A., *Electric Power Systems Analysis, Stability and Protection*, Khanna Publishers, 1998.

Glover, J.D. and M.S. Sarma, *Power System Analysis and Design*, Brooks/core, USA, 2002.

Glover, J.D., M.S. Sarma and T.J. Overbye, *Power System Analysis and Design*, Thomson Learning, 2008.

Greene, S., I. Dobson and F.L. Alvarado, "Sensitivity of Transfer Capability Margin with a Fast Formula", *IEEE Transactions on Power Systems*, Vol. 17, No. 1, pp. 34–40, 2002.

Graigner and Stevenson, *Power System Analysis*, Tata McGraw-Hill, 2003.

Ilic, M., F. Galiana and L. Fink, *Power System Restructuring: Engineering and Economics*, Kluwer Academic Publishers, Boston, MA, 1998.

Kirschen, Daniel S. and G. Strbac, *Fundamentals of Power System Economics*, John Wiley & Sons, 2004.

Know your power, *A Citizens' Primer on the Electricity Sector*, 2nd ed., Prayas Energy Group, Pune.

Kumar A., S.C. Srivastava and S.N. Singh, "A zonal congestion management approach using ac transmission congestion distribution factors", *International Journal of Electric Power Systems Research*, Vol. 72, pp. 85–93, 2004b.

Lai, L.L., *Power System Restructuring and Deregulation Trading, Performance and Information Technology*, John Wiley & Sons, 2001.

Lambert, J.D., *Creating Competitive Power Markets: the PJM Model*, Pennwell, 2001.

Momoh, J.A., *Electric Power System Applications of Optimisation*, Marcel Dekker, Inc., 2001.

Nagrath and Kothari, *Modern Power System Analysis*, Tata McGraw-Hill, 2003.

Paveela, M., D. Ernst and D. Ruiz-vega, *Transient Stability of Power Systems*, Kluwer Academic Publishers, 2000.

Philipson, L. and H. Lee Willis, *Understanding Electric Utilities and Deregulation*, Marcel Dekkers Inc., New York, 1999.

Rau, N.S., Optimisation Principles Practical Applications to Operation and Markets of the Electric Power Industry, Wiley, 2003.

Rothwell, G. and T. Gomez, *Electricity Economics Regulation and Deregulation*, IEEE Press, 2003.

Saadat, H., *Power System Analysis*, Tata McGraw-Hill, 2002.

Schweeppe, F.C., M.C. Caramanis, R.D. Tabors and R.E. Bohn, *Spot Pricing of Electricity*, Kluwer Academic Publishers, Boston, MA, 1998.

S. Dutta and S.P. Singh, "Optimal Rescheduling of Generators for Congestion Management Based on Particle Swarm Optimization", *IEEE Transactions on Power Systems*, Vol. 23, No. 4, pp. 1560–1569, 2008.

Shahidehpour, M. and Muwaffq Alomoush, *Restructured Electrical Power Systems, Operation, Trading and Volatility*, Marcel Dekker, Inc., New York, 2001.

Sheble, G.B., *Computational Auction Mechanisms for Restructured Power Industry Operation*, Kluwer Academic Publishers, Norwell Massachusetts, 1999.

Song, Y.H. and X.F. Wang, *Operation of Market-Oriented Power Systems*, Springer, 2003.

Vadhera, S.S., *Power System Analysis and Stability*, Khanna Publishers, 2004.

Wadhwa, C.L., *Electrical Power Systems*, New Age International, 2009.

Wollenberg, B.F. and A.J. Wood, *Power Generation Operation and Control*, John Wiley & Sons, 2010.

Index